Essentials of Organizational Behavior

Second Edition

To T. K.
For keeping it real.

Essentials of Organizational Behavior

An Evidence-Based Approach

Second Edition

Terri A. Scandura
University of Miami

Los Angeles | London | New Delhi
Singapore | Washington DC | Melbourne

FOR INFORMATION:

SAGE Publications, Inc.
2455 Teller Road
Thousand Oaks, California 91320
E-mail: order@sagepub.com

SAGE Publications Ltd.
1 Oliver's Yard
55 City Road
London, EC1Y 1SP
United Kingdom

SAGE Publications India Pvt. Ltd.
B 1/I 1 Mohan Cooperative Industrial Area
Mathura Road, New Delhi 110 044
India

SAGE Publications Asia-Pacific Pte. Ltd.
3 Church Street
#10–04 Samsung Hub
Singapore 049483

Acquisitions Editor: Maggie Stanley
Content Development Editor: Lauren Holmes
Editorial Assistant: Alisa Nance
Production Editor: Jane Haenel
Copy Editor: Diane Wainwright
Typesetter: Hurix Digital
Proofreader: Jeff Bryant
Indexer: Sylvia Coates
Cover Designer: Candice Harman
Marketing Manager: Amy Lammers

Copyright © 2019 by SAGE Publications, Inc.

Printed in the United States of America.

Library of Congress Cataloging-in-Publication Data

Names: Scandura, Terri A., author. Title: Essentials of organizational behavior / Terri A. Scandura, University of Miami.

Description: Second edition. | Thousand Oaks, California : SAGE, [2018] | Includes bibliographical references and index.

Identifiers: LCCN 2017033151 | ISBN 9781506388465 (pbk. : alk. paper) Subjects: LCSH: Organizational change.

Classification: LCC HD58.8 .S293 2018 | DDC 352.3/67—dc23
LC record available at https://lccn.loc.gov/2017033151

This book is printed on acid-free paper.

18 19 20 21 22 10 9 8 7 6 5 4 3 2

BRIEF CONTENTS

DETAILED CONTENTS

SECTION II: UNDERSTANDING INDIVIDUALS IN ORGANIZATIONS

SECTION V: LEADERS AS CHANGE AGENTS   365

Chapter 14: Organizational Culture   366

PREFACE

After decades of using organizational behavior (OB) textbooks, I realized they were not communicating the right message for today's students. They memorized theories and dutifully wrote them down on exams, but I felt they were missing out on how to apply these theories to become a better leader. Students want takeaway skills they can put into practice immediately. A new approach to teaching OB is needed, and this textbook shows students how to be effective leaders and managers in organizations. With a focus on leadership and management development, students will go beyond memorizing theories and will apply the most-relevant concepts to effectively motivate followers, lead their teams, and champion organizational change.

I have researched leadership for over 30 years. During 5 of those years, I was an acting dean at a major research university undergoing change. With this position, I put OB concepts into practice every day in my administrative position—I hired people, motivated them, set goals, and did annual performance appraisals. I helped employees, students, and faculty cope with organizational change. Based upon my research and the practical experience as an administrator with several direct reports, I began to look at my courses differently. I wanted to translate our rich evidence base into skills that managers can use every day. I also wanted to show how managers can become effective leaders through applications of course concepts. My process to achieve this was to start incorporating more skill-based assessments, role-plays, and team activities into each class meeting. Feedback from students was extremely positive, and many cited these exercises as high points in their learning experience in my course evaluations. I decided to write a textbook that reviewed OB theory and distilled the most relevant concepts for the development of effective leaders in organizations. Keeping a sharp focus on what the evidence base in OB supports, I searched for and developed exercises and activities that reinforce the key takeaways from each area I taught.

This "essentials" book is not a condensed version of a larger OB textbook. It was written with an eye toward the fundamentals every managerial leader needs to know and how to apply them. I used an evidence-based approach, making prescriptions based on research. Theories are reviewed critically, and students are encouraged to think critically about what they read. End-of-chapter assessments and activities make the linkage from theory to practice for students. For example, Chapter 9 includes an activity in which students role-play giving a performance appraisal. Based on my practical experience, performance appraisal is one of the most challenging scenarios a new manager faces. The activity is realistic and encourages students to practice the skill set of how to provide feedback in an effective way. This textbook fills another need by adopting an integrative OB textbook approach with a framework of leadership and management development throughout. Each section begins with a "map" of the field of OB that allows instructors to create integrated learning modules that can be used in courses of varying lengths (for example, 6-week courses and 15-week courses). References are made to other chapters in multiple places so students can see the connections across topics in OB. For example, Chapter 8 discusses core concepts in motivation and refers to the chapter immediately following, which focuses on the role of rewards in motivating followers. As a set, these two chapters compose a learning module on "leaders as motivators."

The cases at the end of each chapter cover a wide range of organizational situations including small business, hospitals, large corporations, and many other types of organizations. My colleagues and I have tested the cases and exercises with students, and they resonate with both MBAs and undergraduates. Regardless of the career paths students choose, they will find these assessments and activities valuable as they develop leadership and management skills.

TARGET AUDIENCES

I have written this book to be appropriate for upper-level undergraduate courses and MBA core courses in OB. Case studies and exercises will prepare students at all levels for today's workplace. The content and activities have been carefully written so students can respond to discussion questions and assessments. For undergraduates, the role-plays and team activities at the end of the chapters are particularly valuable. This experiential approach to learning supports the application of OB fundamentals, and the activities are interesting and fun. Textbook reviews have also indicated that this textbook will work very well in industrial/organizational psychology courses as well as courses in higher education leadership. In writing the textbook, I kept in mind that some OB courses are being offered in hybrid or online formats. The features of this textbook support these formats (for example, all boxed inserts, case studies, activities, and self-assessments have discussion questions that can be answered by students and submitted as assignments).

APPROACH

I always wanted a concise OB textbook that did certain things for my students. This textbook was written with three guiding principles:

1. An *evidence-based management approach* to the field of OB so practice recommendations are grounded in research.

2. Emphasis on *critical thinking* in Chapter 1 and throughout the textbook so students can evaluate the strengths and weaknesses of research before they move to practice applications.

3. A focus on *leadership development* for managers so rather than just memorizing theories, students apply them to cases and a variety of activities at the end of each chapter, including activities, role-plays, case studies, and self-assessments.

Evidence-Based Management

Hundreds of references to classic and current OB research are used in this textbook to build a new way of looking at the research as the foundation for leadership development. The evidence-based management approach is described in detail in Chapter 1. The coverage of research is comprehensive, with a focus on the most important topics managers need to become effective leaders. These are the topics I have selected to teach for over 30 years to undergraduate, MBA, and executive MBA students. This textbook offers a research-based approach that translates theory to practice, focusing on the contemporary approaches rather than the historical/classical approaches. Most students are less interested in historical development of theory and more interested in theories they can apply to be more effective leaders. There is far less emphasis on theories that don't have solid research support than other textbooks that I have used and read. In fairness, certain topics are noted for their contribution to broad-based understanding of OB, followed by a critical assessment of the research support.

Critical Thinking

Over the years, I have heard colleagues lament, "Our students don't think critically." One day while teaching, it occurred to me that I had never actually included a lecture on critical thinking—what it is and why it is important.

It wasn't in my OB textbook. I researched critical thinking and started to lecture on it in my class lectures. I began to see a difference in how my students approached the material in my courses. The quality of classroom discussion improved, and students began to really discuss strengths and weaknesses of theory and develop relevant examples as applications. Their answers on essay questions went beyond memorization to demonstration of understanding concepts, plus providing examples to show they could apply them as managers.

It just makes sense that we teach our students about critical thinking, and this is a major theme of this textbook. Critical thinking is defined and discussed in detail in Chapter 1 so students will understand what it is and why it is important for a managerial leader to think critically.

Leadership Development

I have an extensive background studying the importance of leadership within organizations, in addition to holding positions of leadership at several points in my career. For this reason, leadership is a major theme that flows throughout the textbook. Leadership core concepts are covered in the textbook in Chapter 6; while I believe this is foundational to a leadership and management development approach to OB, this chapter might be assigned earlier as many OB instructors do (this book is written to have such flexibility). In addition to a full chapter on leadership, each chapter includes a section discussing leadership implications in the context of the topic being discussed, as well as end-of-chapter activities and self-assessments designed to enhance students' understanding of leadership and their own leadership styles and tendencies.

Trends in Organizational Behavior

Along with the three guiding principles of evidence-based management, critical thinking, and leadership development, this textbook also touches upon emerging topics in OB. Throughout the chapters, there is an emphasis on globalization and cross-cultural OB. For example, cross-cultural differences in stress are compared in Chapter 15. A number of the chapters include discussions on ethics as well. An example of this theme is found in Chapter 12: Organizational Communication, where the Enron case is discussed as a grapevine effect that led to uncovering major ethical violations. Finally, in a number of places, positive psychology is integrated into the presentation of OB topics. For example, mindfulness is discussed as a coaching strategy for managing emotions and moods in the leadership implications section of Chapter 3.

FEATURES

Learning Objectives

The learning objectives included at the beginning of each chapter highlight the key topics covered in the chapter and note the skills students will develop after reading. These learning objectives are directly tied to main headers within the chapter and can be used to measure and assess students' understanding of chapter material.

Chapter-Opening Vignette

Each chapter begins with a research-based challenge facing managers based upon empirical data, often from national polls or consulting firms. For example, Chapter 7 discusses what it feels like to have power, based on research. These highlights are intended to get the students' attention so they immediately see the relevance of the material in the chapter that follows.

Best Practices and Research in Action Boxes

Within each chapter, there are two types of boxed inserts to enhance the application of the material to the student's development as a leader—"Best Practices" and "Research in Action." Best Practices highlight current applications of OB research in real organizations or consulting examples. One of my favorites is a Best Practices box that teaches students step-by-step how to use perceptual tools to remember people's names. Research in Action vignettes demonstrate how OB research translates to leadership practice. An example is a short discussion of current research on the rise of workplace incivility that asks the question of whether we need to "send in Miss Manners." Included in each of these boxed features are discussion questions to stimulate the student's thinking on the application and can be used for in-class discussion. These discussion questions may be assigned prior to class to encourage students to read and apply the highlighted practice and research in these inserts. These boxed inserts can be integrated into class discussions to show how practice and research use OB theories.

Critical Thinking Questions

To support critical thinking throughout the course, critical thinking questions are integrated within the textbook. These questions encourage students to pause, think about, and then apply the material just covered to an organizational challenge for leaders. For instructors teaching online courses, these questions can be assigned to check the student comprehension of assigned textbook readings.

Key Terms

Key terms featured in each chapter have been set in color throughout the text. Students will be able to quickly search for and locate these key terms.

The Toolkit

Each chapter contains a "Toolkit" in which the student will apply the concepts covered within that chapter. Each chapter's Toolkit contains the following features:

- **Key terms** highlighted within the chapter.

- The **toolkit activities** are team exercises or role-plays in which the students interact with other students to apply the material. I have used these exercises in my classes, and I am pleased to provide them all in one package so you don't have to search for them and copy them for class.

- A short **case study** illustrating one or more concepts from the chapter. These cases are followed by discussion questions that can be assigned prior to in-class case discussion.

- At least one **self-assessment**, including personality tests or leadership assessments. Students learn something about themselves and others, making the concepts relevant to their personal lives and development as a leader.

- Years ago, one of my MBA students asked me if I could compile a list of 10 books that every manager should read. I have included **Suggestions for Further Reading** on the online Instructor Resource Site at **edge.sagepub.com/scandura2e** to encourage further reading on classic and current books on OB topics.

New to This Edition

For this edition, I retained the features that have made *Essentials of Organizational Behavior: An Evidence-Based Approach* successful in its first edition, while updating with current research and strengthening the evidence-based approach.

- *Updated chapter scenarios*—As in the last edition, all the chapters start with a scenario that features research on an interesting real-world problem based on research or practice.

- *Updated Leadership Implications*—The Leadership Implications at the end of each chapter have been retained and expanded.

- *Critical Thinking Questions*—The section on Critical Thinking has been expanded in Chapter 1, and Critical Thinking Questions have been retained and expanded in the second edition.

- *Updated Best Practices and Research in Action boxes*—Best Practices and Research in Action boxes have been retained as features, and new ones have been added for new chapters under the reorganization of the textbook.

- *New Toolkit Activities*—Both instructors and students responded positively to the Toolkit Activities and Self-Assessments, and additional Toolkit items have been added. Based upon feedback from instructors (particularly in the online environment), Discussion Questions have been added for all Toolkit Activities, Case Studies, and Self-Assessments.

- *New and updated Case Studies*—All of the cases have been either replaced or expanded in length. A new feature for the second edition is that each chapter will have one or two longer cases (3,000–5,000 words) selected from SAGE business cases (these cases are provided on the Instructor Resources website).

- *New digital resources*—The second edition also comes with a SAGE coursepack, which houses all of the dynamic digital resources and is specifically designed for your learning management system. A SAGE coursepack is a simple and user-friendly solution for building your online teaching and course management environment. Chapter pretests (25 multiple-choice questions) and posttests (40 multiple-choice questions) and Premium SAGE video tied to assessment questions provide additional critical thinking practice.

- *Premium SAGE videos*—Original SAGE videos have been added to the new edition and are tied to chapter learning objectives to reinforce the evidence-based learning approach.

Updated Chapters

Each chapter has been thoroughly updated to include new developments, new scholarship, and recent events in organizational behavior.

Chapter 1: What Is Organizational Behavior?

- Expanded discussion of the history of OB, and new discussion of additional disciplines contributing to OB (psychology, sociology, anthropology).

- Expanded outcomes of OB now include organizational commitment, organizational citizenship behavior, and employee well-being.

- Expanded coverage of critical thinking and evidence-based management.

- Added coverage of Theory X/Y as an example of how OB influences performance, and a new self-assessment on Theory X/Y.

- New Research in Action box on "How Google Proved Management Matters."

- Revised Leadership Implications section now focuses on critical thinking.

Chapter 2: Personality and Person–Environment Fit

- New chapter that focuses on personality and person–environment fit; the chapter on individual differences has been split into Personality and Person–Environment Fit (Chapter 2) and Emotions and Moods (Chapter 3).

- Updated psychological capital (PsyCap) materials and a new Best Practices box on PsyCap training interventions.

- New section on Machiavellianism and "the Dark Triad."

- Added coverage of additional personality traits (self-monitoring, risk taking, and core self-evaluation) and Holland's personality–job fit theory.

- Person–environment fit has been added to this chapter and includes person–organization and person–job fit.

- New Case Study added: "Who Would You Hire?"

Chapter 3: Emotions and Moods

- New chapter.

- New opening vignette, "Does Lack of Sleep Make You Grumpy?"

- Affective events theory is now presented as an organizing framework for the chapter.

- Expanded coverage of emotional intelligence.

- New material on team emotional contagion, affective climate, the circumplex model (with a new figure), and gratitude.

- The Leadership Implications focus on affective coaching skills.

- New Toolkit Activity, "The 5-minute Gratitude Exercise," and two new Self-Assessments: "The Emotion Regulation Questionnaire (ERQ)" and "Positive and Negative Affect Schedule (PANAS)."

- New Case Study, "Managing Your Boss's Moods and Emotions."

Chapter 4: Attitudes and Job Satisfaction

- Updated opening vignette with 2016 Society of Human Resource Management job satisfaction report data (and a new figure).

- Expanded section on job search attitudes.

- Expanded section on employee engagement, which includes an updated figure on "Employee Engagement and Work Outcomes" to reflect the most recent data from Gallup, and a new figure called "Employee Engagement Improves Financial Results."

- New Self-Assessment, "How Much Career Adaptability Do You Have?"

Chapter 5: Perception, Decision Making, and Problem Solving

- Revised chapter now covers perception, decision making, and problem solving.

- Expanded discussion of wicked organizational problems.

- New Research in Action box that covers "Leading Creativity."

- New Toolkit Activity for decision making, "The Oil Drilling Partnership."

- A new Case Study on SABMiller's decision making has been added.

Chapter 6: Leadership

- Chapter has been split into two chapters (Leadership, Chapter 6, and Power and Politics, Chapter 7).

- Updated opening vignette with new 2016 Edelman Trust Barometer data (and a new figure).

- New figure showing a timeline of the "Development of Modern Leadership Theory."

- New coverage of the trait approach, attributions and leader–member relationships, moral approaches, and the critiques of leadership theory.

- Expanded coverage of situational approaches and path–goal theory in more detail.

- Added discussion of "Attributions and Leader–Member Relationships."

- New Best Practices box on narcissistic leadership.

- A new Toolkit Activity has been added, "Comparing Supervisor Leader–Member Exchange," and two new Self-Assessments, "Mentoring Functions Questionnaire" and "How Trustful are You?"

- Expanded Case Study, "Which Boss Would You Rather Work For?"

Chapter 7: Power and Politics

- New chapter with a new opening vignette on "What Is It Like to Have Power?"

- New discussion of followership has been added in the definition of power and influence.

- Added examples to clarify the Bases of Power section.

- New Research in Action Box, "Can Power Make Followers Speechless?"

- Expanded discussions on organizational sources of power, perceptions and politics, and political skill.

- New Leadership Implications section, "Managing With Power."
- Two new Toolkit Activities: "Politics or Citizenship?" and "What Would You Do?" (which focuses on examples of bosses' unethical use of power).
- New Case Study, "Can You Succeed Without Power?"

Chapter 8: Motivation: Core Concepts

- Added discussion on regulatory goal focus theory has been added to the section on Goal Setting.
- New section on Work Redesign and Job Stress.
- The discussion of expectancy theory has been expanded to include guidelines for leaders.
- Revised Leadership Implications discusses motivation to lead (MTL) research.
- New Toolkit Activity, "Understanding the Pygmalion Effect."

Chapter 9: Motivation: Applications

- Expanded discussion of pros and cons of performance appraisal, and a new example of how companies are getting rid of performance appraisal (Deloitte Consulting).
- New discussion of alternative work arrangements as forms of compensation/rewards (flexible working hours, job sharing, telecommuting, and sabbaticals).
- Expanded Leadership Implications section discusses current trends and the increase in the centrality of the leader to performance management and motivation processes with "Motivating With Rewards."
- Expanded Lilly Ledbetter/Goodyear Tire and Rubber case discusses equal pay, the gender wage gap, and updated statistics on the wage gap.

Chapter 10: Group Processes and Teams

- Reorganized to improve the flow of the topics.
- New opening vignette, "Does Trust Impact Team Performance?"
- Updated section on team creativity now includes innovation.
- Added discussion of social identity theory.
- Expanded section on diversity and multicultural teams covers the challenges and benefits of team diversity.
- Expanded coverage of virtual teams.
- New Case Study on virtual teams.
- New Self-Assessment, "The Team Leadership Inventory (TLI)," has been added.

Chapter 11: Managing Conflict and Negotiation

- New opening vignette with statistics on the costs of workplace conflict.

- Updated and expanded coverage on planned conflict, devil's advocate, the negotiation process, third-party interventions, and workplace incivility.

- New material on abusive supervision, toxic workplaces, and union–management negotiations has been added to this chapter.

Chapter 12: Organizational Communication

- Updated opening vignette on "thin-slicing" includes a discussion of communication networks and recent research on strong versus weak ties.

- Updated sections on electronic communication and nonverbal communication.

- New list of the functions that nonverbal communication serves in organizations has been added.

- Expanded Leadership Implications section on "The Management of Meaning" now includes a list of guidelines for leadership and communication.

- New Case Study on the use of apps at work, "What's App-ening?"

Chapter 13: Diversity and Cross-Cultural Adjustments

- Updated opening vignette on diversity being a key workforce trend.

- Updated coverage of generations at the workplace now includes examples and a new section, "What's Next? Generation Z."

- New discussion of Hofstede's new dimension, indulgence versus restraint.

- Expanded discussion of expatriates and repatriation.

- The Leadership Implications section has been expanded and addresses both diversity and cross-cultural adjustment in "Becoming a Global Leader."

- New Self-Assessment, "Do You Have A Global Mind-Set?"

Chapter 14: Organizational Culture

- New opening vignette, "Culture Change at Verizon: Can You Hear Me Now?"

- New section on markets, bureaucracies, and clans (and a new table).

- Expanded discussions of symbols and language with additional examples.

- Added coverage of ethical culture and onboarding.

- New section on the attraction-selection-attrition model has been added.

Chapter 15: Leading Change and Stress Management

- New opening vignette, "INGs Agile Transformation" (an example of structural change through organizational design), has been added.

- New section on work–school conflict.

- Updated Leadership Implications section has been rewritten to tie together the themes of leading change and stress management in "Helping Employees Cope."

- Updated Toolkit Activities and Self-Assessments reflect both leading change and stress.

- Two expanded case studies: one on leading change, "We Have to Change: Alighting Innovation in the Utility Industry," and one on stress, "The Price of Entrepreneurship."

ONLINE RESOURCES

 Visit edge.sagepub.com/scandura2e

The edge every student needs

SAGE edge for instructors supports teaching by making it easy to integrate quality content and create a rich learning environment for students.

- **Test banks** tied to AACSB standards provide a diverse range of pre-written options as well as the opportunity to edit any question and/or insert personalized questions to effectively assess students' progress and understanding.

- **Sample course syllabi** for semester and quarter courses provide suggested models for structuring one's course.

- Editable, chapter-specific **PowerPoint® slides** offer complete flexibility for creating a multimedia presentation for the course.

- **Lecture outlines** summarize key concepts by chapter to ease preparation for lectures and class discussions.

- Sample **answers to in-text questions** ease preparation for lectures and class discussions.

- Lively and stimulating ideas for **class activities and exercises** that can be used in class and online to reinforce active learning. The activities apply to individual or group projects.

- **Teaching notes for cases** are designed for instructors to expand questions to students, or initiate class discussion.

- EXCLUSIVE! Access to full-text **SAGE journal articles** that have been carefully selected to support and expand on the concepts presented in each chapter to encourage students to think critically.

- **SAGE Business Cases** provide students with real-world cases and discussion questions for additional in-depth analysis.

- **Multimedia content** appeals to students with different learning styles.

SAGE edge for students provides a personalized approach to help students accomplish their coursework goals in an easy-to-use learning environment.

- Mobile-friendly **eFlashcards** strengthen understanding of key terms and concepts.

- Mobile-friendly practice **quizzes** allow for independent assessment by students of their mastery of course material.

- **Chapter summaries** with **learning objectives** reinforce the most important material.

- EXCLUSIVE! Access to full-text **SAGE journal articles** that have been carefully selected to support and expand on the concepts presented in each chapter.

- **SAGE Business Cases** provide students with real-world cases and discussion questions for additional in-depth analysis.

- **Video and multimedia content** appeals to students with different learning styles.

SAGE coursepacks

SAGE coursepacks makes it easy to import our quality instructor and student resource content into your school's LMS with minimal effort. Intuitive and simple to use, **SAGE coursepacks** gives you the control to focus on what really matters: customizing course content to meet your students' needs. The SAGE coursepacks, created specifically for this book, are customized and curated for use in Blackboard, Canvas, Desire2Learn (D2L), and Moodle.

In addition to the content available on the SAGE edge site, the coursepacks include **pedagogically robust assessment tools** that foster review, practice, and critical thinking, and offer a better, more complete way to measure student engagement, including:

- **Diagnostic chapter pretests and posttests** that identify opportunities for student improvement, track student progress, and ensure mastery of key learning objectives.

- **Instructions** on how to use and integrate the comprehensive assessments and resources provided.

- **Assignable video tied to learning objectives, with corresponding multimedia assessment tools** bring concepts to life that increase student engagement and appeal to different learning styles. The **video assessment questions** feed to your gradebook.

- **Integrated links to the eBook version** that make it easy to access the mobile-friendly version of the text, which can be read anywhere, anytime.

Interactive eBook

Essentials of Organizational Behavior 2e is also available as an **Interactive eBook** which can be packaged with the text for an additional $5 or purchased separately. The Interactive eBook offers hyperlinks to licensed videos, additional case studies, as well as carefully chosen articles, all from the same pages found in the printed text. Users will also have immediate access to study tools such as highlighting, bookmarking, note-taking/sharing, and more!

ACKNOWLEDGMENTS

My love of teaching began as a PhD student with the first course I taught. I am excited to bring my perspective on the field of OB as an integrated and evidence-based foundation for the development of leaders to more students. This has truly been a labor of love. I have reflected on the field of OB and realized that we have so very much to offer our students because of the research we have done. I am in awe of my OB colleagues around the world for their theoretical insights and their rigorous research. It is with gratitude and humility that I am offering this book to instructors and their students.

I would like to thank my students Monica Sharif, Ronnie Grant, and Jenny Chin for their assistance with various parts of this project. I am indebted to Stephanie Maynard-Patrick for writing case studies and working with me on the ancillary materials. I cannot express my gratitude enough for all of the authors and publishers that graciously allowed me to reprint their material in this book. I thank my principal mentors George Graen and Belle Rose Ragins for their support and insights throughout my career. I offer thanks to all of my colleagues in OB (too numerous to mention) who provide me with feedback and support on everything I do. My OB colleagues at the University of Miami read drafts of the table of contents and chapters and offered suggestions for the toolkits (and allowed me to test them in their courses): Cecily Cooper, Marie Dasborough, Linda Neider, Chet Schriesheim, and Gergana Todorova. My family and friends suffered through my periods of being a hermit and patiently listened to me talk about this book. I thank my family Laura Scandura Rea, Sandi Kennedy, Deanne Julifs, and Tommy Scandura for always believing in me—and not just with respect to this textbook. I would also like to thank my friends for their practical, down-to-earth advice and for making me laugh at just the right times. Last, but in no way least, I thank the team at SAGE. Alissa Nance kept track of permissions and numerous other details. I greatly appreciate all of the retweets from Lori Hart. I am also grateful to Maggie Stanley and Lauren Holmes for their support throughout the project. They encouraged me to "hear" reviewer feedback but always respected my vison for the book. Special thanks to Cynthia Nalevanko at SAGE for encouraging me to write a textbook and getting me in touch with the right people to discuss this project. Thanks also to Katie Ancheta, Liz Thornton, Erica DeLuca, Ashlee Blunk, Gail Buschman, and Candice Harman at SAGE for their excellent work on this project. Without all of these people in their various ways of supporting me, this book would not have been possible.

I am grateful to the reviewers of this textbook who applied their own critical perspectives to the chapters. They made this textbook better in every way, and I learned from their insightful comments and suggestions what additional research evidence to include. Thanks to the following reviewers for their participation in all stages of this book's development:

Reviewers for the first edition:

Joel Baldomir, Marist College

Nancy Sutton Bell, University of Montevallo

James W. Bishop, New Mexico State University

Michael Buckley, University of Oklahoma

Carrie Bulger, Quinnipiac University

Jim Byran, Fresno Pacific University

Nicholas Capozzoli, Indiana University Kokomo

Eric Chen, University of Saint Joseph

Cecily Cooper, University of Miami

Geni D. Cowan, California State University, Sacramento

Minerva Cruz, Kentucky State University

Roger Dean, Washington & Lee University

Roselynn S. Dow, Empire State College

Mary Lynn Engel, Saint Joseph's College

Leon Fraser, Rutgers University

Mary Ann Gall, Franklin Pierce University

Issam Ghazzawi, University of La Verne

Bruce Gilstrap, University of Southern Mississippi

Daniel E. Hallock, University of North Alabama

Marie Hansen, Husson University

Nell Hartley, Robert Morris University

Carol Harvey, Suffolk University

Chan Hellman, University of Oklahoma

Kimberly Hunley, Northern Arizona University

Carrie S. Hurst, Tennessee State University

Jay Jacobson, Marquette University

C. Douglas Johnson, Georgia Gwinnett College

Charles Kramer, University of La Verne

Kim Lukaszewski, New Paltz SUNY

David McCalman, University of Central Arkansas

DeNisha McCollum, John Brown University

Roberta Michel, Oakland University

Ivan Muslin, Marshall University

Charlena Patterson, Catholic University of America

Jeff Paul, University of Tulsa

Adam Payne, Bentley University—Northeastern University

Mim Plavin-Masterman, Worcester State University

Hannah Rothstein, Baruch College

John Rowe, Florida Gateway College

Carol Saunders, University of Central Florida

Mehmet Sincar, University of Gaziantep

Katherine Sliter, Indiana University—Purdue University

Barbara Stuart, University of Denver

Douglas Threet, Foothill College

Becky J. Timmons, University of Arkansas–Fort Smith

Robert Toronto, University of Michigan-Dearborn

Barbara A. Wech, University of Alabama at Birmingham

Heather Wherry, Bellevue University

Robert Whitcomb, Western Nevada College

Lissa Whyte-Morazan, Brookline College

Lisa V. Williams, Niagara University

Herb Wong, John F. Kennedy University

Jody A. Worley, University of Oklahoma

Chulguen (Charlie) Yang, Southern Connecticut State University

Reviewers for the second edition:

Paul Axelrod, University of San Francisco

Angela Balog, St. Francis University

Carl Blencke, University of Central Florida

Samuel Faught, University of Tennessee

Nancy Hanson-Rasmussen, University of Wisconsin

Christopher Hartwell, Utah State University

Dwight Hite, Cameron University

Julie Hood, Nyack College

Renee Just, Catawba College

William Liang, Brenau University

Stephanie Maynard-Patrick, St. Thomas University

Roberta Michel, Oakland University, Michigan

Terry Nelson, University of Alaska, Anchorage

Charmaine Rose, St. Thomas University

Rebecca Bull Schaefer, Gonzaga University

Pamela Van Dyke, Southern Methodist University

ABOUT THE AUTHOR

Terri A. Scandura is currently a Professor of Management in the School of Business Administration at the University of Miami. From 2007 to 2012, she served as Dean of the Graduate School of the University. Her fields of interest include leadership, mentorship, and applied research methods. She has been a visiting scholar in Japan, Australia, Hong Kong, China, and the United Arab Emirates.

Dr. Scandura has authored or co-authored over 200 presentations, articles, and book chapters. Her research has been published in the *Academy of Management Journal*, the *Journal of Applied Psychology*, the *Journal of International Business Studies*, the *Journal of Vocational Behavior*, the *Journal of Organizational Behavior*, *Educational and Psychological Measurement*, *Industrial Relations*, *Research in Organizational Behavior*, *Research in Personnel and Human Resource Management*, and others.

She has presented executive education programs on leadership, mentoring, leading change, and high-performance teams to numerous organizations such as VISA International, Royal Caribbean Cruise Lines, the Young Presidents Organization, Hewlett-Packard, and Baptist Health Systems.

Dr. Scandura is a Fellow of the Society for Industrial & Organizational Psychology, the American Psychological Association, and the Southern Management Association. She is a member of the Society of Organizational Behavior and the Academy of Management. She is a past associate editor for *Group & Organization Management*, the *Journal of International Business Studies*, the *Journal of Management*, and *Organizational Research Methods*. She currently serves on editorial boards for major journals including *The Leadership Quarterly*, *Organizational Research Methods*, and *Group & Organization Management*.

INTRODUCTION

CHAPTER 1 · What Is Organizational Behavior?

Introduction

Chapter 1: What Is Organizational Behavior?

Understanding Individuals in Organizations

Chapter 2: Personality and Person–Environment Fit

Chapter 3: Emotions and Moods

Chapter 4: Attitudes and Job Satisfaction

Chapter 5: Perception, Decision Making, and Problem Solving

Influencing and Motivating Employees

Chapter 6: Leadership

Chapter 7: Power and Politics

Chapter 8: Motivation: Core Concepts

Chapter 9: Motivation: Applications

Building Relationships

Chapter 10: Group Processes and Teams

Chapter 11: Managing Conflict and Negotiation

Chapter 12: Organizational Communication

Chapter 13: Diversity and Cross-Cultural Adjustments

Leaders as Change Agents

Chapter 14: Organizational Culture

Chapter 15: Leading Change and Stress Management

WHAT IS ORGANIZATIONAL BEHAVIOR?

Learning Objectives

After studying this chapter, you should be able to do the following:

1.1: Define the concept of organizational behavior (OB).

1.2: List and give examples of the four sources of information used in evidence-based management (EBM).

1.3: Define critical thinking, and explain the critical thinking skills leaders need.

1.4: Describe the scientific method used in OB research.

1.5: Discuss five types of outcome variables studied in OB.

1.6: Compare the levels of analysis in OB research.

1.7: Develop plans for using OB research to improve employee job performance.

1.8: Compare and contrast Theory X and Theory Y assumptions.

Get the edge on your studies at **edge.sagepub.com/scandura2e**

- Take the chapter quiz
- Review key terms with eFlashcards
- Explore multimedia resources, SAGE readings, and more!

A CRISIS OF LEADERSHIP?

Recent polls conducted by the Gallup organization show that about 70% of people who hold full-time jobs in the United States either hate their jobs or have "mentally checked out."[1] In December 2015, the majority of workers were "not engaged" (50.8%), while another 17.2% were "actively disengaged." This is a large impact considering that an estimated 100 million people work full time in the United States. Even worse, many of the Gallup survey respondents reported actively engaging in destructive behavior by spreading their dissatisfaction throughout their organizations. Workers who hate their jobs affect the organization's bottom line. One recent analysis estimates that low engagement costs U.S. companies over $350 billion in revenue every year, and disengaged employees are more likely to quit their jobs, resulting in another $11 billion that employers spend to replace them, according to statistics from the Bureau of National Affairs.[2] One of the most important things the Gallup study found is that the source of dissatisfaction is not pay or the number of hours worked, however.

Most employees in Gallup's studies consistently report that the reason for their disengagement from work is their boss. And this is not new. This study was a follow-up of an earlier study conducted since 2010, which showed similar discontent with work and bosses. The graph in Figure 1.1 shows that employee engagement has been stagnant over the years, with no significant improvement. Why? Isn't there something that can be done to improve the well-being, motivation, and productivity of people at work? Is anyone working on addressing the concerns of the workforce? The answer is yes. There is a field of study called **organizational behavior** (or sometimes called OB for short) that studies the challenges leaders face in the workforce. Unfortunately, much of the knowledge that could help leaders improve the experience of work is tucked away in scientific journals that few managers have the time to read.

The goal of this book is to help you become an effective leader—not the kind of leader described in the Gallup poll that produces discontented and unengaged workers. You can choose to be a leader who understands the fundamentals of OB—how to motivate followers, resolve conflicts, lead teams, and even help them manage stress during change. For example, effective communication is essential for leadership, and this is covered in Chapter 12. After reading this textbook, your approach to leading others will be grounded in the most important and current research conducted on organizations.

WHAT IS ORGANIZATIONAL BEHAVIOR?

Learning Objective 1.1: Define the concept of organizational behavior (OB).

OB is defined as the study of individuals and their behaviors at work. It is a multidisciplinary and multilevel research area that draws from applied psychology, cultural anthropology, communication, and sociology. This textbook draws upon all of these areas with a focus on applied social psychology. Social psychologists study the behavior of individuals in groups, so it makes sense that the study of how leaders influence people and their OB is grounded in this field of psychology.

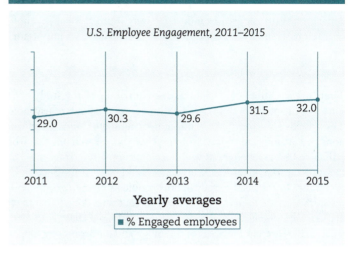

Figure 1.1   Employee Engagement Stagnant

U.S. Employee Engagement, 2011–2015

29.0   30.3   29.6   31.5   32.0

2011   2012   2013   2014   2015

Yearly averages

■ % Engaged employees

Source: Gallup (2016). Employee engagement in U.S. stagnant in 2015. Retrieved from http://www.gallup.com/poll/188144/employee-engagement-stagnant-2015.aspx

OB is a relatively young field in comparison to areas in the field of medicine—and even psychology from which it draws. There were management practices in place since the early 1900s with Frederick Taylor's approach to "scientific management," which was the study of how work could be designed to make production work (particularly assembly lines) more efficient.[3] Most scholars agree, however, that OB originated with the human relations movement[4] ignited by the Hawthorne studies (conducted between 1927 and 1932), which led to a focus on the role of human behavior in organizations. The Hawthorne studies were two studies conducted by Australian-born psychologist Elton Mayo at the Western Electric Company near Chicago.[5]

Mayo spent most of his career at Harvard University and was interested in how to increase productivity in assembly lines. The first study was designed to examine the effects of lighting in the plants on worker productivity. However, the research team had a surprise. Productivity *increased* rather than decreased even though the lights were being dimmed. Perplexed by this finding, the research team interviewed the workers and learned that the workers appreciated the attention of the research team and felt that they were receiving special treatment. And then productivity *declined* after the researchers left the plant. This has been called the **Hawthorne effect** and refers to positive responses in attitudes and performance when researchers pay attention to a particular group of workers.

The second Hawthorne study was designed to investigate a new incentive system. However, instead of the incentive system increasing workers' production, the social pressure from peers took over and had more impact on worker productivity than pay increases. Workers formed into small groups and set informal standards for production, requiring coworkers to reduce their production so pay was more equal among the group members.

The Hawthorne researchers concluded that the human element in organizations was more important than previously thought, and they learned that workers want attention. This is still relevant today. For example, recent work demonstrates that when employers provide gifts to employees (termed *empathy wages*), it elicits feelings of gratitude from them.[6] The "human relations" movement followed the Hawthorne studies, and OB emerged as a distinct field of study in the 1950s. The term *organizational behavior* first appeared in 1957 in a book by Chris Argyris, *Personality and Organization: The Conflict Between System and the Individual.*[7] Today, OB researchers have PhDs from psychology departments (in the area of industrial and organizational psychology) and business schools. They teach from the research base on OB and conduct research that addresses important challenges facing organizational leaders today.

Disciplines Contributing to Organizational Behavior

There are a number of disciplines that contribute to the study of OB. Studies of individual differences such as personality (Chapter 2 of this textbook) draw from the fields of psychology and industrial and organizational psychology. These fields also contribute to our understanding of human performance. Individual reactions to work, such as emotions and attitudes, also draw from psychology research but also from social psychology. Motivation theory has been influenced by psychology as well as economics. Understanding decision making (Chapter 5) draws from economic theory. Research on leaders as influencers and motivators (Section III) draws from applied social psychology. **Applied social psychology** is the study of how people interact in groups and addresses significant challenges facing leaders as organizations use teams more regularly to get things done (Chapter 10). Trends such as the need to compete in a global marketplace, organizational restructuring, and rapid changes in technology have resulted in the need to lead through change. Research in the areas of sociology and anthropology help us understand organizational culture and leading change. OB is an applied field of study aimed at problem solving for organizational leaders. Thus, OB is a multidisciplinary field that draws upon the best ideas and research from several disciplines.

The goal of OB as a field is to improve the functioning of the organization and how employees experience their work. For example, OB researchers study how job satisfaction affects employee well-being. Another example is how a leader's vision affects follower motivation and performance toward goals. A third example is how perceptions of politics at work might lead to an employee quitting the organization (this is called *turnover*). Low productivity and turnover cost organizations millions of dollars. Beyond the impact on costs, employee well-being is a major concern for forward-thinking organizations today. OB researchers develop guidelines that directly address such challenges. Based on research, leaders can make better decisions to make their organization more effective and better places to work. It's important for OB researchers to translate their evidence into practical guidelines for managers to follow. Next, the journey from theory to practical applications will be discussed.

From Theory to Practice

OB is an applied science, so first it is necessary to briefly review what science is all about. The goals of science—any science—are as follows:

1. **Description:** What does the process look like?

2. **Prediction:** Will the process occur again? And when?

3. **Explanation:** Why is this happening?

4. **Control:** Can we change whether or not this happens?

For example, the forecasting of extra workers needed for a toy store during the holiday season is an important process for ensuring the best customer service. Human resource managers have an understanding of how many customers will visit the store based upon prior holiday seasons (in other words, a theory) and can describe their need for extra workers. This theory is also fairly high on explanation since the store managers have some understanding of why customers visit their store and when volume increases. Prediction is important since managers need to project with some accuracy how many extra seasonal workers they will need to hire to ensure that customers will be served and not have long wait times at the cash registers. However, hiring forecasts are not always accurate, resulting in unhappy customers or the hiring of too many seasonal workers that wait idly for customers to visit. In this example, the science is moderate for prediction. For control, one could say that the science is low because there are many reasons why customers may not visit the store that are outside of the organization's control (e.g., customers may be able to purchase the toys online). This example illustrates why theories are so important to applied science. The better the initial understanding of how many workers will be needed, the better the store manager should be able to predict how many seasonal workers to hire for the season and for how long. Theories are important to OB as a science since theory is translated into practical advice for managers, and this is illustrated by Google's Project Oxygen in the boxed insert.

The phrase "there is nothing as practical as a good theory" has been attributed to social psychologist Kurt Lewin. Theories build upon prior research and extend into new areas of importance to leaders. A researcher generates hypotheses about human behavior in organizations and then gathers data to test it. Research eliminates the guesswork about what will work (or not work), and this helps leaders solve the problems they face every day. The ability to translate research to practice has been termed **evidence-based management (EBM)**.

RESEARCH IN ACTION

How Google Proved Management Matters

Google faced a challenge. Ever since the company started, it's highly trained and self-motivated engineers questioned whether they needed managers. In the high-technology culture, employees actually believed that managers did more harm than good. But Google grew rapidly and by 2013 had 37,000 employees with just 5,000 managers, 1,000 directors, and 100 vice presidents. The organizational structure was flat rather than hierarchical. How could Google's managers convince its skeptical employees that they needed managers to operate effectively and remain competitive?

Google launched Project Oxygen to prove that managers don't make a difference (this was their hypothesis). "Luckily, we failed," said project co-lead Neal Patel. To accomplish the goal, they hired several PhD researchers to form a people analytics team. As with everything Google does, they applied hypothesis-driven research methods to analyze the "soft skills" of managers. Project Oxygen was a multiyear research study designed to uncover the key management behaviors that predict employee satisfaction and organizational effectiveness. One part of the project was an employee survey about their managers' behaviors. The research team also interviewed employees

who were quitting about the behaviors of their managers and why they were leaving Google. The team discovered that there was less turnover on teams with the best managers. They also documented a statistical relationship between high-scoring managers' behaviors and employee satisfaction. So they concluded that managers did matter and then conducted another study to learn specifically what Google's best managers did.

Here's what they found. Project Oxygen identified eight behaviors shared by high-scoring managers:

- Is a good coach
- Empowers the team and does not micromanage
- Expresses interest in, and concern for, team members' success and personal well-being
- Is productive and results-oriented
- Is a good communicator — listens and shares information
- Helps with career development
- Has a clear vision and strategy for the team
- Has key technical skills that help him or her advise the team

Because this project was evidence-based, the sceptical engineers were convinced that the best managers did make a difference. In describing

(Continued)

Project Oxygen, David A. Garvin from the Harvard Business School notes: "Data-driven cultures, Google-discovered, respond well to data-driven change." Google now offers training and feedback to low-scoring managers. However, they learned that the best approach is to have panels of highly rated managers tell their stories about how they coach and empower their teams. Rather than being told what to do by upper management, they get advice from their colleagues.

Discussion Questions:

1. Why did they use an evidence-based approach? Describe the type(s) of evidence Google used in their research.
2. Are you convinced that managers matter? Why or why not? What additional evidence would you like to see?
3. Create a brief description of the design for the next steps in Project Oxygen to further develop Google's managers.

Source: Garvin, D. A. (2013). How Google sold its engineers on management. Retrieved from https://hbr.org/2013/12/how-google-sold-its-engineers-on-management; Kamensky, J. M. (2014). Does management matter? Retrieved from http://www.business ofgovernment.org/blog/business-government/does-management-matter

EVIDENCE-BASED MANAGEMENT

Learning Objective 1.2: List and give examples of the four sources of information used in evidence-based management (EBM).

The term *evidence-based* was originally employed in the field of medicine to guide how doctors make decisions regarding patient care. EBM improves a leader's decisions by disciplined application of the most relevant and current scientific evidence. Although many definitions of EBM are available, this is the most frequently quoted and widely used:[8] EBM means making decisions about the management of employees, teams, or organizations through the conscientious, explicit, and judicious use of four sources of information:

1. **The best available scientific evidence**—for example, research published on OB
2. **The best available organizational evidence**—for example, interviews or surveys completed by people in an organization
3. **The best available experiential evidence**—for example, the intuition of the leader and his or her expert opinions
4. **Organizational values and stakeholders' concerns**—for example, stock price or groups that focus on whether the organization employs environmentally friendly practices

How can a leader use these sources of evidence to make better decisions? First, leaders must have the ability (basic skills and competencies), motivation (behavioral beliefs, behavioral control, and normative beliefs), and opportunity (support that overcomes barriers) to practice EBM.[9] For example, EBM was applied to an operational problem in a hospital. Researchers tracked the process through interviews. An EBM decision process was implemented by a physician manager. This research concluded that the "fit" between the decision maker and the organizational context enables more effective evidence-based processes.[10] Leader involvement at all levels is essential for EBM to work in practice,[11] as well as collaboration with researchers.[12]

The following standards may be applied by leaders using EBM to ask questions and challenge their thinking about their organizations:[13]

1. **Stop treating old ideas as if they were brand new.** This has resulted in a cynical workforce that may view innovations from leaders as short-term fads (e.g., positive changes such as total quality management, teams, and engagement). Progress cannot be made by treating old ideas as new ones; cynicism could be reduced by presenting ideas that have been able to "stand the test of time" as best practices rather than new ideas.

2. **Be suspicious of "breakthrough" studies and ideas.** Question whether some new ideas in management are really breakthroughs, and be wary of claims about new management principles that may be either overstated or understated.[14]

3. **Develop and celebrate collective brilliance.**[15] In theory, a diverse collection of independent decision makers (although not expert) makes better predictions on the average compared to an expert decision maker. In a sense, this is how the "ask the audience" lifeline works on the game show *Who Wants to Be a Millionaire?* A contestant can ask the audience for the answer to a question and the audience votes. The contestant then sees the percentages of people who chose each answer. It's interesting to see that often the audience is right. The contestant is thus gathering the collective brilliance of a random group of decision makers. See the following box for another method that may be used to develop collective brilliance: the Delphi decision-making method.

4. **Emphasize drawbacks as well as virtues.** An interesting example of this is the marketing of an energy drink called Cocaine. Cocaine contains three and a half times the amount of caffeine as Red Bull. It was pulled from U.S. shelves in 2007 after the FDA declared that its producers, Redux Beverages, were marketing their drink as an alternative to street drugs, and this was determined to be illegal. The FDA pointed to the drink's labeling and advertising, which included the statements "Speed in a Can" and "Cocaine—Instant Rush." Despite the controversy, Redux Beverages continued to produce and market the beverage in limited markets and online.[16]

5. **Use success (and failure) stories to illustrate sound practices but not in place of a valid research method.** For example, Circuit City went bankrupt in 2009 but was a "great company" in the now-classic book *Good to Great*. What happened to Circuit City? Alan Wurtzel, the former CEO and the son of the founder, saw the threats coming from Best Buy and Amazon in the early 2000s, and he knew the company was headed for decline. "After I left, my successors became very focused on the bottom line—the profit margin," Wurtzel told a group at the University of Richmond. "They were too focused on Wall Street. That was the beginning of the end," said the former CEO as he recalled the rise and fall of the great company.[17] The lesson here is that no matter how great a company is, care must be taken not to simply copy what they do in today's changing business environment. There is no substitute for a careful analysis and diagnosis before embarking on a search for solutions.

6. **Adopt a neutral stance toward ideologies and theories.** An example of this is that most management "gurus" are from North America (e.g., Peter Drucker, Tom Peters, Ken Blanchard). This is not to say that their ideology isn't useful. However, in a global world, EBM demands that we question whether ideology developed in North America applies abroad. EBM would also suggest that we search for theories developed overseas to locate experts from other countries with important ideas.

BEST PRACTICES

Using the Delphi Method to Harness Collective Brilliance

The Delphi method is a systematic decision-making technique that employs a panel of independent experts. It was developed by the RAND Corporation in the 1950s by Olaf Helmer and Norman Dalkey to systematically solicit the view of experts related to national defense. The term *Delphi* originates from Greek mythology. Delphi was the site of the Delphic oracle, where people would go to get insight from the gods. Thus, the method was thought of as brainstorming by a panel of experts.

Here's how it works. An expert panel is chosen and given a proposal. Members of the group are selected because they are experts or they have information related to the problem. Next, a series of questionnaires or surveys are sent to the experts (the Delphi group) through a facilitator who oversees the process. The group does not meet face-to-face. All communication is normally in writing (typically e-mail). Experts are given a proposal and complete an assessment of it over several rounds. These experts can be co-located or they can be dispersed geographically and submit their ideas from anywhere in the world electronically. The responses are collected and analyzed to determine conflicting viewpoints on each point. The process continues in order to work toward synthesis and building consensus. After each round, a facilitator provides an anonymous summary of the experts' predictions or problem solutions from the previous round as well as the rationale each expert provided. Participants are encouraged to revise their earlier solutions in light of the replies of other members of the group. Over time, the expert panel converges on the best solution or prediction. This technique allows a leader to gather information from a wide range of expert sources to make better decisions, thereby utilizing the wisdom of many (or collective brilliance).

The success of this process depends upon the facilitator's expertise and communication skills. Also, each response requires adequate time for reflection and analysis. The major merits of the Delphi process are

- elimination of interpersonal problems,
- efficient use of experts' time,
- diversity of ideas, and
- accuracy of solutions and predictions.

Discussion Questions:

1. How should experts used in a Delphi decision-making process be selected? Would paying experts influence their participation in the process and/or the outcome?

2. To harness collective brilliance using Delphi, how many decision makers do you think should

   be invited to participate? In other words, is there a minimum number to gain a broad-enough perspective? How many is too many?

3. Do you feel that this process is worth the time and effort to improve a decision? Why or why not?

Sources: Delbecq, A. L., Van de Ven, A. H., & Gustafson, D. H. (1975). *Group techniques for program planning: A guide to nominal group and Delphi processes.* Glenview, IL: Scott, Foresman; Clark, D. R. (2010). Delphi decision making technique. Retrieved from http://nwlink.com/~donclark//perform/delphi_process.html; Hsu, C. C., & Sandford, B. A. (2007). The Delphi technique: Making sense of consensus. *Practical Assessment, Research & Evaluation, 12*(10), 1–8.

In making important organizational decisions, the leader may include information gathered from one or all four of the sources described previously in the definition of EBM. This can result in a lot of information. So how can a leader sort through it all and determine what is most relevant to the problem at hand? The answer lies in critical thinking, a process that has been developed for over 2,500 years, beginning with the ancient Greeks and the Socratic Method, which is the process of learning by questioning everything. Critical thinking skills are applied to sort through all of the information gathered and then prioritize it (and even discard evidence that appears to be invalid or irrelevant to the problem).

WHAT IS CRITICAL THINKING?

Learning Objective 1.3: Define critical thinking, and explain the critical thinking skills leaders need.

Critical thinking can be defined as follows: "Critical thinking calls for persistent effort to examine any belief or supposed form of knowledge in the light of evidence that supports it and the further conclusions to which it tends."[18] Critical thinking is a mode of thinking about a problem we face where the problem solver improves the quality of the process by taking control of it and applying rigorous standards. The process has been described as having three interrelated parts:

1. the *elements of thought* (reasoning);

2. the *intellectual standards* that applied to the elements of reasoning; and

3. the *intellectual traits* associated with a cultivated critical thinker that result from the consistent and disciplined application of the intellectual standards to the elements of thought.[19]

Critical thinking involves using justification; recognizing relationships; evaluating the credibility of sources; looking at reasons or evidence; drawing inferences; identifying alternatives, logical deductions, sequences, and order; and defending an idea. Critical thinking requires the decision maker in an organization to apply a complex skill set to solve the problem at hand. A set of guidelines for critical thinking is shown in Table 1.1.[20] Critical thinking is, in short, self-directed, self-disciplined, self-monitored, and self-corrective thinking. It requires rigorous standards of problem solving and a commitment to overcome the inclination to think that we have all of the answers.[21] A recent study demonstrated that students' attitudes toward and beliefs about critical thinking skills is related to their GPA due to effective argumentation and reflective thinking. [22]

Table 1.1 Critical Thinking Skills

No one always acts purely objectively and rationally. We connive for selfish interests. We gossip, boast, exaggerate, and equivocate. It is "only human" to wish to validate our prior knowledge, to vindicate our prior decisions, or to sustain our earlier beliefs. In the process of satisfying our ego, however, we can often deny ourselves intellectual growth and opportunity. We may not always want to apply critical thinking skills, but we should have those skills available to be employed when needed.

Critical thinking includes a complex combination of skills. Among the main characteristics are the following:

Skills	We are thinking critically when we do the following:
Rationality	• Rely on reason rather than emotion • Require evidence, ignore no known evidence, and follow evidence where it leads • Are concerned more with finding the best explanation than being right, analyzing apparent confusion, and asking questions
Self-awareness	• Weigh the influences of motives and bias • Recognize our own assumptions, prejudices, biases, or point of view

(Continued)

Table 1.1 (Continued)	
Honesty	• Recognize emotional impulses, selfish motives, nefarious purposes, or other modes of self-deception
Open-mindedness	• Evaluate all reasonable inferences • Consider a variety of possible viewpoints or perspectives • Remain open to alternative interpretations • Accept a new explanation, model, or paradigm because it explains the evidence better, is simpler, or has fewer inconsistencies or covers more data • Accept new priorities in response to a reevaluation of the evidence or reassessment of our real interests • Do not reject unpopular views out of hand
Discipline	• Are precise, meticulous, comprehensive, and exhaustive • Resist manipulation and irrational appeals • Avoid snap judgments
Judgment	• Recognize the relevance and/or merit of alternative assumptions and perspectives • Recognize the extent and weight of evidence
In sum:	• Critical thinkers are by nature skeptical. They approach texts with the same skepticism and suspicion as they approach spoken remarks. • Critical thinkers are active, not passive. They ask questions and analyze. They consciously apply tactics and strategies to uncover meaning or assure their understanding. • Critical thinkers do not take an egotistical view of the world. They are open to new ideas and perspectives. They are willing to challenge their beliefs and investigate competing evidence.

Critical thinking enables us to recognize a wide range of subjective analyses of otherwise objective data and to evaluate how well each analysis might meet our needs. Facts may be facts, but how we interpret them may vary.

By contrast, passive, noncritical thinkers take a simplistic view of the world. They see things in black and white, as either/or, rather than recognizing a variety of possible understanding. They see questions as yes or no with no subtleties, they fail to see linkages and complexities, and they fail to recognize related elements.

Source: Kurland, D. (2000). Critical thinking skills. Retrieved from www.criticalreading.com

When it comes to asking questions, some of the best ideas come from a book by Ian Mitroff called *Smart Thinking for Crazy Times: The Art of Solving the Right Problems.*[23] Mitroff warns us about solving the wrong problems even though leaders solve them with great precision in organizations. This happens because they don't ask the right questions. Mitroff provides advice to managers who fall into the trap of solving the wrong problems by spelling out why managers do it in the first place. The five pathways to error are

1. picking the wrong stakeholders by not paying attention to who really cares about the problem;

2. selecting too narrow a set of options by overlooking better, more creative options;

3. phrasing a problem incorrectly by failing to consider at least one "technical" and one "human" variation in stating a problem;

4. setting the boundaries of a problem too narrowly by ignoring the system the problem is embedded in; and

5. failing to think systemically by ignoring the connection between parts of the problem and its whole.

So what questions should a manager be asking? Mitroff provides the following list of the basic questions facing all organizations (and ones we should be asking frequently if we expect to gain buy-in from employees for the implementation of their solutions):

- What businesses are we in?

- What businesses should we be in?

- What is our mission?

- What should our mission be?

- Who are our prime customers?

- Who should our customers be?

- How should we react to a major crisis, especially if we are, or are perceived to be, at fault?

- How will the outside world perceive our actions?

- Will others perceive the situation as we do?

- Are our products and services ethical?

In OB, there is a systematic method to answer questions. As the field was developing, scholars adopted much of their methodological approach from the social sciences, which were following research methods from the physical sciences. These methods are applied to address problems and opportunities faced by organizational leaders.

> **Critical Thinking Questions:** Why does asking these questions improve employee buy-in for the implementation of plans? Are there other questions you feel are important to ask?

THE SCIENTIFIC METHOD

Learning Objective 1.4: Describe the scientific method used in OB research.

How do OB researchers know what they know? As discussed earlier, it begins with a problem to solve. For example, a problem might be a leader's concern that only about 50% of their employees are satisfied with their work. First, the leader reviews the available knowledge on job satisfaction (i.e., the scientific evidence from EBM) and learns that the way supervisors treat followers may improve job satisfaction. Based on theory, the leader forms hypotheses, or predictions, regarding what might improve job satisfaction. An example of a hypothesis is "A leader's appreciation of workers' efforts will lead to increased job satisfaction." The next step is to collect observations from the organization. This might be, for example, through interviews with employees or surveys completed by employees. Once data are collected, the hypothesis is tested with statistical techniques. For additional information on the research designs that are used by open researchers, refer to the Appendix of this textbook.

The basic research process described previously is depicted in Figure 1.2. As the figure shows, research is an ongoing process that begins with observations that lead to interesting questions. Next, hypotheses and testable predictions are formulated. Data are collected to test these predictions and are then refined, altered, expanded, or rejected (the center of the figure). Based on these results, additional predictions and data collections follow until general theories of OB begin to emerge. These theories then lead us to frame additional observation, and the research cycle continues. As noted in the introduction to this chapter, OB is an applied field, and this is underscored by the typical outcome variables

Figure 1.2   The Scientific Method as an Ongoing Process

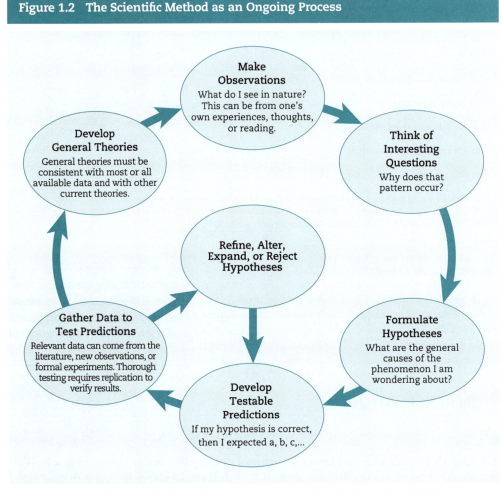

Make Observations
What do I see in nature? This can be from one's own experiences, thoughts, or reading.

Think of Interesting Questions
Why does that pattern occur?

Develop General Theories
General theories must be consistent with most or all available data and with other current theories.

Refine, Alter, Expand, or Reject Hypotheses

Formulate Hypotheses
What are the general causes of the phenomenon I am wondering about?

Gather Data to Test Predictions
Relevant data can come from the literature, new observations, or formal experiments. Thorough testing requires replication to verify results.

Develop Testable Predictions
If my hypothesis is correct, then I expected a, b, c,...

Source: Garland, T., Jr. (2016). *The scientific method as an ongoing process.* Riverside: University of California. Archived from the original on August 19, 2016.

that are studied. Researchers focus on outcomes that are of interest to leaders in organizations, such as employee job satisfaction and productivity. Next, the types of outcomes typically studied in OB research will be reviewed.

OUTCOME VARIABLES IN ORGANIZATIONAL BEHAVIOR

Learning Objective 1.5: Discuss five types of outcome variables studied in OB.

In the preceding example, leader appreciation of workers is the independent variable. Worker engagement is the dependent variable (i.e., it *depends* on the independent variable: leader appreciation). Since OB is an applied science, the outcome variables studied are typically variables that leaders are interested in improving. There are five broad groups of outcome variables studied: performance, work-related attitudes, employee well-being, motivation, and employee withdrawal.

Performance

Productivity (or **job performance**) is one of the most important outcomes in OB. Performance can be actual performance as collected in organizational records (e.g., the number of forms correctly processed in an insurance company) or it may be rated by supervisors and/or peers (e.g., the supervisor rates the follower's work quality on a scale of 1 to 7, with 1 being poor and 7 being outstanding). **Organizational citizenship behavior (OCB)** is the worker's willingness to go above and beyond what is required in his or her job description to help others at work.[24,25] OCB is considered to be performance beyond the expectations of a person's job description—extrarole performance. While OCB is often studied as an important performance outcome variable, it has also been shown that OCB predicts individual and organizational outcomes as well. A large-scale review of the OCB literature found that OCB predicts employee performance, reward-allocation decisions, and a variety of withdrawal-related criteria (employee turnover intentions, actual turnover, and absenteeism).[26]

Work-Related Attitudes

The measurement of work-related attitudes is an important aspect of OB research, and job satisfaction has long been studied as an outcome variable. For example, there is a measure of **job satisfaction** dating back to 1935 that is still employed in organizational studies today: the Hoppock Job Satisfaction Blank shown in Table 1.2.[27] Loyalty to an organization, known as **organizational commitment**, is another key attitude that has proven to be important because it is related to job satisfaction and is one of the strongest predictors of turnover.[28,29,30] Organizational commitment is an employee's relationship with the organization he or she works for.[31] In other words, OB researchers can measure a person's loyalty, and this predicts whether or not they will quit in the future. Also, lack of loyalty results in people being absent from work more often. Uncommitted workers are less motivated and perform at lower levels.[32] Another contemporary outcome variable that is

Table 1.2 A Measure of Job Satisfaction: The Hoppock Job Satisfaction Blank

A. Which **one** of the following shows how much of the time you feel satisfied with your job?
1. Never.
2. Seldom.
3. Occasionally.
4. About half of the time.
5. A good deal of the time.
6. Most of the time.
7. All the time.

B. Choose **one** of the following statements that best tells how well you like your job.
1. I hate it.
2. I dislike it.
3. I don't like it.
4. I am indifferent to it.
5. I like it.
6. I am enthusiastic about it.
7. I love it.

C. Which **one** of the following best tells how you feel about changing your job?
1. I would quit this job at once if I could.
2. I would take almost any other job in which I could earn as much as I am earning now.
3. I would like to change both my job and my occupation.
4. I would like to exchange my present job for another one.
5. I am not eager to change my job, but I would do so if I could get a better job.
6. I cannot think of any jobs for which I would exchange.
7. I would not exchange my job for any other.

D. Which **one** of the following shows how you think you compare with other people?
1. No one dislikes his job more than I dislike mine.
2. I dislike my job much more than most people dislike theirs.
3. I dislike my job more than most people dislike theirs.
4. I like my job about as well as most people like theirs.
5. I like my job better than most people like theirs.
6. I like my job much better than most people like theirs.
7. No one likes his job better than I like mine.

Source: Hoppock, R. (1935). *Job satisfaction.* New York, NY: Harper; McNichols, C. W., Stahl, M. J., & Manley, T. R. (1978). A validation of Hoppock's job satisfaction measure. *Academy of Management Journal, 21*(4), 737–742.

gaining research attention is employee engagement.[33] Employee engagement can be defined as "a relatively endur-ing state of mind referring to the simultaneous investment of personal energies in the experience or performance of work."[34] In Chapter 4 of this book, you will learn more about these and other work attitudes and how they are studied in OB research.

Employee Well-Being

In addition to job satisfaction, researchers are also interested in other indicators of **employee well-being**. Some studies examine outcomes such as emotional exhaustion, psychosomatic health complaints, and physical health symptoms.[35] Recent research has shown that leaders not doing their job (i.e., passive leadership) undermines employee well-being because having a weak leader increases role stress and depletes employees' psychological resources for coping with the stress.[36] Another study found that being asked to do an illegitimate task predicted lower employee well-being (lower self-esteem and job satisfaction with increased anger and depression). An illegitimate task is one that is outside of the boundaries of a person's job: "For example, an administrative assistant asked to care for an executive's child, while the executive attends a meeting may be feeling 'this is not my job!'"[37] The recommendations from these two studies for leaders seem clear: Being passive will affect your followers' well-being negatively, but so will giving them tasks that are inappropriate. Well-being has emerged as an important outcome variable in OB, and some studies have added engage-ment as another indicator of well-being.

Motivation

Classic views on motivation describe both extrinsic and intrinsic motivation as being equally important. Extrinsic motivation is based on the rewards from the organization's compensation system such as pay and bonuses. Intrinsic motivation, on the other hand, is related to the value of the work itself.[38] As with attitudes, motivation has been studied as an outcome variable but also as an independent variable that predicts productivity. Prosocial motivation is a new concept of motivation[39] that assesses the degree to which employees behave in a way that benefits society as a whole. You will learn more about motivation and rewards in Chapters 8 and 9 of this textbook.

Employee Withdrawal

As noted earlier, an employee quitting the organization is costly in terms of the money and time spent to recruit, hire, and train replacements. There is much research in OB on the reasons why employees think about quitting (**turnover intentions**) and actual **turnover**.[40] The availability of outside employment opportunities is a factor, but thoughts of quit-ting may be related to other outcomes such as lower job satisfaction and engagement. And if the economy improves and the job market improves with it, workers may eventually leave for other opportuni-ties. Another costly form of employee withdrawal is **absenteeism**, since workers may not come to work when they are dissatisfied and there are few alternative jobs available.

> Critical Thinking Questions: Is employee productivity the most important outcome variable? If not, what outcome(s) do you think is/are more important?

LEVELS OF ANALYSIS IN ORGANIZATIONAL BEHAVIOR

Learning Objective 1.6: Compare the levels of analysis in OB research.

Individual behavior in an organization may be influenced by processes at different levels in the organization. The most basic level is the **individual level**. For example, an individual's personality and experiences would explain much of their behavior, and differences in these variables among people would help explain why people behave differently. Other differences between people's behavior occur at the dyad (or two-party) level. An example would be a mentor and a protégé. Still, other sources include group- and **team-level** influences on individual behavior. An example would be a team that has high-performance norms that encourage a team member to perform at his or her best. Additional influences on individual behavior may come from the **organizational level.** For example, in organizations with strong cultures, the cultural characteristics can have a profound influence on an individual member's behavior. To illustrate this, one needs to look no further than the U.S. Marine Corps. The Marine Corps has a strong culture that includes pride, and this inspires Marines to excel (this is evident in their recruiting ads: "The few, the proud, the Marines"; you will learn more about organizational culture in Chapter 14 of this book). There is also the **industry level** of analysis where comparisons are made across different industries (this is more typical for research in strategic management than OB). However, this level is included here to provide a complete listing of levels of analysis in organizational research. All levels may influence employee performance in organizations, and this is discussed in the next section.

HOW OB RESEARCH INCREASES EMPLOYEE PERFORMANCE

Learning Objective 1.7: Develop plans for using OB research to improve employee job performance.

The chapters in this book will address all of the levels that may influence individual behavior and show how processes at one level may affect processes at another level. For example, a positive organizational culture may increase the commitment of individuals to their work and, in turn, their performance. Table 1.3 provides examples of hypotheses at the different levels of analysis discussed previously. This table illustrates how OB research at all levels may help leaders improve employee performance.

As this table illustrates, understanding OB has strong influences on employee performance. Thus, understanding behavior in organizations is every manager's job. But some managers engage in behaviors that decrease employee performance. One of the reasons why managers do this is because they hold subconscious assumptions regarding employees' willingness to work hard. An important theory of such managerial assumptions emerged in the 1960s and suggested that managers' assumptions regarding their followers' motivation affects the way they treat them. If a manager assumes that followers are lazy and will perform poorly, they treat them in ways that control their behavior and decrease creativity. In contrast, if a manager assumes that their followers are smart and motivated, they allow them to participate in decisions and give them goals that stretch their talents. This theory described two sets of leader behaviors related to these assumptions—Theory X and Theory Y. This theory provides a good opportunity to apply your critical thinking skills.

> Critical Thinking Question: Which level(s) do you think have the most influence on individual behavior in organizations and why?

Table 1.3 Examples of How Organizational Behavior Research Relates to Performance

Level	Example Organizational Behavior Hypothesis
Individual	The personality characteristic of conscientiousness is positively related to employee performance.
Dyad	High-quality relationships with bosses lead to higher employee performance.
Group and team	Team conflict is negatively related to employee performance.
Organizational	A strong, positive organizational culture is positively related to employee performance.
Industry	Employee performance is higher in the financial services industry compared with government organizations.

THEORY X AND THEORY Y

Learning Objective 1.8: Compare and contrast Theory X and Theory Y assumptions.

One of the most influential books in OB is *The Human Side of Enterprise* by Douglas McGregor.[41] This book is important because it presents the idea that leader behaviors are influenced by fundamental assumptions and beliefs about human nature. Most managers are not aware of their underlying assumptions; thus, their influence on behavior is pervasive yet hard to detect. These assumptions are divided into pessimistic (Theory X) and optimistic (Theory Y) views of human nature. **Theory X** leaders assume that people are basically lazy, don't like to work, and avoid responsibility. This type of manager's related behaviors include being directive, engaging in surveillance, and coercion. In contrast, **Theory Y** leaders assume that people are internally motivated, like to work, and will accept responsibility. These managers' related behaviors are to allow discretion, participation, and the encouragement of creativity on the job.

Although McGregor proposed Theory X and Y over 55 years ago, most quantitative research did not emerge until relatively recently. However, research findings on these managerial assumptions are interesting. For example, one study showed that Theory Y assumptions were more related to participative decision-making by leaders. Further, participative decision-making is actually perceived as a threat by Theory X managers because it reduces their power. Theory Y managers viewed participation differently and saw it as a positive influence on their power and effectiveness.[42] Another study of 50 military leaders and 150 of their followers found that the Theory Y management style was significantly and positively associated with subordinates' satisfaction with the leader, organizational commitment, and organizational citizenship behaviors. The Theory X management style had a significantly negative impact on subordinates' satisfaction with the leader but no significant impact on commitment and organizational citizenship behavior.[43] The findings of this study in the military environment are interesting because they suggest that Theory Y relates to satisfaction but may not always relate to commitment and performance. The authors concluded that Theory X/Y assumptions provide unique insights into leadership behavior and outcomes.

One of the key themes of this textbook is to encourage you to think critically about the theories and approaches presented. Theory X/Y is no exception. Over the years, Theory X/Y has been criticized for being too simple and not considering the situation leaders and followers find themselves in.[44,45] For a long time, research was also hindered because good measures of Theory X/Theory Y did not exist. However, Richard Kopelman and his associates have developed a measure of Theory X and Y that shows promise for the valid assessment of these diverse management philosophies.[46] Their measure appears in the Toolkit at the end of this chapter (Self-Assessment 1.1), and you can learn about your own Theory X and Y assumptions by completing it. Despite its critics, McGregor's book *The Human Side of Enterprise* was voted the fourth most influential management book of the 20th century in a poll of top management scholars.[47] McGregor's theory continues to hold an important position in OB research due to the implication that it is important for leaders to understand their subconscious fundamental assumptions about how human beings relate to work. It appears that the assumptions of Theory X and Theory Y are worthy of further study.

> **Critical Thinking Questions:** Why do you think that Theory X/Y has had such a strong influence on understanding leadership? Can you think of other assumptions that managers may hold in their subconscious mind that influence how they treat their followers?

PLAN FOR THIS TEXTBOOK

There are numerous challenges facing leaders of organizations today. Most organizations are experiencing rates of change unlike anything we have seen in the past.[48] External pressures have been created from mergers, downsizing, restructuring, and layoffs as organizations strive to remain competitive or even survive. Other external forces are global competition, product obsolescence, new technology, government mandates, and demographic changes in the workforce itself. Internally, leaders must effectively communicate to followers, peers, and bosses. Managing poor performance is one of the most challenging tasks a manager must do. As noted at the beginning of this chapter, addressing the pervasive problem of worker disengagement will be a challenge for leaders in the years ahead. The changes organizations have undergone have resulted in followers who are filled with cynicism and doubt about their leaders and organization.[49] Ethics scandals in business have fueled the perception that leaders have lost the credibility to lead their organizations in a principled way.

By now, you have realized that OB is a problem-focused discipline aimed at making organizations more effective. Your ability as a leader will be enhanced through knowledge of the theory and applications from OB research. Each chapter will review the essential and most current theory and research, and relate it to how you can develop your leadership skills. At the end of each chapter, there are tools for your "toolkit," where you will directly apply the theories through cases, self-assessments, and exercises. At the end of this chapter, Toolkit Activity 1.1 is a personal leadership development plan where you can apply the concepts and research covered in the textbook to your own development as a leader by setting goals and specific behavior strategies to meet them. For example, a student who set a specific goal to improve their coaching of other students that they tutor in accounting would formulate specific coaching behaviors and commit to engaging in them once per week. To gain feedback, the student would have the tutored students rate their coaching behavior by providing a yes or no answer to the following statement after each tutoring session: My tutor provides specific knowledge that has improved my accounting performance. Since leaders are expected to be coaches, this process should help the student improve their coaching skills for the future.

The figure on page 1 (Section I opening page) shows an overview of the entire book and how the material is tied together to impact the challenges of shaping organizational culture and leading change. Leadership is a theme that runs through the textbook with each chapter concluding with implications for leaders. This introductory chapter has provided an overview of EBM and critical thinking that should be applied to all of the following chapters. Next, the importance of understanding individuals in organizations is covered in Chapters 2 through 5, including personality, emotions and moods, job attitudes as well as perception, and decision making. The next section addresses the leader's role as an influencer and motivator (Chapters 6 through 9). First, leadership is covered, highlighting evidence-based recommendations for you to follow to become effective. Organizations are political entities, and the role of power and politics is discussed in Chapter 7. The role of leaders as motivators is covered next in Chapters 8 and 9. Following this, the role of leaders as relationship builders is covered in Chapters 10 through 13, which builds upon the core leadership theories covered in Chapter 6 (leadership). Section IV addresses the topics of teams, conflict, organizational communication, diversity, and leading across cultures. Finally, the role of leaders as change agents is discussed in Chapters 14 and 15, which discuss organizational culture, leading change, and stress management. As you read this book, refer back to this figure as a map of how to organize the vast amount of theory and research on OB that has been generated for decades. It won't seem so overwhelming if you can place the material in the four broad groupings as shown in the figure. This textbook generally follows the levels of analysis noted in the current chapter: individuals, dyads (leadership and influence), groups, and organizations.

LEADERSHIP IMPLICATIONS: THINKING CRITICALLY

The goal of this book and your OB course is for you to become a more effective leader in organizations. To accomplish this, you will need to learn to think critically about the material you encounter. This may go against your intuition, which tells you to "see what you want to see" and confirm what you already believe. For example, you may think that OB is just all "touchy-feely" stuff that has no practical value. Try to keep an open mind and overcome any biases or preconceived ideas you may have about leadership or management. Linda B. Nilson, author of several books including *Creating Self-Regulated Learners: Strategies to Strengthen Students' Self-Awareness and Learning Skills*, suggests that you ask the following questions about your readings:[50]

- What is your interpretation/analysis of this argument?

- What are your reasons for favoring that interpretation analysis? What is your argument?

- How well does your interpretation/analysis handle the complexities of the reading/data/argument?

- What is another interpretation/analysis of the reading/data/argument? Any others?

- What are the implications of each interpretation/analysis?

- Let's look at all the interpretations/analyses and evaluate them. How strong is the evidence for each one?

- How honestly and impartially are you representing the other interpretations/analyses? Do you have a vested interest in one interpretation/analysis over another?

- What additional information would help us to narrow down our interpretations/analyses?

Let's practice critical thinking. Try to apply these questions to your results for the Theory X/Y Self-Assessment 1.1. In completing the Theory X/Y Self-Assessment, you learned that your subconscious assumptions about human nature will influence how you treat your followers. Interpret your results and check your arguments by asking the questions above. If you are Theory X, try to develop an alternative explanation for your results. Examine your Theory Y scores to determine if you have some tendency to believe that workers are self-motivated. If you are Theory Y, look at your Theory X scores to better understand the strength of your Theory Y assumptions. If you are a strong Theory Y leader, you are on your way to creating a participative and empowering work environment for your followers. In every chapter of this textbook, you will have the opportunity to take additional self-assessments that will challenge you to examine your own assumptions, attitudes, and behaviors by applying the critical thinking questions above. Through this understanding, you will be able to adjust your leadership style to become more effective.

A critical thinking filter has already been applied to the OB literature since this book includes the most relevant and evidence-based theory and research. You will need to think critically yourself and decide whether this approach will be a useful one for you to adopt into your management skill set. Throughout this textbook, you will be challenged to apply your own critical thinking skills based upon your own experiences with behavior in organizations and your study of this book. This is the **evidence-based approach** to learning OB. For example, Self-Assessment 1.2 tests your experiential evidence—what you already know about OB. To aid in this process, you will find Critical Thinking Questions to challenge you to think critically about the material throughout the book. You may choose to read further from the Suggestions for Further Reading or conduct your own research on topics you find particularly interesting. Complete the activities in the Toolkit sections to apply the material to your own leadership development. In this chapter, the activity is for you to start a Personal Leadership Development Plan where you can log the most useful approaches and develop plans to track your progress. The Case Studies found at the end of each chapter encourage you to apply organizational science to a real-world problem. By studying the chapters and completing the activities, this book should serve as a point of departure for your growth as you become an effective organizational leader with a comprehensive understanding of behavior in organizations.

 **edge.sagepub.com/scandura2e**

Want a better grade? Go to **edge.sagepub.com/scandura2e** for the tools you need to sharpen your study skills.

KEY TERMS

absenteeism, 14

applied social psychology, 4

critical thinking, 8

employee well-being, 14

evidence-based approach, 18

evidence-based management (EBM), 5

TOOLKIT ACTIVITY 1.1: Personal Leadership Development Plan

As you study the evidence-based research in this textbook, use the following development plan to tie the concepts to specific action plans and measurable outcomes that you find most useful.

Name: _____

Date: _____   _____

Leadership Development Plan

Goal	Connection to Course	Behavior Strategies and Frequency (fill in below)	Measurable Outcome
1	1A	1B	• 1C.1
		1B	• 1C.2
2	2A	2B	• 2C.1
		2B	• 2C.2
3	3A	3B	• 3C.1
		3B	• 3C.2

Plan Detail

Complete the following for each of the goals listed previously.

1. **Goals:** This section is where you enter your development objectives. These objectives should be written so they read as goals you desire to achieve—for example, "I want to improve my team communication skills."

    A. **Connection to course material:** This section is where you tie each of your development objectives into the material you learned in this course. This will reinforce course material and help translate it into practice. For example, you would write a few paragraphs relating the exercises or material on communication to why you find your listening skills to need development. Be specific (e.g., cite exercises, articles, material from text or lecture). Fill out this chart: 1A to 3A.

    B. **Behavior strategies and frequency:** This section is the "how" portion. How will you achieve your goals? How often will you perform these tasks? This is the heart of your development plan. You should create specific strategies that will push you toward the completion of your goals—for example, "Practice active listening once a day." Fill out this chart for each goal: 1B to 3B.

GOAL: 1B

TimeFrame	Behavior Strategy to Practice	Time Required
All the time	❏	
Weekly	❏	
Biweekly	❏	
Monthly	❏	

GOAL: 2B

TimeFrame	Behavior Strategy to Practice	Time Required
All the time	❏	
Weekly	❏	
Biweekly	❏	
Monthly	❏	

GOAL: 3B

TimeFrame	Behavior Strategy to Practice	Time Required
All the time	❏	
Weekly	❏	
Biweekly	❏	
Monthly	❏	

C. **Measurable outcome:** This section helps you measure your success toward each goal.

Note: You can have more than three goals in your plan. Just be sure to complete all sections.

Discussion Questions

1. If you are achieving your goal, how would you notice the change in your leadership?

2. Specifically what will improve?

3. How will you measure it? Develop or find a metric—for example, "I will have the person who I listen to fill out an evaluation of my listening skills, rating them on a 1 (poor) to 5 (excellent) scale" (1C to 3C).

CASE STUDY 1.1: Organizational Science in the Real World

The skills and techniques of research are valuable to an organization's leaders. The following case study illustrates how research can be used to solve a challenge facing a government organization. Imagine that you are the leader in this organization. As you read the case, consider how you might use the four sources of EBM rather than your own intuition to solve the pressing problems.

The state of Florida implemented the federal government's decree that individuals applying for or renewing their driver's license must provide a number of documents to verify their identity. Resulting from the REAL ID Act of 2005, these measures were set forth by the federal government to help develop a national identity database through the Department of Motor Vehicles (DMV; or Bureau of Motor Vehicles [BMV] depending on the state) to not only prevent identity theft but also prevent terrorists and illegal immigrants from accessing identities. Phase 1 of the act had to be completed by 2014, with the target completion of all the phases by 2017. This was clearly an important mandate, and attention to the details of implementation was essential to ensure both compliance and success.

The mandate to make these changes came at a challenging time. This requirement was not the only major change Florida was making to its driver's license processes. Prior to this, the state of Florida merged the state's DMV with each county's tax collector. County tax collectors are often small organizations with 100 employees or fewer working at a handful of offices in each county to serve their patrons. Previously, tax collectors' offices handled vehicle registration, license plates, property taxes, and hunting and fishing licenses. The DMV handled only driver's licenses and identification cards. The purposes of this merger were to save money for the state, save time for citizens, and make the entire process easier. Thus, most DMV employees were not retained when the organizations were merged. So the organization had already undergone downsizing, and remaining employees were nervous about their jobs. Also, tax collector employees had to be trained on a variety of new processes and procedures within a short period of time.

After these initiatives were rolled out statewide, the general manager of one county's tax collector offices noticed a number of changes. Employees were discontented and turnover skyrocketed. Large numbers of employees began to quit where previously they worked for the organization until they retired. Similarly, only 1 of 6 new hires was retained for more than 6 months after the changes. Retaining a skilled workforce became a major concern for the offices.

Customer service declined. Before the merger, customers typically handled their transactions within half an hour or less. However, driver's licenses take significantly longer. Because the REAL ID Act requires documentation to be scanned into state and nationwide databases, it takes about an hour to apply for or renew licenses if there are no problems or delays. This has resulted in excessive wait times for customers. The tax collector tried to address this issue with requiring appointments for those seeking driver's licenses. However, not all patrons made appointments; instead, they continued to just show up, creating delays for those with appointments. While these patrons were denied and offered to schedule an appointment, they often became belligerent and sometimes verbally abusive to the staff.

Customers were often upset and irritated not only by the excessive wait time but also by the amount of documentation they had to produce. They were also upset by having to renew driver's licenses in person whereas previously they could renew by mail or the Internet. Tax collector employees were still friendly and polite with customers, but there was definitely some underlying tension resulting from the more complicated transactions. The camaraderie and morale among employees deteriorated; employee engagement was low.

Now it is your turn. Imagine that you are the office manager and are trying to solve the organization's problems. You simply can't revert the business back the way it was before the state's mandated changes, and you're not sure what needs to be fixed and where to go in the future.

Discussion Questions

1. How could research help this small organization? What would you hope to gain as the leader?

2. What dependent variables should you, as the leader, consider researching? Why?

3. Review the sources of EBM discussed in this chapter. Which ones would you rely most on and why?

4. Think about the research designs discussed in the Appendix on Research Designs used in OB at the end of the book. Which one(s) do you think would be appropriate for the manager to use? Would there be any benefit to using multiple methods, and if so, in what order would you conduct the research studies?

SELF-ASSESSMENT 1.1: Are You Theory X or Theory Y?

This self-assessment exercise identifies whether your leadership philosophy is Theory X or Theory Y as determined by research. The goal of this assessment is for you to learn about your general assumptions about people and work, and to understand how this may affect how you lead them. There are no right or wrong answers, and this is not a test. You don't have to share your results with the others unless you wish to do so.

Part I. Taking the Assessment

For each of the statements below, circle the number that indicates the degree to which you agree or disagree.

Statements	Strongly Disagree	Disagree	Neutral	Agree	Strongly Agree
1. Most people will try to do as little work as possible.	1	2	3	4	5
2. Most people are industrious.	1	2	3	4	5
3. Most people are lazy and don't want to work.	1	2	3	4	5
4. People naturally like to work.	1	2	3	4	5
5. Most employees will slack off if left alone by managers.	1	2	3	4	5
6. Most employees are capable of providing ideas that are helpful to the organizations where they work.	1	2	3	4	5
7. Employees possess imagination and creativity.	1	2	3	4	5
8. Employees' ideas are generally not useful to organizations.	1	2	3	4	5
9. Most employees lack the ability to help the organizations where they work.	1	2	3	4	5
10. Most employees are trustworthy.	1	2	3	4	5

Part II. Scoring Instructions

In Part I, you rated yourself on 10 questions. Add the numbers you circled in each of the columns to derive your score for Theory X and Theory Y. During class, we will discuss each approach, its strengths and weaknesses, and how this may affect your leadership style.

Theory X	Theory Y
1. _____	2. _____
3. _____	4. _____
5. _____	6. _____
7. _____	8. _____
9. _____	10. _____
Total _____	Total _____

Source: Adapted from Kopelman, Prottas, and Falk (2012).

Interpretation

If your Theory X score is greater than 12, your assumptions are more in line with Theory X.
If your Theory Y score is greater than 12, your assumptions are more in line with Theory Y.

Discussion Questions

1. Were you surprised by your results? What does this tell you about how you view human nature?

2. Compare your scores with five other students in the class. Do you believe that most people are more Theory X or Theory Y?

3. How will your X/Y assumptions relate to how you may listen to the ideas of your followers and allow them to participate in decisions you are responsible for?

SELF-ASSESSMENT 1.2: Assessing Your Experiential Evidence Base

Some students think OB is common sense. Are the following statements true or false? The answers follow.

	True	False
1. A happy worker is a productive worker.	_____	_____
2. Larger teams perform better because there are more people to do the work.	_____	_____
3. Performance appraisals have high accuracy.	_____	_____
4. People perform better when asked to do their best.	_____	_____
5. When trust is broken with your leader, it is best to take the blame and apologize.	_____	_____
6. Money is the best motivator.	_____	_____
7. Leaders should treat everyone the same in their work group.	_____	_____
8. A work group can be "moody."	_____	_____
9. Group spirit improves team decisions.	_____	_____
10. Conflict in organizations should be minimized.	_____	_____
11. Models developed in the United States will work anywhere.	_____	_____
12. It's best to commit to a course of action and follow through no matter what.	_____	_____

Answers

1. True. What is important is what the worker is happy about. But generally, happier people are more productive. You'll learn why in Chapter 4.

2. False. No. In fact, larger teams underperform due to increased conflict, free-riding, and other group dysfunctions. Research shows that there is an optimal group size for high performance, and you will learn what it is in Chapter 10.

3. False. No. There are a number of perceptual biases that can affect how a leader evaluates followers. You need to be aware of them so you can guard against these errors, and you will know about them after reading Chapter 5.

4. False. While this seems intuitive, people actually achieve higher performance when the leader gives them a specific goal rather than a "do your

best goal." You will read more on the motivating properties of goals in Chapter 8.

5. False. No. Research on trust repair shows that admitting guilt may not be the best strategy. You will learn what the research shows you should do in Chapter 6.

6. False. While this may surprise you, pay may actually decrease intrinsic motivation. You will learn about how to best reward employees in Chapter 9.

7. False. Research on the leader–member exchange (LMX) model of leadership shows that effective leaders treat each follower differently based upon their skills, motivation, and need for development on the job. You will read more about this in Chapter 6.

8. True. What? Yes, it can. Multilevel research has shown that negative affect (a "blue" mood) can be aggregated to the group level—and it affects group functioning. You will learn more about this in Chapter 3.

9. False. While cohesion can be a positive force in teams, it does not always result in the best decisions. Too much group spirit can result in groupthink and impair a group's decision making. You will read about this and other group dysfunctions in Chapter 10.

10. False. Actually, research shows that some conflict can be healthy since it can generate interest and challenge for followers. In Chapter 11, you will learn more about how to harness conflict and channel it toward increased motivation.

11. False. Research on cultural differences indicates that we need to consider cultural values before we generalize research findings from one country to another. You will learn about cross-cultural differences in Chapter 13.

12. False. While it is important to commit to goals, research shows that escalation of commitment to a failing course of action is a decision trap. Learn how to avoid this and other traps in Chapter 5.

Discussion Questions

1. How did you do? Were you surprised by some of the research evidence on these topics?

2. Which of these topics are particularly of interest to you? Why?

3. Did you feel that you had to guess at some of these?

OB research takes the guesswork out of being an effective leader! So keep reading!

UNDERSTANDING INDIVIDUALS IN ORGANIZATIONS

CHAPTER 2 · Personality and Person–Environment Fit

CHAPTER 3 · Emotions and Moods

CHAPTER 4 · Attitudes and Job Satisfaction

CHAPTER 5 · Perception, Decision Making, and Problem Solving

Introduction

Chapter 1: What Is Organizational Behavior?

Understanding Individuals in Organizations

Chapter 2: Personality and Person–Environment Fit

Chapter 3: Emotions and Moods

Chapter 4: Attitudes and Job Satisfaction

Chapter 5: Perception, Decision Making, and Problem Solving

Influencing and Motivating Employees

Chapter 6: Leadership

Chapter 7: Power and Politics

Chapter 8: Motivation: Core Concepts

Chapter 9: Motivation: Applications

Building Relationships

Chapter 10: Group Processes and Teams

Chapter 11: Managing Conflict and Negotiation

Chapter 12: Organizational Communication

Chapter 13: Diversity and Cross-Cultural Adjustments

Leaders as Change Agents

Chapter 14: Organizational Culture

Chapter 15: Leading Change and Stress Management

CHAPTER TWO

PERSONALITY AND PERSON–ENVIRONMENT FIT

Learning Objectives

After studying this chapter, you should be able to do the following:

2.1: Define *personality*, and discuss the role of heredity.

2.2: Discuss the benefits and limitations of using the Myers-Briggs Type Indicator in organizations.

2.3: List and explain the five factors in the Big Five theory of personality.

2.4: Compare and contrast the Type A and Type B behavior pattern.

2.5: Develop an example of a job that would benefit from risk taking.

2.6: Summarize the elements of psychological capital.

2.7: Explain the effects of positive and negative core self-evaluations.

2.8: Compare and contrast person–organization fit and person–job fit.

Get the edge on your studies at **edge.sagepub.com/scandura2e**

- Take the chapter quiz
- Review key terms with eFlashcards
- Explore multimedia resources, SAGE readings, and more!

THE RIGHT STUFF AT THE WRONG TIME?

On July 1, 2013, Mark Pincus, the founder and CEO of Zynga, resigned as CEO of the Internet gaming company and announced that he had "fired himself." The Internet gaming company was a rising star due to the success of the innovative game Words With Friends but experienced difficulties maintaining market share following its IPO in December 2011. Pincus hired Don Mattick, former head of Microsoft's Xbox division, to replace him.[1] While Pincus remained at Zynga as chairman and chief product officer, the organization needed a different type of leadership style to address the persistent company problems of a company culture that was widely viewed as toxic with employees quitting in droves. Research conducted by Noam Wasserman, who studied founder–CEO succession, concluded that founders often find it difficult to remain as CEO as the company grows and the organization grows and adds employees.[2] A different leadership skill set is needed to manage others, and 80% of the time the founder is not able to make the adjustment to leader of a larger and more complex organization. For example, he or she may keep the original management team on board and be reluctant to make changes to ensure long-term market success and continued growth. The technical guru with the brilliant idea for an Internet start-up like Pincus might not have the right personality for the demands of leading a large organization, which include leadership and political skills. However, in 2015, Pincus returned to Zynga after 2 years of lackluster stock performance under Mattick. To survive against competitors like King (Candy Crush), Zynga needed to become nimble and innovative again. Some questioned whether Pincus's leadership style could change.[3] And after only 11 months, Pincus again stepped down as CEO in March 2016 after its stocks got slammed under his watch.[4] It seems that Pincus had the right personality and risk-taking traits for a start-up but had difficulty leading a larger organization. From this example, it is clear that understanding personality is essential for being an effective leader.

WHAT IS PERSONALITY?

Learning Objective 2.1: Define *personality*, and discuss the role of heredity.

Understanding your own **personality**—and the personalities of others—is critical. This is because personality and other individual differences are relatively stable over the life course. For example, personality has been generally defined as "regularities in feeling, thought and action that are characteristic of an individual."[5] Also, personality matters because it is linked to social behavior in organizations. Personality may affect our work habits and how we interact with our coworkers. However, personality and most individual differences aren't like other areas of organizational behavior (OB) where the manager can influence the outcomes by intervention. Individual differences are aspects of OB that must be *understood*, and leaders must often work with them rather than try to change people. This is why we often hear people speak about two people who just don't get along as a "personality clash." As the example of Marc Pincus suggests, a real question for Zynga is whether they will be able to name a successor with the right personality traits to lead the organization and be innovative again. Next, we will discuss research that addresses whether personality can change.

The Role of Heredity

Can a brilliant engineer who is introverted change his personality and become an extraverted visionary leader? In other words, are personality traits inborn or learned? This question has been addressed by the famous **Minnesota twin studies.** To conduct this research, twins born in Minnesota from 1936 through 1955 were asked to join a registry.[6] Identical twins (monozygotic and dizygotic reared apart, MZAs and DZAs, respectively) were confirmed through birth records, and 80% of the surviving intact pairs were located and recruited for participation in various psychological studies. Some twins were reared apart for various reasons (e.g., adoption). These twins tell us a great deal about the contribution of heredity compared to the child-rearing environment. A study showed that 50% of the variation in occupational choice (whether a person is a dentist or a soldier, for example) is due to heredity.[7] Most people are surprised to learn this. Another study of MZA and DZA twins showed that 40% of the variance in values related to work motivation could be attributed to heredity, whereas 60% was due to the environment (and measurement error).[8] The implications for a leader are that while personality might change, most psychologists believe that it is a relatively stable individual difference. Instead of trying to change a coworker's personality, it is perhaps better to learn about personality differences, understand how different personalities operate at work, and then learn to work effectively with different types. Psychologists have developed inventories (personality tests) to assess personality differences. These tests are useful in training programs on conflict resolution and team building.

MYERS-BRIGGS TYPE INDICATOR

Learning Objective 2.2: Discuss the benefits and limitations of using the Myers-Briggs Type Indicator in organizations.

The Myers-Briggs Type Indicator (MBTI) is the most often administered personality test to nonpsychiatric populations (i.e., the "well population").[9] The publishers of the MBTI, Consulting Psychologists Press, report that over 2 million people take the MBTI every year. Because it was developed and normed on "well people," it has been a popular approach with organizations and is used by Hallmark, GE, and many other large organizations in their leadership training and development programs. The MBTI was developed by a mother and daughter team, Katherine Briggs and

RESEARCH IN ACTION

Leaders: Are They Born or Made?

With the research on the twins reared apart and evidence from the Big Five personality theory relating personality traits to leader emergence in groups, one question that arises is whether leaders are born to greatness or if leadership can be acquired by anyone. There are arguments on both sides of this issue among scholars of OB. For example, research suggests genetic factors contribute as much as 40% to the explanation of transformational leadership. This suggests that much of charismatic, visionary leadership is an inborn trait. On the other hand, many people believe that transformational leadership can be learned, and experimental research has shown that leaders can be trained to exhibit charismatic behaviors. Also, followers responded positively to leaders that have been trained, and their performance increased. An integrative perspective suggests that leaders have certain inborn traits that predispose them to self-select into leadership positions. For example, an employee who exhibits extraversion might be more likely to pursue a high-level position in an organization. Once hired into a leadership role, these people may respond to leadership training more than those who are not as interested in becoming leaders. The best thinking on this at present is that leadership is most likely a combination of inborn traits and learned behavior. The implications for organizations are to carefully select those hired into leadership and then provide the training needed to enhance leader effectiveness. Those with innate leadership skills have an advantage, but an individual may be able to enhance his or her leadership capabilities by learning about the behaviors that comprise effective leadership and then practicing the behavioral skills needed.

Discussion Questions:

1. In your opinion, is leadership born (hereditary) or learned (through training, for example)? Support your position.
2. If leadership is both born and made, as some researchers believe, what do you think is the best way to identify leadership potential?
3. What type of leadership training would you recommend to complement the selection process?

Sources: Arvey, R. D., Rotundo, M., Johnson, W., Zhang, Z., & McGue, M. (2006). The determinants of leadership role occupancy: Genetic and personality factors. *Leadership Quarterly, 17*, 1–20; Howell, J., & Frost, P. (1989). A laboratory study of charismatic leadership. *Organizational Behavior and Human Decision Processes, 43*, 243–269; Judge, T. A., & Long, D. M. (2012). Individual differences in leadership. In D. V. Day & J. Antonakis (Eds.), *The nature of leadership* (pp. 179–217). Thousand Oaks, CA: Sage.

Isabel Myers-Briggs, following World War II and is based upon the personality theories of Carl Jung.[10] The MBTI is based upon four general personality preferences:

- **Introversion (I) vs. extraversion (E):** Extraverts tend to be outgoing; introverts tend to be shy.

- **Sensing (S) vs. intuition (N):** Sensing types tend to be practical; intuitive people tend to be "idea people."

- **Thinking (T) vs. feeling (F):** Thinking types tend to use logic; feeling types tend to use emotion.

- **Judging (J) vs. perceiving (P):** Judging types tend to make quick decisions; perceiving types tend to be more flexible.

People who take the MBTI are grouped into 16 personality "types" based on these characteristics. For example, an ENTP would be extraverted, intuitive, thinking, and perceiving. This person might be attracted to starting their own business, for example. In contrast, an INTJ is introverted, intuitive, thinking, and judging, and may be attracted to a scientific career. ISTJs are detail-oriented and practical, where ESTJs are organizers and may be comfortable in managerial roles.

Limitations of the Myers-Briggs Type Indicator

There has been limited research support for the reliability and validity of the MBTI. If you take the test again, you may not receive the same score, and the matter of whether people are actually classifiable into the 16 categories is questionable.[11,12] However, the MBTI remains the most popular personality test in use for organizations. Also, it is important to note that the MBTI has not been validated for selection; in other words, its publisher makes it clear that you should not use the MBTI to hire people for particular jobs in an organization.[13]

> Critical Thinking Question: Given the limited research support for the MBTI, what are the concerns regarding organizations continuing to use it?

How the Myers-Briggs Type Indicator Is Used in Organizations

The best uses for the MBTI appears to be for conflict resolution and team building, and this is where it is most often used in management training programs and classrooms. The value of the MBTI is to enable people in organizations to discuss personality differences in their approach to work in a nonjudgmental way. All of the labels in the MBTI are neutral; it is not better or worse to be judging or perceiving, for example. Briggs and Myers-Briggs titled their book *Gifts Differing*, and this captures the essence of this approach to understanding personality. At the workplace, everyone has something to offer, and it takes all types of people for teams and organizations to be effective. For a leader, this underscores the importance of understanding individual differences because to build effective teams, everyone needs to feel valued to be engaged. The MBTI is, of course, not the only personality assessment available; next, will discuss another personality theory that has had more research support (although it is currently not as well-known as the MBTI to most practicing managers and the general population). This personality assessment is known as the "Big Five" personality theory.

"THE BIG FIVE"

Learning Objective 2.3: List and explain the five factors in the Big Five theory of personality.

After much research examining personality inventories, the developers of the Big Five theory of personality concluded that personality could be summarized using five factors: **openness**, **conscientiousness**, **extraversion**, **agreeableness**, and **neuroticism**.[14] These factors and their definitions are summarized in Table 2.1. Note that the table is organized such that the first letters of these personality traits are an acronym that spells *OCEAN*, and this will help you to remember them.

Openness is a person's willingness to embrace new ideas and new situations. *Conscientiousness* represents the characteristic of being a person who follows through and gets things done. *Extraversion* is a trait of a person who is outgoing, talkative, and sociable as well as enjoys social situations. *Agreeableness* is being a nice person in general. Finally, *neuroticism* represents a tendency to be anxious or moody (this trait is often referred to by its opposite: emotional stability). There has been a good deal of research on whether these five traits predict job performance, and results indicate that the conscientiousness dimension best predicts performance on the job (it makes sense

Table 2.1 The Big Five Personality Characteristics

Trait	Description
Openness	Being curious, original, intellectual, creative, and open to new ideas
Conscientiousness	Being organized, systematic, punctual, achievement oriented, and dependable
Extraversion	Being outgoing, talkative, sociable, and enjoying social situations
Agreeableness	Being affable, tolerant, sensitive, trusting, kind, and warm
Neuroticism	Being anxious, irritable, temperamental, and moody

Source: Barrick, M. R., & Mount, M. K. (2005). Yes, personality matters: Moving on to more important matters. *Human Performance, 18*, 359–372.

that people who are achievement-oriented and dependable would be better employees and also better leaders).[15] This translates into success; conscientiousness is related to job satisfaction, income, and higher occupational status (e.g., being an executive, business owner, or professional).[16] While conscientiousness is the big one in terms of job performance, extraversion also has a moderate but significant relationship to performance, particularly in sales.[17]

Other Big Five traits relate to other positive work outcomes. Research has also shown that emotional stability relates to the ability to cope with stress, and those with higher openness adjust better to organizational change.[18] Given the strong research support for the relationships of the Big Five personality variables and relevant performance and career outcomes, leaders need to know that instruments such as the Big Five inventories successfully predict performance and can be used as one component in making hiring decisions. For this reason, personality research has a great deal of practical utility for organizations. You can learn what your scores are on the Big Five personality dimensions by taking Self-Assessment 2.1 at the end of this chapter.

> **Critical Thinking Question:** What are the fairness issues involved in using personality tests for selection of new employees?

PERSONALITY TRAITS AND HEALTH RESEARCH

Learning Objective 2.4: Compare and contrast the Type A and Type B behavior pattern.

We have heard the phrase stress kills, but is there any truth to this? Some years ago, cardiologists showed a link between a personality trait called Type A behavior and cardiovascular heart disease. Their theory was based on observing patients in their waiting room; some sat patiently reading a magazine, for example. Others sat on the edge of their seats and got up frequently (they literally wore out the edges of the chairs and armrests!). The doctors conducted a study over a long period of time and asked questions such as the following:

- Do you feel guilty if you use spare time to relax?

- Do you need to win in order to derive enjoyment from games and sports?

- Do you generally move, walk, and eat rapidly?

- Do you often try to do more than one thing at a time?

Study respondents were then classified into one of three groups: **Type A** (competitive, aggressive), **Type B** (relaxed, easygoing), or **Type C** (nice, hardworking people who try to appease others). By the end of this long-term study, 70% of the men who were classified as Type A had coronary heart disease. This study had several limitations, including that it was only conducted on men who were middle-aged, and the researchers didn't take into account other factors such as the dietary habits of the study participants. However, this study generated media interest and led to additional research. A review of this research indicated that there is an association between Type A behavior (particularly hostility) and heart disease.[19] Examples of hostility-related questions are "Do you get irritated easily?" and "Are you bossy and domineering?"[20] And research has shown that the Type A behavior pattern (i.e., "stress energized") is exhibited in samples of women also.[21]

More recently, researchers have discussed an additional personality type and its relationship to health risks: the **Type D** personality. The Type D, also called *the distressed personality*, is a combination of negative affect ("I feel unhappy") and social inhibition ("I am unable to express myself"). Research has indicated that the rates of recovery were lower for coronary heart disease patients with Type D personality.[22] A review of 10 studies of Type D personality have concluded that "Type D patients are also at increased risk for psychological distress, psychosocial risk factors, impaired quality of life, and seem to benefit less from medical and invasive treatment."[23] Thus, while research on personality and health risk continues, there seems to be a clear association between certain personality traits and higher risk of disease, suppressed immune system functioning, and slower recovery from illnesses.

Figure 2.1 summarizes the four personality types, and you can reflect on the checklists in each cell to get a sense of whether you may fall into Type A, B, C, or D. This may be scary news if you think you may have Type A or D personality characteristics. However, there is some good news. Being able to express your emotions may also reflect a "healthy" Type A pattern.[24] It is important for people with a Type A personality to be able to talk to another person about the stress they are experiencing. Second, research has shown that having a "hardy" personality (e.g., letting stress roll off of your back rather than ruminating on your problems) has been shown to reduce the potential for personality type to affect health.[25,26] Also, social support from family, friends, and coworkers can alleviate some of the detrimental effects of personality traits on health.[27]

> **Critical Thinking Questions:** How might knowledge of whether you have the Type A personality affect your decision about taking a job in a high-stress environment? If you were to accept such a position, how would you plan to cope with the stress?

OTHER RELEVANT PERSONALITY TRAITS

Learning Objective 2.5: Develop an example of a job that would benefit from risk taking.

Machiavellianism

The trait of **Machiavellianism** (sometimes abbreviated Mach) refers to a person who believes that the "ends justify the means." In other words, such a person will do whatever it takes to win. The trait is named for Niccolo Machiavelli, who wrote a book called *The Prince*,[28] which detailed his strategies for gaining and holding onto power in the 16th century. High Mach individuals believe that other people can be manipulated and that it is permissible to do so to realize their goals. Recent research has conceptualized Mach as being comprised of a complex set of characteristics: a tendency to distrust others, a willingness to engage in amoral manipulation, a desire to accumulate status for oneself, and a desire to maintain interpersonal control (see Figure 2.2). Thus, Mach appears to involve behaviors as well as internal beliefs and motivations.[29] This research also found that high Mach employees engage in counterproductive work behaviors (for example, purposely wasting office supplies). However, they reported

Figure 2.1   Personality Types A, B, C, and D

TYPE A	TYPE B
_____ Hard-driving	_____ Enjoys the moment
_____ Competitive	_____ Relaxed
_____ Status-conscious	_____ Laid back
_____ Driven to succeed	_____ Patient
_____ Seemingly achievement-addicted	_____ Not competitive
_____ Can be hostile	_____ Not aggressive

TYPE C	TYPE D
_____ Cooperative	_____ Feels unhappy
_____ Not assertive	_____ Tends to worry
_____ Predictable and dependable	_____ Easily irritated
_____ Loyal	_____ Finds it hard to express opinions
_____ Suppresses negative emotions	_____ Reserved
_____ Complies with authority	_____ Doesn't like many people around

Sources: Adapted from Denollet, J. (1998). Personality and risk of cancer in men with coronary heart disease. *Psychological Medicine, 28*(4), 991–995; Denollet, J. (2000). Type D personality: A potential risk factor refined. *Journal of Psychosomatic Research, 49*(4), 255–266; Riggio, R. E. (2012). Are you a Type A or Type B personality? Cutting edge leadership. Retrieved from https://www.psychologytoday.com/blog/cutting-edge-leadership/201206/are-you-type-or-b-personality

lower job satisfaction and experienced more stress on the job. The relationship of Mach and task performance was interesting: High Mach employees' performance improved over time, suggesting that they need time to learn the organization's political system and work themselves into power networks. Despite the positive long-term relationship with task performance, Mach has been related to negative outcomes for others. High Mach behavior has been linked to workplace bullying[30] and abusive supervision.[31] Abusive supervision is even more prevalent when supervisors perceive that they have a great deal of power over their employees. Recent experiments have demonstrated that when individuals perceive that they are in a rivalry situation, their high Mach behavior increased and they falsely inflated their own performance and even deceived their rival for self-gain.[32] Therefore, the high Mach personality may engage in unethical behavior to achieve their goal. Remember—they believe that the end justifies the means, even if it involves lying to manipulate others.

Researchers have added to our understanding of high Mach behavior by articulating a combination of personality traits known as the Dark Triad. The **Dark Triad** is comprised of Machiavellianism, narcissism, and psychopathy.[33] **Narcissism** is the expression of grandiosity, entitlement, dominance, and superiority.[34] Narcissists can therefore appear charming or pleasant in the short term but in the long term, they have difficulty trusting others and fail to develop effective working relationships.[35] **Psychopathy** has been described as impulsivity and thrill seeking combined with low empathy and anxiety.[36] Such individuals lack feelings of guilt, are impulsive, and seek

Figure 2.2   The Structure of Machiavellianism

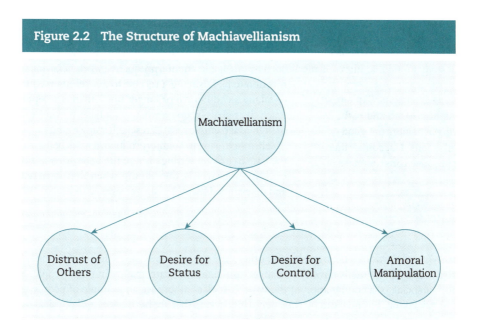

Source: Dahling, J. J., Whitaker, B. G., & Levy, P. E. (2009). The development and validation of a new Machiavellianism scale. *Journal of Management, 35*(2), 219–257.

immediate gratification of their needs.[37] A study of Dark Triad personality and the exercise of power at work found that psychopathy and Machiavellianism were associated with the use of hard tactics such as threats and manipulation. However, Machiavellianism and narcissism were related to reliance on soft tactics such as charm, ingratiation, and giving compliments. This study also found that the Dark Triad pattern results in men using hard tactics (being forceful).[38] You might be wondering if such toxic employees or "bad guys" win at work. A study of 793 employees in their early careers found that narcissism was positively related to salary and Machiavellianism was positively related to leadership position and career satisfaction; however, psychopathy was negatively related to all career outcomes. Thus, the Dark Triad as a combination did not predict career satisfaction and success, but individual traits may have a relationship to higher salary.[39]

Self-Monitoring

Have you ever known someone who had a chameleon-like personality and adapted to a situation they were in? Such individuals are keenly sensitive to the cues they see in every situation they are in and adapt their behavior to fit in. This is known as **self-monitoring** and is defined as "self-observation and self-control guided by situational cues to social appropriateness."[40] High self-monitors are very adaptable to situations, and low self-monitors are not able to pretend that they are someone that they are not. In other words, low self-monitors are true to themselves and don't take cues to change their behavior from social situations. They are consistent in their display of feelings and attitudes regardless of the situation. For example, a person may give others honest feedback, even if it is hurtful. High self-monitors pay more attention to the actions of others and adjust to fit the situation.[41] For example, this type of person will withhold negative feedback to allow the other person to "save face." In the workplace, high self-monitors receive higher performance ratings and become leaders but have lower organizational commitment.[42] They do, however, develop better working relationships with bosses than low self-monitors, and this helps explain the higher performance ratings they receive.[43] Not surprisingly, they achieve more rapid career mobility since they are able to attain central positions in the powerful networks in the organization.[44] Despite the positive outcomes associated with self-monitoring behavior, there may be a downside to this trait. A research study found that high self-monitors may engage in counterproductive work behavior toward the organization (e.g., falsifying a receipt to get reimbursed for more money, or taking an additional or longer break than is acceptable). They may reach their goals by doing whatever it takes to win (similar to behavior of high Mach employees). A research study found that the relationship of self-monitoring to counterproductive work behaviors was especially the case in private settings where the behavior was not visible to others.[45] In other words, they do this when they have read the situation and determined that they can get away with it.

> Critical Thinking Questions: Explain why you think high Mach and high self-monitoring behaviors are good or bad for organizations. List some other positive and negative consequences of these traits.

Risk Taking

Some people are naturally prone to taking risks, and others are risk-averse. **Risk taking** is a personality trait defined as "any purposive activity that entails novelty or danger sufficient to create anxiety in most people. Risk taking can be either physical or social, or a combination of the two."[46] Rock climbers are an example of people who assume the physical aspect of risk taking. Firemen can be considered risk-takers that are both social and physical because they risk physical harm, but it is to help others so it has a social component. Entrepreneurs can be considered social risk-takers but not physical. Entrepreneurs have been found to have a higher risk-taking propensity than general managers. Moreover, there are larger differences between entrepreneurs whose primary goal is venture growth versus those whose focus is on producing family income.[47] Risk taking has been examined in the general population and across cultures, and the evidence is interesting. Survey data from 77 countries (147,118 respondents) suggests that risk taking declines across the life span—as we get older, we take fewer risks. However, there are differences across countries. In countries in which hardship (e.g., social unrest and economic strife) exists, risk does not decline as the people get older. These findings suggest that when resources are scarce, people must continue to assume risk to compete for resources, so risk taking does not decline as they age.[48]

Research on risk taking found that there were some changes over the life span (from age 15 to 85). So this does suggest that some personality traits may change or be malleable over a long period of time. The discussion about Mach and self-monitoring revealed that some traits may not always be desirable, so you may be wondering if there is any theory or research in OB that suggests that personality traits can change. Some scholars believe that certain personality characteristics are state-like instead of trait-like. **Trait-like** implies that the personality characteristic is relatively stable over time. **State-like**, on the other hand, refers to personality characteristics that are relatively changeable, and a person can develop (or reduce) them through either self-awareness and/or training. New research suggests that **psychological capital (PsyCap)** characteristics are more stable than fleeting states of mind, but they are open to change. This is an emerging area of study within the movement called positive psychology, and research is showing promising results.

PSYCHOLOGICAL CAPITAL

Learning Objective 2.6: Summarize the elements of psychological capital.

Positive organizational behavior (POB), borrowed from Positive Organizational Scholarship, is an emerging field. POB is "the study and application of positive-oriented human resource strengths and psychological capacities that can be measured, developed, and effectively managed for performance improvement in today's workplace."[49]

In POB, only positive psychological capacities are included. Being state-like versus trait-like, these positive aspects could be developed through performance improvement solutions such as training programs and other engagement interventions (see boxed insert for an example of a training program to increase PsyCap). PsyCap has been shown to be positively related to employee empowerment and engagement.[50] Fred Luthans and his colleagues have articulated a four-part explanation of PsyCap. Just like we have financial capital, these state-like qualities represent the *value of individual differences* at the workplace. In other words, PsyCap is more than "what you know" or "who you know." It is focused on "who you are" and "who you are becoming."[51] These four characteristics are as follows:

- **Efficacy:** a person's belief that they have the ability to execute a specific task in a given context

- **Optimism:** a positive outcome outlook or attribution of events, which includes positive emotions and motivation

- **Hope:** the *will* to succeed and the ability to identify and pursue the *path* to success

- **Resiliency:** coping in the face of risk or adversity; the ability to "bounce back" after a setback[52]

BEST PRACTICES

Can Psychological Capital Be Acquired Through Training?

Fred Luthans and his colleagues implemented a training program for management students at the University of Nebraska designed to increase PsyCap. Participants in the training program were first asked to identify personally valuable goals that would be used throughout the session. Once they recorded these goals, the facilitator explained the process to implement their goals: (1) concrete end points to measure success, (2) an approach which allows participants to positively move toward goal accomplishment, and (3) the importance of identifying subgoals to reap the benefits of small "wins." To increase optimism, participants were asked to anticipate potential obstacles and then create alternative pathways to minimize the obstacles. Worst-case scenarios were anticipated and preparations were put in place. To build confidence (self-efficacy), the facilitator engaged participants to experience and model success in accomplishing the personal goals set earlier in the session. This efficacy-building process elicited positive emotions

and built up the participants' confidence to generate and implement their plans to attain goals. To affect participants' resiliency, asset factors, risk factors, and influence processes were discussed. Assets refer to factors that increase levels of resiliency (e.g., a good education). Risk factors are those factors that lead to lower levels of resilience, such as a lack of mentors. Participants then identified recent personal setbacks. This could be major (receiving a D in a course) or minor (having a computer that is slow). Participants were then instructed to write their immediate reactions to the identified setbacks. The facilitator then elaborated on a realistic view of reality and how to mentally reframe a setback. Throughout the training program, participants discussed their goals and PsyCap with others to share ideas and get feedback.

The results of the training program were promising. Participants' PsyCap was measured before and after the training program for both the training group and a control group that participated in a non-PsyCap

(Continued)

(Continued)

group exercise. The training significantly increased the students' level of PsyCap by 3%. The control group, on the other hand, showed no increase in their level of PsyCap. The training was next implemented in a sample of managers from all types of organizations who volunteered to participate in the training. The managers' PsyCap significantly increased about the same as the student sample (3%). Another study in a very large high-tech manufacturing firm with a sample of engineering managers resulted in a slightly lower, but still significant, increase in PsyCap. The authors projected that the improvements in productivity from increased PsyCap could be estimated at $73,919.

Discussion Questions:

1. Do you think that things such as hope and optimism can be increased through training? Explain your position.
2. Which of the four PsyCap variables do you think accounted for the results the most (hope, optimism, self-efficacy, and/or resiliency)? Explain your choice(s).
3. Why do you think that the results for the high-tech manufacturing firm were slightly lower than the student and manager group?

Source: Luthans, F., Avey, J. B., Avolio, B. J., Norman, S. M., & Combs, G. M. (2006). Psychological capital development: Toward a micro-intervention. *Journal of Organizational Behavior, 27*(3), 387–393.

While research on PsyCap is relatively new as an area of study for individual differences, initial results show that the four elements predict job performance and satisfaction.[53] Some might argue that high performance causes people to be more optimistic, hopeful, resilient, and believing more in their own abilities, but a longitudinal study found that PsyCap predicts performance and not the other way around.[54] Training interventions may increase PsyCap.[55] Thus, PsyCap is important for human development, but it is also related to an organization's competitive advantage due to its impact on job performance.[56] Figure 2.3 summarizes the relationships of the four PsyCap elements and organizational outcomes that relate to the competitive advantage of organizations.

PsyCap variables are relatively stable but can change. However, there is research in OB on states or things that change frequently—over the course of a day or even hours. These are known as emotions and moods, and research demonstrates that they also significantly impact OB. For example, a study of PsyCap and organizational change showed that efficacy, hope, optimism, and resiliency were related to positive emotions at work, which in turn affected the acceptance of organizational change.[57] Experiencing positive emotions enhanced the role of PsyCap in explaining *why* employees were less cynical and showed more citizenship during the change. PsyCap involves self-efficacy, which is our belief in our own ability to execute a specific goal. Another personality trait that relates to our self-concept is core self-evaluation, which represents a more generalized positive self-view and is covered next.

CORE SELF-EVALUATIONS

Learning Objective 2.7: Explain the effects of positive and negative core self-evaluations.

Core self-evaluations (CSE) are defined as "fundamental premises that individuals hold about themselves and their functioning in the world."[58] People who have a high core self-evaluation see themselves as competent and in control. An experimental study found that management students who scored high on core self-evaluations chose more complex tasks.[59] Core self-evaluations relate to job satisfaction, and this is, in part, due to high CSE employees taking on

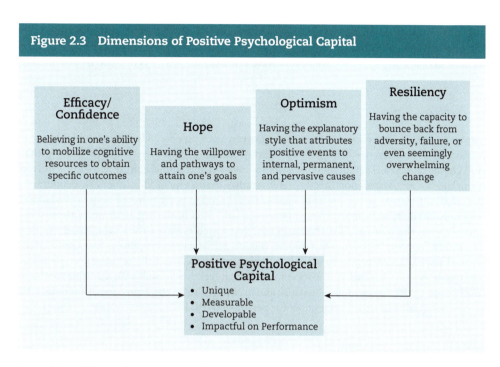

Figure 2.3 Dimensions of Positive Psychological Capital

Efficacy/ Confidence

Believing in one's ability to mobilize cognitive resources to obtain specific outcomes

Hope

Having the willpower and pathways to attain one's goals

Optimism

Having the explanatory style that attributes positive events to internal, permanent, and pervasive causes

Resiliency

Having the capacity to bounce back from adversity, failure, or even seemingly overwhelming change

Positive Psychological Capital

- Unique
- Measurable
- Developable
- Impactful on Performance

Source: Adapted from Luthans, F., & Youssef, C. M. (2004). Investing in People for Competitive Advantage. *Organizational Dynamics, 33*(2), 152.

more challenging tasks and seeing their work as personally fulfilling. Having a positive core self-evaluation predicts employee voice; in other words, such individuals are more likely to speak up and make suggestions about how to improve the work situation.[60] Core self-evaluations have also been related to job performance in a meta-analysis of 81 studies including thousands of employees.[61] For example, a study of 1,486 employees and 145 managers in grocery store departments found that core self-evaluations were positively related to managers' service quality orientation, even after dimensions of the Big Five model of personality were taken into account.[62] Given the relationships of CSE and job performance, it is not surprising that the research evidence shows a positive relationship between CSE and higher salaries. However, this relationship holds when the manager had strong networking relationships with select mentors rather than lots of relationships.[63] CSE has implications for your career as well. Core self-evaluations have also been strongly related to both persistence in job search behavior and success.[64] Higher core self-evaluations are associated with early job success as well as higher career success over time.[65] In sum, the evidence on CSE shows that your concept of self-worth will likely translate into net worth. To learn about your own core self-evaluations, complete Self-Assessment 2.3 in the Toolkit at the end of this chapter.

PERSON–ENVIRONMENT FIT

Learning Objective 2.8: Compare and contrast person–organization fit and person–job fit.

Research on **person–environment (PE) fit** has shown that when an individual's personality is aligned with his or her environment, it results in job satisfaction, organizational commitment, and better performance on the job. Also, employees that fit their work environment are less likely to quit.[66] There are different forms of how a person fits into his or her work environment, and two types of PE fit are important: person–organization (PO) fit, which is the match between the person and the organization, and person–job (PJ) fit, which is the match between the person and the job.[67]

Person–Organization Fit

Person–Organization (PO) fit is viewed as the match between a person's individual values and those of the organization they work for. PO fit is often considered in the context of recruiting employees who will "fit in" with the organizational culture.[68] Organizations seek applicants that embrace their organizational culture and values. Job candidates are interested in working for an organization that has values similar to their own. This is because people are attracted to and trust others that they view as being similar to themselves.[69] Good fit is the result of better communication among employees, increased predictability, interpersonal attraction, and trust in the organization, with trust being the key component that explains the positive outcomes of PO fit.[70] Research evidence shows that good PO fit is positively related to job satisfaction, organizational commitment, and job performance. Employees feel a sense of psychological ownership for their work because they feel a sense of belonging and experience the organization as a place that makes them feel comfortable, positive, and safe.[71,72] Also, employees that feel they fit well with the values of the organization are also less likely to quit.[73] PE fit is multidimensional, and in addition to PO fit, employees want to feel that they have a job that fits their personality as well. This is known as person–job (PJ) fit.

Person–Job Fit

One study found that the lack of fit between the person and the job they do significantly relates to higher job burnout and physical symptoms. Thus, poor fit may be detrimental to employee well-being. The authors offer the following scenarios:

> Imagine an accountant who actually is an outgoing person, enjoys being in company and seeks closeness in her social relationships. However, at her workplace, she most of the time works on her own with hardly any contact with colleagues or clients. Thus, her job does not offer many opportunities to socialize and to be in a trusting mutual exchange with other people. And now imagine another employee, a mid-level manager, who is expected to take on responsibility for his team, motivate and supervise his staff members, find compromises between conflicting interests, make personnel decisions, in short, to influence on other people. When at his workplace, though, he is out of his element as he does not like to take center stage and actually feels awkward in his role as a leader. As different, at first sight, the situation of these two employees might seem, there is one commonality between them: their motivational propensities with respect to the two social motives, namely affiliation and power, do not match with the demands and opportunities their job offers them, that is, a motivational person-environment misfit exists.[74]

The above examples demonstrate poor person–job fit. Good **person–job (PJ) fit** occurs when job characteristics are aligned with employees' personalities, motivations, and abilities. The concept of PJ fit also includes the fit with the work group and the supervisor.[75] PJ fit is comprised of two forms. The first is **demands–abilities (DA) fit**, which refers to the compatibility between the employee's knowledge, skills, and abilities, and the demands of the job. In other words, the job characteristics are neither too easy nor too difficult for the abilities of the employee; they match. The second type of fit refers to the extent to which the job supplies the employee's needs and is therefore called **needs–supplies (NS) fit**.[76] This form of PJ fit addresses whether the job fulfills the employee's needs for interesting work and a sense of meaning in their work.

One of the best researched theories of PJ fit is John Holland's **personality–job fit theory**. He discovered six different personality types and examined occupations that match these types. As shown in Figure 2.4, the personality types are Realistic (R), Investigative (I), Artistic (A), Social (S), Enterprising (E), and Conventional (C). This is sometimes referred to as the RIASEC model, and this acronym is helpful in remembering these personality types. Holland developed a questionnaire known as the Vocational Preference Inventory to assess these personality types and their match to 160 occupational titles. Research evidence supports these six personality types.[77] Personality types that are closer to one another on the hexagon shown in the figure are more similar. Types that are opposite are

Figure 2.4 Personality–Job Fit Theory

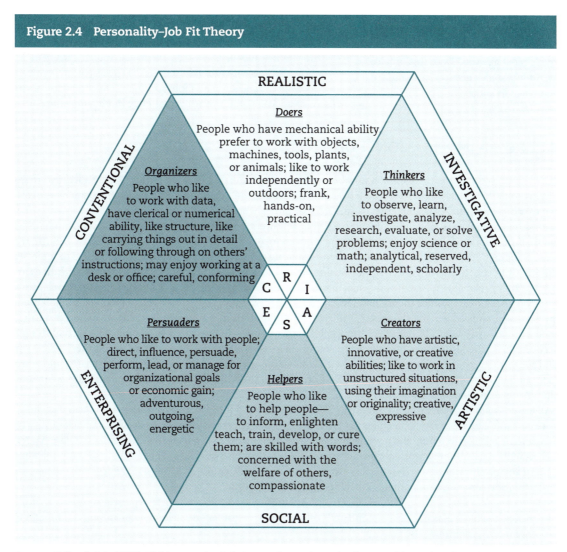

Sources: Holland, J. L. (1997). *Making vocational choices: A theory of vocational personalities and work environments.* Odessa, FL: Psychological Assessment Resources; Psychological Assessment Resources, Inc. from Making Vocational Choices, copyright 1973, 1985, 1992 by Psychological Assessment Resources, Inc. All rights reserved.

most dissimilar. For example, realistic people may be more introverted, and they are practical people that get things done. Investigative people are analytical and may enjoy research work. Artistic types are imaginative and may best match with being a musician or writer. Social individuals are more extroverted and may enjoy teaching or social work. Enterprising people are confident and energetic and may match with being a lawyer or small business ownership. Conventional people are conforming and might best match with accounting or corporate management.

> Critical Thinking Questions: Evaluate the personality–fit theory by explaining why you think the personalities adjacent to one another in the hexagon are most similar. Which personality type is most like you? Does this provide insight into which occupations you might best fit with?

A recent meta-analysis of 92 studies found that the match between personality traits and job demands significantly predicts job performance.[78] In addition, the research evidence found that PJ fit job knowledge relates to lower turnover intentions.[79] When personality is aligned with the work that we do, it increases our goal direction, vigor, and persistence, resulting in high motivation—this is true for both academic and job performance.[80] The "Fitting in Somewhere Great!" activity (Toolkit Activity 2.1) gives you an opportunity to locate an organization and job, and then reflect on your personality traits and how well you will experience PO fit and PJ fit.

LEADERSHIP IMPLICATIONS: UNDERSTANDING OTHERS

In this chapter, you have learned about a number of different personality characteristics. You also learned that personality is something that is relatively stable over the life course (the exception might be PsyCap, since research has shown that these personality characteristics are state-like and may be changed through training). As a leader, you may not be able to change the personalities of your boss, your followers, or your peers. Since some of the research evidence (recall the Minnesota twin studies) suggests that personality may be in part hereditary or determined at birth, trying to change another person's personality traits might be a futile effort. Thus, it is important for leaders to understand others and work effectively with different personality types. Leaders can do two important things. One is to examine each applicant's personality type and vocational interests when making hiring decisions. The robust research program on Holland's personality–job fit theory has demonstrated that congruence between the person and the job predicts job performance and reduces the chances that the person will quit. Paying attention to the RIASEC traits during the interview process may help a leader select the applicant that best fits the demands of the job. The second thing that leaders can do is to assess personality characteristics of their team members. The assessments in the Toolkit will be helpful for this purpose (Big Five, Type A, and CSE); however, there are others that can be purchased and administered by an industrial/organizational psychologist. For example, the MBTI is often used by organizations for conflict resolution and team building.

All leaders want followers who are agreeable and conscientious. However, this chapter has revealed that there are some personality traits that are challenging for a leader to work with on a day-to-day basis. Difficult personality traits are Machiavellianism, narcissism, and perhaps the Type A behavior pattern when taken to an extreme. These types may engage in bullying, explode at work, throw tantrums, and yell. Connie Merritt, a registered nurse and public health nurse, and author of the book *Too Busy for Your Own Good: Get More Done in Less Time—With Even More Energy*, offers the following advice for disarming these difficult personalities at work:[81]

1. Adopt a neutral stance. Picture an inflated balloon that you just let go . . . fssuuuu all around the room. Do not interrupt or touch the person.

2. Rise slowly if you are seated; make eye contact, cross your arms or make a "stop sign" gesture.

3. Snap them out of it by saying their name.

4. Ask for a solution. Say, "Al, I can see this is a big problem for you. What can we do together to help solve it?"

5. Ask them to leave. Say, "I feel overwhelmed right now. I would like you to come back when you're less angry."

6. Leave. Say, "I'm going to leave now, and I'll come back when we can talk about this in a more productive way."

Merritt cites a book by Jim Grigsby, *Don't Tick Off the Gators*, who suggests that after you have addressed the outburst from a difficult personality, ask yourself:

- Did I cause or contribute to the problem by not knowing enough about the other person?

- Did I create the environment that allowed the situation to flourish by ignoring it or hoping it would go away?

- Was the cause of the problem a lack of communication or bad information?

- How did I respond to each event? Did I know when to "hold 'em and when to fold 'em"?

- Can this situation be prevented in the future? What can I learn from this experience?

As a leader, you'll encounter difficult personalities sooner or later. By taking the actions above, you should be able to diffuse the situation. Asking the questions listed and thinking critically about the answers may help you to avoid negative encounters with difficult personality types in the future. It's important to own your contributions to the negative behaviors of a person that exhibits the dark side of personality at work.

Personality has the potential for both positive and negative contributions to the workplace. Understanding personality differences is thus essential for leader effectiveness. Personality is like a diamond and has many facets. This chapter has reviewed the personality traits that are most relevant to the workplace. As a leader, you may not be able to change personality, but it is important to assess personality traits of your followers, coworkers, and boss. Then be ready to take action and develop an individualized relationship with them that is based upon their unique personality. If the follower has a difficult personality, be ready to disarm it using the steps above. Difficult personalities may have negative moods and engage in emotional outbursts. The next chapter (Chapter 3) discusses the role that emotions and moods play in the workplace.

edge.sagepub.com/scandura2e

Want a better grade? Go to **edge.sagepub.com/scandura2e** for the tools you need to sharpen your study skills.

KEY TERMS

agreeableness, 29
conscientiousness, 29
core self-evaluation (CSE), 36
Dark Triad, 32
demands–abilities (DA) fit, 38

extraversion, 29
Machiavellianism, 31
Minnesota twin studies, 27
narcissism, 32
needs–supplies (NS) fit, 38

neuroticism, 29
openness, 29
personality, 27
personality–job fit theory, 39
person–environment (PE) fit, 37

person–job (PJ) fit, 38
person–organization (PO) fit, 38
psychological capital (PsyCap), 34
psychopathy, 32

risk taking, 34
self-monitoring, 33
state-like, 34
trait-like, 34

Type A behavior, 31
Type B behavior, 31
Type C behavior, 31
Type D behavior, 31

TOOLKIT ACTIVITY 2.1: Fitting In Somewhere Great!

1. Explain the difference between person–job fit and person–organization fit.

2. Select a small, medium, or large organization you would like to work for and explain why you would be a good fit there (person–organization fit). For example, you can search for great organizations to work for using search engines or the glassdoor.com best places to work list:

   https://www.glassdoor.com/Best-Places-to-Work-LST_KQ0,19.htm

3. What would be your ideal position in this organization? Again, you can search jobs within the organization using search engines or the glassdoor.com list. Explain why this would be a good fit for you (person–job fit).

4. In your responses to 2 and 3 above, include a discussion of personality traits covered in this chapter, including things such as:

   • Big Five Personality Test (Self-Assessment 2.1 results)

   • Type A/Type B Behavior Pattern (Self-Assessment 2.2 results)

   • Core Self-Evaluations (Self-Assessment 2.3 results)

   • Self-Monitoring

   • Risk-Taking

   • PsyCap (optimism, hope, self-efficacy, resiliency)

   • RIASEC (Realistic, Investigative, Artistic, Social, Enterprising, Conventional)

   For this activity, you will need a high level of self-awareness and also do some insightful research into the job and organization you select.

Discussion Questions

1. Why did you select the organization that you would like to work for? What factors did you consider after doing your research on what working there would be like?

2. Why did you select the job that you would like to hold? Did you consider factors other than how you would fit in there such as location, pay, or benefits?

3. Which personality traits do you feel are most important regarding how well you would fit in with the organization and job you selected?

Source: Adapted from an exercise developed by Marie Dasborough, University of Miami.

CASE STUDY 2.1: Who Would You Hire?

Worldwide Manufacturing Inc. has just weathered intense scrutiny after it was investigated and fined for violations of improper chemical storage and waste disposal. Worldwide is a special-order manufacturer that makes plastic products in whatever shapes and sizes a customer specifies. In order to do so, it makes special molds for each project for pouring and shaping the plastic into the forms requested by customers. Each order takes retooling and reorganizing of the manufacturing floor. To help prevent further issues in the future, the company has decided to add a compliance department that will ensure that not only are EPA regulations followed but also other legal regulations, from proper accounting to ensuring everything is in compliance with OSHA. You have been promoted to be the firm's compliance officer and are now looking to hire several new members of the compliance department, including a compliance manager, compliance analyst, as well as an auditor and inspector.

You decide to begin with filling the compliance manager position. A compliance manager is a professional that keeps the legal and ethical integrity of a company intact through policy enforcement and program planning. He or she makes sure all departments of a business are complying with the rules and regulations the company is required to uphold and should regularly meet with managers in the areas of finance and accounting, cybersecurity, human resources, and operations. Compliance managers are responsible for keeping up to date with changing laws that affect the corporate world and are responsible for preparing reports to present to their upper management detailing these laws and how the policies of the company are ensuring that employees are following them. After advertising for 2 weeks on indeed.com and Monster.com, you've begun to look through resumes. You have two promising candidates who have made it through initial phone interviews, and you have flown them out to meet with you and see the headquarters and manufacturing operations. Now you have to review what you have learned about each candidate and make your decision.

Aarya Song

Aarya Song grew up on military bases and joined the military after completing high school. Over a 15-year career, Aarya worked with base operations managers on a team that handled everything needed for running a base. Aarya worked in supply chain management, both in procurement and disposal, in facilities planning, inventory management, and even in operations planning for setting up new bases. All of these positions required great organization and time-management skills. In addition, part of Aarya's job was to ensure everything was to regulation and followed local regulations as well. While serving in the military, Aarya earned a bachelor's degree in logistics and later an MBA.

After leaving the military with highest honors, Aarya worked as the transportation manager for an international manufacturer of wind turbines. However, after talking on the phone during the first round of interviews, you have learned that Aarya is now looking for a new job that will provide new challenges.

During the onsite interview, Aarya excitedly chatted with you about how Worldwide could ensure compliance and start building interorganizational teams to ensure companywide compliance. Aarya shared the logic behind these ideas, which you found impressive and well thought out. Your only concern is that Aarya seems to be very direct and no-nonsense, and while a zero tolerance stance on policy violations is likely needed after the investigation, it may be too rigid for the organization's existing culture.

Francis Simmonne

Francis grew up in an industrial city and began working in manufacturing while in high school at a plant that made various rubber-based components for automobile assembly. After attending a regional university to learn about engineering for product design, Francis began working as a designer for a firm that designed and manufactured toys. However, Francis was better at helping the men and women on the manufacturing floor fix the problems that arose with making the first batches of new toys. After a few moderately successful products, Francis was promoted to production manager because of the skills he demonstrated on the shop floor. Three years later, Francis started working on an MBA and ended up taking a materials manager position with a construction firm. It was very important in this position that all materials were to code, and Francis took that responsibility very seriously. Five years later, Francis took a position as a work site inspector for the construction company, examining work sites and ensuring all health and safety policies as well as building codes were being followed. While these later positions had increasing responsibility, he did not have any direct reports.

Francis is getting married and is looking to move to the city Worldwide calls home, and so has applied for the compliance manager position. When you spoke on the phone, Francis seemed practical yet reserved, a perception you had reinforced during the site interview. Francis relies on instinct more than evidence to make decisions, which helps to quickly provide a course of action. However, you have concerns that Francis might not be a firm-enough manager as he likes to work with the production teams and crews and has had very little direct management of teams or departments.

So now you have a choice: Simmonne or Song? Both candidates have strong points and weak points, and both could do the job.

Discussion Questions

1. Identify each candidate's personality characteristics using the Big Five and the Myers-Briggs typology.

2. Based on personality, is there a candidate that you think would fit the position better?

3. Why is it important to consider personality in hiring? What other individual differences should you consider in hiring?

SELF-ASSESSMENT 2.1: The Big Five Personality Test

Introduction

This is a personality test; it will help you understand why you act the way that you do and how your personality may be structured. Please follow the instructions below. The scoring and interpretation follow the questions. There are no right or wrong answers. You don't have to share your results with others if you do not wish to do so.

Instructions

In the following table, for each statement 1 through 25, rate each with the following scale of 1 through 5:

Statements	Strongly Disagree	Disagree	Neutral	Agree	Strongly Agree
1. I feel comfortable around people.	1	2	3	4	5
2. I have a good word for everyone.	1	2	3	4	5
3. I am always prepared.	1	2	3	4	5
4. I often feel blue.	1	2	3	4	5
5. I believe in the importance of art.	1	2	3	4	5
6. I make friends easily.	1	2	3	4	5
7. I believe others have good intentions.	1	2	3	4	5
8. I pay attention to details.	1	2	3	4	5

9. I dislike myself.	1	2	3	4	5
10. I have a vivid imagination.	1	2	3	4	5
11. I am skilled in handling social situations.	1	2	3	4	5
12. I respect others.	1	2	3	4	5
13. I get chores done right away.	1	2	3	4	5
14. I am often down in the dumps.	1	2	3	4	5
15. I enjoy hearing new ideas.	1	2	3	4	5
16. I am the life of the party.	1	2	3	4	5
17. I accept people as they are.	1	2	3	4	5
18. I carry out my plans.	1	2	3	4	5
19. I have frequent mood swings.	1	2	3	4	5
20. I am interested in abstract ideas.	1	2	3	4	5
21. I know how to captivate people.	1	2	3	4	5
22. I make people feel at ease.	1	2	3	4	5
23. I make plans and stick to them.	1	2	3	4	5
24. I panic easily.	1	2	3	4	5
25. I have excellent ideas.	1	2	3	4	5

The question numbers are shown in parentheses below. Write your score (1 to 5) on the blank following the question. For example, if you answered question (1) with a score of 2, write 2 on the blank.

O = (5) ___ + (10) ___ + (15) ___ + (20) ___ + (25) ____ = ____ (Openness to Experience)
C = (3) ___ + (8) ___ + (13) ___ + (18) ___ + (23) ___ = ____ (Conscientiousness)
E = (1) ___ + (6) ___ + (11) ___ + (16) ___ + (21) ___ = ____ (Extraversion)
A = (2) ___ + (7) ___ + (12) ___ + (17) ___ + (22) ___ = ____ (Agreeableness)
N = (4) ___ + (9) ___ + (14) ___ + (19) ___ + (24) ____ = ____ (Neuroticism)

The scores you calculate for each personality characteristic should be between 5 and 25. Scores from 5 to 10 can be considered lower, and scores above 10 can be considered higher.

Following is a description of each trait.

Openness to Experience (O) is the personality trait of seeking new experience and intellectual pursuits. High scorers may daydream a lot. Low scorers may be very down-to-earth.

Conscientiousness (C) is the personality trait of being honest and hardworking. High scorers tend to follow rules and prefer clean homes. Low scorers may be messy and cheat others.

Extraversion (E) is the personality trait of seeking fulfillment from sources outside the self or in community. High scorers tend to be very social, while low scorers prefer to work on their projects alone.

Agreeableness (A) reflects that many individuals adjust their behavior to suit others. High scorers are typically polite and like people. Low scorers tend to "tell it like it is."

Neuroticism (N) is the personality trait of being emotional.

Discussion Questions

1. Discuss your personality profile based upon the results of the Big Five personality assessment.

2. Are there any traits that you would like to improve upon (for example, low openness to experience)? How will you go about improving on them?

3. How will you use the results of the assessment to become a more effective leader?

Source: Adapted from the NEO Big 5 Scales at http://ipip.ori.org. Finholt, T. A., & Olson, G. M. (1997). From laboratories to collaboratories: A new organizational form for scientific collaboration. *Psychological Science, 8*(1), 28–36.

SELF-ASSESSMENT 2.2: Type A/Type B Behavior Pattern

This assessment measures the extent to which you are a Type A or Type B personality. There are no right or wrong answers, and this is not a test. You don't have to share your results with other classmates unless you wish to do so.

Part I. Taking the Assessment

For each of the statements below, circle the number that indicates the degree to which you agree or disagree.

Statements	Strongly Disagree	Disagree	Neutral	Agree	Strongly Agree
1. Having work to complete "stirs me into action" more than other people.	1	2	3	4	5
2. When a person is talking and takes too long to come to the point, I frequently feel like hurrying the person along.	1	2	3	4	5
3. Nowadays, I consider myself to be relaxed and easygoing. (reversed)	1	2	3	4	5
4. Typically, I get irritated extremely easily.	1	2	3	4	5
5. My best friends would rate my general activity level as very high.	1	2	3	4	5
6. I definitely tend to do most things in a hurry.	1	2	3	4	5
7. I take my work much more seriously than most.	1	2	3	4	5
8. I seldom get angry. (reversed)	1	2	3	4	5
9. I often set deadlines for myself workwise.	1	2	3	4	5
10. I feel very impatient when I have to wait in line.	1	2	3	4	5
11. I put much more effort into my work than other people do.	1	2	3	4	5
12. Compared with others, I approach life much less seriously. (reversed)	1	2	3	4	5

Part II. Scoring and Interpretation

Subtract your answers to questions 3, 8, and 12 (marked *reversed*) from 8, with the difference being your new score for those questions. For example, if your original answer for question 12 was 3, your new answer is 5 (8 – 3). Then add up your answers for the 12 questions. Compare your answer to the following scale:

53 or above	Type A	You may perceive higher stress in your life and be susceptible to health.
52 or below	Type B	You experience less stress in your life, and you are less sensitive to stress you do experience.

Discussion Questions

1. Are you Type A or Type B? Are you concerned about your results? Give some examples from your daily life that are consistent with your type (for example, do you get impatient waiting in line)?

2. If you are Type A, list some coping strategies that you will use to start to address the stress based upon the reading in this chapter.

3. If you are Type B, find a friend or classmate that is Type A and explain to them how you react to stressful situations.

Source: Jenkins, C. D., Zyzanski, S. J., & Rosenman, R. H. (1971). Progress toward validation of a computer-scored test for the Type A coronary-prone behavior pattern. *Psychosomatic Medicine, 22,* 193–202. Reprinted with permission of Lippincott, Williams and Wilkins.

SELF-ASSESSMENT 2.3: Core Self-Evaluations Assessment

This self-assessment exercise identifies your core self-evaluations. There are no right or wrong answers, and this is not a test. You don't have to share your results with the class unless you wish to do so.

Part I. Taking the Assessment

You will be presented with some questions representing how you might see yourself. For each of the statements below, circle the number that indicates the degree to which you agree or disagree.

Statements	Not Like Me At All	Not Much Like Me	Somewhat Like Me	Mostly Like Me	Very Much Like Me
1. I am confident I will get the success I deserve in life.	1	2	3	4	5
3. When I try, I generally succeed.	1	2	3	4	5
5. I complete tasks successfully.	1	2	3	4	5
7. Overall, I am satisfied with myself.	1	2	3	4	5
9. I determine what will happen in my life.	1	2	3	4	5
11. I am capable of coping with most of my problems.	1	2	3	4	5

	Very Much Like Me	Mostly Like Me	Somewhat Like Me	Not Much Like Me	Not Like Me At All
2. Sometimes I feel depressed.	1	2	3	4	5
4. Sometimes when I fail I feel worthless.	1	2	3	4	5
6. Sometimes I do not feel in control of my work.	1	2	3	4	5
8. I am filled with doubts about my competence.	1	2	3	4	5

(Continued)

	Very Much Like Me	Mostly Like Me	Somewhat Like Me	Not Much Like Me	Not Like Me At All
10. I do not feel in control of my success in my career.	1	2	3	4	5
12. There are times when things look pretty bleak and hopeless to me.	1	2	3	4	5

Part II. Scoring Instructions

1. For questions 1, 3, 5, 7, 9, and 11, assign the following points:

   5 = Very much like me   3 = Somewhat like me   1 = Not like me at all

   4 = Mostly like me   2 = Not much like me

2. For questions 2, 4, 6, 8, 10, and 12, assign the following points:

   1 = Very much like me   3 = Somewhat like me   5 = Not like me at all

   2 = Mostly like me   4 = Not much like me

In Step 1, you rated yourself on 12 questions. Add the numbers you circled in each of the columns to derive your score for your core self-evaluations.

Part 1	Part 2
1. _____	2. _____
3. _____	4. _____
5. _____	6. _____
7. _____	8. _____
9. _____	10. _____
11. _____	12. _____
Part 1 Total _____ +	Part 2 Total _____ = Your Score _____

Interpretation

Your scores can range from 12 to 60. In general, scores from 12 to 24 can be considered having low core self-evaluations and scores above 25 can be considered higher core self-evaluations.

Discussion Questions

1. If your core self-evaluation (CSE) was low, how can you improve it? If it was high, can you cite experiences that you have had that have led to this positive self-evaluation?

2. Compare your results with a friend or another student in the class. Were your results similar or different? What experiences do you share that provide insight into how you developed your CSE? If your results are different, learn about the other person's experiences and compare them to your own.

3. List some ways that you will gain control over your work and schoolwork to increase your CSE.

Source: Adapted from Judge, T. A., Erez, A., & Bono, C. J. (2003). The core self-evaluations scale: Development of a measure. *Personnel Psychology, 56*(2), 303–331.

CHAPTER THREE

EMOTIONS AND MOODS

Learning Objectives

After studying this chapter, you should be able to do the following:

3.1: Illustrate, with an example, the differences between emotions and moods.

3.2: Summarize the affective events theory with an example.

3.3: Explain how affective climate (positive and negative) of a work group relates to team conflict.

3.4: Demonstrate with an example how positive and negative state affect relates to customer service.

3.5: Demonstrate understanding of emotional labor by providing examples of jobs that require "surface acting" and "deep acting."

3.6: Discuss the case for training in emotional intelligence in the workplace.

3.7: Explain how positive and negative emotions can spread from one individual to a group through the emotional contagion process.

3.8: Explain affective neuroscience and provide an organizational example.

Get the edge on your studies at
edge.sagepub.com/scandura2e

- Take the chapter quiz
- Review key terms with eFlashcards
- Explore multimedia resources, SAGE readings, and more!

DOES LACK OF SLEEP MAKE YOU GRUMPY?

Have you ever stayed up late studying and then noticed that the next day everything seemed to go wrong? You get stuck in traffic, and you find your classmate who asks to see your notes annoying. However, this might be more due to your own emotions and mood than other people. Research has shown that the lack of sleep has a dramatic influence on emotions. Sleep researchers conduct experiments to figure out how the lack of sleep affects emotions and moods. Researchers bring people into their laboratories and keep them up all night. Would you do this for science? This research evidence has documented that when people are sleep deprived they feel more irritable, angry, and hostile. Loss of sleep is even associated with feeling more depressed: A meta-analysis of the literature found that sleep deprivation depresses mood.[1] Also, sleep deprivation results in people reacting more emotionally—especially when something doesn't go well for them. So your angry feelings about classmates asking to see your notes for days they missed class might be due to your lack of sleep. Sleep loss leads to increased negative mood and a reduction in the ability to regulate anger due to biochemical changes that occur in the brain.[2] Even small changes in normal nightly sleep inhibit the ability to regulate emotions at work the next day.[3]

We have all heard stories about employees who didn't get enough sleep and then subjected their coworkers to a cranky mood the following workday.[4] Organizational behavior (OB) research has found that sleep loss results in lower self-control and higher workplace deviance (e.g., dragging out work to get more overtime pay).[5] A fascinating study found that lack of sleep by managers led them to be more likely to abuse their followers.[6] Insomnia has been related to lower job satisfaction.[7] A recent study found that the use of smartphones late at night rather than sleeping soundly resulted in lower work engagement the next day.[8] So how much sleep should you be getting? According to the National Sleep Foundation, adults aged 18 to 64 should aim to get around 7 to 9 hours of sleep each night.[9] So put that smartphone or computer down at night start getting your Zs!

EMOTIONS AND MOODS AT WORK

Learning Objective 3.1: Illustrate, with an example, the differences between emotions and moods.

Unfortunately, we have all had the experience of being treated rudely by someone—a coworker, supervisor, or a clerk in a retail store. We wonder, "Why is this person such a crab?" One reason, as noted above, might be that they didn't get enough sleep. But what are other reasons for negative emotions and moods at work? Research on emotions at work seeks to address these questions.

Despite the clear implications of employee feelings about the experience of work, emotions and moods were largely ignored in most early OB literature.[10] It was assumed that employees left their feelings at home when they came to work in the morning. Yet we can all think of situations in which people react based on their emotions at work and don't act rationally. And as you saw in Chapter 1, the measure of job satisfaction (how employees feel about their work) contains strong emotion, since the first item asks employees how they feel about their job and has "I hate it" as a possible response.

With the exception of job satisfaction, emotions at the workplace were not regularly studied until relatively recently. This is likely because societal expectations of leaders are that—in order to be most effective—they should be logical, detached, and rational decision makers. Showing one's feelings or caring about the feelings of followers and coworkers was attributed to weakness and not sound leadership. However, in the mid-1980s and the 1990s, organizational researchers began studying the effects of emotions and moods on behavior in organizations. By 2003, scholars referred to this research as "the affective revolution" in OB.[11] **Affect** is a general term that refers to the range of feelings that employees experience at work. Affect is comprised of emotions and moods.[12] **State affect** refers to feelings experienced in the short term, and fluctuate over time, whereas **trait affect** refers to stable individual differences. **Emotions** are triggered by specific events and are brief but intense enough to disrupt a person's thinking—lasting only seconds or minutes. Some emotions are internal to a person, such as pride and love.[13] Other emotions emerge in relationships with others, such as shame and guilt.[14] **Moods**, on the other hand, are general feeling states that are not related to a specific event, but they are not intense enough to interrupt regular thought patterns or work.[15] Emotions are more fleeting than moods. In other words, a felt emotion, such as anger at your boss, may pass. But being in a foul mood may last for hours. Moods aren't typically caused by a person or something that happens to us. However, emotions are directed at another person or situation (i.e., we are happy to see our coworkers when they come back from a vacation). Obviously, emotions and moods are related—being in a good mood can result in the experience of feeling happy (an emotion). The relationship between affect and emotions and mood is shown in Figure 3.1.

As noted above, the study of emotions and moods has revolutionized thinking about OB. Next, we turn to the key foundation for studying emotions at work: the affective events theory (AET). This framework will be a useful reference for you to follow as you read further about research on emotions and moods.

> Critical Thinking Questions: Do you think a leader should suppress their emotions and moods to be effective? Why or why not?

AFFECTIVE EVENTS THEORY: AN ORGANIZING FRAMEWORK

Learning Objective 3.2: Summarize the affective events theory with an example.

Affective events theory provides a useful roadmap for the material we cover in this chapter.[16] This framework integrates

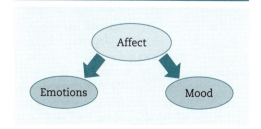

Figure 3.1 The Relationship Between Affect and Emotions and Mood

Source: Adapted from Watson, D. (2000). *Mood and temperament.* New York, NY: Guilford Press.

personality, emotions, and moods, and considers the impact of the work environment and events that may trigger emotional reactions (positive and negative affect). Areas in the work environment that leaders should pay close attention to are the characteristics of the job (e.g., is it boring or interesting?), the job demands (e.g., is the job just too difficult for the person to handle?), and the requirements for emotional labor (e.g., does the person have to interact with the public and be courteous to irate customers?). Notice that in Figure 3.2, these work environment factors lead to work events such as daily hassles and uplifts (uplifts are moments when everything is going just great). Personality and moods play a role in how people react to hassles and uplifts. For example, a person low on emotional stability may have a stronger reaction to a daily hassle. Taken together, the work environment, events, personality, and moods combine to evoke emotional responses—positive or negative. This, in turn, leads to job satisfaction and performance. Affective events explain the development of effective working relationships between leaders and followers.[17] A review of AET discusses the large number of studies that have supported the AET and considers it to be a "classic" OB model.[18] This review summarizes what we know about affective events at work:

- **Satisfaction is not emotion**. Research has demonstrated that emotions influence outcomes such as job performance and turnover independent of job satisfaction. The fluctuating experiences of emotions and moods are not the same thing as a judgment of job satisfaction. For example, a person can be satisfied with their work in general, but their negative emotions can reduce their ability to attend to details in their work.

- **Events cause emotions**. This is a distinct aspect of AET from other OB theories. Both job-related and non-job-related events can instigate emotional states at work and therefore have work consequences. For example, being treated negatively by a coworker can cause an employee to have negative affect (job-related). Also, getting into an argument with a person's spouse can cause an employee to experience negative affect all day at work (non-job-related).

- **Affect-driven behaviors are different from judgment-driven behaviors**. Affect-driven behaviors are decisions and judgments that have (relatively) immediate consequences. In comparison, judgment-driven behaviors are decisions, or judgments, that are driven by more long-term attitudes about the job or organization. For example, an affect-driven behavior occurs when a person feels negative about being treated badly by a customer and then raids the department's refrigerator and eats a coworker's donut (immediate consequence).

- **Affective experiences change over time**. This is important since research has shown that a person is more likely to perform better when he or she is happy than when he or she is less happy.[19] For example, a person could come to work experiencing negative affect, but they receive a compliment from their boss in the late morning that lifts them up and they perform better in the afternoon.

- **Affect is structured as emotions and moods**. As noted above, AET specifies that emotions are distinct from moods. This distinction is important since moods lack a specific causal event, whereas emotions are reactions to something that provokes a person at work. For example, a person can be in a bad mood for no reason, but when they get into an argument with a coworker, they also experience negative affect.

Research on AET sometimes asks employees to keep diaries of their emotions and moods at work. An example of such a study[20] asked 218 employees to keep diaries of negative and positive events at work. Positive events were when they were enthusiastic, and negative events were when they were worried or angry. Most positive events were related to goal attainment and task success. Also, praise and appreciation generated enthusiasm. Negative events were most related to hindrances and obstacles encountered at work. Also, employees reported managerial problems and poor organizational climate as generating worry or anger. Decades of research supports the relationships shown in Figure 3.2. AET serves as an evidence-based and useful way to summarize what we cover in this chapter. This theory really puts it all together for us.

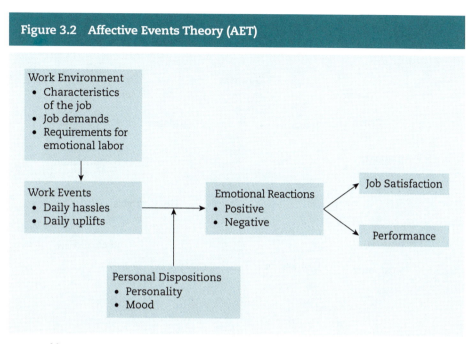

Figure 3.2 Affective Events Theory (AET)

Work Environment
- Characteristics of the job
- Job demands
- Requirements for emotional labor

Work Events
- Daily hassles
- Daily uplifts

Emotional Reactions
- Positive
- Negative

Job Satisfaction

Performance

Personal Dispositions
- Personality
- Mood

Source: Ashkanasy, N. M., & Daus, C. S. (2002). Emotion in the workplace: The new challenge for managers. *Academy of Management Executive,* 16(1), 77.

One of the key aspects in AET is the work environment. Research has found that the overall emotional climate of the work group matters. This is known as the affective climate.

AFFECTIVE CLIMATE

Learning Objective 3.3: Explain how affective climate (positive and negative) of a work group relates to team conflict.

Affective climate refers to the shared affective experience of a work group or team.[21] The climate, or tone, of the group can be considered feelings that arise from, or in, groups.[22] Affective climates are typically referred to as being affectively "positive" or "negative."[23] For example, a positive affective climate includes "participation, warmth, social rewards, cooperation."[24] The range of emotions that may be experienced has been summarized in the circumplex model of affect shown in Figure 3.3. This model locates specific emotions in the conceptual space defined by two orthogonal primary dimensions: pleasantness (pleasure–displeasure) and arousal (low activation–high activation). Affective climate is described as having different facets as shown in the figure.[25] A study using the circumplex model examined team conflict in 156 bank branches and found that disagreements about the work (task conflict) and difficulties with other team members (relationship conflict) were significantly related to the creation of a tension affective climate. This climate is characterized as the group mood being nervous, tense, and anxious rather than enthusiastic.[26]

A positive affective climate in the work group enhances the effects of good leader–member relationships. Research has shown that leader–member relationships result in more friendships at work, but the positive affective climate in the work group enhances this relationship. A feeling that team members are friends was related to more effective teamwork.[27] Another study of 97 teams in a car factory in Belgium found that positive team affective climate reduced

Figure 3.3　The Circumplex Model of Group Affective Climate

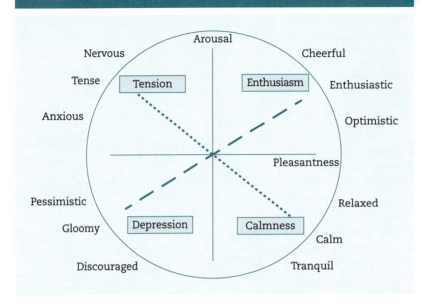

Source: Gamero, N., González-Romá, V., & Peiró, J. M. (2008). The influence of intra-team conflict on work teams' affective climate: A longitudinal study. *Journal of Occupational and Organizational Psychology, 81*(1), 47–69.

psychological distress. All team members benefited from a positive affective climate, even those workers who had a negative perception of their emotional work environment.[28] Affective climate is related to team creativity, especially when the groups work together effectively (for example, by asking a lot of questions of one another).[29]

As studies of affective climate have shown, emotions can have a positive impact within a group. They may also build over time into positive cycles of emotions. This happens because positive emotions change a person's outlook and how they see other people with whom they work. This is explained in the broaden-and-build model of emotions.

The Broaden-and-Build Model of Emotions

Emotions serve to both broaden employee experiences and then allow them to build better functioning in organizations. This is known as the **broaden-and-build model**.[30] Positive emotions such as pride in one's work can transform organizations and the people in them.[31] This is because positive emotions open people's minds and they begin to build personal and social resources, which enable them to work more effectively. Positive emotions can be contagious: A person's positive outlook at work affects the emotional reactions of their coworkers.[32] Also, positive workers are more likely to have positive interactions with customers. The broadening and building of emotions has also been linked to creativity at work (see the boxed insert).

Being grateful is an example of an emotion that may broaden and build positive spirals of positive emotion and behaviors at work.[33] **Gratitude** has been studied as a trait (in other words, some people are more grateful than others). Trait gratitude is defined as "a generalized tendency to recognize and respond with grateful emotion to the roles of other people's benevolence in the positive experiences and outcomes that one obtains."[34] Gratitude may also be a state

RESEARCH IN ACTION

Affect and Creativity

A study by Teresa Amabile of Harvard University and her colleagues found a link between positive emotions and creativity. Creativity is affectively charged, and complex cognitive processes are shaped by both emotions and moods. Creativity may be particularly susceptible to affective influence, mainly because positive affect leads to the sort of thought processes that stimulate creativity. Consider these emotional reactions to creative outputs cited in Amabile's research study:

> I figured out why something was not working correctly. I felt relieved and happy because this was a minor milestone for me. (Female participant in a high-tech company)

> I smashed that bug that's been frustrating me for almost a calendar week. That may not be an event to you, but I live a very drab life, so I'm all hyped. No one really knows about it; three of the team that would be involved are out today—so I have to sit here rejoicing in my solitary smugness. (Male participant in a high-tech company)

Both of these individuals are expressing positive emotions resulting from their creativity. This qualitative analysis showed that positive affect as a consequence of creative thought events, as well as occurring alongside the creative process, result in an affect–creativity cycle. This research identified positive affect as an antecedent of creative thought, with incubation periods of up to 2 days. In other words, creativity both evokes and accompanies creative performance. Positive affect has three primary effects on creativity. First, positive affect makes additional information available for processing by increasing the number of associations that can be made. Second, it leads to more complex contexts by defocusing people's attention on one solution, and this increases the number of things that are treated as relevant to the problem. Third, it increases cognitive flexibility by increasing the probability that diverse cognitive elements will become associated with one another. These processes generate more positive affect, and this, in turn, has a positive influence on creativity. As noted earlier in this chapter, the broaden-and-build model of positive emotion suggests that positive emotions, such as joy and pride, broaden a person's available repertoire of thoughts and actions. The experience of positive emotions leads people to pursue more novel ideas. Positive emotions broaden the scope of attention and the scope of ideas during the creative problem-solving process. Thus, positive affect leads to greater variation and thus increases the probability of creativity occurring.

Discussion Questions:

1. Discuss the impact of affect on creativity.
2. Recall an experience where you felt that you had produced a creative work. What emotions did you experience during the time you were being creative?
3. How can leaders create work environments where affect leads to enhanced creativity? Provide an example of this process.

Sources: Amabile, T. M., Barsade, S. G., Mueller, J. S., & Staw, B. M. (2005). Affect and creativity at work. *Administrative Science Quarterly, 50*(3), 367–403; Frederickson, B. L. (1998). What good are positive emotions? *Review of General Psychology, 2,* 300–319; Isen, A. (1999). On the relationship between affect and creative problem solving. In S. W. Russ (Ed.), *Affect, creative experience and psychological adjustment* (pp. 3–18). Philadelphia, PA: Brunner/Mazel.

that is related to being in a particular work situation. For example, state gratitude at work would result from a person having a job that gives them a sense of purpose, which evokes positive emotions.[35] Feeling grateful for having a purpose in your work creates additional positive emotions that result in higher motivation and performance.

An example of gratitude[36] in action happened when Sherilyn Joseph, who works at World Duty Free Group's Tampa gift shop at Tampa International Airport, was on duty when a passenger came in asking for help finding her coat and gloves. The passenger was about to board a flight to New York when she realized she had lost them. After airport officials were unable to find the coat, Sherilyn gave her own jacket to the woman. "I just felt I should do something to help her," Sherilyn said in a news release. "I wanted her to be warm and have a blessed trip." Company officials said Joseph showed exceptional customer service with her compassionate deed. Joseph received a letter of gratitude from the customer: "If not for your giving nature and helping another in a time of need, I would have walked into LaGuardia Airport shivering and looking to purchase a coat in the middle of the night!" And in addition to the gratitude from the customer, the company expressed its gratitude as well. Sherilyn was rewarded with a trip to London, including round-trip airfare, accommodations, and $1,000 in spending money.

Sherilyn may not have expected to receive gratitude, but this may create positive expectations of being thanked for her and other employees. The expectation that others will show gratitude at work motivates employees to help others.[37] Research has also shown that employees that have an orientation toward the well-being of others are more likely to expect gratitude, and this expectation increased their job performance.[38] Meta-analytic research has concluded that the positive emotion of gratitude is enhanced by training interventions in which people practice feeling grateful for what they have, and this increases their well-being.[39] You can learn to practice feeling the emotion of gratitude by following the steps in the 5-minute gratitude exercise in the Toolkit at the end of this chapter (Activity 3.1).

In addition to emotions, people may experience moods throughout the workday that affect their relationships with others and performance. The next section discusses the importance of individual moods at work.

MOODS

Learning Objective 3.4: Demonstrate with an example how positive and negative state affect relates to customer service.

Moods are generally more enduring than emotions. Positive and negative state affect are the most studied moods at the workplace (i.e., being happy or sad). **Positive state affect** (PA) is defined as the extent to which a person feels enthusiastic, active, and alert. High PA is a state of high energy, full concentration, and pleasurable engagement. In contrast, **negative state affect** is defined as a general dimension of subjective distress and unpleasant engagement that subsumes a variety of aversive mood states. These states may be anger, contempt, disgust, guilt, fear, and nervousness.[40] Research has shown that happier people perform better and have higher incomes.[41,42,43] Mood at the start of the workday (i.e., "waking up on the wrong side of the bed") related to perceptions of customer emotions in a call center, and this affected the employees' moods after the calls.[44] Positive affect was, in turn, related to performance quality, whereas negative affect was negatively related to productivity. The results of this research study are summarized in Figure 3.4. The start-of-workday mood affected their perceptions of customers' moods, which in turn affected their own moods. These moods were related to performance quality and quantity. So if you get up on the wrong side of the bed in the morning, pay attention to your mood. You just might be less productive that day. Self-Assessment 3.1 provides you with the opportunity to learn about your own tendencies toward having positive or negative affect.

Emotions play an important role in the workplace. To this point, much of our discussion has been focused on relationships among coworkers. However, how leaders and employees interact with those outside the organization

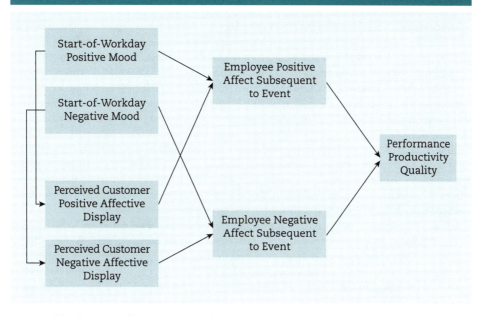

Figure 3.4   The Effects of Mood, Work Events, and Employee Affect on Performance

Start-of-Workday Positive Mood

Start-of-Workday Negative Mood

Perceived Customer Positive Affective Display

Perceived Customer Negative Affective Display

Employee Positive Affect Subsequent to Event

Employee Negative Affect Subsequent to Event

Performance Productivity Quality

Source: Rothbard, N. P., & Wilks, S. L. (2011). Waking up on the right or wrong side of the bed: Start-of-workday mood, work events, employee affect, and performance. *Academy of Management Journal, 54*(5), 959–980.

(including customers) is also important to organizational success. This is the focus of another area where there has been significant research: the study of emotional labor.

EMOTIONAL LABOR

Learning Objective 3.5: Demonstrate understanding of emotional labor by providing examples of jobs that require "surface acting" and "deep acting."

As noted above, employees feel a range of emotions and moods during the course of the workday. However, they don't always show it. For example, if you have ever had a service job such as a waiter or waitress, you knew that you had to smile and be pleasant regardless of your emotions ("I am disgusted by your table manners!") or moods ("It's raining outside and I just feel blah."). Jobs that require employees to suppress affect (emotions and moods) are said to require emotional labor. Other jobs require you to express affect. **Emotional labor** is defined as "the management of feeling to create a publicly observable facial and bodily display."[45] In other words, it is the effort required to effectively manage emotions to be successful on the job. The feeling of having to act differently than true emotions creates emotional dissonance for employees. **Emotional dissonance** is the result of the difference between the organizationally expected emotions and an employee's inner or "real" emotions.[46] In other words, employees are told to "fake it until they make it." All jobs have this requirement to some extent, but some have higher requirements than others (e.g., flight attendants, salespeople, customer service representatives, and nurses).

The concept of emotional labor was introduced by sociologist Arlie Hochschild,[47] who investigated flight attendants and demonstrated that a significant part of their job was attending to the emotions of passengers. Emotional labor has been studied with convenience store clerks and customers. Clerks had differing expectations of their roles and followed scripts (like actors in a role) to control customer service interactions.[48] This is known as "deep acting" since the employees actually feel the emotions they are acting out. **Deep acting** happens when a desired emotional expression is achieved by changing one's underlying felt emotion. For example, a college professor may "psych himself up" to present a lecture to students after learning of a family member's illness. The professor actually becomes more enthusiastic. In contrast, **surface acting** refers to producing a desired outward emotional expression without modifying the underlying emotions.[49] Research has, however, shown that surface and deep-level acting occur simultaneously.[50] Such acting may come with costs, however. Surface acting emotional labor (acting out service roles) has been related to emotional exhaustion and burnout.[51,52] The emotional exhaustion from surface acting may be reduced by team members' positive actions.

When team members engage in deep acting, the deep acting spreads to their team members. Thus, not every person in a team needs to deep act—there is an emotional division of labor that occurs in teams. **Emotional division of labor** is defined as any explicit or implicit division of roles in which individuals vary in their requirement to use emotional abilities.[53] For example, in a car dealership, the general manager, customer service representatives, and sales representatives need to have high emotional abilities, but the service technicians don't.[54]

Team leaders should engage in positive deep acting and encourage key team members to do the same. Research has demonstrated that some people are better at emotional labor (surface and deep acting) than others.[55] However, training programs can discuss the benefits of deep acting and provide strategies for genuinely changing one's feelings during difficult situations to reduce the stress of emotional labor.[56] Training can also help individuals be more aware of their emotions and employ different emotional labor strategies.[57] Emotional labor has a bright side: It may have positive outcomes when organizations grant more autonomy and adopt norms that call for the expression of positive emotions.[58] For example, allowing a call-center employee to work without being watched increases her motivation to help customers.

This overview of emotional labor further illustrates that emotions and feelings at work do matter. Emotional labor causes stress; however, when properly managed, it increases performance. To engage in emotional labor, an employee needs to be sensitive to their own emotions and those of others. Some people are more adept than others at reading the emotions and/or moods of coworkers or customers. There has been a great deal of research and practitioner interest in recent years on understanding **emotional intelligence (EI),** and next we will review EI research and practice.

EMOTIONAL INTELLIGENCE

Learning Objective 3.6: Discuss the case for training in emotional intelligence in the workplace.

Research from the field of psychology shows emotional regulation may be a form of intelligence.[59,60] Organizational leaders and human resource professionals find this concept, EI, relevant to the workplace. In fact, having EI abilities may be essential to be an effective leader.[61] EI is considered to have four aspects:[62]

1. Ability to perceive emotion in self and others (e.g., correctly identifying a perceived emotional expression as fear)

2. Ability to use emotion to facilitate cognitive activities like thinking and problem solving (e.g., knowing how to capitalize on a happy mood swing to engage in a creative task)

3. Ability to understand emotional information (e.g., understanding how two emotions can blend into a third emotion)

4. Ability to manage emotion in self and others (e.g. detaching from fear states that interfere with one's functioning)

Emotion regulation is one of the important abilities that high EI people possess. To determine your emotional regulation, you can take Self-Assessment 3.2, the Emotion Regulation Questionnaire (ERQ).

EI is related to job performance.[63] This is especially true in jobs that have high emotional labor requirements.[64] However, EI becomes a stronger predictor of performance and organizational citizenship behavior (OCB) when intelligence is lower.[65] In other words, employees with lower intelligence perform tasks correctly and engage in OCBs frequently if they are also emotionally intelligent. This may be explained by the results of a study that found that employees with high EI are better able to control and reduce the counterproductive outcomes of challenging developmental job experiences (EI reduced the unpleasant feelings associated with demanding tasks that required new learning). Taking on these difficult tasks resulted in employees being seen as having more advancement potential.[66] In a study of retail stores, store managers' EI increased team cohesiveness, which resulted in higher sales volume.[67] A study conducted with U.S. Air Force recruiters found that EI was related to success in meeting recruiting quotas.[68] In addition, a study of more than 300 managers at Johnson & Johnson found that managers who scored higher on a measure of EI were rated as more effective by their followers.[69] Meta-analyses have shown that leaders' EI relates to follower job satisfaction.[70,71] Another meta-analysis review of 2,168 individuals reported significant positive correlation between EI and performance.[72] Other benefits of EI demonstrated by research are enhanced employee creativity,[73] teamwork effectiveness,[74] and the ability to resolve conflict.[75] Given the benefits of EI in the workplace, organizations are interested in whether EI measures can be used for personnel selection. In other words, can leaders be confident in using EI to decide who to hire for a job (or who to promote to a higher one)? Based upon a meta-analytic review, researchers offer the evidence-based practical advice for using EI for hiring employees shown in Table 3.1.[76]

Table 3.1 Practical Advice for Using Emotional Intelligence Measures for Selection

1. *Choose your EI measure carefully.* There are two distinct definitions of the term *emotional intelligence*: (a) ability to perform emotional tasks and (b) a grab bag of everything (mixed models). It is critical to distinguish these two because measures based on the two EI definitions do not have the same content, prediction, or subgroup differences.

2. *Exercise extreme caution when using mixed EI measures.* Grab-bag measures of EI (i.e., self-report mixed measures) appear to exhibit some incremental validity over cognitive ability and personality measures on average (based on nine studies), but it is not clear why. As such, use of these measures for personnel decisions may be difficult to defend without extensive local validation.

3. *Know that ability EI measures may add little to the selection system.* On average, ability-based measures of EI (performance-based and self-report) exhibit little incremental validity over cognitive ability and personality.

4. *Base the decision to use an EI measure on the job type (i.e., consider the emotional labor content of the job).* For high emotional labor jobs (jobs that require positive emotional displays), all EI measures predict performance over intelligence and personality.

5. *Be aware of subgroup differences on EI.* Although more data are needed, preliminary evidence suggests that performance-based EI measures favor women and Whites, which may produce adverse impact against men and African Americans.

Source: Adapted from Joseph, D. L., & Newman, D. A. (2010). Emotional intelligence: An integrative meta-analysis and cascading model. *Journal of Applied Psychology, 95*(1), 54–78.

Can Emotional Intelligence Be Learned?

Given the interest of organizational leaders in EI, there has been research to determine if the attributes of EI can be learned. In other words, can we send employees to a training program to increase their EI and improve their ability to get along with others? Many scholars believe that EI can be learned. First, people need to develop emotional literacy and be able to label their emotions. Second, they need to learn how to manage or regulate their emotions.[77] Research has compared managers who received EI training to a group receiving no training (a control group). After the training, managers showed higher EI, and they also reported lower work-related stress, higher morale, and treated one another in a more civil manner.[78,79]

EI training programs vary in their content; however, they include both emotional awareness exercises and emotion regulation strategy practice. For example, people are shown a series of photos of faces and then asked to identify the emotions expressed in the photos (emotional awareness). An example of an emotion regulation strategy exercise is the Stop! Technique in which participants are asked to shout the word *stop* in their mind whenever an anxious or troubling thought appears. Then they replace it with a word like *calm*.[80] While the research on training interventions in organizations is not extensive, a review of training interventions from diverse fields including OB, education, mental health, and sports concluded that "it is possible to increase emotional intelligence and that such training has the potential to lead to other positive outcomes."[81]

Limitations of Emotional Intelligence

EI has supporters. Yet researchers disagree on its definition. Some researchers believe that EI is a *trait* or ability similar to IQ.[82] Others argue that EI is a *mixed combination* of intelligence, personality traits, and affect (they use grab-bag measures of EI that have a number of different measures of personality traits and EI combined).[83] A third approach is that EI is an *ability* that can be learned.[84] Due to differences in definitions and a great number of researchers interested in EI, there are various measures of EI, and they don't converge.[85] Some scholars even argue that the concept is too vague and can't be measured at all.[86,87,88] A critical review of the literature on EI in the workplace concluded initial claims of the predictive value of EI may have been overstated.[89]

How Emotional Intelligence Is Used in Organizations

Despite its critics, the EI concept has definitely impacted the workplace through EI training programs, specialized EI consultants, and articles in the business press and popular press.[90,91] For example, the FedEx Global Leadership Institute is charged with continuously updating and innovating in keeping with Fred Smith's call for continuously "raising the standards." FedEx Express implemented a training program for new managers in action-based EI that had three steps for using emotional intelligence on a day-to-day basis:

- **Know Yourself**—increase self-awareness of emotions and reactions (Competencies: Enhance Emotional Literacy and Recognize Patterns).

- **Choose Yourself**—shift from unconscious reaction to intentional response (Competencies: Apply Consequential Thinking, Navigate Emotions, Engage Intrinsic Motivation, and Exercise Optimism).

- **Give Yourself**—align the moment-to-moment decisions with a larger sense of purpose (Competencies: Increase Empathy and Pursue Noble Goals).

Results of the training at FedEx indicated an 8% to 11% increase in EI competencies from before to after the training, which was a statistically significant difference. By supporting new managers in this way, FedEx gains by having more competent leaders and also by showing employees that the company puts its values into action. This training models the kind of people-centered leadership that FedEx expects from all managers. One of the key principles of the EI training at FedEx is: "Emotions drive people, people drive performance."[92]

The following summarizes what we can safely conclude about EI:[93]

1. EI is distinct from, but positively related to, other intelligences (such as IQ).

2. EI is an individual difference, where some people are more endowed and others are less so.

3. EI develops over a person's life span and can be enhanced through training.

4. EI involves, at least in part, individuals' abilities to effectively identify and perceive emotion (in themselves and others), as well as possession of the skills to understand and manage those emotions successfully.

> Critical Thinking Questions: Do you believe that training can improve EI? Why or why not? What are the limits on the degree to which a person with low EI can change?

EI may also improve employees' ability to cope with stressful situations. A study conducted in a law enforcement setting found that coping strategies such as venting, denial, and disengagement might be adaptive for short-term performance. Organizations could manage employee emotions via awareness of appropriate coping responses for jobs that involve emotions (i.e., jobs that require emotional labor).[94] The Best Practices box describes some strategies that have been found to be effective in regulating emotions.

BEST PRACTICES

Regulating Emotions Through Affect Spin, Relabeling, and Reappraisal

Emotion regulation theory is "the processes by which individuals influence which emotions they have, when they have them, and how they experience and express these emotions."[95] Emotional regulation focuses on the causes, responses, and/or mechanisms through which employees respond to emotional events at work.[96] For example, a bill collector may encounter an angry person on the phone, which raises the emotional labor required to interact with the person. Suppressing emotions in responding to the angry person is needed for the bill collector to perform their job well. Research has shown that customer service employees can reduce feelings of burnout by engaging in affect spin. Affect spin is the ability to vary responses to emotional events by knowing which people are more reactive than others to both internal and external events. In other words, employees with higher affect spin ability can read other people's emotions and change their reaction to fit the

person's expressed emotions. A study of restaurant servers found that affect spin buffered the servers from the fatigue caused by difficult customers.[97] Another effective emotion regulation strategy is to relabel and reappraise an undesirable situation. Affect relabeling is verbally labeling the initial reaction of something negative (e.g., I am angry) and then relabeling it to be less intense (e.g., I am annoyed). Reappraisal is intentionally decreasing the intensity of an emotional response to a situation or reinterpreting it in a positive way. For example, reappraisal occurs when the person "looks for the silver lining" in a bad situation.[98]

This line of research has clear evidence-based best practice implications. An individual can regulate his or her emotional responses to work by reading others and adapting to their emotional response to reduce the impact of fatigue (affect spin). Also, when encountering a negative or undesirable situation, they can relabel it

(Continued)

(Continued)

as something less upsetting and then look for something good that may come from the situation (i.e., treat it as a learning experience). As noted above, emotional regulation has been shown to be an important component of EI, and it is also necessary for the surface-level acting requirements of emotional labor.

Discussion Questions:

1. Recall a negative situation that was upsetting to you. How did you respond? Did it make the situation better or worse? Why?
2. What could you have done differently in the situation you described above? Apply the techniques of affect spin, affect relabeling, and reappraisal to the situation.
3. Based on what you have learned about emotion regulation, what strategies will you use to diffuse emotional situations you encounter in the future? Be specific.

Sources: Beal, D. J., Trougakos, J. P., Weiss, H. M., & Dalal, R. S. (2013). Affect spin and the emotion regulation process at work. *Journal of Applied Psychology, 98*(4), 593–605; Burklund, L. J., Creswell, J. D., Irwin, M., & Lieberman, M. (2014). The common and distinct neural bases of affect labeling and reappraisal in healthy adults. *Frontiers in Psychology, 5,* https://doi.org/10.3389/fpsyg.2014.00221; Gross, J. J. (1998). The emerging field of emotion regulation: An integrative review. *Review of General Psychology, 2*(5), 271–299; Grandey, A. A. (2000). Emotional regulation in the workplace: A new way to conceptualize emotional labor. *Journal of Occupational Health Psychology, 5*(1), 95–100.

EMOTIONAL CONTAGION

Learning Objective 3.7: Explain how positive and negative emotions can spread from one individual to a group through the emotional contagion process.

Even groups can be in a bad mood. Emotional labor is essential for high performance in certain jobs, but may also result in stress for employees who must suppress their own emotions and moods. For example, consider whether the magical people at Walt Disney World always feel magical. Such stress may cause coworkers to complain to one another because they have to hold in negative emotions toward customers. When this happens, an **emotional contagion** effect may occur, which is defined as the negative mood of one employee spreading to others in their group. Negativity spreads like a virus; employees "catch" the negative moods of others.[99] Positive moods are also contagious.

By adding up responses to measures of mood from individuals in groups, researchers have discovered that mood can be defined for a group, and it is consistent. In other words, groups can be characterized as having a negative mood.[100] Also, the "group mood" spreads to the moods of individuals in the group. In other words, if a group is positive, then members of the group typically experience positive mood states as well. This happens because of the linkages that emerge among group members. For example, **convergent linkage** occurs when individuals share the interpretations of emotional events. **Divergent linkage** occurs when interpretations of emotional events differ. **Complementary linkage** occurs when the other person is the stimulus. In other words, one individual identifies with another person and this identification causes the emotions to spread, as in "misery loves company." To assess the degree that emotional contagions may be affecting a work group, leaders should ask the following questions:[101]

- To what extent are people on the same side of the table?

- What events and environmental conditions do they tend to face together?

- What are the hot buttons to which a lot of people are reacting?

- Even when people share the same viewpoint, how do they interpret what is going on around them?

- Do people converge in their interpretation, or do people disagree in terms of their reactions?

Leaders have a strong influence on how emotional contagions emerge and spread from individuals to teams, and the organization as a whole.[102] The spread of negative emotions in groups has a "ripple effect," and the emotional contagion reduces team cooperation and creates conflict.[103] But keep in mind that positive moods are also infectious—when an employee smiles at a coworker, their positive mood spreads.[104,105] Research has demonstrated that the contagion of positive emotions is associated with higher teamwork engagement. The sharing of positive emotions between team members leads the team to feel fully absorbed in their work, elevating feelings of pride and joy.[106] A study found that leaders created positive emotional contagion in their work groups, and followers responded by spreading the positive emotions.[107] In longitudinal studies of large social networks, researchers have shown that the spread of emotions is likened to infectious diseases, influencing the experience of positive affect for large numbers of individuals. In other words, the spread of happiness moves through social networks through social ties.[108] The same happens for negative emotions. For example, one study found that when employees feel a climate of job insecurity, safety outcomes were negatively impacted (i.e., there were more injuries and accidents).[109]

Another new development in the field of emotions and mood is the idea that we might be able to understand emotions and moods (for example) by studying the ways that our brains function biologically. Next, we will discuss an emerging field—brain science (or neuroscience)—which may help us understand affect in new ways.

AFFECTIVE NEUROSCIENCE

Learning Objective 3.8: Explain affective neuroscience and provide an organizational example.

You might have read about the case of Phineas Gage in your psychology courses. Phineas was a railroad worker who survived a 3-foot, 7-inch, 13½-pound iron bar being blown right through his skull by an explosion. The bar removed part of the frontal lobe in his brain. It is remarkable that he survived the explosion given the level of medical care available for such an injury in 1848. But he did—and what happened next gave rise to research that examines the effects of the brain on personality and emotions: brain science. Before the accident, Phineas was one of the most capable and reliable workers. He was well liked and professionally successful. But after a portion of his brain was accidentally removed, he became "fitful, irreverent, and grossly profane, showing little deference for his fellows" and unable to keep his job.[110] His case is widely cited as a breakthrough in understanding that the brain has an influence on emotions and moods. Today, brain science is being applied to OB.

An emerging topic to understand affect is **organizational neuroscience**, which is the study of how understanding the functions of the brain may enhance prediction of OB, and an area of research known as **affective neuroscience** has emerged. Affective neuroscience is the study of the neural mechanisms of emotion. This interdisciplinary field combines neuroscience with the psychological study of personality, emotion, and mood.[111] There is not a great deal of research in this area in OB yet, but research in psychology is demonstrating that affect may be the result of brain chemistry. Understanding how networks of brain systems operate may finally allow researchers to enter the "black box" to understand what happens in the brain when emotions such as anger and gratitude are experienced by people in organizations. For example, mirror neurons (brain processes that regulate a person's ability to imitate another person, either consciously or unconsciously) may increase understanding of role modeling and learning through watching others at work.[112] Experimental data suggest key roles of drive and motivation in the wanting, liking, and learning processes underlying the pleasure cycle supporting survival of individuals' reactions to rewards they receive.[113] Some emotions may be embedded in a deeper part of the brain, making them implicit rather than explicit. For example, being fearful of organizational change may be rooted in an older and deeper part of our brains, making employees react automatically rather than logically to change. Neuroscience will increase our understanding of the range of emotions shown in the circumplex model of affect (shown in Figure 3.3 in this chapter).[114] For example, research has already determined that pleasure and displeasure are located in different regions of the brain.[115]

Ethical Issues in Neuroscience

Debates have already begun regarding the ethics of applying brain science to OB, and there are clearly issues that will need to be addressed.[116] One can imagine that knowledge of a person's brain chemistry may be employed to justify their promotion. On the other hand, this same knowledge might be employed to fire them. Would it be an invasion of privacy to be asked to submit to a brain scan in order to be hired for a position? Organizational neuroscience represents a potentially exciting field that would integrate OB theories with biology. However, the ethical concerns clearly need attention before this field moves from prediction to control and applications in organizational settings.

Neuroscience represents perhaps the deepest level of understanding emotions and moods since it focuses on biological differences that underlie emotional expressions. For example, a researcher on leadership concludes that "research at the nexus of biology and psychology should yield interesting and high-impact research: It is likely that leadership researchers will start venturing further into this very fertile research landscape."[117] One study found that a mindfulness meditation reduced negative affect and was associated with prefrontal cortical regulation of affect through labeling of negative affective stimuli.[118] In other words, practicing mindfulness resulted in changes in the brain. Next, we discuss the leadership implications of being mindful.

> Critical Thinking Questions: Should there be governmental regulations on the applications of neuroscience in OB? Why or why not?

LEADERSHIP IMPLICATIONS: AFFECTIVE COACHING

We have all had the experience of asking someone what's wrong and they reply, "Nothing, I'm fine." But we know from their tone of voice and body language that they are upset about something. People have a tendency to deny their emotional pain. For example, they may feel worthless, rejected, not listened to, or even invisible. There are a number of reasons why people conceal their hurt emotions, but what these reasons all have in common is fear. In other words, people conceal their emotions because they don't want to feel weak and powerless. The bottom line, according to psychologist Leon F. Seltzer, is that people don't trust others to respond in caring, supportive ways.[119] What are organizations doing to increase the levels of trust so that employees can discuss their emotions? And what can we do as leaders?

Companies such as Aetna, Google, General Mills, and Goldman Sachs now provide training and meditation rooms for their employees. David Gelles, author of the book *Mindful Work*, states that mindful meditation programs resulted in a 28% reduction in employee stress levels, a 20% improvement in sleep quality, and a 19% reduction in pain. Employees who participated in the programs also became more effective on the job, gaining an average of 62 minutes per week of productivity each, which Aetna estimates is worth $3,000 per employee per year. This may not seem like a lot, but considering that about one fourth of Aetna's 50,000 employees have participated in the program, this works out to be about $37,500,000 per year. And Gelles reports that the classes continue to be full and are overbooked.[120]

Mindfulness is a new area of research in psychology, and it is being applied to the study of emotion regulation in the workplace. A study of employees who engaged in surface acting found that mindfulness training reduced emotional exhaustion.[121] **Mindfulness** is a state of open attention on what is happening in the present without thinking about the past or worrying about the future. When a person is in a mindful state, they look at their emotions and moods without labeling them as bad or good. On the other hand, much behavior in organizations may be "mindless." To assess *mindlessness*, some of the following questions are asked:[122]

- I forget a person's name almost as soon as I've been told it for the first time.

- I find myself listening to another person with one ear and doing something else at the same time.

- I find myself preoccupied with the future or the past.

Being mindful is significantly related to well-being. Are you mindful or mindless in how you go about your study, work, or life in general? Being mindful is related to the EI aspect of being self-aware (recognizing emotions when you experience them), but it is more than this. By focusing on the present, we can learn about the individual differences of followers and also be attentive to their emotions and moods. Research has shown that mindfulness training increases empathy (the ability to feel what another person is feeling).[123]

Here are mindfulness guidelines from the Mayo Clinic that may help a leader understand followers and coach more effectively. The first three steps help prepare for a coaching session with a follower:*

1. **Make the familiar new again.** Even if you have worked with someone for a long time, learn one new thing about them. As you become more aware of this person, you will be able to identify what their personality type might be. Are they a Type A person? Are they conscientious?

2. **Focus on your breathing when you are preparing to listen to another person.** Sit in a quiet place and pay attention to your nostrils as the air moves in and out. Notice how your abdomen expands and contracts with each breath. Remember that you are not trying to accomplish anything. You are just becoming aware of your breathing and mentally preparing yourself to hear the other person's words.

3. **Prepare to pay attention.** Get in the habit of delaying judgment and/or the urge to "categorize" them (e.g., don't be too quick to put them in the in-group or the out-group). Plan to focus on the person and what they have to say—their words and the meaning of their words. Don't forget to also be ready to pay attention to emotions or moods that may get expressed, since we have learned that they matter as well.

Next, begin the coaching session by following steps from the Center for Creative Leadership for mindful leadership coaching:[124]

1. **Based on your preparation, start with an empty mind.** Try not to judge or think about what the person *should* have done in the past or *should* do in the future.

2. **Be nonreactive.** Remember that during this coaching session "no reaction is required, regardless of the provocation." Create a safe emotional space for the person to express himself or herself.

3. **Practice permissive attention.** Try to draw the person into moments of connection where distractions disappear (cell phones, street noise, or anything else that might impair their ability to focus). Try to stay focused for more than a moment on one serious line of thought, perception, judgment, or action that you might observe. Draw the person's attention to what is important (but not in a coercive way).

With a bit of practice, leaders should be able to create an affective coaching environment where they attend with a focus on their followers' emotions. Athletes refer to this as being "in the zone" where you are focused and behavior seems effortless.[125] A great coach can evoke this state from a follower and maintain it so that the person can hear their feedback without becoming defensive. Thus, mindful coaching is about preparation and execution of a few steps in

---

* Reprinted with permission, courtesy of Mayo Clinic.

each phase. Research has shown that people can be trained to experience mindfulness and that this state is related to increased attention (alerting, orienting, and conflict monitoring).[126] Like any skill, with practice, a leader can become more mindful and then use this skill to understand the entire range of the emotions and moods expressed by their followers. Leaders can then develop the ability to react and then do so in an appropriate way to reduce emotional exhaustion and enhance their followers' well-being.

In this chapter, you have learned about the importance of affect (emotions and moods) to job performance and employee well-being. Affective events theory serves as a guide and overall framework to understand how emotions and moods influence workplace outcomes. Emotional intelligence has emerged as a major area of research as well as practice applications through EI training such as that conducted at FedEx Express. Emotions (both positive and negative) can spread through groups and organizations through the emotional contagion process, so it's important to understand them and keep them positive. Finally, the role of brain science and the potential for affective neuroscience to shed light on how emotions and moods influence OB has been discussed. In sum, emotions are a relatively new area of OB, but an "affective revolution" has taken place in the field, which has led to new implications for effective leadership.

SAGE edge™   **edge.sagepub.com/scandura2e**

Want a better grade? **Go to edge.sagepub.com/scandura2e** for the tools you need to sharpen your study skills.

KEY TERMS

affect, 51
affect spin, 61
affective climate, 53
affective neuroscience, 63
broaden-and-build model, 54
complementary linkage, 62
convergent linkage, 62
deep acting, 58
divergent linkage, 62

emotion regulation, 61
emotional contagion, 62
emotional dissonance, 57
emotional division of labor, 58
emotional intelligence (EI), 58
emotional labor, 57
emotions, 51
gratitude, 54
mindfulness, 64

moods, 51
negative state affect, 56
organizational neuroscience, 63
positive state affect, 56
self-awareness, 60
state affect, 51
surface acting, 58
trait affect, 51

TOOLKIT ACTIVITY 3.1: The 5-Minute Gratitude Exercise

Everyone at one time or another experiences problems that consume them. Some examples are:

- Schoolwork challenges

- Work problems

- Health issues

- Financial challenges

The list is numerous. These issues grab hold and overwhelm you and your energy, sometimes so much so that you are exhausted from the problem. They grab so tight you wonder if you will ever move forward. How do you lessen the grasp your challenges have on you and your energy? What if something could have you seeing a way of positive change? The 5-Minute Gratitude Exercise just may be what you have been looking for. The practice of acknowledging gratitude lessens the heaviness issues have on you, your energy, and your inability to see through your challenges. With slack on the problem, you create space for new and more harmonious views on the situation.

The exercise takes 5 minutes and has seven steps.

1. For 1 minute, ponder the issue that has consumed your energy.

2. Focus on how you are feeling as you think about the problem.

3. For the second minute, think of something you are grateful for around that issue. Some examples might be:

   • My best friend and I are having difficulties at the moment. I am grateful for my best friend, as I can call and talk with her and feel I have someone with whom I can share my feelings. Focus on something you love about your best friend.

   • I received a C on an exam. I felt that I studied hard, but I don't do well on multiple-choice exams. I am grateful that the course has other assignments where I can shine. I am really good at writing papers.

   • The workload on my job has been heavy, and I am stressed about it. I worry about whether or not I will be able to keep up. I am thankful to have a job that pays my bills and gives me the opportunity to learn new things.

   These are just examples to get you going. Think of what is in your life around the issue that you can honestly be grateful for, even though the issue seems to hold you so. There's always something to be grateful for, even in a difficult situation. It may require a bit of searching, but it's there.

4. Once you have identified that for which you are grateful, close your eyes and focus on it. Let your thoughts wander, and soon other things for which you are grateful in other areas of your life will begin to speak up. Positive thoughts attract positive thoughts.

5. As these thoughts speak to you, imagine there is a volume knob inside your head, a physical knob like the one on a car radio, not the digital one. Now, envision reaching out and turning up the volume on these thoughts of gratitude to a point where it is comfortable but stretches you a little bit.

6. Just like that song that you crank up the volume to because it feels good, let this volume of gratitude fill you with that same sense.

7. Notice how you feel. Hold onto this feeling, and when you feel yourself stuck by the situation, go find this feeling and think of another thought of gratitude to add. When you find yourself being sucked down into the "woe is me" syndrome, or consumed by your problems, stop for 5 minutes and practice gratitude with this exercise.

Discussion Questions

1. Did you find it difficult to let go of your "woe is me" negative feelings? Why or why not?

2. How did you feel when you "turned up the volume" on your thoughts of gratitude?

3. Explain how the 5-minute gratitude exercise broadens and builds your psychological capital (PsyCap). Describe your feelings of hope, optimism, self-efficacy, and resiliency after doing the exercise (for definitions of PsyCap, refer back to Chapter 2).

Source: Adapted from The 5-Minute Gratitude Exercise. Retrieved from http://www.livingwhole.net/uploads/1/3/0/7/13072851/the_5_minute_gratitude_exercise.pdf

CASE STUDY 3.1: Managing Your Boss's Moods and Emotions

Ted is a forensic accountant at the law firm of Chambers, Bergweitz, and Rowe. He has worked there for 10 years and is called in on cases when his unique skills are needed by the different attorneys and partners. He reports to Richard, who has been his boss for 8 years. Richard is responsible for all of the specialized personnel used on cases, not just the forensic accountants. He has been a decent boss—fair with clear standards for performance and what it takes to get promotions, raises, and bonuses. However, Richard suffered a heart attack last month and is going to be taking early retirement in order to take care of his health. As a result, the specialists under Richard are now being divided out to the different department heads they serve until a replacement can be hired in a few months (as Richard is on medical leave, he can't be replaced in his position for legal reasons at this time).

Ted now reports to Margret, the head of the divorce department, and finds her a difficult boss to work for on most days. She always seems to start her day in a bad mood, where she denies any subordinates' requests or finds that the requests (as well as requestor) are stupid if she is approached before 11 a.m. Whereas Richard had a clear process for assigning cases to the accountants, Margret seems to let her emotions guide her choices. For instance, when Seeru, another forensic accountant, was late getting Margret a report because he had to get an emergency crown repair, Margret was angry with him. She seemingly retaliated by dumping three cases on him in one week and left Ted with nothing to do. She also required Seeru to complete his analysis of all the cases by Monday, thus requiring him to work the weekend. However, when Ted and Seeru's work helped a client get a large divorce settlement, and thus the firm a large cut of the settlement, she was pleased and gave both of them Friday off on a whim so they could enjoy a long weekend. Additionally, Ted has found her sobbing in her office on more than one occasion when he has gone to get files or clarification on cases from her. To make matters worse, Margret often screams at her assistant and other employees outside of her office, which disturbs those in nearby offices and cubicles.

Margret's emotionally charged behaviors are very disruptive to Ted and Seeru's work. It is hard for them to concentrate when she is yelling, and they do not feel comfortable working in their cubicles because they never know when she is going to have an outburst that makes it impossible to have a phone conversation or to have clients, clients' financial managers, or other attorneys over for meetings. They also can't get information they need from her when she is in a rage or fit of despair, as they don't dare go near her.

Ted would like to request a transfer to the partner that handles corporate trials and investigations. He has talked to some of the attorneys in that department, and it seems a much nicer working environment. However, until he can get transferred over, he and Seeru are employing a number of strategies to deal with their boss and her volatile moods. These include:

- **Avoidance.** The guys work out of the office when possible by meeting with clients and their financial managers at their homes or offices. When they have to work in the office, they try to work in the archives, libraries, or conference rooms away from Margret.

- **Gray Rocking.** By not emoting, even when Margret's emotions are affecting their own feelings, Ted and Seeru are not fueling her fire. Oftentimes they have seen her react even more harshly if someone cried or yelled back, and so do their best to not only not say anything but not have any facial expressions that could communicate how they are feeling.

- **Gifting and complimenting.** In the last few weeks, the guys have brought what they consider peace offerings whenever they go see Margret—from coffees to bagels or bars of chocolate. Whenever she gets these little things, Margret perks up and is a bit easier to get information from or permission to use company resources.

- **Overdelivering.** After getting that Friday off for doing good work, and knowing what can happen if they don't deliver on time, the guys work hard to ensure they do excellent work and beat deadlines.

Discussion Questions

1. What other strategies might you employ in dealing with Margret or your own moody boss? Are there any actions or behaviors you should avoid?

2. What can Ted and Seeru do to help themselves not catch their boss's negative emotions and moods, and cope with the emotional stress and turmoil working for Margret causes?

3. Why do you think working for Margret is so emotionally stressful?

4. Think about the legal and ethical ramifications of the behavior of bosses like Margret. Organizations in the United States have the legal obligation to provide safe workplaces, including ones that are safe from harassment. What would you do if you were Margret's boss or another leader in the organization, and why do you think she was even hired for this position?

SELF-ASSESSMENT 3.1: Positive and Negative Affect Schedule (PANAS)

This scale consists of a number of words that describe different feelings and emotions. There are no right or wrong answers, and this is not a test. You don't have to share your results with other classmates unless you wish to do so.

Part I. Taking the Assessment

Read each item and then list the number from the scale below next to each word. Indicate to what extent you feel this way right now, that is, at the present moment **OR indicate the extent you have felt this way over the past week** (circle the instructions you followed when taking this measure):

(Circle one):

Momentary: I feel this way right now (state affect)
Weekly: I have felt this way over the past week (trait affect)

Statements	Strongly Disagree	Disagree	Neutral	Agree	Strongly Agree
1. Interested	1	2	3	4	5
2. Distressed	1	2	3	4	5
3. Excited	1	2	3	4	5
4. Upset	1	2	3	4	5
5. Strong	1	2	3	4	5
6. Guilty	1	2	3	4	5
7. Scared	1	2	3	4	5
8. Hostile	1	2	3	4	5
9. Enthusiastic	1	2	3	4	5
10. Proud	1	2	3	4	5
11. Irritable	1	2	3	4	5

(Continued)

(Continued)

Statements	Strongly Disagree	Disagree	Neutral	Agree	Strongly Agree
12. Alert	1	2	3	4	5
13. Ashamed	1	2	3	4	5
14. Inspired	1	2	3	4	5
15. Nervous	1	2	3	4	5
16. Determined	1	2	3	4	5
17. Attentive	1	2	3	4	5
18. Jittery	1	2	3	4	5
19. Active	1	2	3	4	5
20. Afraid	1	2	3	4	5

Part II. Scoring and Interpretation

	Positive Affect	Negative Affect
	1 _____	2 _____
	3 _____	4 _____
	5 _____	6 _____
	9 _____	7 _____
	10 _____	8 _____
	12 _____	11 _____
	14 _____	13 _____
	16 _____	15 _____
	17 _____	18 _____
	19 _____	20 _____
Totals	_____	_____
Averages	Divide by 10 _____	Divide by 10 _____

Positive Affect Score: Add the scores on items 1, 3, 5, 9, 10, 12, 14, 16, 17, and 19. Scores can range from 10 to 50, with higher scores representing higher levels of positive affect. You can compare your scores to the following norms:

Mean Scores: Momentary = 29.7 (SD = 7.9); Weekly = 33.3 (SD = 7.2)

Negative Affect Score: Add the scores on items 2, 4, 6, 7, 8, 11, 13, 15, 18, and 20. Scores can range from 10 to 50, with lower scores representing lower levels of negative affect. You can compare your scores to the following norms:

Mean Score: Momentary = 14.8 (SD = 5.4); Weekly = 17.4 (SD = 6.2)

Source: Copyright ©1988 by the American Psychological Association. Reproduced with permission. Watson, D., Clark, L. A., & Tellegan, A. (1988). Development and validation of brief measures of positive and negative affect: The PANAS scales. *Journal of Personality and Social Psychology,* 54(6), 1063–1070.

Discussion Questions

1. Overall, do you display more positive or negative affect? Do you think your results would be different if you had chosen another time frame (momentary vs. weekly)? Explain.

2. How did you compare to the average scores on this self-assessment? Are you above or below average in positive and negative affect?

3. Explain how your knowledge of your own mood states may influence how you interact with others at work. How can you use this information to change your behavior?

SELF-ASSESSMENT 3.2: Emotion Regulation Questionnaire (ERQ)

We would like to ask you some questions about your emotional life, in particular, how you control (that is, regulate and manage) your emotions. The questions below involve two distinct aspects of your emotional life. One is your emotional experience, or what you feel like inside. The other is your emotional expression, or how you show your emotions in the way you talk, gesture, or behave. Although some of the following questions may seem similar to one another, they differ in important ways. For each item, please answer using the following scale:

Statements	Strongly Disagree	Disagree	Somewhat Disagree	Neutral	Somewhat Agree	Agree	Strongly Agree
1. When I want to feel more positive emotion (such as joy or amusement), I change what I'm thinking about.	1	2	3	4	5	6	7
2. I keep my emotions to myself.	1	2	3	4	5	6	7
3. When I want to feel less negative emotion (such as sadness or anger), I change what I'm thinking about.	1	2	3	4	5	6	7
4. When I am feeling positive emotions, I am careful not to express them.	1	2	3	4	5	6	7
5. When I'm faced with a stressful situation, I make myself *think about it* in a way that helps me stay calm.	1	2	3	4	5	6	7
6. I control my emotions by *not expressing them.*	1	2	3	4	5	6	7
7. When I want to feel more *positive* emotion, I *change the way I'm thinking* about the situation.	1	2	3	4	5	6	7
8. I control my emotions by *changing the way I think* about the situation I'm in.	1	2	3	4	5	6	7
9. When I am feeling *negative* emotions, I make sure not to express them.	1	2	3	4	5	6	7
10. When I want to feel less *negative* emotion, I *change the way I'm thinking* about the situation.	1	2	3	4	5	6	7

Scoring

Cognitive Reappraisal	Expressive Suppression
1 _____	2 _____
3 _____	4 _____
5 _____	6 _____
7 _____	9 _____
8 _____	
10 _____	
Totals _____	_____
Averages Divide by 6 _____	Divide by 4 _____

Source: Gross, J. J., & John, O. P. (2003). Individual differences in two emotion regulation processes: Implications for affect, relationships, and well-being. *Journal of Personality and Social Psychology, 85,* 348–362. https://spl.stanford.edu/resources

Note: Cognitive reappraisal is a form of cognitive change that involves construing a potentially emotion-eliciting situation in a way that changes its emotional impact. For example, during an admissions interview, one might view the give-and-take as an opportunity to find out how much one likes the school rather than as a test of one's worth. Items 1, 3, 5, 7, 8, and 10 make up the Cognitive Reappraisal facet. *Expressive suppression* is a form of response modulation that involves inhibiting ongoing emotion-expressive behavior. For example, one might keep a poker face while holding a great hand during a card game. Items 2, 4, 6, and 9 make up the Expressive Suppression facet.

The scoring takes the average of all the scores (i.e., the score lies between 1 and 7). The table below shows the averages of 1,483 undergraduate students around 20 years of age.

Score on	Men	Women
Cognitive reappraisal	4.60	4.61
Expressive suppression	3.64	3.14

Source: Emotion Regulation Questionnaire. Retrieved from http://www.psytoolkit.org/survey-library/emotional-regulation-erq.html

Discussion Questions

1. Which of the two strategies do you rely on most (cognitive reappraisal or expressive suppression)? Give an example of when you used this strategy.

2. How do your results compare to the averages (male or female)? Were you surprised by your results? Explain why or why not.

3. How can you use the results of this self-assessment to improve your strategies for emotion regulation?

CHAPTER FOUR

ATTITUDES AND JOB SATISFACTION

JOB SATISFACTION: AN UPWARD TREND

The Society of Human Resource Management (SHRM) conducts a survey each year of employee attitudes toward their work. In November and December of 2015, they surveyed about 600 U.S. employees to track their job satisfaction and factors that contribute to their satisfaction at work. The trends for job satisfaction over time show an interesting pattern. As shown in Figure 4.1, overall job satisfaction (the global rating of how much a person is "somewhat satisfied" or "very satisfied" with their job) experienced a positive trend from 2005 to 2009. Job satisfaction peaked at 86% of workers saying they were very satisfied with their jobs in 2009. However, the following few years saw a downward trend, with only 81% of respondents indicating high job satisfaction in the years 2012 and 2013. This may have been due to the economic stress and uncertainty resulting from the recession of 2008. It appears that job satisfaction recovered from this slump, with 88% of the respondents reporting that they were very satisfied with their jobs in 2015—the highest level in 10 years. The survey also looked at the reasons *why* people are satisfied with their jobs. Respectful treatment of employees at all levels was the most important contributor (67% of respondents reported this was "very important"). Overall compensation and pay was second with 63% of respondents rating this is very important to them, with 60% also listing benefits as very important. Trust between employees and senior management emerged as fourth most important (55% of respondents), and opportunities to use their skill and abilities at work was equally rated (55%). Consistent with research on leadership (covered in Chapter 6 of this textbook), having a positive relationship with the boss was a close sixth factor contributing to job satisfaction (53%).

> **Critical Thinking Questions:** Why do you think job satisfaction has been increasing in recent years? Explain why respectful treatment is more important to employees than pay or benefits. What can a leader do to increase employee job satisfaction by allowing followers to use their skills and abilities at work (give a specific example)?

Learning Objectives

After studying this chapter, you should be able to do the following:

4.1: Define the concept of an attitude, and know its three components.

4.2: Understand why the measurement of attitudes is important for the workplace.

4.3: Define *job satisfaction*, and know what the consequences of dissatisfaction are.

4.4: Explain the role of job attitudes and core self-evaluation in the job search process.

4.5: Discuss the concept of organizational commitment and its three components.

4.6: Define *perceived organizational support* (POS), and explain its relationship to fairness at the workplace.

4.7: Explain psychological empowerment and its relationship to job performance.

Get the edge on your studies at **edge.sagepub.com/scandura2e**

- Take the chapter quiz
- Review key terms with eFlashcards
- Explore multimedia resources, SAGE readings, and more!

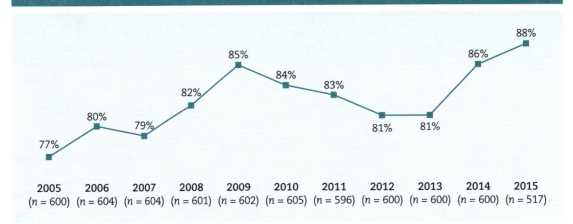

Figure 4.1 Employee Job Satisfaction 2005–2015

| 2005 | 2006 | 2007 | 2008 | 2009 | 2010 | 2011 | 2012 | 2013 | 2014 | 2015 |
| (n = 600) | (n = 604) | (n = 604) | (n = 601) | (n = 602) | (n = 605) | (n = 596) | (n = 600) | (n = 600) | (n = 600) | (n = 517) |

Source: Employee Job Satisfaction and Engagement (SHRM, 2016). Retrieved from https://www.shrm.org/hr-today/trends-and-forecasting/research-and-surveys/pages/job-satisfaction-and-engagement-report-revitalizing-changing-workforce.aspx

Note: Figure represents those employees who answered "somewhat satisfied" or "very satisfied" with their current job.

Job satisfaction is the most often studied work attitude. In this chapter, we review research on job satisfaction and other important work attitudes. First, the concept of attitude is defined followed by a discussion of why attitudes matter for both individuals and the organizations they work for.

WHAT IS AN ATTITUDE?

Learning Objective 4.1: Define the concept of an attitude, and know its three components.

Captain Jack Sparrow in *Pirates of the Caribbean* utters "the problem is not the problem; the problem is your *attitude* about the problem. Do you understand?" Most people have an idea of what an attitude is from such statements in films and Dilbert cartoons that parody concepts such as empowerment. Attitudes have been researched in psychology for many years and are one of the earliest concepts studied. From the outset, researchers maintained that it is possible to measure attitudes but also recognized that attitudes are complex.[1] It has been noted that the concept of attitude is indispensable to the study of social psychology.[2] An **attitude** is defined as "a psychological tendency that is expressed by evaluating a particular entity with some degree of favor or disfavor."[3] Attitudes are, thus, a person's evaluation of something else. These evaluations have three components: cognitive, affective, and behavioral.[4] The existence of this three-component structure has generally been supported by research.[5,6] The **cognitive** component of an attitude is a statement of belief about something—for example, "My boss is a mean person" reflects a person's statement that they believe to be factual. The **affective** component of an attitude is the emotional part. As we learned in Chapter 3, emotions often have a powerful effect on employee motivation and work behaviors—for example, an affective statement related to the previously stated cognitive component might be, "I am angry because my boss is mean." The **behavioral** component of an attitude refers to an intention to act based upon the cognitions and affect experienced—for example, "I am going to go to the Human Resources department and report my mean boss."

This three-part conceptualization of an attitude helps us understand that attitudes are complicated; it isn't just that we think something and believe it to be true. We also experience feelings related to our beliefs, and we contemplate taking actions based on them. These components are all related to one another, as shown in Figure 4.2. This figure provides an additional example of the three-component model. The cognitive component is that the person thinks their job is boring. Therefore, they don't like the job (the affect part). This results in a behavioral intention to withdraw from the work by planning to spend more time on Facebook during work hours rather than working on things that are boring, and they don't like being bored (the behavioral intention).

While this three-part conceptualization is useful in explaining the complexity of attitudes, the three components are typically closely related and converge.[7] In other words, cognitions may not cause affect or vice versa; these components move in the same direction. This is actually useful for a leader to recognize since research has shown that behavior does not always follow an attitude. In fact, thoughts and feelings can be changed by changing behaviors first. For example, having followers state their perceptions

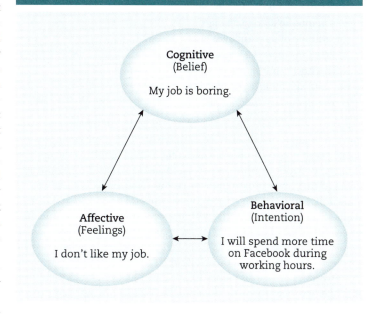

Figure 4.2 Three Components of an Attitude

Cognitive
(Belief)

My job is boring.

Affective
(Feelings)

I don't like my job.

Behavioral
(Intention)

I will spend more time on Facebook during working hours.

of the mission of the organization during a team meeting may have the effect of changing their belief that the mission is worthwhile, and they may also change the way they feel about the mission. Another example would be to have students read the honor code statement to change their thoughts ("cheating is not okay") and feelings ("I would be embarrassed if I were caught cheating"). This is because when behaviors don't line up with thoughts and feelings, cognitive dissonance may occur.

Critical Thinking Question: Give an example of three parts of an attitude that you have experienced at either work or school (cognitive, affect, and behavioral intention).

Cognitive Dissonance

Cognitive dissonance is the incompatibility between two or more attitudes or between attitudes and behavior.[8] This creates stress for an individual, and the person will be motivated to resolve the stress by making a change in one or both of the other components. Our thoughts (cognitions) need to be consistent with our feelings (affective), and these need to line up with our behavioral intentions. In other words, thoughts, feelings, and behaviors need to be aligned. Very few people can completely avoid dissonance in their lives. For example, you may be reminded of this when a child corrects you for swearing because you have told them not to do this in the past. Festinger proposed that the degree to which people are motivated to resolve dissonance is related to the importance of what creates it and how much influence the person has over it.[9] The final motivating element is reward. So one of the best ways to learn to stop swearing is to have your children remind you, because it is important to you and you do have influence

Critical Thinking Questions:
How can the theory of cognitive dissonance be used to change the attitude of the employee depicted in Figure 4.2? In other words, how can a leader reduce the time an employee spends on Facebook during work hours?

over what you say. The reward from swearing isn't all that much, so you are probably willing to change it to be a positive role model for your child, which is more rewarding.

DO ATTITUDES MATTER?

Learning Objective 4.2: Understand why the measurement of attitudes is important for the workplace.

As noted in Chapter 1, work-related attitudes are often key outcome variables in organizational behavior (OB) research. In some cases, these same attitudes are employed as predictors. As in social psychology, attitudes have become indispensable to the understanding of people's reactions to their work and leaders. Attitudes are, thus, important in and of themselves. Knowing how satisfied people are with their work or how engaged they are is important because this contributes to their well-being and life satisfaction. Also, OB research has shown that attitudes are related to behaviors that organizations care about, such as job performance and turnover. A meta-analysis and additional research were conducted to examine the link between attitudes and behaviors that relate to productivity.[10] The findings strongly suggest that job satisfaction and organizational commitment are significantly related to job performance and turnover. The authors conclude that job attitudes are one of the most important things for a leader to know about their followers.

Attitudes make a difference in employee behaviors such as job performance. However, there are contingency factors that have been found to influence the relationship between attitudes and behavior.[11] The importance of an attitude and the correspondence between the attitude and the behavior increases the prediction of behavior.[12] In other words, more specific attitudes predict more specific behaviors. For example, it is better to ask an employee how much they trust the boss rather than how much they trust all of the leaders in the organization to predict job performance. **Social pressure** from others may also strengthen the relationship of an attitude toward behavior. A meta-analysis of research examining the link between attitudes and behavior found that how accessible an attitude is makes a difference, as well as how stable the attitude is over time.[13] For example, having direct experience with an attitude such as having a job you love increases the relationship to performance. Also, being asked frequently about an attitude increases the link to behavior (stability). Organizations that implement yearly employee attitude surveys may actually be increasing the awareness of favorable aspects of the work, and this might decrease turnover.

OB research has identified and researched dozens of work-related attitudes. The following sections discuss the best-researched attitudes and how they significantly and positively affect outcomes for organizations, such as higher job performance and lower turnover.

JOB SATISFACTION

Learning Objective 4.3: Define *job satisfaction*, and know what the consequences of dissatisfaction are.

As suggested in the research conducted by SHRM at the beginning of this chapter, most people are satisfied with their jobs, and this is showing an upward trend. Job satisfaction is defined as "a pleasurable or positive emotional state resulting from the appraisal of one's job or job experience."[14] Job satisfaction can be measured as an overall (or global) concept as shown in Chapter 1, Table 1.2 (in fact, the Hoppock Job Satisfaction Measure is one of the oldest measures from OB research dating back to the 1930s). Job satisfaction is viewed as one part of a person's reactions to their life resulting in happiness and life satisfaction.[15] Current perspectives on positive OB suggest that it is important for organizations to care about the well-being and health of their employees, even if this is unrelated to performance and other outcomes.[16] Thus, job satisfaction is important because it shows how positive an employee is

RESEARCH IN ACTION

The Curious Case of Post-9/11 Job Satisfaction

Can a public event change how satisfied government workers are with their jobs? Job satisfaction in the public sector may not only depend on facets such as pay, coworkers, and supervisor satisfaction but may also depend on larger national events or crises.[17] Van Ryzin proposed that the image of public service in times of crisis may become more positive since citizens look to government institutions for security, leadership, and a sense of national purpose. Government workers may see themselves as heroes following a crisis and view their work as more meaningful. This increase in the positive image of the public sector boosts the everyday morale of government workers. Also, government workers may find renewed meaning and purpose in their work since the government responds to a crisis, and this has a positive effect on their job satisfaction. The

researcher compared job satisfaction data from the General Social Survey (GSS) for a sample of government workers compared to private sector workers from the years 2000 to 2010. The findings indicate that the national crisis of 9/11 may have boosted government workers' job satisfaction 5 to 10 percentage points, representing 1 to 2 million additional satisfied government workers in the United States. These results suggest that people found more meaning in their work since national crises remind them of the important role that they play in the lives of other people. These feelings appeared to influence government workers' job satisfaction. It's important to remember that job satisfaction is complex, and may be affected by the employee's personality but also external events may influence the thoughts and feelings people have regarding their work.

Discussion Questions

1. This study was conducted for government employees. Do you think that the results would be different for employees in the business sector? Why or why not?
2. Police officers are an example of government employees who would likely be affected by a

   national crisis. Provide some other examples and explain them.
3. List and discuss two other factors outside of the job that may affect job satisfaction.

Source: Van Ryzin, G. G. (2014). The curious case of the post 9-11 boost in government job satisfaction. *American Review of Public Administration, 44*(1), 59–74.

regarding their work. This translates into better performance. For example, one study found that frontline employee job satisfaction is significantly related to customer satisfaction and engagement.[18]

Job satisfaction may change over time. A study of 132 newcomers with data collected at four time periods showed a curvilinear pattern for job satisfaction, such that satisfaction increased after they started their jobs and then decreased as they settled into their jobs at the 1-year point.[19] A research study of new employees earning a college or graduate degree in a recession or an economic boom found that the recession had lasting effects on job satisfaction. Across three studies, well-educated graduates who entered the workforce during economic downturns were more satisfied with their current jobs than those who entered during more prosperous economic times.[20] Another study conducted for an even longer period of time—40 years—examined survey data from 21,670 participants in nationally representative samples. Results found interesting patterns for age and organization tenure. People appeared to become less satisfied as their tenure within a given organization increased. However, as people became older and moved to different organizations, their satisfaction increased. This finding is, in part, explained by pay increases over time.[21] Thus, external factors such as the economy or a national crisis may influence job satisfaction (see the boxed insert for an example of how a national event influenced job satisfaction).

Job satisfaction has been examined across cultures. Typically, studies seek to understand whether U.S.-based models of job satisfaction hold in other cultures. For example, a study of over 70,000 employees in four cultural regions (Asia, Europe, North America, and Latin America) found employees' sense of achievement from work was related to job satisfaction in all regions.[22]

A review of cross-cultural research on job satisfaction concluded that the relationship of job satisfaction to performance in a number of other cultures was similar to that in the United States, with an average correlation of .20 (the review included studies from India, Poland, Australia, Canada, Israel, and South Africa).[23] However, international research was more likely to focus on nonwork attitudes such as adaptive behaviors. In addition, job satisfaction was found to be related to life satisfaction and withdrawal behaviors (lateness and absenteeism) in other cultures.

Job Satisfaction Facets

It is recognized that it is possible for a person to be satisfied with one aspect of their work but dissatisfied with others. In other words, an employee might love the work they do but dislike their gossiping coworkers. Thus, measures of facet job satisfaction have been developed. One of the most widely known measures of facet satisfaction is the Job Descriptive Index (JDI).[24] This measure includes different scales that measure various aspects of the work experience: pay, promotions, supervision, coworkers, and the work itself. Examples of items from the JDI are shown in Table 4.1. Research has suggested the strongest relationship of these facets to overall job satisfaction is the work itself, followed by supervision and coworker satisfaction. While it may be surprising, satisfaction with pay has the lowest relationship to overall job satisfaction.[25,26] You will learn more about the role of extrinsic rewards such as pay on motivation in Chapter 9. Toolkit Activity 4.1 gives you the opportunity to evaluate what workers want from various aspects of their jobs.

If work is the most important component of job satisfaction, then you may be wondering what the relationship is between pay and job satisfaction. In a review study including over 90 samples, researchers found that pay was only weakly related to job satisfaction. In fact, employees who were highly paid were just as satisfied as those who made less. The results of their study are summarized in Figure 4.3. Once a person reaches an income level where they can live

> Critical Thinking Questions: Why do you think that the most important aspect of job satisfaction is the work itself? Which aspect is most important to you?

Figure 4.3 The Relationship Between Average Pay in a Job and Job Satisfaction

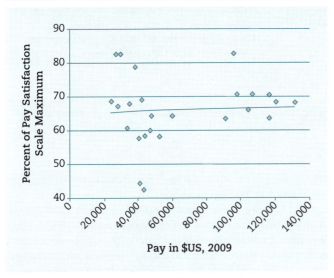

Source: Judge, T. A., Piccolo, R. F., Podsakoff, N. P., Shaw, J. C., & Rich, B. L. (2010). The relationship between pay and job satisfaction: A meta-analysis of the literature. *Journal of Vocational Behavior, 77*(2), 157–167.

comfortably (around $40,000 in the United States), the relationship between income and job satisfaction goes away. A recent study examined pay over a wider range and found that the relationship between pay and job satisfaction may be more complex. Researchers obtained data from 25,465 working adults in the United States using the company rating website www.careerbliss.com. They found that income and pay satisfaction had a significant curvilinear relationship such that people began reporting decreased pay satisfaction above income levels of $260,000.[27] These findings suggest that income is not related to job satisfaction once we achieve a comfortable standard of living but that when we attain very high salaries, we become dissatisfied. More research is needed to understand this intriguing finding.

Job satisfaction matters because progressive organizations care about the well-being of their workforce. It is also important because it is related to other work attitudes, which we review next in this chapter (such as organizational commitment and engagement). The research is clear that job satisfaction increases performance on the job: A meta-analysis including over 300 samples showed that job satisfaction is significantly and positively related to performance.[28] But what happens when employees are dissatisfied?

Dissatisfaction with work produces four possible responses that are summarized in Figure 4.4. As shown in this figure, these responses can either be **active** or **passive**.[29] Thus, the employee can actually do something about it or choose not to respond in an active way. The second dimension is whether the response is **constructive** or **destructive**. The employee who is dissatisfied can respond by trying to do something positive or negative about the situation. There are thus four reactions shown in the figure, and their definitions follow:

- **Exit.** The employee can search for another job and leave. This response is active and destructive.

- **Voice.** The employee can discuss their dissatisfaction with their supervisor, making suggestions for improvement. This is an active and constructive response to being dissatisfied.

- **Loyalty.** The employee can wait for the situation to improve, showing loyalty and trust in the management to address it in time. This is a passive response, but it is constructive.

- **Neglect.** The employee allows the situation to get worse and may be late or absent from work and put in less effort on the job. This is a passive response that is destructive.

Table 4.1 Sample Items From the Job Descriptive Index

Think of the work you do at present. How well does each of the following words or phrases describe your work? In the blank beside each word or phrase, write the following:

Y for "Yes" if it describes your work

N for "No" if it does NOT describe it

? for "?" if you cannot decide

Pay Satisfaction

___ Well paid

___ Bad

___ Barely live on income

Promotion Satisfaction

___ Regular promotions

___ Promotion on ability

___ Opportunities somewhat limited

Supervision Satisfaction

___ Knows job well

___ Around when needed

___ Doesn't supervise enough

Coworker Satisfaction

___ Stimulating

___ Smart

___ Unpleasant

Satisfaction With the Work Itself

___ Fascinating

___ Pleasant

___ Can see my results

Source: The Job Descriptive Index, © Bowling Green State University (1975, 1985, 1997).

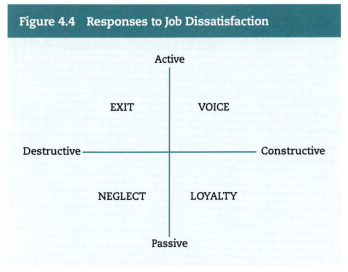

Figure 4.4   Responses to Job Dissatisfaction

Active

EXIT   VOICE

Destructive ————————————— Constructive

NEGLECT   LOYALTY

Passive

Source: Rusbult, C. E., Farrell, D., Rogers, G., & Mainous A. G., III. (1988). Impact of exchange variables on exit, voice, loyalty, and neglect: An integrative model of responses to declining job satisfaction. *Academy of Management Journal, 31*(3), 599–627.

This framework is also known as the EVLN (Exit-Voice-Loyalty-Neglect) approach to job dissatisfaction. Research has shown that voice leads to turnover—when employees speak out about their concerns they are more likely to quit. However, this research also found that leaders who allowed participation and provided support were able to prevent turnover from occurring.[30] This effect is even more pronounced when leaders and followers agree on the extent to which followers voice their concerns. By leaders having open discussions with followers regarding what makes their input valuable, followers are able to get their concerns addressed. This may also avoid potential negative consequences for being out of sync with follower perceptions and the destructive responses of exit or neglect.[31] For followers, it isn't just a matter of speaking up (voice); it is also a matter of *being heard*.

The previous sections reviews research that shows that attitudes make a difference on the job. But what happens when a person is looking for a job? The next section discusses how having a positive attitude about oneself and the job search process can lead to a higher degree of success in finding a great job.

JOB SEARCH ATTITUDES

Learning Objective 4.4: Explain the role of job attitudes and core self-evaluation in the job search process.

OB research has shown that the job search is like a "roller coaster," with ups and downs in attitudes during the process.[32] Perceived progress, experienced affect, and the belief that a job will be found may vary on a day-to-day basis during the job search process. In this research, individuals were asked about how confident they were that they would find another job. The researchers asked questions such as the following:

1. Will you find a job if you look?

2. Will you get a good paying job?

3. Will you find a job that you like?

4. Will you land a job as good as or better than the one you left?

This research found that it is important to keep a positive attitude and maintain a positive self-image during a job search. This positive attitude about oneself is known as *core self-evaluations*, which you learned about in Chapter 2 of this textbook. A recent study found that career adaptability was related to university graduates' beliefs that they would have a great career and their success in finding a job. **Career adaptability** has been defined as "a psychosocial construct that denotes an individual's resources for coping with current and anticipated tasks, transitions, traumas in their occupational roles."[33] It is comprised of the adaptive resources of concern, control, curiosity, and confidence (known as the 4 Cs).[34] A meta-analysis of 90 studies found that career adaptability is significantly associated with measures of adaptability (e.g., optimism), adapting responses (e.g., career planning), and outcomes (e.g., higher organizational commitment, lower job stress, and life satisfaction).[35] Keep in mind, however, that some forms of flexibility may have a downside with respect to finding a good career match. Another research study examined **flexible job search behavior (FJSB)** with three general forms: flexibility with respect to pay/hierarchical level, skill use, and commuting time. Researchers found

BEST PRACTICES

Your Attitude May Derail Your Job Search

Those seeking employment need to pay attention to their attitudes. Your attitudes may manifest themselves in how you conduct yourself during the process. Bob McIntosh, a career trainer who leads job search workshops and an authority on the job search process, offers the following advice:

1. Don't be arrogant. People don't appreciate being looked down upon.
2. "Dress for success." Make sure you are well groomed and presentable when you might be in contact with a potential employer or someone who could help you.
3. Your countenance matters. Try not to look down at the floor or frown. Be positive and upbeat.
4. Be outgoing (or at least fake it). Use every opportunity you can to network. Don't view networking as only formal, arranged events.
5. Mind your manners. Remember to say thank you as well as something such as, "It was great seeing you."

6. Don't appear desperate and despondent. People will want to help you, but don't look like you are giving up. If you doubt yourself, it will show, and then others will begin to doubt you.
7. Hide your anger. Keep your composure at all times. If you are angry about how you were treated unfairly in your last job, don't show this in an interview. Also, if you are frustrated with the job search, try to focus on the positive things that are happening.

Here is some sound advice from McIntosh:

Simply put, your job search is ongoing. You are being judged wherever you go. Those who try to help you take into account the aforementioned aspects of your overall attitude. Be mindful at all times how you appear to others.

Discussion Questions

1. How many people could you let know that you are searching for a job? List their names and how you know them (e.g., your internship mentor or a former boss).

2. How would you ask them to help you in a positive and upbeat way? Write a brief speech or e-mail with your job search request.

Source: McIntosh, B. (2013). 7 things you need to consider about your attitude when looking for work. Retrieved on February 10, 2014, from http://thingscareerrelated.com/2013/12/23/6-things-you-need-to-consider-about-your-attitude-when-looking-for-work

that this FJSB may result in poor person–job fit, so it's important to balance flexibility with finding the best match.[36] To summarize, keep a positive attitude about both yourself and the job search process, which have both been related to job search success. Also, remain flexible and curious about different career options and jobs, but remember to look for a job that is a good match. Self-Assessment 4.1 provides you with the opportunity to learn about how adaptable you are with respect to your career search.

In addition to core self-evaluations, work-related attitudes are important because they reflect an employee's reactions to work and serve as an important barometer of how well the organization is attending to employee needs. The next section discusses job satisfaction, which is one of the most often studied work-related attitudes.

Critical Thinking Questions: What limitations do you see on the effect of being positive in the job search process? What is the right balance between optimism and being realistic?

ORGANIZATIONAL COMMITMENT

Learning Objective 4.5: Discuss the concept of organizational commitment and its three components.

Organizational commitment is another work-related attitude that has proven to be important in OB. Reviews (including several meta-analyses) have shown that organizational commitment relates to turnover.[37,38,39] OB research has also shown that people who are not committed to their jobs are absent more often, less motivated, as well as perform at lower levels.[40] *Organizational commitment* is a psychological state that describes an employee's relationship with their organization and a propensity to continue the relationship with the organization.[41] It links an individual to the organization because of their identification with the organization's values and goals.[42] A three-component model of organizational commitment captures different aspects of this work attitude.[43] First, **affective commitment** refers to an employee's emotional attachment to an organization (they stay because they care about the organization and are loyal to it). Second, **continuance commitment** is the degree to which an employee is aware of the costs of leaving the organization (they stay because they are not able to leave). Third, **normative commitment** is the moral obligation to stay with the organization (they stay because it is the right thing to do). Employees that are more committed to the organization are less likely to engage in organizational deviance (e.g., overly long breaks, intentionally poor work quality) and interpersonal deviance (e.g., gossiping about peers, making fun of others).[44]

Job Involvement

Job involvement is how much an employee identifies with his or her job and views their performance at work as an essential part of their self-esteem. Job involvement has been related to employee turnover,[45] organizational citizenship, and job performance.[46]

By combining organizational commitment and job involvement, we can better understand the relationship of these variables to employee withdrawal behaviors (absenteeism and turnover).[47] This relationship is shown in Figure 4.5. As this figure shows, when organizational commitment and job involvement are both high, employees can be viewed as institutionalized "Stars" because their efforts are focused on both the task and the group they belong to. The other extreme case is when both organizational commitment and job involvement are low. In this case, employees are "Apathetics" because they don't put forth much effort on the task and are not concerned about the maintenance of group norms of goals. The other two quadrants represent interesting scenarios in which "Lone Wolves" are involved with their jobs to a high degree and have a task focus, but they are not concerned about the maintenance of the group. They prefer to "go it alone" and are more likely to leave the organization than the final group, "Corporate Citizens." Corporate Citizens are not focused on the task, but they do

Critical Thinking Question: Which component of organizational commitment do you feel is most related to turnover (and why)?

Figure 4.5 The Relationship of Organizational Commitment and Job Involvement to Employee Turnover

Organizational Commitment

	High	**Low**
High (Job Involvement)	**Institutional "Stars"** • Least likely to be absent or leave • Focus on work itself and future with the organization, satisfaction with pay, coworkers, and supervision	**"Lone Wolves"** • More likely to leave voluntarily than corporate citizens • Focus on work itself, satisfaction with working conditions and pay
Low (Job Involvement)	**Corporate Citizens** • Less likely to leave voluntarily than lone wolves • Focus on satisfaction with coworkers	**Apathetics** • Most likely to leave voluntarily • Focus on satisfaction with rewards

Source: Blau, G. J., & Boal, K. B. (1987). Conceptualizing how job involvement and organizational commitment affect turnover and absenteeism. *Academy of Management Review*, 12(2), 288–300. Adapted from p. 293.

attend to the maintenance of the group. They may not be star performers, but they are loyal to the organization and the group. The figure also indicates suggestions for what aspects of satisfaction are important for each type of employee. For example, the Corporate Citizen is most concerned with coworker satisfaction to maintain their organizational commitment. In contrast, if the leader has a Lone Wolf in their group, they should focus more on the satisfaction with the work itself, working conditions, and pay to avoid absenteeism and turnover.

Employee engagement has emerged as an important concept due to research conducted by both OB professors and consultants. Engagement appears to be distinct from job involvement and adds to our understanding of the relationships of attitudes such as job satisfaction.

Employee Engagement

Employee engagement is related to job involvement and enthusiasm for the work performed.[48] Engagement has been defined as "the investments of an individual's complete self into a role." A study of 245 firefighters and their supervisors found that engagement plays a key role in the relationship between **perceived organizational support (POS)** (discussed in the next section) and job performance. This study included job involvement, but engagement explained additional variance in performance. A large-scale study of 7,939 business units in 36 companies found that engagement was related to customer satisfaction, productivity, profit, employee turnover, and safety (fewer accidents).[49] Improving employee engagement may increase business-unit outcomes including profit since disengaged employees cost organizations due to low motivation, poor customer service, and higher turnover.

Gallup estimates that these actively disengaged employees cost the United States between $450 billion and $550 billion each year in lost productivity."[50] In 2012, Gallup conducted its eighth meta-analysis on their engagement measure (the Q12) using 263 research studies, including 49,928 business and work units, with almost 1.4 million employees. Gallup researchers statistically analyzed business- and work-unit-level relationships between employee engagement and performance outcomes. In 2016, this meta-analysis was repeated and the results were similar to the prior analysis (shown in Figure 4.6). Median differences between top-quartile and bottom-quartile units were 10% in customer loyalty ratings, 21% in profitability, 20% in sales production, –24% in turnover (high-turnover organizations), –59% in turnover (low-turnover organizations), –70% in safety incidents, –28% in shrinkage, –41% in absenteeism, –58% in patient safety incidents, and –40% in quality (defects).[51]

Given these positive findings, many organizations are implementing formal engagement programs. The Aberdeen Group, a Boston-based research organization that identifies best-in-class practices by working with industry practitioners, conducted a study that compared companies that have engagement programs with those that don't. Their analysis found that companies that have a formal engagement program reduce the loss of customers due to better responsiveness. In fact, customer referrals actually increased. As shown in Figure 4.7, additional outcomes of engagement were higher revenues, sales teams meeting their quotas more often, and improved cost savings.[52]

Engaged employees feel valued by their organization. A longitudinal panel study found employee perceptions of how much they were valued by the organization were related to changes in affective commitment.[53] Also, the resources employees feel that they have on their job positively relate to engagement. A research study found that three job resources in particular relate to engagement: performance feedback, social support from colleagues, and supervisory coaching.[54] Another study found that resources of supervisor support, innovativeness, appreciation, and organizational climate mattered even more when the demands of a job were high.[55] Thus, employees respond positively to the work

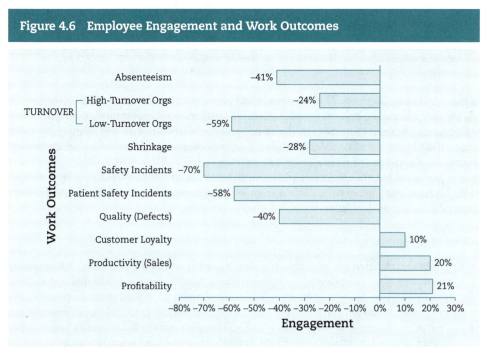

Figure 4.6 Employee Engagement and Work Outcomes

Source: Gallup. (2016). The relationship between engagement at work and organizational outcomes. 2016 Q12 meta-analysis (9th ed.). Retrieved from http://www.gallup.com/services/191489/q12-meta-analysis-report-2016.aspx

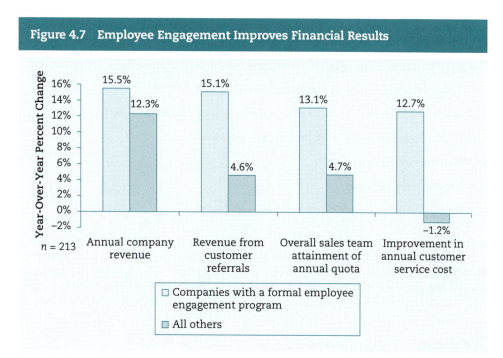

Figure 4.7   Employee Engagement Improves Financial Results

Source: Minkara, O. (2015). Employee engagement and customer satisfaction: "Why" and "how" to bridge the gap. Retrieved from http://v1.aberdeen.com/launch/report/research_report/13091-RR-Employee-Engagement.asp

environment when they feel their supervisors and organization support them. This attitude—POS—is discussed next.

PERCEIVED ORGANIZATIONAL SUPPORT

Learning Objective 4.6: Define *perceived organizational support* (POS), and explain its relationship to fairness at the workplace.

> **Critical Thinking Questions:** Do you see a significant difference between the concepts of job involvement and employee engagement? If so, what is this difference?

An emerging line of research suggests employees pay attention to whether the organization values their contributions and cares about their well-being: POS.[56] Organizational justice and fair rewards are important to the perception of organizational support.[57] A review of over 70 studies of POS indicate that there are three major categories of beneficial treatment: fairness, supervisor support, and organizational rewards along with favorable job conditions.[58] The supervisor also plays an important role in the perception of POS, and it is important for employees to feel that they have a voice in decisions.[59] Employees with higher POS engage in more citizenship behavior and are less likely to show up late for work.[60] A meta-analysis of studies found strong positive effects of POS on job satisfaction and organizational commitment, a moderate positive effect on employee performance, and a strong negative effect on intention to leave.[61] More than 20 years of research suggests that POS appears to be distinct from other attitudes and adds to understanding why some employees perform at higher levels than others. Robert Eisenberger and his colleagues note that leadership drives POS and provide eight evidence-based tactics for increasing POS in organizations to enhance employee engagement.[62]

- Implement supportive workforce services that are discretionary—"Don't just do the things you are required to do."

- Be fair and equitable in the making, monitoring and enforcement of all management practices.

- Set achievable goals and reward proportionately.

- Offer individualized benefits—"Learn and provide the type of support your workers and workforce need."

- Support supervisors so they will foster POS in their subordinates.

- Train subordinates to be supportive.

- Promote strong social networks.

- Begin organizational support prior to the start of employment.

Research on POS indicates that employees respond positively when they feel the organization values them. Such employees want to have a voice in decisions that affect them. Feeling a sense of power to have an impact at work is another work attitude that has been researched in recent years, with results indicating strong relationships to other work attitudes and organizational effectiveness. The next section discusses the research findings for psychological empowerment.

PSYCHOLOGICAL EMPOWERMENT

Learning Objective 4.7: Explain psychological empowerment and its relationship to job performance.

Psychological empowerment refers to "intrinsic task motivation manifested in a set of four cognitions reflecting an individual's orientation to his or her work role: competence, impact, meaning, and self-determination."[63] These four cognitions are defined as follows:

- **Meaning**—how much work goals align with your personal standards (i.e., how well the work "fits" your values)

- **Competence** (or self-efficacy)—your belief in your capabilities to show mastery in your work role

- **Self-Determination**—the degree to which you feel that you have a choice in your work and autonomy to carry it out according to your own preferences

- **Impact**—refers to how much you believe that you can influence important work outcomes (e.g., administrative policies at work)

Research has shown that psychological empowerment is positively related to managerial effectiveness, innovation,[64] and organizational commitment.[65,66] Empowerment is related to lower stress as well.[67] *Meaning* is the driver of psychological empowerment; however, all four components make unique contributions to outcomes. For example, *competence* is most related to ratings of managerial effectiveness. Today, more than 70% of organizations have adopted some kind of empowerment initiative.[68] It is important for leaders to allow their followers to experience meaning in their work but also feel that they have an

> **Critical Thinking Question:** Researchers suggest that meaning is the driver of psychological empowerment. Why do you think this is the case?

impact. Also, leaders should coach followers to develop their sense of competence and allow them discretion in how they do their work. A study of leaders who coached their teams found that team members felt more empowered, and this translated into higher team performance.[69] Self-Assessment 4.2 provides you with feedback on how empowered you feel in your work or school projects.

As noted previously, leaders can develop their followers' feelings of empowerment. They may also create positive attitudes through developing a **sense of meaning** with respect to the work performed. By creating a sense of meaning, leaders may be able to activate other positive attitudes about work and improve employee motivation.

LEADERSHIP IMPLICATIONS: CREATING MEANING AT WORK

Research on attitudes and job satisfaction shows that attitudes relate to important workplace outcomes such as improved job performance and lower turnover. Moreover, positive attitudes at work give people a sense that their work has meaning. A research study found that, over time, individuals who feel committed to their career derive more meaning from their work and are more satisfied with their jobs. These individuals believed that they were living a "calling" rather than going to work for money every day.[70] The sense of having a calling in work also predicts goal-directed effort (work effort and career strategies) and psychological career success (life meaning and career adaptability) over time.[71] The questions used to measure the meaning of work are shown in Table 4.2.[72]

Leaders must recognize that attitudes can change and that the behaviors of leaders affect attitudes. They should think about how they can increase followers' responses to these questions by engaging in empowering leadership and increasing engagement. First, leaders can discuss how their followers' work relates to developing a meaningful career over the long term (positive meaning). Second, leaders should delegate challenging work to their followers to increase their sense of meaning (meaning-making through work). Third, leaders can point out ways that their followers' work impacts others in a positive way (greater-good motivations). When people experience these three aspects of their work, they will be more engaged and should also experience a higher level of well-being.

Certain leadership styles influence the degree to which work is perceived as meaningful.[73,74] A review of the literature on finding meaning in work concluded, "leaders can imbue work with meaningfulness by prompting employees to transcend their personal needs or goals in favor of those tied to a broader mission or purpose."[75] Empowering leadership increases work engagement by giving followers a sense of work meaningfulness.[76] Research on leadership similarly shows that developing high-quality working relationships with followers relates to higher levels of job

Table 4.2	The Work as Meaning Inventory (WAMI)

Positive meaning

- I have found a meaningful career.
- I understand how my work contributes to my life's meaning.
- I have a good sense of what makes my job meaningful.
- I have discovered work that has a satisfying purpose.

Meaning-making through work

- I view my work as contributing to my personal growth.
- My work helps me better understand myself.
- My work helps me make sense of the world around me.

Greater-good motivations

- My work really makes no difference to the world (reversed).
- I know my work makes a positive difference in the world.
- The work I do serves a greater purpose.

Source: Steger, M. F., Dik, B. J., & Duffy, R. D. (2012). Measuring meaningful work: The work and meaning inventory (WAMI). *Journal of Career Assessment*, 1–16.

satisfaction, organizational commitment, and empowerment.[77] In sum, leaders play a powerful role in creating meaning for their followers by developing high-quality relationships and then sharing the organization's overall mission with followers. This provides followers with a sense of meaning in their work, which has been shown to relate to job satisfaction.[78] In turn, employees respond with high levels of engagement and job performance.

Top managers play a role in the development of meaning as well. OB research has demonstrated that work meaningfulness trickles down from strategic leaders to mid-level leaders to employees through visionary leadership. This effect is even more prevalent for followers that are new to an organization.[79] Followers with a transformational leader are more committed because they experience psychological empowerment at work.[80] A recent study found that CEOs who make work interesting for followers by encouraging innovation increase their followers' work meaningfulness.[81] Such charismatic leaders increase their followers' commitment by (1) promoting higher levels of intrinsic motivation through goal accomplishment, (2) emphasizing the linkages between follower effort and goal achievement, and (3) creating a higher level of personal commitment by leader and followers to a common vision, mission, and organizational goals.[82] In sum, feeling part of the larger mission of the organization increases followers' meaning in their work and their organizational commitment.

 **edge.sagepub.com/scandura2e**

Want a better grade? Go to **edge.sagepub.com/scandura2e** for the tools you need to sharpen your study skills.

KEY TERMS

active, 79

affective, 74

affective commitment, 82

attitude, 74

behavioral, 74

career adaptability, 80

cognitive, 74

cognitive dissonance, 75

constructive, 79

continuance commitment, 82

destructive, 79

employee engagement, 83

flexible job search behavior (FJSB), 81

job involvement, 82

normative commitment, 82

passive, 79

perceived organizational support (POS), 83

psychological empowerment, 86

sense of meaning, 87

social pressure, 76

TOOLKIT ACTIVITY 4.1: What Do Workers Want From Their Jobs?

Objective: To identify what satisfies people at work.

Instructions: Rank each item under the column titled "Individual Factors" from 1 to 10, with 1 being the most important and 10 being the least important.

When you have completed the ranking, meet with a group of four to five classmates and calculate the average individual weights within the group. Rank the 10 items under the column titled "Group Factors." Discuss your answers with your group before reading further.

Individual Factors	Group Factors	What Do People Want From Their Jobs?
_____	_____	Promotion in the company
_____	_____	Tactful discipline
_____	_____	Job security
_____	_____	Help with personal problems
_____	_____	Personal loyalty of supervisor
_____	_____	High wages
_____	_____	Full appreciation of work being done
_____	_____	Good working conditions
_____	_____	Feeling of being in on things
_____	_____	Interesting work

This same scale has been given to thousands of workers across the country. Supervisors ranked the items in this order:

1. High wages
2. Job security
3. Promotion in the company
4. Good working conditions
5. Interesting work
6. Personal loyalty of supervisor
7. Tactful discipline
8. Full appreciation of work being done
9. Help with personal problems
10. Feeling of being in on things

However, when employees were given the same exercise, their rankings tended to follow this pattern:

1. Full appreciation of work being done
2. Feeling of being in on things
3. Help with personal problems
4. Job security
5. High wages
6. Interesting work
7. Promotion in the company
8. Personal loyalty of supervisor
9. Good working conditions
10. Tactful discipline

Discussion Questions

1. In comparing the different ratings, what might account for the different opinions between you and your group?

2. What might be the cause of the supervisors' rankings being so different from the employees?

3. Do you think the results of this survey will change over time?

Source: Kovach, K. A. (1987). What motivates employees? Workers and supervisors give different answers. *Business Horizons, 30*(5), 58–65. Retrieved from http://www.nwlink.com/~donclark/leader/want_job.html#sthash.86o3taW7.dpuf

CASE STUDY 4.1: A Crisis in Nursing

Los Rayos del Sol Medical Center is a hospital and surgery center located in Florida. Its main facility has 500 beds and several outpatient centers, it employees 2,600 people, and has recently partnered with the Mayo Clinic. Despite this seeming success, Los Rayos is experiencing high turnover amidst its nursing staff. The nurse average turnover rate is 14% for hospitals,[83] while Los Rayos has a turnover rate of 21%. New graduate nurses turn over at a rate of 27% within their first year, with an additional 37% of those new nurses wanting to leave, according to a survey conducted nationwide.[84] At Los Rayos, new-nurse turnover is 40%. The hospital spends an average of 13 weeks[85] to fill a vacant position and thousands of dollars per hire.[86] Turnover often leaves units understaffed, which creates poor patient experiences, nurse burnout, and lower quality of care. It also cuts into the firm's bottom line.

Why are the nurses leaving? Los Rayos strives to provide the highest quality in patient care, but it also has to manage costs and comply with the new government regulations from the Affordable Care Act. Thus, over the last 10 years, Los Rayos has made a number of changes.

- Ten years ago, Los Rayos changed the staffing model. All units had two licensed nurses and a housekeeper. Housekeepers were minimum-wage staff that helped the nurses do things like wash linens and stock the nurses' station with basics. These tasks can take a lot of time away from the normal nurses' job duties of doing rounds, required charting, administering doctors' orders, and helping patients. Los Rayos promoted the housekeepers to health techs, which were supposed to do more patient care tasks, but most were not equipped with the skills needed to do these advanced tasks and were not given training by the hospital. At the same time, Los Rayos reduced the number of nurses per unit by one. This raised staffing ratios from 12 patients to one nurse to 24 patients to one nurse.

- Eight years ago, Los Rayos cut the annual employee picnic and Christmas party in order to save money.

- Five years ago, Los Rayos expanded nurses' jobs to engage in activities like cost cutting and quality control. It required nurses to provide three to five cost saving ideas per year or they would be negatively evaluated on their performance appraisals. The next year, the firm put a cap on each position's wage brackets, which resulted in nurses with greater than 12 years of service not receiving raises.

- Three years ago, Los Rayos removed the intake coordinator position from all units except the ER and laboratory. This means that unless a patient is admitted to the hospital in the ER or immediately after laboratory testing, the nurse(s) on the unit has to complete the admission paperwork when the patient is brought to the unit.

- Two years ago, Los Rayos began using tablets for patients' charts and tracking and dispensing medicine. To prevent drug theft, medicine carts were equipped with a new security system that requires nurses to scan a patient's hospital bracelet with the tablet, select the medication, and confirm the order before the tablet will send the information to the cart and unlock the needed medicine. The process often has technical problems or delays and causes frustration to both nurse and patient.

- A year ago, Los Rayos began requiring all its nurses to take turns developing, planning, and presenting continuing education courses to reduce training costs. Nurses are required to complete 60 hours of continuing education annually for license renewal. The nurses did not receive any additional compensation for the training they developed, nor were they given any nonmonetary rewards.

- Six months ago, Los Rayos changed from 8- to 12-hour shifts to reduce costs and to allow patients to be closer to their caretakers. However, patients from the maternity and geriatrics wards have complained about only seeing nurses at the start and end of shift and have negatively rated their hospital experience on surveys. Some employees like 12-hour shifts; however, most employees agree these shifts are exhausting, and the nurses often state they don't have the time and energy to "go the extra mile" for colleagues and patients.

Discussion Questions

1. How do you think the changes Los Rayos made affected nurses' attitudes? What problems to the business may poor nurse attitudes cause in addition to turnover?

2. Which of the job attitudes from the chapter do you feel is the biggest contributor to nurse turnover? The smallest contributor? Why do you think so?

3. How might leadership and personality of managers and administrators be affecting the situation?

4. If you were the director of a hospital and going to do a survey of employee attitudes, which attitudes would you want to know?

SELF-ASSESSMENT 4.1: How Much Career Adaptability Do You Have?

Part I. Taking the Assessment

Different people use different strengths to build their careers. No one is good at everything; each of us emphasizes some strengths more than others. Please rate how strongly you have developed each of the following abilities using the scale below each question.

Statements	Strongly Disagree	Disagree	Neutral	Agree	Strongly Agree
1. I think about what my future will be like.	1	2	3	4	5
2. I am aware of the educational and career choices that I must make.	1	2	3	4	5
3. I prepare for the future.	1	2	3	4	5
4. I plan how to achieve my goals.	1	2	3	4	5
5. I make decisions by myself.	1	2	3	4	5
6. I take responsibility for my actions.	1	2	3	4	5
7. I do what's right for me.	1	2	3	4	5
8. I count on myself.	1	2	3	4	5
9. I look for opportunities to grow as a person.	1	2	3	4	5

(Continued)

(Continued)

	1	2	3	4	5
10. I investigate options before making a choice.	1	2	3	4	5
11. I observe different ways of doing things.	1	2	3	4	5
12. I am curious about new opportunities.	1	2	3	4	5
13. I learn new skills.	1	2	3	4	5
14. I work up to my ability.	1	2	3	4	5
15. I overcome obstacles.	1	2	3	4	5
16. I solve problems.	1	2	3	4	5

Part II. Scoring Instructions

In Step I, you rated yourself on 16 questions. Add the numbers you circled in each of the columns to derive your scores for four aspects of Career Adaptability. Add your scores to determine your overall Career Adaptability score.

Concern	Control	Curiosity	Confidence
1. _____	5. _____	9. _____	13. _____
2. _____	6. _____	10. _____	14. _____
3. _____	7. _____	11. _____	15. _____
4. _____	8. _____	12. _____	16. _____
Total _____	_____	_____	_____

Interpretation

Your scores can range from 4 to 20 for each dimension. A score above 15 can be considered a strength. For your overall Career Adaptability, your scores can range from 16 to 80. An overall score over 60 suggests that you have a strong level of Career Adaptability.

The Four Cs:

Concern helps individuals look ahead and prepare for what might come next.

Control enables individuals to become responsible for shaping themselves and their environments to meet what comes next by using self-discipline, effort, and persistence.

Curiosity prompts a person to think about self in various situations and roles.

Confidence increases aspirations so that the person can actualize choices to implement their life design.

Discussion Questions

1. What are your greatest strengths related to your ability to adapt to your career? Your greatest weaknesses?

2. Overall, do you feel that being adaptable to your career is a positive thing? How will you balance your flexibility with finding a good fit to an organization and a job?

3. What did you learn about yourself from this self-assessment, and how will you use it to be more strategic in your career search?

Source: Adapted from Savickas, M. L., & Porfeli, E. J. (2012). Career Adapt-Abilities Scale: Construction, reliability, and measurement equivalence across 13 countries. *Journal of Vocational Behavior, 80*(3), 661–673. p. 672.

SELF-ASSESSMENT 4.2: Do You Experience Empowerment?

This self-assessment exercise provides feedback on how empowered you feel at work. If you don't have work experience, consider how you feel working on team projects for your classes. There are no right or wrong answers, and this is not a test. You don't have to share your results with others unless you wish to do so.

Part I. Taking the Assessment

You will be presented with some questions representing how you feel about your work.

Statements	Strongly Disagree	Disagree	Somewhat Disagree	Neutral	Somewhat Agree	Agree	Strongly Agree
1. The work I do is very important to me.	1	2	3	4	5	6	7
2. I am confident about my ability to do my job.	1	2	3	4	5	6	7
3. I have significant autonomy in determining how I do my job.	1	2	3	4	5	6	7
4. I have a large impact on what happens in my department.	1	2	3	4	5	6	7
5. My job activities are personally meaningful to me.	1	2	3	4	5	6	7
6. I am self-assured about my capabilities to perform my work activities.	1	2	3	4	5	6	7
7. I can decide on my own how to go about doing my work.	1	2	3	4	5	6	7

(Continued)

(Continued)

Statements	Strongly Disagree	Disagree	Somewhat Disagree	Neutral	Somewhat Agree	Agree	Strongly Agree
8. I have a great deal of control over what happens in my department.	1	2	3	4	5	6	7
9. The work I do is meaningful to me.	1	2	3	4	5	6	7
10. I have mastered the skills necessary for my job.	1	2	3	4	5	6	7
11. I have considerable opportunity for independence and freedom in how I do my job.	1	2	3	4	5	6	7
12. I have significant influence over what happens in my department.	1	2	3	4	5	6	7

Part II. Scoring Instructions

In Step I, you rated yourself on 12 questions. Add the numbers you circled in each of the columns to derive your score for empowerment.

Meaning	Competence	Self-Determination	Impact
1. _____	2. _____	3. _____	4. _____
5. _____	6. _____	7. _____	8. _____
9. _____	10. _____	11. _____	12. _____
Total _____	_____	_____	_____

Note: *Meaning*—how much work goals align with your personal standards (i.e., how well the work "fits" your values); *Competence (or self-efficacy)*—your belief in your capabilities to show mastery in your work role; *Self-Determination*—the degree to which you feel that you have a choice in your work and autonomy to carry it out according to your own preferences; *Impact*—refers to how much you believe that you can influence important work outcomes (e.g., administrative policies at work).

Information on the empowerment profiles for different contexts and norm data for the empowerment dimensions can be found in Spreitzer (2001). Norm data for each of the four dimensions and the total empowerment scale (for each dimension, divide by 3 and divide your total score by 12 to compare your results) are shown in the following table.

Empowerment Norming Scores

	Meaning	Competence	Self-Determination	Impact	Empower
Lowest 5%	3.67	4.33	3.67	2.00	4.17
10%	4.67	4.50	4.33	2.67	4.50
15%	4.80	4.75	4.67	3.00	4.69
20%	5.00	5.00	4.75	3.33	4.83
25%	5.25	5.25	4.85	3.67	5.00
30%	5.33	5.33	5.00	4.00	5.08
35%	5.50	5.51	5.30	4.33	5.19
40%	5.67	5.67	5.33	4.67	5.33
45%	5.75	5.71	5.50	4.82	5.42
50%	5.91	5.75	5.67	5.00	5.50
55%	6.00	5.82	5.72	5.03	5.58
60%	6.11	6.00	5.75	5.33	5.67
65%	6.22	6.25	5.93	5.50	5.8
70%	6.33	6.33	6.00	5.67	5.88
75%	6.50	6.50	6.08	5.78	6.00
80%	6.67	6.67	6.33	6.00	6.08
85%	6.78	6.75	6.38	6.35	6.19
90%	6.89	6.91	6.67	6.50	6.38
Highest 95%	7.00	7.00	7.00	7.00	6.58

Source: Spreitzer, G. M. (2001). Psychological Empowerment Instrument. Retrieved from http://webuser.bus .umich.edu/spreitze/Pdfs/12-item%20empowerment%20instrument%2002-2015.pdf

Discussion Questions

1. Which of the four factors contributing to empowerment was highest for you? Do you feel that your work (or schoolwork) has meaning?

2. How much control (impact) do you have over your work (or schoolwork)? How can you increase the amount of influence you have? List two strategies.

3. Compare your scores to the norm data shown in the previous table. Are you in the top 80% on any dimension? The bottom 20%? Where does your overall score fall compared with the norms?

Sources: Spreitzer, G. M. (1995). Psychological empowerment in the workplace: Dimensions, measurement, and validation. *Academy of Management Journal, 38*(5), 1442–1465; Spreitzer, G. M. (1996). Social structural characteristics of psychological empowerment. *Academy of Management Journal, 39*(2), 483–504; Spreitzer, G. M., & Quinn, R. E. (2001). *A company of leaders: Five disciplines for unleashing the power in your workforce.* San Francisco, CA: Jossey-Bass.

PERCEPTION, DECISION MAKING, AND PROBLEM SOLVING

Learning Objectives

After studying this chapter, you should be able to do the following:

5.1: Illustrate common perceptual biases with examples.

5.2: Explain how self-fulfilling prophecies affect job performance.

5.3: Provide two examples of how decision making affects organizational performance.

5.4: Explain the rational decision-making model and bounded rationality.

5.5: Demonstrate understanding of prospect theory and the impact of framing on decisions with an example.

5.6: Describe the role of intuition in decision making.

5.7: List and explain three major decision traps and how to avoid them: hindsight, hubris, and escalation of commitment.

5.8: Discuss the elements in Amabile's three-component model of creativity.

Get the edge on your studies at **edge.sagepub.com/scandura2e**

- Take the chapter quiz
- Review key terms with eFlashcards
- Explore multimedia resources, SAGE readings, and more!

WOULD YOU BE HAPPIER IF YOU WERE RICHER?

This question was investigated in a survey of working women, asking them to estimate the amount of time they were in a bad mood the previous day.[1] Respondents were then asked to estimate the percentage of time people were in a bad mood with pairs of high- and low-income situations. These estimates were compared to the actual reports of mood provided by high- and low-income participants. The researchers learned that the women in the study exaggerated the bad moods of other people with low-income levels. The average person estimated that people with incomes below $20,000 per year spend 58% of their time in a bad mood, compared with 26% for those with incomes above $100,000 per year. However, the actual percentages were 32% and 20%, respectively. This perception bias can be explained as the focusing illusion, which is the tendency to overestimate the effect of a single factor on one's life satisfaction (in this example, the factor tested was income). Income actually has less effect on a person's moments of pleasurable experience than on their response to questions about their overall well-being. Why? The authors cite research suggesting that material goods are not all that strongly related to general well-being. Also, income is seen as relative (as others in a society get richer, people shift their reference point with respect to life satisfaction and income). Finally, research shows that with higher income, people spend more time working and commuting to and from work (often reported as the low points of the day) rather than spending time with family or doing other pleasurable activities. They also report higher levels of stress. So the focusing illusion explains why people in general are not more satisfied if they are richer. If people focus only on income and ignore other factors related to well-being, they feel less satisfied with their lives.

Perception is the process through which people organize and interpret their sensory information (what they hear and see) to give meaning to their world. Perception plays a large role in how people view their work, their coworkers, their boss, and the overall organization they work for. Unlike individual differences, such as personality traits and cross-cultural differences, research shows that perceptions can change. Given the example above, and now that you understand the focusing illusion, will you look at your income differently? In this chapter, other perceptual biases are covered, as well as individual decision making. Group decision making is covered in the chapter on Group Processes and Teams in this textbook. We begin with perception because understanding why people perceive situations differently is essential for a leader to be effective in making decisions. It is important to a leader to remember that *perceptions are the reality experienced by followers.*

Critical Thinking Questions: How can leaders employ the focusing illusion to improve follower satisfaction with pay and benefits? What aspects of the job can employees focus on besides pay and benefits?

UNDERSTANDING WHY PEOPLE DON'T SEE EYE TO EYE

Learning Objective 5.1: Illustrate common perceptual biases with examples.

People may see things differently in organizations because they make perceptual errors. **Perceptual errors** are defined as flaws in perception due to mental shortcuts people make to simplify information that is processed. These errors matter for a number of reasons. First, they affect interpretations of leaders' and coworkers' behavior. Second, perceptual errors (or biases) affect how job applicants are seen in interviews. Third, they affect performance appraisals. Thus, leaders need to know about these perceptual biases and guard against them. Examples of important decisions leaders make that may be affected by perceptual errors include hiring the best person for a job and making an ethical choice. This chapter covers perceptual biases that have been most studied in workplace settings and are most relevant to effective leadership. These biases can be remembered with the acronym PRACH for *primacy, recency, availability, contrast,* and *halo.*

The Primacy Effect

We have heard the statement "you never get a second chance to make a good first impression." But do first impressions really matter? There is a significant body of research that suggests they do, and this is the **primacy effect** or "belief perseverance."[2] For example, if a person smells like smoke when met by an interviewer who doesn't smoke, this impression may last and influence whether they get the job. Once a person has formed an initial impression, they maintain it even when presented with concrete evidence that it is false. Classic experimental research in psychology has demonstrated that this affects problem solving[3] and the persistence of **stereotypes.**[4] Specifically, order-effects research confirms that information presented early in a sequence affects judgments made later.[5] This may be due to fatigue or not paying attention. People discount information presented later due to the need to confirm their first impressions. They seek only consistent information and rule out alternatives that conflict with their initial impression.[6] More recently, experimental research has shown that the primacy effect persists due to **belief updating**, where initial information affects the conclusion one draws, and this conclusion then impacts later judgments.[7]

How quickly do we form a first impression? It may be much faster than you might think. In experimental research, subjects were shown a photograph of a person's face for only a tenth of a second.[8] Based on this flash photo of a face, people gave ratings of the person's attractiveness, likeability, trustworthiness, competence, and aggressiveness. Moreover, when the exposure time was increased, there was no change in the assessments. The authors concluded increased exposure time only seems to bolster a person's initial first impressions.

What can be done to address the primacy effect? An experimental study found that accountability influences a person's vigilance and improves processing of all information presented.[9] When people are asked to justify their decisions to others, they are more likely to process all of the information available. So a leader should keep this in mind when

> Critical Thinking Question: If you make a bad first impression in an interview, what would you try to do to change it? Provide examples of the specific behaviors you would engage in.

making important decisions. Imagine that you would have to justify a decision to your boss or in public (you never know—you might end up having to do so). Second, based upon research on belief updating, the leader should be willing to "hit the reset button" and look at a situation as if they had no prior exposure to it. From this review, it seems clear that primacy is important and first impressions do matter.

The Recency Effect

Not only do people remember what they experience first, they also remember the most recently presented items or experiences. This perceptual bias is called the **recency effect**. For example, if you are given a long list of names to remember, you will probably remember the ones you heard last and forget the ones in the middle. Actually, in terms of free recall on tasks, there is a U-shaped pattern in which the primacy effect results in the first words that are mentioned being remembered, followed by a decline in the middle words presented, then a steep increase, and then leveling off (an S-shaped curve) for the words presented last.[10] For example, after a job interview, it is important to end on a positive note by showing the interviewer appreciation for their time.

The recency effect is pervasive.[11] Recency may affect performance appraisals (the manager remembers their direct reports' most recent behavior rather than behavior in the middle of the evaluation period). In experimental studies involving role-plays of performance appraisal sessions, recency effects were present regardless of whether the appraisal was made at the end of each task or at the end of the entire rating process.[12] However, people can improve their short-term memory by employing control processes that affect how information is stored and retrieved.[13] So how can a leader guard against the recency effect?

First, **rehearsal,** or repetition of information, has been shown to improve recall (think about how you might repeat a phone number you hear over and over in your mind several times to remember it until you can write it down). **Coding** is another technique, in which you link the information you need to remember to something familiar and easily retrievable (e.g., you remember passwords by creating combinations of your pet's name with other alphanumeric characters and symbols). Another example is mnemonic coding, in which you create acronyms to remember information (such as PRACH to remember these perceptual biases: primacy, recency, availability, contrast, and halo). Another technique to improve recall is called **imaging**, in which verbal information is linked to visual images. For example, a person would visualize an image that is associated with a word that sounds like the person's name, so someone named D. J. who is a finance professor could be remembered as Dow Jones. These types of memory techniques have been shown to improve short-term memory of long lists of information significantly.[14] By now, you have probably realized research on recency and memory improvement has implications for how you can improve your study habits and performance on exams!

The Availability Bias

Sometimes, a person's judgments are based upon what most readily comes into a person's mind. In the most frequently cited study of the **availability bias,** subjects were read two lists of names, one presenting 19 famous men and 20 less-famous women, and the other presenting 19 famous women and 20 less-famous men.[15] When asked, subjects reported that there were more men than women in the first list but more women than men in the second list, even though the opposite was true (by a difference of one). Presumably, the famous names were easier to recall than the nonfamous ones, resulting in an overestimate. In fact, subjects were able to recall about 50% more of the famous than of the non-famous names. Another study conducted by the same researchers found that people tended to overestimate the number of words that began with the letter r but to underestimate the number of words that had r as the third letter.[16] The first letter likely prompts people to remember more words; however, there are actually more words in the English language that have r as the third letter.

BEST PRACTICES

Remember Every Name Every Time

According to Benjamin Levy, who has trained thousands of executives to improve their memory, there is nothing as pleasant to another person as hearing their own name spoken. For leaders to really connect with a large constellation of different people, they need to be able to remember their names. Research on perception has indicated there are some tricks you can employ to remember people's names. Levy suggests the FACE method for remembering names: FACE stands for "Focus, Ask, Comment, and Employ."[17]

Focus: Lock in on the person's face. Lean forward and turn your head slightly to one side. You should give the other person your ear (literally).

Ask: Inquire about his name (Is it Robert or Bob? What is the origin of your last name?). Ask or clarify that you heard the name correctly. Genuinely pay attention, and show that you really care.

Comment: Say something about the name, and cross-reference it in your head ("My best friend in high school's name was Bob"). Or relate the name to a famous movie star; for example, if the person's name is Benjamin, ask if they like to be called "Ben" like Ben Affleck.

Employ: Put the name to use right away: "Great to meet you, Bob!" A great aid to memory is to teach material to someone else. You can introduce the person to another person in the room to further fix the name in your mind. At the end of the conversation, use the name again: "It's a pleasure to meet you, Ben."

Once you master the FACE technique, you can learn the NAME technique. NAME stands for "Nominate, Articulate, Morph, and Entwine."

Nominate: Pick a feature of the person's face and then nominate it as the feature you will use to link the name to the face. Try to focus on the eyes, nose, lips, ears, chin, or eyebrows.

Articulate: Silently make a note to yourself of what is unique about the feature you have nominated. For example, Ben's eyes are green.

Morph: Change the name into another word you can remember, but retain an element of the original name. For example, Ben becomes a Lens.

Entwine: You nominated a physical characteristic of a person you just met. Then you articulated a mental description of the person. Third, you morphed the name into a sound-alike word. Try to create as vivid an image as you can. For example, think of Ben wearing large, funny glasses with green lenses (LENS = BEN, a person with GREEN EYES).

These tips are only the basics of how to learn to remember names every time. More detail can be found in his book *Remember Every Name, Every Time*. Does it work? Benjamin Levy stuns corporate training audiences by remembering the names of 100 to 150 people! With practice, you can learn his techniques to enhance your ability to connect with others—an essential leadership skill.

Discussion Questions

1. Explain how the primacy effect helps you remember people's names during the focus phase of the FACE technique.
2. Practice remembering names by developing memory aids using the NAME technique for the following names: Laura Ray and Kevin Rankin.
3. Give an example of a situation when you will need to remember people's names using this technique.

Source: Levy, B. (2002). *Remember every name, every time: Corporate America's memory master reveals his secrets.* New York, NY: Fireside Books.

Both the ease and difficulty of recall affects how well people remember information.[18] In addition to information that is readily available, information that is more difficult to recall is more likely forgotten. There is evidence that shows events are judged to be more common when instances more *easily* come to mind, even when a smaller absolute *number* of instances are generated. For example, a lot of people have a fear of flying because incidents of plane crashes make headlines and high-profile news reports. However, the probability that one will die in a plane crash is much lower than in a car crash (a chance of 1 in 108 for a car accident compared to 1 in 7,229 for a plane crash based on data reported by the National Safety Council). This is a demonstration of the availability heuristic.

How can a leader guard against making the availability bias mistake? First, they can make the things that are desired for decision making (perhaps at a later date) vivid and very easy to bring to mind (e.g., with repetition and visualization). They can also try to minimize things that influence decisions by making them more difficult to recall by using vague, abstract, complex, or uncomfortable language to describe them. Increasing the number of counter-explanations reduces the persistence of the availability bias.[19, 20] Elaborative interrogation increases the willingness to let go of preconceived notions and learn material that challenges beliefs. Elaborative interrogation requires people to generate their own explanations of factual statements that are presented to them.[21] For example, a leader can write out a statement challenging their decision and then generate arguments for why this statement is false to check their thinking and perhaps avoid the availability bias effect.

When making important decisions, pause and think why you are making the decision. Is it because of information you see frequently? What is the source of the information? What motivated the person to provide it? It's important to keep in mind that we rely on what is familiar and most readily available, but taking shortcuts when making important decisions can have serious negative consequences. Another shortcut happens when we make comparisons based upon what has happened just before we make a decision or judgment: the contrast effect. Contrast effects are among the most significant decision biases for a leader to guard against.

> Critical Thinking Question: How can elaborative interrogation be used to change perceptions of a follower who does not like to work on a team?

Contrast Effects

Figure 5.1 shows the Ebbinghaus illusion as an example of a perceptual contrast effect. The center circle is exactly the same size in Groups 1 through 3, but it looks larger in Group 1 than in Group 2 because the circles that surround it are small in Group 1 and large in Group 2. Contrast effects also happen in organizational decision making. For example, a leader's performance evaluation of a person is affected by comparisons with other people recently encountered who rank higher or lower on the same characteristics.

Figure 5.1 The Ebbinghaus Illusion

Group 1   Group 2   Group 3

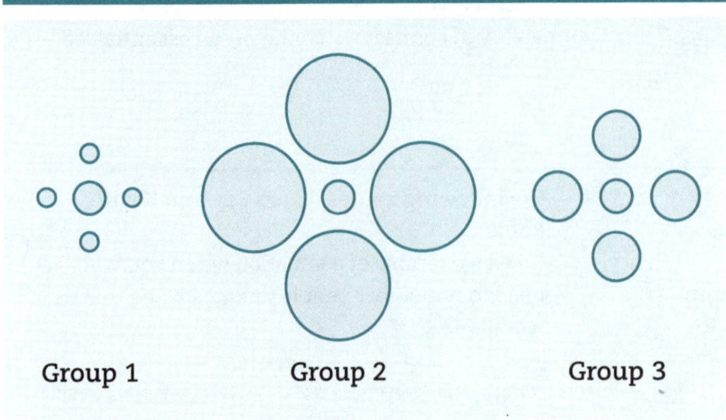

Experimental research has demonstrated that contrast effects influence performance evaluations. When a leader has followers who are poor performers, they tend to give very high ratings to average-performing subordinates. On the other hand, when all subordinates were high performers, fewer rewards and lower performance ratings were given—even to the most outstanding performers.[22,23] The contrast effect has been found in real organizational settings as well. The greater the proportion of engineers who had low performance ratings (unsatisfactory), the more likely supervisors were to assign favorable ratings and provide rewards to just average performance engineers.[24] Thus, the poor performance of other engineers generated a contrast effect in which a satisfactory performer stood out even though they were not actually stellar. Leaders need to focus on individual performance and avoid comparisons that may result in the contrast effect.

Another potential contrast effect may happen in the interviewing process. An applicant for a position may be rated more favorably if they follow a sequence of poor applicants, although they may not be the best person for the job. Training managers to eliminate biases including the contrast effect results in improved evaluations.[25] There is some indication that becoming aware of the contrast effect may help a leader reduce the bias when making hiring decisions and performance appraisals. In addition, using a structured interview process may reduce the contrast effect.[26] A structured interview should have the following elements:

1. Use standard and numerical score sheets.

2. Use behavioral and situational questions.

3. Ask the same questions in the same order for each applicant.

4. Avoid questions that are unrelated to the position you are interviewing for.

Training and the use of structured interviews may also reduce another pervasive decision error that may affect managerial judgments of all types, including performance appraisals and hiring decisions: the **halo error** effect.

Halo Error

Halo error (or its opposite **horns error**) occurs when the rater's overall positive (or negative in the case of horns) impression or evaluation strongly influence ratings of specific attributes.[27] For example, wearing a fraternity or sorority pin to an interview may invoke a positive impression if the interviewer is a person who assumes membership in the organization translates to high performance. Research on halo errors in rating can be traced back to early organizational behavior (OB) research,[28] and there has been steady interest in its study over time.[29,30] Some researchers consider halo error to be ubiquitous in organizations and perhaps the most serious of rating errors that are made by managers.[31] A meta-analytic review of research on halo effects in ratings of job performance concluded that halo error "substantially" increased both supervisory and peer ratings of performance.[32] Halo error results in an overall positive impression of a follower that clouds evaluation of actual performance because it is assumed that if a follower is good at one aspect of the job, they are good at everything.

Halo effects in OB may occur for many reasons. A manager might form a general impression after having seen a few successful task accomplishments, and subsequent judgments may be heavily influenced by this first impression (i.e., the primacy effect + halo error resulting in a strong influence on perception). Some managers may be too busy and stop paying attention to a follower's performance. Another manager may strive to make later ratings consistent with earlier ratings to prove they are right. Halo effects may also be compounded by the contrast effect in which a previously rated person interviewed influences the ratings of those interviewed later (halo + contrast). As noted earlier for contrast effects, training and the use of structured interviews may be effective in reducing halo error. Another recent study found that providing feedback to interviewers regarding how their ratings compared with average ratings of others (norms) reduced halo and horn errors (leniency and severity).[33]

> Critical Thinking Question: What are your perceptions of leaders? Provide an example of a situation where leaders are believed to have the power to make major changes in society.

The evidence reviewed above demonstrates that perceptions play a role in how leaders view their followers' performance. But do perceptions play a role in how a job applicant is viewed before they are hired? The research described next suggests that how potential employers perceive you influences whether or not you will get the job.

EMPLOYABILITY: SELF-FULFILLING PROPHECIES DURING THE APPLICATION PROCESS

Learning Objective 5.2: Explain how self-fulfilling prophecies affect job performance.

Recent research on **employability** suggests the degree to which you are perceived as employable may determine whether or not you are hired for a position. The ability to gain a job in a formal organization is an emerging area in OB research.[34] Employability is defined as "an attribution employers make about the probability that job candidates will make positive contributions to their organizations."[35] An important question, then, is what determines employer's perceptions of whether or not a job applicant has this potential and is employable by their organization. There are three important aspects to an applicant's profile that affect employers' perceptions and subsequent attributions about employability, as shown in Figure 5.2. What matters to employers is proposed to be the candidate's social or interpersonal compatibility, which leads to the perception that the candidate will have positive interactions with others on a daily basis. Next, abilities, expertise, and know-how lead to the perception that the candidate is able to do the job. Finally, ambition, work ethic, and drive lead to the perception that the candidate is willing to work hard. These factors combine to form the employer's attribution of employability and therefore relates to whether or not the applicant gets a job offer. Once hired, perceptions of employability explain who gets mentored and subsequently experiences career success and a higher number of promotions.[36]

Research examined individual differences believed to be related to employability, such as openness to change at work and optimism. The next question you may be wondering is "How do I know if I am employable as perceived by employers?"[37] To see your ratings on the dimensions of employability, complete Self-Assessment 5.1 at the end of this chapter. While research on employability is relatively new, it is a very important concept that offers practical advice for students preparing for their job search. Applicants for positions need to pay attention to how they present their qualifications so employers make the attribution that they are employable and will become a significant contributor to the organization's success.

Figure 5.2 Determinants of Employability

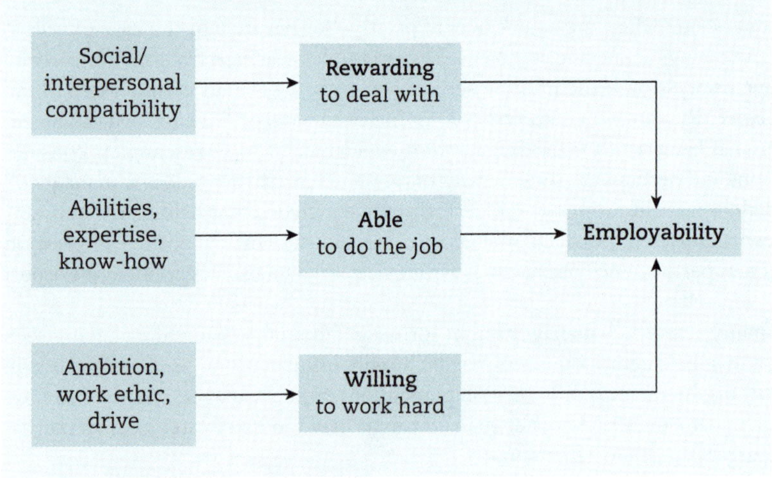

Source: Hogan, R., Chamorro-Premuzic, T., & Kaiser, R. B. (2013). Employability and career success: Bridging the gap between theory and reality. *Industrial and Organizational Psychology, 6*(1), 3–16.

> **Critical Thinking Questions: How can you use the knowledge of employability to improve your chances of getting hired? What dimensions of employability will you focus on?**

INDIVIDUAL DECISION MAKING

Learning Objective 5.3: Provide two examples of how decision making affects organizational performance.

Business leaders make decisions every day, but are there some decisions that have a defining impact on the future of an organization? This question is addressed in the book *The Greatest Business Decisions of All Time*.[38] Based on the author's analysis, the greatest business decisions follow:

1. Henry Ford's decision to double the salaries of Ford's workforce to attract top talent and increase income so that people could afford his cars

2. The Apple board's decision to bring back Steve Jobs after he had been fired 10 years earlier, leading to innovations that have created the most valuable brand in the world

3. Sam Walton's decision to hold Saturday morning all-employee meetings for Walmart to create a culture of information sharing and rapid decision making, creating one of the largest retailers in the world

4. Samsung's decision to create a sabbatical program that allows their top performers to travel all over the world, which continues to be one of the secrets to their global brand success

5. Jack Welch's decision to create Crotonville, a training and development center that produced hundreds of great leaders who practice the "GE Way"

From these examples, it's clear that making the right decisions plays a large role in leader effectiveness. The next sections cover both classic and contemporary research on decision making that every leader must know to make the right decisions—at the right time.

> **Critical Thinking Question:** What is it about each of these decisions that caused them to be listed as the most important business decisions? Propose a recent business decision that is a candidate for this list.

Decision Processes and Organizational Performance

The greatest business decisions discussed previously suggest that decision making affects firm performance. For example, decision rationality is related to the success of strategic decisions ranging from restructuring to the introduction of new products or processes. Managers who collect information and use analytical techniques make decisions that are more effective and profitable. However, political behavior on the part of managers is negatively related to decision effectiveness. The use of power or hidden agendas hinders sound decisions. The bottom line is that good information and analysis are more important than politics for effective decision making.[39]

Decision making is central in Mintzberg's classic analysis of the nature of managerial work.[40] He found that managers have four decisional roles, including **entrepreneur** (looking for new ideas and opportunities), **disturbance handler** (resolving conflicts and choosing strategic alternatives), **resource allocator** (deciding how to prioritize the direction of resources), and **negotiator** (protecting the interests of the business by interacting within teams, departments, and the organization). Decision making is a fundamental part of a leader's job, and followers expect leaders to make the right decisions.[41] As a manager, you will likely be promoted on the basis of your track record for making decisions that positively impact the organization (enhancing profitability, for example).

Why Some People Can't Make Decisions

Indecisiveness is when a person cannot prioritize activities in order of importance. The book *Why Quitters Win* reports that effective leaders weigh both sides of an issue, decide quickly, and then work to gain support from those on both sides for effective execution.[42] The author, Nick Tasler, believes that it is possible to improve decisiveness through training by encouraging decisive action. People need a clearly defined starting and ending point so that they feel empowered to move forward. Also, providing incentives for decision making may boost the speed of decisions made by leaders. Tasler cites the case of the CEO of Agilent Technologies who created a "speed to opportunity" metric in which leaders in the organization are regularly rated by their followers on decisiveness. This approach makes leaders aware that decisions are valued by the organization.

Why are some people more indecisive than others? Personality traits play a role. Less emotionally stable leaders who fear upsetting others allow debates to drag on for too long and make compromise decisions that are not optimal.[43] Feeling out of control and pessimism also lead to indecisiveness. Low self-esteem predicts indecisiveness, as well as attributing events to external causes and irrational beliefs.[44] Indecisiveness may also affect students faced with the decision of which job offer to take. **Career indecision** "refers to the difficulties preventing individuals from making a career decision."[45] Career indecision is related to personality characteristics of neuroticism and agreeableness but lower extroversion and openness to experience (the Big Five personality theory is discussed in Chapter 2). Also, students' tendencies toward perfectionism are related to career indecision.

Constraints on Individual Decision Making

Indecisiveness may also be due to the complex nature of situations leaders face in today's rapidly changing environment. Three situational factors may hinder decision making: lack of information, unclear or conflicting goals, and the uncertainty of outcomes.[46] There may be constraints on decisions due to time, rewards, and regulations. Also, stakeholders within and outside of the organization are invested in a leader's decisions. These stakeholders may have conflicting interests that must be balanced. Decision making is arguably at the core of leadership, but it is not always easy. Leaders must often make decisions under pressure and with incomplete information.

Employees as well as leaders may suffer from indecisiveness, which may be a source of frustration for a leader. Some employees are able to support their decisions with facts and evidence. However, others rely on historical precedents or personal experiences. In addition, employees are confronted by an overload of information that is nearly impossible to sort through and often under time constraints. The results are often poorly researched and supported decisions that waste company resources and possibly risk the effectiveness of the organization.

THE RATIONAL DECISION-MAKING MODEL

Learning Objective 5.4: Explain the rational decision-making model and bounded rationality.

One prevalent model of decision making presents a series of logical steps decision makers follow to determine the optimal choice.[47,48] For example, optimization involves maximizing value and/or minimizing cost. The six-step process for rational decision making is shown in Figure 5.3.[49] In this model,

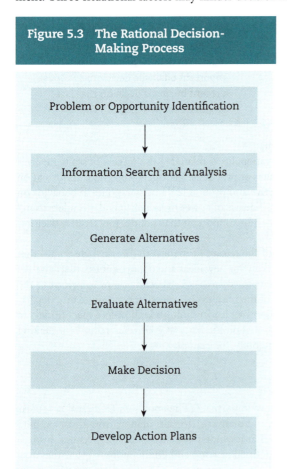

Figure 5.3   The Rational Decision-Making Process

Problem or Opportunity Identification

↓

Information Search and Analysis

↓

Generate Alternatives

↓

Evaluate Alternatives

↓

Make Decision

↓

Develop Action Plans

the problem (or opportunity) is defined, and then information is gathered and analyzed. Based on this information, a broad set of alternatives or possible courses of action are identified. Next, these alternatives are analyzed in terms of the feasibility, costs, and benefits. A decision is based upon the analysis of the alternative courses of action (i.e., the decision with the lowest costs and greatest benefit). The final step is to develop a specific set of action steps for the implementation of the decision. This model includes a number of assumptions. Decision makers must have complete information, be able to develop an exhaustive list of alternatives, weight them, and then choose a decision with the highest value and/or lowest cost to the organization. As you may have noticed, this rational model is often emphasized in business schools through the case study method to learn the decision-making process.

Limitations of the Rational Model

Managers sometimes fail to identify the problem correctly at the start of the decision-making process.[50] Also, some only consider a few alternatives rather than a broad set of possible options. They may only consider the most obvious alternatives and not brainstorm creative solutions (creative problem solving is discussed later in this chapter). Managers sometimes suboptimize rather than choose an optimal alternative resulting in lose-lose decisions.[51,52] Finally, decisions are sometimes made without complete information due to the lack of availability of information relevant to the problem or time pressure. For example, a recent study found that entrepreneurs were

> **Critical Thinking Question:** In your opinion, do leaders follow the rational decision-making model in practice? Give an example of when the process is followed and an example when it is not followed. Compare and contrast the outcomes of these decisions.

unable to accurately assess the quality of potential venture capital partners in an information-sparse environment.[53] Decision makers have limits on their ability to assimilate large amounts of information, and this is known as **bounded rationality**.

Bounded Rationality

Human beings have a limited capacity to process large amounts of information in the context of decision making to make optimal decisions. In many instances, people **satisfice**—in other words, they make a decision that is satisfactory but perhaps not optimal. Decision makers operate within bounded rationality rather than perfect rationality.[54] What this means is that decision makers simplify complex problems to limit the amount of information processing needed. Within the boundaries of this simplified model, they behave rationally.[55] In addition to limiting the information analyzed, they also limit the number of alternatives considered. They accept the first acceptable alternative they encounter rather than continue their information search, analysis, and alternative generation until they find an optimal one.

Decision making is susceptible to the perceptual errors discussed in the first part of this chapter: Primacy, recency, availability, contrast, and halo errors may all affect how information is presented to decision makers and processed.[56] In sum, bounded rationality in decision making is the result of organizational factors (e.g., political behavior around a decision), individual limits on the ability to process information (e.g., limiting the information search), and perceptions (e.g., perceptual errors related to the limited availability of information to make a decision).

Bounded rationality is also the result of two guesses the decision maker must address: (1) a guess about uncertain future consequences and (2) a guess about uncertain future preferences.[57] In other words, the decision maker at the time of the decision can't know the future, nor can they know what they would like to see happen in the future. So the decision-making process may be influenced by other organizational processes such as the situation, interpersonal gaming, and the need to justify prior decisions. This perspective highlights the importance of uncertainty and risk to the decision-making process. The next section explains **prospect theory**, which is one of the most important frameworks for decision making under risk and uncertainty.

PROSPECT THEORY

Learning Objective 5.5: Demonstrate understanding of prospect theory and the impact of framing on decisions with an example.

Daniel Kahneman won the Nobel Prize in Economics in 2002, in part for his work with Amos Tversky on the prospect theory of decision making. Their work focused on the risk perceptions in decisions people make. The authors conducted studies in which subjects were asked to make decisions when given two monetary options that involved prospective losses and gains. Consider the following options used in their studies:[58]

1. You have $1,000, and you must pick one of the following choices:
    Choice A: You have a 50% chance of gaining $1,000 and a 50% chance of gaining $0.
    Choice B: You have a 100% chance of gaining $500.

2. You have $2,000, and you must pick one of the following choices:
    Choice A: You have a 50% chance of losing $1,000 and a 50% chance of losing $0.
    Choice B: You have a 100% chance of losing $500.

Choosing B indicates that the person is more risk averse than someone choosing A. If you chose B for question 1 and A for question 2, you are like the majority of people who are presented with these decision scenarios. If people made decisions according to rational decision-making norms, they would pick either A or B in both situations (i.e., they should be indifferent because the expected value of both outcomes is the same). However, the results of this study showed that an overwhelming majority of people chose B for question 1 and A for question 2. Why? People are willing to settle for a reasonable gain (even if they have a reasonable chance of earning more) but are willing to engage in risk-seeking behaviors where they can limit their losses. In other words, losses weigh more heavily emotionally in decision making than an equivalent gain.

The Importance of How Decisions Are Framed

Prospect theory explains why decisions are sometimes irrational. People put more emphasis on gains rather than losses; they make decisions that increase their gains and avoid loss. According to the theory, people treat the two types of risk (gain versus loss) in a completely different way to maximize their perceived outcome. However, this may result in irrational decisions that are not based on a correct calculation of expected utility.

Framing refers to whether questions are presented as gains or losses. Leaders must pay attention to how decisions are framed when they are presented. As the examples of monetary choices under losses and gains illustrated, decisions may be affected by how options are presented (people are more risk averse when decisions are framed in terms of loss). Table 5.1 shows real-world examples to illustrate the role of framing in decision making and highlights the importance of considering both the probability of an outcome and the associated gain or loss from the decision. For example, in scenario A, as a manager you might take a risk on an idea that is outside of the box. There is a low probability that it would pan out, but the gains would be huge. In scenario B, a business owner sells off a business that is doing well to avoid potential losses from new entrants into the market. For scenario C, there is a high probability of gain, so a business in expansion mode sells delayed invoices to a financial institution for 70% to 80% of their value just to get cash needed to grow the business. In scenario D, there is a high probability of loss, so an entrepreneur in a failing business ignores advice to divest the business and increases efforts to succeed. So it is important for managers to recognize risk as a part of business decision making that is essential for innovation. Järrehult states the following:

Table 5.1 Risk Behavior Regarding Gains and Losses at High and Low Probability

	Gains	Losses
High Probability	**C.** Big chance to win a lot Fear of getting disappointed RISK AVERSE Accepting unfavorable settlement *Example: Court case*	**D.** Big risk to lose a lot Hoping to avoid loss RISK SEEKING Rejecting favorable settlement *Example: Casino evening*
Low Probability	**A.** Small chance to win a lot Hoping for a great gain RISK SEEKING Rejecting favorable settlement *Example: Lottery*	**B.** Small risk to lose a lot Fear of large loss RISK AVERSE Accepting unfavorable settlement *Example: Insurance*

Source: Järrehult, B. (n.d.). The importance of stupid, irrational decisions. Retrieved from www.innovationmanagement.se/2013/09/06/the-importance-of-stupid-irrational-decisions

Doing what is rational is usually good, but if we *only* would be rational, we would miss out on many of the "Black Swans." The trick is to strike the appropriate balance between the few expensive rational decisions we need to take and the inexpensive, but plentiful, irrational decisions that we take more on a gut feeling.[59]

Note: A "black swan" is a highly consequential but unlikely event that is easily explainable, but only in retrospect.[60]

It is important to consider how information regarding risk and uncertainty is presented. Decision makers expect uncertainty and can effectively use information on uncertainty to make better decisions. In one study, college students made daily decisions about whether or not to order roads to be salted to prevent ice on roads during several winter months. Decisions were based on actual archived forecasts of the nighttime low temperature. In one condition, participants used the nighttime low temperature alone (i.e., the conventional deterministic forecast). In the other condition, students were also provided with the probability of freezing. Participants were given a budget of $30,000. The salt treatment cost $1,000 per application, but if they didn't decide to salt the roads and the temperature dropped below freezing, they were penalized $6,000. Participants were informed of the outcome each day (the temperature). At the end of the experiment, participants were paid based upon their remaining budget (about $10), so they had an incentive to make good decisions. Results of these experiments indicated that people can make good use of probability information in making decisions if they are provided with it during the decision process and if it is presented in a way that they can use. The authors concluded: "Our view is that not only do people need explicit uncertainty information to make better, more individualized decisions, but also they can understand it as long as some care is taken in how it is presented."[61]

The book *Thinking Fast and Slow* examines two modes of thinking that psychology has labeled System 1 and System 2 Thinking.[62] System 1 Thinking represents automatic and effortless decision making that is often involuntary. System 2 Thinking is complex thinking that demands mental effort, including complex calculations.

> **Critical Thinking Questions:** How can you use knowledge of prospect theory to improve your chances of getting a good deal during a negotiation? What role do you think framing of options as gains or losses plays in negotiations?

System 2 Thinking is what is most often taught in business schools to prepare students to be effective decision makers. Yet System 1 Thinking represents intuition, which has received research attention as well as a great deal of interest in the popular press.

INTUITION

Learning Objective 5.6: Describe the role of intuition in decision making.

Blink: The Power of Thinking Without Thinking popularized the idea that intuition may play an important role in decision making.[63] Author Malcolm Gladwell noted that people learn by their experiences; they may not know why they know things, but they are certain they know them. He acknowledges the influences of the unconscious mind on decisions and put forth the premise that there can be value in a decision made in the "blink of an eye" rather than months of analysis. Gladwell introduced the idea of "thin-slicing" in which the unconscious mind finds patterns in situations and behaviors based upon very narrow experiences. However, he cautioned there may be errors made when thin-slicing is used to make decisions. Such quick decisions may be affected by perceptual errors discussed in this chapter or by stereotypes about people, and leaders need to be aware of these biases.

Intuition has been described as follows: "The essence of intuition or intuitive responses is that they are reached with little apparent effort, and typically without conscious awareness. They involve little or no conscious deliberation."[64] Four characteristics comprise intuition: "a (1) nonconscious process (2) involving holistic associations (3) that are produced rapidly which (4) result in affectively charged judgments."[65] Intuition may be a potential means of helping managers make both fast and accurate decisions. While research on such unconscious thought processes is new, available evidence supports the idea that intuitive processes should be considered part of a leader's decision making.

Intuition is not the same thing as common sense. Intuition is perception without conscious thinking and can seem like common sense. However, intuition varies greatly from basic gut feelings to complicated judgments like a physician's quick diagnosis. According to Simon, "intuition and judgment—at least good judgment—are simply analyses frozen into habit and into the capacity for rapid response through recognition."[66] In other words, intuition is the unconscious operation in the brain formed by freezing sensing and judgment. By contrast, common sense is not typically repetitive; it is a more simplified thought process. Another major difference is intuition is individual and common sense is often social (i.e., what the majority of people think as a consensus).[67]

Benefits of Intuition

Leaders often rely on their gut feelings or instincts in making important decisions, particularly related to innovation.[68] In-depth interviews with 60 professionals across a variety of industries and occupations revealed the role that intuition plays in decision making.[69] Professionals often rely on their intuition and report the following benefits:[70]

- **Expedited decision making**—quicker decisions that get the job done; adapting to a changing environment.

- **Improvement of the decision in some way**—provides a check and balance; allows for fairness; avoids having to rework the decision; causes one to pay more attention.

- **Facilitation of personal development**—gives one more power; develops instincts; helps to apply one's experiences; allows for positive risk taking.

- **Promotion of decisions compatible with company culture**—helps make decisions in accord with the organization's values.

Intuition in decision making has a bad reputation, but most managers acknowledge that it plays a role in their decisions. It may be risky to apply intuition to certain types of organizational problems, because they are complex and changing decision scenarios that leaders are facing with more frequency. Such problems have been termed **wicked organizational problems**.

> **Critical Thinking Questions:** What are the risks of relying on intuition to make decisions? What can a leader do to address these risks and gain the benefits from intuition?

Wicked Organizational Problems

It is important for managers to know when to "think" (i.e., rely on analysis), "blink" (i.e., rely on intuition), or "smink" (employ heuristics and algorithms). An example of a **heuristic** is the way credit scores are computed and used to determine interest rates. An important consideration is the complexity of the task. For example, if the task is simple, rely on analysis. Such problems have learning environments that are "kind" in that they can be structured so analysis or **heuristics** can be applied. Other problems are "wicked" because they are complex, dynamic, and constrained, so there are limits to whether analysis or heuristics can be applied. Also, stakeholders disagree on the preferred solution. Wicked organizational problems have the following characteristics:[71]

- There are no clear boundaries, many actors, and high connections to other problems.

- They require holistic strategies—piecemeal solutions do not work.

- They have nonlinear cause-effect relationships that are difficult to determine.

- They lack finality of resolution.

- Patterns continually emerge, so predictability is impossible.

- They lack ultimately "right" answers; situational factors mean every solution is temporary.

The complexity of wicked organizational problems increases the likelihood that leaders will fall into decision traps if they are not careful. The next sections review common decision errors leaders make when they are faced with wicked organizational problems. Leaders need to be aware of these traps and know how to avoid them.

> **Critical Thinking Question:** Give an example of a wicked organizational problem (one that is complex, dynamic, and constrained with most of the characteristics listed above).

DECISION TRAPS

Learning Objective 5.7: List and explain three major decision traps and how to avoid them: hindsight, hubris, and escalation of commitment.

Hindsight Bias

Hindsight bias, also commonly referred to as the **I-knew-it-all-along effect**,[72] is well established and has been shown to have far-reaching effects. Hindsight bias is defined as "the tendency for individuals with outcome knowledge (hindsight) to claim they would have estimated a probability of occurrence for the reported outcome that is higher than they would have estimated in foresight (without the outcome information)."[73] Four processes underlie this belief. First, the person recalls the old event and responds consistently with the memory of it. Second, the person focuses on the outcome and adjusts their belief, pretending that they didn't know the outcome. Third, the belief is reconstructed based upon what the judgment would have been prior to the outcome. Research shows people do this by first sampling evidence related to the judgment from their long-term memories and the external world. Once an outcome is known, people seek out and retain evidence that fits the outcome rather than evidence that contradicts it. The fourth process is based upon a person's motivation to present themselves favorably to others. People want to be seen as accurate, and they claim when something happens that they "knew it all along." A meta-analysis of 90 studies of hindsight bias showed moderate support for the effect.[74]

Hindsight bias is a process that may influence how outcomes of decisions are interpreted after the fact and lead to poor decision making since a leader may ignore important information in the present and then reconstruct the past as if they had the knowledge. Thus, a leader's ability to learn from past mistakes is compromised by hindsight bias. This may be compounded if the leader is also overconfident in their decision-making ability, and this is another decision trap.

Overconfidence

British Petroleum (BP) executives were confident that there were no serious risks with their Deepwater Horizon oil well in the Gulf of Mexico. They repeatedly assured government regulators that an accident was almost impossible. Several months later, one of their oil rigs exploded. Eleven people were killed and 17 were injured. The leak spread to over a mile, resulting in one of the worst disasters in recent history, with damage to the natural environment and the wildlife that relies on the Gulf for survival (over 8,000 animals were reported dead 6 months after the spill). Top decision makers had engaged in a long-standing practice of inattention to safety precautions. Investigations reveal that this accident could have been prevented with more attention to mitigation and preparation for oil spills of this nature.[75] How could decision makers fail to accurately assess the risks involved with operating these oil rigs? One reason for the Deepwater Horizon oil rig explosion has been attributed to **overconfidence bias** (sometimes referred to as *hubris*).[76] Overconfidence bias is an inflated confidence in how accurate a person's knowledge or estimates are.[77]

As we have seen with the rational decision-making model and bounded rationality, the ability to estimate probable outcomes is critical to a leader's ability to make sound decisions in organizations. For example, accurate forecasting is significantly related to a leader's ability to create an effective vision for their organization.[78] However, leaders with more power are more likely to exhibit the overconfidence bias.[79] Those higher in the organizational hierarchy feel more empowered and overestimate their ability to accurately forecast the future. Hiring experts to assist with making decisions may not be the answer either, because experts sometimes fail to make accurate predictions.[80] In one study, experts in information technology (IT) were as likely to make errors due to overconfidence as novices (people with little expertise in IT).[81]

How can leaders avoid the overconfidence bias? Leaders may keep the overconfidence bias in check by assigning a trusted follower to critique the decisions (i.e., play the devil's advocate role), by being open to different opinions, and by placing limits on their power by having someone else approve decisions (a peer, for example). Reminding oneself of past decision-making errors might be an effective way to keep the power effect on overconfidence in check.[82]

Overconfidence can result in poor decision making and can even result in serious disasters, as in the BP oil spill case. It is estimated that the oil spill cost BP over $100 billion, and Tony Hayward, the CEO, was moved to a role in the company with much less power. A recent analysis of four studies found that overconfidence significantly predicts another decision trap that is called the **escalation of commitment**.[83]

Escalation of Commitment

Escalation of commitment occurs when individuals continue a failing course of action after receiving feedback that shows it isn't working. In effect, they try to turn the situation around by investing more after a setback.[84] People continue to invest in failing courses of action to recoup their losses to show they had made the right decision all along. One experiment found that decision makers continued to invest in research and development (R&D) of a failing company when they had personal responsibility for the negative outcomes.[85] This occurs because of self-justification, or the need to demonstrate that one's actions are rational. In addition to self-justification, escalation may be caused by risk perceptions (prospect theory), group decision-making dysfunctions, and an organization's tendency to avoid change.[86] This is sometimes called the **sunk costs fallacy** because the continued commitment is because a person has already invested in this course of action and does not recognize what they invested initially is sunk (or gone). Lunenburg provides the following example:

> Denver's International Airport set out to add a state-of-the-art automated baggage handling system to its airport construction. The project was never completed, which caused a delay in the opening of the airport by nearly two years and $2 billion over budget.[87]

Figure 5.4 shows the reasons why leaders may engage in escalation of commitment. Instead of viewing the money already spent as sunk costs, decision makers focus on how much they have already spent.[88] Also, leaders want a sense of completion; they have the need to finish what they have started, and this may also contribute to escalation.[89] Leaders may also let their ego get in the way, and the feeling of pride in their own decision-making ability (or the need to avoid "losing face") may lead to increased investment in poor decisions. Finally, being unsure of oneself may increase the need to "prove" to others they were right.

There are other examples of poor decisions due to escalation. Venture capitalists sometimes continue to invest in start-up companies even after results indicate the ideas are not panning out in the marketplace.[90] Supervisors of clerical workers in a large public-sector organization provided positively biased performance evaluations for the workers they originally supported hiring or promoting.[91] Senior bank managers escalated commitment to loans they initiated by retaining them even after the loans were not being paid on time.[92] Finally, a study of Wall Street analysts found that radical stock picks were followed with more extreme earnings projections after a company's yearly earnings reports showed their initial forecasts were wrong.[93] These examples illustrate that escalation, or "throwing good money after bad," is a serious decision trap leaders may fall into because they want to avoid regret.[94] What can a leader do to avoid escalation?

The following four antidotes to escalation have been proposed:[95]

1. **Separate the initial decision maker from the decision evaluator**. In other words, remove the ego of the decision maker from the evaluation of it.

2. **Create accountability for decision processes only, not outcomes**. Ask employees to explain or justify their decision processes (i.e., how they made the decision in the first place).

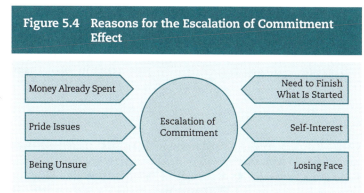

Figure 5.4   Reasons for the Escalation of Commitment Effect

Money Already Spent — Escalation of Commitment — Need to Finish What Is Started

Pride Issues — Escalation of Commitment — Self-Interest

Being Unsure — Escalation of Commitment — Losing Face

Source: Adapted from Staw, B. M. (1981). The escalation of commitment to a course of action. *Academy of Management Review, 6*(4), 577–587.

3. **Shift attention away from the self**. Make a balanced assessment by considering the impact of the decision on other people.

4. **Be careful about compliments**. Try not to inflate the decision maker's ego. Research has shown positive feedback increases the risk of becoming overconfident about one's decisions.

CREATIVE PROBLEM SOLVING

Learning Objective 5.8: Discuss the elements in Amabile's three-component model of creativity.

Albert Einstein wrote the following famous quote on creativity:

> Imagination is more important than knowledge. For knowledge is limited to all we now know and understand, while imagination embraces the entire world, and all there ever will be to know and understand.

Albert Szent-Gyorgyi, the Hungarian chemist who won the Nobel Prize for Medicine in 1937, defined **creativity** as follows: "Discovery consists of seeing what everybody has seen and thinking what nobody has thought." A contemporary definition of creativity is "the tendency to generate or recognize ideas, alternatives, or possibilities that may be useful in solving problems, communicating with others, and entertaining ourselves and others."[96] In the organizational context, applied creativity is a process "occurring in a real-world, industrial, organizational, or social context; pertaining to the finding or solving of complex problems; and having an actual behavioral creative product (or plan) as the final result."[97] There is a growing consensus that creativity can be defined as "production of a novel and appropriate response, product, or solution to an open-ended task."[98] Given the challenges of organizational change and the need to remain competitive, leaders desire more creative problem solving in all aspects of the work followers perform.[99] You have the opportunity to test your creative problem-solving skills and assess your creativity in Self-Assessment 5.2 at the end of this chapter.

Certain personality traits are related to creativity—particularly openness to experience.[100] Also, intelligence (general mental ability, known as "g") relates to creativity. In a meta-analysis, creativity was compared for both academic and work performance. Ratings of creativity were a faculty member's or work supervisor's evaluation of a person's creativity or potential for creative work. The implications of this study are that selecting students or workers on the basis of their intelligence may also result in scholars and employees who are creative and have high potential.[101]

Going With the "Flow"

Creative experiences are linked to emotional states called **flow**—when a person experiences a challenging opportunity aligned with their skills.[102] In other words, when both challenges and skills are high, a person may learn more during the experience. A study of 78 individuals' flow states during both work and leisure found most flow experiences are reported when working, not during people's leisure time.[103] Moreover, a recent study found that employees that were more motivated during flow reported more work engagement.[104] Csikszentmihalyi believes that creativity results from the interaction of a supportive culture for innovation.[105] For example, an employee brings a novel idea for product packaging to their work and a group of marketing experts validates the idea as a worthwhile innovation.

Despite some evidence that personality traits and intelligence relate to creativity, many experts believe most people can learn to be more creative with training.[106,107] There are a number of misconceptions about creativity in the book *The Myths of Creativity: The Truth About How Innovative Companies and People Generate Ideas*, which challenges commonly held "myths" about creative people and innovation processes.[108] This book addresses common misunderstandings about how innovative organizations actually encourage creativity. For example, rather than the lone genius working alone in a laboratory all night, creative ideas are more likely to come from teams that work on problems—especially teams that have a leader who provides a supportive climate for innovation to flourish.

Three-Component Model of Creativity

One of the most important models of creativity in organizations is the three-component model of creativity developed by Teresa Amabile from Harvard University.[109] As shown in Figure 5.5, creativity is a function of three intersecting components: expertise, creative thinking skills, and motivation. Expertise refers to knowledge (technical, processes, and academic). Creative thinking skills are how adaptable and imaginative individuals in the organization are. Finally, motivation refers to the intrinsic form of motivation—the urgent need to solve the problem faced and not the monetary rewards expected. Given that the person has the expertise related to the problem, their creative thinking skills can be enhanced through training. In addition, leaders can create the right processes and workplace climates to enhance creativity. For example, leaders can give followers challenging problems to work on and allow them the freedom to innovate (see the boxed insert for a summary of research on leading creativity). Support from the organization also matters—for creativity to thrive, people need resources, a positive work group climate, and encouragement.

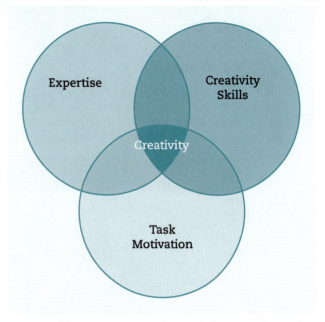

Figure 5.5 Three Component Model of Creativity

Expertise

Creativity Skills

Creativity

Task Motivation

Source: Amabile, T. M. (1998, September-October). How to kill creativity. *Harvard Business Review, 77–87.*

LEADERSHIP IMPLICATIONS: MAKING ETHICAL DECISIONS

As we have shown throughout this chapter, perceptions can be flawed and they can impact the quality of a leader's decisions. Decision shortcuts are convenient, but they result in perceptual errors that guide leaders in the wrong direction. Perceptual biases may lead to unethical decisions, and leaders need to be on guard against them.[110] This chapter reviews perceptual errors and decision theory and provides tools that have proven to improve the quality and effectiveness of decision making. Also, the traps that leaders may fall into have been

RESEARCH IN ACTION

Leading Creativity

Creativity expert Min Basadur states:

The most effective leaders of the 21st century will help individuals and teams to coordinate and integrate their differing styles to drive change through a process of applied creativity that includes continuously discovering and defining new problems, solving those problems, and implementing the new solutions.[111]

Figure 5.6 The Creative Leadership Model

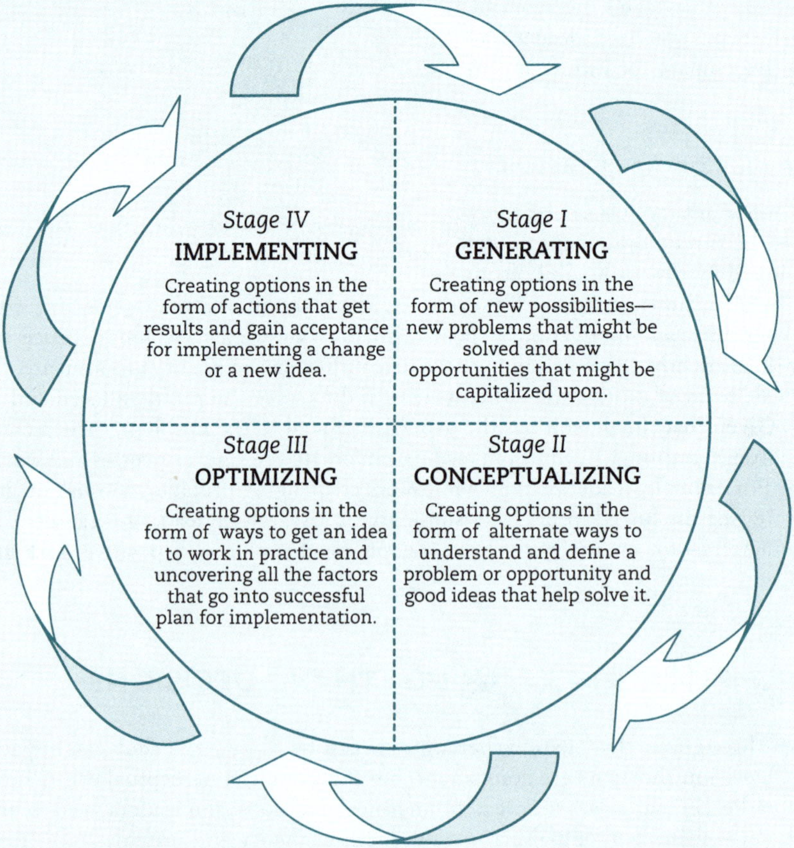

Stage IV
IMPLEMENTING
Creating options in the form of actions that get results and gain acceptance for implementing a change or a new idea.

Stage I
GENERATING
Creating options in the form of new possibilities—new problems that might be solved and new opportunities that might be capitalized upon.

Stage III
OPTIMIZING
Creating options in the form of ways to get an idea to work in practice and uncovering all the factors that go into successful plan for implementation.

Stage II
CONCEPTUALIZING
Creating options in the form of alternate ways to understand and define a problem or opportunity and good ideas that help solve it.

Source: Basadur, M. S. (1995). *The power of innovation: How to make innovation a way of life and put creative solutions to work.* Pitman Professional Publishing, available at www.basadur.com

He has conducted numerous field experiments over many years and demonstrated that training in creative problem-solving skills, attitudes, and behaviors improves creative performance.[112,113] Leaders can create the right conditions for creativity to occur in organizational settings.[114]

Basadur's model of leading people to think creatively in organizations involves three creative activities: problem finding (which has two separate phases), problem solving, and solution implementation. He pointed out the first step is to use creative problem-solving skills to articulate the problem correctly. Next, engage in problem solving, and creativity must also apply to the implementation of solutions.

The problem-finding phase is split into two phases: problem generating (creating new possibilities) and problem conceptualizing (defining the problem). Next, alternative solutions to the problem are generated in the optimizing phase. Basadur also suggests that creative problem-solving attitudes, skills, and behaviors must be applied during implementation to generate options for how the solution will be implemented and for how the needed support in the organization will be obtained. Basadur's four-phase model is shown in Figure 5.6. This is a comprehensive model of problem solving and how leaders can influence all four steps of the process by modeling the desired behaviors and providing necessary support and encouragement to followers.

Discussion Questions

1. What phase of the creative leadership model do you think is the most important and why?
2. Why do you think it is important to separate idea generation and conceptualizing from optimizing? Why is it necessary to create options in the implementation phase also?
3. Explain how the creative leadership process cycles from the implementing stage (Stage IV) back to the generating stage (Stage I) by providing an example.

identified, including hindsight, overconfidence, and escalation of commitment. Leaders need to carefully plan their decision process and follow the rational decision-making model presented in this chapter as closely as possible.

Guidelines for effective planning include referencing your moral compass. Three fundamental ethical philosophies guide ethical decisions in organizations.[115] First, **utilitarianism** is the consideration of decisions that do the most good for the most people. A person who believes that the "ends justify the means" is advocating the utilitarian approach. When using this approach, the decision maker tries to maximize the satisfaction of the most people. Second, **individual rights** protect individuals, such as the right to appeal a decision that affects them. These rights include such things as the right of free consent, the right to privacy, the right to freedom of conscience (i.e., not having to do something that violates their moral standards), the right of free speech, and the right to due process. For example, allowing employees to have a voice in decisions that affect them is a decision process that reflects individual rights. Third, **justice** emphasizes social justice. In following this approach, decision makers are guided by equity, fairness, and impartiality. For example, rewards should be distributed fairly by compensating individuals based on their efforts and not on arbitrary factors. In addition to these three philosophies, the **ethics of care** focuses on the need to maintain relationships with others, and connections to others guide decisions.[116] For example, in following the ethics of care, a decision maker considers the damage that might be done to a relationship if a decision is made that they feel is unfair. Most individuals follow one of these philosophies in making decisions; however, the utilitarian approach is the most common among business leaders.[117] Despite the best of intentions, however, leaders do succumb to external forces such as economic conditions, scarce resources, and competition, and make decisions that are unethical.[118] Recent research has shown that excessively focusing on the desired outcome (i.e., career advancement and monetary gain) results in selfish and unethical behavior.[119]

Some unethical decisions may be unintended. Leaders may have **bounded ethicality**: an unconscious psychological process that hinders the quality of decision making. In other words, ethicality is limited in ways that are not visible. Similar to bounded rationality discussed earlier in this chapter, bounded ethicality refers to systematic and predictable ethical errors due to the limited capacity to process information.[120] For example, a leader may not be able to articulate the ethical challenge in a decision to rate followers' performance lower because there is a limited salary pool. Research has shown that people may even lie to get more money while feeling honest about it.[121] Under conditions of bounded ethicality, people make unethical decisions that they are unaware of and then engage in self-justification to explain their behavior. Leaders may lack awareness of ethical violations (bounded awareness), and they need to develop systems that uncover violations in their organization.[122]

Guidelines for creating awareness and encouraging ethical decisions follow:[123]

1. Talk "ethics"—make it a part of your workplace culture.

2. Publish your guiding principles.

3. Select, train, and retain employees who behave ethically.

4. Make ethical behavior part of business and performance reviews.

5. Work on increasing moral sensitivity from as many different perspectives as possible.

6. Attach consequences to desired behavior and measure its occurrence.

7. Assure that structure and resources exist to monitor and enforce commitment to an ethical climate.

8. Invite external review by an ethics audit team.

9. Establish a set of criteria to evaluate your own actions and share those with others.

10. Encourage, model, and help others establish a method to discuss actions and increase alertness to the ethical issues in everyday decisions.

Following these guidelines should increase awareness of ethics in your organization and help avoid decision traps leading to compromised ethics. Another theme of this chapter is leading creativity. The ability to avoid decision traps and bounded ethicality often requires keeping one's mind open and being able to view problems from a variety of perspectives. Thus, the ability to think creatively may help avoid making decision errors and avoid unethical decisions due to bounded ethicality. A leader must be willing to hear the truth—no matter how difficult it may be. Ethical leadership has emerged as a research area of great interest in the past decade. The next chapter (Chapter 6) discusses leadership theories, and you will learn that several of them have a moral component.

 **edge.sagepub.com/scandura2e**

Want a better grade? Go to **edge.sagepub.com/scandura2e** for the tools you need to sharpen your study skills.

KEY TERMS

availability bias, 98
belief updating, 97
bounded ethicality, 116
bounded rationality, 105
career indecision, 104
coding, 98
contrast effect, 100
creativity, 112
disturbance handler, 103
elaborative interrogation, 100
employability, 102
entrepreneur, 103
escalation of commitment, 110
ethics of care, 115

flow, 112
framing, 106
halo error, 101
heuristic, 109
hindsight bias, or I-knew-it-all-
    along effect, 109
horns error, 101
imaging, 98
individual rights, 115
justice, 115
negotiator, 103
overconfidence bias, 110
perception, 96
perceptual errors, 97

primacy effect, 97
prospect theory, 105
recency effect, 98
rehearsal, 98
resource allocator, 103
satisfice, 105
solution implementation, 115
stereotypes, 97
sunk costs fallacy, 111
utilitarianism, 115
wicked organizational
    problems, 109

TOOLKIT ACTIVITY 5.1: The Oil Drilling Partnership

Part 1

Your company has acquired a good-sized lease position within a well-known North American basin. The position was acquired at a cost of $235,000. The company has recently drilled a 50 bopd (barrels of oil per day) discovery well on the lease. The acreage position is such that a minimum of five more wells can be drilled. The drilling partnership provides a $1 million budget for the five subsequent wells. The budgeted cost per well is $400,000 ($200,000 drilling cost; $200,000 completion cost). You have been given the final authority to authorize all expenditures on this project. The discovery well has proven out both your original exploration approach and associated geophysical data. However, the confirmation well was a $200,000 dry hole. Your total cost for this nonproducing well is, thus, $200,000 (because you do not incur the completion costs).

1. On a scale from 0 to 100, how likely is it that if faced with this situation, you would authorize another $200,000 to drill the next well in the program? Circle the chances of your making the decision to authorize drilling the next well.

0	50	100
Definitely would not authorize	Even chance	Definitely would authorize

2. Regardless of how you answered the previous question, what is your perception of the likelihood that the next well to be drilled on this prospect would produce 50 or more bopd? (This is about the smallest yield that would produce a reasonable return on investment.)

0	50	100
Definitely would not produce 50 or more bopd	Even chance	Definitely would produce 50 or more bopd

Part 2

Assume that you decided to drill the second well and it turned out to be another $200,000 dry hole. Your total expenditure for the two dry holes has been $400,000.

1. On a scale from 0 to 100, how likely would you be to authorize another $200,000 to drill the next of the remaining wells in the program? Circle the chances of your making the decision to authorize drilling the next well.

0	50	100
Definitely would not authorize	Even chance	Definitely would authorize

2. Regardless of how you answered the previous question, what is your perception of the likelihood that the next well to be drilled on this prospect would produce 50 or more bopd? (This is about the smallest yield that would produce a reasonable return on investment.)

0	50	100
Definitely would not produce 50 or more bopd	Even chance	Definitely would produce 50 or more bopd

Discussion Questions

1. Did you consider the total amount of your expenditures when you made your decision on the next well to be drilled? Why or why not?

2. Assume that you decided to drill the third and fourth holes and they also turned out to be dry. Your total expenditures are now $800,000. Will you authorize the fifth hole (on the same scale of 1 to 100 as above)? What are the chances that the fifth hole will produce 50 or more bopd (on the same scale of 1 to 100 as above)?

3. How does the concept of escalation of commitment explain your decision process? Circle all that apply.

Money already spent	Need to finish what is started
Pride issues	Self-interest
Being unsure	Losing face

4. How enthusiastic were you about the prospects of producing an acceptable return on investment? Did you continue to drill even though you thought the chances of the third and fourth holes would not produce a good investment (i.e., 50 or more bopd)? Or, if you stopped authorizing the investment, when and why did you stop? What factors did you consider in your decision?

Source: Adapted from Garland, H., Sandefur, C. A., & Rogers, A. C. (1990). De-escalation of commitment in oil exploration: When sunk costs and negative feedback coincide. *Journal of Applied Psychology, 75*(6), 721–727.

CASE STUDY 5.1: Do You Have to Spend Money to Make Money?

That is the question SABMiller, the world's second-largest brewing company that controls about 90% of the South African market, is asking itself. Looking for ways to gain greater sales and increase market share, SABMiller is trying to generate more sales by attracting women in South Africa to drink its beers. The company makes Brutal Fruit Mango-Goji Fusion Beer and Flying Fish Premium Flavored Beer, which are sweeter and generally preferred by female customers.

The problem is that most women in South Africa don't frequent bars and pubs—and with good reason. For many years, the country's major religions, Christianity and Islam, kept most South African women out of bars, as drinking did not fit in with their religious principles. These days, religion has little impact on a woman's decision to visit bars, but the attractiveness, cleanliness, and safety of the establishments certainly do. Leftover from the days of apartheid, illegal shebeens (informal bars often with just a few plastic chairs set up in the proprietor's front room) have transitioned to licensed bars but have yet to lose their unclean appearance. Most former shebeens would be considered dives in the United States, with no toilets and ramshackle conditions. Thus, going out to a bar to drink doesn't appeal to "respectable" women.

SABMiller sees women as a way to generate more money in a market with increasing competition from Heineken and Diageo. There are 17 million women of legal drinking age in South Africa. But how can the company get them to frequent bars, SABMiller's preferred sales avenue, and spend money? SABMiller's managing director in Johannesburg, Mauricio Leyva, thinks the answer can be found by working with the 6,000 bar and tavern keepers to make their establishments more attractive to women. Leyva wants to finance $5 million in bar renovations that include adding or updating bathrooms, painting, and redesigning the establishments' seating arrangements. The company is also considering buying bar supplies, such as beer glasses, because focus groups have revealed that many women don't like drinking from bottles.

You're the director of African and Asian sales and Leyva's boss. It's your decision to approve or deny Leyva's idea of helping establishments upgrade their look to appeal to women customers.

Discussion Questions

1. What are the key issues regarding the decision? What information are you going to want to find out before you decide on this investment?

2. Recall from the chapter the four key decision-making approaches (rational decision-making model, intuition, wicked organizational problems, and creative problem solving). Try to come to a decision for the organization using the tenets of each of these styles.

3. What differences in the results do you see?

4. What personal biases might have influenced you?

5. What elements of the situation might have made the decision easier or harder to make?

6. How do you think making a decision with others would have influenced the decisions and decision-making process? How might have others' perspectives, pressure, and persuasion influenced you?

Source: Developed from Kew, J., & Fletcher, C. (2014, May 29). SABMiller cleans up South Africa's bars to attract women. Retrieved from http://www.businessweek.com/articles/2014-05-29/sabmiller-cleans-up-south-africas-bars-to-attract-women

SELF-ASSESSMENT 5.1: Employability—Perceptions of Prospective Employers

This self-assessment exercise suggests your level of employability as measured by OB researchers. There are no right or wrong answers, and this is not a test. You don't have to share your results with others unless you wish to do so.

Part I. Taking the Assessment

You will be presented with some questions representing different approaches to work. If you are not currently employed, answer the questions as you would if you were employed. There is no "one best" approach. All approaches have strengths and weaknesses, and the goal is for you to be adaptable to different change situations.

Statements	Strongly Disagree	Disagree	Somewhat Disagree	Neutral	Somewhat Agree	Agree	Strongly Agree
1. I am optimistic about my future career opportunities.	1	2	3	4	5	6	7
2. I feel changes at work generally have positive implications.	1	2	3	4	5	6	7
3. I stay abreast of developments in my company.	1	2	3	4	5	6	7
4. I have participated in training or schooling that will help me reach my career goals.	1	2	3	4	5	6	7
5. I define myself by the work that I do.	1	2	3	4	5	6	7
6. I feel that I am a valuable employee at work.	1	2	3	4	5	6	7
7. I feel that I am generally accepting of changes at work.	1	2	3	4	5	6	7
8. I stay abreast of developments in my industry.	1	2	3	4	5	6	7
9. I have a specific plan for achieving my career goals.	1	2	3	4	5	6	7
10. I am involved in my work.	1	2	3	4	5	6	7
11. I have control over my career opportunities.	1	2	3	4	5	6	7
12. I would consider myself open to changes at work.	1	2	3	4	5	6	7
13. I stay abreast of developments relating to my type of job.	1	2	3	4	5	6	7
14. I have sought job assignments that will help me obtain my career goals.	1	2	3	4	5	6	7
15. It is important to me that others think highly of my job.	1	2	3	4	5	6	7
16. My past career experiences have been generally positive.	1	2	3	4	5	6	7
17. I can handle job and organizational changes effectively.	1	2	3	4	5	6	7
18. It is important to me that I am successful in my job.	1	2	3	4	5	6	7
19. I take a positive attitude toward my work.	1	2	3	4	5	6	7

Statements	Strongly Disagree	Disagree	Somewhat Disagree	Neutral	Somewhat Agree	Agree	Strongly Agree
20. I am able to adapt to changing circumstances at work.	1	2	3	4	5	6	7
21. The type of work I do is important to me.	1	2	3	4	5	6	7
22. In uncertain times at work, I usually expect the best.	1	2	3	4	5	6	7
23. It is important to me that I am acknowledged for my successes in the job.	1	2	3	4	5	6	7
24. I always look on the bright side of things at work.	1	2	3	4	5	6	7
25. I am a believer that "every cloud has a silver lining" at work.	1	2	3	4	5	6	7

Part II. Scoring Instructions

In Part I, you rated your approaches to work on 25 questions. Add the numbers you circled in each of the columns to derive your score for the five different aspects of employability. During our session, we will discuss each approach—its strengths and weaknesses—and how you can develop employer perceptions of your employability based on this research.

Employability Approaches

Work and Career Resilience	Openness to Changes at Work	Work and Career Proactivity	Career Motivation	Work Identity
1. _____	2. _____	3. _____	4. _____	5. _____
6. _____	7. _____	8. _____	9. _____	10. _____
11. _____	12. _____	13. _____	14. _____	15. _____
16. _____	17. _____			18. _____
19. _____	20. _____			21. _____
22. _____				23. _____
24. _____				
25. _____				
Total _____	_____	_____	_____	_____

Work and career resilience—Individuals with work and career resilience possess some combination of the following attributes: optimistic about their career opportunities and work, feel that they have control over the destiny of their careers, and/or feel that they are able to make genuinely valuable contributions at work. Scores can range from 8 to 56. In general, a lower score is from 8 to 24; a higher score is above 25.

Openness to changes at work—Individuals who are open to changes at work are receptive and willing to change and/or feel that the changes are generally positive once they occur. Scores can range from 5 to 35. In general, a lower score is from 5 to 14; a higher score is above 15.

Work and career proactivity—A proactive career orientation reflects people's tendencies and actions to gain information potentially affecting their jobs and career opportunities, both within and outside their current employer. Scores can range from 3 to 21. In general, a lower score is from 3 to 11; a higher score is above 12.

Career motivation—Individuals with career motivation tend to make specific career plans and strategies. People in this category are inclined to take control of their own career management and set work or career-related goals. Scores can range from 3 to 21. In general, a lower score is from 3 to 11; a higher score is above 12.

Work identity—Work identity reflects the degree to which individuals define themselves in terms of a particular organization, job, profession, or industry. Work identity is characterized by a genuine interest in what one does, how well it is done, and the impression of others. Scores can range from 6 to 42. In general, a lower score is from 6 to 18; a higher score is above 19.

To determine your overall level of employability, add together your scores for the five dimensions above. This total employability score can range from 25 to 175. In general, a lower score is from 25 to 75; a higher score is above 76.

Discussion Questions

1. What was your overall level of employability? Which of the five dimensions did you score highest on? Lowest?

2. How can you increase your employability based on these results? What specific strategies will you work on (for example, being more proactive)?

3. Ask someone who is currently working to complete this assessment about you and compare your perceptions of your employability to theirs. Do you see any differences? How can you explain them?

Source: Adapted from Fugate, M., & Kinicki, A. J. (2008). A dispositional approach to employability: Development of a measure and test of implications for employee reactions to organizational change. *Journal of Occupational and Organizational Psychology, 81*(3), 503–527.

SELF-ASSESSMENT 5.2: How Would You Rate Your Creativity?

Creative people have a lot in common. This self-assessment tool identifies the characteristics of creative people. Check it out for yourself to see how you rate. Just by completing it you will get some ideas for improving your creativity.

Please indicate your level of agreement or disagreement with each of the following statements using a scale from 1 to 5, where 1 means strongly disagree and 5 means strongly agree, by writing the number in the corresponding box. There are no right or wrong answers. Just choose the one that best represents your view of yourself. You don't have to share your results with others unless you wish to do so.

Statements	Strongly Disagree	Disagree	Neutral	Agree	Strongly Agree
1. I go beyond the obvious to the new, different, and unusual.	1	2	3	4	5
2. I generate many ideas and come up with several possible solutions to a problem.	1	2	3	4	5
3. I can expand and work out details for an idea or a solution.	1	2	3	4	5
4. I can hold conflicting ideas and values without undue tension.	1	2	3	4	5
5. I can go beyond commonly accepted ideas to the unusual.	1	2	3	4	5
6. I can see the "whole picture"; I hold a wide range of interests.	1	2	3	4	5
7. I am aware of my own inner feelings and the feelings and thoughts of others.	1	2	3	4	5
8. I have the capacity for play, the desire to know, and openness to new ideas and experiences.	1	2	3	4	5
9. I can think for myself and make decisions; I am self-reliant.	1	2	3	4	5
10. I can put ideas into action and help shape that with which I am involved.	1	2	3	4	5
11. I can work consistently with deep concentration; I get lost in a problem.	1	2	3	4	5
12. I proceed with determination when I take on a task or project and do not give up easily.	1	2	3	4	5
13. I am able to work intensively on a project for many hours.	1	2	3	4	5
14. I am not afraid to try something new; I like adventure.	1	2	3	4	5
15. I have a keen sense of humor. I often see humor in situations that may not be seen as humorous to others.	1	2	3	4	5
16. I believe in my ability to be creative in a given situation.	1	2	3	4	5
17. Insightful and intuitive, I am able to see relationships and make mental leaps.	1	2	3	4	5
18. I am open to the ideas of others.	1	2	3	4	5
19. I can produce new products or formulas; I bring about change in procedures and organizations.	1	2	3	4	5
20. I am highly confident in my abilities.	1	2	3	4	5
21. I enjoy challenging tasks; I have a dislike for doing things in a prescribed way.	1	2	3	4	5
22. I do not depend on others to maintain my interest level; I am a self-starter.	1	2	3	4	5
23. I am artistic.	1	2	3	4	5
24. I am sensitive to beauty; I attend to aesthetic characteristics of things.	1	2	3	4	5
25. I am involved in the arts, theater, music, dance, and/or design.	1	2	3	4	5

Significance of This Assessment

We are all creative but in varying degrees depending upon many factors and experiences in our lives. Perhaps the most important aspect of who has creative capabilities is dependent on the encouragement or discouragement of the use of these capabilities by others and the motivation and efforts exerted by the individuals themselves. Dozens of research studies, combined with informed opinions, point to one conclusion about creative people: Creative people may be nonconformist, but they certainly have a lot in common.

The purpose of this assessment is to evaluate creative predispositions in adults. The statements of characteristics are based on research found to be common and recurrent among creatively productive people. The statements are inclusive of behaviors, traits, interests, values, motivation, and attributes of creative people.

Completion of this assessment will help you determine which of the characteristics you already possess and which you may want to develop further if you would like to be a more creative person. Research has shown that creativity can be learned, developed, and nurtured.

Use this assessment to determine actions to improve your lowest scores. Examine the underlying reasons for the results. Discuss your results with someone who knows you well and who can act as a coach or buddy in helping you further develop these areas.

Your Results

First, add your scores for each column, then add the columns together for your total score. If your raw score is over 90: Congratulations! By your own assessment, you possess the characteristics of highly creative people. It is important that you continue to look for opportunities to tap into your creativity and create an environment for yourself where your creativity can continue to flourish. The bad news is that creative people can have habits or dispositions that can upset others. Researchers have narrowed these down into seven categories: egotistical, impulsive, argumentative, childish, absentminded, neurotic, and hyperactive. In business or a professional setting, the highly creative person will need to maintain patience and understanding of others if they want to be successful.

If your raw score is between 75 and 90: By your assessment, you are a fairly creative person. It is important, at this point, that you continue to nurture these creative characteristics and further develop the ones where you had a lower score. Take a look at the end of this section to see a further breakdown of the test and identify the characteristics you want to develop further.

If your raw score is between 50 and 75: It is important to celebrate the fact that you possess some of the characteristics of a creative person; however, additional development of the characteristics—where you are not so strong—would go a long way. Take a look at the end of this section to see a further breakdown of the test and identify the characteristics you want to develop further. There are many books and courses to help develop your creativity.

If your score is below 50: Don't fret. Perhaps you have not been in an environment that nurtured your creativity or you were told as a child that you were not creative and have held that belief ever since. The truth is that creative attitudes and personality traits can be strengthened. Take a look at the end of this section to see a further breakdown of the test and identify the characteristics you want to develop further. There are many books and courses to help develop your creativity.

Further Interpretation of the Test

Recurrent Characteristics of Creative People Found in the Literature	
Question(s) From the Test:	**Creative Characteristic**
16	Awareness of creativeness
5	Original
9, 20, 22	Independent

Question(s) From the Test:	Creative Characteristic
14	Risk taker/adventurous
10, 12, 19	Highly energetic
13	Thorough: must finish
6, 8	Curiosity
15	Sense of humor
4, 21	Attracted to complexity, ambiguity
23, 24	Artistic, aesthetic interests
18	Open minded
17	Perceptive: intuitive
7	Emotional: sensitivity, empathy
25	Capacity for fantasy
11, 13	Need for some privacy; alone time
2	Cognitive abilities important to creative thinking
Question From Test:	**Creative Ability**
1	Flexibility
2	Fluency
3	Elaboration
5	Originality
11	Concentration

Source: Davis, G. A. (1998). *Creativity is forever.* Dubuque, IA: Kendall/Hunt.

Discussion Questions

1. Were you surprised by your results? Do you consider yourself to be a creative person?

2. Which of the aspects of creativity did you score highest on? What specific characteristics and cognitive abilities do you exhibit?

3. How can you use the results of this self-assessment to develop your creative abilities?

INFLUENCING AND MOTIVATING EMPLOYEES

CHAPTER 6 · Leadership

CHAPTER 7 · Power and Politics

CHAPTER 8 · Motivation: Core Concepts

CHAPTER 9 · Motivation: Applications

Introduction

Chapter 1: What Is Organizational Behavior?

↓

Understanding Individuals in Organizations

Chapter 2: Personality and Person–Environment Fit

Chapter 3: Emotions and Moods

Chapter 4: Attitudes and Job Satisfaction

Chapter 5: Perception, Decision Making, and Problem Solving

Influencing and Motivating Employees

Chapter 6: Leadership

Chapter 7: Power and Politics

Chapter 8: Motivation: Core Concepts

Chapter 9: Motivation: Applications

Building Relationships

Chapter 10: Group Processes and Teams

Chapter 11: Managing Conflict and Negotiation

Chapter 12: Organizational Communication

Chapter 13: Diversity and Cross-Cultural Adjustments

Leaders as Change Agents

Chapter 14: Organizational Culture

Chapter 15: Leading Change and Stress Management

CHAPTER SIX

LEADERSHIP

Learning Objectives

After studying this chapter, you should be able to do the following:

6.1: Define *leadership*, and explain the difference between being a manager and being a leader.

6.2: Describe how the trait approach differs from other theories of leadership.

6.3: Explain the difference between initiating structure and consideration.

6.4: Demonstrate the role of leaders in the motivation process using path–goal theory (PGT).

6.5: Illustrate the leader–member exchange (LMX) model with an example.

6.6: Explain why trust is important and how to repair it.

6.7: Compare and contrast the elements of transactional and transformational leadership.

6.8: Illustrate the role of morality in ethical, servant, and authentic leadership.

Get the edge on your studies at **edge.sagepub.com/scandura2e**

- Take the chapter quiz
- Review key terms with eFlashcards
- Explore multimedia resources, SAGE readings, and more!

HAVE LEADERS LOST THEIR FOLLOWERS' TRUST?

Each year, Richard Edelman conducts a global survey on which people and institutions we trust and how much we trust them.[1] Edelman is the president and CEO of the world's largest public relations company. In 2016, they surveyed over 33,000 respondents in 28 countries around the world and measured their trust in institutions, industries, and leaders. This year, the Global Results Report highlights why trust matters. As shown in Figure 6.1, when people distrust companies, they share negative opinions about the company (26%), criticize the company online (42%), and even refuse to buy products and service (48%). In contrast, when a company is trusted, people share positive experiences online (41%), recommend the company to a friend or colleague (59%), and chose to buy the trusted company's products and services (68%). Interestingly, the most trusted content creators online were friends and family. And the most trusted media source was online search engines like Google. There appears to be a "trust gap" because many organizations are no longer trusted to do the right thing. Within organizations, followers have lost trust in their leaders. Given these findings, it is no surprise that trust has emerged as a major concern for research in organizational behavior (OB). The key role of trust and how to repair it when it is broken is covered later in this chapter.

As mentioned in Chapter 1, the objective of this textbook is to develop leadership skills. In this chapter, we review the essential theories of leadership—both classic and contemporary—that you will use to guide your thinking about influencing and motivating followers. The next chapter discusses power and influence tactics to round out your leadership skill set. It is important that you grasp these core leadership concepts since they are essential for motivating your team, which is covered in Chapter 10. This chapter will not cover all theories of leadership, but it focuses on the ones that have the strongest research base and/or best applicability to OB today. For a more comprehensive treatment of leadership theories, you can read a textbook by Peter Northouse.[2]

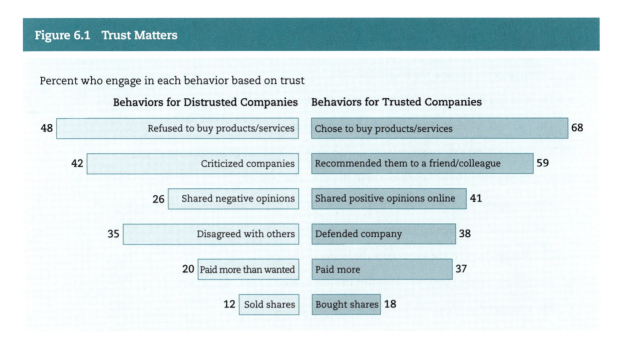

Figure 6.1 Trust Matters

Percent who engage in each behavior based on trust

Behaviors for Distrusted Companies		Behaviors for Trusted Companies	
48	Refused to buy products/services	Chose to buy products/services	68
42	Criticized companies	Recommended them to a friend/colleague	59
26	Shared negative opinions	Shared positive opinions online	41
35	Disagreed with others	Defended company	38
20	Paid more than wanted	Paid more	37
12	Sold shares	Bought shares	18

Source: Edelman, R. (2016). 2016 Edelman Trust Barometer Global Results. http://www.edelman.com/insights/intellectual-property/2016-edelman-trust-barometer/global-results/

WHAT IS LEADERSHIP?

Learning Objective 6.1: Define *leadership*, and explain the difference between being a manager and being a leader.

Yukl[3] has reviewed various definitions of leadership over the past 50 years and offers the following synthesis:

> Leadership is the process of influencing others to understand and agree about what needs to be done and how to do it, and the process of facilitating individual and collective efforts to accomplish shared objectives.

This definition captures the essence of leadership as an influence process (power and influence tactics are covered in the next chapter). It also has the idea that leadership involves directing individuals and groups toward organizational goals. Yukl notes that there has been confusion in the literature about the difference between leadership and other terms like *management*—so a distinction regarding whether or not management is the same as leadership is needed.

Differentiating Management and Leadership

In his classic book *On Becoming a Leader*, Warren Bennis composed a list of the differences between being a manager and being a leader:[4]

- The manager administers; the leader innovates.

- The manager is a copy; the leader is an original.

- The manager maintains; the leader develops.

- The manager focuses on systems and structure; the leader focuses on people.

- The manager relies on control; the leader inspires trust.

- The manager has a short-range view; the leader has a long-range perspective.

- The manager asks how and when; the leader asks what and why.

- The manager has his or her eye always on the bottom line; the leader's eye is on the horizon.

- The manager imitates; the leader originates.

- The manager accepts the status quo; the leader challenges it.

- The manager is the classic good soldier; the leader is his or her own person.

- The manager does things right; the leader does the right thing.

Zalesnick also posed the question, "Leaders and managers: Are they different?"[5] He made an important point that both managers and leaders are needed for an organization to function optimally. The manager is a day-to-day problem

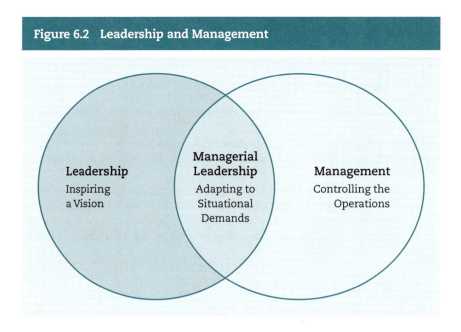

Figure 6.2   Leadership and Management

Leadership
Inspiring
a Vision

**Managerial
Leadership**
Adapting to
Situational
Demands

Management
Controlling the
Operations

solver, and the leader is focused on developing new approaches and options for the future. To some extent, leaders must engage in some problem-solving activities, and in reality, the two overlap (see Figure 6.2). As shown in the figure, leadership is about inspiring others to follow their vision for the organization. Managers, on the other hand, are concerned with controlling the operations of the organization so things run efficiently. Both are needed, and some managers have the adaptability to do both and switch between the roles of leader and manager as the situation demands. These are managerial leaders as shown in the figure where the two roles overlap.

TRAIT APPROACHES

Learning Objective 6.2: Describe how the trait approach differs from other theories of leadership.

Leadership has been of interest to human beings dating back to the days of the Ancient Greeks. Modern theory and empirical research, however, began in the early 1900s with the "great man" theory, also known as the trait approach. Figure 6.3 shows a timeline with the general dates for the periods of the development of modern leadership theory. The dates are approximate, and research on these approaches continues to the present. For example, interest in researching leader traits was abandoned but has now seen recent interest by OB researchers. In the **trait approach**, it is believed

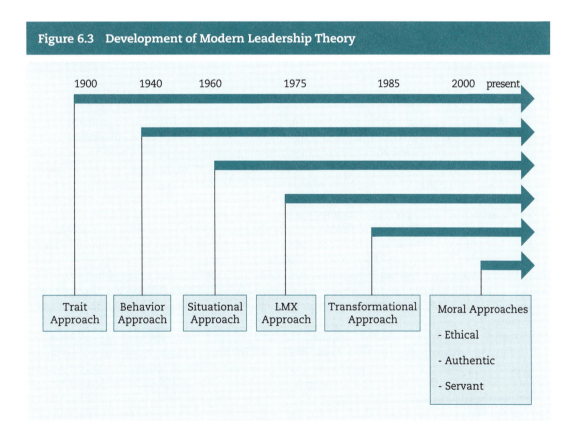

Figure 6.3   Development of Modern Leadership Theory

that leaders are born with the talent and abilities for leadership. This is in contrast with most other leadership theories, which propose that leadership can be learned. The focus on traits suggests that the best way to ensure effective leadership is to select the right people for leadership positions rather than to train them. Leaders are believed to be different than followers because they hold special attributes that make them great leaders. Early research identified traits such as drive, vigor, and originality in people that held leadership positions.[6] The trait-based perspective of leadership has a long history, and dozens of traits have been studied. Trait approaches were largely dismissed by OB researchers because they didn't show reliable differences between leaders and followers. Interest in traits lessened when the behavioral approaches began (described in the next section). But interest in traits resurfaced when a review from the early 1990s urged scholars to reconsider traits and suggested that the following traits do matter for leadership: drive (achievement, ambition, energy, tenacity, initiative), leadership motivation, honesty, integrity, self-confidence (including emotional stability), cognitive ability (IQ), and knowledge of the business.[7] Recently, OB researchers found that the personality trait of extraversion helps us to understand leadership emergence and effectiveness.[8] A review of decades of research on traits suggests that it may be the combination of traits rather than a single one that best explains how traits may influence leadership.[9]

When the trait approach did not fully explain leadership in the 1940s and 1950s, researchers turned their focus on what leaders do. The behavioral approaches followed and are covered in the next section. These approaches represent those that are focused on understanding the behavior of leaders rather than their inborn traits and talents. In contrast to trait theories, the leader behavior approach assumes that leaders are made and not born. In other words, anyone can learn the behaviors needed to be an effective leader.

LEADER BEHAVIORS

Learning Objective 6.3: Explain the difference between initiating structure and consideration.

The best-known research program on leader behaviors was conducted at Ohio State University in the late 1950s.[10] Researchers asked followers to describe what their leaders did and created a list of over a thousand leader behaviors but were able to combine them into two broad categories using statistical analyses. These two categories were labeled *Initiating Structure* and *Consideration*.[11] **Initiating structure** refers to defining tasks for employees and focusing on goals. **Consideration** is the degree to which the leader shows trust, respect, and sensitivity to employees' feelings. These two leader behaviors have been studied for decades, and a meta-analytic review of over 150 studies found that both consideration and initiating structure have moderately strong relationships with outcomes. Consideration was more strongly related to follower satisfaction (with the leader and job), motivation, and leader effectiveness. Initiating structure was slightly more strongly related to leader job and group performance.[12] A recent review expanded the behaviors of leaders to include three task-oriented behaviors (enhancing understanding, strengthening motivation, and facilitating implementation) and three relation-oriented behaviors (fostering coordination, promoting cooperation, and activating resources). Task-oriented behaviors are directed toward the accomplishment of shared objectives; however, relation-oriented behaviors support the coordinated engagement of team members.[13]

Which leader behavior is more effective? It appears that what matters is behavioral flexibility and knowing when to engage in the right behavior at the right time. The ability to switch leadership behaviors when needed is highlighted in the contingency approaches to leadership. Behavioral approaches were critiqued because they did not consider the influence of the followers or the situation on the emergence of leadership. The next phase in the development of leadership theory was the contingency or situational approach. For example, the situational leadership theory considers the "readiness" of followers in terms of their ability, motivation, and confidence to perform a task.[14] The leader changes their behavior based upon how able and willing a follower is to perform a specific task. One of the best researched situational theories of leadership is the path–goal theory (PGT), which is discussed next.

PATH–GOAL THEORY

Learning Objective 6.4: Demonstrate the role of leaders in the motivation process using **path–goal theory (PGT)**.

Leaders motivate followers to accomplish goals by establishing the *paths* to the *goals*.[15] Specifically, leaders increase the quality and number of payoffs from reaching goals and then make the path to the goals clear by removing obstacles.[16] PGT specifies four different motivating leadership behaviors:

1. **Directive leadership**—giving followers specific instructions about their tasks, providing deadlines, setting standards for performance, and explaining rules

2. **Supportive leadership**—showing consideration, being friendly and approachable, and paying attention to the well-being of followers

3. **Participative leadership**—allowing followers to have a voice in decisions that affect them, sharing information, inviting followers' ideas and opinions

4. **Achievement-oriented leadership**—challenging followers to perform at high levels, setting standards for excellence, showing confidence in followers' ability to reach goals

Adapting to the Situation

The leader should be flexible and adapt their leadership behavior to followers and the situation. PGT incorporates a number of considerations, but it is useful because this model reflects key aspects of followers and the situation that leaders need to consider to increase motivation. The expectancy theory of motivation is employed to explain the motivation process. As shown in the PGT model in Figure 6.4, motivation is represented as the follower path perceptions that have three elements. First, the E->P Expectancy is the follower's effort path to performance (in other words, if a person tries, they will achieve their goal). The performance-to-outcome expectation (P->O) is the belief that the leader will provide a reward that is wanted, and these rewards are of value to the follower, or valences (Vs). Thus, the leader's behavior affects follower motivations to assure the leader will provide the rewards that are valued. The leader learns of obstacles that the follower faces and helps by removing them. For example, a follower may need market data from the research department in the organization to complete a report. The leader can help by calling the department and asking them to expedite the requested report. The removal of barriers and strengthening of expectancies and instrumentalities results in follower satisfaction, effort, and performance. Expectancy theory is covered in more detail in Chapter 8.

A key aspect of the situation that the leader needs to consider is follower ability—the leader must adjust expectations in relation to a person's ability to complete a task. As we learned in Chapter 2, individual differences matter, including personality. For example, some followers have a higher need to socialize with others at work. Other followers may have a higher need for control or a preference for more structure in their work. The PGT framework also considers aspects of the situation including the task itself; if the task is not clear, the leader must explain what needs to be done. In highly repetitive tasks, leaders can show concern for followers' well-being (supportive leadership). The formal authority system is another situation characteristic to consider. In other words, if the formal authority system is strong, the leader can enforce rules. Finally, the norms of the work group may influence individual motivation, and the leader can build cohesion to support the followers' expectancies (the effects of work-group norms on performance is discussed further in Chapter 10).

Research on PGT has shown support for propositions of the model.[17,18] However, its strength lies in the application of motivation theory (expectancy theory, in particular) to leadership. When you read about expectancy theory, recall that no other leadership theory makes such a direct linkage to motivation. The framework informs leaders about what aspects of followers and the situation to consider when setting up pathways to their goals. The model is practical in that

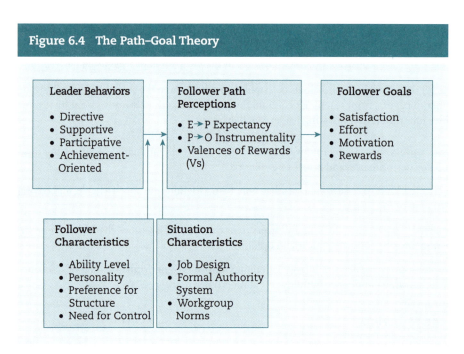

Figure 6.4 The Path–Goal Theory

Leader Behaviors

- Directive
- Supportive
- Participative
- Achievement-Oriented

Follower Path Perceptions

- E→P Expectancy
- P→O Instrumentality
- Valences of Rewards (Vs)

Follower Goals

- Satisfaction
- Effort
- Motivation
- Rewards

Follower Characteristics

- Ability Level
- Personality
- Preference for Structure
- Need for Control

Situation Characteristics

- Job Design
- Formal Authority System
- Workgroup Norms

Sources: House, R. J. (1971). A path–goal theory of leadership effectiveness. *Administrative Science Quarterly, 16,* 321–328; House, R. J., & Mitchell, T. R. (1974). Path–goal theory of leadership. *Journal of Contemporary Business, 3,* 81–97.

it helps leaders to clarify the motivational aspects of their expectations of goals and performance. It is also important that PGT stresses the removal of barriers to effective performance.

Critical Thinking Question: Explain how a leader can intervene using PGT if followers are having difficulty getting help from the purchasing department to get the supplies they need to do their job.

Path–goal theory and other theories focusing on leader behavior were criticized because they assumed that leaders treated all followers the same. Research in the 1970s found that this was not the case. In fact, leaders develop unique relationships with each of their followers. A theory emerged that focuses on these unique working relationships that develop between the leader and each follower called **leader–member exchange (LMX)**, and this approach is discussed next.

LEADER–MEMBER EXCHANGE

Learning Objective 6.5: Illustrate the leader–member exchange (LMX) model with an example.

Should a boss treat everyone alike? Leaders treat subordinates differently based upon their unique abilities and contributions to the work group and organization. LMX is defined as the quality of the working relationship developed with each follower and is characterized by more delegation of authority to those with high-quality LMX.[19] In a relatively short period of time, leaders decide on their **in-group members** and **out-group members**. Out-group members perform to the specifications in their job descriptions, but they don't go above and beyond and don't take on extra work.

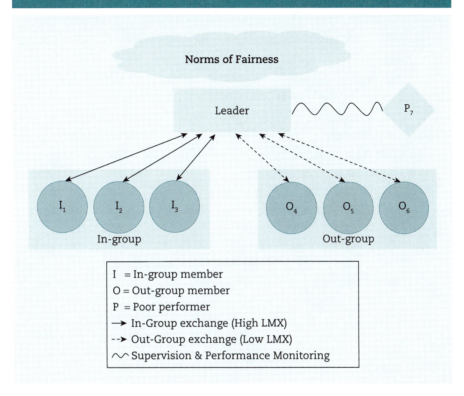

Figure 6.5   Leader–Member Exchange in a Work Group With Seven Direct Reports

Norms of Fairness

Leader

P_7

I_1 I_2 I_3

In-group

O_4 O_5 O_6

Out-group

I = In-group member
O = Out-group member
P = Poor performer
→ In-Group exchange (High LMX)
--→ Out-Group exchange (Low LMX)
∿ Supervision & Performance Monitoring

In-group members do. A diagram of what in-groups and out-groups might look like in a seven-person work group is shown in Figure 6.5.

Note that there is a poor performer in the work group (labeled P7). This is a different type of relationship where the supervisor is monitoring performance and attempting to get the minimally accepted level of performance. The first goal would be to move this person to the out-group where they are perform-ing to the basic expectations of the job. If performance does not improve, in time, they may be transferred to another work group (where they get a second chance) or dismissed from the organization altogether.

> Critical Thinking Questions: Is the LMX process fair? Should managers treat all followers alike? Why or why not?

The other important thing the diagram shows is that norms of fairness must pervade this entire process.[20,21] Fairness must be established to avoid possible negative effects on the performance of the entire work team. Table 6.1 contains the questions that are used by leadership researchers to assess the follower's evaluation of their relationship with their boss (known as the LMX7 measure). A meta-analytic review study found that follower answers to these questions strongly relate to their performance on the job.[22] A recent meta-analysis of 3,327 studies with over 930,000 observations demonstrated that LMX consistently predicts performance compared to other theories of leadership. This study underscores the importance of LMX relationships for understanding what contributes to individual performance at work.[23]

Table 6.1 Leader–Member Exchange Questions

The following questions ask about **your relationship with your immediate boss**—that is, **the person you report to.** Circle your answers.

Do you know where you stand with him or her? Do you usually know how satisfied he or she is with what you do?

1	2	3	4	5
Rarely	Occasionally	Sometimes	Fairly often	Very often

How well does he or she understand your job problems and needs?

1	2	3	4	5
Not a bit	A little	A fair amount	Quite a bit	A great deal

How well does he or she recognize your potential?

1	2	3	4	5
Not at all	A little	Moderately	Mostly	Fully

Regardless of how much formal authority he or she has built into his or her position, what are the chances that he or she would use his or her power to help you solve problems in your work?

1	2	3	4	5
None	Small	Moderate	High	Very high

Again, regardless of the amount of formal authority he or she has, what are the chances that he or she would "bail you out" at his or her expense?

1	2	3	4	5
None	Small	Moderate	High	Very high

I have enough confidence in him or her that I would defend and justify his or her decision if he or she were not present to do so.

1	2	3	4	5
Strongly disagree	Disagree	Neutral	Agree	Strongly agree

How would you characterize your working relationship with him or her?

1	2	3	4	5
Extremely ineffective	Worse than average	Average	Better than average	Extremely effective

Source: Adapted from Scandura, T. A., & Graen, G. B. (1984). The moderating effects of initial leader–member exchange status on the effects of a leadership intervention. *Journal of Applied Psychology, 69,* 428–436.

Leader–Member Exchange Development

So how do effective LMX relationships develop? There are three steps in the process: role taking, role making, and role routinization.[24] In role taking, the boss tests the commitment of the follower by offering extra work. Through this testing and response, the boss forms an overall assessment of whether the follower is in-group or out-group. It is important to pay attention to the boss's signals when a person takes a new job or has a new boss. If a person wants the benefits of more challenging work, promotion potential, or higher salary, they need to respond in a way that the boss views positively. During the process of role making, mutual expectations of the working relationship are established, and the follower's role is clearer. The final step is role routinization. Once roles are made, they become stable since the leader and follower both know what to expect. For example, relationships develop best when the leader is able to delegate tasks to the member.[25] Therefore, everyone who reports to a boss (and that's most of us) should be concerned with managing the relationship and developing a relationship by being dependable. The next sections focuses on how to manage your boss and develop a high-quality relationship.

Managing Your Boss

Critical Thinking Questions: Develop an example by having two people you know complete the LMX questionnaire in Table 6.1. What do you see when you compare their responses? Do you see differences in the quality and effectiveness of the working relationships?

Research on the LMX model of leadership has demonstrated that an effective working relationship with your boss predicts all of the outcomes of OB that we have discussed in Chapter 1 (performance, job satisfaction, organizational commitment, motivation, well-being, and lower turnover). Outcomes of interest to many students include career progress, and LMX predicts promotions and salary increases. A classic *Harvard Business Review* article[26] termed the upward exchange process *managing your boss* and described how to develop an effective working relationship with the boss: understanding your boss, understanding yourself through self-assessment, and developing a compatible working relationship. Remember that leaders and their followers depend upon one another for success, and it is the follower's responsibility to ensure that an effective working relationship develops.[27] Jean Kelley[28] offers the following guidelines for effectively managing the boss:

1. **Find out from your boss what "good" looks like and who is involved in measuring good.** Make sure you are meeting everyone's expectations.

2. **Ask your boss what kind of follow-up he or she wants for his or her comfort level.** Take the initiative to set expectations for every project you are assigned.

3. **Examine your boss's style and adjust to that style.** Is your boss a reader or a listener? Does your boss want data before you talk (a reader)? Or does your boss want to talk through the project and gather the data later (a listener)?

4. **Muster up the courage to tell your boss when you feel you haven't been fully heard.** It's your responsibility to speak up when you feel you are not being heard. Use *I* instead of *you*—for example, "I was really upset by you not hearing me" rather than "You don't listen to me."

5. **Become aware of other managers' styles, especially when they have a stake in the outcome of a project.** Do you have more than one boss or person who evaluates your work? Ask each one what is most important so that you can focus your efforts.

6. **Manage up.** No matter how poorly you may have managed your relationship with your boss in the past, the good news is that you can start over with a new project. It's about understanding your boss and teaching your boss how to work with you.

Some people may have a negative reaction to this process, feeling that it is manipulative. It is important to point out that this is not about flattering the boss or becoming a "pet" employee. Rather, this is a process of developing an effective working relationship based upon mutual expectations. Focus on your strong points—what you can offer your boss to make them more effective. This is where relationship compatibility comes in. For example, if your boss is quiet and reserved and you are more outgoing, you could be his go-to person for making public contacts and networking.

Critical Thinking Question: Do you feel that the process of "managing your boss" is manipulative or just being a smart and dependable employee? Explain your position.

Follower Reactions to Authority

Part of being able to adjust to your boss's style is your understanding of how you feel about authority. Some people resent authority and being told what to do (**counterdependent**). Others are compliant and give in all of the time (**overdependent**). According to Gabarro and Kotter, the best approach is to avoid these two extremes and recognize that most followers are dependent on their boss to some extent. Ideally, you will be able to create a working relationship where you feel **interdependent** (you depend on one another to get things done in the group and organization). In developing an effective working relationship, you should be dependable and honest above all, keeping your boss informed (but also using their time wisely). Effective working relationships with the boss can permeate the entire organization. Leaders with great boss relationships have more resources to exchange with their own followers and therefore develop more effective working relationships with them.[29] Thus, the leader in the middle is viewed as a "linking pin" between upper management and followers below, sharing important information about the organization's vision and goals with followers. These linking-pin leaders become valuable members of the organization, and they gain power and influence due to their position in organizational networks.

In developing a working relationship with each follower, leaders make judgments regarding the reasons for their behaviors, particularly in the case of poor performance. These judgments may or may not be accurate, but they have a strong influence on whether or not a follower will become a member of the leader's in-group. Thus, it is important to understand what causes these judgments (known as *attributions*) to guard against inaccuracies. Leadership research has examined the attributions that leaders make about the causes of follower poor performance, and this is addressed next.

Attributions and Leader–Member Relationships

There is a great deal of OB research that shows that the attributions of what causes behavior in organizations matter. **Attributions** represent a person's attempt to assign a cause to a behavior or event they observe. **Attribution theory** proposes that the attributions people make about events and behavior can be either internal or external.[30] In organizational settings, attributions are particularly important when events are important, novel, unexpected, and negative. Attributions are particularly important when a follower fails to meet performance expectations of the leader.[31] In the case of an **internal attribution**, people infer that an event or a person's behavior is due to his or her own character traits or abilities. If a person makes an **external attribution**, they believe that a person's behavior is due to situational factors. For example, Damon is late to class. If the professor believes the tardiness happened because of Damon's lack of motivation to attend class, he is making an internal attribution. On the other hand, if the professor believes Damon is late because he could not find a parking space in overcrowded university lots, he is making an external attribution. Thus, internal attributions will lead the professor to infer that Damon is a poor student.

Research on attribution theory has demonstrated attributions can bias how we process information and make decisions. The first way this occurs is called the **fundamental attribution error**. This is the tendency to attribute other people's behavior to internal factors such as character traits or abilities, but when explaining one's own behavior, people tend to attribute the cause to the situation.[32] The second way attributions may cloud judgment is the **self-serving bias** that occurs when a person attributes successes to internal factors and failures to situational factors. And the further an event is in the past, the more likely the cause of a failure will be attributed to the situation. For example, Mindy gets a poor grade on a quiz and attributes her failure to unfair test questions rather than not

> **Critical Thinking Questions:** Why do you think the just-world hypothesis is so pervasive? Why do you think leaders might believe that people get what they deserve?

studying for the quiz. The third way attributions may affect judgment is the **just-world hypothesis,** which is the need to believe that the world is fair and that people get what they deserve. This gives people a sense of security, particularly when they encounter a challenging situation. For example, Manny gets laid off at work due to downsizing, and his coworkers attribute the layoff to him being an argumentative person rather than the business situation or a bad economy.

How can a leader avoid attribution bias? When we ascribe a cause to behavior, we should gather additional information. By paying attention to overall patterns of behavior, we make more accurate conclusions by considering the following:

1. **Consensus information**—information about how other people would behave if they were in the same situation. High consensus means others would behave the same way. Low consensus means other people would behave differently.

2. **Distinctiveness information**—information about how the individual behaves the same way in different situations. Low in distinctiveness means the individual behaves the same way to different situations. High in distinctiveness means the individual behaves a particular way toward a particular situation only.

3. **Consistency information**—information about how the individual behaves toward a certain stimuli across time and circumstances. High in consistency means the individual behaves the same way almost every time they are in a particular situation.

Based on this perspective, if a leader wants to improve judgments and avoid the attribution error, they should consider how well other people would do in the same situation. For example, do all employees make the same mistake when filling out forms for customers? If so, maybe the form needs to be revised. Second, how distinctive is the behavior? For example, does the employee behave rudely to all coworkers or just one in particular? Finally, how consistent is the behavior? For example, over time, the leader observes that an employee does not pay close attention to their work every Friday afternoon, and this is a consistent pattern. Attending to these three possibilities alerts the leader to investigate and gather additional information before making a definitive conclusion about the cause of behavior. This is important because attributions play a role in how leader–member relationships develop.

Attributions play a clear role in the development of work relationships between leaders and followers.[33,34] A dyadic (two-party) relational approach to attribution theory is shown in Figure 6.6.[35] As shown in the figure, an internal or an external attribution might be made as we have previously discussed—for example, "I did not get a positive performance review" could be attributed to "I did not put in enough effort" (internal) or "The human resources department is incompetent" (external). A relational attribution offers a third and potentially powerful explanation: "My boss and I don't have a positive relationship." The actions a person might take to remedy the situation will vary depending upon the attribution. In the case of an external attribution (the most likely according to the fundamental attribution error), the person may feel helpless to change it except for finding another job. However, if a relational attribution is made, the person might try to improve the working relationship with the boss. Thus, relational attribution theory offers another way a person might improve their work situation by changing what they attribute the causes of an event to. If it is the relationship (and not internal or external), actions can be taken to improve the working relationship.

When the right attributions are made, the working relationship between a leader and follower will develop into a high-quality one. Next, we turn to how you can increase investment in the LMX relationship with your boss so that it develops into a mentoring relationship, which has also been shown to relate to performance and positive career outcomes for the junior person, or mentee.

Figure 6.6   Relational Attributions in Response to Negative Achievement-Related Events

	Internal attribution	Relational attribution	External attribution
	Self	**Self in relation to other**	**Other person/ situation**
"I did not get a positive performance review because...	... I did not put in enough effort over the past few weeks."	... my boss and I don't have a positive relationship."	... my boss is incompetent."
"I was not chosen as the team leader because...	... I have poor communication skills."	... my boss and I do not communicate well with each other."	... it was my coworker's turn—people are selected based on a policy of rotating responsibility."
"I did not meet the project's deadline because...	... I did not ask for additional help soon enough."	... my coworker and I did not give each other frequent enough updates."	... I had to redo all the work my coworker turned in."

Source: Eberly, M. B., Holley, E. C., Johnson, M. D., & Mitchell, T. R. (2011). Beyond internal and external: A dyadic theory of relational attributions. *Academy of Management Review, 36*(4), 731–753.

The Mentor Connection

Mentoring is defined as follows:[36]

> Mentoring is an intense developmental relationship whereby advice, counseling, and developmental opportunities are provided to a protégé by a mentor, which, in turn, shapes the protégé's career experiences.

One of the best things that can happen is when the boss becomes a mentor. Career mentoring from a boss contributes to performance, promotions, and salary increases above and beyond a high-quality LMX relationship.[37] Research on mentoring in organizations shows that having a mentor can have a powerful impact on your career, and the boss is an important place to begin. You want to show him or her that you want to be a trusted member of the in-group and that you are willing to take on more responsibility. Hopefully, he or she will then view you as a mentee—someone worth the investment of time and energy to develop. There are many cases where a boss gets promoted and a trusted in-group member is promoted along with him. So you want to be sure to do an inventory of what you have to offer your boss in exchange for career investment. For example, you might offer to take on a challenging problem that the boss has been working on (particularly if it fits your strengths). Or you might lead the team meeting while your boss is out of town (and be sure to keep them informed with a summary of how the meeting went).

Mentors provide two general types of support to protégés: (1) career support and (2) social support.[38] In addition, mentors may serve as role models to mentees. Cultivating a mentoring relationship enhances your job satisfaction and performance.[39] Mentoring is now seen as a network of developmental relationships[40] including peers, managers other than your boss, and people outside of the organization. However, keep in mind that research has demonstrated that the boss is a key node of your mentoring network since supervisory mentoring has been associated with higher potential, productivity, and organizational commitment.[41] Belle Rose Ragins, mentoring expert, points out that mentoring relationships can become transformative and "change the way we view our careers, our environment, and ourselves."[42]

She further notes that mentoring relationships are characterized by a willingness to be vulnerable and trust one another. For a high-quality relationship to mentees, expect the mentors to be trustworthy and dependable. A study of 315 health care workers found that health care managers' mentoring behaviors influenced worker perceptions of their trustworthiness in terms of ability, integrity, and benevolence.[43] Trust is at the heart of all effective working relationships—with bosses, mentors, and peers. Next, we discuss research on trust, which is essential for a leader to understand to be effective, and address the "trust gap" highlighted at the beginning of this chapter.

THE IMPORTANCE OF TRUST

Learning Objective 6.6: Explain why trust is important and how to repair it.

The following definition of trust is often cited: "the willingness to be vulnerable."[44] Trust is related to important outcomes, including risk taking and job performance.[45] A review of the various definitions of trust offers the following summary:[46] Trust is a psychological state comprising the intention to accept vulnerability based upon positive expectations of the intentions or behavior of another. A meta-analytic study found that trust is related to LMX as well as job satisfaction and performance.[47] Several other theories of leadership mention trust (e.g., servant leadership, which is discussed later in this chapter). Trust is therefore fundamental to the development of effective working relationships with bosses (and others).

There are some helpful frameworks to organize your thinking about how trust operates in organizations. A three-part view of trust is a useful way to think about trust development with another person: calculus-based, knowledge-based, and identification-based.[48] Each of these forms is explained in detail in the following sections.

Calculus-Based Trust

Calculus-based trust (CBT) is a form of trust based upon keeping records of what another person does for you and what you do for them. It is an "arm's length" form of trust in which neither party really becomes that vulnerable to the behavior of the other person. The expectations are like contracts, and the consequences of violating trust are punishment or the severing of the relationship. An example of CBT (sometimes called deterrence-based trust) in an organization is a leader telling a follower to perform a task because it is in their job description and reminding them that they are paid to do it (in other words, "Do it or you are fired!"). Many relationships in organizations (and in our daily lives) operate on this level. For example, this is the type of relationship most people have with the person who they hire to cut their grass. It is a straightforward transaction. If the person shows up, cuts the grass, and it looks good, you pay them. If not, you don't.

Knowledge-Based Trust

In this framework, the second level of trust is called **knowledge-based trust (KBT)**. This level of trust is grounded in how predictable the other person is. Over time, through interactions where benefits are exchanged between two parties, people come to expect the other person to come through for them. It is based upon information gathered about the other person in a variety of circumstances. An example of this form of trust in an organization would be a follower becoming the go-to person for the boss in terms of creating her PowerPoint decks for important presentations. The boss can jot down a list of bullet points in a document and send them to the follower. Within a day, the boss receives a professional-looking presentation deck to review and edit. The boss does not have to remind the person that it is in their job description (and it may or may not be). They just make the request, and it happens because the follower's behavior is predictable.

Identification-Based Trust

Finally, the highest degree of trust in this model is called **identification-based trust (IBT).** This form of trust is characterized by the leader and follower sharing the same goals and objectives. In other words, the follower identifies with the leader's vision. There is no need for record keeping, and the predictability of the follower's behavior is assumed. The follower sees the work group and organization in the same way that the leader does and will perform the right tasks without being asked. For example, a trusted follower would step in and resolve a conflict with another work-group member for the leader. IBT becomes a highly efficient form for the leader since followers take care of details while the leader focuses on the strategic vision or negotiating resources for the group with her boss (i.e., working the "linking pin," as suggested by the LMX model).

Lewicki and Bunker built upon Shapiro et al.'s work and described the process through which trust develops over time.[49] As shown in Figure 6.7, trust may transform over time and develop different "faces" as it matures. In other words, the types of trust build upon one another over time based on the nature of the working relationship. CBT develops to a point (J1), and the trust level becomes KBT as the behavior of the parties becomes predictable. As noted in the figure, most relationships in organizations fall into the KBT range of trust. Once stable, a few relationships will reach the next point (J2) and will become stable IBT relationships. At this point, both parties fully understand what the other party cares about, and there is a level of empathy that emerges (i.e., the ability to put oneself in the boss's place and see the organization the way they do). As noted previously, at this level, the follower becomes able to act effectively for the boss. There is a sense of harmony in thoughts, emotions, and behavior. Activities that strengthen IBT are the creation of joint projects, shared goals, and shared work values.

The development of trust is viewed as "tactical climbing" in which there are increasing levels of risk and vulnerability over time. A longitudinal study of new hires found that the cues that are perceived early in employment predict the emergence of trust. In fact, information attended to in the first hours on a job is crucial.[50] Trust becomes stable, but

Figure 6.7 The Development of Trust

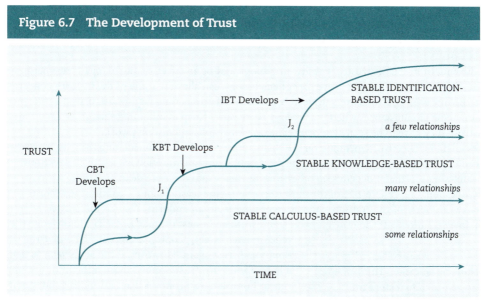

Source: Lewicki, R. J., & Bunker, B. B. (1996). Developing and maintaining trust in work relationships. In R. M. Kramer & T. R. Tyler (Eds.), *Trust in organizations: Frontiers of theory and research.* Thousand Oaks, CA: Sage.

it is important to remember that trust is vulnerable. Even in high-quality leader–follower relationships, IBT can revert to the CBT stage, so followers and bosses must be careful about maintaining relationships.[51] According to this model, movements between the stages of trust can be smooth and incremental or they can be dramatic and transformational. Remember that the development of trust takes time and that trust does require testing to see how durable it is.

Critical Thinking Questions: Describe how calculus-based trust explains how people view their jobs. How can a leader move a person to the two higher levels of trust?

From the examples provided, you can see the critical role that trust plays in the development of working relationships with bosses (and others, including peers) in the organization. It's hard to imagine an organization that could function without trust. So it's important to understand what you need to do should you damage trust with your boss (of course, the best strategy is to never damage trust, but it can happen). Research on trust repair has examined what strategies work to get the relationship back on track.

Repairing Broken Trust

There are three important questions to ask after a trust violation has occurred (the trustee is the person who is the target of the trustor's trust):[52]

1. Is the trustee innocent or guilty of committing the transgression?

2. If the trustee is guilty of the transgression, should this be attributed to the situation or to the person?

3. If the transgression is attributed at least in part to the person, is the personal shortcoming fixable or is it an enduring characteristic of the trustee?

These questions are important because they offer guidance for repairing trust. Regarding question 1, if a trustee is actually innocent, they should emphasize lack of guilt through denial and offer any available exonerating information.[53] Not addressing the issue—remaining reticent (e.g., saying "no comment")—can be risky because people usually assume the worst.[54]

Regarding question 2, if the trustee is guilty, an apology may be an effective way to repair trust because the expressions of remorse and repentance, which are part of an apology, can alleviate some of the trustor's concerns. However, the way the apology is given also matters. Research shows that if extenuating factors also played a role, there is benefit to mentioning these circumstances when the apology is offered.[55] Keep in mind that though explanations and excuses can restore trust, they have to be seen as adequate; incomplete explanations don't work.[56]

Excuses might be effective, depending on the characteristics of the person violating the trust and the relationship quality, but adding reparations (i.e., attempts to "make it right") increase the effectiveness of explanations.[57,58] However, further research suggests that it depends on other contingencies, and these are described next.

Finally, question 3 represents one of the most important—but least obvious—contingencies for trust repair. Will the trustor see the cause of the transgression as stemming from an enduring flaw in the trustee or something the trustee can, in fact, address? If the transgression stems from an honest mistake or lack of knowledge (i.e., a compe-

Critical Thinking Question: Think of a time when you tried to restore trust after it was broken. Based on this section, what would you do differently?

tence-related issue), people are more likely to give the benefit of the doubt and trust again. However, if the act is seen as demonstrating a lack of integrity, trust is much more difficult (if not impossible) to repair. For example, promises may restore trust but not if the trust is broken because the person has initially lied. Lying is one of the most damaging behaviors.[59] If someone feels deceived, trust may not be restored, even if apologies, promises, and repeated trustworthy actions follow the deception. Even more "substantive" (rather than verbal) responses such as offering reparation or paying a personal cost are limited in their effectiveness when questions of integrity are at the center of the issue.[60]

If you are interested in becoming a leader at the top levels of an organization or starting your own business, you will tend to be interested in research on transformational and visionary leadership. You may view yourself as charismatic. However, for those of you who view yourselves as managers who sometimes take the leadership role, you will also benefit from knowledge about leadership. Leadership is a "full range" of behaviors, and the next section discusses both management (i.e., transactional behaviors) and leadership (i.e., transformational behaviors).

FULL-RANGE LEADERSHIP DEVELOPMENT

Learning Objective 6.7: Compare and contrast the elements of transactional and transformational leadership.

The full-range leadership development model is based upon over 25 years of research on **transformational leadership**.[61,62,63] People are more engaged when their leaders behave in certain ways at the highest end of the full-range model. The full-range model starts at the lower end of leadership, which is termed **transactional leadership**. Leadership is a continuum, with transactional leadership being the foundation upon which transformational leadership is built. These behaviors range from passive to active and ineffective to effective as depicted in Figure 6.8. The specific elements of transactional and transformational leadership are described in the following sections.

Transactional Leadership

Transactional leadership is defined as behaviors that motivate followers through rewards and corrective actions. The transactional leader behaviors are (from worst to best):

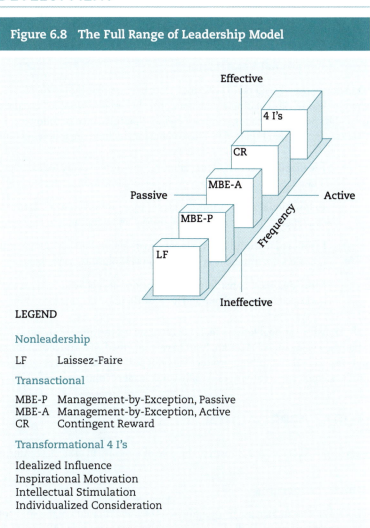

Figure 6.8 The Full Range of Leadership Model

LEGEND

Nonleadership

LF Laissez-Faire

Transactional

MBE-P Management-by-Exception, Passive
MBE-A Management-by-Exception, Active
CR Contingent Reward

Transformational 4 I's

Idealized Influence
Inspirational Motivation
Intellectual Stimulation
Individualized Consideration

Source: Bass, B. M., & Avolio, B. J. (1994). *Improving organizational effectiveness through transformational leadership.* Thousand Oaks, CA: Sage.

- **Nonleadership/laissez-faire leadership.** This is the "near-avoidance of leadership,"[64] the least active and least effective of all of the leadership styles in the full-range model.

- **Management by exception.** This has two forms: active and passive. In management by exception, active (MBE-A), the leader looks for the follower to make errors and then corrects them. In management by exception, passive (MBE-P), the leader does not actively look for errors or deviations from work standards, but when noticed, they take corrective action.

- **Contingent reward.** This is promising or delivering rewards to followers contingent on their performance.

There are times when a manager must use the transactional approach. For example, if they have a low-performing employee, a leader may need to employ the management-by-exception approaches. At the next level in the full-range model are the transformational leadership behaviors.

Transformational Leadership

Transformational leadership is defined as behaviors that mobilize extra effort from followers through emphasis on change through articulating a new vision for the organization. As noted earlier, it is this set of behaviors that is most related to positive attitudes, commitment, and performance of followers. Leadership is active, and this leads to effectiveness, as shown in Figure 6.8. These behaviors include the following (known as the *four I*s):

- **Idealized influence.** Being admired and respected by followers is the core of this leadership component. They are seen as change agents in the organization.

- **Inspirational motivation.** Leaders inspire others to work hard toward organizational goals by providing challenge. They are positive and upbeat and get others to feel optimistic.

- **Intellectual stimulation.** Transformational leaders encourage innovation and new ideas. They listen to followers openly and don't criticize novel solutions to problems.

- **Individualized consideration.** Transformational leaders treat each follower as a unique person. They get to know people one-on-one and mentor them.

Transformational leaders increase intrinsic motivation by aligning followers' tasks with their own interests and what they value most. Meta-analyses have confirmed that transformational leadership behaviors are positively and significantly related to both productivity and performance ratings by supervisors.[65] Transformational leadership also predicts employee creativity, especially when leaders communicate high expectations for creative behaviors.[66]

MORAL APPROACHES

Learning Objective 6.8: Illustrate the role of morality in ethical, servant, and authentic leadership.

Ethical Leadership

There has been an increase in attention to ethics and morality in the study of leadership in the past 10 years. Following the scandals of Enron, Wells Fargo, and others, researchers in OB responded by working on new theories that incorporate a moral component and placing followers first. These theories discuss the **ethical leadership** role and how leaders today must be authentic and serve followers rather than their own goals exclusively. These emerging theories are a good example of how OB research responds to current challenges organizations face and how researchers generate new knowledge to guide leaders. The study of ethics and morality in leadership will continue to be of interest to OB researchers as they continue to demonstrate relationships of ethical leadership with employee well-being and performance. Development of these new approaches now appears in textbooks for students and in corporate training programs to sensitize the next generation of managers to ethical aspects of leadership and improve leadership practice.

Leadership and ethics are intertwined; the tests described in the boxed insert must be applied. Ethical decision making is important to the practice of leadership, and contemporary theories of leadership address morality. Research on ethical leadership has found four components:

- Moral sensitivity involves recognizing that our behavior *impacts* others.

- Moral judgment involves determining the right decision.

- Moral motivation is having the need to do the right thing.

- Moral action.[67]

Ethical leadership has been found to be positively related to work-group-level ethical behavior and negatively related to relationship conflict among coworkers.[68] A review of the research on ethical leadership concludes:

The research quite consistently shows that if employees indicate that their leaders are ethical and fair role models who communicate and reward ethical behavior, there is less deviance and more cooperative behavior, and employees perform better and are more willing to both expend effort and report problems to management.[69]

If leaders at the top of the organization are viewed as ethical by their followers, then ethics have a cascading effect throughout the organization; lower-level employees also view their manager as ethical.[70] Thus, ethical leadership at the top of an organization has a trickle-down effect to lower organizational levels. The moral component is emerging as a key aspect of contemporary leadership theories. Next, we discuss two other recent approaches to leadership that directly incorporate aspects of morality: servant and authentic leadership.

Servant and Authentic Leadership

As indicated previously, there is a "new wave" of leadership research that emphasizes morality. In addition to ethical leadership, two other theories have emerged: **servant leadership**[71] and **authentic leadership**.[72,73] While research on these theories is relatively new, findings indicate that followers respond positively to these leader behaviors. Servant leadership dates back to the 1970s when Robert Greenleaf was inspired about leadership while reading Herman Hesse's *Journey to the East*. In this novel, a group of men undertake a long journey. A servant named Leo sings to them and inspires them while doing his tasks. Leo disappears along the way, and the group falls into chaos and cannot complete their journey. The basic idea is that followers are first rather than leaders. Greenleaf's definition of the servant leader is as follows:

The servant-leader *is* servant first. . . . It begins with the natural feeling that one wants to serve, to serve *first*. Then conscious choice brings one to aspire to lead. That person is sharply different from one who is *leader* first, perhaps because of the need to assuage an unusual power drive or to acquire material possessions.[74]

Researchers have recently developed measures of servant leadership, and it has been shown to relate to positive attitudes and performance of followers.[75] Seven servant leadership dimensions have been identified: emotional healing, creating value for the community, conceptual skills, empowering, helping subordinates grow and succeed, putting

BEST PRACTICES

Is Narcissism Good or Bad for Business?

When many people think of a successful CEO these days, they imagine someone with a take-charge personality who is self-centered and ruthless. This seems at odds with the research findings on humble leadership. According to Christian J. Resick and his colleagues, "narcissism is broadly defined as an exaggerated, yet fragile self-concept of one's importance and influence." Lolly Daskal, a well-known leadership coach, points out that a narcissistic CEO has the following traits:

1. A sense of entitlement and superiority.
2. A strong need for attention.
3. A single-minded focus on themselves.
4. A lack of empathy for others.
5. Constant criticism of others.
6. High levels of aggression.
7. An unwillingness to hear feedback.

There seem to be pros and cons to narcissistic leadership. Such a CEO may drive high performance and achieve bottom-line results during times of rapid change. John Stahl-Wert and Kenneth Jennings, authors of the book *The Serving Leader*, explain why self-serving leaders are bad for business. First, they may fail to serve the customer because they focus too much on themselves. CEOs receive high compensation and may become greedy. Also, they may inhibit innovation because they prefer their own ideas and don't listen to input from others. They may even avoid learning new things needed to stay abreast of trends.

Narcissistic behavior, in the long term, may have more cons than pros, and such leaders may need to keep their ego in check for the benefit of followers and the organization. Followers must be aware of the potential negative aspects of this behavior pattern and pay attention to how the narcissistic leader may be affecting their own well-being.

Discussion Questions

1. Provide an example of a leader that demonstrates narcissism.
2. Discuss the impact of the narcissistic behavior on others in the organization. Does this affect the organization's performance?
3. What can organizations do to guard against the impact of a narcissistic leader?

Sources: Daskal, L. (2015). How to deal with a narcissistic leader. Retrieved from http://www.inc.com/lolly-daskal/how-to-deal-with-a-narcissistic-leader.html; Tenney, M. (2016). Why egos are bad for business, and what to do about it. Retrieved from http://www.huffingtonpost.com/matt-tenney/why-egos-are-bad-for-business-and-what-to-do-about-it_b_9090098.html; Resick, C. J., Whitman, D. S., Weingarden, S. M., and Hiller, N. J. (2009). The bright-side and the dark-side of CEO personality: Examining core self-evaluations, narcissism, transformational leadership, and strategic influence. *Journal of Applied Psychology, 94,* 1365–1381; Wales, W. J., Patel, P. C., & Lumpkin, G. T. (2013). In pursuit of greatness: CEO narcissism, entrepreneurial orientation, and firm performance variance. *Journal of Management Studies, 50*(6), 1041–1069.

subordinates first, and behaving ethically.[76,77] Servant leaders facilitate team confidence, affirming the strengths and potential of the team and providing developmental support.[78] This developmental support is also characteristic of **humble leadership**, where a leader's humility allows them to show followers how to grow as a result of work. This leads followers to believe that their own developmental journeys are legitimate in the workplace.[79] A recent study found that leader humility creates shared leadership in teams by encouraging proactive team members to take responsibility.

Shared leadership was most strongly related to team performance when team members had high levels of task-related competence.[80]

Critical Thinking Questions: Compare and contrast ethical, servant, and authentic leadership. What do they have in common, and what are the key differences?

Authentic leadership involves knowing oneself and behaving in a way that is consistent with what is intuitively right.[81] Authentic leaders are most effective when they develop an effective vision that relates to the shared interests of their team. Dan Vesella (CEO of the pharmaceutical company Novartis) is an example of such a leader because he is successful but also demonstrates compassion by assisting people suffering from life-threatening diseases.[82] Authentic leadership has four dimensions:[83]

- **Self-awareness**—for example, seeks feedback to improve interactions with others.

- **Relational transparency**—for example, says exactly what he or she means.

- **Internalized moral perspective**—for example, demonstrates beliefs that are consistent with actions.

- **Balanced processing**—for example, solicits views that challenge his or her deeply held positions.

These leadership theories seem to sound alike, but they also have some differences so it is important to compare and contrast them. Table 6.2 shows a comparison of transformational leadership (which we discussed earlier in this chapter under Full-Range Leadership Development), ethical leadership, authentic leadership, and servant leadership. As you can see from the table, there are some similarities among these approaches to leadership, but there are also some key differences. Transformational leadership is probably the most unique but does share some aspects of servant leadership. A recent study conducted several meta-analyses to compare these approaches and found that authentic and ethical leadership may not offer unique contributions to understanding the relationship of leadership to employee performance, organizational citizenship behaviors, and attitudes. However, servant leadership did appear to be significantly different than transformational leadership.[84]

Table 6.2   Comparison of Authentic, Transformational, Ethical, and Servant Leadership Theories

Theoretical Components	Authentic Leadership	Ethical Leadership	Transformational Leadership	Servant Leadership
Leader self-awareness	✓			✓
Relationship transparency	✓		*	
Internalized moral perspective	✓	✓	✓	
Balanced processing	✓		*	
Moral person	✓	✓	✓	✓
Moral manager	*	✓	*	✓
Idealized influence	*	✓	✓	
Inspirational motivation			✓	

(Continued)

Table 6.2 (Continued)

Theoretical Components	Authentic Leadership	Ethical Leadership	Transformational Leadership	Servant Leadership
Intellectual stimulation			✓	
Individualized consideration		*	✓	
Emotional healing				✓
Value for community				✓
Conceptual skills	*		✓	✓
Empowering			*	✓
Helping subordinates grow and succeed			✓	✓
Putting subordinates first			✓	✓
Behaving ethically		✓		✓
Relationships	✓		✓	✓
Servanthood				✓

✓ = focal component, * = minor or implicit component

Source: Adapted from Walumbwa, F., Avolio, B., Gardner, W., Wernsing, T., & Peterson, S. (2008). Authentic leadership: Development and validation of a theory-based measure. *Journal of Management, 34,* 89–126.

CRITIQUES OF LEADERSHIP THEORY

A key theme of this textbook is to apply critical thinking. Despite the proponents of leadership, there have been some important critiques that have been supported. Some researchers have criticized the emphasis on the leader and their behavior. An alternative view is that leadership is in the eyes of the follower. In other words, leadership is an attribution that a follower makes about another person. These perspectives include the implicit leadership theory and romance of leadership, which are addressed next.

Implicit Leadership Theory

Implicit leadership theory (ILT) examines how attributions about leadership affect follower perceptions of who you are in the role of leader. Research has shown people have **implicit leadership schemas** (or models) in their minds about what constitutes an effective leader.[85] These models are traits and characteristics that a person thinks are being linked to a leader. For example, a person might believe all leaders are tall and highly intelligent. Followers find such models of leaders to be an effective way to categorize leaders and interpret their behavior.[86] For example, followers can accurately recall neutral leadership behaviors, but they exaggerate or distort either positive or negative leadership behaviors.[87] Such implicit assumptions about what an effective leader is serve as a benchmark for how the leader's behavior is interpreted.[88] The models then affect how followers respond to the leader and the way that the relationship develops.[89] To apply this idea, assume that you thought all leaders should be supportive of followers. But you have a leader who is not supportive, which results in a discrepancy, and you don't respond positively to the leader's request for extra effort on a task. This may affect your job performance and evaluation in the future. Changing your assumptions and responding to a task-oriented leader may be difficult to do since this approach assumes leadership is in the "eye of the beholder"—the followers.

Attributions may affect how we process information and lead to errors in judgment. Also, they affect how we develop leader–member relationships with followers and others at work. Attributions may also affect the way that we view leaders in general. Research has found that people make significant attributions about the power of leaders, which is called the *romance of leadership*. In other words, leaders are not powerful because of their expertise or behaviors, but their power is derived from follower attributions of their influence over events.

Romance of Leadership

The **romance of leadership** perspective represents a critique of all leadership research. This perspective articulates why people credit leaders for their influence to change organizations and even societies.[90] This approach highlights the fact that leaders are often the most favored explanation for both positive and negative outcomes in organizations. There is an overemphasis on the importance of the leader: People value performance results more highly when those results are attributed to leadership. Moreover, if an individual is perceived to be an effective leader, his or her personal shortcomings and even poor organizational performance may be ignored. Thus, the romance of leadership perspective challenges the public's apparent fascination with leaders and leadership in which leaders are portrayed as heroes and heroines even when there is no real evidence to support this level of admiration. Leadership is viewed as an attribution by the followers rather than a trait or behavior of the leader. This perspective is not "antileadership," but it does place an emphasis on the follower and the situation. This helps explain why some leaders exercise so much power in organizations.

LEADERSHIP IMPLICATIONS: FLEXIBILITY MATTERS

A key takeaway from this chapter is that leaders need to stay flexible and adapt to both followers and the situation they are in. This chapter covers the essential core leadership theories that are best supported by research. Effective leaders understand the manager role and build upon it to create vision and move the organization toward the future. Leadership represents a full range of behaviors, and this is perhaps best represented by the full-range leadership model. Leaders engage in both transactions and transformation, and the importance of behavioral flexibility is a theme in the chapter. This adaptability has been supported by research on the path–goal theory of leadership and other situational approaches. This chapter discusses emerging perspectives on leadership that all emphasize morality, including ethical, authentic, and servant leadership. While research on these perspectives is new, it shows much promise for understanding a new role for leaders that places integrity at the forefront.

In adapting to the situation, leaders should follow these steps based on leadership research:

1. **Assess your followers' individual differences in terms of abilities and motivation**. Get to know followers individually and develop one-on-one relationships with them. Some followers are motivated by pay and other monetary incentives such as bonuses. Others desire more challenging work and a chance to learn new things. Some followers prefer more structure and want direction, and others need relatively more support. Some followers may need both direction and support. Consider their personality differences (you learned about personality in Chapter 2). Consider their Big Five characteristics, and have them complete the Big Five Personality Test found in the Chapter 2 Toolkit (Openness, Conscientiousness, Extroversion-Introversion, Agreeableness, and Neuroticism/Emotional Stability). If they are Type A, they may need to feel a sense of control over their work, and you can help them cope with stress. Remember, not everyone is alike, and leaders need to adapt to followers, as the path–goal theory prescribes.

2. **Assess the situation**. Is the work structured or unstructured? In other words, is there only one way to perform a task, or can multiple solutions address the problems they are working on? How much power do you have in the situation? How important is it for you to balance your use of power with maintaining positive work relationships? Finally, consider your entire team. How will the development of in-group relationships with some members affect those in the out-group? Develop plans for engaging those in the out-group and offering them

the opportunity to join your in-group. Do members of your work group stick together as a group? Do they have shared goals of performing at a high level?

3. **Pay attention to follower behaviors, and take corrective actions and apply rewards as suggested by the full-range model of leadership**. Assess the need for transformational leadership. Consider whether the organization is going through change and if you need to articulate a vision and inspire your followers. If so, implement the four *Is* of idealized influence, inspirational motivation, intellectual stimulation, and individualized consideration (individualized consideration also addresses Step 2—treat each follower as a unique individual).

4. **Assess the moral component of every leadership decision you make**. Start to view your role as a leader as a servant, as suggested by the servant leadership theory. In your interactions with your followers, be yourself (be authentic). Apply ethical guidelines to your interactions with your followers. This will go a long way toward building relationships that are based on trust. This chapter reviews theories that relate to the development of trust and what to do to repair it.

Leadership is a relationship that is built on trust that develops over time. Guidelines for taking responsibility for managing the boss are discussed. Some leader–member relationships develop into mentoring relationships, and the follower can behave in ways that increase the chances of becoming a mentee and experiencing a transformational work relationship. It is important to understand the dynamics of leader–follower relationships, and the role of attributions in relationship development is highlighted.

Leadership is important to the topics covered in all of the chapters in this textbook. Leaders need to understand individual differences such as personality (Chapter 2) and manage emotions and moods (Chapter 3). Leaders can change follower attitudes and improve job satisfaction (Chapter 4). An important leadership role is the decision-making role, and leaders are problem solvers (Chapter 5). To motivate effectively, leaders need to build trust and establish high-quality relationships with their followers (Chapters 8 and 9). You will learn that leadership matters in teams (Chapter 10) as well. One of the most important things a leader must do is resolve conflict and negotiate with others effectively (Chapter 11). Effective leaders know how to communicate one-on-one as well as in large groups[91] (Chapter 12). Leaders today must understand diversity and cultural differences that may affect how employees interact with one another at work (Chapter 13). Organizational culture is, in part, shaped by the leader (Chapter 14). Leaders play an important role in the implementation of organizational change through transformational leadership and helping employees cope with change (Chapter 15). Leadership is a two-way influence process, and the next chapter discusses power as well as influence and politics (Chapter 7).

edge.sagepub.com/scandura2e

Want a better grade? Go to **edge.sagepub.com/scandura2e** for the tools you need to sharpen your study skills.

KEY TERMS

achievement-oriented leadership, 133
attributions, 138
attribution theory, 138
authentic leadership, 147
calculus-based trust (CBT), 142
consideration, 132
counterdependent, 138

directive leadership, 133
ethical leadership, 146
external attribution, 138
fundamental attribution error, 138
humble leadership, 148
identification-based trust (IBT), 143
implicit leadership schemas, 150

implicit leadership theory (ILT), 150
in-group members, 134
initiating structure, 132
interdependent, 138
internal attribution, 138
just-world hypothesis, 139
knowledge-based trust (KBT), 142

TOOLKIT ACTIVITY 6.1: Applying the Full-Range Leadership Development Model

These short cases provide an opportunity to practice applying the full-range leadership development model. For each case, select the leadership approach you would take and explain why.

Case 1

Because of organizational restructuring directives from your boss, your department must reassign team members to new project teams. You are thinking of asking a highly capable and experienced member of your work group to handle these reassignments. This person has always been dependable and a high performer. She also has positive working relationships with other team members. She is very willing to help with the reassignments. What would you do? Circle it.

A. Do nothing and hope the problem takes care of itself.

B. Allow your follower to complete the reassignments and tell her she may have the afternoon off when it is completed.

C. Allow your follower to complete the reassignments and only intervene if you notice a problem.

D. Allow your follower to complete the reassignments and watch to see if she makes mistakes, and then intervene to correct them.

E. Mentor your follower one-on-one and discuss how doing this task will help her learn new skills. Remind her of how important the restructuring is to the overall vision and strategy of the organization, and be a positive role model.

Discussion Questions

1. Identify the approach from the full-range leadership development model (e.g., transactional/MBEP or transformational/four *Is*).

2. Explain why you would use this approach, citing the full-range leadership development model.

Case 2

You have noticed that one of your team members is not following through on the part of a project assigned to her. She is very motivated and has told you she wants a promotion; however, her recent actions are contradictory to her goal. The current staffing situation does not allow you to reassign the project to someone else in your work group. What would you do? Circle it.

A. Do nothing and hope the problem takes care of itself.

B. Tell her that if she wants the promotion she will need to finish the project in 1 week.

C. Allow your follower to complete the task, and only intervene if you notice a problem.

D. Allow your follower to complete the task and watch to see if she makes mistakes, and then intervene to correct them.

E. Mentor your follower one-on-one and discuss how doing this task will help her learn new skills. Remind her of how important the project is to the overall vision and strategy of the organization, and be a positive role model.

Discussion Questions

1. Identify the approach from the full-range leadership development model (e.g., transactional/MBEP or transformational/four *Is*).

2. Explain why you would use this approach, citing the full-range leadership development model.

3. Compare your responses to the two case studies. Are you consistent with your leadership style, or do you adopt a contingency approach to leadership by changing your leadership style based upon the circumstances?

Source: Cases adapted from Hersey, P., & Blanchard, K. H. (1988). *Management of organizational behavior: Utilizing human resources.* Englewood Cliffs, NJ: Prentice-Hall.

TOOLKIT ACTIVITY 6.2: Comparing Supervisor Leader–Member Exchange

Locate a manager who will complete the following form about three of their direct reports. He or she can indicate their followers by using initials, first names only, or even fabricated names. Ask the manager to think about *their relationship with the member(s) of their staff.* Then have them indicate the extent to which they disagree or agree with each statement using the 1 to 5 scale with respect to each of the staff listed by circling their answers.

Statement	Staff	Strongly Disagree	Disagree	Neutral	Agree	Strongly Agree
1. Regardless of how much power I built into my position, I would be personally inclined to use my power to help him/her solve problems in his/her work.	Name 1 Name 2 Name 3	1 1 1	2 2 2	3 3 3	4 4 4	5 5 5
2. I would be willing to "bail out" him/her, even at my own expense, if he/she really needed it.	Name 1 Name 2 Name 3	1 1 1	2 2 2	3 3 3	4 4 4	5 5 5
3. I think that I recognize his/her potential.	Name 1 Name 2 Name 3	1 1 1	2 2 2	3 3 3	4 4 4	5 5 5
4. I have enough confidence in him/her that I would defend and justify his/her decisions if he/she were not present to do so.	Name 1 Name 2 Name 3	1 1 1	2 2 2	3 3 3	4 4 4	5 5 5
5. I think that I understand his/her problems and needs.	Name 1 Name 2 Name 3	1 1 1	2 2 2	3 3 3	4 4 4	5 5 5

6.	I usually let him/her know where where he/she stands with me.	Name 1	1	2	3	4	5
		Name 2	1	2	3	4	5
		Name 3	1	2	3	4	5
7.	How would you describe your relationship with him/her?	Name 1	1	2	3	4	5
		Name 2	1	2	3	4	5
		Name 3	1	2	3	4	5

Source: Scandura, T. A., & Graen, G. B. (1984). The moderating effects of initial leader–member exchange status on the effects of a leadership intervention. *Journal of Applied Psychology, 69,* 428–436.

Discussion Questions

1. What patterns do you see in the working relationships that the manager rated? Did they rate everyone the same, or did they give higher scores (4s and 5s) to some followers? Followers with higher scores are the in-group.

2. Did your manager have any out-group members? If so, which questions indicated that they were in the out-group? Explain why the person was in the out-group. What do you think they could do to improve their working relationship with their boss?

3. Were all working relationships equally effective (question 7)? Follow up with the manager and ask them to tell you who they trust most to delegate work to.

CASE STUDY 6.1: Which Boss Would You Rather Work For?

José works for a transportation company in Miami. He works on the loading dock but has been taking business courses part time at a local community college. He was married recently and has a baby on the way. He is a good performer but is interested in moving up in the organization. He approached his boss, Kim, and asked how he could learn new skills that would prepare him for the next level, which would be a supervisory position with oversight of seven workers on the dock. His boss listened to his situation and asked questions regarding José's specific job-related interests and career plans. José told his boss that he had been taking courses, including an organizational behavior course in which he learned leadership skills. Kim was surprised since she didn't know that José was attending college and he never missed work. She promised to meet with the general manager and discuss José's increasing qualifications and interests. After discussion, management decided to pay for José's tuition but encouraged him to wait until he completed his bachelor's degree so that he could focus on building his management and leadership skills. They promised to consider him for a promotion when he completed his degree. José

was somewhat disappointed but was even more motivated to finish school and appreciated the tuition support. José became even more dedicated to his job and the organization. He became one of the best employees in the company and the informal leader of the dock workers. He proactively advocated and protected the reputation of the company outside the organization. For example, another worker was stealing from the boxes on the loading dock and José stopped him and reported it to Kim. Two years later, José completed his degree and the company held a party for him and his family celebrating his achievement. As promised, when a supervisor left the company, José was promoted into a management position. He always remembered Kim's encouragement and treated his followers the same way—by listening and supporting their goals.

Paula recently graduated from college with a bachelor's degree in accounting and landed her dream job as an accountant/analyst at a financial services company. Paula was excited about the new opportunity to showcase her skills and contribute to the company. On her first day, Paula arrived early to make a good impression. Her new boss, Jennifer, wasn't there to see her arrive early. When she did arrive, she breezed past Paula's cubicle without saying anything. Paula noticed that other people in the office acted the same way that Jennifer did. No one in the office acknowledged Paula's presence or introduced themselves to her. Paula thought that the cubicle environment was sterile. She had not seen it before starting the job since she had been interviewed in a conference room. Jennifer immediately put Paula to work, however. Her first assigned task was to prepare a bank reconciliation. She had completed a similar assignment in an accounting class, but this was somewhat different and more complex. Paula began working on it but reached a point where she needed help to finish it. She went to Jennifer for help, but Jennifer told her to figure it out by herself. She remarked, "I am so busy right now, I just don't have time to teach you what you should already know how to do." Paula was shocked at Jennifer's response and felt overwhelmed by her new job. She returned to her desk and continued to

work on the reconciliation, which took her 3 days to complete. Although she was proud of herself for completing it, she was still concerned that her boss wouldn't help her and began to doubt herself and whether she was qualified for the job. Over the next year that Paula worked for the company, Jennifer gave Paula low-level tasks that were not challenging and didn't provide any opportunities to learn. Also, Jennifer never provided Paula with feedback on her work. Paula received no training beyond the online orientation and videos on company policies required by corporate headquarters. As a result, Paula spent most of her days alone in her cubicle and even ate her lunch there, which she packed and brought from home. She did her job but put in minimal effort and spent her time looking for another job. Her first performance appraisal by Jennifer was mostly negative, and she was told that she didn't perform to standards and did not show initiative. After this appraisal, Paula took a job at another company for less money.

Discussion Questions

1. Compare the experiences of the two employees (José and Paula). Which boss would you rather work for? Why?

2. Think about the path–goal theory that was covered in this chapter and determine which leadership styles are exemplified in the two scenarios. Which ones should have been used?

3. What steps could Paula have taken to develop a higher-quality LMX relationship or "manage her boss" more effectively? Do you think this would have worked in this case?

4. What were the outcomes for each of the employees and companies in these two scenarios? Thinking about these outcomes, why is it important for organizations to have effective leaders?

SELF-ASSESSMENT 6.1: Mentoring Functions Questionnaire

Think of a person who is or has devoted special time and consideration to helping you with your career. Answer the following questions to determine the type(s) of mentoring you are receiving from this person. This person can be a boss, former boss, professor, former teacher, peer, or family member. Write your responses on the line to the left of the question. There are no right or wrong answers, and you do not have to share your results with others unless you wish to do so.

Statements	Strongly Disagree	Disagree	Neutral	Agree	Strongly Agree
1. My mentor takes a personal interest in my career.	1	2	3	4	5
2. My mentor helps me coordinate professional goals.	1	2	3	4	5
3. My mentor has devoted special time and consideration to my career.	1	2	3	4	5

4. I share personal problems with my mentor.	1	2	3	4	5
5. I exchange confidences with my mentor.	1	2	3	4	5
6. I consider my mentor to be a friend.	1	2	3	4	5
7. I try to model my behavior after my mentor.	1	2	3	4	5
8. I admire my mentor's ability to motivate others.	1	2	3	4	5
9. I respect my mentor's ability to teach others.	1	2	3	4	5

Scoring and Interpretation

You rated your mentoring on nine questions. Add the numbers you circled in each of the columns to derive your score for each dimension of mentoring. Then add your scores to determine your total mentoring score.

Career Development	Social Support	Role Modeling	Total Mentoring Score
1. _____	4. _____	7. _____	
2. _____	5. _____	8. _____	
3. _____	6. _____	9. _____	
Total _____ +	_____ +	_____ +	= _____

Discussion Questions

1. Which mentoring function was the highest? If it was role modeling, do you know this person? If not, can you create a relationship with them?

2. Career development mentoring has been most consistently related to career outcomes for mentees. Evaluate your score on this measure. What can you do to increase your career development mentoring?

3. Do you think your results would have been different if you had chosen a different person as your mentor? For example, if you chose a peer, would the results be different if you had chosen a boss or a professor? Explain.

Sources: Adapted from Pellegrini, E. K., & Scandura, T. A. (2005). Construct equivalence across groups: An unexplored issue in mentoring research. *Educational & Psychological Measurement, 37,* 264–279; Hu, C., Pellegrini, E. K., & Scandura, T. A. (2011). Measurement invariance in mentoring research: A cross-cultural examination across Taiwan and the U.S. *Journal of Vocational Behavior, 78,* 274–282.

SELF-ASSESSMENT 6.2: How Trustful Are You?

This self-assessment exercise identifies your propensity to trust others. The goal is for you to learn about yourself. There are no right or wrong answers, and this is not a test. You don't have to share your results with others unless you wish to do so.

Instructions: Circle the response that best describes your behavior.

Statements	Strongly Disagree	Disagree	Neutral	Agree	Strongly Agree
1. I usually give people the benefit of the doubt if they do something that seems selfish.	1	2	3	4	5
2. Most people can be counted on to do what they say they will do.	1	2	3	4	5
3. I tend to trust people I have just met.	1	2	3	4	5
	Strongly Agree	Agree	Neutral	Disagree	Strongly Disagree
4. People will take advantage of you if you are not paying attention.	1	2	3	4	5
5. Most people would tell a lie if they could gain by telling it.	1	2	3	4	5
6. I am typically cautious with people until they have proven they can be trusted.	1	2	3	4	5
7. Most people pretend to be more honest than they actually are.	1	2	3	4	5
	Strongly Disagree	Disagree	Neutral	Agree	Strongly Agree
8. In general, I believe that most people are trustworthy.	1	2	3	4	5

Scoring: Add your responses to the eight questions to compute your total propensity to trust others:

Question 1 ___ + 2 ___ + 3 ___ + 4 ___ + 5 ___ + 6 ___ + 7 ___ + 8 ___ = _____

Interpretation

Score

27–40   **Trusting.** You tend to trust all people in most situations you encounter, regardless of whether or not they have earned your trust. You believe that other people are honest most of the time.

14–26   **Cautious.** You are cautious about trusting others, and people often have to demonstrate that they are trustworthy before you trust them. You are guarded and don't believe everything you hear; you evaluate it.

Below 14   **Skeptic.** You generally don't trust other people and may not even trust them after they have proven trustworthy. You are skeptical and think that people lie a lot.

Discussion Questions

1. Evaluate your level of trust in general, considering at least two different situations in which you behaved in a way that is consistent with your overall range.

2. Are there some situations in which you are more trusting than others? Explain why you tend to trust more in certain circumstances.

3. Compare your trust assessment results with a classmate. Are your scores similar or different? If they are similar, discuss why you see things the same way. If they are different, discuss why you differ with respect to how much you trust other people.

Source: Adapted from Mayer, R. C., & Davis, J. H. (1999). The effect of the performance appraisal system on trust for management: A field quasi-experiment. *Journal of Applied Psychology, 84*(1), 123–136.

CHAPTER SEVEN

POWER AND POLITICS

Learning Objectives

After studying this chapter, you should be able to do the following:

7.1: Define *power* and *influence*, and provide an example of each.

7.2: Compare and contrast the five bases of power.

7.3: Demonstrate understanding of the three lines of power in organizations by providing examples.

7.4: Identify the most effective influence strategies.

7.5: Compare and contrast "minimizing bad" and "maximizing good" impression management strategies.

7.6: Define *perceptions of organizational politics* (POP) and evaluate the negative outcomes for employees having this perception.

7.7: Explain why political skill is important for a leader to be effective.

Get the edge on your studies at **edge.sagepub.com/scandura2e**

- Take the chapter quiz

- Review key terms with eFlashcards

- Explore multimedia resources, SAGE readings, and more!

WHAT IS IT LIKE TO HAVE POWER?

Researchers have long asked the question: "What is it like to have power?"[1] The research evidence shows that having power has strong effects on a person's thoughts (cognitions), affect (emotions and moods), and their behavior. A review of research summarized research findings on the effects of power on the person who holds it. Table 7.1 shows the results of this review. For example, a person's thoughts are changed, resulting in more optimism, risk taking, and confidence. However, those with a lot of power do not always consider the perspectives of other people and tend to rely on stereotypes of others. With respect to affect, they may have greater emotional displays (such as enthusiasm and pride). However, those in power may be less compassionate and unable to take the perspective of others. They lack empathy and cannot feel the suffering of others. They feel more distant than others. On the flip side, people who feel powerless express more discomfort and fear when asked to discuss controversial subject matter.[2] Organizational behavior (OB) researchers are particularly interested in the effects of power on behavior, and research has shown that power affects behaviors also. Powerful individuals are more likely to take action, pursue rewards, and initiate negotiations. However, they may also be corrupt and less likely to conform to norms. One study found that powerful individuals have been found to experience less guilt, even when they know that they are violating social norms,[3] and they are more likely to be good liars.[4] Another study found that having powerful individuals in a team harms team performance. When working together in groups, high power groups performed worse than did other groups; individuals who were randomly assigned power in an initial task were less creative.[5] Power affects us in our personal lives as well. An interesting study of consumer spending found that powerful individuals may be more selfish than others and spend more money on themselves.[6] In sum, this line of research clearly demonstrates that having power changes people. As you move up in the organization in your career, will power change you?

Table 7.1 Effects of Power on the Power Holder

Finding	Defining Property		
	Cognition	Affect	Behavior
Power influences emotional display		X	
Power promotes stereotypical social perceptions	X		
Powerful individuals are better at remembering individuating info	X		
High power promotes more touching behavior			X
High power participants are more likely to act			X
Power holders are more likely to approach rewarding outcomes			X
Power holders use stereotypes when they're relevant to the context	X		
Experiencing power increases optimism and risk-taking behavior	X	X	X
Power can reduce the taking of additional perspectives into account	X		
Power leads to global processing and prevents distraction by details	X		
Power increases perceptions of confidence	X		
Power induces a selective processing of information	X		
Power holders exhibit a greater propensity to initiate a negotiation			X
Power holders experience less compassion toward others' suffering		X	
Power promotes individuating and ease of information retrieval	X		
Power increases optimism and the perception of personal control	X	X	
Power is associated with rule-based moral thinking	X		
Power can increase perspective taking	X		
Power motivates self-regulation toward effective performance	X		
Powerful individuals spend more money on themselves			X
Power provides a reason to doubt the purity of others' favors	X	X	
High power individuals are more prone to being corrupt			X
High power individuals feel more distant from others	X	X	
Power holders demonstrate less nonnative behavior			X

Source: Adapted from Sturm, R. E., & Antonakis, J. (2015). Interpersonal power: A review, critique, and research agenda. *Journal of Management*, 41(1), 136–163.

POWER AND INFLUENCE

Learning Objective 7.1: Define *power* and *influence*, and provide an example of each.

Ana Guinote, author of a large-scale review of how power affects people, notes: "Power is admired and fought over by those who desire it and often feared by those who lack it. It is ubiquitous and affects the fate of many."[7] Decades ago, Bertrand Russell observed that "the fundamental concept in social science is Power, in the same sense in which Energy is the fundamental concept in physics."[8,9] It can be said that power is the other side of the leadership coin. Without power, leadership cannot be effective. If you think about it, leadership requires some form of deference to a leader: "If leadership involves actively influencing others, then followership involves allowing oneself to be influenced."[10] Yet leaders are reluctant to admit that they want power, and power and politics have been called the "last dirty words."[11] **Power** is defined as "having the discretion and the means to asymmetrically enforce one's will over others."[12] Nearly all definitions of leadership include the idea of influencing others, and power is the source of **influence**. A useful distinction between power and influence follows:[13]

Power is the *potential* of one person (or group) to influence another person or group. Some people have a lot of power but they don't need to actually exercise it. For example, a police officer sitting on the side of the interstate affects your behavior (and those ahead of you!). You remove your foot from the accelerator and slow down. It is the officer's potential power to write you a ticket and not the actual behavior of writing it that changes your behavior. This is important to keep in mind. You don't always have to demonstrate your power—if you attain a managerial position and have others who report to you, it is unspoken. Often, power is best executed when it is done so in a subtle manner. Influence, in turn, is the exercise of power to change the behavior, attitudes, and/or values of that individual or group.

Critical Thinking Question: What is the difference between power and influence? Provide an example of each.

Influence can, therefore, be thought of as *power in use*. We first discuss where power comes from followed by how power and influence are effectively used in organizations.

BASES OF POWER

Learning Objective 7.2: Compare and contrast the five bases of power.

Five bases of power in organizations have been described.[14] Some forms of power come with a person's position in the hierarchy: **position power**. Other power may come from the personal characteristics of the person and may have no relationship to their position in the organization: **personal power**. Position power includes the following:

- **Coercive power**—the ability to punish, and can include threats. For example, a supervisor threatens to write a memorandum to an employee's file for being late all the time.

- **Reward power**—the ability to provide incentives or other things valued, such as pay raises, bonuses, and promotions.[15] For example, an employee receives a merit pay increase.

- **Legitimate power**—the ability to make a request and get a response due to the nature of the roles between two people (e.g., boss and direct report, a favor-doer and a favor-recipient), it is based upon structural level in the organization and/or a feeling of obligation. For example, an employee completes a sales report for their boss, and such reports are in their job description.

While coercive power is on the list of bases of power, most leaders in organizations say that they rarely, if ever, use it. French and Raven warned that the use of coercion may result in employee resistance and other forms of dysfunctional behavior on the part of the follower. Another example of dysfunctional behavior is when followers talk badly about the boss behind his or her back. The personal sources of power are not tied to position but can be generated by anyone in the organization. They help explain why many people in organizations have a great deal of power although they don't have important-sounding titles and are not at the upper levels in the organizational hierarchy. These personal power sources are as follows:

- **Expert power**—the ability to influence others due to knowledge or a special skill set or expertise. For example, the information technology department has special skills to troubleshoot computer problems for a manager.

- **Referent power**—the ability to influence based upon others' identification with the individual and followers' desire to emulate them, it is based on liking, respect, and admiration. For example, volunteers work hard for a political candidate that they admire.

A study of college coaches found that expert power was most related to athletes' satisfaction with the coach, coaches' general influence, training effort, and the team's belief in their abilities (collective efficacy). Coaches' use of other bases of power had mixed results, however.[16] A study of Malaysian employees found that expert, referent, and reward power were positively related to satisfaction with the supervisor, but legitimate and coercive power were not.[17] A meta-analytic review[18] found that legitimate power exerts little influence on either job satisfaction or performance. Similarly, reward power does not significantly affect satisfaction, but it does have a positive influence on performance. In contrast, coercive power seems unrelated to performance but does negatively affect satisfaction. With regard to the personal power bases, referent power most strongly influences satisfaction, and expert power positively influences both satisfaction and performance.

As noted previously with respect to coercion, these power bases may result in different reactions from followers. Three possible outcomes of an influence attempt can be distinguished:[19]

- **Commitment**— also known as internalization; a strong effort made and enthusiastically carries out the request. Both attitudes and behaviors change.

- **Compliance**—willing to complete the request but does so in an apathetic manner giving minimal effort; only behavior changes.

- **Resistance**—opposed to the request and refuses to do it. They may explain why they can't complete it, try to change it, get superiors to change it, delay it, or even sabotage the task by doing it wrong; no change in attitude or behavior toward the request.

Figure 7.1 summarizes the bases of power and shows the likely responses from followers. Coercive power may be met with resistance, but referent power, in contrast, may result in commitment to the leader's vision. Compliance can be expected from legitimate power and the ability of the leader to reward followers for their work. Expertise may also result in compliance, but it is higher than legitimate power since some may admire expertise and it may have some impact on commitment. The figure also depicts another important concept with respect to power: the **zone of indifference**.[20]

There exists a "zone of indifference" in each individual within which orders are acceptable without conscious questioning of their authority. . . . The zone of indifference will be wider or narrower depending upon the degree to which the inducements exceed the burdens and sacrifices which determine the individual's

Figure 7.1 Bases of Power and Follower Responses

Follower Engagement Level	Power Base Used (Follower Response)	Follower Reaction to Directives
Commitment	Referent "I admire you"	High motivation and performance
	Expert "I need your help"	
Compliance	Legitimate "It's my job"	"Zone of indifference"
	Reward "I'm in it for the money"	
Resistance	Coercive "I resent being treated this way"	Low performance and sabotage

Sources: French, J. R. P., & Raven, B. (1960). The bases of social power. In D. Cartwright & A. Zander (Eds.), *Group dynamics* (2nd ed., pp. 607–623). New York, NY: Harper & Row; Barnard, C. (1938). *Functions of the executive.* Cambridge, MA: Harvard University Press.

adhesion to the organization. It follows that the range of orders that will be accepted will be very limited among those who are barely induced to contribute to the system.

As shown in Figure 7.1, the zone of indifference falls between reward power and expert power, and is centered on legitimate power. In most cases, followers will comply with directions from leaders because they fall within the zone in which they are indifferent. Followers become dissatisfied and resist when coercive tactics are employed. However, working within the zone does not produce high levels of commitment or engagement, which are now needed for organizations to function most effectively. To gain high levels of engagement and commitment, the leader should develop and use expert power at a minimum and try to develop referent power through being a positive role model and getting followers to respond in an emotionally positive way to his or her influence. For example, a new graduate negotiates his salary when offered employment by a consulting company. At the outset, the graduate focuses on long-term financial benefits. But after the graduate is hired, he begins to become more committed to the mission of the consulting firm and admires his mentors. Over time, pay becomes less important, and he makes sacrifices by working long hours for the company.

ORGANIZATIONAL SOURCES OF POWER

Learning Objective 7.3: Demonstrate understanding of the three lines of power in organizations by providing examples.

Power is based on how much people depend upon others for necessary resources.[21] A leader's control over resources has been linked with follower perceptions of their power and outcomes of more hope and lower turnover.[22] Rosabeth Moss Kanter described power as a property of organizational systems rather than individuals.[23] She presented the following **three "lines" of power** for leaders in organizations to tap into to gain productive power:

RESEARCH IN ACTION

Can Power Make Followers Speechless?

A series of laboratory experiments was conducted to examine the impact of how much the formal leader of a group talks on the reactions of team members. MBA students were assigned to work on a leadership simulation. The first experiment showed that leaders who felt powerful were more likely to verbally dominate discussions, and this decreased perceptions of their openness. As a result, team performance was lower. The second experiment replicated these findings and further demonstrated the important role of team members' reactions to leaders' behavior. Specifically, although subjective feelings of power increased leaders' autocratic tendencies, their formal role determined team members' willingness to give in to them. The third experiment replicated the findings from Studies 1 and 2 with respect to formal leaders. This study also found that teams with powerful formal leaders reported higher levels of their leader talking, lower team open communication, and lower team performance. This only occurred when leaders were not reminded of how important their team member input was for success. When leaders were reminded that all team members had the potential to contribute to team success, these effects did not emerge. These findings show that a leaders' awareness of the importance of their team members motivates them to overcome their tendency to discount others' perspectives and input. In other words, the negative effect of power on team open communication is eliminated. A summary of these research findings is shown in Figure 7.2.

Figure 7.2 Power and Talking Affects Team Communication and Performance

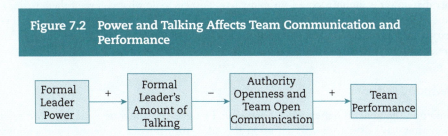

Discussion Questions:

1. Why do you think that being assigned as a formal leader results in the person dominating team discussions?
2. Have you ever held back communication in a team when the leader behaved autocratically? Explain why the leader's amount of talking suppresses team members' open communication.
3. How can organizations implement the idea that reminding a leader of the importance of team open communication is important for team performance?

Source: Tost, L. P., Gino, F., & Larrick, R. P. (2013). When power makes others speechless: The negative impact of leader power on team performance. *Academy of Management Journal*, 56(5), 1465–1486.

1. **Lines of supply.** Leaders bring in the things that their group needs, such as materials, money, and resources such as rewards and even prestige.

2. **Lines of information.** Leaders need to know what is happening in the organization that may affect their group's goals. Having access to information from all areas of the organization is an important source of power. Also, knowing who to share information with (and not share it with) is an essential skill that leaders need to develop.

3. **Lines of support.** A leader needs to be able to innovate to have an impact on the organization. He or she needs support that allows for risk taking beyond typical organizational routines. Leaders also often need the backing of other influential managers in the organization to get things done.

Structural power comes from a person's position and the communication networks they are in. This view of power suggests that sometimes power arises from "being in the right place at the right time." Organizational sources of power result in part from being in a position of authority within an organizational hierarchy.[24] For example, a leader may be in a place to resolve uncertainty for the organization or bargain across departments, which may also result in being powerful. For example, purchasing agents may have a great deal of power because they operate between engineering, production scheduling, and marketing within the organization and outside vendors. They can use their position to influence other departments and gain preferential treatment in exchange for expedited purchasing orders.[25] Also, a person's position in an organization determines with whom they communicate and what information they have access to. These sources of power exist in organizations regardless of one's individual personality or leadership style.[26] That being said, some people are more adept at using influence strategies to attain their goals than others. A clever person might even be able to generate sources of power, including supply, information, and support.

Remember that power is simply a stored-up ability to get others to do what you want them to do, and that some power will come from the position you have in the organizational hierarchy. However, what happens if you don't have formal authority over another person and you need them to commit to your goals? Research on influence without authority addresses this important question.

Influence Without Authority

Power is based upon the general dependence postulate: The greater someone depends upon another person, the more power they have over them. Based upon this idea, to influence someone over whom you have no formal authority, you need to assess whether and how much they may depend upon you.[27] A model of *influence without authority* can be used in wide variety of situations.[28] The model is based upon the **law of reciprocity** first articulated by Gouldner: the nearly universal belief that if someone does something for you, they should be paid back.[29] The influence without authority process is depicted in Figure 7.3. It begins with assuming the other person is your ally and wants to exchange with you. You need to be clear about what your goals are and then understand the other person's situation (showing empathy). Then you identify what you have to exchange (i.e., the currencies) and what you need from them. Dependence is created when you control resources that are important, scarce, and cannot be substituted by others.[30] Examples of such resources are support, loyalty, and extra effort on the job. In their model, Cohen and Bradford call these resources the "currencies of exchange," and others include supporting the vision, gaining additional resources, providing visibility, giving personal support, and showing gratitude. It is important to assess the quality of the relationship (if it is a supervisor, you can use the

> Critical Thinking Questions: Do you think the "influence without authority" approach contains risks? If not, why? If so, what are they?

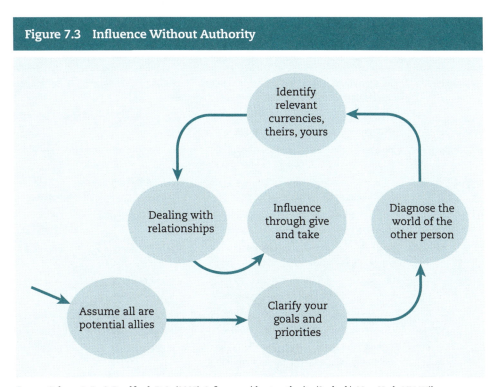

Figure 7.3 Influence Without Authority

Identify relevant currencies, theirs, yours

Dealing with relationships

Influence through give and take

Diagnose the world of the other person

Assume all are potential allies

Clarify your goals and priorities

Source: Cohen, A. R., & Bradford, D. L. (2005). *Influence without authority* (2nd ed.). New York, NY: Wiley.

LMX7 measure from Chapter 6 to assess relationship quality). Finally, influence the person and emphasize the give-and-take as shown in the figure.

Next, we turn to more research evidence on how power is used in organizations and the specific strategies (tactics) that have been shown to work (and those that don't).

INFLUENCE STRATEGIES

Learning Objective 7.4: Identify the most effective influence strategies.

Social influence is one of the oldest experimental topics in the behavioral sciences, dating back to Triplett's[31] investigation of how cyclists become more competitive in the presence of other cyclists—their behavior changed compared to when they rode alone.[32] Much more recently, Gary Yukl presented a typology of **proactive influence tactics** based upon his decades of research. While other typologies exist,[33] Yukl's typology is comprehensive and has been researched employing a wide variety of research methods including "critical incidents, diaries, questionnaires, experiments, and scenarios."[34] He and his colleagues developed an assessment for use in research called the Influence Behavior Questionnaire.[35,36] These tactics may be used alone or in combinations, and some are more effective than others.[37] Research has also shown that there are cross-cultural differences in perceptions of the effectiveness of influence tactics.[38] For example, U.S. managers prefer rational persuasion, whereas Chinese managers prefer coalitions.[39] In all cases, a careful diagnosis of the person you are trying to influence and the situation is necessary. These tactics are shown in Table 7.2.

Table 7.2　Proactive Influence Tactics

Tactic	Definition
Rational persuasion	The agent uses logical arguments and factual evidence to show a proposal or request is feasible and relevant for attaining important task objectives.
Apprising	The agent explains how carrying out a request or supporting a proposal will benefit the target personally or help advance the target person's career.
Inspirational appeals	The agent makes an appeal to values and ideals or seeks to arouse the target person's emotions to gain commitment for a request or proposal.
Consultation	The agent encourages the target to suggest improvements in a proposal or to help plan an activity or change for which the target person's support and assistance are desired.
Collaboration	The agent offers to provide relevant resources and assistance if the target will carry out a request or approves a proposed change.
Ingratiation	The agent uses praise and flattery before or during an influence attempt or expresses confidence in the target's ability to carry out a difficult request.
Personal appeals	The agent asks the target to carry out a request or support a proposal out of friendship or asks for a personal favor before saying what it is.
Exchange	The agent offers an incentive, suggests an exchange of favors, or indicates willingness to reciprocate at a later time if the target will do what the agent requests.
Coalition tactics	The agent seeks the aid of others to persuade the target to do something or uses the support of others as a reason for the target to agree.
Legitimating tactics	The agent seeks to establish the legitimacy of a request or to verify authority to make it by referring to rules, policies, contracts, or precedent.
Pressure	The agent uses demands, threats, frequent checking, or persistent reminders to influence the target to carry out a request.

Source: Yukl, G. (2013). *Leadership in organizations* (6th ed.). Boston, MA: Pearson.

Which Influence Strategies Are the Most Effective?

So what does research show with respect to which tactics work and with whom? As noted earlier, followers may respond to an influence attempt with commitment, compliance, or resistance. OB research has demonstrated that the different influence strategies used have different reactions from followers and other targets of influence.[40,41,42]

Rational persuasion is a tactic commonly employed by leaders, and it is very effective—particularly if the leader is viewed as an expert. Apprising involves persuading the target of influence that complying will advance his or her career. It is more likely to be used with peers or followers than with the boss. Inspirational appeals try to arouse followers' emotions and can work with all targets of influence. It may be particularly useful during times of organizational change. Consultation invites the person to be involved with a proposed idea and may be used in any direction as well. It may be particularly effective with peers in cross-functional teams, for example. Exchange is based on the quid pro quo in organizational life. It may be direct or indirect, but it will involve the idea that the exchange of favors will occur between the parties. This tactic has been shown to be more effective with peers than with bosses. Collaboration is an offer to provide assistance or resources to the person being asked to do something. It is used least with superiors in the organization but can be very effective with peers and followers.

Ingratiation is compliment-giving or acting deferential. This tactic must be used with caution because if it is overdone or comes across as insincere, it can fail entirely. Personal appeals are based on friendship or loyalty and may be more appropriate with a peer or someone outside the organization than with bosses or subordinates. Asking someone to do something based on a personal friendship may be a risky strategy. Legitimating tactics remind the target of their role in the organization in relation to the person making the request—for example, "I am asking you to do this because it is your job." This works with followers better than other targets. Pressure tactics are threats and relate to coercion. For this reason, pressure tactics should be used sparingly—even with followers, where they are most commonly found. Finally, coalition tactics involve gaining the support of others. They are more likely to be used with peers or bosses, but the idea is that there is "strength in numbers" and should be used carefully, especially with supervisors or those higher in the organization. A meta-analysis of 8,987 respondents[43] examined the impact of influence tactics and task (e.g., performance) and relationship outcomes (e.g., trust). Rational persuasion, inspirational appeal, apprising, collaboration, ingratiation, and consultation were positively related to both task and relationship effectiveness. Pressure was negatively related to both outcomes. Rational persuasion is the only tactic that held stable positive relationships with both task and relationship outcomes.

Ingratiation is an influence tactic in which flattery is used to create a favorable impression, but are there other ways to change the way others see you? Research on impression management addresses this question, and the next sections addresses how people manage impressions of others in organizational settings.

IMPRESSION MANAGEMENT

Learning Objective 7.5: Compare and contrast "minimizing bad" and "maximizing good" impression management strategies.

People in organizations care about what others think about them. Social psychologists have researched self-presentation and the motivations that people have to present themselves in a positive way to others.[44] Impression management is a set of behaviors that people use to protect their self-image or change the way they are seen by others (or both).[45,46,47] People are motivated to manage impressions for three reasons: the relevance of the goal of the impressions, the value of these goals, and the difference between their desired and current image. For example, a person is motivated to manage impressions when they see their image as important for achieving a goal, such as a promotion or pay raise. Research has also shown that when people feel there is a discrepancy between the way they hope to be seen and how they are currently seen, they are more motivated to manage impressions. For example, if an employee thinks they are not liked by their coworkers, they may begin to compliment them (ingratiation).[48] It is important to keep in mind that impression management may be an inauthentic representation of the self, so it's important not to be seen as insincere when engaging in these behaviors.[49] Research has found that when presenters engaged in internal self-enhancement they were viewed as immoral, unintelligent, and unfriendly.[50]

Impression management has been shown to affect interviews, performance appraisals, and career success.[51] A wide range of impression management tactics have been studied, and there are two different goals for using them. One goal is to use them defensively to avoid blame for poor performance or ask for forgiveness ("minimizing bad"), and the other goal is to generate respect and liking from other people ("maximizing good").[52] This view of impression management includes these maximizing good tactics: self-promotion, whereby individuals point out their abilities or accomplishments in order to be seen as competent by observers; ingratiation, whereby individuals do favors or use flattery to elicit an attribution of likability from observers; and exemplification, whereby people self-sacrifice or go above and beyond the call of duty in order to gain the attribution of dedication from observers. The minimizing bad tactics include: intimidation, where people signal their power or potential to punish in order to be seen as dangerous by

Table 7.3 Examples of Impression Management Strategies

Goal	Strategy	Example
Minimizing bad	Apologies	Saying you are sorry when you violate a coworker's trust
	Excuses	Not taking responsibility for your failures
	Justifications	Blaming poor performance on another department's failure to respond
Maximizing good	Exemplification	Trying to appear busy, even when things are slower at work
	Ingratiation	Using flattery to make your coworkers like you more
	Self-Promotion	Hanging your diplomas on your office wall so that people are aware of your accomplishments

Sources: Adapted from Bolino, M. C., Kacmar, K. M, Turnley, W. H., & Gilstrap, J. B. (2008). A multi-level review of impression management motives and behaviors. *Journal of Management, 34*(6), 1080–1109.

Critical Thinking Questions: Do you think that impression management strategies are ethical? Why or why not? Can you think of situations where these tactics could be abused?

---

observers; and **supplication**, where individuals advertise their weaknesses or shortcomings in order to elicit an attribution of being needy from observers.[53] For example, supplication would be telling your team members that you didn't do well in statistics courses to elicit their help on a team project. This is an example of trying to influence teammates to see you as needing help. An example of "maximizing good" is exemplification in which a person stays late at work so that others know they are a hard-working employee. This approach was later modified by researchers, and Table 7.3 shows examples of impression management strategies in which some additional "minimizing bad" tactics were added, such as apologies, excuses, and justifications.[54] Impression management strategies have been found to be job-focused (e.g., exemplification), supervisor-focused (e.g., ingratiation), or self-focused (e.g., self-promotion).[55] Despite the large number of impression management tactics discovered, the strategies most relevant for leaders are the ones that maximize good intentions: exemplification, ingratiation, and self-promotion.[56] In Self-Assessment 7.1 at the end of this chapter, you can learn the degree to which you would use some of the "maximizing good" impression management strategies.

Managing Impressions With Body Language

Making direct eye contact and having a relaxed facial expression predict whether a person is viewed as having power.[57] Recent research by Amy Cuddy and her colleagues has indicated a person's body language is also an important aspect of impression management. For example, holding an expansive posture may make a person feel more confident and, in turn, influences how they are perceived by others.[58] For example, think about the stance of Wonder Woman with her arms on her hips and legs planted firmly apart. In the research, "power poses" were not superhero stances but were expansive—either sitting with one's arms behind the head and legs up on a table or leaning forward on a table with arms spread apart. Another example of powerful body language is extending one's hand with the palm down for a handshake. This communicates dominance. Examples of the power poses used in this research are shown in Figure 7.4. The researchers conducted experiments in which subjects were asked to hold a power pose for 2 minutes. Following the power pose, subjects self-rated themselves higher on how powerful they felt (compared to subjects that held low poses) and were more likely to take risks in a gambling task.[59] Another study found that subjects who did the power poses prior to a job interview did better and were more likely to be hired.[60] These subjects were asked to stand with their hands on their hips and feet apart for about 5 minutes while they prepared

Figure 7.4   Power Poses

Source: Carney, D. R., Cuddy, A. J. C., & Yap, A. J. 2010. Power posing: Brief nonverbal displays affect neuroendocrine levels and risk tolerance. *Psychological Science,* 21(10), 1363–1368.

for an interview (i.e., the Wonder Woman pose). A meta-analysis of 55 studies found that power posing appears to be related to feelings of power, including emotions, affect, mood, and evaluations, attitudes, and feelings about the self.[61] According to Cuddy, "poses are powerful . . . it's about becoming so comfortable and feeling you have so much control over how you present yourself that you become more your authentic self."[62]

This discussion suggests that exercising power and influence effectively requires both planning and skill. OB research has identified three important political skills: Leaders need to understand the perceptions of organizational politics, have **political skill**, and must use power ethically (see the boxed insert for specific guidelines to help in making ethical decisions regarding the use of power). The next section describes organizational political skills and how you can develop your leadership through political acumen.

BEST PRACTICES

Power and Ethics: Making Tough Choices

Perhaps the most important point about the use of influence in organizations is the ethical use of power and politics for leaders. We only need to think of the scandal where a Manhattan jury found Dennis Kozlowski and Mark Swartz guilty of stealing more than $150 million from Tyco through fraud in the sale of company shares and falsification of company records. Leaders must apply ethical tests to every action they take in the organization using the tactics in this chapter. *How Good People Make Tough Choices* provides a nine-step checklist you may use to determine if they are being ethical in their dealings with others:[63]

1. Recognize that there is a moral issue.
2. Determine the actor (and the players) in the issue.
3. Gather the facts.
4. Test for right vs. wrong: four tests.
   - Is it legal?
   - Does it feel right at the gut level?
   - Would you want to see this on the front page?
   - What would your mother/family think?
5. Test for right vs. right (when both options seem moral): e.g., truth vs. loyalty (hard decisions).
6. Apply the appropriate ethical principles (e.g., utilitarian, rights, justice).

(Continued)

(Continued)

7. Is there a third way through the dilemma?
8. Make the decision.

9. Revisit and reflect.

Discussion Questions

1. Provide an example of the utilitarian approach in organizations (think of a decision that does the most good for the most people).
2. How does the utilitarian approach in your example differ from focusing on individual rights? What

would you do differently if focusing on individual rights?
3. What approach do you think most leaders use in practice?

Source: Kidder, R. M. (2003). *How good people make tough choices: Resolving the dilemmas of ethical living.* New York, NY: HarperCollins.

PERCEPTIONS OF ORGANIZATIONAL POLITICS

Learning Objective 7.6: Define *perceptions of organizational politics* (POP) and evaluate the negative outcomes for employees having this perception.

Organizational politics have been defined as unsanctioned influence attempts that seek to promote self-interest at the expense of organizational goals.[64,65] Behaving politically is not prescribed in an employee's job description or formal role, but people engage in these behaviors to gain advantage over others.[66] Research has shown that employees vary in the degree to which they perceive behaviors of others as constituting organizational politics as being self-serving and at the expense of others. Negative political behaviors are a pressing problem for organizations and can create "corrosive political climates."[67] **Perceptions of organizational politics (POP)** is defined as an individual's subjective appraisal of the extent to which the work environment is characterized as self-serving of various individuals and groups, to the detriment or at the cost of other individuals or groups.[68] This is an employee's perceptual evaluation of a behavior as being political, and this may or may not reflect reality. POP consists of *general political behavior,* which includes the behaviors of individuals who act in a self-serving manner to obtain valued outcomes; *going along to get ahead,* which consists of a lack of action by individuals (e.g., remain silent) in order to secure valued outcomes; and *pay and promotion policies,* which involves the organization behaving politically through the policies it enacts.[69] Sometimes it can be difficult to determine whether or not a given behavior is political—Toolkit Activity 7.1 will allow you to assess how you might react to a political situation in an organization.

How would you answer the following?

1. People in this organization attempt to build themselves up by tearing others down.

2. There has always been an influential group in this department that no one ever crosses.

3. Agreeing with powerful others is the best alternative in this organization.

4. Telling others what they want to hear is sometimes better than telling the truth.

5. Favoritism, rather than merit, determines who gets good raises and promotions around here.

6. Inconsistent with organizational policies, promotions in this organization generally do not go to top performers.[70]

These questions are taken from the measure used to assess POP. If you found yourself agreeing or strongly agreeing with these questions, you view your organization as having a great deal of organizational politics. The first two questions are general political behavior, the second two questions are going along to get ahead, and the last two questions are pay and promotion policies. These perceptions of organizational politics have been associated with decreased job satisfaction, increased anxiety and stress, increased turnover, and reduced performance.[71] These results have been shown to be consistent over the past 30 years of research. A meta-analytic study[72] found POP has strong negative relationships with job satisfaction and organizational commitment. However, POP had moderately positive relationships with job stress and turnover intentions. There was no relationship between POP and job performance. A second meta-analysis involving a larger sample of 44,560 participants found that POP is positively related to stress, burnout, turnover intentions, and counterproductive work behavior, and negatively related to job satisfaction, citizenship behavior, and job performance.[73]

Research has identified some potential causes of POP including job ambiguity, scarcity of resources, and a poor trust climate.[74] Other causes include highly centralized decision making, lack of formality in procedures, and low procedural justice (unfairness). In addition, career-related events such as lack of advancement opportunities may trigger POP. Mistrust in management and low leader-member exchange (LMX, described in Chapter 6) also influence POP. In other words, out-group members are more likely to view the work environment as being political. Personality factors such as having a high Mach personality (see Chapter 2 for discussion of the Mach personality) and negative affect (see Chapter 2 for discussion of negative affect) influence POP. [75,76,77,78] A summary of these factors and the outcomes of POP is shown in Figure 7.5. Research has shown that the job/work context factors have the most influence on POP (i.e., things like the lack of career opportunities and development, mistrust, and low LMX).[79] As the figure shows, POP is related to job anxiety (stress), lower job satisfaction, increased turnover, and lower job performance, as the meta-analytic studies reviewed have shown. However, how much control a person has over their work and understanding of what is happening in the organization reduces the effects of POP on stress and job satisfaction.[80] It is important for a leader to build effective working relationships with all of the members of their work group and be fair to avoid the emergence of POP. As Chapter 6 discusses, trust really matters in organizations, and POP is yet another outcome of the lack of trust in management.

Organizational politics can bring out the "dark side" of power. You have probably heard of Bernard Madoff, who almost always tops the list of leaders who have abused their power. Madoff ran an investment securities firm that delivered high percentage returns over a long period of time. But a lot of people were suspicious of Madoff's ability to deliver such returns compared to the markets. It turns out that he ran a $50 billion Ponzi scheme that, when discovered, ruined the life savings of many people. It's not yet clear how many people at Bernard L. Madoff Investment Securities knew of the scam, but it's clear that Madoff was the mastermind.[81] He was clearly a Machiavellian personality, and his company lacked the formal checks and balances that would have uncovered the scandal sooner. The Madoff example shows how a leader's abuse of power becomes political and unethical.

Another influence on POP is unethical leader behavior. A study of 136 pairs of matched leaders and followers found that when ethical leadership is lacking, there may be increased POP. This study also found that political skill reduced the negative effects of POP on the helping behaviors and how promotable followers were seen by supervisors.[82] Political acumen may mitigate the perceptions that behaviors are politically self-serving. Next, we turn to research on political skill.

Figure 7.5   Influences on Perceptions of Organizational Politics

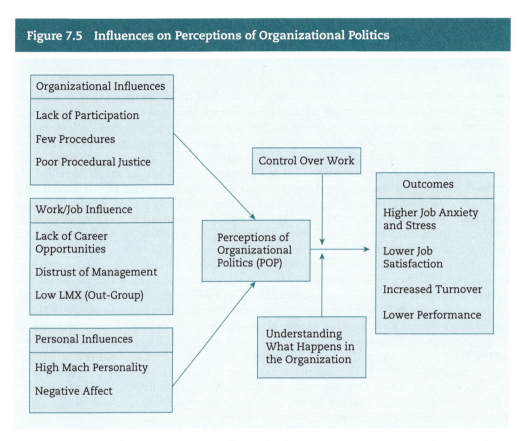

Source: Adapted from Atinc, G., Darrat, M., Fuller, B., & Parker, B. W. (2010). Perceptions of organizational politics: A meta-analysis of theoretical antecedents. *Journal of Managerial Issues*, 494–513; Ferris, G. R., Perrewé, P. L., Daniels, S. R., Lawong, D., & Holmes, J. J. (2016). Social influence and politics in organizational research: What we know and what we need to know. *Journal of Leadership & Organizational Studies, 24*(1), 5–19.

POLITICAL SKILL

Learning Objective 7.7: Explain why political skill is important for a leader to be effective.

The power bases and influence tactics described in this chapter may be viewed by others in an organization as political. Political skill has been defined as follows:

The ability to effectively understand others at work, and to use such knowledge to influence others to act in ways that enhance one's personal and/or organizational objectives.[83]

Political skills are comprised of four sets of behaviors. First, *networking ability* is the ability to create a diverse constellation of contacts both inside and outside of the organization. Second, *social astuteness* is being able to accurately interpret the behavior of others through attentive observation. Third, *interpersonal influence* is having the ability to adapt influence strategies to different situations. Fourth, *apparent sincerity* is appearing to others as genuine and honest.[84] The Toolkit Self-Assessment 7.2 at the end of this chapter contains a self-assessment that you can complete to assess your political acumen with respect to these four behaviors.

A meta-analysis of 120 unique samples[85] found that political skill is positively related to self-efficacy, job satisfaction, organizational commitment, work productivity, organizational citizenship behavior, career success, and personal reputation. In this study, political skill was also found to be negatively related to stress due to physiological strain. Employees higher in political skill benefit when leaders have in-groups and out-groups. Politically skilled employees reap the benefits of in- and out-groups since they enjoy higher LMX and relative (i.e., to their peers) LMX quality. Those with political skills are also rated higher by their supervisors with respect to job performance and organizational citizenship.[86] Research has shown that political skill increases the effectiveness of impression management. Individuals who are high in political skill have the ability to create better supervisor impressions when they use impression management. However, individuals who engage in high levels of impression management are viewed less favorably when they are low in political skill. If lacking political skill, a person should avoid using impression management tactics.[87]

Having Both the Will and the Skill for Politics

Research shows that individuals need to have the "will" as well as the "skill" for political acumen. Being proactive combined with political skill was most related to career satisfaction in a recent study.[88] Research has demonstrated how "will" and "skill" combine: Having a strong power motive is related to being viewed as a formal leader in a group, but political skill is related to higher perceptions of leadership performance.[89] The relationship between will and skill is now considered to be more complex and can best be described as an inverted U-shaped relationship between will and job performance. In other words, having the will to use political skills will improve job performance—to a point. However, the will can go too far because if a person engages in too much political activity, it may actually harm their job performance.[90]

This relationship is shown in Figure 7.6. For example, if a leader constantly displays apparent sincerity, people may begin to question whether or not they are genuine. Or the leader may switch their influence style so often that they appear inconsistent to others. So scholars in the area of political skill offer a word of caution: It is important not to take your will and political skill behaviors to extremes.

To mitigate the negative outcomes associated with perceptions of political behavior, there are two main approaches. The first is to develop political skill, and the second is to consider the ethical implications of organizational politics. Political skill is the first tool essential for making all of the tactics described in this chapter work. The second approach to mitigate the negative impact of perceptions of politics is to ask whether the use of power, influence, and/or political skill in an organization to obtain outcomes that you prefer is ethical. It may depend,

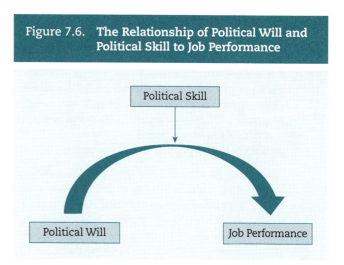

Figure 7.6. The Relationship of Political Will and Political Skill to Job Performance

Political Skill

Political Will

Job Performance

Source: Adapted from Harris, J. N., Maher, L. P., & Ferris, G. R. (2016). The roles of political skill and political will in job performance prediction: A moderated nonlinear perspective. In E. Vigoda-Gadot & A. Drory (Eds.), *Handbook of organizational politics: Looking back and to the future* (pp. 15–39). Northampton, MA: Edward-Elgar. (p. 27.)

Critical Thinking Question: In addition to the goals and objectives of an influence attempt, what are other ethical concerns regarding the use of political skills in organizations? Develop an example of a leader taking political skills too far and being seen as dishonest or not genuine.

in part, on the goals and objectives being pursued. However, the ends don't justify the means. It is also important to treat others ethically and fairly.

LEADERSHIP IMPLICATIONS: MANAGING WITH POWER

An effective leader needs to understand the difference between power and influence. Based upon the research evidence presented in this chapter, it is important to recognize that there are structural as well as personal sources of power. Every leadership position will have some positional sources of power due to location in the organizational hierarchy. By virtue of position, a leader will also have access to information through communication networks (communication systems are discussed in Chapter 12 of this textbook). Generating power and storing it for future use is important. The skillful leader understands how to use this stored power to get things done and solve problems in the organization. Jeffrey Pfeffer of Stanford University, an expert on power in organizations and author of the best-selling book *Managing With Power*, offers the following guidelines for managing with power[91] (with notes on how the guidelines relate to the updated research covered in this chapter).

1. Recognize that every organization has varying interests, and the leader needs to first diagnose the political landscape. Understand these interests and whom they belong to. Perceptions are not necessarily reality, but they do influence thoughts, feelings, and behaviors. Understand that perceptions of politics matter and affect employees' satisfaction, performance, and stress levels. Develop political acumen by understanding that political skill can be learned and may reduce the perceptions of politics in the organization.

2. Figure out what point of view various individuals and units have on issues of concern to the leader. The secret to success is to get those who hold different views from your own on board with what we need and want them to do. In general, the personal sources of power (expert and referent) get the most positive responses from people in organizations. However, reward power can also be used effectively.

3. Understand that to get things done, you need power—so you need to understand where power comes from and how the sources of power can be developed. Be willing to do things that build your sources of power. Know that power comes from position as well as individual personality and leadership style. Develop strategies for "maximizing good" impression management, as well as effective use of body language to convey that you have power. Assess whether you have the "will" to demonstrate political "skill" but be careful not to take political skills to an extreme or you may be viewed as a fake.

4. Understand the strategies and influence tactics through which power is developed and used in organizations. These include influence strategies discussed in this chapter, but also the timing, the use of structure, and the social psychology of commitment. This requires an understanding that the target of your influence strategies may respond with commitment, compliance, or resistance. As shown in this chapter, there is a zone of indifference, where compliance may be gained by making legitimate requests. However, the most effective response is commitment, where the target of your influence attempt internalizes your goals and responds by changing both their attitude and behavior.

Effective leaders use power, influence, and politics to get things done. It is part of every manager's job to generate and use power. This chapter opens with a discussion of how power changes people, so as you advance to higher levels in an organization, be mindful of the impact that being more powerful is having on your thoughts, feelings, and behaviors. Having political skills can have positive outcomes for a leader personally as well as benefitting their organization. Political skills may reduce negative perceptions of politics. The relationships of political skills to career satisfaction, job satisfaction, and performance have been established, but be careful not to take them to an extreme. Remember that it is important to influence others ethically. A nine-step checklist has been provided for a leader to check all influence attempts to ensure they follow ethical guidelines. This chapter highlights the importance of using power, influence, and politics in an ethical way.

edge.sagepub.com/scandura2e

Want a better grade? Go to **edge.sagepub.com/scandura2e** for the tools you need to sharpen your study skills.

KEY TERMS

apprising, 168
coalition tactics, 169
coercive power, 162
collaboration, 168
commitment, 163
compliance, 163
consultation, 168
exchange, 168
exemplification, 169
expert power, 163
impression management, 169
influence, 162

ingratiation, 169
inspirational appeals, 168
intimidation, 169
law of reciprocity, 166
legitimate power, 162
legitimating tactics, 169
organizational politics, 172
perceptions of organizational
    politics (POP), 172
personal appeals, 169
personal power, 162
political skill, 171

position power, 162
power, 162
pressure tactics, 169
proactive influence tactics, 167
rational persuasion, 168
referent power, 163
resistance, 163
reward power, 162
self-promotion, 169
supplication, 170
three "lines" of power, 164
zone of indifference, 163

TOOLKIT ACTIVITY 7.1: Politics or Citizenship?

Instructions

Put yourself in the situation described in this scenario and then answer the questions that follow:

Smitheson & Company was founded in 1989 in a small Chicago suburb. Since its creation, the company has grown from a small printing company to a midsized printing and distribution enterprise that provides services to corporate customers as well as to private individuals. Smitheson & Co. presently employs 51 individuals. The company is set up so that there is one supervisor in charge of the employees in each of three departments: design, printing, and sales/distribution. Each of the three supervisors report directly to the president of the company.

Most people who work as Smitheson would agree that it is the kind of work environment where it is important to find out right away which people can help you get ahead and which people not to cross. Even for people who aren't the hardest workers, trying to impress the boss seems to be beneficial in terms of getting promotions and pay raises. All in all, it's the kind of place where it is more important to impress the boss than to be the best at doing your job. Smitheson supervisors do not use a formal system to evaluate their employees' performance: Pay raises and promotions are rewarded every year in December based on managers' informal assessments of "employees' contributions."

You have worked at Smitheson for the past 2 years in the printing department as a "printing worker." There are 15 other people who also work in the printing department under Cory, the printing supervisor. You enjoy your job on most days, mostly because of your fascination with the printing process and the enjoyment you get from mastering the operation of the various machines. Your job involves four main work tasks: Consulting with the design department, preparing for printing (choosing materials and programming machines), printing itself, and inspection. At the beginning of each workday, each of the employees in the department is given a list of the projects that they are expected to complete that day.

Kris is another employee who works in the printing department and was hired at about the same time you were. Kris is an average performer; in fact, you would guess that the quality of Kris's work is about the same as yours. Even though it's not required, Kris has attended and made suggestions at three company workforce development meetings (you have noticed that he has never attended one of these meetings when he knows Cory won't be there). Twice you noticed that when other printing workers fell behind in production, Kris slid over to their production stations to help them get back on track. Both times he did this, Cory was right there in the production room, able to witness Kris's good deeds. When a new employee started recently, Kris went to Cory and volunteered to "show him the ropes" and answer any questions that he might have.

When pay raises and promotions are announced, you learn that Kris has been promoted from "printing worker" to "project coordinator." The promotion means that Kris will be given more of the important corporate projects to work on and, as a result, will get a pay raise.

Imagine that you work in Kris's department and were passed over for the promotion and pay raise. Answer these questions:

1. In this department, the pay and promotion policies are applied politically.

   Yes _____ No _____ Not sure _____

2. The pay increase and promotion was inconsistent with the published policies.

   Yes _____ No _____ Not sure _____

3. I did not receive a raise that was consistent with the policies on how raises should be determined.

   Yes _____ No _____ Not sure _____

4. In this department, the stated pay and promotion policies had nothing to do with how pay raises and promotions are determined.

   Yes _____ No _____ Not sure _____

5. When it comes to pay raise and promotion decisions, policies were irrelevant.

   Yes _____ No _____ Not sure _____

6. Promotions in this department are not valued much because how they are determined is so political.

   Yes _____ No _____ Not sure _____

If you answered "Yes" to four or more of these questions, you are experiencing POP related to *pay and promotion policies*. If you answered "not sure" to more than four of these questions, you may have difficulty discerning political behavior from citizenship behavior in organizations. In other words, you believe that the same behavior could be interpreted different ways. However, participants in the research study cited below could detect that Kris's behaviors were "self-serving."

Form a group of four to five classmates and compare your answer to the questions about POP above. Discuss the following questions and be prepared to report your consensus on them to the class.

Discussion Questions

1. Why do you think Kris got promoted, even with average performance? How do you feel about being passed over for the promotion and Kris getting it?

2. Do you feel that Kris's behavior was altruistic (i.e., being a good organizational citizen)? Or do you view the behavior as self-serving and political? Will POP change your job satisfaction? Your performance?

3. What aspects of "maximizing good" impression management was Kris exhibiting? Would you behave this way to gain a promotion?

Sources: Vignette from Farrell, S. K., & Finkelstein, L. M. (2011). The impact of motive attributions on coworker justice perceptions of rewarded organizational citizenship behavior. *Journal of Business and Psychology, 26*(1), 57–69. Used with permission. POP questions on pay and promotion policies adapted from Kacmar, K. M., & Carlson, D. S. (1997). Further validation of the perceptions of politics scale (POPS): A multiple sample investigation. *Journal of Management, 23*(5), 627–658.

TOOLKIT ACTIVITY 7.2: What Would You Do?

Read the following situations and make some brief notes about what you would do in the situation. After you have completed making your notes, join a group of four to five classmates and discuss your reactions and planned behaviors.

1. You walk by your boss's office and hear him asking his spouse how their sick child is doing.

2. You see your boss taking a box of pens from the storeroom and putting it in her purse on the way out of the office.

3. Your boss asks your opinion about a nice purse on eBay. She shows it to you on her computer after your meeting.

4. You overhear your boss making calls to advance his part-time freelance business.

5. You hear your boss making abusive remarks to a coworker who made mistakes on a report. She yells at your coworker, "Why are you so stupid?"

6. You are reviewing expense reports submitted by your boss, and you notice that one of the documents submitted has been Photoshopped to make the expense look greater than it was.

Discussion Questions

1. Do you think that any of the above behaviors are acceptable? Which ones? Did you decide to "do nothing" in any of the cases. Explain why.

2. Rank the behaviors of your boss in terms of the degree to which they violate ethics. Explain your ranking.

3. When you discussed these situations with your classmates, did differences of opinion on what to do and what was/was not unethical emerge? Explain your reactions to your classmates' decisions.

CASE STUDY 7.1: Can You Succeed Without Power?

Scoria is a company that helps provide colleges and universities the tools needed to offer degree programs online. The firm's basic package provides services like the learning management system (LMS), tech support for the system, and online application management. However, it also offers packages with marketing, recruitment specialists, student services specialists and at-risk student support, course-building assistance, textbook and materials management, and human resource services for adjuncts. Depending upon the services a university chooses, Scoria charges 30% to 80% of the revenues the university makes from each online student.

Scoria recently entered a partnership with Daily University, a fairly well-known private university in the southeastern United States. Daily wants to offer its MBA, master of education, and master of professional studies degrees online. The reason driving this decision is that there are many students in the state's rural areas that want to earn a degree but live more than 60 miles from the campus and are not able to make the drive after work each night or want to give up their weekends in all-day intensive sessions. Daily decides to use the learning management and online teaching tools, course-building services, student recruitment and admission services, and textbook and materials management services. The contract is drawn up, and it is agreed that Scoria will receive 50% of the revenues generated from the students in the online program.

However, now that the contract is signed, a number of issues are arising that are causing Daily University and its faculty problems. Academic regulatory agencies require that courses be developed and taught by individuals with proper degree credentials. So in this partnership, Daily faculty develop the course content and send it to the team at Scoria that build the course in the LMS. Once the courses are built, Scoria does not allow changes to be made for causes like poor student feedback or changing book editions. So the faculty have the authority to develop their courses but lack the ability to make interesting changes to the courses based upon what they think is happening. This really bothers one faculty member, Dr. Kelly, who wants to pull in different current articles each week when she is teaching the course. However, she cannot do so, and Scoria is not willing to

find a way to work around the current system to find a solution that would benefit both the faculty and students. Several other faculty members share Dr. Kelly's desire.

But Daily University personnel are not the only ones having a hard time in this partnership. Scoria is providing recruitment and admission services for Daily by ensuring students have a complete application, including any test scores, before sending an application to Daily's admission office. This is a benefit to Daily as then they are only processing complete applications. However, to the employees at Scoria that are working as admissions specialist, the process of application review by Daily is too long and frustrating for students and Scoria staff. The current process is for the admission team to review the application materials and transfer them to Daily's system. The system then kicks the application to the dean of the program the applicant has applied to for review. As deans are busy people, this can take a few days, if not a week. To further bog down the process, Scoria has forbidden the deans from contacting applicants or their references, and so the deans don't have a way to get clarification for any questions arising from the materials. Thus, on borderline or questionable applications, it can take the deans extra time to consider and make a decision regarding a candidate. However, to Scoria's employees, they feel that Daily should be able to make a decision within 48 hours and constantly are asking for updates.

Finally, Daily's IT department is having issues in the partnership as well. Scoria and Daily use different systems that don't interface with each other. The administrators have been discussing options for solving the problem, such as adding new lines of code that should help one system drop data into the other system, having Daily upgrade and change its systems, having Scoria provide staff that enters the data into Daily's system using remote access and Daily's software licenses, and hiring more staff on Daily's end to enter the data from Scoria. However, none of the solutions are that ideal to either party, and so the IT administrators are looking to the provost of Daily and the vice president at Scoria to come up with an amicable solution.

So far, this partnership is off to a rocky start, but it is early in the relationship and there is hope that the relationship can be saved.

Discussion Questions

1. Identify the different power issues going on in the case. What types of power do the different parties have? Explain.

2. How are individuals reacting to their power or lack thereof?

3. What types of influence techniques could be used to help in any of these situations to reach commitment by both parties? Identify and justify at least three.

SELF-ASSESSMENT 7.1: Your Impression Management Strategies

This self-assessment exercise identifies your impression management strategies for maximizing good impressions. There are no right or wrong answers, and this is not a test. You don't have to share your results with others unless you wish to do so.

Part I. Taking the Assessment

You will be presented with some questions representing different strategies. If you don't currently have a job or boss, then answer the questions with respect to what you would likely do.

Statements	Strongly Disagree	Disagree	Somewhat Disagree	Neutral	Somewhat Agree	Agree	Strongly Agree
1. I talk proudly about my experience or education.	1	2	3	4	5	6	7
2. I compliment my colleagues so they'll see me as likeable.	1	2	3	4	5	6	7
3. I try to appear like a hardworking, dedicated employee.	1	2	3	4	5	6	7
4. I make sure people are aware of my talents or qualifications.	1	2	3	4	5	6	7
5. I take an interest in my colleagues' personal lives to show them that I am friendly.	1	2	3	4	5	6	7
6. I stay at work late so people will know that I'm hardworking.	1	2	3	4	5	6	7
7. I let others know that I am valuable to the organization.	1	2	3	4	5	6	7
8. I praise my colleagues for their accomplishments so that they'll think I'm nice.	1	2	3	4	5	6	7
9. I try to appear busy, even when things are slower.	1	2	3	4	5	6	7

(Continued)

(Continued)

Statements	Strongly Disagree	Disagree	Somewhat Disagree	Neutral	Somewhat Agree	Agree	Strongly Agree
10. I let others know that I have a reputation for being competent in certain areas.	1	2	3	4	5	6	7
11. I use flattery and favors to make my colleagues like me more.	1	2	3	4	5	6	7
12. I arrive at work early in order to look dedicated.	1	2	3	4	5	6	7
13. I make sure people are aware of my accomplishments.	1	2	3	4	5	6	7
14. I do personal favors for my colleagues to show them that I'm friendly.	1	2	3	4	5	6	7
15. I come to the office at night or on the weekends to show my dedication.	1	2	3	4	5	6	7

Part II. Scoring Instructions

In Part I, you rated yourself on 15 questions. Add the numbers you circled in each of the columns to derive your score for your impression management strategies. We will discuss each approach—its strengths and weaknesses—and how you can improve impressions others have of you. Scores on each dimension below can range from 5 to 35. In general, a lower score is from 5 to 14; a higher score is above 15.

Self-Promotion	Ingratiation	Exemplification
1. _____	2. _____	3. _____
4. _____	5. _____	6. _____
7. _____	8. _____	9. _____
10. _____	11. _____	12. _____
13. _____	14. _____	15. _____
Total _____	_____	_____

Source: Adapted from Bolino, M. C., & Turnley, W. H. (1999). Measuring impression management in organizations: A scale development based on the Jones and Pittman taxonomy. *Organizational Research Methods, 2*(2), 187–206.

Notes: **Self-Promotion**—pointing out your abilities or accomplishments in order to be seen as competent by observers; **Ingratiation**—doing favors or using flattery to elicit an attribution of likability from observers; **Exemplification**—self-sacrificing or going above and beyond the call of duty in order to gain the attribution of dedication from observers.

Discussion Questions

1. Compare your scores for self-promotion, ingratiation, and exemplification. Provide an example of the strategy when you used impression management for the tactic with your highest score.

2. Examine your lowest score. Explain whether or not you would use this tactic in practice and why.

3. Do you feel that using these tactics is faking? How does this relate to being authentic (authentic leadership was covered in Chapter 6)?

SELF-ASSESSMENT 7.2: What's Your Level of Political Acumen?

This self-assessment exercise identifies your level of political acumen in four areas determined by research. There is no "one best" approach; all approaches have strengths and weaknesses, and the goal is for you to learn about your political skill and think of ways to improve it. There are no right or wrong answers, and this is not a test. You don't have to share your results with others unless you wish to do so.

Part I. Taking the Assessment

Instructions: Circle the response that best describes your behavior.

Statements	Strongly Disagree	Disagree	Somewhat Disagree	Neutral	Somewhat Agree	Agree	Strongly Agree
1. I spend a lot of time and effort at work networking with others.	1	2	3	4	5	6	7
2. It is important that people believe I am sincere in what I say and do.	1	2	3	4	5	6	7
3. I always seem to instinctively know the right thing to say or do to influence others.	1	2	3	4	5	6	7
4. It is easy for me to develop good rapport with most people.	1	2	3	4	5	6	7
5. At work, I know a lot of important people and am well connected.	1	2	3	4	5	6	7
6. When communicating with others, I try to be genuine in what I say and do.	1	2	3	4	5	6	7
7. I have good intuition or savvy about how to present myself to others.	1	2	3	4	5	6	7
8. I am able to make most people feel comfortable and at ease around me.	1	2	3	4	5	6	7
9. I am good at using my connections and networks to make things happen at work.	1	2	3	4	5	6	7
10. I try to show a genuine interest in other people.	1	2	3	4	5	6	7
11. I am particularly good at sensing the motivations and hidden agendas of others.	1	2	3	4	5	6	7
12. I am able to communicate easily and effectively with others.	1	2	3	4	5	6	7

Part II. Scoring Instructions

In Part I, you rated yourself on 12 questions. Add the numbers you circled in each of the columns to derive your score for the four political skills. Your scores for each skill can range from 3 to 21. Scores above 12 can be considered higher.

Networking Ability	Apparent Sincerity	Social Astuteness	Interpersonal Influence
1. _____	2. _____	3. _____	4. _____
5. _____	6. _____	7. _____	8. _____
9. _____	10. _____	11. _____	12. _____
Total _____	_____	_____	_____

Source: Adapted from Ferris, G. R., Treadway, D. C., Kolodinsky, R. W., Hochwarter, W. A., Kacmar, C. J., Douglas, C., & Frink, D. D. (2005). Development and validation of the political skill inventory. *Journal of Management, 31,* 126–152.

Discussion Questions

1. Which political skill are you most adept at (what were your highest scores)?

2. Which political skills(s) do you need to develop (what were your lowest scores)? Develop strategies to improve upon your lowest scores.

3. Discuss apparent sincerity in terms of impression management. Do you feel that someone could fake being sincere for political purposes? Is this ethical?

CHAPTER EIGHT

MOTIVATION
Core Concepts

DO YOU HAVE GRIT?

Do you think that perseverance is as important as intelligence (IQ)? This is the question that Angela Duckworth, professor of psychology, has been investigating. She calls a high level of effort and persistence "grit" and defines it as "perseverance and passion for long-term goals."[1] Grit is the ability to stick to a goal and not give up, even in the face of adversity. Research has shown that grit may be as important as intelligence. There are a lot of smart people who don't achieve, and Duckworth's research found students who had more grit but were not as intelligent as their peers worked harder and had higher GPAs. Another study Duckworth conducted was at West Point, and cadets who had the highest levels on the "grit scale" were the most likely to succeed in the rigorous summer training program known as "Beast Barracks." Grit mattered more than intelligence, leadership ability, or physical fitness. In a third study, she found that participants in the National Spelling Bee contest who had higher levels of grit were ranked higher. This study revealed that success was, in part, due to participants with more grit spending more hours practicing for the contest. Two work-related studies found that soldiers who reported having more grit were more likely to complete a special operations selection course, and grittier sales employees were more likely to keep their jobs.[2] In Duckworth's research, grit was not related to IQ, but it was related to the Big Five personality trait *conscientiousness*. Perseverance pays off since conscientiousness has been significantly and positively related to motivation in numerous studies.[3] A meta-analysis[4] of 88 independent samples representing 66,807 individuals found that grit is moderately correlated with performance and retention (for example, not dropping out of school) and that grit is very strongly correlated with conscientiousness. The perseverance of effort was related to performance even when conscientiousness was accounted for. Duckworth's advice for people with a desire to achieve is: "If it's important for you to become one of the best people in your field, you are going to

Learning Objectives

After studying this chapter, you should be able to do the following:

8.1: Identify and discuss the three parts of the motivation process.

8.2: Compare and contrast Maslow's hierarchy with McClelland's need theory.

8.3: Produce an example of a SMART goal.

8.4: Describe the job characteristics theory (JCT) and why growth needs matter.

8.5: Explain why fairness is a necessary condition for leadership using equity theory and the four types of organizational justice.

8.6: Discuss how the expectancy theory of motivation predicts effort.

8.7: Summarize how self-fulfilling prophecies affect motivation.

Get the edge on your studies at
edge.sagepub.com/scandura2e

- Take the chapter quiz
- Review key terms with eFlashcards
- Explore multimedia resources, SAGE readings, and more!

have to stick with it when it's hard. Grit may be as essential as talent to high accomplishment."[5] If you would like to learn how much perseverance you have, you can take the perseverance assessment found in Self-Assessment 8.1 at the end of this chapter.

As suggested by the research on grit, motivation is important for leaders to understand; thus, there is a large evidence base on motivation in organizational behavior (OB). The next two chapters focus on the role of the leader as motivator. This chapter reviews theories of motivation that have received research support and provide evidence-based guidance for practice. The next chapter (Chapter 9) reviews research on applications of motivation concepts including rewards in organizations and how to design reward systems that motivate.

> **Critical Thinking Question:** What do you think is more important: IQ or perseverance? Explain why.

WHAT IS MOTIVATION?

Learning Objective 8.1: Identify and discuss the three parts of the motivation process.

The word *motivation* comes from the Latin word for *movement* (*movere*).[6] Motivation has been defined as "what a person does (direction), how hard a person works (intensity), and how long a person works (persistence)."[7] An overview of the motivation process is shown in Figure 8.1. This figure depicts motivation as a process that follows three stages. First, a leader must energize their followers' behavior by activating underlying needs and drives. For example, an employee may have a strong need for personal growth and want to learn new things on the job. Once energized, the leader then directs the energized behavior toward goals that are important to the employee and the organization. In this chapter, we explore models of motivation that activate and direct behavior (for example, by setting the right type of goals). The third step in the figure is sustaining behavior. This is often done through the provision of rewards that employees value (such as a pay raise). Research shows that reward systems are necessary to sustain behavior over the long term, and the next chapter addresses rewards as motivation in practice. Finally, for motivation to be effective, feedback is needed so that the processes of energizing and directing behavior stay on track. Feedback is essential in a number of theories of motivation, including goal setting. Feedback is also a central part of the design of performance management systems.

NEED THEORIES

Learning Objective 8.2: Compare and contrast Maslow's hierarchy with McClelland's need theory.

Early theories of motivation address the first part of Figure 8.1 by focusing on what needs or drives motivate people. The most well-known theory of need motivation is the Maslow hierarchy of needs.[8] The theory was the first to point out that there are individual differences in motivation. The first level in the hierarchy of needs is physiological needs (e.g., hunger, sex, and other bodily needs). The next level is safety needs (e.g., the need for protection from physical harm). At the third level of the hierarchy are a person's social needs (e.g., belongingness and friendship). The fourth level is esteem needs (e.g., status and recognition from others). Finally, at the top of the hierarchy is what Maslow termed **self-actualization**, which is the drive to meet our fullest capacity (e.g., growth and feeling fulfilled as a person). Physiological and safety needs are lower-order needs, and social, esteem, and self-actualization are higher-order needs, according to the theory. When a need is not satisfied, it becomes dominant. For example, if a person's safety is threatened, they focus on finding a place where there is no threat of physical harm.

Despite the popularity of Maslow's hierarchy due to its simplicity and intuitive appeal, it has not been supported by research evidence.[9] Needs are not arranged in this particular hierarchy, and there is no evidence that unsatisfied needs become dominant and induce motivation. However, this theory remains a commonly mentioned theory by many practicing managers, so it is important to be aware of it.

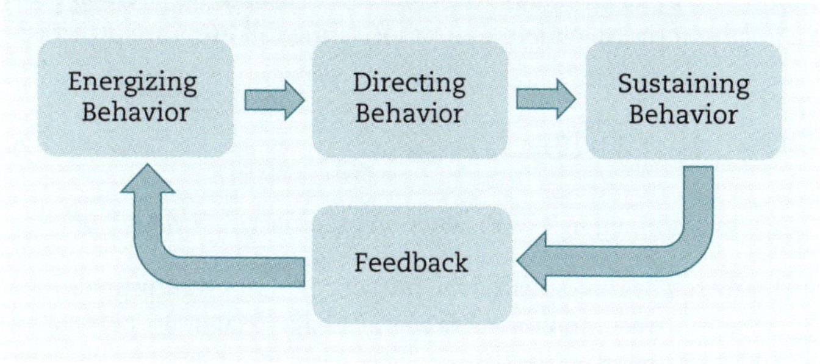

Another need theory considers three fundamental needs:[10]

Figure 8.1 The Motivation Process

- **Need for achievement (nAch)**—the drive to succeed at high levels

- **Need for power (nPow)**—the need to influence others to do what you want

- **Need for affiliation (nAff)**—the need for close personal relationships

Most of the fundamental need research was on nAch. There is some research support for the idea that people who have a higher need to achieve do perform at higher levels and people with a higher nAch may be more successful entrepreneurs.[11] However, a high need to achieve is not necessarily related to being an effective leader, since those with higher nAch may be more interested in their own attainment rather than coaching others to succeed. McClelland's theory has received more research support than other need theories; however, the application of the theory to motivate followers is limited because these needs are believed to be learned at a young age (in other words, it may not be possible to increase an adult's nAch).

The **two-factor theory** relates to lower- and higher-order needs, and relates them to job satisfaction (which is discussed in Chapter 4).[12] This is also called the **motivator–hygiene theory** and sought to answer the question of what people really want from their work. When people think about what makes them dissatisfied with work, they think of things like supervision, pay, company policies, and the working conditions, which are called **hygienes**. On the other hand, when people think of what *satisfies* them, they are more likely to think of things like advancement, recognition, and achievement, called **motivators**. Hygiene factors can only bring a person's satisfaction to the level of "no dissatisfaction" (in other words, they stop complaining about their pay). To motivate people, leaders need to focus on the motivators, such as providing people with a sense of achievement.

As with Maslow's theory, Herzberg's two-factor theory is widely cited, but it has not received much research support.[13] For example, the methods used in this research have been criticized because it was all self-reported data based on limited samples. Also, the relationship of satisfaction to job performance was assumed in his research but never tested.

This brief review of research on need theories is a cautionary tale. Overall, research on need theories has not provided strong research evidence for how to motivate people. In the following sections, theories aimed at understanding what directs a person's behavior toward outcomes, such as high job performance, are discussed. Recalling the

> Critical Thinking Questions: Explain the relationship between high self-actualization (Maslow) and nAch. Next, explain the relationship between high self-actualization and motivators.[14]

research on grit in the introduction to this chapter, we know that persistence plays a role in understanding how individuals attain high levels of performance. Once people set a goal, perseverance (grit) measures their ability to stick to it until it is attained. There has been a great deal of research on goal setting in OB, and some of the most practical and well-substantiated guidelines for motivating followers are provided by this research.

GOAL SETTING

Learning Objective 8.3: Produce an example of a SMART goal.

OB research has investigated the properties of motivating goals in numerous laboratory and field experiments.[15,16] For goals to motivate employees, they must have certain properties.[17] These goal-setting principles can be remembered with the acronym *SMART* for specific, measurable, actionable, relevant, and time-based goals.

"SMART" Goals

1. **Specific:** A specific goal has been shown to be more motivating than a "do your best" goal. Answer these questions: Who is involved? What do I want to accomplish? Where will this need to occur? When will it happen? Why am I or we doing this?

2. **Measurable:** Set concrete criteria for measuring progress toward the attainment of each goal. Measuring progress provides feedback and keeps people on track. Answer these questions: How much? How many? How will I know this goal is attained?

3. **Attainable:** Goals need to be challenging, but they also need to be seen as attainable by the person setting them. When people identify goals that matter to them, it energizes them and motivates a search for ways to perform. This may require new skills or resources. Answer these questions: Is this goal realistic? Do I have the skills and abilities to achieve it? Do I have the resources needed to achieve it? Have I attained something similar in the past?

4. **Relevant:** The goal you set needs to matter—to the individual setting it and/or the organization. Goals that are relevant are more likely to gain the support and the resources needed. Relevant goals (when met) drive the team, department, and organization forward. A goal that supports or is in alignment with other goals would be considered a relevant goal. Answer these questions: Does this matter? Is this the right time to do this? How does this fit in with the broader mission of the organization?

5. **Time based:** To be motivating, goals should have a specific time frame. This creates a sense of urgency and encourages benchmarking toward the attainment of the goal. Ask yourself these questions: When do I need to attain this goal? Are there minigoals or benchmarks I can set to monitor progress toward the goal?

For example, a not-so-smart goal would be the following: "Improve your punctuality." In comparison, an example of a SMART goal would be as follows: "Be at work by 8:30 a.m. every day this month because everyone being at work on time contributes to our team's productivity." Toolkit Activity 8.1 contains a goal-setting exercise where you write a letter to your "future me" and can apply SMART goal setting to your own life and career.

In practice, SMART goal setting has been applied using **management by objectives (MBO)**. MBO is a performance appraisal program where leaders meet with their direct reports and set specific performance objectives jointly.

Progress toward objectives is periodically reviewed, and rewards are allocated on the basis of that progress.[18] Performance appraisal is discussed in more detail in Chapter 9.

The degree to which a person is committed to a goal influences their willingness to persist and attain it. Also, motivation is higher when an employee is more committed to challenging goals compared with easy goals.[19] It is not clear whether allowing a person to participate in setting their own goals makes a difference; research findings are mixed.[20] However, if the goal is set by the leader, it is important for the leader to focus on the relevance of the goal to the person and the organization.

> **Critical Thinking Question: Why would allowing followers to participate in setting their own goals make a difference? Provide an example.**

Regulatory Goal Focus

Regulatory focus theory (RFT) is an alternative approach to understanding how individuals strive to meet their goals. According to RFT, individuals who are promotion-focused are oriented toward growth and development, and becoming their ideal. In contrast, individuals who are prevention-focused are oriented toward the things they feel that have to do and focus on their job responsibilities.[21] It's important to ensure that the person's regulatory orientation (i.e., whether they are promotion- or prevention-focused) fits the situation they are in. For example, a **promotion-focused** person will want to be provided with goals that stretch their abilities. Promotion-focused individuals have a need for achievement, focus on advancement, and set learning goals. In contrast, a person who is **prevention-focused** would be stressed out by such stretch goals and should be given goals that are within their job description. A prevention focus is a tendency to aim for getting to an end because of a fear of an undesirable alternative. Prevention-focused individuals are vigilant and careful, emphasize fears, focus on avoiding threats, and set prevention goals. The motivating force of a prevention focus is the avoidance of pain. Research has shown that the match between regulatory focus and the situation results in fewer negative emotions and more self-regulation in working toward the goals.[22] If there is a mismatch, then the person may feel negative about their work and not pursue the goal. In contrast, promotion-focused individuals tend to have a **learning goal orientation (LGO)**; they want to learn new things at work and see themselves as adaptable.[23,24] A meta-analysis[25] reviewed over 20 years of research on learning goal orientation and found that it predicts job performance. This is likely because employees with a learning goal orientation are more persistent, ask for feedback, and set their own goals. As a result, employees with a learning goal orientation report higher-quality relationships (LMX) with their supervisors.[26] Organizations should provide training to educate leaders about the motivational orientations of their employees so that they can better shape work experiences and challenges in ways that allow employees to attain their orientation-related goals.[27] Research on goal orientation suggests that leaders respond to goal setting by followers, and they play a significant role in the goal-setting process.

The Role of Leaders in Goal Setting

An example of successful implementation of goal setting is how they do it at Microsoft.[28] Goal commitment is so important that they changed the name of the process from "goal setting" to "goal commitment." Also, the leaders are actively involved in the process of developing commitments from followers. Each leader is expected to do the following:

1. Discuss and document the commitments of all employees.

2. Revisit and refresh commitments over time.

3. Agree to success metrics for each commitment, including the "how" behind execution (e.g., the plans to be used to attain the commitments), not just the "what."

4. Align commitments across the company by cascading commitments, beginning with Microsoft's commitments and connecting to organizational, team, and ultimately individual commitments.

5. Drive management team calibration discussions so interdependencies and metrics are vetted across individuals.[29]

This case example shows that leaders play an important role in negotiating mutual goals one-on-one with each of their direct reports. This process assures alignment with the organization's goals, commitments, and accountability for results. Psychologists have demonstrated that goals operate at the subconscious level and that cues for high performance result in high performance.[30] Thus, the leader can set challenging goals to obtain higher performance from followers.

Research on goal setting has also demonstrated that employees who receive **feedback** on their progress achieve higher levels of performance than those who don't.[31] Feedback on goals guides performance and allows the person to correct behaviors that may not be working or to try different performance strategies. Further, research has indicated that if employees are allowed to generate their own feedback, it may be more motiving than feedback from an outside source such as their supervisor.[32] Goal setting has been criticized due to the fact that goal setting may undermine creativity and the flexibility of employees to adapt to changing situations. For example, focusing on only one criterion for success may preclude looking at other opportunities to improve.[33] However, despite this concern, proponents of the theory maintain that the benefits of goal setting outweigh the limitations.[34] A SMART goals worksheet that can be used to set goals for yourself or for your followers is provided in Toolkit Activity 8.2 at the end of this chapter. As we have seen, feedback is essential to the process of motivation. In addition to setting SMART goals and learning feedback on performance, an employee may gain feedback from the work itself. Another major theory of motivation is the job characteristics theory (JCT), which looks at the motivating properties of work. We turn to this core theory of motivation next.

JOB CHARACTERISTICS THEORY

Learning Objective 8.4: Describe the job characteristics theory (JCT) and why growth needs matter.

The work itself may have characteristics that have the potential to motivate people to higher levels of performance.[35] Also, people are more satisfied when their work is interesting, and they may be less likely to quit. JCT is shown in Figure 8.2. In this theory of motivation, jobs can be designed so that people are more motivated and satisfied, as well as perform better.

The Motivating Potential of Work

First, the JCT specifies five core job dimensions. These dimensions combine to produce the critical psychological states that enhance motivation:

1. **Skill variety**—the extent to which people use different skills and abilities at work. The employee is not doing the same repetitive tasks over and over.

2. **Task identity**—the task is one that people experience from beginning to end. In other words, they identify with an entire work product.

3. **Task significance**—the degree to which the job is seen as having an impact on others. The work does something good for society.

4. **Autonomy**—the employee has the freedom to plan and perform his or her own work. The employees have discretion about their work and are not intensely supervised.

5. **Feedback**—the job provides information on how effective the employee's work is. Just doing the work itself provides performance feedback.

Skill variety, task identity, and task significance combine in the job characteristics model to produce a sense of meaningfulness of the work. For example, autonomy increases a person's responsibility for the work they perform. As in goal setting, feedback provides knowledge of the actual results of a person's work. These states experienced from the nature of the work performed translate into high work motivation, work performance, satisfaction, and lower absenteeism and turnover.

As Figure 8.2 shows, the growth needs of employees affect the degree to which a person experiences meaningfulness, responsibility, and knowledge of results from their work. **Growth need strength** refers to a person's need to learn new things, grow, and develop from working. People vary in this need; some people have a high desire to grow as a result of their work, and others do not. This need also

> Critical Thinking Questions: How do growth needs relate to higher-order needs as described in the need theories earlier in this chapter? How can a leader identify growth needs in followers?

Figure 8.2   The Job Characteristics Model

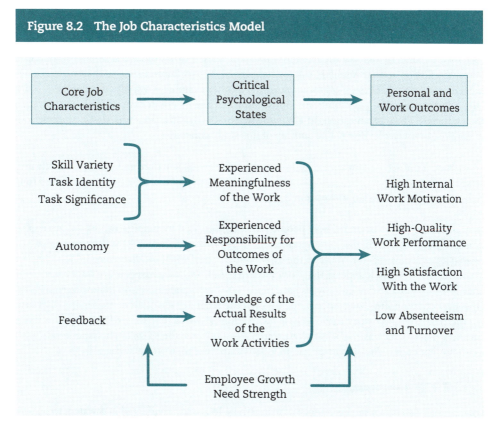

Source: Hackman, J. R., & Oldham, G. R. (1980). *Work redesign.* Reading, MA: Addison-Wesley.

affects performance. In other words, if a person's job is interesting, he or she may not have higher motivation and performance if he or she doesn't really need to grow from the work. Employees who prefer challenging work experience have less stress after their work is redesigned.[36]

Designing Work to Be Motivational

Based on the research on the job characteristics model, organizations have implemented work redesign to enhance the motivating potential of work.[37] The basic idea is to load jobs with more of the core job characteristics that have been shown to motivate. This job loading may be horizontal (e.g., adding different tasks at the same level) or vertical (e.g., adding decision-making responsibility). Recall that it is important to consider the growth needs of employees when redesigning work since these employees will respond more positively to the redesign of their work. These strategies have been referred to as job enrichment, and some examples follow.[38]

Job rotation involves cross-training or allowing workers to do different jobs. This increases the skill variety, task identity, and possibly the task significance. For example, a person who works on an assembly line is rotated to a clerical position in which he or she learns the purchasing process for supplies needed on the line 1 day a week. This provides variety and also allows the worker to see more of the "big picture" of what is needed to perform the work. In addition to job rotation, work may be designed to create natural work units by combining tasks. For example, a worker who drills holes for a door handle of a car would also learn to install the handle. Job rotation and combining tasks must be supported by adequate training and coaching for employees as they learn new skills on the job. Job rotation and combining tasks are examples of horizontal job loading.

Jobs may also be loaded vertically by allowing employees to establish client relationships in which workers can interact directly with clients to increase the meaningfulness of work. For example, the human resources manager for the Applied Systems Group at Spar Applied Systems redesigned the work into teams so that most workers interacted with customers to increase the focus on customer needs.[39] Another example is a study of callers requesting donations that found the callers were more persistent and motivated when they were in contact with undergraduate students funded by their efforts.[40] Thus, organizations might increase employee motivation by designing interactions with those who benefit from the employee's efforts. The authors of this study conclude:

> Consider the back room accountant who never meets the clients who benefit from her work. Merely introducing her to these clients may allow her to perceive her impact on them and feel affectively committed to them and thereby enable her to maintain her motivation.[41]

This form of motivation is based on how people may be motivated by helping others—prosocial motivation, which has emerged as an important outcome variable in OB as noted in Chapter 1.[42,43] A meta-analytic review found that the prosocial aspects of work contribute to the explanation of performance, turnover, and job satisfaction beyond that of job characteristic.[44] Thus, it appears that both the work itself and social aspects are important to motivation.

Work may be redesigned so that employees have more autonomy and discretion in how they perform their work to increase the level of autonomy experienced. Finally, opening feedback channels so that employees can learn more quickly about the results of their work may increase motivation (as we have seen, feedback is an important aspect of motivation in other theories such as goal setting). Research has supported the job characteristics model by demonstrating that job enrichment does reduce turnover and increases employee motivation and satisfaction.[45,46,47,48,49,50]

Work Redesign and Job Stress

The design of jobs may also lessen the experience of work stress. In a study conducted in Sweden, work was redesigned to improve the quality of work life, and this intervention alleviated work stress.[51] Another study found that when workers are able to create their own job designs to solve problems in their work, they experience less fatigue.[52] Employees

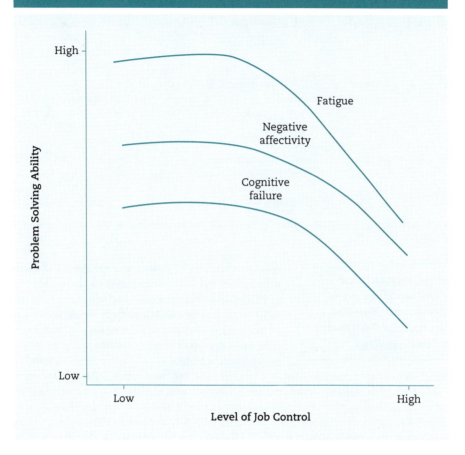

Figure 8.3   The Relationship Between Job Control, Fatigue, Negative Affectivity, and Cognitive Failure

Fatigue

Negative affectivity

Cognitive failure

Problem Solving Ability

Low

High

Low

High

Level of Job Control

Source: Daniels, K., Beesley, N., Wimalasiri, V., & Cheyne, A. (2013). Problem solving and well-being: Exploring the instrumental role of job control and social support. *Journal of Management, 39*(4), 1016–1043. p. 1033.

felt they had more job control, which is the authority to make decisions about their job on a day-to-day basis. The study also measured negative affectivity (being pessimistic) and cognitive failure, and the results are shown in Figure 8.3. This study also found asking for social support and executing job control to solve problems encourages further job redesign. Thus, work redesign appears to reduce stress—particularly when followers are empowered to make changes to their work to solve the problems they face.

Job Crafting

Recent work on job design has examined **job crafting**, or the extent to which individuals can demonstrate initiative in designing their own work. The term *job crafting* is used "to capture the actions employees take to shape, mold, and

Table 8.1 Forms of Job Crafting

Form	Example	Effect on Meaning of Work
Changing the number, scope, and type of job tasks	Design engineers engaging in relational tasks that move a project to completion	Work is completed in a more timely fashion; engineers change the meaning of their jobs to be guardians or movers of projects
Changing the quality and amount of interaction with others encountered in job	Hospital cleaners actively caring for patients and their families, integrating themselves into the workflow of their floor units	Cleaners change the meaning of their jobs to be helpers of the sick; see the work of the floor as an integrated whole of which they are a vital part
Changing cognitive task boundaries	Nurses take responsibility for all information and "insignificant" tasks that may help them to care more appropriately for a patient	Nurses change the way they see the work to be more about patient advocacy, as high-quality technical care

Source: Wrzesniewski, A., & Dutton, J. E. (2001). Crafting a job: Revisioning employees as active crafters of their work. *Academy of Management Review, 26*, 179–201. p. 185.

> **Critical Thinking Questions: What limitations (if any) would you put on allowing followers to craft their own work? What are the risks of not putting any limitations on job crafting?**

redefine their jobs."[53] Jobs vary in the degree of discretion that they offer, but in many cases, employees may be able to design aspects of their own work. Outcomes include changes to the work itself as well as interactions with others that may enhance the meaningfulness of the work performed.[54] A three-wave longitudinal study[55] of 368 police officers found that job crafting was positively associated with engagement, adaptability, and fewer stress demands during change. However, change communication was important too since it increased job crafting behaviors for promotion-focused employees. An example of job crafting would be a team member who is working on a marketing research project designing a set of team-building activities and implementing them to improve the way that the team works together on the project. Additional examples of job crafting are shown in Table 8.1. A review of the job design literature states the following: "Job crafting is an exciting area of research."[56] However, the authors caution that there may be dysfunctional consequences from employees designing their own work that need research. For example, an employee might redesign their work to include extraneous meetings with other department members that cause them to be away from the office, resulting in work disruptions to coworkers.

There has been much research on motivation that has provided specific guidelines for leaders to follow: Setting SMART goals and designing work to be motivational are key takeaway concepts. Despite effective goals and challenging work, however, motivation may be lower if employees have strong negative reactions based on how rewards are distributed or how they are treated. To effectively motivate followers and avoid costly absenteeism and turnover, leaders must follow principles of **organizational justice**.

The next sections address this concern.

THE IMPORTANCE OF FAIRNESS

Learning Objective 8.5: Explain why fairness is a necessary condition for leadership using equity theory and the four types of organizational justice.

Despite our parents telling us that "life is not fair," employees expect the workplace to be fair. This is, in part, due to the "just-world hypothesis," or the belief that people should get what they deserve. There are situations in which employees experience anger when they don't receive what they believe they deserve on a performance evaluation and subsequent pay raise. It has been proposed that the need for fairness is a universal motive.[57] For example, an employee may feel that he should have been promoted to a higher position instead of a coworker. Employees may react to even lesser outcomes, such as who in the work group gets an office that has a window. As these examples illustrate, concerns for fairness permeate the workplace, and effective leaders need to be aware of how followers might react to their decisions.

Equity Theory

Equity theory focuses on **distributive justice** (what people receive as a result of their knowledge, skills, and effort on the job).[58] As shown in Figure 8.4, equity theory suggests that people may become demotivated or put forth less effort when they feel that what they give and what they get is not in balance. According to the theory, a person (the focal person, or FP) compares himself to the coworker (or CO). Next, he compares his inputs (skills, abilities, effort on the job) to his outcomes (e.g., a merit raise). Three situations can occur in this comparison:

1. **The inputs and outcomes for the FP equal the inputs and outcomes for the CO.** What this means is that the FP puts in effort and receives a certain pay raise. This is compared with a CO who puts in more effort and receives a higher pay raise. There is balance because the FP recognizes that the CO works harder and gets a higher raise.

2. **The inputs and outcomes for the FP are _lower_ than the inputs and outcomes for the CO.** For example, the FP views the ratio of his inputs and outcomes as less than the CO. The FP realizes that they are "underpaid," and this causes dissonance or stress for the FP. In this situation, the FP may become demotivated (reduce inputs or efforts) to bring the ratios back to balance. If the situation persists, they may leave the situation entirely (find another job that pays better). This is referred to as **underpayment inequity**.

3. **The inputs and outcomes for the FP are _higher_ than the inputs and outcomes for the CO.** For example, the FP makes the comparison of inputs to outcomes and views their ratio of inputs to outcomes as higher than his CO. The FP realizes that he is being "overpaid" for his contributions compared to his CO. This situation is interesting because while we might expect the FP to work harder, this typically does not happen. People are more likely to distort the perceptions of inputs and/or outcomes to justify or rationalize their relative **overpayment inequity**. For

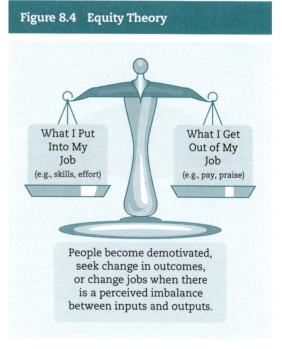

Figure 8.4   Equity Theory

What I Put Into My Job
(e.g., skills, effort)

What I Get Out of My Job
(e.g., pay, praise)

People become demotivated, seek change in outcomes, or change jobs when there is a perceived imbalance between inputs and outputs.

Source: Adapted from Adams, J. S. (1965). Inequity in social exchange. In L. Berkowitz (Ed.), *Advances in experimental social psychology* (Vol. 2, pp. 267–299). New York, NY: Academic Press.

example, they may point to their degree being from a better business school or adjust their view of their CO's input downward.

Inequitable comparisons affect employee attitudes such as job satisfaction.[59] For example, employees in underpayment conditions engage in behavior to adjust or compensate for the inequity (theft, for example).[60] Also, employees who experience unfair situations don't help their coworkers out (organizational citizenship).[61,62] There is strong research support indicating that perceptions of fairness affect motivation. However, research has also shown that equity may be viewed differently depending on whether or not a person has a positive or negative relationship with their comparison other.[63] In other words, if we like our coworker and they get a raise, then we are happy for them and less likely to experience a sense of inequity. On the other hand, if we don't like them, we may perceive the raise as unjust. Given the limited resources a leader has to distribute (particularly monetary compensation), leaders need to work at being perceived as fair. Research on equity (or distributive justice) was expanded to include other forms of justice that help explain how employees come to view their leader as fair.

Organizational Justice: Expanding Fairness

The concept of equity was expanded to consider broad concerns for organizational justice at the workplace.[64] Organizational justice is the "members' sense of the moral propriety of how they are treated."[65] When people feel an event is unfair, they may even experience **moral outrage**, which is a severe reaction to the perceived injustice (including strong emotions such as anger and resentment).[66] One study found that followers even engaged in sabotage when they perceived situations to be unfair.[67] Given that OB researchers have documented the importance of fairness perceptions (particularly underpayment inequity) on demotivation, researchers became interested in how other forms of justice might somehow address fairness concerns. When leaders follow fair procedures, followers are more willing to accept distributive outcomes and their formal authority—even if they receive less.[68] Research on organizational justice turned to the development of additional forms of fairness, broadening the concept into the overall umbrella term *organizational justice*.

Organizational justice is now considered to have four components: distributive (equity), procedural, interactional, and informational.[69] As noted earlier, distributive justice refers to the fairness of decisions made as perceived by followers as described above.[70] **Procedural justice** is the perception of how fair the process was in making decisions that affect employees. There are certain rules of fair process that are expected by employees.[71,72] For example, employees want to have a voice in decisions that affect them. They also want some form of an appeal process or way to correct something they see as unfair. Third, they want procedures to be consistent across people and over time. They also want the process to be unbiased and to represent the concerns of everyone affected by the decision. Finally, procedures need to be based on accurate information. Procedural justice has been shown to be more important than distributive justice in how followers respond to the decisions of their leaders in two meta-analytic studies that included a variety of organizational and occupational samples.[73,74]

Interpersonal justice refers to how employees are treated by their leaders, including respect and propriety (which refers to whether the leader refrains from offending the follower with comments that are inappropriate).[75,76] The final form of justice is **informational justice**, which refers to the perceived fairness of the communications made by leaders during a process. Informational justice includes full explanations of processes and the perception that the leader is being truthful.[77,78] For example, during the great recession of 2008, many organizations had zero pay raises. When this happened, leaders provided explanations for why raises were zero for hardworking employees because of the economic situation. Figure 8.5 summarizes the four components of organizational justice and provides a sample item from an organizational justice measure to illustrate each aspect of justice.

Given the central role of fairness in motivation, OB theory and research has described how a leader can change the perceptions of their followers that they are being fair. Research has shown a clear relationship between fairness and effective leadership. This research is described in the following section, as well as the process through which a leader can develop a reputation in the organization for being fair.

RESEARCH IN ACTION

Who Cares About Fairness?

Equity sensitivity is an individual difference which affects how different people react to inequity.[79] Individuals can be thought of as being along a continuum as either benevolents (tolerant of underpayment), equity sensitives (adhere to equity norms), or entitleds (tolerant of overpayment). Benevolents don't get stressed when they experience underpayment or overpayment, but people who are equity sensitive do. Equity sensitivity may also affect the types of rewards that people prefer: Entitled employees prefer monetary rewards, whereas benevolents prefer intrinsic rewards such as the ability to learn something new on the job.[80] Equity sensitivity has also been associated with motivation: Benevolence is related to job performance and

organizational citizenship.[81,82] Intriguing experimental research found benevolent individuals report the highest pay satisfaction, pay fairness, and lowest turnover intentions.[83] However, entitled individuals did *not* report lower overall pay satisfaction, perceived pay fairness, or higher turnover intentions than benevolents. The overrewarded condition was also very interesting: All three equity sensitivity groups preferred being overrewarded to being fairly rewarded and were distressed when underrewarded. These findings support equity theory for underpayment. Yet overpayment is enjoyed by everyone, regardless of whether they are sensitive to equity or not. So whether we care about equity may depend on whether we are being overpaid or underpaid.

Discussion Questions

1. Given the descriptions just given, do you consider yourself to be equity sensitive? In other words, do you believe that employees should be rewarded relative to their contributions?

2. Explain why overpayment satisfies employees regardless of whether they are equity sensitive or not.

3. Why is it important for a manager to consider the equity sensitivity of their followers?

Sources: Bing, M. N., & Burroughs, S. M. (2001). The predictive and interactive effects of equity sensitivity in teamwork-oriented organizations. *Journal of Organizational Behavior, 22*(3), 271–290; Blakely, G. L., Andrews, M. C., & Moorman, R. H. (2005). The moderating effects of equity sensitivity on the relationship between organizational justice and organizational citizenship behaviors. *Journal of Business & Psychology, 20*(2), 259–273; Huseman, R. C., Hatfield, J. D., & Miles, E. W. (1987). A new perspective on equity theory: The equity sensitivity construct. *Academy of Management Review, 12*(2), 222–234; Miles, E. W., Hatfield, J. D., & Huseman, R. C. (1994). Equity sensitivity and outcome importance. *Journal of Organizational Behavior, 15*(7), 585–596; Shore, T. H. (2004). Equity sensitivity theory: Do we all want more than we deserve? *Journal of Managerial Psychology, 19*(7), 722–728.

Developing a Fair Reputation

Fairness is a necessary (but not sufficient) condition for effective leadership.[84] The ability to develop high-quality relationships depends upon following norms of procedural justice and ensuring that outcomes are fairly distributed. Interpersonal and informational justice are both important; leaders must respect followers and provide truthful explanations of how they make decisions. Fairness is pivotal to relationships between leadership and employee work attitudes, relationships with coworkers, and employee turnover.[85] And employees with good relationships with their boss also engage in more organizational citizenship when they perceive a fair climate in the work group.[86] Fairness issues emerge at the group level when followers compare their relationships with their boss (in-group or out-group) and the outcomes they receive. Thus, the procedural justice climate that a leader creates is essential to being effective in motivating followers and avoiding costly turnover.

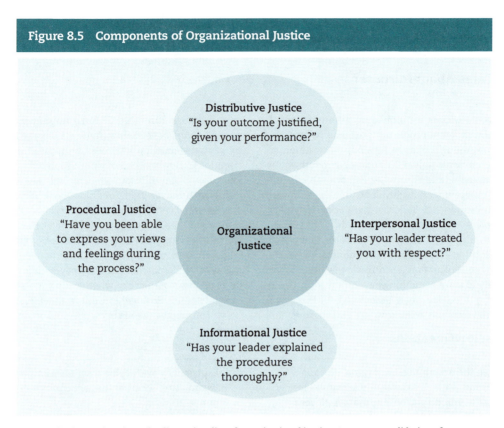

Source: Colquitt, J. A. (2001). On the dimensionality of organizational justice: A construct validation of a measure. *Journal of Applied Psychology, 86*(3), 386–400.

Leaders can develop followers' perceptions that they are being fair—a fair identity.[87] When a follower presents the boss with an unfair situation, it is a predicament for the boss. For example, a coworker gets assigned to a more lucrative client; however, another direct report feels they deserved the assignment. What should the leader do to resolve this? First, the leader should have empathy and see the situation from the follower's perspective. The leader then has options to respond to the follower, but these should be carefully thought through because they have consequences for the continued trust and development of the relationship.

> **Critical Thinking Question:** Do you believe that other forms of justice can compensate for distributive justice (what people get)? Provide an example of when this happens.

One set of options are verbal; the leader can deny the unfairness, show regret, or admit that it was not fair to the follower. These actions may damage the trust in the working relationship. Other options are to provide explanations to justify the action by making excuses or apologies. While these verbal responses represent better options for the maintenance of the working relationship, the follower may still not be satisfied. Finally, the leader can take actions to address the concern, such as restoring the benefit (in the example just given, the leader could assign the follower to join

The Importance of Leader Attention for Employee Motivation

A survey conducted by *McKinsey Quarterly* asked 1,047 executives, managers, and employees from a range of industries what practices were the most effective motivators. While most people expect financial incentives such as cash bonuses and increases in base pay to be the biggest motivators, the research indicated that this was not the case. Despite the survey findings that financial incentives are frequently used (e.g., 68% of those surveyed indicated that their organization used cash bonuses), they are not the most effective.

Praise and commendation from leaders was cited as the most effective motivator with 67% reporting that this was effective, followed by attention from leaders at 63%. In addition, opportunities to lead projects or task forces were reported effective (62%). According to Dewhurst, "these themes recur constantly in most studies on ways to motivate and engage employees."[88] With many organizations cutting back on financial incentives, now may be the best time to begin to work on more effective leadership as a motivational tool for effective motivation.

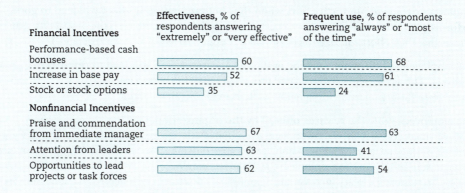

Source: Dewhurst, M. (2009). Motivating people: Getting beyond money [Commentary]. *McKinsey Quarterly*. Retrieved on January 2, 2014, from http://www.mckinsey.com/insights/organization/motivating_people_getting_beyond_money

Discussion Questions

1. Explain why praise from the immediate supervisor was the most effective motivator using the principle of feedback discussed in this chapter.
2. Use the motivator–hygiene theory to explain why financial incentives were less related to effective motivation than nonfinancial incentives such as praise, leader attention, and opportunities to lead projects.

the coworker in working with the lucrative client). Another action would be to provide alternative recompense; assign the follower an equally valuable client to work with. A fair identity and reputation for being fair is thus negotiated and must be monitored carefully.

This example shows that leaders play a large role in follower perceptions of fairness, which may avoid demotivation and withdrawal behaviors such as absenteeism and turnover. In essence, organizational justice theory addresses what has happened in the past. Leaders also help employees understand how they will be rewarded in the future. The next section discusses theory and research on expectancy theory and how leaders motivate by articulating the pathways to goals.

EXPECTANCY THEORY

Learning Objective 8.6: Discuss how the expectancy theory of motivation predicts effort.

Valence-instrumentality-expectancy (VIE) theory was one of the most influential approaches to motivation in the 20th century.[89] A review of research on expectancy theory noted the following: "Expectancy theory has become a standard in motivation, as reflected by its incorporation as a general framework for a wide variety of research."[90] The expectancy theory of motivation has received mixed research support but does provide insight into the process of motivation.[91] The theory has three basic principles:[92]

1. **Employees decide to put forth effort when they believe that their effort will lead to good performance.** This is called the effort à performance relationship, which is the probability that a person believes that their effort will lead to performance (designated as the E → P expectancy).

2. **The employee's performance will be evaluated accurately and will lead to rewards (e.g., pay raises, bonuses).** This is the follower's estimated probability that if they perform well, they will actually receive the reward from the organization (designated as the P → O instrumentality).

3. **The employees value the rewards offered by the organization.** One level of performance may have multiple outcomes (such as a salary increase *and* a bonus) (designated as the list of valences, Vs, which can be either positive or negative). For example, a negative outcome associated with high performance might be having to stay late at work to accomplish a task and the employee misses his daughter's violin solo at a school concert. So receiving a salary increase and a bonus has a positive (+) valence. At the same time, having to work late has a negative (–) valence.

In the original formulation of expectancy theory, these components were multiplied to predict effort.[93] Later, these three aspects of motivation were shown to each directly predict effort (rather than needing to be multiplied together).[94,95] For example, a person's belief that he or she can perform affects performance ("I can do the task"). The person's belief in the organizational reward system also affects his or her performance ("My leader will provide me with a bonus if I perform well"). Finally, the degree to which rewards are valued also affects performance ("I really want that bonus!"). A summary of the expectancy theory of motivation is shown in Figure 8.6. Expectancy theory highlights the role that a leader plays in motivating followers by strengthening their perception that they can perform a task—their self-efficacy (you learned about efficacy as part of PsyCap in Chapter 2).[96] Also, the leader can reassure followers that if they perform, they will be rewarded. Finally, the leader can engage in candid conversations with followers regarding what rewards they value most (and therefore, most motivating). In sum, leaders can take several actions to motivate employees based upon VIE theory:[97]

- First, leaders should ensure that their employees expect that they can achieve whatever goals are set. This begins with selecting employees who have the knowledge, skills, and ability (KSA) to perform the goals.

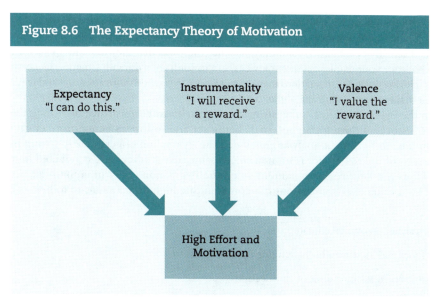

Figure 8.6 The Expectancy Theory of Motivation

Expectancy
"I can do this."

Instrumentality
"I will receive
a reward."

Valence
"I value the
reward."

High Effort and
Motivation

Source: Vroom, V. H. (1964). *Work and motivation.* New York, NY: Wiley.

- Second, leaders should offer rewards that employees value (positive valences). Keep in mind that employees may not value the same things as leaders and managers.

- Third, leaders should make a strong linkage between goal attainment and valued rewards. Employees must also perceive this linkage; don't assume that they see the association between performance and rewards.

Leader transformational behavior is related to the degree to which followers set goals that are related to authentic values.[98] This goal setting translates into job performance, initiative, self-direction, and innovation on the job. Leaders influence follower motivation and performance.

A leader may also influence follower performance by having positive expectations of them. In other words, how a leader views their followers may become a motivating force. There is much research on the Pygmalion effect, which shows that performance expectations by a leader play a significant role in improving follower motivation and performance.

> **Critical Thinking Questions:** Apply expectancy theory to explain whether a talented junior football player should go to a professional football league or stay and finish his college degree. What are the valences, expectancies, and instrumentalities the player might have?

THE PYGMALION EFFECT

Learning Objective 8.7: Summarize how self-fulfilling prophecies affect motivation.

Perceptions sometimes result in the self-fulfilling prophecy, or Pygmalion effect, in which the high expectations of performance by leaders actually create conditions in which followers succeed. Named after a George Bernard Shaw play, effect was first studied by Robert Rosenthal in an elementary classroom setting.[99] In his experiments, he told teachers that some of their students had the capability to be leading performers—or as he called them "intellectual bloomers."[100] The teachers, unknowingly, gave these students more learning opportunities and more positive feedback. These students had actually been chosen randomly, but the result was that they did end up performing better. As a leader, you may challenge your employees or empower them to confront a difficult situation by persuading them into positive thoughts. Having positive expectations may cause a leader to provide more attention and feedback to followers and, in turn, result in them performing at a higher level.

Research on the Pygmalion effect suggests managers can boost performance by raising their expectations of followers.[101] This occurs through higher goals being set and followers being more engaged and striving to learn more on the job.[102] A meta-analysis concluded the Pygmalion effect is fairly strong in organizations, but the work context of the research was limited since many early studies were conducted in military settings with men.[103,104] However, later research demonstrated the Pygmalion effect in nonmilitary settings and with women as well.[105,106] Leaders in organizations can communicate high expectations to followers in the following four ways:[107]

1. Create a warmer emotional climate.

2. Provide more and increasingly challenging opportunities to learn.

3. Invite followers to ask questions of clarification.

4. Provide feedback on performance.

What about a person's expectations of himself or herself? The **Galatea effect** is present when an individual sets high expectations for themselves and then performs to these expectations. Such a follower already has high self-esteem and believes in his or her ability to succeed. The Galatea effect was examined by conducting an experiment where subjects' self-esteem was boosted by a series of positive feedback messages.[108] This intervention resulted in improved self-esteem, motivation, and an impact on performance. Thus, leaders need to provide ongoing feedback and challenging assignments to increase follower expectations. The Galatea effect suggests followers may even exceed the leader's expectations when they have confidence in their ability to succeed.

As might be expected, expectations may also work in the opposite direction where lower expectations lead to lower performance, and this is called the **Golem effect**. Golem comes from the Hebrew slang for *dumbbell*. Bosses can "kill" followers' motivation by having low expectations. A 2-year study was conducted of 50 boss–subordinate pairings; the managers were asked to differentiate high performers from low performers. Within 5 minutes of meeting and working with new employees, managers could easily evaluate their future performance. They unanimously stated that the low performers were passive, less motivated, less proactive, and so on. Some followers were classified as not having potential; therefore, the managers spent less time providing them with instructions on how to do their jobs. The managers viewed the low performers as weak and, thus, did not assign challenging tasks to them where they could learn new skills. When the "weak" performers began to notice the bosses' treatment, they became disengaged, their performance deteriorated, and they ended up matching the bosses' expectations. In effect, these bosses set the followers up to fail.[109] It is possible, through training, to reverse the Golem effect ("de-Golemization") in which supervisors can change their expectations of low performance to higher performance, and followers respond positively with more effort.[110,111] Based upon the long stream of research on Pygmalion effect in organizations, it is clear that high expectations play a role in enhancing job performance. Toolkit Activity 8.3 provides you with the opportunity to check your understanding of the Pygmalion effect.

> **Critical Thinking Question:** Based on what you have learned about the Galatea effect, how can you use the concept to improve your grades? Develop two or three positive feedback messages that will impact your performance.

LEADERSHIP IMPLICATIONS: WHO WILL LEAD?

This chapter has discussed how leaders serve as motivators for their followers. But is everyone equally motivated to be a leader? Research on **motivation to lead (MTL)** has addressed this interesting question. The MTL is defined as "an individual differences construct that affects a leader's or leader-to-be's decisions to assume leadership training, roles, and responsibilities and that affect his or her intensity of effort at leading and persistence as a leader."[112] This research has found that people have different reasons for wanting to be a leader. There are three basic reasons, based on the measurement of MTL:

- **Affective-identity MTL**—the natural tendency to lead others—reflects the value an individual places on a leadership role and most directly reflects leadership self-efficacy and experience. For example, how would you respond to the statement "Most of the time I prefer to be a leader rather than a follower when working in a group"?

- **Social-normative MTL**—the tendency to lead because of a sense of duty or responsibility—is associated with general attitudes toward social norms. For example, how would you respond to the statement "I feel that I have a duty to lead others if I am asked"?

- **Noncalculative MTL**—where people agree to lead without calculating the costs and benefits of assuming leadership—is associated with an individual's level of altruism. For example, how would you respond to the statement "I am only interested in leading a group if there are clear advantages for me"? (If your answer is no, you tend to have a higher noncalculative MTL.)[113]

Of course, these reasons can combine to produce stronger MTL. For example, a person might have a natural tendency to lead others and also feel a sense of duty to lead them. They may also not be interested in the advantages that being a leader provides. While people vary in their motivation to lead, scholars believe that MTL results from experiences that shape a person's motivation to assume leadership roles. In other words, MTL is learned through experience. For example, a person with MTL may pay more attention when leadership is covered in an OB course, or they may sign up for leadership training provided by their organization. MTL may be affected by regulatory focus. For example, affective-identity MTL is more related to promotion (advancement) focus, whereas social-normative MTL is more related to prevention-focus because such individuals do things out of necessity (to avoid pain).[114] A study of students participating in team projects found that those who were high in affective-identity MTL became leaders in leaderless discussions, while high social-normative MTL individuals assumed leadership roles in long-term project teams.[115] Thus, the particular reason why a person is motivated to lead influences the type of leadership roles they assume. A study of 215 Israeli military recruits found that those with higher MTL were more likely to display effective teamwork and emerge as team leaders; however, intelligence combined with MTL to predict leader emergence.[116] A follow-up study of 60 recruits conducted 1 year later found that MTL predicted which ones became commanders (i.e., formal leaders). Another study of 100 leaders in an experimental simulation of a manufacturing organization found that MTL was related to perceptions of leader effectiveness as rated by followers, after taking personality traits into account.[117] In other words, MTL cannot be explained by whether a person is an extrovert or not. The results of these studies suggest that organizations can influence MTL by providing training in leadership and leadership development opportunities to build a person's belief in their own leadership abilities (known as leader self-efficacy).

Some people will follow, and some will lead. Leadership is an identity that emerges through social interactions with others.[118] People hold images in their minds of what a leader is and they compare themselves to those images to determine whether they have a leader identity, but the degree of leader self-efficacy is also important. Congruence between a person's self-image with images of great leaders and leader self-efficacy relate to MTL.[119] If you aspire to be a leader, it is important to understand your motivations for being a leader. Once you understand your own motivations, you will be better able to lead others. Take opportunities to assume leadership roles to gain experience to build your leader self-efficacy.

Leaders play a major role in how motivated their followers are to perform at high levels. First, leaders must assure that followers understand their goals and are committed to their goals. Second, leaders can design more motivating work or allow followers some discretion to craft their own work (aligned with work unit and organizational objectives). Leaders must negotiate a fair identity with their followers so that followers don't become unmotivated by perceptions of inequity. Finally, leaders strengthen followers' expectations that they can perform at a high level (expectancy) and that they will receive rewards they value for performing (instrumentality). Holding high expectations of followers can induce the positive effects of a Pygmalion effect on follower motivation. Finally, leaders need to talk to their followers to understand their motives and what rewards they value. The next step is to provide those rewards. The next chapter discusses the motivating properties of rewards and reward systems in organizations.

 **edge.sagepub.com/scandura2e**

Want a better grade? Go to **edge.sagepub.com/scandura2e** for the tools you need to sharpen your study skills.

KEY TERMS

autonomy, 192
combining tasks, 192
distributive justice, 195
equity theory, 195
feedback, 190
Galatea effect, 202
Golem effect, 202
growth need strength, 191
horizontal, 192
hygienes, 187
informational justice, 196
interpersonal justice, 196
job crafting, 193
job enrichment, 192

job rotation, 192
learning goal orientation
 (LGO), 189
management by objectives
 (MBO), 188
moral outrage, 196
motivation to lead (MTL), 203
motivator–hygiene theory, 187
motivators, 187
need for achievement (nAch), 187
need for affiliation (nAff), 187
need for power (nPow), 187
organizational justice, 194
overpayment inequity, 195

prevention-focused, 189
procedural justice, 196
promotion-focused, 189
prosocial motivation, 192
Pygmalion effect, 201
regulatory focus theory
 (RFT), 189
self-actualization, 186
self-efficacy, 200
two-factor theory, 187
underpayment inequity, 195
valences, 200
vertical, 192
work redesign, 192

TOOLKIT ACTIVITY 8.1: Future Me Letter

Gary Wood has developed a motivational technique called "Future Me." You write a letter to yourself in the future. You give yourself thoughtful advice and encouragement like you would to a good friend. We learned about self-fulfilling prophecies in this chapter—the Galatea effect—in which a person sets high expectations for themselves and then their performance meets these expectations. In a sense, writing a letter to your future self is creating a self-fulfilling prophecy.

Here are the steps:

1. **Start by outlining some ideas of how you want things to be in your life in 6 months.** According to Wood, 6 months should allow you to focus on medium-term goals and goals that are not so ambitious that they can't be attained in a reasonable amount of time.

2. **Recall the properties of SMART goals.** Write out specific, measurable, actionable, realistic, and time-based statements (for the 6-month time frame).

3. **Write the letter to yourself.** Be realistic, and give yourself sound advice and encouragement on how great it is that you reached your goals. For example, this can be tangible like landing a new job if you are 6 months from graduation. Your goals might also be more intangible such as increasing your emotional intelligence (EQ).

4. **Print the letter.** Place the letter in an envelope and seal it. Write your name on the envelope and the date 6 months from when you wrote it. Put it in a safe place. You may want to put a reminder in your calendar to open the letter.

5. **When you open the letter, reflect on your achievements, personal learning, and growth over the 6 months.** If you reached any of your goals, give yourself positive feedback and add a reward (a nice dinner out or a trip to the mall to get that jacket you have been wanting). For things you may not have attained, reflect on why and set new goals. If this is important to you, remember the concept of "grit." Stick with it!

Source: Adapted from Wood, G. (2013). Future me—Write yourself a letter from the you in six months time. Retrieved from http://psycentral.wordpress.com/2013/08/09/future-self-letter-goals-dr-gary-wood-life-coach-birmingham

TOOLKIT ACTIVITY 8.2: SMART Goals Template

SMART goals help improve achievement and success. A SMART goal clarifies exactly what is expected and the measures used to determine if the goal is achieved and successfully completed.

A SMART goal is as follows:

- **Specific (and strategic):** It is linked to job description, departmental goals/mission, and/or overall company goals and strategic plans. It answers these questions: Who? What?

- **Measurable:** The success toward meeting the goal can be measured. It answers this question: How?

- **Attainable:** Goals are realistic and can be achieved in a specific amount of time and are reasonable. It answers this question: Is this reasonable?

- **Relevant (results oriented):** The goals are aligned with current tasks and projects and focus in one area; it includes the expected result. It answers this question: Why?

- **Time based:** Goals have a clearly defined time frame, including a target or deadline date. It answers this question: When?

Examples:

This is not a SMART goal:

- Employee will improve their writing skills.

This does not identify a measurement or time frame, nor identify why the improvement is needed or how it will be used.

This is a SMART goal:

- The department has identified a goal to improve communications with administrative staff by implementing an online newsletter. Jane will complete a business writing course by January 2015 and will publish the first monthly newsletter by March 2015. She will gather information and articles from others in the department and draft the newsletter for supervisor review. After approval by supervisor, Jane will create an e-mail distribution list and send the newsletter to staff by the 15th of each month.

SMART Goal Planning Form
Specific—WHO? WHAT?
Measurement/Assessment—HOW?
Attainable/Achievable—IS THIS REASONABLE?
Relevant—WHY?
Time (Due Date)—WHEN?

TOOLKIT ACTIVITY 8.3: Understanding the Pygmalion Effect

It is a scientific fact that people perform, to a large degree, according to the expectations others have for them. If deep down a manager believes his or her subordinates are incompetent and irresponsible, the chances are good that the employees will act that way. Conversely, if a manager treats employees as competent and responsible, the employees will generally live up to those expectations.

This exercise provides an opportunity to explore various scenarios that might occur within a work environment. Each scenario involves a manager and one or more employees. Divide into groups of two or three. Each group will be assigned one of the scenarios and explore the discussion questions listed after the scenarios.

Scenario 1

Jim is the production floor manager at Acme Cabinets. He supervises over 100 assemblers who work on the company's day shift assembling audiovisual cabinets. He has noted a recent decline in productivity and an increase in error rate. In order to improve performance, Jim has posted a chart in the lunchroom. This chart contains the names of all the employees as well as their daily performance (by number of cabinets assembled) and their error rate (by number of mistakes).

Scenario 2

Lynn is the director of a nonprofit organization that works with local children and teachers to build their arts education programs. She has recently hired several individuals who previously worked as classroom teacher aides. Her intent was to have them do clerical tasks for her professional staff. However, one of the aides has shown an exceptional talent for painting and sculpture. Lynn has asked this aide to design a program that would introduce preschool children to art and, in order to help train the aide, has enrolled her in a child development class at a local college.

Scenario 3

Gina is the newly appointed manager of marketing communications for a large corporation. She is responsible for the activities of seven employees—all of whom have been with the company for several years and are experienced, creative, and competent at their jobs. In an effort to appear strong and managerial, Gina has "laid down the law" in her new department. She has asked everyone to account for their time by project and to submit a weekly report of their activities. In addition, she has installed a sign in/sign out board to keep track of employee breaks and lunch hours.

Scenario 4

Jill recently returned to her job as executive assistant after 2 months of maternity leave. Her boss, Susan, is thrilled to have Jill back because the temp assigned to cover for Jill left a lot to be desired. However, in the past week, Susan has noticed that Jill is very tired and is spending a lot of time on personal calls. While Jill's work is getting done and the quality hasn't suffered, Susan voices her concerns. Jill confesses that her babysitter isn't working out and that the baby is keeping her up at night. Susan explains that while she is sympathetic, it is important that Jill reduce the number of personal calls she is making and be more alert on the job. She also asks Jill to take on the added responsibility of a special research project because "no one else in the company is capable of finishing it on time."

Discussion Questions

1. Is the manager communicating high or low expectations to the employee by his or her behavior?

2. How do you think the employee(s) will react to the manager's behavior? Choose several adjectives that you believe describe this reaction (e.g., angry, motivated).

3. If low expectations are being communicated by the manager in the scenario, answer this question: If you were the manager in this scenario and wanted your employee(s) to respond in a positive manner, what would you have done differently?

4. If high expectations are being communicated by the manager in the scenario, discuss what benefits might result. For the sake of contrast, pretend the manager in the scenario held low expectations for the employee(s). What might that low expectation manager have done in these scenarios, and what would be the result?

Source: CRM Learning. (2009). Pygmalion effect training activity. Retrieved from http://www.crmlearning.com/blog/index.php/2009/08/pygmalion-effect-training-activity

CASE STUDY 8.1: Building Motivation

Construction Products Inc. sells construction products to various retail and wholesale markets across the United States. Its only office is in Illinois, and so it sends sales representatives on the road to different territories to obtain orders and develop relationships with retailers. You are the newest sales representative and have been assigned to the Southeast territory. A typical workday for a sales rep involves stopping at numerous stores and talking with general managers while visiting the retail stores to view how products are marketed and displayed. On these visits, sales reps try to increase wholesale orders by improving the sales of Construction Products. Also, they complete market reports that are used by the Illinois main office for future forecasting of product demand. Most territories are responsible for about 50 retail stores and about a dozen wholesale accounts. Sales reps are expected to spend a lot of time in the stores focusing on optimizing product location within the store, training employees, and educating customers about the benefits

of the company's products. For example, a sales rep typically tries to get larger space in the store for plywood so that more can be sold. Employees and customers need to be educated on the different grades of plywood and how to match them with building projects. This is important since the stores carry competitors' products in the stores.

After 6 months on the job, your boss has tasked you with increasing sales in your territory by 20%. You plan to meet this goal by explaining the benefits of your product and why it should be the product of choice. During store visits, you socialize with store employees but realize quickly that getting everyone on the same page is not going to be as easy as anticipated. You learn that most employees don't really care if the customer gets the best material for their project. They get their paycheck regardless of how much of your products are sold. They listen politely but are not enthusiastic about your ideas. Among the 50 retail stores that you are assigned to, there are seven that agree to help you with increasing sales in their store. You plan to track the sales in these stores compared to the others that did not agree to help. After a month, you see only slight increases in the sales in the seven stores but you are encouraged. Sales are about the same in the other 43 stores. You realize that focusing on the seven stores will not meet your boss's goal of increasing sales by 20%.

The next month, you try a different approach in your other 43 stores. In those stores, you spend time teaching employees about various building products so they can educate their customers. They seem to grasp an understanding of the benefits your product could bring to the customers compared to competitors' products. They also seem to understand the applications and how to match your products with customers' building needs. But when you ask them to teach customers what you had shown them, you were met with looks of confusion and aggravation. Although a bit reluctant, they agree to give it a try.

Checking the weekly sales figures over the next month, you notice that there has been little improvement in the sales of your product at these 43 stores. You

ask your boss for advice, and he suggests that you speak with the manager of one of the retail stores to gain an understanding for the lack of motivation. You show him a printout of the sales numbers and how much income your products bring to the store as well as ask for his help getting employees on board with promoting the products. Since the store manager's main concern is revenue for the store, he quickly agreed and offered his full support.

The store manager calls a meeting where he, the store employees, and you discussed techniques for product presentation and how employees can effectively pitch the product to customers. You left feeling confident that the employees would be effective since the goal was reinforced by their boss. However, on the next review, not only had there been no improvement in sales but the employees' attitudes toward you had drastically declined. They either avoided you or were unfriendly when you tried to speak to them.

You realize you must come up with a completely different plan of attack to be successful and spend the next Monday morning considering your courses of action.

Discussion Questions

1. Relate the motivation techniques described in the case to those covered in this chapter. What have you tried already? What do you think should still be tried?

2. How is it different trying to motivate people who work directly for you compared to those who work for someone else (as in the situation with the store employees in the case)?

3. Explain the role that the retail store manager plays in motivating these retail employees. What can you do to encourage more support from the managers?

4. As a follow-up to this case, you started offering financial incentives (bonuses) to employees that met the desired sales increase. Discuss the pros and cons of using incentives to increase sales.

SELF-ASSESSMENT 8.1: How Much Perseverance Do You Have?

This self-assessment exercise identifies your degree of perseverance. There are no right or wrong answers, and this is not a test. The purpose of this assessment is for you to learn about yourself. You don't have to share your results with other classmates unless you wish to do so.

Part I. Taking the Assessment

Directions for taking the perseverance scale: Please respond to the following eight items. Be honest. There are no right or wrong answers! You will be presented with some questions representing different characteristics that may or may not describe what kind of person you are.

As an example, the answer to a question could look like this:

I enjoy solving complex puzzles.

Statements	Not much like me at all	Not much like me	Somewhat like me	Mostly like me	Very much like me
1. I don't quit a task before it is finished.	1	2	3	4	5
2. I am a goal-oriented person.	1	2	3	4	5
3. I finish things despite obstacles in the way.	1	2	3	4	5
4. I am a hard worker.	1	2	3	4	5
5. I don't get sidetracked when I work.	1	2	3	4	5

Statements	Very much like me	Mostly like me	Somewhat like me	Not much like me	Not much like me at all
6. I don't finish what I start.	1	2	3	4	5
7. I give up easily.	1	2	3	4	5
8. I do not tend to stick to what I decide to do.	1	2	3	4	5

Add up all the points. The maximum score on this scale is 40 (extreme perseverance), and the lowest score on this scale is 8 (not much perseverance).

Part 1	Part 2	
1. _____	6. _____	
2. _____	7. _____	
3. _____	8. _____	
4. _____		
5. _____		
Part 1 Total _____ +	Part 2 Total _____	= Total Score _____

Sources: Adapted from the Perseverance-Persistence scale at http://ipip.ori
.org/newVIAKey.htm#Industry_Perseverance_Persistence; Finholt, T. A., &
Olson, G. M. (1997). From laboratories to collaboratories: A new organizational
form for scientific collaboration. *Psychological Science, 8*(1), 28–36.

Part II. Interpreting Your Scores

Total Score	Interpretation
8–15	Low perseverance: You may be giving up too often or letting obstacles get in the way. You get sidetracked from tasks by other things.
16–23	Fair perseverance: You might sometimes give up, but you do work hard and try to remove obstacles. You may get sidetracked.
24–32	High perseverance: You don't quit very often, and you finish things despite the obstacles. You tend to stick with a task and finish most of the time. You don't get sidetracked very often.
33–40	Very high perseverance: You are not a quitter. You stay with tasks to the finish and overcome obstacles. You stay focused and don't get sidetracked.

CHAPTER NINE

MOTIVATION
Applications

Learning Objectives

After studying this chapter, you should be able to do the following:

9.1: Demonstrate understanding of OB mod by providing an example.

9.2: Describe the four steps in the modeling process articulated in social learning theory.

9.3: Compare and contrast intrinsic and extrinsic rewards.

9.4: Discuss the guidelines for using monetary rewards effectively.

9.5: Illustrate the methods of performance management with examples.

9.6: Critique the performance review process.

9.7: Explain how feedback seeking by employees relates to more accurate perceptions of performance.

Get the edge on your studies at
edge.sagepub.com/scandura2e

- Take the chapter quiz
- Review key terms with eFlashcards
- Explore multimedia resources, SAGE readings, and more!

THE MEANING OF MONEY

We all have logo-imprinted gifts from universities, employers, or customer gifts. But do people value such tchotchkes more than money? Why doesn't your organization just give you cash instead of an engraved set of glasses with the company logo? Nobel laureate George Akerlof, a pioneer in the field of behavioral economics, found the answers by studying gift exchange at the workplace. Gifts are viewed as acts of kindness by an employer, which carries more meaning than cash. But will people work harder for gifts?

This premise was studied in a German university that needed to catalog books in their library.[1] Students were employed to catalog books, and some were told they would receive a bonus of 20% more than base pay. Another group was told they would receive a gift-wrapped water bottle. A third group didn't receive any bonus at all to establish the baseline for productivity. The results are shown in the accompanying chart. The cash bonus had no effect on the speed or accuracy of cataloging the books. But those receiving the water bottle increased their data entry rate by 25% (a productivity increase that more than offset the 7 euro cost of the water bottle). It was the thought that seemed to matter; we know from research on engagement (discussed in Chapter 4) that most employees are searching for meaning in their work. This was reinforced by a second study done by the authors. Money was delivered as a bonus but either as cash or a cute origami folded shirt with a two-euro coin that had a smiley face painted on it. The origami money gift resulted in the highest increase in productivity of all (even more than the wrapped water bottle). Another study found that paying higher wages had no effect on productivity in jobs with no future employment opportunities. However, when a portion of the wage was given as an unexpected gift (offering a bonus raise after the employee accepted the contract for temporary work), it led to higher productivity for the duration of the job.[2] The implications of these studies illustrate an important point for leaders. Even a slight gesture of appreciation may increase motivation (even if it involves a cash bonus). However, gifts seem to work best when they are personalized to the employee.

So what does money really mean? Money has symbolic meaning for employees, and it represents nonmonetary aspects of life such as achievement, success, competence, autonomy, security, and power.[3] Some people feel that money may even bring many friends. Employees pay attention to money and compare what they make to their peers. Perceived pay inequity motivates employees to take action, and compensation is often the focus of employee grievances and lawsuits regarding fairness. The essentials of reward systems and how they are administered are discussed in this chapter. First, the fundamentals that underlie the philosophy of reward systems as they are used in organizations are reviewed.

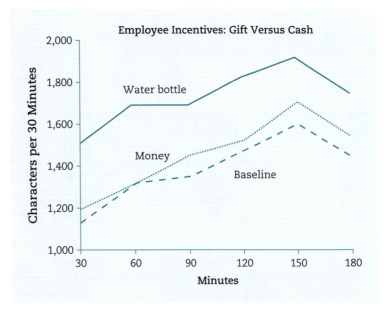

Source: Kube, S., Maréchal, M. A., & Puppe, C. (2012). The currency of reciprocity: Gift-exchange in the workplace. *American Economic Review*, 102(4), 1644–1662. Retrieved from HBR.org.

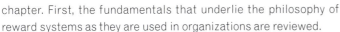

Critical Thinking Questions: The research on gifts described previously was conducted in Germany. Do you think that this would work in the United States or the culture you are from? Explain why or why not. Can you think of any potential limitations to the motivating potential of gifts?

REINFORCEMENT THEORY

Learning Objective 9.1: Demonstrate understanding of OB mod by providing an example.

Reinforcement theory is based upon the **law of effect**, which states that past actions that led to positive outcomes tend to be repeated, whereas past actions that led to negative outcomes will diminish.[4] The law of effect led to the development of **operant conditioning** (sometimes referred to as **reinforcement theory**).[5] In this approach to motivation, individual personality, thoughts, and attitudes don't motivate behavior. Instead, the emphasis in operant conditioning is on the environment. The goal of reinforcement theory is to explain learned behavior. B. F. Skinner is the psychologist most associated with this approach. He conducted experiments with animals to understand how behavior could be shaped by setting up systems of rewards and punishments. These rewards (or punishments) were contingent on the response of the animals he studied (probably the most well-recognized studies are those of rats who were taught to run mazes through the shaping of their behavior with pellets of food as rewards).

Reinforcers

Reinforcement is any event that strengthens or increases the behavior it follows. Skinner's research found there are **reinforcers** that increase behavior and those that decrease behavior. The two kinds of reinforcement that *increase* behavior are as follows:

1. Positive reinforcement is a favorable event or outcome presented after the behavior (e.g., praise or a bonus).

2. Negative reinforcement is the removal of an unpleasant event or outcome after the display of a behavior (e.g., ending the daily criticism when an employee shows up for work on time).

Punishment

Punishment, in contrast, is the presentation of an adverse event or outcome that causes a *decrease* in the behavior it follows. There are two kinds of punishment:

1. Punishment by application is the presentation of an unpleasant event or outcome to weaken the response it follows (e.g., writing a letter to an employee's file for failing to meet a deadline).

2. Punishment by removal (also called extinction) is when a pleasant event or outcome is removed after a behavior occurs (e.g., withholding praise when an employee does not perform well).

> Critical Thinking Questions: Explain why punishment may not be the most effective way to encourage learning. What would you do to encourage learning instead?

A summary table of these contingencies of reinforcement is shown in Figure 9.1; it is important to consider whether the reward is applied or withheld and whether the event is pleasant or unpleasant. Figure 9.1 and the previously given definitions and examples refer to the type of reward or punishment that is applied or removed. For example, a pleasant event that is applied would be a manager praising an employee when he or she completes an excellent project report (a positive reinforcement).

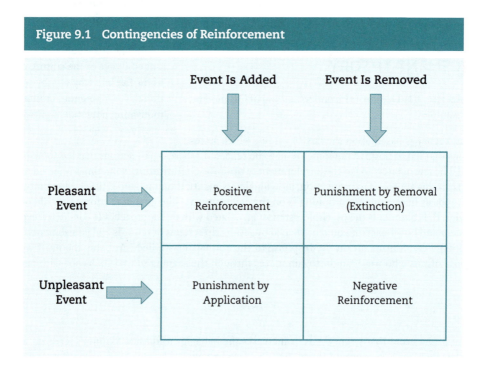

Figure 9.1   Contingencies of Reinforcement

	Event Is Added	Event Is Removed
Pleasant Event	Positive Reinforcement	Punishment by Removal (Extinction)
Unpleasant Event	Punishment by Application	Negative Reinforcement

Figure 9.2 Schedules of Partial Reinforcement

	Interval	Ratio
Fixed	Reinforced after a certain amount of time has passed	Reinforced after a certain number of responses have occurred
Variable (Random)	Reinforced after an average amount of time has passed	Reinforced after an average number of responses have occurred

Schedules of Reinforcement

Skinner's research also found how often a reward (or punishment) is applied also predicts learning and motivation. He referred to this as the **schedules of reinforcement**.[6] The first schedule is continuous—a specified behavior is rewarded or punished every time it occurs. This is not seen often in organizations; however, it is useful during the learning process (e.g., when an employee is learning to use a new computer program). In this example, the employee would be allowed to leave work one-half hour early (a positive event) each time he completes a module of a computer training program successfully. Once the employee has attained an acceptable level of mastery, they are moved to a partial reinforcement schedule. For example, the employee is no longer rewarded or punished every time, but they are rewarded (punished) on a more random basis as described next.

As illustrated in Figure 9.2, the schedules of partial reinforcement are based on time (interval) or the number of times the response is given by the employee (ratio). Also, the schedule can be fixed or variable (random). These two dimensions result in four possible schedules of partial reinforcement as shown in the figure:

1. **Fixed-interval schedules are those where the first response is rewarded only after a specified amount of time has elapsed.** This schedule causes high amounts of responding near the end of the interval. An example of this in a work setting is the way pay is typically disbursed—every 2 weeks or every month, for example. After a fixed amount of time, the employee receives a paycheck.

2. **Variable-interval schedules occur when a response is rewarded after an unpredictable amount of time has passed.** This schedule produces a slow, steady rate of response. An example of this would be bringing in bagels for breakfast once a week for employees but varying which day they are brought in (e.g., sometimes on Monday and sometimes Wednesday). The employees never know when they will be treated to bagels, so the element of surprise is motivating and they may come to work on time regularly so they don't miss out.

3. **Fixed-ratio schedules are those where a response is reinforced only after a specific number of responses.** This schedule produces a high, steady rate of responding. An example of a fixed-ratio schedule

would be payment to employees based upon the number of items they produce (a piece-rate pay system). In piece-rate systems, the employee is paid for each article produced; for example, a worker sewing zippers into jeans is paid for each zipper correctly sewn in.

4. **Variable-ratio schedules occur when a response is reinforced after an unpredictable number of responses.** This schedule creates a high, steady rate of responding. Gambling and lottery games are good examples of a reward based on a variable ratio schedule. This is why gambling results in such long-term and persistent behavior (it's the element of chance that motivates the behavior). In a work setting, this might be offering praise to an employee for good performance after one time and then again after four times and then another time after two times.

Partial schedules are more motivating than continuous reinforcement (e.g., the employee may become accustomed to praise from the leader so it loses its motivating power on behavior). Of the partial reinforcement schedules, research has demonstrated that the variable-ratio schedule of partial reinforcement produces the most persistent, long-term effects on behavior.[7] Receiving rewards in a random fashion tends to increase effort until the reward is received.

As the previously given examples indicate, reinforcement is used in organizations in a variety of ways to increase employee motivation and performance. It is also used to extinguish undesirable behaviors. Given the strong research base supporting the principles of reinforcement theory, it represents a powerful tool most leaders use to motivate performance.[8] The application of reinforcement theory in organizational behavior (OB) is known as **organizational behavior modification (OB mod).**

Organizational Behavior Modification

OB mod has been employed to increase performance and reduce absenteeism. Figure 9.3 shows how to apply OB mod using the principles of reinforcement theory. As shown in the figure, the first step is to pinpoint the specific behavior that needs to be changed. For example, coming to work on time every day is an example of a behavior that needs intervention

> **Critical Thinking Questions:** Discuss why the biweekly paycheck form of payment is not the most motivating schedule based upon the principles of reinforcement. Provide an example of a method of payment that would be more motivating.

Figure 9.3   Applied Behavior Modification

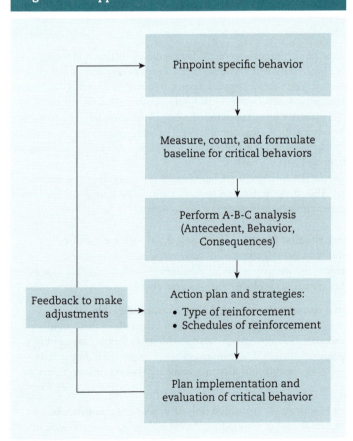

if an employee is not doing it. Second, measure the baseline: How many days per month is the employee on time? Third, perform an **A-B-C analysis**. This stands for *antecedents*, *behavior*, and *consequences*:

- **Antecedents:** What is causing the behavior? Consider both internal and external factors.

- **Behavior:** What is the current behavior? What is the desired behavior?

- **Consequences:** What is currently reinforcing the behavior? What needs to be changed?

Fourth, develop an action plan based on reinforcement theory strategies to apply (using the contingencies of reinforcement and the schedules). Implement the plan and then evaluate the plan comparing the behavior to the baseline (after compared to before). This will provide feedback, and the plan may need to be changed or another behavior targeted for the future. A comprehensive review of OB mod interventions[9] stressed the importance of following up after interventions to ensure the long-term durability of the intervention. Also, the authors concluded that follow-up is needed to provide the feedback necessary to adjust the intervention if warranted. Leaders use the principles of OB mod to change employee behaviors by meeting with followers to discuss their performance. In some cases, this discussion takes place during performance management reviews (this process is discussed later in this chapter).

An example of applied OB mod for an employee who is late to work frequently is shown in Figure 9.4. As this example shows, the specific behavior targeted is that the employee arrives at work on time (say, 8:30 a.m. each day).

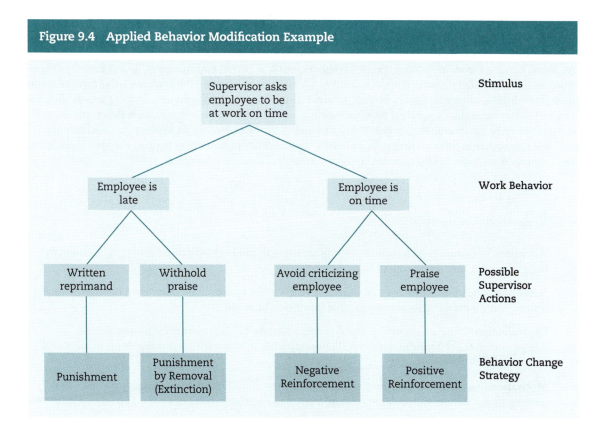

Figure 9.4 Applied Behavior Modification Example

If the employee is on time, the supervisor can praise them (positive reinforcement) or withhold criticism (this only works if the supervisor has consistently criticized the employee's tardiness prior to the day they arrive on time, of course). If the employee is late, the objective is to decrease the behavior, so the supervisor can withhold praise to produce extinction of the behavior (punishment by removal), or write a reprimand and put it in the employee's file, which is unpleasant (punishment). Of course, the supervisor can use more than one behavior change strategy and should eventually move the employee to a variable interval or ratio schedule (i.e., apply or remove the reinforcement more randomly) once the employee is coming to work consistently on time.

Proponents of behavior modification argue that it has a strong research base and applies to all employees regardless of individual difference and national culture.[10] A meta-analysis found that OB mod increased task performance by 17%; however, results of interventions using OB mod were stronger in manufacturing than service organizations.[11] Critics of operant conditioning and OB mod have argued that the results can be explained using theories that involve cognitions (thoughts) of employees.[12] Also, some people may react negatively to the use of operant conditioning to control the behavior of employees, feeling that it is manipulative. In response to criticisms of behavior modification, subsequent research incorporated thought processes into reinforcement theory. **Social learning theory** extends operant conditioning to consider the fact that people can learn from watching other people succeed or fail.

SOCIAL LEARNING THEORY

Learning Objective 9.2: Describe the four steps in the modeling process articulated in social learning theory.

Albert Bandura presented social learning theory, and it is perhaps the most influential theory of learning today.[13] Bandura believed that operant conditioning (reinforcement) was useful but did not explain all of the ways a person can learn. Social learning theory introduced the social element into how people acquire new skills and described the ways that people learn by watching other people. Known as **observational learning** (or modeling), this form of learning explains much behavior in organizations. Second, external reinforcements are not the only factors that influence motivation. Intrinsic reinforcement is related to pride, satisfaction, and a sense of accomplishment in learning something new. Social learning theory considers people's thoughts as well as their perceptions of others (a social cognitive theory). While reinforcement theorists maintained external rewards create permanent behavioral changes, social learning theory proposes that people can learn things but not necessarily change their behavior.

The Modeling Process

The modeling process has four steps:

1. **Attention.** To learn, a person has to be paying attention to another's behavior. People pay attention to things that are either interesting or new.

2. **Retention.** The information must be stored for access in the future. This is important to observational learning since a person must remember what they have observed.

3. **Reproduction.** Once information is noted and retained, the next step is that the person imitates (i.e., performs) the behavior that they recall. Repeating the behavior (i.e., practicing) leads to improved performance.

4. **Motivation.** For observational learning to work, the person needs motivation to imitate. Thus, social learning theory discusses the roles of reinforcement and punishment. For example, if you see another

student rewarded with extra credit points for participating in class every day, you might begin to do the same.

As noted previously, not all reinforcement comes from external rewards such as pay. OB researchers became interested in the motivational power of both external (extrinsic) as well as internal (intrinsic) reinforcement on motivation at work. The next section discusses these two forms of motivational rewards and what the research has shown regarding their effectiveness.

INTRINSIC VERSUS EXTRINSIC REWARDS

Learning Objective 9.3: Compare and contrast intrinsic and extrinsic rewards.

Expectancy theory (covered in Chapter 8) includes both intrinsic and extrinsic work motivation.[14,15] **Intrinsic motivation** is when someone works on a task because they find it interesting and gain satisfaction from the task itself. **Extrinsic motivation** involves the performance to outcome instrumentality between the task and a tangible reward. Satisfaction does not come from the task itself but rather from the extrinsic outcome to which the activity leads (e.g., working extra hours to earn a bonus). Work should be set up in a manner so effective performance leads to both intrinsic and extrinsic rewards to produce job satisfaction.[16] There are other sources of motivation in addition to intrinsic and extrinsic such as the enhancement of self-concept and the degree to which a person internalizes the goals of the organization.[17]

Does paying someone to do a job reduce their intrinsic motivation? Intrinsic motivation refers to their internal reasons for doing something such as enjoying the task or being interested in it. For example, are you reading this because you want to get a good grade (extrinsic), or are you interested in learning more about motivation (intrinsic)? The answer can be both, but OB researchers designed experiments to see what would happen if people were paid for doing something they enjoy. Extrinsic rewards can lead to reduction in intrinsic motivation. For example, in an experimental study, paying money was found to undermine college students' intrinsic motivation to perform a task.[18] These experiments were replicated in work organizations.[19]

Rewards should be administered so that they are contingent upon effective performance. However, research on the impact of paying someone to do something that they enjoy showed surprising findings. While it appears counterintuitive, pay may not motivate people to perform at the highest levels. Also, extrinsic motivation plus intrinsic motivation (for example, pay plus challenging work) may not always combine to produce the highest motivation (see the boxed insert for further discussion of this effect).

> **Critical Thinking Questions:** Explain why paying someone to do something they like doing reduces their intrinsic motivation. What steps can a leader take to address this situation?

Relationship Between Intrinsic and Extrinsic Rewards

There can be synergistic effects between intrinsic and extrinsic motivation, and there are two psychological mechanisms that illustrate this. First, "**extrinsics in service of intrinsics**"[20] refers to how extrinsic rewards may support an employee's sense of competence if they don't undermine autonomy (self-determination). For example, a reward can be more time to work on creativity projects. This has been implemented at Google, where engineers and project managers are given 20% of their work time to work on something that they are passionate about. In other words, one day per week they can work on anything they like, even if it falls outside of the scope of their job or is unrelated to the mission of the company.[21] A second mechanism is the **motivation–work cycle match**. This is

RESEARCH IN ACTION

Why the "Carrot and Stick" May Not Always Work

Daniel Pink (2009), in his book *Drive: The Surprising Truth About What Motivates Us,* discusses three forms of motivation as "operating systems." Motivation 1.0 was humankind's inherent need to survive. The next operating system, Motivation 2.0, was the carrot-and-stick approach (or the rewards and punishments we discussed in reinforcement theory research). Pink is critical of the carrot-and-stick approach, pointing out the carrot and the stick can produce results that are the opposite of what leaders are looking for because rewards can transform an interesting task into drudgery; they can turn play into work. Traditional "if-then" rewards (if you do this, then you will get that) cannot produce high levels of motivation for seven reasons, according to Pink:

- It extinguishes intrinsic motivation.
- It diminishes performance.
- It crushes creativity.
- It crowds out good behavior.
- It encourages cheating and unethical behavior.
- It becomes addictive.
- It fosters short-term thinking.

Pink considered these to be bugs in human beings' current operating systems. For those driven by intrinsic motivation, the drive to do something because it is interesting and challenging is essential for high creativity and motivation. Goals that people set for themselves for mastering a skill are healthy. But goals imposed by others such as sales targets, quarterly returns, and standardized test scores can sometimes have the seven dangerous side effects listed previously. Pink presented what he believes is the next operating system for human motivation—Motivation 3.0, which goes beyond the carrot-and-stick approach and centers on intrinsic motivation. He believes there are three important aspects to this new operating system based on psychological empowerment: autonomy, mastery, and purpose. Pink highlighted autonomy as one of the most important motivating factors at work. He said that people want control over the task (what they do), time (when they do it), team (who they do it with), and technique (how they do it).[22] These three new elements of motivation are fueled by intrinsic and not extrinsic rewards.

Discussion Questions

1. Discuss Pink's premise in light of what you have learned about the effectiveness of positive reinforcement. Why are these criticisms valid (or not)?
2. Do you agree that intrinsic motivation is a preferable way to influence performance? Why or why not? Why is autonomy so important to intrinsic motivation?
3. What other factors do you think are important for increasing intrinsic motivation?

Source: Pink, D. H. (2009). *Drive: The surprising truth about what motivates us.* New York, NY: Penguin Books.

the understanding that innovation occurs in phases and intrinsic motivation may be more important during the idea-generation phase. However, when the project is being implemented, extrinsic rewards may be needed to ensure that deliverables are produced on time and within the budget. A longitudinal study found support for this idea in study of project teams.[23] Team members reported higher levels of radical creativity in early phases of a project compared to incremental creativity at later phases. Thus, one type of motivation may not suit all types of project work. A meta-analysis of over 40 years of research on intrinsic and extrinsic motivation found that intrinsic motivation predicts quality of performance, whereas extrinsic motivation (incentives) is a better predictor of quantity of performance.[24] These findings may be surprising since most people think that money matters more than other rewards. In fact, paying people money for doing something they enjoy may actually *reduce* their motivation.[25] Edward Deci and his colleagues developed the theory of **self-determination** to explain why this happens.

Critical Thinking Questions: Use reinforcement theory to explain why extrinsic rewards may not produce long-term effects on motivation. What should a leader do instead to motivate workers based on the relationship between intrinsic and extrinsic motivation?

Self-Determination Theory

Intrinsic motivation is a function of a person's needs for autonomy and **competence** in the theory of self-determination (also known as **cognitive evaluation theory**).[26] *Autonomy* is the need to work alone without constant surveillance. *Competence* is the sense of mastery an employee has over their job. A large-scale meta-analytic study of 99 studies of self-determination theory (119 distinct samples) found that these needs for autonomy and competence significantly predict employee psychological growth, internalization (the shift of motivation from extrinsic to intrinsic), and well-being.[27]

The effects of a reward depend on how the person views the reward's effect on their autonomy and competence. Rewards that diminish these perceptions tend to decrease intrinsic motivation. The issue with extrinsic rewards like money is that such rewards might be interpreted by employees as controlling by the boss rather than indicators of their competence. If the reward is seen as controlling, then the individual's need for autonomy is challenged, and this undermines intrinsic motivation. If a reward is seen as useful feedback and informational, then it increases motivation. For example, setting limits for employees could be seen as either informational or controlling depending on the relationship with the boss.[28] Managers can create a climate of trust that alters whether a person views their rewards as controlling or good feedback.[29] For example, a leader can communicate a pay raise without compromising motivation by emphasizing the informational aspect of the raise as valuable feedback rather than just money. Self-determination theory views rewards as a continuum from the lack of motivation to intrinsic motivation as shown in Figure 9.5. Extrinsic motivation is seen as complex and ranges from external regulation (rewards and punishments) to feelings of self-worth derived from job performance (introjected regulation). At the higher end of extrinsic motivation, identified regulation means employees realize that the goals of the organization are important. At the highest level for extrinsic motivation, the employee identifies with the values and integrates them into automatic performance (integrated regulation). This continuum helps the manager understand that extrinsic motivation can play an important role in encouraging employee performance. However, as shown in the figure, intrinsic motivation reflects the enjoyment of work, and extrinsic rewards may not be needed to maintain high levels of performance.[30] Therefore, with respect to performance, incentives and intrinsic motivation are not necessarily antagonistic and are best considered simultaneously. So it is important to keep in mind that extrinsic rewards can motivate, but they also have limitations. The next section discusses what money can and cannot do in terms of motivation.

WHAT MONEY CAN AND CANNOT DO

Learning Objective 9.4: Discuss the guidelines for using monetary rewards effectively.

There are pros and cons of using money as a motivational tool.[31] On the one hand, organizations that appropriately tie pay to performance and pay more have higher rates of return.[32] A study of hospitals showed that pay-level practices and pay structures combined to affect resource efficiency, patient care outcomes, and financial performance. On the other

Figure 9.5   The Self-Determination Continuum of Rewards

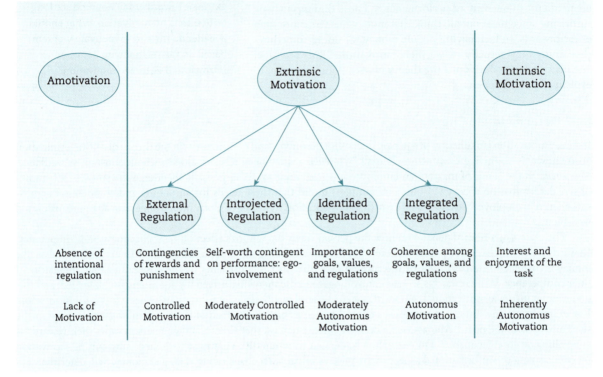

Source: Gagné, M., & Deci, E. L. (2005). Self-determination theory and work motivation. *Journal of Organizational Behavior, 26*(4), 331–362.

hand, tying pay directly to performance can have dysfunctional or even unethical consequences.[33] For example, Green Giant, a producer of frozen and canned vegetables, implemented a pay system that rewarded employees for removing insects from vegetables. It was later discovered that employees were bringing insects from home and putting them into the vegetables to receive the monetary rewards.[34]

Pay Dispersion

Another caveat regarding money as a motivational tool is that care must be taken when implementing systems in which employees receive different levels of rewards for individual efforts. This results in **pay dispersion**, which can cause jealously among employees or harm team performance. If pay dispersion creates **pay inequity** due to discrimination, it may result in litigation under the Equal Pay Act of 1963 (see Case Study 9.1 for an example of a pay dispersion lawsuit and an update on legislation related to equal pay at the workplace).

To summarize, there are five evidence-based guidelines for money as a motivator: (1) define and measure performance accurately, (2) make rewards contingent on performance, (3) reward employees in a timely manner, (4) maintain justice in the reward system, and (5) use monetary and nonmonetary rewards.[35] These evidence-based guidelines are summarized in Table 9.1.

Table 9.1 Research-Based Recommendations on How to Use Monetary Rewards Effectively

Principles	Implementation Guidelines
1. Define and measure performance accurately.	• Specify what employees are expected to do, as well as what they should refrain from doing. • Align employees' performance with the strategic goals of the organization. • Measure both behaviors and results. But the greater the control over the achievement of desired outcomes, the greater the emphasis should be on measuring results.
2. Make rewards contingent on performance.	• Ensure pay levels vary significantly based on performance levels. • Explicitly communicate that differences in pay levels are due to different levels of performance and not because of other reasons. • Take cultural norms into account. For example, consider individualism–collectivism when deciding how much emphasis to place on rewarding individual versus team performance.
3. Reward employees in a timely manner.	• Distribute fake currencies or reward points that can later be traded for cash, goods, or services. • Switch from a performance appraisal system to a performance management system, which encourages timely rewards through ongoing and regular evaluations, feedback, and developmental opportunities. • Provide a specific and accurate explanation regarding why the employee received the particular reward.
4. Maintain justice in the reward system.	• Only promise rewards that are available. • When increasing monetary rewards, increase employees' variable pay levels instead of their base pay. • Make all employees eligible to earn rewards from incentive plan. • Communicate reasons for failure to provide promised rewards, changes in the payouts, or changes in the reward system.
5. Use monetary and nonmonetary rewards.	• Do not limit the provision of nonmonetary rewards to noneconomic rewards. Rather, use not only praise and recognition but also noncash awards consisting of various goods and services. • Provide nonmonetary rewards that are needs-satisfying for the recipient. • Use monetary rewards to encourage voluntary participation in nonmonetary reward programs that are more directly beneficial to employee or organizational performance.

Source: Adapted from Aguinis, H., Joo, H., & Gottfredson, R. K. (2013). What monetary rewards can and cannot do: How to show employees the money. *Business Horizons,* 56(2), 241–259.

As the previous review of monetary and nonmonetary rewards shows, the ability to assess employee performance is essential to the successful implementation of any reward system. Most organizations today employ pay for performance incentive systems, which include individual merit pay.[36] A review of this research concludes with this: "Job performance is perhaps the most central construct in work psychology."[37] The approaches to performance evaluation and guidelines for effective practice are covered next.

PERFORMANCE MANAGEMENT

Learning Objective 9.5: Illustrate the methods of performance management with examples.

As noted previously, performance management is essential for the determination of compensation and other outcomes such as promotions. But there are other objectives that are equally important. The performance management session is an opportunity to regularly discuss an employee's performance and results. The leader can identify the follower's strengths, weaknesses, and areas for improvement. The process supports pay equity in which followers are paid according to their inputs and results, and it supports a climate of organizational justice. Performance management, thus, provides essential feedback for followers. Importantly, it can recognize exceptional performance and document weak performance. Also, it can lead to effective goal setting for future performance and identify training that may be needed to improve skills. Most organizations use the performance management process for compensation decisions and performance improvement as well as to provide feedback to employees.[38] Next, we discuss the sources and methods used by organizations to evaluate employee performance—who rates performance and how it is managed.

Sources of Performance Management Ratings

In most organizations, the immediate supervisor is involved in the performance appraisal and often is the only person conducting the review. This appraisal is often reviewed by the human resources department. In some cases, the process is reviewed by a manager one level above the supervisor. However, recent trends have included ratings from higher management, peers (coworkers), the employee's followers, and customers. Performance appraisal may also include self-ratings in which the employee rates his or her own performance, and this becomes a part of the file. However, self-ratings are typically used for development purposes and not for compensation or promotion decisions because they suffer from self-interest bias and they don't agree well with supervisor ratings.[39] In a **360-degree performance appraisal**, the input from a number of these sources is included to provide a more comprehensive view of an employee's performance. The research evidence on 360 degree suggests it increases the perspectives that provide input into the review process.[40,41] The challenge with 360-degree reviews is that organizations don't often provide necessary training for peers to provide constructive feedback. Peers, for example, tend to be more lenient than supervisors in rating their coworkers.[42,43] Despite these challenges, 360-degree feedback has been implemented successfully in numerous organizations.

An example of a successful implementation is Starwood Hotels and Resorts Worldwide. The executive team wanted to provide their managers with valuable feedback on their strengths and areas for development. They used the viaPeople 360-degree feedback system along with a proprietary, internally developed, and validated competency model, and this process produced the following individual and organizational benefits:[44]

Individual Benefits

- A simple, easy-to-use 360-degree feedback tool

- A "self-paced" 360-degree feedback report complete with targeted questions to guide the leader through the process of uncovering strengths and development areas

- Specific interpretive tables and graphs in the feedback report that helped leaders analyze their data

- A downloadable discussion guide for report recipients and their managers—what to focus on, how to lead and focus the discussion, and how to deal with emotions/defensiveness

Organizational Benefits

- Competency/skill strengths and development areas across division and employee level

- Better understanding the skill mix across the organization, Starwood was able to more effectively leverage the leadership strengths and refocus efforts where developmental opportunities may exist

- Data specific for each division provided (by viaPeople) allowed Starwood to target local training efforts, thereby saving precious resources

- Each divisional leader received analysis of their division's results so they could take specific actions on the data and have a better understanding of the team strengths/development areas.

Performance Management Methods

It is best to avoid rating traits such as having a positive attitude since they may not relate to actual performance.[45] Most organizations use a standard form to evaluate employee performance. There may be an overall global rating for performance, but there are also specific dimensions that are rated. These ratings are typically on a graphic rating scale having multiple points along a continuum. Here is an example:

Outstanding	Performance is consistently superior.
Exceeds expectations	Performance is routinely above job requirements.
Meets expectations	Performance is regularly competent and dependable.
Below expectations	Performance fails to meet job requirements on a frequent basis.
Unsatisfactory	Performance is consistently unacceptable.

An example of a graphic rating scale is shown in Toolkit Activity 9.2 at the end of this chapter. You have the opportunity to practice using this commonly-used performance management tool in the role-play exercise.

Another approach is to use **behaviorally anchored rating scales (BARS)** in which a vertical scale is presented with specific examples of performance provided. For example, for an executive assistant, a BARS might look like this:

Performance Dimension: Knowledge of Company Policies	
Outstanding	Knows details of all policies and procedures from memory, recommends updates, and communicates policies to all employees in the office
Exceeds expectations	Maintains organized files and can look up policies; maintains updates and communications to all employees in the office
Meets expectations	Has familiarity with policies and can locate them on the organization's website, including updates; communicates policies to most employees in the office.
Below expectations	Is not familiar with policies or updates, and does not communicate policies to employees in the office.
Unsatisfactory	Makes errors in locating or interpreting policies or updates; communicates incorrect information to employees in the office.

As this table shows, the creation and updating of BARS can be time consuming, but they can be more effective because they focus on specific behaviors rather than general statements such as "knowledge of work."

Some organizations use a forced-ranking method in which all employees in the work group are ranked relative to one another. This approach was made famous by Jack Welch at GE, where he committed to firing the bottom 10% of the workforce each year.[46] Even if the bottom 10% is not fired, such forced-ranking systems may make managers uncomfortable and create a culture of competition. Recently, such forced-ranking systems have come under scrutiny by large corporations. Microsoft, for example, has done away with their long-standing practice of forced rankings. According to research conducted by the Institute for Corporate Productivity, only 145 companies surveyed in 2011 reported that their appraisal process included forced rankings—down from 49% in 2009.[47] See the boxed insert for an update on why many organizations are doing away with forced rankings due to their limitations.

> **Critical Thinking Questions:** Do you agree that forced rankings should be eliminated in evaluating performance? Why or why not? Discuss the positive side of having competition in the organization.

PROBLEMS WITH PERFORMANCE REVIEWS

Learning Objective 9.6: Critique the performance review process.

There are issues related to performance appraisals that a leader needs to know about. Some employees view the appraisal process as unfair and showing favoritism. Others may fear the appraisal process and view it as punitive.[48] There are perceptual biases that may affect the rater's ability to accurately rate follower performance (from Chapter 5, major perceptual errors are primacy, recency, availability, contrast, and halo). These errors have been shown by research to affect the performance rating process. In addition, there may be a tendency for a rater to be too lenient (or too strict) in their ratings.[49] They might have a **central tendency error** in which they rate all dimensions of performance as average (e.g., rating every dimension as 3 on a 5-point scale). Cultural values such as power distance and collectivism may influence how a rater assesses the performance of another person.[50] Performance appraisals should be supported by training for those making the ratings to avoid these errors and increase sensitivity to the perspectives of employees from different cultural backgrounds.

These perceptual biases may be avoided by rewarding for results rather than behaviors. For example, in **profit-sharing plans**, employee bonuses are based upon reaching a financial target such as return on assets or net income. **Stock options** are a variation of profit sharing where employees are given stock options as part of their compensation package. **Gain-sharing plans** are another alternative, in which compensation is tied to unit-level performance (e.g., the employees receive a percentage of the sales increase or cost savings for efficiency improvements). These plans tend to increase performance.[51] However, the pay may be too variable for employees to rely solely on these plans for their total compensation. Also, the focus on results may encourage unethical behaviors to reach the targets.[52]

Other Forms of Compensation

Other benefits that employees may value as rewards include **flexible working hours**, which research has shown relates to employee satisfaction and motivation. Flexible working hours may be formal (i.e., allowing employees to arrive later to work and stay later) or informal (i.e., a supervisor being flexible regarding an employee's need to pick up children from school). Another variation on flexible hours is **job sharing**, or splitting one full-time job into two jobs.[53] Another benefit that many employees value is **remote working** (also known as telecommuting), or the ability to work from home—or anywhere. A study of 2,617 employees in four organizations[54] found that remote working and flexible hours were related to organizational commitment. This commitment translated into higher job performance. Another reward that progressive organizations are offering is **sabbaticals** from work. A sabbatical is a leave taken from work to "recharge one's batteries" or take care of family responsibilities. In some cases sabbaticals are paid and others are unpaid. For example, Genentech, a San Francisco, California, breast cancer research firm, offers a 6-week paid sabbatical after 6 years of continuous service with the company. In 2015, 1,100 employees took advantage of the program, in addition to their 18 paid vacation days.[55]

Some managers feel that performance appraisals offer little benefit relative to the time involved. Some are not comfortable with face-to-face confrontation over difficult performance issues. Finally, there is an inherent conflict in the role of the supervisor as evaluator and at the same time performance coach. Despite this discomfort on the part of supervisors, research has shown employees are satisfied with their performance evaluation when the process combines development with administrative reward purposes.[56] Moreover, employees reported higher intentions to use developmental feedback when rewards were also discussed. One study found that all employees are unhappy with receiving negative feedback—even those with a strong learning orientation.[57] It appears that negative feedback does not help employees learn more from their jobs.

Another criticism that has been leveled at the performance management process is that by focusing on individual achievement, effective teamwork is discouraged.[58, 59] While the critics of individual performance management have made important points, team-based reward systems also have drawbacks. Most employees prefer that their pay be based on individual merit rather than group output.[60] This preference is strongest among the most productive and achievement-oriented employees.[61,62] Thus, if pay is based on group performance, an organization's best performers

BEST PRACTICES

Rethinking the Review: For Whom the Bell Curve Tolls

The logic behind forced-ranking systems is that employee performance falls on a bell-shaped curve—the normal distribution, as you learned in your statistics courses. Thus, only a small percentage of employees fall into the outstanding category, and an approximately equal number fall into the unsatisfactory category. Most employees are considered average in terms of their performance and need further coaching and/or training to improve. Large organizations have recently been questioning whether such systems work. Concerns have been raised that forced rankings are demotivating and harm cooperation and teamwork. Some companies, including Microsoft and Adobe Systems, have even removed numerical ratings from their evaluation systems after learning that employees stop listening after they get their number and don't hear the essential feedback they need to improve their performance. Shelly Carlin, senior vice president of human resources at Motorola Solutions, agrees: "In a traditional review, the employee listens until he hears the rating and then tunes out because he's doing the calculation in his head about how that will affect his bonus."[63] At Adobe Systems, Donna Morris, the senior vice president of human resources, noticed that turnover increased each year after the performance review process. There has also been a trend toward more frequent reviews—quarterly or monthly—rather than the traditional 1-year review.[64] Morris stated the following:

> We came to a fairly quick decision that we would abolish the performance review, which meant we would no longer have one-time-of-the-year formal written review. What's more, we would abolish performance rankings and levels in order to move away from people feeling like they were labeled.[65]

The company changed to a process where check-in conversations that focus on ongoing feedback were instituted instead of numerical ratings each year.[66] In addition to reducing turnover, increasing regular feedback, and improving teamwork, many organizations feel that the performance review process must change because organizations themselves have changed. According to the founder and principal at Bersin by Deloitte, a research-based provider of human resource systems, "Organization structures have changed and companies need to be more agile. We have a shortage of key talent and the keys to success now focus on regular alignment, coaching, creating passion and engagement, and continuous employee development."[67]

Discussion Questions

1. List the pros of performance appraisals. Provide an example of when a performance appraisal has a positive benefit.
2. List the cons of performance appraisals. Provide an example of when a performance appraisal has a negative outcome.
3. Based on motivation theory, we know that employees need feedback to perform well. Describe an alternative to performance appraisal that provides necessary feedback.

Sources: Bersin, J. (2013). Is it time to scrap performance appraisals? Retrieved on December 2, 2013, from http://www.forbes.com/sites/joshbersin/2013/05/06/time-to-scrap-performance-appraisals; McGregor, J. (2013). For whom the bell curve tolls. Retrieved on November 20, 2013, from http://www.washingtonpost.com/blogs/on-leadership/wp/2013/11/20/for-whom-the-bell-curve=tolls; Morris, D. (2013). Forget reviews, let's look forward. Retrieved on November 20, 2013, from http://blogs.adobe.com/conversations/tag/donna-morris; Ramirez, J. C. (2013). Rethinking the review: After 50 years of debate, has the time come to chuck the performance review? Retrieved on November 20, 2013, from www.hronline.com/HRE/view/story.jhtmal?id=534355695&.

Critical Thinking Questions: Explain how the management of individual performance may harm team performance. How can this be addressed?

may become frustrated and seek other jobs. It's best to offer mixed or aggregate compensation systems, which include individual merit pay, group incentives, and gain sharing to offset the advantages and disadvantages of the different approaches.

A research report from McKinsey Consulting summarizes recent trends that reflect changes to traditional performance appraisals in organizations. These trends include the following:

- Some companies are rethinking what constitutes employee performance by focusing specifically on individuals who are a step function away from average—at either the high or low end of performance—rather than trying to differentiate among the bulk of employees in the middle.

- Many companies are also collecting more objective performance data through systems that automate real-time analyses.

- Performance data are used less and less as a crude instrument for setting compensation. Indeed, some companies are severing the link between evaluation and compensation, at least for the majority of the workforce, while linking them ever more comprehensively at the high and low ends of performance.

- Better data back up as a shift in emphasis from backward-looking evaluations to fact-based performance and development discussions, which are becoming frequent and as-needed rather than annual events.[68]

What should a leader do to improve motivation given these trends in performance management? A leader should focus on what is important to the employee and what they learned from mistakes. Performance management should be about employee growth and development. Leadership consultant Jose Luis Romero suggests that growth means two things:

1. To help employees possess the needed skill level to achieve desired performance; and

2. To help employees develop the ability to exceed desired performance and move to greater levels of more complex performance.[69]

HR consultant Earl Silver notes that ratings can be demotivating, so it is important for a leader to separate discussions of growth and development from salary increases. He reminds leaders to make an investment in making their performance management process work effectively to motivate employees.[70] Toolkit Activity 9.1, at the end of this chapter, provides some additional tips for conducting an effective performance appraisal. Then practice your skills in developing a plan for growth and development by completing the role-play exercise in Toolkit Activity 9.2.

As noted previously, one of the primary goals of the performance evaluation process is to provide feedback to employees on their performance. Research has shown that some employees seek feedback from their supervisors to enhance their performance that does not depend on the formal performance management process. Thus, the formal appraisal review process is not always enough to provide followers with the feedback they need to perform well. Research on feedback seeking by followers has demonstrated that accuracy of follower perceptions of their performance is improved by more frequent feedback from leaders.

FEEDBACK SEEKING

Learning Objective 9.7: Explain how feedback seeking by employees relates to more accurate perceptions of performance.

As noted previously, performance management systems have been criticized for emphasis on categorizing employees and failure to address the followers' need for feedback on their work on a day-to-day basis.[71] As shown in Figure 9.6,

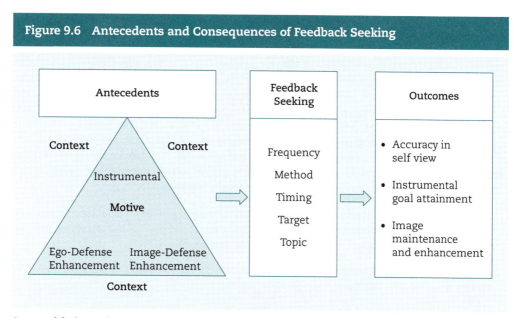

Figure 9.6   Antecedents and Consequences of Feedback Seeking

Antecedents

Context | Context

Instrumental

Motive

Ego-Defense Enhancement | Image-Defense Enhancement

Context

Feedback Seeking

Frequency

Method

Timing

Target

Topic

Outcomes

- Accuracy in self view
- Instrumental goal attainment
- Image maintenance and enhancement

Source: Ashford, S. J., Blatt, R., & Vandewalle, D. (2003). Reflections on the looking glass: A review of research on feedback-seeking behavior in organizations. *Journal of Management, 29*(6), 773–779. p. 775.

the situation affects the person's motives for **feedback seeking**. People may either want to defend their self-perception or image (ego or image defense). Alternatively, their goal may be to enhance their self-perception (or image) in the eyes of others (by asking for feedback on something they knew they did a good job on, for example). There are five patterns of feedback seeking that matter: (1) how frequently people seek feedback, (2) how they seek it (observing, comparing, or asking for it), (3) the timing, (4) whom they ask for feedback from (i.e., the target), and (5) what they ask for feedback about (e.g., success on an task assignment).[72] Outcomes from feedback seeking are a more accurate perception of one's own performance and progress on goal attainment by gaining feedback when needed. Also, one's self-perception and image may be enhanced through the five strategies of feedback seeking. Research on feedback seeking suggests seeking negative feedback does improve an employee's image (unless the feedback seeker is a poor performer). However, seeking positive feedback can be detrimental to a *leader's* image as seen by subordinates.

> **Critical Thinking Questions:** Can you explain why it isn't a good idea for a leader to seek feedback from followers? Do you agree or disagree? Why or why not?

LEADERSHIP IMPLICATIONS: MOTIVATING WITH REWARDS

Leaders play an important role in managing follower motivation and performance. Research has shown that the relationship between and leader and follower (i.e., leader–member exchange [LMX]) is an important factor in the performance appraisal process. A study found that perceptions of performance management process fairness matter to individuals, and high LMX employees tend to see the process as being fairer than low LMX employees.[73] Leaders need to pay close attention to the extent to which followers perceive that the performance appraisal process is procedurally fair. The authors conclude that "*all* employees need to feel cared for and supported."[74] Leaders should ask their followers how they feel about the organization's performance appraisal procedures and practices on an informal basis. Suggestions for improving the process should be taken seriously. Good supervisor–subordinate relationships create a social context that substantially influences the performance management discussion and how followers respond to their feedback.[75]

A longitudinal study[76] found that employee voice during the performance management session (procedural justice) influenced the reactions to receiving negative feedback. In this study, the relationship with the supervisor (LMX) was more important than the differences in performance ratings. What this study suggests is that followers will accept feedback when they are rated lower than their peers if they have a trusting and high-quality relationship with their boss, and they have a voice during the process. A case study of a performance appraisal process supported this finding. Followers who trusted their leaders were more satisfied with the performance appraisal process in their organization.[77]

An example of how the leader plays an important role is shown in a study of performance management conducted at Deloitte Consulting by a team of consultants.[78] To see performance at the individual level, consultants asked team leaders not about the *skills* of each team member but about their *own future actions* with respect to that person. At the end of every project (or once every quarter for long-term projects), they asked team leaders to respond to four future-focused statements about each team member. These questions were designed to clearly highlight differences among individuals and reliably measure performance. Here are the four questions:

1. Given what I know of this person's performance, and if it were my money, I would award this person the highest possible compensation increase and bonus (*measures overall performance and unique value to the organization on a five-point scale from "strongly agree" to "strongly disagree"*).

2. Given what I know of this person's performance, I would always want him or her on my team (*measures ability to work well with others on the same five-point scale*).

3. This person is at risk for low performance (identifies problems that might harm the customer or the team on a yes-or-no basis).

4. This person is ready for promotion today (*measures potential on a yes-or-no basis*).

In effect, team leaders were asked what they would *do* with each team member rather than what they *think* of that individual. Completing these assessments after each project produces a rich stream of information for leaders' discussions of what they, in turn, plan for each follower in terms of their growth and development as well as promotions. This process shifts the role of the leader from evaluator to coach and provides followers with feedback on a more frequent basis (after each project or quarterly) rather than once per year.

This chapter has shown that research supports how leaders can motivate followers using rewards. Knowing reinforcement and social learning basics is essential to understanding how reward systems operate in organizations. Based on the self-determination theory, it is important for leaders to recognize that follower needs for autonomy and competence play an important role in intrinsic motivation and well-being. It is also important to become thoroughly familiar with the performance management in your organization so that it can be used effectively to provide the necessary feedback to motivate employees to high levels of performance. Research has shown that the process must be perceived as fair, and employees need to be able to voice their concerns during the process. People are more likely to accept feedback, even if it is negative, if they trust their leader. Feedback-seeking research has demonstrated that employees need feedback far more often than yearly performance management reviews. Leaders should encourage their followers to seek feedback so they can stay on track toward reaching their goals. A number of organizations, including GE, Microsoft, Netflix, and Google, have redesigned their performance management systems to provide fluid and frequent feedback that emphasizes the role of the leader as coach.[79] Some organizations are even experimenting with apps that provide real-time feedback to employees.[80] The process of motivating employees is evolving, but current trends indicate that the leader will play an even more central role in the performance management process in the future.

edge.sagepub.com/scandura2e

Want a better grade? Go to **edge.sagepub.com/scandura2e** for the tools you need to sharpen your study skills.

KEY TERMS

A-B-C analysis, 215
behaviorally anchored rating scales
   (BARS), 223
central tendency error, 224
cognitive evaluation theory, 219
competence, 219
extrinsic motivation, 217
"extrinsics in service of
   intrinsics," 217
feedback seeking, 227
fixed, 213
flexible working hours, 224
gain-sharing plans, 224

interval, 213
intrinsic motivation, 217
job sharing, 224
law of effect, 211
motivation–work cycle
   match, 217
observational learning, 216
operant conditioning, 211
organizational behavior
   modification (OB mod), 214
pay dispersion, 220
pay inequity, 220
profit-sharing plans, 224

ratio, 213
reinforcement theory, 211
reinforcers, 211
remote working, 224
sabbaticals, 224
schedules of reinforcement, 213
self-determination, 219
social learning theory, 216
stock options, 224
360-degree performance
   appraisal, 222
variable, 213

TOOLKIT ACTIVITY 9.1: Performance Appraisal Do's and Don'ts

Refer to these guidelines the next time you have to conduct performance appraisals.

Do's

- Reassure your staff member by building on strengths; give him or her confidence. Set the stage for a two-way conversation. Relieve tension and facilitate dialogue by communicating up front your review process agenda. Let the employee know they have input.

- Use a "we" approach when discussing problems. Talk about their strengths and challenge areas. Deliver the negative (avoid sugarcoating), but make sure the employee knows what he or she can do about it.

- Be specific when discussing performance appraisal. Identify what success looks like for the coming year given the organization's objectives. Create an employee development plan with specific goals and tasks.

- Keep the interview on track. Start the process by letting employees assess themselves. What are they most proud of, and what do they consider areas for development?

- Draw him or her out by asking thought-provoking questions (not the yes or no type); then listen. Restate or reflect the follower's statements. Listen with warmth, frankness, and real interest.

- Talk about job results, not activities. Seize the opportunity to acknowledge what you like and appreciate about how the employee performs.

- Function as a coach, not as inspector. Counsel—don't advise. Focus on the employee. Be truly present. Listen and make a genuine attempt to understand concerns and any feedback.

- Close properly, summarize, and plan for improvements and changes. Write down the results.

Don'ts

- Don't use negative words or too many negative criticisms. Everyone has room for improvement. Even the most talented individuals want to know how they can reach the next level. Refusing to identify issues, challenges for improvement, or not holding the individual accountable does not foster growth. When you avoid giving tough, direct feedback, you are not doing them (or you) any favors.

- Don't hammer on negatives. Don't shred personal self-esteem by telling them every negative thing you've ever noticed. Reinforce that it is behaviors and actions you want changed and that you have confidence in the person.

- Don't give insincere or excessive praise.

- Don't use generalities that cannot be backed up by examples.

- Don't dominate the conversation. Don't offer challenging feedback in general terms. Many people are told during performance appraisals that they need to improve "communication." Most people have no idea what this means. Identify how you and the follower will know that he or she met your expectations for improvement.

- Don't place emphasis on personality traits. Don't make it personal. Stick to behavior specifics.

- Don't be fussy, picky, or hurried. Don't make assumptions about how the employee is receiving the feedback. Emotionally charged situations often foster misunderstanding. Probe for understanding reactions, including confirmation of the critical points of the review.

- Don't rush or talk too much. Reviews should be interactive. Don't let whatever "form" you use dictate your process; it's not about the form. If you are doing all the talking, you've probably lost them.

Discussion Questions

1. Which of the do's for performance appraisal would you find most difficult to do? Explain why.

2. Which of the don'ts for performance appraisal would you find most difficult to refrain from doing? Explain why.

3. Provide an example of how you would specifically coach a follower on how to improve their communication with coworkers. What would you say to them?

Source: Basking, K. (2013). Performance appraisal do's and don'ts. Retrieved from www.evaluationforms.org/tips/performance-appraisal-dos-and-donts

TOOLKIT ACTIVITY 9.2: Performance Management Role-Play

In this exercise, you will role-play a performance management session with another student in the class. One of you will play the role of the leader, and the other will play the role of the follower. On the next pages, you will find the leader role and the follower role. You and your partner should select a role and take 10 minutes to study the information and review the performance appraisal form. It is Monocle's practice to have the follower provide a self-assessment, so both of you should complete the form. After you have completed the form, you will conduct the performance appraisal session for 30 minutes. It is important that you both sign the performance appraisal document.

Refer back to Toolkit Activity 9.1 on the do's and don'ts for conducting a performance appraisal, and try to follow these guidelines during the session.

Leader Role: You have an MBA from a prestigious university and have worked for Monocle Software for 20 years. Monocle conducts enterprise resource planning (ERP), which is the process of examining business functions and installing software that allows an organization to use a system of integrated software applications to manage the business and automate functions. ERP software integrates all facets of an operation, including product planning, development, manufacturing processes, sales, and marketing. ERP software typically consists of a variety of modules that are individually purchased based on what best meets the specific needs and technical capabilities of your clients. Each ERP module is focused on one area of business process, such as human resources or project management. You are conducting an appraisal with one of your team leaders. He or she has been responsible for the accounting application. There have been a number of complaints from the client regarding the software taking too long to customize and some functions that do not work. The employees in the client company are frustrated, and they have commented that the new software doesn't work as well as what they had before. The members of this follower's team have complained that the client did not know what they wanted and has unrealistic expectations about what the software would be able to do. They have told you that they were not involved as a team in the early stages and did not have input into what was promised to the client. You observed your follower's behavior in the initial meeting and felt that he or she may not have fully understood the threats to the employees' sense of security and potential resistance to change during an ERP implementation. This contract is several million dollars, and you are concerned that the complaints are spreading throughout the client organization, and other software applications are being questioned recently. Unfortunately, you are finding out about these problems from the client and your follower's team members. He or she has not been communicating with you regularly regarding the situation. You hope to provide feedback that will turn the situation around.

Follower Role: You have a master's degree in computer science from a top regional university. You have worked for Monocle Software for 10 years and have worked your way up from a software developer; you were promoted 6 months ago to project team leader. You took over a project that was nearing completion at the time of your promotion and saw it through to a successful implementation. Your current assignment is your first full implementation from beginning to end. You met with the clients in the accounting area and conducted the needs assessment following Monocle's protocols. Your supervisor asked you if you needed assistance or if you wanted another team leader with more experience to sit in on some of the early meetings with the client, but you assured your boss that you were ready to handle the client on your own. There have been some difficulties with the project, and some of the programmers on your team have complained that the client did not know what they wanted and has requested numerous changes to the applications. The project is not on schedule for successful completion with the other modules, and you have had to request overtime payments for your team to complete the modules on time. Your supervisor has been reluctant to approve the overtime payments due to concerns about the overall budget for the implementation and complaints about too much weekend work by your team. You realize that there have been some client complaints, but you have tried to address their concerns by convincing them that the overall structure of the software is sound and has worked in many other companies. You have added additional features that they only learned they wanted after they had experienced the new software. Members of your team have been complaining about the clients' demands and blaming one another for the failure to complete the necessary changes during normal working hours. They are tired of being asked to work on weekends and trying to shift responsibility to one another. Despite the challenges, you remain confident that with 2 additional weeks and overtime budget approval you will complete the project on time.

Monocle Software Job Performance Management Form

Supervisor Name: _____

Employee Name: _____

Evaluation Period: _____

Title: _____ Date: _____

Performance Planning and Results

Performance Review

- Rate the person's level of performance, using the definitions that follow.

- Review with employee each performance factor used to evaluate his or her work performance.

- Give an overall rating in the space provided, using the following definitions as a guide.

Performance Rating Definitions

The following ratings must be used to ensure commonality of language and consistency on overall ratings. There should be supporting comments to justify ratings of "outstanding," "below expectations," and "unsatisfactory."

Outstanding	Performance is consistently superior.
Exceeds expectations	Performance is routinely above job requirements.
Meets expectations	Performance is regularly competent and dependable.
Below expectations	Performance fails to meet job requirements on a frequent basis.
Unsatisfactory	Performance is consistently unacceptable.

Rate the employee's behavior on the dimensions on the following form. There is space on the form to add comments that are specific to each dimension of performance. Also, complete the sections on strengths, areas for improvement, and plans for improved performance.

A. Performance Factors

Administration—Measures effectiveness in planning, organizing, and efficiently handling activities and eliminating unnecessary activities	Outstanding ❏
	Exceeds expectations ❏
	Meets expectations ❏
	Below expectations ❏
	Unsatisfactory ❏
	N/A ❏
Knowledge of work—Considers employee's skill level, knowledge, and understanding of all phases of the job and those requiring improved skills and experience	Outstanding ❏
	Exceeds expectations ❏
	Meets expectations ❏
	Below expectations ❏
	Unsatisfactory ❏
	N/A ❏
Communication—Measures effectiveness in listening to others, expressing ideas—both orally and in writing—and providing relevant and timely information to management, coworkers, subordinates, and customers	Outstanding ❏
	Exceeds expectations ❏
	Meets expectations ❏
	Below expectations ❏
	Unsatisfactory ❏
	N/A ❏

Teamwork—Measures how well this individual gets along with fellow employees, respects the rights of other employees, and shows a cooperative spirit	Outstanding	❏
	Exceeds expectations	❏
	Meets expectations	❏
	Below expectations	❏
	Unsatisfactory	❏
	N/A	❏
Decision making/problem solving—Measures effectiveness in understanding problems and making timely, practical decisions	Outstanding	❏
	Exceeds expectations	❏
	Meets expectations	❏
	Below expectations	❏
	Unsatisfactory	❏
	N/A	❏
Expense management—Measures effectiveness in establishing appropriate reporting and control procedures; operating efficiently at lowest cost; staying within established budgets	Outstanding	❏
	Exceeds expectations	❏
	Meets expectations	❏
	Below expectations	❏
	Unsatisfactory	❏
	N/A	❏
Independent action—Measures effectiveness in time management; initiative and independent action within prescribed limits	Outstanding	❏
	Exceeds expectations	❏
	Meets expectations	❏
	Below expectations	❏
	Unsatisfactory	❏
	N/A	❏
Job knowledge—Measures effectiveness in keeping knowledgeable methods, techniques, and skills required in own job and related functions; remaining current on new developments and work activities	Outstanding	❏
	Exceeds expectations	❏
	Meets expectations	❏
	Below expectations	❏
	Unsatisfactory	❏
	N/A	❏
Leadership—Measures effectiveness in accomplishing work assignments through subordinates; establishing challenging goals; delegating and coordinating effectively; promoting innovation and team effort	Outstanding	❏
	Exceeds expectations	❏
	Meets expectations	❏
	Below expectations	❏
	Unsatisfactory	❏
	N/A	❏

(Continued)

(Continued)

Managing change and improvement—Measures effectiveness in initiating changes, adapting to necessary changes from old methods when they are no longer practical, identifying new methods, and generating improvement in performance	Outstanding	❏
	Exceeds expectations	❏
	Meets expectations	❏
	Below expectations	❏
	Unsatisfactory	❏
	N/A	❏
Customer responsiveness—Measures responsiveness and courtesy in dealing with internal staff, external customers, and vendors; employee projects a courteous manner	Outstanding	❏
	Exceeds expectations	❏
	Meets expectations	❏
	Below expectations	❏
	Unsatisfactory	❏
	N/A	❏
Employee's responsiveness—Measures responsiveness in completing job tasks in a timely manner	Outstanding	❏
	Exceeds expectations	❏
	Meets expectations	❏
	Below expectations	❏
	Unsatisfactory	❏
	N/A	❏

B. Employee Strengths and Accomplishments
Include those that are relevant during this evaluation period. This should be related to performance or behavioral aspects you appreciated in their performance.

C. Performance Areas That Need Improvement:

D. Plan of Action Toward Improved Performance:

E. Employee Comments:

F. Signatures:

Employee _____ Date _____
(Signature does not necessarily denote agreement with official review and means only that the employee was given the opportunity to discuss the official review with the supervisor.)

Evaluated by _____ Date _____

Reviewed by _____ Date _____

Discussion Questions

1. If you were the leader giving the appraisal, discuss whether it was difficult to give negative feedback. What emotions did you experience? If you were the follower, was it difficult to hear negative feedback? What emotions did you experience?

2. Did you find that you rated all aspects of performance the same (e.g., all "meets expectations"),

or did you vary your responses? Explain why you did your ratings the way that you did.

3. Discuss the areas that you feel need improvement. Did you agree or disagree with your leader/ follower? If you disagreed, did you come to an agreement during the performance appraisal? Why or why not?

CASE STUDY 9.1: Pay Inequity at Goodyear Tire and Rubber

One evening when she came to work to start the night shift, Lilly Ledbetter found an anonymous note in her mailbox at the Goodyear Tire & Rubber plant in Gadsden, Alabama. She had worked for Goodyear for 19 years as a manager and was shocked at what she read. On the note, her monthly pay ($3,727) was written along with the pay (which ranged from $4,286 to $5,236) of three of her male colleagues who started working for Goodyear the same year that she did and did the same job. Ledbetter (2012) stated, "My heart jerked as if an electric jolt had coursed through my body." She filed a gender pay discrimination lawsuit under the 1964 Civil Rights Amendment and was awarded $3 million in back pay and other benefits she lost due to pay discrimination (e.g., contributions to her retirement).

Lilly's case was appealed to the U.S. Supreme Court, which ruled against Ledbetter. In the case of *Ledbetter v. Goodyear Tire & Rubber Co., 550 U.S. 618 (2007)*, the U.S. Supreme Court decided that the statute of limitations for presenting an equal-pay lawsuit begins on the date that the employer makes the initial discriminatory wage decision, not at the date of the most recent paycheck. Lilly became famous after she lost the Supreme Court case. While she did not win the case, it did result in new legislation regarding when an equal-pay lawsuit can be filed. This court decision ultimately led to the *Lilly Ledbetter Fair Pay Act of 2009* (Pub.L. 111–2, S. 181), which states the 180-day statute of limitations for filing an equal-pay lawsuit resets with each new paycheck affected by discrimination. The act is a federal statute and was the first

bill signed into law by President Barack Obama in 2009. Lilly's website states the following:

> For 10 years, Lilly Ledbetter fought to close the gap between women's and men's wages, sparring with the Supreme Court, lobbying Capitol Hill in a historic discrimination case against Goodyear Tire and Rubber Company. . . . Ledbetter will never receive restitution from Goodyear, but she said, "I'll be happy if the last thing they say about me after I die is that I made a difference." (www.lillyledbetter.com)

The Lilly Ledbetter case shows that employees care a great deal about the rewards they receive from an organization, and these rewards must be fair. Lilly learned of the pay disparity with her male coworkers after a number of years on the job. She experienced a sense of moral outrage and filed a lawsuit to address the unfairness. As you learned, fairness is one of the guidelines for the effective implementation of reward systems in organizations. Employees pay attention to rewards—particularly what they are paid. Pay inequity may cause employees to feel undervalued by the organization and may reduce motivation. As seen in this case, unfair pay practices may also result in litigation. The federal statute based on Lilly's case is clear that pay discrimination lawsuits may be based on every paycheck that a person receives throughout their employment. Equal pay for equal work is a concept that individuals in the same workplace be given equal pay for doing the same work.

This concept is most commonly applied with respect to the gender pay gap—it was once estimated that women are paid 77.5% of men's earnings (U.S. Census Bureau, 2008). On the seventh anniversary of the passage of the Lilly Ledbetter Fair Pay Act, the Council of Economic Advisors[81] published an update on the wage gap between men and women. In 2014, median earnings for a woman working full-time all year in the United States totaled only 79% of the median earnings of a man working full-time all year. Phrased differently, women earned 79 cents for every dollar that men earned. The gender wage gap has many causes and contributors, including differences in education, experience, occupation and industry, and family responsibilities. But even after accounting for these factors, a gap still remains between men's earnings and women's earnings. Organizations should be proactive in examining their pay policies to ensure equal pay for men, women, and minorities. Employers must design reward systems that are fair and follow organizational justice guidelines to avoid litigation—but also because it is the right thing to do.

Discussion Questions

1. What are the implications of the Ledbetter case for the performance management system?

2. Explain Lilly Ledbetter's reaction to learning she was being paid less than her coworkers based upon pay dispersion.

3. How do you feel about Ledbetter never receiving compensation from Goodyear for her lower wages for 10 years?

4. Referring back to Chapter 7, relate this case to what you learned about organizational justice. What type(s) of justice does the case illustrate?

Sources: Council of Economic Advisors. (2016, January). The gender pay gap on the anniversary of the Lilly Ledbetter Fair Pay Act. Retrieved on April 20, 2017, from http://digitalcommons.ilr.cornell.edu/key_workplace/1580/; Ledbetter, L. (with Isom, L. S.). (2012). *Grace and grit: My fight for equal pay and fairness at Goodyear and beyond.* New York, NY: Crown Archetype; Bishaw, A., & Semega, J. (2008, August). Income, earnings, and poverty data from the 2007 American Community Survey [U.S. Census Bureau, American Community Survey Reports, ACS-09]. Washington, DC: U.S. Government Printing Office, p. 14.

SELF-ASSESSMENT 9.1: Work Values Checklist

Every day, we make choices—some without careful consideration. Whether we realize it or not, often our career choice is based on values rather than the work. Values are the beliefs, attitudes, and judgments we prize. Are you aware of your values? Do you act on them?

Use this checklist to get a better idea of what's important to you. It's divided into three categories related to intrinsic, extrinsic, and lifestyle values.

Intrinsic Values

These are the intangible rewards—those related to motivation and satisfaction at work on a daily basis. They provide the inner satisfaction and motivation that make people say, "I love getting up and going to work!"

How important (on a scale of 1 to 5, with 5 being most important) are these intrinsic values to you?

Statements	Very Unimportant	Somewhat Unimportant	Neutral	Somewhat Important	Very Important
1. Have variety and change at work	1	2	3	4	5
2. Be an expert	1	2	3	4	5
3. Work on the frontiers of knowledge	1	2	3	4	5
4. Help others	1	2	3	4	5

Statements	Very Unimportant	Somewhat Unimportant	Neutral	Somewhat Important	Very Important
5. Help society	1	2	3	4	5
6. Experience adventure and excitement	1	2	3	4	5
7. Take risks or have physical challenges	1	2	3	4	5
8. Feel respected for your work	1	2	3	4	5
9. Compete with others	1	2	3	4	5
10. Have lots of public contact	1	2	3	4	5
11. Influence others	1	2	3	4	5
12. Engage in precision work	1	2	3	4	5
13. Gain a sense of achievement	1	2	3	4	5
14. Have opportunities to express your creativity	1	2	3	4	5
15. Work for a good cause	1	2	3	4	5

Extrinsic Values

These are the tangible rewards or conditions you find at work, including the physical setting, job titles, benefits, and earnings or earning potential. Extrinsic values often trap people into staying at jobs they don't like, saying, "I just can't give up my paycheck!" They are commonly called *golden handcuffs*.

How important (on a scale of 1 to 5, with 5 being most important) are these golden handcuffs to you?

Statements	Very Unimportant	Somewhat Unimportant	Neutral	Somewhat Important	Very Important
1. Have control, power, or authority	1	2	3	4	5
2. Travel often	1	2	3	4	5
3. Be rewarded monetarily	1	2	3	4	5
4. Be an entrepreneur	1	2	3	4	5
5. Work as a team	1	2	3	4	5
6. Work in a fast-paced environment	1	2	3	4	5
7. Have regular work hours	1	2	3	4	5
8. Set your own hours/have flexibility	1	2	3	4	5
9. Be wealthy	1	2	3	4	5
10. Have prestige or social status	1	2	3	4	5
11. Have intellectual status	1	2	3	4	5
12. Have recognition through awards, honors, or bonuses	1	2	3	4	5
13. Wear a uniform	1	2	3	4	5
14. Work in an aesthetically pleasing environment	1	2	3	4	5
15. Work on the edge, in a high-risk environment	1	2	3	4	5

Lifestyle Values

These are the personal values associated with how and where you want to live, how you choose to spend your leisure time, and how you feel about money.

How important (on a scale of 1 to 5, with 5 being most important) are these lifestyle values to you?

Statements	Very Unimportant	Somewhat Unimportant	Neutral	Somewhat Important	Very Important
1. Save money	1	2	3	4	5
2. Vacation at expensive resorts	1	2	3	4	5
3. Have access to educational/cultural opportunities	1	2	3	4	5
4. Live close to sports or recreational facilities	1	2	3	4	5
5. Be active in your community	1	2	3	4	5
6. Entertain at home	1	2	3	4	5
7. Be involved in politics	1	2	3	4	5
8. Live simply	1	2	3	4	5
9. Spend time with family	1	2	3	4	5
10. Live in a big city	1	2	3	4	5
11. Live abroad	1	2	3	4	5
12. Have time for spirituality or personal growth	1	2	3	4	5
13. Be a homeowner	1	2	3	4	5
14. Live in a rural setting	1	2	3	4	5
15. Have fun in your life and at work	1	2	3	4	5

Once you have completed all three checklists, write down all the values you rated as 5s. If you have less than five, add the values you rated as 4s to the list. If your list of 4s and 5s has more than 20 values, you need to stop and prioritize your list. To prioritize, select no more than four or five values from each category.

Discussion Questions

1. Analyze which of the three categories is most important to you. How is each reflected in the work or schoolwork you currently do? Are there overlaps in your values that seem to go together, such as "be wealthy" from Extrinsic Values and "save money" from Lifestyle Values?

2. If there is no overlap or compatibility between categories (or if everything is important to you), then what are your top 10 values? What are your top five values you absolutely need both on and off the job?

3. Write two or three sentences describing or summarizing how your values will translate into your ideal job. Knowing what's important will help you prepare for your next interview or help you find increased satisfaction with the job you have. What motivates you (are your rewards already a part of your lifestyle)? What can you do to incorporate your values into your lifestyle?

Source: Adapted from Boer, P. (n.d.). Work values checklist. Retrieved on February 5, 2015, from http://career-advice.monster.com/job-search/career-assessment/work-values-check-list/article.aspx

BUILDING RELATIONSHIPS

Introduction

Chapter 1: What Is Organizational Behavior?

Understanding Individuals in Organizations

Chapter 2: Personality and Person–Environment Fit

Chapter 3: Emotions and Moods

Chapter 4: Attitudes and Job Satisfaction

Chapter 5: Perception, Decision Making, and Problem Solving

Influencing and Motivating Employees

Chapter 6: Leadership

Chapter 7: Power and Politics

Chapter 8: Motivation: Core Concepts

Chapter 9: Motivation: Applications

Building Relationships

Chapter 10: Group Processes and Teams

Chapter 11: Managing Conflict and Negotiation

Chapter 12: Organizational Communication

Chapter 13: Diversity and Cross-Cultural Adjustments

Leaders as Change Agents

Chapter 14: Organizational Culture

Chapter 15: Leading Change and Stress Management

CHAPTER TEN

GROUP PROCESSES AND TEAMS

Learning Objectives

After studying this chapter, you should be able to do the following:

10.1: Explain the difference between a working group and a team.

10.2: Illustrate the relationship between team purpose and performance by using a team charter.

10.3: Compare and contrast the five-stage and team performance curve models of team development.

10.4: Describe the three main aspects of team effectiveness.

10.5: Demonstrate how to assess the cohesion of your team.

10.6: Compare and contrast consensus decision making and the nominal group technique (NGT).

10.7: Generate an example of how a team leader can reduce social loafing.

10.8: Discuss the challenges and benefits of team diversity.

Get the edge on your studies at **edge.sagepub.com/scandura2e**

- Take the chapter quiz
- Review key terms with eFlashcards
- Explore multimedia resources, SAGE readings, and more!

DOES TRUST IMPACT TEAM PERFORMANCE?

How much time do you spend building trust with your team members? New research[1] shows that leaders would do well to spend more time creating trusting partnerships among team members. A meta-analysis of 112 studies representing over 7,700 teams found that the degree to which team members trust one another increases team performance (achieving shared goals). Trust makes a significant difference. This study also revealed how trust works and the team situations when it matters most. Trust within a team setting reduces the feelings of vulnerability that members experience, and this helps them to work more effectively together to achieve team goals. In other words, when trust is present, team members are more likely to admit they don't know something and critique one another's ideas. They are more likely to share creative ideas and resolve conflict. But the opposite holds true as well. When there is a lack of trust, people are more defensive and work at odds with the team goals. They also avoid criticism and don't provide constructive feedback. This defensiveness impairs the team from optimal functioning. The findings of this study are summarized in Figure 10.1.

Another interesting finding from this study is that trust among team members is perhaps more important than trust in the team leader or past success. Team situations when trust matters the most are when the members must depend upon one another and when leaders depend upon followers to make decisions (rather than only one person making the decision). The bottom line from this study is that if you are interested in enhancing the performance of your team, pay attention to how much team members trust one another and create opportunities to strengthen trust.

Research on teams at work is not new. Beginning in the 1960s, organizations experimented with teams in the workplace, and there was an explosion in interest in team-based organizations in the 1980s. At the same time, research on teams in organizations began to expand rapidly and has increased significantly since 2005.[2] Some employees were skeptical and viewed teamwork as a "fad" that would

Figure 10.1 How Might Trust Impact Team Performance?

WHEN WE TRUST

We expect others to behave positively towards us . . . → So, we may tolerate more vulnerability & uncertainty . . . → . . . and tend to work better with others and stay focused on team goals.

WHEN WE DON'T TRUST

We might be more suspicious of how others may act toward us . . . → We can become defensive, trying to reduce our vulnerability . . . → We may lose sight of team goals and focus on personal interests.

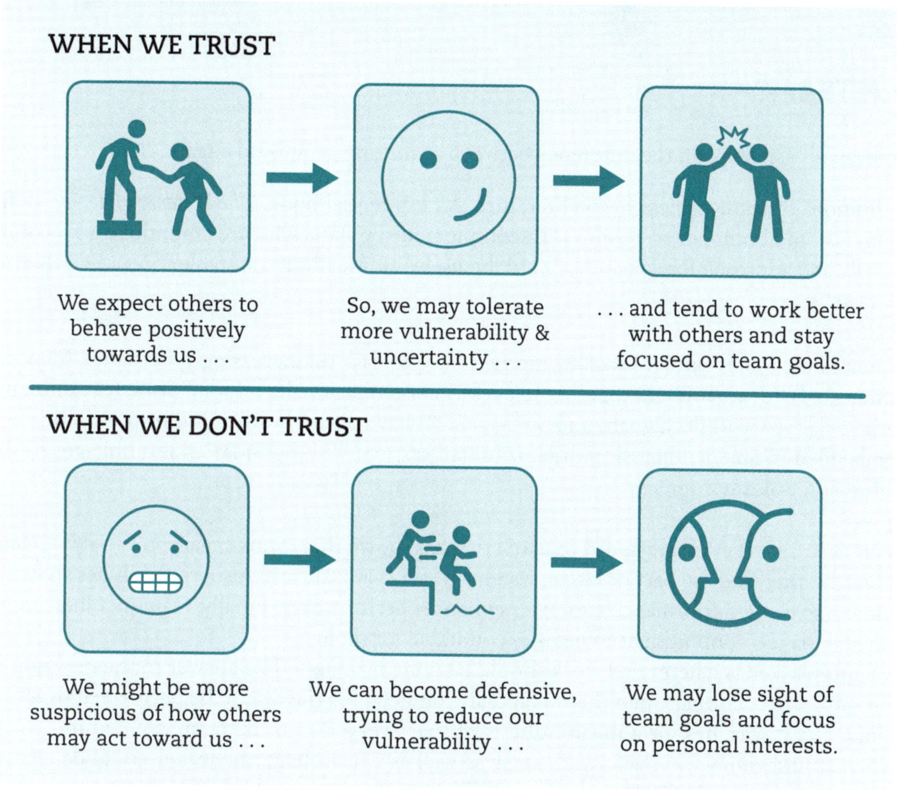

Source: Hirsch, W. (n.d.). Trust: Does it impact team performance . . . or not? Retrieved on March 21, 2017, from: http://scienceforwork.com/blog/trust-impact-team-performance/

go away. However, it is now clear that teamwork is here to stay, and most organizations employ teams to make significant decisions and develop new ideas. After the downsizings of the 1980s and 1990s, leaders needed a way to get more done with fewer people. Teams turned out to be one answer to this challenge. By the 1990s, the digital age had arrived, and leaders looked for new ways to structure and manage work flows. Team-based work arrangements created much-needed flexibility and became even more common.[3] The competitive landscape has become increasingly global and complex requiring more teamwork. One study found that the time spent by managers and employees in collaborative teamwork has increased by more than 50% over the last 2 decades.[4] Teams allow for more creative solutions and build commitment to the implementation of innovative ideas. Teamwork revolutionized the world of work.[5] It is thus essential for a leader to understand team basics and how to lead teams effectively.

This chapter reviews the essential research on small groups from social psychology and discusses current approaches to **work teams**. The emphasis is on leading teams, since this is a core competence given that most organizations now use work teams to maximize organizational performance. As we learn in this chapter, teams are also one of the best forums for learning, since employees share their skills and expertise with one another. Teams are now often charged with making important decisions, and a variety of techniques for team decision making are discussed.

WHAT IS A TEAM?

Learning Objective 10.1: Explain the difference between a working group and a team.

Numerous definitions of teams appear in the literature. An influential book, *The Wisdom of Teams*, defines a team as follows: "A team is a small number of people with complementary skills who are committed to a common purpose, performance goals, and approach for which they hold themselves mutually accountable."[6] Another often-cited research definition of a team is

(a) Two or more individuals who; (b) socially interact (face-to-face or, increasingly, virtually); (c) possess one or more common goals; (d) are brought together to perform organizationally relevant tasks; (e) exhibit interdependencies with respect to workflow, goals, and outcomes; (f) have different roles and responsibilities; and (g) are together embedded in an encompassing organizational system, with boundaries and linkages to the broader system context and task environment.[7]

These definitions reflect evidence-based research that has shown that teams engage in social interaction, members depend upon one another, and are part of larger systems (i.e., organizations). Also, research has shown that commitment to a common goal and performance strategies enhances performance. Finally, team members must accept relevant team goals and make a commitment to being accountable for them.

A question often asked is whether all work should be done by teams. The answer to the question is *no*. In many cases, teams become dysfunctional when there is actually no need for the task to be performed by a team at all. The team may flounder as it searches for a meaningful goal that everyone on the team can commit to. Teams should not be used when an individual can perform the task as well as a team (e.g., the leader could delegate the ordering of supplies to one person rather than having a team discussion about it). Also, if a performance goal can be met by adding up individual contributions (known as an **additive task**), then members of the work unit can work independently and their efforts can be combined later. The right time to use teams is when a performance goal requires **collective effort** and a work project that reflects the contributions of everyone on the team. To accomplish a team goal, different skill sets, perspectives, or experiences are often needed.[8] So sometimes a work group is needed, and other times, a team is needed. There is an important distinction between a work group and a team, and this is discussed next.

> **Critical Thinking Questions:** In addition to the type of task, provide some other factors that influence whether a work group or a team is needed. Provide an example of a task in which a team is not needed.

Work Group Versus Team

Some of the literature on groups and teams is confusing because the terms *group* and *team* are used interchangeably. To clarify this, the distinction between the group and team has been articulated.[9] A work group interacts primarily to share information with other members (e.g., members of a work group attend a monthly staff meeting and share what they are working on). They are not responsible for a collective work effort, or their individual contributions can be added up to create something. An example of a work group is the service department of an automobile dealership, which consists of a service manager and 12 service advisers who report to the manager. Each service adviser meets with their own customers independently, and the contributions are summed for an overall customer rating of the dealership's service department. If conflicts arise in work groups, the group typically looks to the leader to resolve them.

A work team, in contrast to a work group, depends on one another, and they must interact to create something that no one person on the team could create. There is **synergy** on the team, which means that the team can produce something beyond the sum of individual member contributions. An example of a work team is a task force assembled to brainstorm ideas for improving patient safety in a hospital. The team depends highly on the participation of all members for success since each member contributes a unique perspective that influences the quality of the suggestions for patient safety. If conflicts emerge within a work team, the members manage it internally since there may be no designated leader. Some work groups can become teams, and a strong purpose or performance challenge sets a work group on the path to becoming a real team.

TEAM PURPOSE

Learning Objective 10.2: Illustrate the relationship between team purpose and performance by using a team charter.

Setting goals for teams is just as important as it is for individuals. As discussed in Chapter 8, goal setting increases both motivation and performance. It's important to keep in mind that team goals should also be SMART (specific, measurable, actionable, relevant, and time based). Effective teams have a sense of shared purpose, and it is one of the components of the definition of a team. Specific team goals predict specific team performance (e.g., setting challenging goals for quantity results in higher team output). Also, feedback on performance affects the allocation of resources when individuals strive to accomplish both individual and team goals. For example, allowing team members to decide on how resources are distributed (a team regulatory process) increases team performance. Also, feedback on team performance is essential for teams to make the correct allocation of resources for future team performance.[10] Team members who receive no team-level feedback can't effectively set team goals and, as a result, set completely unrealistic goals.[11] Once a team has established its purpose, **team norms** emerge and have a powerful effect on team member attitudes and behaviors.

Team Norms

Team norms are defined as informal and interpersonal rules that team members are expected to follow.[12] These standards may be explicit and formally stated by the leader or members of the team. But norms may also be implicit. They are not written down, and communication of the norms to team members depends on the ability of the leader (or team members) to effectively convey the expected behaviors. Norms have a strong influence on team members' behavior, and they are often difficult to change. For example, some teams allow team members to miss team meetings, and this disrupts the flow of work. While this isn't written down anywhere that it's OK to miss meetings, it just starts happening. One team member misses without an excuse, and since there is no penalty, others start to miss too. This is an example of an implicit norm. Implicit norms are tricky in that they are difficult to detect, and it is easy to misinterpret them. Of course, norms can have a positive influence on team member behavior as well. An example of the power of team norms was demonstrated by the results of research conducted by Google's People Operations department who set out to study teams with the goal of building the perfect team.[13] The project was code-named Project Aristotle, and hundreds of Google teams were studied to learn what made some more effective than others.

No matter how they analyzed the data, the composition of the teams did not matter (nothing showed that demographics or personality combinations created a great team). What the analysts learned was that team norms made the difference. These "unwritten rules" defined the team performance culture. The specific norms they identified were communication and empathy. High-performing teams engaged in conversational turn-taking in which all members spoke in roughly equal proportions (communication). The second norm was that high-performing team members had high social sensitivity—they were good at interpreting team members' feelings based on their tone of voice and facial expressions (empathy). The Google research team shared their findings about communication and empathy with Google employees to make these implicit norms more explicit. Explicit norms are written down and discussed. One way to make norms explicit is by developing a team charter.

The Team Charter

One of the best ways that a leader can make norms explicit and clearly communicate them to team members is by engaging the team to develop a **team charter**. In creating a team charter, not only is the team purpose clarified but the expectations for behavior are set forth (e.g., required on-time attendance at meetings). Norms provide an important regulatory function in teams. Once they are developed through a charter and agreed upon, misunderstandings should be fewer and a team member violating a norm (e.g., missing meetings) can be reminded of the group's commitment to attendance. Some groups even apply sanctions to the violation of norms, such as small fines or social ostracism. However, sanctioning systems are ineffective if they are not applied consistently. In other words, it is important to be fair and apply the principles of organizational justice described in Chapter 8 if sanctions are included in a team charter.

The influences of having a team charter and performance strategies of 32 teams of MBA students were studied using a business strategy simulation.[14] Taking the time to develop a high-quality team charter and performance strategies paid off in terms of more effective team performance over time. Teams that had high-quality charters and strategies outperformed teams with poor-quality charters and strategies. Charters are an important tool the leader can use to get their team off to a good start by developing a sense of purpose and performance strategies. Toolkit Activity 10.1 contains specific guidelines for developing a team charter.

Strong team norms give rise to shared understandings within teams, known as **team mental models (TMMs)**. These models and why they are important for team process and performance are discussed next.

Team Mental Models

TMMs "are team members' shared, organized understanding and mental representation of knowledge about key elements of the team's relevant environment."[15] TMMs are related to effective team processes and performance[16] because they serve a number of functions, including (1) allowing team members to interpret information similarly, (2) sharing expectations concerning the future, and (3) developing similar reasoning as to why something happens.[17] Teams with highly developed TMMs are fundamentally "on the same page" with respect to sharing a common view of what is occurring in the team. This makes decision making more efficient and enhances team performance.[18] A summary of how TMMs affect performance and other team outcomes is shown in Figure 10.2. The shared similarity and/or accuracy of TMMs translates demographic factors, skills, and training into shared norms, effective team processes, and higher performance. A meta-analysis of 65 studies of TMMs and performance found that teams with shared mental models interacted more frequently, were more motivated, had higher job satisfaction, and were rated as more productive by others.[19]

TMMs affect a team's purpose and team processes, including how team members back one another, coordination, and communication. For example, shared understandings emerge in TMMs, which determine how much participation by members is allowed. Team purpose, norms, and mental models are typically established in the early stages of a team's development. Teams then follow predictable patterns over their life cycles. Team development is discussed in the following section.

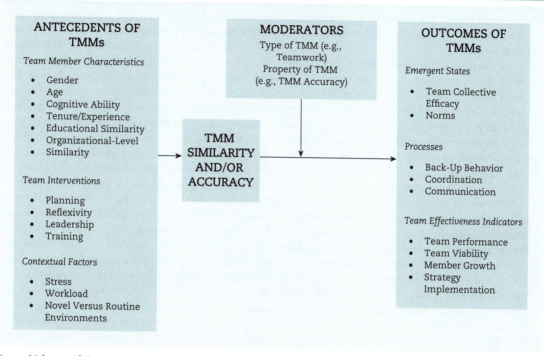

Figure 10.2 Team Mental Models and Outcomes

ANTECEDENTS OF TMMs

Team Member Characteristics

- Gender
- Age
- Cognitive Ability
- Tenure/Experience
- Educational Similarity
- Organizational-Level Similarity

Team Interventions

- Planning
- Reflexivity
- Leadership
- Training

Contextual Factors

- Stress
- Workload
- Novel Versus Routine Environments

TMM SIMILARITY AND/OR ACCURACY

MODERATORS
Type of TMM (e.g., Teamwork)
Property of TMM (e.g., TMM Accuracy)

OUTCOMES OF TMMs

Emergent States

- Team Collective Efficacy
- Norms

Processes

- Back-Up Behavior
- Coordination
- Communication

Team Effectiveness Indicators

- Team Performance
- Team Viability
- Member Growth
- Strategy Implementation

Source: Mohammed, S., Ferzandi, L., & Hamilton, K. (2010). Metaphor no more: A 15-year review of the team mental model construct. *Journal of Management, 36*(4), 876–910. p. 892.

TEAM DEVELOPMENT

Learning Objective 10.3: Compare and contrast the five-stage and team performance curve models of team development.

Teams don't emerge just by putting individuals together. Teams go through a process of development over time, and success is not guaranteed. Research on teams recognizes the role of time in the development of the team. Next, two important models of team development are discussed: the **five-stage model** and the **team performance curve**.

Five-Stage Model

A classic model of team development is the five-stage model, which includes five stages: **forming, storming, norming, performing**, and **adjourning**.[20],[21] During the forming stage, team members may experience stress due to the uncertainty of not knowing the other team members and understanding their role on the team. Initial interactions may be tentative as team members "test" one another to determine what the norms and expectations will be. The team leader should clarify the team purpose and set up ground rules through a team charter, as previously discussed. As the team interacts on project work, conflicts begin to emerge regarding the goals and contributions of team members, and the team enters the storming stage. There may be challenges to the leader of the group (either a formally assigned leader or an informal one). The team leader should openly address conflict and maintain a focus on the team purpose and ground rules established in the charter. At the end of this stage, the leadership question is typically resolved, and it is clear who will lead the group. Also, a status hierarchy, or pecking order, may be established. If the storming phase does not destroy the team and result in abandonment of the team by all of its members, the team moves to the next stage of development, which is called norming. In this stage, the members of the team form a cohesive unit and close relationships among team members develop. The group establishes additional implicit norms regarding what is acceptable behavior (beyond that specified in the team charter). For example, if the team members who show up late for meetings are called out by their teammates, then lateness is unacceptable and the tardy members start to show up on time. During the norming phase, the leader should remind the followers of the ground rules and address deviations constructively. Once norms are established, the team should be performing by producing collective work products. The group shifts from relationship development and norm articulation to the work itself and goal attainment. For a work group or a task force that is permanent, the performing stage is the last stage. In this phase, the team leaders should celebrate success along the way to achieving the team goal. However, in some cases, teams are temporary and have a specific goal to accomplish. When this is the case, the team finalizes their work in the adjourning stage and disbands. The team leader should arrange a celebration activity such as a party or dinner to reward the members for achieving the team goals.

While the model proposes that teams move through the phases smoothly, in actuality, the team may regress to a previous stage or runs the risk of adjourning at any stage. For example, the level of conflict during the storming stage may result in team members deciding it's just easier to work alone. Even after the norming stage, the group is at risk of adjournment if the performance norms are repeatedly violated and the team determines that members aren't really committed.

In many student project teams—and also at work—teams are temporary and have a clear deadline. Teams don't follow the typical stages of development in such teams. In fact, there is a transition between an early phase of inactivity followed by a second phase of significant acceleration toward task completion. This process is called **punctuated equilibrium**.[22] There is an initial meeting in which the group's goals are discussed. Following this meeting, not much gets done until about halfway to the deadline. This midpoint transition occurs regardless of the total time allowed for the project. In other words, it doesn't matter whether the total time for the project is 1 hour or 6 months. At about halfway toward the completion of a project, team members begin to revisit goals and discuss how to get the group moving toward finishing the task. Following this midpoint discussion, there is a burst of new activity as team members scramble to reach their goals in time.

You may be able to relate to this by recalling times when you and your team pulled an "all-nighter"—a meeting that lasts hours and is intense right before your team project is due for a class. It is important to recognize that this doesn't apply to all types of teams; the punctuated equilibrium effect appears to be most prevalent in temporary teams with a fixed deadline.[23] The takeaway message from this research is clear: Try not to procrastinate when a team project is assigned. The team leader should get the momentum going early by setting benchmarks to avoid having to rush at the end of the project.

> Critical Thinking Question: How can you keep a team from procrastinating on the start of a project? Describe what you would do specifically.

Not all team development follows an upward pattern of productivity. A second model of team development addresses the potential performance losses that may occur during the initial storming or procrastination phases. This model is known as the team performance curve.

Team Performance Curve

Like the punctuated equilibrium model, the team performance curve recognizes that team performance over the course of the life of the team is not always linear, and performance does not always increase over time.[24] Figure 10.3 combines the five-stage model with the team performance curve and shows there may be a performance decrease as the team goes through the storming phase. A working group is a collection of people without a common sense of purpose. As the figure shows, this produces a certain level of performance, and some tasks are appropriate for a working group

Figure 10.3 The Stages of Group Development

Source: Adapted from Katzenbach, J. R., & Smith, D. K. (1993). *The wisdom of teams: Creating the high-performance organization.* New York, NY: Harper Business; Tuckman, B. (1965). Developmental sequence in small groups. *Psychological Bulletin, 63,* 384–399; Tuckman, B., & Jensen, M. (1977). Stages of small-group development revisited. *Group & Organization Studies, 2*(4), 419–427.

because they are additive. The team leader may attempt to transform his or her group into a team by introducing a common goal—particularly a challenging one. As team members organize to attain the goal, storming occurs and the team performance may actually *decline* for a period of time. Some working groups remain at this point as a pseudoteam because they are not on the path toward becoming a high-performance team. If the team gets past the storming and establishes productive norms, they reach a point where they can be considered a potential team. At this stage, the team has the potential to become a real team, which exhibits the characteristics of the definition of a team (i.e., they are committed to a common purpose, performance goals, and approach for which they hold themselves mutually accountable). A small number of teams become high-performance teams, which have all of the characteristics of real teams plus team members are deeply committed to the growth and development of the other team members. For example, a team member would teach another member how to use new presentation software. Research has shown that team leaders play a critical role in the development of high-performance teams (also known as *intense teams*). During the launch phase, the team leader must emphasize the vision and establish trust. The second phase is focused on sustaining trust between team members and creating a team identity. In the third phase, team members collaborate and begin performing and evaluating their work compared to their goals.[25] A high-performance team is enabled by six key factors:

1. team member competencies;

2. skills, processes, tools, and techniques;

3. interpersonal skills, communication, understanding personality differences;

4. a shared value system;

5. shared vision, purpose, goals, direction; and

6. supporting organizational values including openness.[26]

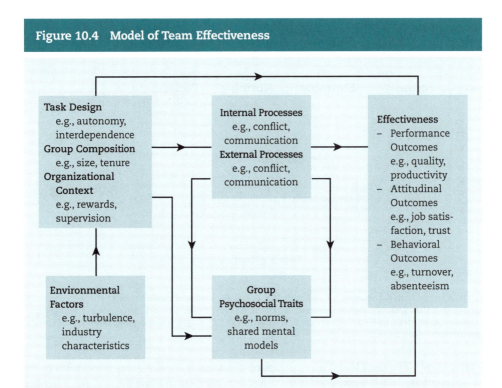

Figure 10.4 Model of Team Effectiveness

Task Design
e.g., autonomy, interdependence
Group Composition
e.g., size, tenure
Organizational Context
e.g., rewards, supervision

Internal Processes
e.g., conflict, communication
External Processes
e.g., conflict, communication

Effectiveness
– Performance Outcomes
e.g., quality, productivity
– Attitudinal Outcomes
e.g., job satisfaction, trust
– Behavioral Outcomes
e.g., turnover, absenteeism

Environmental Factors
e.g., turbulence, industry characteristics

Group Psychosocial Traits
e.g., norms, shared mental models

Source: Cohen, S. G., & Bailey, D. E. (1997). What makes teams work: Group effectiveness research from the shop floor to the executive suite. *Journal of Management, 23*(3), 239–290.

> **Critical Thinking Questions:** How can the use of a team charter help a team get through the storming phase? How could it help establish team norms and lead to high performance?

Thus, in high-performance teams, team interests become more important than individual interests. High-performance teams are rare. If you think about it, this would mean that team members would celebrate the success of a teammate receiving a promotion rather than feeling jealous. They would do everything to help their teammate be successful in the new position. Given that high-performance teams are rare yet essential for organizations, the next sections discusses team performance effectiveness and how it is defined and measured.

TEAM EFFECTIVENESS

Learning Objective 10.4: Describe the three main aspects of team effectiveness.

The question of how to know if a team is effective is an important one. Team effectiveness has a number of dimensions. The input-process-output model defines the different aspects of team effectiveness.[27] First, input refers to the individual characteristics of team members (e.g., skills and abilities) and the resources they have at their disposal. Inputs may also refer to knowledge and personality. For example, a study of 51 teams found that both general mental ability (IQ) and personality (particularly conscientiousness, agreeableness, extroversion, and emotional stability) increased team performance.[28]

Process is the second aspect of team effectiveness and refers to how the team interacts. Examples of process include team development and patterns of participation. Also, trust, cross-training, and coordination relate to team effectiveness.[29],[30] Third, the most obvious measure of team effectiveness is team output—the collective work product generated from the team (team performance). Output has three components: (1) performance as rated by those outside of the team, (2) how well team member individual needs are met, and (3) the willingness of team members to stay on the team.[31]

Team effectiveness reflects three broad categories: performance, behaviors, and attitudes as shown in Figure 10.4.[32] The figure indicates important inputs to team processes such as the organization environment and design of the task. On the output side, performance is the team's productivity, quality, or innovation as examples (i.e., the collective work effort). Behaviors are what individual team members do, such as going the extra mile for the team. "Extra milers" engage in more helping behaviors outside of their roles than other team members. A study of these extra milers found that they influence team processes and, ultimately, team effectiveness beyond the influences of all the other members.[33]

An important team process that has received much research attention is team conflict, which is covered in Chapter 11. Attitudes are team members' reports on their experience in the team, such as team satisfaction. These attitudes and behaviors matter because organizational behavior (OB) research has demonstrated that team behaviors relate to team outcomes such as job performance and satisfaction. For example, motivating and confidence building are teamwork processes that develop and maintain members' motivation and confidence that the team will accomplish its goals.[34]

Team Metrics

In addition to the team charter, it is also important to have measures (or metrics) to assess how a team is performing over time and to provide feedback to team members. Metrics are important to assess team effectiveness. There are three types of metrics for teamwork:

1. **Task metrics.** These are the "what" of teamwork. They relate to the actual work the team is performing. For example, task metrics might be goals for quantity and/ or quality and deadlines for the project completion. It is important to set 30-day targets as minigoals toward task completion so team members have a sense of forward momentum.

> Critical Thinking Questions: Provide additional examples of task, process, and individual development metrics. Next, create an example of an organization-level metric related to teamwork.

2. **Process metrics.** These are the "how" of teamwork. These metrics are assessment of how the teamwork is operating. For example, process metrics might be assessments of team communication or who is participating. Teams often focus on task goals to the exclusion of process goals, but they are important because the process affects task performance.

3. **Individual development metrics.** These metrics relate to how much individuals are developing new skills and learning through teamwork. For example, individual development metrics might be how well one team member is developing leadership abilities from working with the team. Individual development is important to track, since the hallmark of a high-performance team is when team members genuinely care about the development of their teammates.[35]

As indicated, team process metrics are important indicators of team effectiveness. In addition to team affect and viability, team learning is another outcome that reflects team process effectiveness. Also, team creativity and innovation are additional outcomes of effective team process. These team effectiveness outcomes are emerging as important outcomes of teamwork and are covered in the following sections.

Team Learning

Individual development of team members is an important metric for teams and defines a high-performance team. Team learning is now considered essential and has received a considerable amount of research. Viewing teams as a forum for learning began with the publication of the influential book *The Fifth Discipline: The Art and Practice of the Learning Organization*. Author Peter Senge views teamwork as one of the key experiences that lead to employee learning:

> When you ask people about what it is like being part of a great team, what is most striking is the meaningfulness of the experience. People talk about being part of something larger than themselves, of being connected, of being generative. It becomes quite clear that, for many, their experiences as part of truly great teams stands out as singular periods of life lived to the fullest. Some spend the rest of their lives looking for ways to recapture that spirit.[36]

> **Critical Thinking Question:** Describe a situation in which you learned something from interacting with others on a team (this can be related to task, process, or your individual development).

Team learning is an ongoing process through which teams acquire, combine, and apply knowledge.[37] For example, asking questions, seeking feedback, improvising, discussing errors, challenging underlying assumptions, and reflecting on specific results or unexpected outcomes increases a team member's knowledge.[38] Team learning originates in individual intuitions, is amplified through interpretation, and emerges at the team level as collective thoughts and actions. Teams that have a higher learning orientation (a proactive climate toward learning) outperform teams that don't.[39] Research has identified two related but distinct types of personal learning that can occur in work settings: relational job learning and personal skill development. Relational job learning refers to an "increased understanding about the interdependence or connectedness of one's job to others," whereas personal skill development refers to the "acquisition of new skills and abilities that enable better working relationships."[40] Transformational leadership predicts team members' personal learning.[41] Research has also shown that team learning significantly affects team performance.[42] One key factor for team learning to translate into performance is the degree to which team members agree that they feel a sense of **psychological safety** for taking risks.[43]

Team psychological safety allows members to take risks and be more creative and innovative. In addition to learning, research has also shown that teams enhance creativity and innovation. Creativity as a result of teamwork is recognized as essential to make high-quality decisions that relate to organizational effectiveness.[44] The next section discusses research on team creativity and innovation.

Team Creativity and Innovation

In Chapter 5, you learned that individual creativity is a key aspect of the problem-solving process. Research has shown that creativity in teams is essential to the innovation process. In fact, research has shown that teams produce more new knowledge than individuals.[45] Due to synergy, team creativity is not just the additive sum of individual team member creativity. Team creativity involves both processes and outcomes of developing new ideas for innovation. Team creativity encompasses what team members do behaviorally, cognitively, and emotionally as they define problems, generate ideas, and attempt new ways of doing their work.[46] Communication of new ideas and sharing information with diverse others leads to higher creativity.[47] The sharing of information increases team innovation, and this is facilitated by the leader being positive.[48] The positive behaviors of leaders should be directed at individuals but also at the entire team. Expressing positive affect supports being a transformational leader and stimulates creativity both in the team as well as in individuals.[49] Also, shared team goals result in higher creativity. In a study of project teams, more creative teams recognized that there was a need to be creative to be successful, and they valued participation by all team members. Interestingly, more creative teams also spent more time socializing with each other, both inside and outside of work.[50]

For creativity to flourish, it is important that the team does not have too much structure or bureaucratic red-tape to get through. A study of 100 research and development (R&D) teams found that a team's ability to improvise is enhanced by knowledge sharing and the minimum amount of structure needed to manage the innovation process. Team improvisation can be assessed by asking the following questions:

- Is the team good at dealing spontaneously with unanticipated problems?

- Is the team capable of responding extemporaneously to unexpected opportunities?

- Does the team have a strong capability to creatively improvise?[51]

In addition to knowledge sharing within teams, it is also important that teams share knowledge with other teams in the organization to enhance innovation. This helps avoid the problem of "reinventing the wheel" but also creates a culture of innovation where diverse knowledge is shared throughout the entire organization.[52] In a study of 397 R&D employees (consisting of 68 teams), benevolent R&D leaders who treated their team like a family facilitated innovative behavior at the individual level through creating strong identifications with the team. These leaders also enhanced cross-team innovative behavior at the team level via identification with the R&D department.[53] Thus, leaders influence both within-team and cross-team innovative behavior.

As this review has shown, team effectiveness has many dimensions and includes performance, learning, and innovation. A review of the research on team effectiveness concluded that team performance is the most commonly studied outcome. However, recent studies have considered team viability to be an important indicator of effectiveness. **Team viability** is a collective sense of belonging similar to team cohesion.[54] **Cohesion** is the "team spirit" experienced in high-performing teams and is discussed next.

COHESION

Learning Objective 10.5: Demonstrate how to assess the cohesion of your team.

Cohesion is defined as "the resultant of all the forces acting on the members to remain part of the group."[55] These forces depend on the attractiveness (or unattractiveness) of the prestige of the group, the group members, and/or the group's activities. Cohesion becomes a state in which a group tends to stick together and unite in the pursuit of team goals.[56] The mutual attraction of the member to the group is the most important determinant of cohesion.[57] Also, the degree to which people feel that being in a team where they fit in (i.e., a climate of inclusiveness) influences cohesion.[58] Cohesion influences the behaviors of team members. Behavioral indicators of cohesiveness are team members attending meetings more often, being on time, sitting closer to one another, making more eye contact, being less likely to quit, and even engaging in longer group hugs.[59] When cohesion is strong, the group is motivated to perform and is better able to coordinate activities for success. In cohesive teams, there is a sense of "we-ness" since team members tend to use *we* rather than *I* to describe the team and its activities.[60] A three-wave longitudinal study of 188 project teams found that team cohesion leads to group members being engaged in the task, which in turn had a positive effect on team creative performance.[61] Meta-analytic studies have found that team cohesion and team performance are positively and significantly related.[62,63] For example, one review reports the average cohesive team performed 18% higher than the average noncohesive team.[64] Since cohesion and performance influence one another (in other words, high performance can lead to more cohesion), a study was designed to determine which comes first—cohesion or performance. The results of this longitudinal study[65] of 205 members of 57 student teams competing in a complex business simulation over 10 weeks

> **Critical Thinking Question:** Explain why cohesion in teams may not always be a good thing. Discuss the potential downside of a team being too cohesive.

found that cohesion causes performance, and this effect became stronger over time. This study also found that the leader makes a difference as well: Teams that shared leadership had higher cohesion and performance.

You may be working in a team for a project for your OB course (or another course). The extent to which your team is cohesive can be assessed by asking the following questions:[66]

- How well do members of your group get along with each other?
- How well do members of your group stick together (i.e., remain close to each other)?
- Would you socialize with the members of your group outside of class?
- How well do members of your group help each other on the project?
- Would you want to remain a member of this group for future projects or in future courses?

A sense of cohesion in a team may also be due to a person's allegiance to the social groups they belong to. **Social identity** was introduced as a way to explain how people view their own place in society through membership in various groups.[67]

Social Identity Theory

Social identity is "the individual's knowledge that he belongs to certain social groups together with some emotional and value significance to him of this group membership."[68] People belong to different groups (e.g., a student can also be a coworker, a friend, and a member of a church), and these categorizations comprise their social identity.[69] Also, these groups exist in relation to other groups, so people derive meaning by relating their membership in a group by comparison to other groups. Think about the team spirit we feel when our football team defeats one of its longtime rivals. We feel a sense of belonging to our university and purchase a new shirt with our team's logo to show the world we are members of that university. Leaders should increase the sense of group cohesion, or solidarity, to stay in power and motivate followers to high performance.[70] Social identity binds people to a group—especially if the group has higher status or is distinctive and motivates people to behave in a manner that is consistent with the norms of the group.[71] Thus, the self-attributions of who people believe themselves to be (i.e., the social identity) are an important consideration for leaders. Leaders are also members of the groups they lead and can communicate with their followers as a member of the group. This plays a key role in followers' perceptions of their leaders' effectiveness. Viewing the leader as being "one of us" increases followers' positive endorsements of the leader due to their social identity with the team. When followers' identification with the group is important to them, and followers trust the leader's orientation to the group, they are more likely to be motivated, perform at high levels, and are more willing to accept change.[72]

RESEARCH IN ACTION

Coaching for Cohesion

Sports teams represent a unique place for the effects of cohesion to take hold due to their well-defined structures, tasks, and roles.[73] A review of the relationship between cohesiveness and team performance concluded that in 83% of the studies, team cohesiveness was significantly and positively related to team performance.[74] Research on sports psychology has examined the relationship between coaching style and team cohesion. When coaches exhibit training, being democratic, supporting, and giving feedback, team cohesion is higher.[75] An in-depth interview study of male and female athletes in college sports plus a case study of a Division I college football team was conducted to determine the effects of coaching styles on team cohesion.[76] This study found that using abusive language, treating the relationship as a superior or subordinate one, being unfair, lacking communication, and ridiculing players all related to lower team cohesion. Motivational coaching (being inspirational, having a personal relationship with athletes, showing support, and having dedication) was related to higher team cohesion. A case study of a football team indicated that players felt that bragging about the abilities of their teammates, talking about the quality of their opponent, giving motivational speeches, and conducting a team prayer increased feelings of team cohesion. This was confirmed by a meta-analysis[77] examining coaching style and team cohesion that included 288 effects from 24 studies that used the same sports leadership scale. The leadership scale was the Leadership Scale for Sport (LSS) and is composed of five leadership dimensions for a coach's behaviors: (1) training and instruction, which emphasizes athletes' development of skills, tactics, and physical performance; (2) democratic, which focuses on motivating athletes to make decisions on their goals, training objectives, and game strategies; (3) autocratic, which focuses on authority and independent decision making; (4) social support, which emphasizes interpersonal relationships with athletes outside of practice; and (5) positive feedback, which focuses on rewarding and praising athletes for outstanding performance. Overall, a moderate relationship was found between leadership and cohesion, and a large relationship was found between leadership and satisfaction, with training being the highest contributor for both. The gender composition of the athletic teams was also important. When coaches displayed a high frequency of positive behavior, teams comprised of females or coed teams showed an increase in players' satisfaction; however, this effect was not as strong for teams composed of only male athletes. It is important to recognize the influence of leadership behaviors on team cohesion, especially as sports evolve to be more competitive. This interesting research on coaching shows that being inspirational and developing the skills of your followers will likely enhance your team's cohesion.

Discussion Questions

1. To what extent can these findings for sports teams be applied to teams at work? What are the limitations of using sports examples?
2. In these studies, training, being democratic, showing support, and giving feedback were important in developing team cohesion. Which do you think is most important and why?
3. Based on the meta-analysis, why do you think that coaches' positive behaviors were more important for the satisfaction of female and coed teams but not for male teams?

Sources: Jowett, S., & Chaundy, V. (2004). An investigation into the impact of coach leadership and coach–athlete relationship on group cohesion. *Group Dynamics: Theory, Research and Practice, 8*(4), 302–331; Kim, H. D., & Cruz, A. B. (2016). The influence of coaches' leadership styles on athletes' satisfaction and team cohesion: A meta-analytic approach. *International Journal of Sports Science & Coaching, 11*(6), 900–909; Pescosolido, A. T., & Saavedra, R. (2012). Cohesion and sports teams: A review. *Small Group Research, 43*(6), 744–758; Widmeyer, W. N., Carron, A. V., & Brawley, L. R. (1993). Group cohesion in sport and exercise. *Handbook of Research on Sport Psychology*, 672–692; Turman, P. D. (2003). Coaches and cohesion: The impact of coaching techniques on team cohesion in the small group sport setting. *Journal of Sport Behavior, 26*(1), 86–104.

Despite the best efforts to form an effective team by using a charter and establishing norms that result in cohesion, teams still encounter challenges. In fact, cohesion may work against the team and result in what is known as **groupthink**.

Groupthink

Groupthink is a team decision-making challenge that arises due to a high degree of cohesiveness and group norms that result in conformity.[78] Groupthink is defined as the conformity-seeking tendency of the group, which results in compromised decision making. Due to group pressure, the team does not survey all alternatives, and expressions of views that go against the majority of team members are suppressed. Team members apply direct pressure on dissenters and urge them to go along with the majority. The symptoms of groupthink are as follows:

1. **Group rationalization.** The team members generate explanations that support their preferred course of action.

2. **Direct pressure.** Those who speak out against the group decision are pressured into conformity.

3. **Suppression.** Members with differing views don't share them with the group for fear of ostracism and/or ridicule.

4. **Illusion of unanimity.** The team members believe that they are in agreement. But in fact, they are not. Dissenting views have been suppressed. Not speaking is interpreted as support for the team decision.

Groupthink occurs most often in highly cohesive groups and when the group is confident about their course of action early in the process.[79] Initial research on groupthink involved case studies of public policy decisions including the Bay of Pigs invasion of Cuba and the attack on Pearl Harbor.[80] Experimental research has partially supported the theory.[81] For example, an experiment tested groupthink and found support for the ideas that direct pressure from leaders increased the symptoms of groupthink.[82] Teams with directive leaders proposed and discussed fewer alternatives than groups with leaders who encouraged member participation. These teams were also willing to comply with the leaders' proposed solutions when the leaders stated their preferences early in the group discussion. The *Challenger* space shuttle disaster case has been interpreted using groupthink.[83] In this scenario, the decision by NASA to launch the space shuttle when temperatures were too low for O-rings to function properly resulted in the death of six astronauts and a civilian teacher. The analysis concludes that directive leadership and time pressure contributed to the impaired decision-making process of NASA engineers.

> Critical Thinking Questions: Why is directive leadership the strongest antecedent to groupthink? What else can leaders do to prevent putting undue pressure on a group to conform to their decision preferences?

To minimize groupthink, the leader can avoid being too directive and encourage everyone to participate fully in team discussions. The leader can assign a member of the team to play the devil's advocate, which is a role that challenges team assumptions and decisions throughout the process.

Most students recognize groupthink symptoms since they have probably occurred in student project teams. Think about a time when you felt like disagreeing with your team but stayed silent because the team was cohesive or you didn't want to create conflict. You may have been a victim of groupthink.

Groupthink represents deterioration in the effectiveness of team decision making. Fortunately, research has also indicated how groupthink can be prevented. For example, leaders can employ a variety of decision-making techniques instead of always relying on consensus decision making to provide more structure and avoid conformity. OB research has investigated other important techniques for the effectiveness of decision-making processes. These techniques are essential for a leader to know since decision quality may be affected by how the decision is made by the team. For example, involving followers in decisions by allowing participation is one important aspect of team decision making. The next sections discuss participation, brainstorming, consensus, multivoting, **nominal group technique (NGT)**, and the stepladder technique.

TEAM DECISION MAKING

Learning Objective 10.6: Compare and contrast consensus decision making and the nominal group technique (NGT).

Participation in Team Decisions

Leadership research has long recognized that leaders have options with respect to the degree of participation they allow their followers when making team decisions.[84] Table 10.1 shows the **normative decision-making model**, which shows that team decisions fall on a continuum ranging from leaders making the decision themselves to **delegating** the decision to the team.[85] Between these two points, there are **consultative** modes of decision making. The manager can consult followers one-on-one or as a group. They also have the option of serving as the **facilitator** of a group decision. Involving the right people in group decision making has been shown to result in higher quality decisions and more support for decision implementation.[86,87] However, key elements of the situation are important to consider when applying the normative decision-making model of participation. These factors include the following:[88]

1. How significant is the decision?

2. How likely is it that your team members will disagree?

Table 10.1 The Normative Decision-Making Model

Decide	Consult (Individually)	Consult (Group)	Facilitate	Delegate
You make the decision alone and either announce or "sell" it to the group. You may use your expertise in collecting information—from the group or others—that you deem relevant to the problem.	You present the problem to group members individually, get their suggestions, and then make the decision.	You present the problem to group members in a meeting, get their suggestions, and then make the decision.	You present the problem to the group in a meeting. You act as facilitator, defining the problem to be solved and the boundaries within which the decision must be made. Your objective is to get concurrence on a decision. Above all, you take care to ensure that your ideas are not given any greater weight than those of others simply because of your position.	You permit the group to make the decision within prescribed limits. The group undertakes the identification and diagnosis of the problem, developing alternative procedures for solving it, and deciding on one or more alternative solutions. While you play no direct role in the group's deliberations unless explicitly asked, your role is an important one behind the scenes, providing needed resources and encouragement.

Source: Vroom, V. H. (2003). Educating managers for decision making and leadership. *Management Decision, 41*(10), 968–978.

3. Do you (or your team) have the knowledge necessary to make the decision?

4. Do you need commitment from your team?

5. How likely is it that you will have commitment from your team?

6. Is there a time constraint?

7. Is team interaction difficult or impossible?

8. Do your team members function effectively as a team?

9. Is development of your team members important?

10. Do members of your team agree with your goals (and those of the organization)?

Employees value being able to participate in group decisions, and research has shown involving them in decisions increases their satisfaction and the chances of success.[89,90] Results from a study of over 400 decisions that had been made by managers in medium to large organizations found that over half of the decisions failed (they were either never implemented or fell apart within 2 years).[91] While some decisions failed due to technical issues such as the problem being defined wrong, the best predictors of success were the involvement and participation of key stakeholders. Specifically, decisions that used participation to foster implementation succeeded more than 80% of the time.

Participation is the foundation for decision-making effectiveness. Balanced participation of team members is needed for the following decision-making techniques, beginning with the process of brainstorming.

Brainstorming

Brainstorming is one of the most common forms of team decision making.[92] Brainstorming should be used when the team needs to produce a creative solution. It enhances the creative process because idea generation is separated from idea evaluation. Members are trained not to critique ideas but just to write them down as the group generates solutions to a problem. Ideas are typically written on flip-chart paper or a whiteboard so that everyone can see them. The team meets in a separate session to evaluate the ideas generated and decide on a course of action. IDEO is a successful product design company, and their rules for brainstorming are shown in the boxed insert.

Consensus

Consensus decision making is another technique that is commonly used in organizations. In many cases, consensus is preferable to voting (although voting is more common). Voting creates winners and losers, and may result in a lack of commitment to implement the decision. In a consensus decision-making process, everyone can say they have been heard and will support the final decision. The following steps are suggested for reaching consensus:[93]

1. **Introduction.** It typically takes fewer than 5 minutes and covers the following:

   - Why are we talking about this? Why does it matter?

   - History of the issue (including results of any previous meetings on it).

   - Goal for this item at this particular meeting (a report, decision, to gather input, etc.).

   At the end of the initial presentation, others who have factual knowledge of the issue are sometimes invited to add in further bits about the issue—as long as it doesn't go on for too long.

IDEO's Rules for Brainstorming

1. **Defer judgment.** Creative spaces don't judge. They let the ideas flow so that people can build on each other and foster great ideas. You never know where a good idea is going to come from. The key is to make everyone feel like they can say the idea on their mind and allow others to build on it.

2. **Encourage wild ideas.** Wild ideas can often give rise to creative leaps. In thinking about ideas that are wacky or out there, we tend to think about what we really want without the constraints of technology or materials. We can then take those magical possibilities and perhaps invent new technologies to deliver them.

3. **Build on the ideas of others.** Being positive and building on the ideas of others take some skill. In conversation, we try to use *and* instead of *but* . . .

4. **Stay focused on the topic.** We try to keep the discussion on target; otherwise, you can diverge beyond the scope of what we're trying to design for.

5. **Have one conversation at a time.** There are lots of conversations happening at once, which is great! Always think about the topic and how the ideas could apply.

6. **Be visual.** In live brainstorms, we use colored markers to write on Post-it notes that are put on a wall. Nothing gets an idea across faster than drawing it. It doesn't matter how terrible of a sketcher you are! It's all about the idea behind your sketch. You could also try your hand at sketching it out or mocking it up on the computer. We love visual ideas as the images make them memorable. Does someone else's idea excite you? Maybe make them an image to go with their idea.

7. **Go for quantity.** Aim for as many new ideas as possible. In a good session, up to 100 ideas are generated in 60 minutes. Crank the ideas out quickly.

Discussion Questions

1. Provide an example of how a team leader can train team members to defer judgment.

2. Evaluate the IDEO guideline for quantity of ideas. Do you feel that generating 100 ideas in 60 minutes is realistic? Why or why not?

3. What do you think a team leader should do after brainstorming? In other words, how should the final decision be made?

Source: OpenIDEO. (2011). 7 tips on better brainstorming. http://www.openideo.com/blog/seven-tips-on-better-brainstorming

2. **Clarifying questions.** These are simple questions just to make sure everyone in the room fully understands what has been presented or proposed.

3. **Discussion.** This is the exploratory phase, where people are invited to ask further questions, show the full diversity of perspectives, raise challenges and concerns, and so on. Agreements and disagreements on general direction are noted and the reasons for them examined—not just what the positions are but why and any underlying value conflicts they represent.

4. **Establish basic direction.** What is the sense of the meeting, in terms of basic direction on this issue? Here we seek general or philosophical agreement—an agreement in principle.

5. **Synthesize or modify proposal (as needed).** Integrate what's been shared, and make it as specific as needed, recognizing that some details will always be left to implementation. Again, notice agreements and disagreements (this time on the specifics of the proposal), and work with the underlying reasons, then generate ideas for addressing and resolving concerns, emerging with a proposal that has substantial group support. Periodically, the facilitator may ask, "Are there any remaining unresolved concerns?"

6. **Call for consensus.** The facilitator clearly restates the proposal and then asks people to indicate where they are.

7. **Record.** The note taker reads back the decision to the group. In addition, they record any implementation information needed (tasks, who's responsible, timelines, etc.).
   At the point that the facilitator calls for consensus (Step 6), participants typically have the following options:

Agreement: "I support this proposal and am willing to abide by and help implement it."

Stand Aside: "I have major concerns with the proposal and agree to stand aside and let the group proceed with it." The choice to stand aside may be based on (but is not limited to) any of the following:

- Disagreement with the proposal or the process used to reach the decision

- Personal values or principles

- Personal impact or need—for example, "I can't afford this" or "I'd have to leave the group."

If someone stands aside, their name and reason are traditionally recorded in the minutes. That person is relieved of lead implementation responsibilities yet is still bound to follow the decision.

Blocking: "I believe this proposal would be majorly detrimental to our group, because either it goes against our fundamental principles or it would lead to a disastrous outcome." Note that none of the following are appropriate reasons to block:

- To get your way or because you prefer a different proposal, or no proposal

- Because you'd have to leave the group if the proposal passed

- Tradition: Because things have always been done a certain way

- Because the proposed action doesn't fit your personal needs (or finances)

- To fulfill your personal moral values or how you want to live

In order to function and prevent tyranny of the minority, consensus-based groups rely on having a robust response to inappropriate blocks. The form of this response varies but usually includes both procedural and cultural elements.

Abstain: "I choose not to participate in the making of this decision." It is typically used because a participant feels uninformed or not ready to participate.

> Critical Thinking Question: Explain why following the consensus guidelines will result in more support for the implementation of a decision rather than simply voting on it.

Some groups include other options, such as consent with reservations: "I support the basic thrust of this proposal and have one or more minor unresolved concerns."

Consensus is one of the most commonly used and effective decision-making processes in organizations. The previously given guidelines should be followed in situations in which the support of all members of a team is needed for effective implementation of the decision.

Multivoting

In practice, it is often required that votes be taken. Given that voting has a number of disadvantages, including dissatisfaction with decisions and lack of commitment, the leader should know that multivoting is another decision-making option. The steps for multivoting follow.[94] As with other team decision-making techniques, you need a flip chart or whiteboard, marking pens, plus five to 10 slips of paper for each individual, and a pen or pencil for each individual.

1. **Display the list of options.** Combine duplicate items. Organize large numbers of ideas, and eliminate duplication and overlap. List reduction may also be useful.

2. **Number (or letter) all items.**

3. **Decide how many items must be on the final reduced list.** Decide also how many choices each member will vote for. Usually, five choices are allowed. The longer the original list, the more votes will be allowed—up to 10.

4. **Working individually, each member selects the five items (or whatever number of choices is allowed) he or she thinks most important.** Then each member ranks the choices in order of priority, with the first choice ranking highest. For example, if each member has five votes, the top choice would be ranked five, the next choice four, and so on. Each choice is written on a separate paper, with the ranking underlined in the lower right corner.

5. **Tally votes.** Collect the papers, shuffle them, and then record the votes on a flip chart or whiteboard. The easiest way to record votes is for the note-taker to write all the individual rankings next to each choice. For each item, the rankings are totaled next to the individual rankings.

6. **If a decision is clear, stop here. Otherwise, continue with a brief discussion of the vote.** The purpose of the discussion is to look at dramatic voting differences, such as an item that received both 5 and 1 ratings, and avoid errors from incorrect information or understandings about the item. The discussion should not pressure anyone to change his or her vote. Also, if a team member or members feel strongly that an option should be considered, the team can put it back in the voting process.

7. **Repeat the voting process in Steps 4 and 5.** If greater decision-making accuracy is required, this voting may be done by weighting the relative importance of each choice on a scale of 1 to 10, with 10 being most important. As can be seen from this process, multivoting allows for multiple rounds and discussion as the list gets reduced. It allows team members to have more of a voice in the final decision through a series of votes rather than just one.

> Critical Thinking Questions: What are the advantages and disadvantages of multivoting? Would you consider using this technique? Why or why not?

Nominal Group Technique

The NGT is a more structured process that may be effective if there are status differences in the team or if the team has one or more dominating participants. The group meets face-to-face, but the discussion is more restricted than in brainstorming or consensus decision making. This process reduces status differentials since participants write their ideas on index cards and they are collected by a facilitator. This process is particularly effective when the team has a dominating participant who shuts down the team discussion with criticism. Research has indicated that NGT works better than brainstorming.[95] NGT is often used by senior management teams as a preparation tool for productive strategy meetings. The steps for the NGT follow:[96]

1. Each team member independently writes their ideas on the problem on 3×5 cards or slips of paper.

2. Each member presents one idea to the team. The cards are collected by the facilitator who can either read them

or redistribute them randomly to the team members who then read the ideas on the card. This way, no one is identified with a particular idea.

3. The discussion continues until all ideas are heard and recorded.

4. The team discusses the ideas and asks questions to clarify them.

5. Each team member then silently ranks the ideas independently. The idea with the highest total ranking is the final decision.

Stepladder

The stepladder technique is a newer technique and may also be an effective way to combat the challenge of dominating participants in the team. It has five basic steps:

1. **Present the task.** Before getting together as a group, present the task or problem to all members. Give everyone sufficient time to think about what needs to be done and to form their own opinions on how to best accomplish the task or solve the problem.

2. **Two-member discussion.** Form a core group of two members. Have them discuss the problem.

3. **Add one member.** Add a third group member to the core group. The third member presents ideas to the first two members *before* hearing the ideas that have already been discussed. After all three members have laid out their solutions and ideas, they discuss their options together.

4. **Repeat, adding one member at a time.** Repeat the same process by adding a fourth member and so on to the group. Allow time for discussion after each additional member has presented his or her ideas.

5. **Final decision.** Reach a final decision only after all members have been brought in and presented their ideas.[97]

An experiment was conducted to see if the stepladder technique resulted in higher-quality decisions compared to consensus decision making.[98] Stepladder groups produced significantly higher-quality decisions than did conventional groups in which all members worked on the problem at the same time. Stepladder group decisions surpassed the quality of their best individual members' decisions 56% of the time. In contrast, conventional group decisions surpassed the quality of their best members' decisions only 13% of the time. Since all members must contribute in the step-ladder process, it is suggested as a way to help teams address the challenge of social loafing. This and other team challenges are discussed in the following sections.

TEAM CHALLENGES

Learning Objective 10.7: Generate an example of how a team leader can reduce social loafing.

Social Loafing

A group challenge that is common in student project teams is **social loafing**. You will recognize this one if you have ever been in a team where you (or a subgroup of team members) did all the work but others got the credit and didn't contribute. Social loafing is defined as the reduction in motivation and effort when individuals work collectively compared with when they work individually or coactively (i.e., they work with others but do not combine inputs into a group product).[99] Social loafing occurs more often in larger teams where individuals can hide in the team.[100] When there is skill redundancy, some team members may feel that their contributions are not valued. If others are slacking, then team members may stop contributing. Team members may not see the goal as valuable or agree with it, so they don't contribute. There are individual differences as well: Research has shown men are more likely to social loaf than women, and those from individualistic cultures are more likely to loaf.[101] Leaders can prevent social loafing by doing the following:

1. Keep teams small (four to six members).

2. Set meaningful team goals.

3. Set clear roles for team members.

4. Eliminate redundancy.

5. Select members with high motivation and affinity for teamwork.

6. Provide feedback and coaching to members who social loaf.

Virtual Teams

Today, more work is being conducted through the Internet in virtual teams. Virtual teams are defined as "functioning teams that rely on technology-mediated communication while crossing several different boundaries."[102] Such teams rely on technology to communicate, and this has significantly changed how teamwork is conducted. It has been suggested that virtual teams have more challenges in developing the TMMs needed to be effective.[103] In many cases, virtual team members are geographically dispersed and may even be working in different countries and time zones. A comparison of computer-mediated teams to face-to-face teams in a longitudinal study found the relationship between technology and performance depended on experience with the technology.[104] The results also suggested the newness of the medium to team members and not the newness of the group led to poorer task performance for computer groups. Another study found that communication apprehension and poor typing ability negatively influenced the quality and quantity of communication in virtual teams, and this determined who emerged as the team leader.[105] A review of studies on computer-mediated groups reported computer-based groups generated more ideas but had more limited interactions and took longer to complete their work compared with teams that met face-to-face.[106] Research has shown that trust is essential for knowledge sharing to occur in virtual teams.[107] However, virtual teams may have less social support and direct interaction among team members, which are needed to build trust.[108] A meta-analysis of more than 5,000 teams found virtual teams share less information.[109] Also, virtual work and the use of e-mail in combination may change the distribution of information within an organization and change knowledge flows.[110]

Leaders play a central role in virtual team functioning since they influence how a team deals with obstacles and how the team ultimately adapts to the unique challenges they face.[111] A study of student teams was conducted in which the leaders of virtual teams were compared with those in face-to-face teams.[112] Researchers found that leader behaviors focusing on the task and monitoring of performance significantly impacted the performance of virtual teams. Leaders can enhance the effectiveness of virtual teams by establishing trust, carefully monitoring e-mail, attending to team progress, and by sharing the team's work with others.[113] Establishing team goals early in the life cycle of the team also improves virtual team cohesion and effectiveness.[114] Advanced information technology (IT) will have a significant impact on leadership in organizations in the future, and leaders must be aware of the impact for leading virtual teams.[115] Additional guidelines for leading virtual teams are shown in Table 10.2.

One of the advantages of virtual teams is that team members can be geographically dispersed. Members can contribute to teamwork

> **Critical Thinking Question:** Provide an example of a type of work that cannot be done by a virtual team. Why do you think this would be the case?

Table 10.2　Practices of Effective Virtual Team Leaders

Leadership Practices of Virtual Team Leaders	How Do Virtual Team Leaders Do It?
1. Establish and Maintain Trust Through the Use of Communication Technology	• Focusing the norms on how information is communicated • Revisiting and adjusting the communication norms as the team evolves ("virtual get-togethers") • Making progress explicit through use of team virtual workspace • Equal "suffering" when setting up meetings across different time zones
2. Ensure Diversity in the Team Is Understood, Appreciated, and Leveraged	• Prominent team expertise directory and skills matrix in the virtual workspace • Virtual sub-teaming to pair diverse members and rotate sub-team members • Allowing diverse opinions to be expressed through use of asynchronous electronic means (e.g., electronic discussion threads)
3. Manage Virtual Work-Cycle and Meetings	• Idea divergence between meetings (asynchronous idea generation) and idea convergence and conflict resolution during virtual meetings (synchronous idea convergence) • Use the start of virtual meeting (each time) for social relationship building • During meeting—ensure through "check-ins" that everyone is engaged and heard from • End of meeting—ensure that the minutes and future work plan is posted to team repository
4. Monitor Team Progress Through the Use of Technology	• Closely scrutinize asynchronous (electronic threaded discussion and document postings in the knowledge repository) and synchronous (virtual meeting participation and instant messaging) communication patterns • Make progress explicit through balanced scorecard measurements posted in the team's virtual workspace
5. Enhance External Visibility of the Team and Its Members	• Frequent report-outs to a virtual steering committee (comprised of local bosses of team members)
6. Ensure Individuals Benefit From Participating in Virtual Teams	• Virtual reward ceremonies • Individual recognition at the start of each virtual meeting • Making each team member's "real location" boss aware of the member's contribution

Source: Malhotra, A., Majchrzak, A., & Rosen, B. (2007). Leading virtual teams. *Academy of Management Perspectives*, 21(1), 60–70. p. 62.

from anywhere in the world. In many cases, virtual teams are diverse and comprised of members from different cultures. In addition to being virtual, cultural differences affect teams. Diversity is a challenge for teams but it also offers opportunities to increase team performance. Diversity within teams is addressed next, considering its challenges and benefits.

TEAM DIVERSITY

Learning Objective 10.8: Discuss the challenges and benefits of team diversity.

Challenges of Team Diversity

Consider the following hypothetical product development team at a leading manufacturer of industrial and medical products:

This four-member team is composed of one mid-level female accountant, one newly hired female biomedical engineer, one established male executive vice-president (VP) of marketing and one male mid-level production manager with a degree in industrial engineering. The biomedical engineer is passionate about biomedical innovation, while the production manager is equally committed to incrementally improving the company's existing products for the gas and oil industry. Team members have a variety of in-house connections: the biomedical engineer meets regularly with other medical staff to discuss new products, the production manager meets weekly with other industrial engineers from the manufacturing department to coordinate workflow and the VP of marketing has executive meetings to plan marketing strategies. During lunchtime, the two females get together in the office and the two males join their old-time group of friends. Top management considers medical marketing core to business growth, whereas accounting and engineering on the industrial side are perceived as less competitive functions.[116]

How will the diversity of this team affect its processes and outcomes? For over 20 years, researchers have been studying the effects of diversity in teams. The previous example reflects diversity that is related to the functional areas and gender of the team members. There has also been a great deal of research on the effects of cultural differences in multicultural teams. This research has high relevance for team leaders since teams have become increasingly diverse, with individuals from different cultural backgrounds working closely with one another both in virtual as well as face-to-face teams.

Not all team processes translate cross-culturally. One study surveyed members of 461 **self-managed work teams (SMWTs)** in four countries: the United States, Finland, Belgium, and the Philippines.[117] Resistance to SMWTs was affected by cultural values of collectivism and power distance. **Collectivism** is group orientation, and **power distance** is respect for authority. Also, the degree of **determinism** (i.e., the belief that "people should not try to change the paths their lives are destined to take") affected reactions to the implementation of SMWTs. Employees in the Philippines were significantly more likely to reject self-management compared to employees in the United States. Caution should be exercised when implementing SMWTs and other forms of participation in countries with high power distance. Individuals in high power distance cultures respect authority and expect the leader to have all the answers. They may be confused by a leader who asks for their input and make the attribution that the leader is not competent to make the decision alone. Similar reactions to the offer of participation might be found in Russia and Mexico.[118,119] Participation in countries with high power distance may not be appropriate, and managers should check cultural assumptions before offering participation to multicultural teams. Diversity presents a challenge to the team leader in that there is a greater need to manage conflict. But it appears to be worth the effort since benefits can be realized through increased creativity and satisfaction in diverse teams.

Benefits of Team Diversity

Diverse teams can accomplish great things. For example, in the wake of the earthquake and tsunami in Japan, rescue professionals from different countries had to come together quickly to fulfill critical rescue missions. These international teams, which possessed different professional capacities, did not have the luxury of negotiating clear formal leadership before undertaking time-critical, life-saving tasks at ground zero.[120] Thus, these international teams had to be self-managed, and research has shown that there are certain characteristics of team members that enable self-managed multicultural teams to perform well. A longitudinal study of multicultural MBA project teams found that teams performed better when members had more tolerance for uncertainty and were more relationship-oriented.[121]

Diversity may enhance team creativity, and this is considered one of the benefits of having a diverse workforce. For example, different abilities are related to particular cultures: British inventiveness, for example, or Japanese pragmatism. According to the head of R&D at Hitachi Europe, the underlying consideration in the internationalization of R&D is the conviction that mixing western and Japanese mentalities achieves high-quality R&D results faster.[122] This belief is supported by evidence from a study[123] of 574 R&D multicultural team members, their leaders, and their leaders' managers in 82 co-located teams in a Chinese branch of a large German global organization. Multicultural team leaders with high global identity leveraged cultural diversity to promote innovative goals, which further enhanced team communication, inclusion, and its positive impact on team innovation.

Diversity in teams can increase flexibility, creativity, and problem solving.[124] A meta-analysis of team diversity and team performance found having members with diverse skill sets and backgrounds enhances team creativity and innovation.[125] Specifically, differences in functional expertise, education, and organizational tenure were most related to team performance. A second meta-analysis of 108 studies in 10,632 teams found cultural diversity leads to process losses through task conflict.[126] Effective team leaders credit diversity for being a key reason for team creative outputs that directly impact organizational success.[127] There is some evidence that diversity training enhances creativity. An experimental study compared the creativity of teams that attended nationality diversity training to teams that did not have the training (controls). Results of the study indicated that for teams with less positive diversity beliefs, diversity training increased creative performance when the team's nationality diversity was high.[128]

Leadership makes a difference in how well diverse teams perform. Throughout this chapter, a clear theme is that the leader can set up groups for success by directing the group toward a meaningful goal, selecting the right decision-making tools, and preventing groupthink. In the concluding section of this chapter, the importance of empowering team leadership is discussed further.

LEADERSHIP IMPLICATIONS: EMPOWERING THE TEAM

Research has shown that team leaders engage in certain behaviors that enhance team performance. The focus of team leadership has shifted from the leader to the team, and this is called *team-centric leadership*. One review notes that: "Team-centric leadership research has exploded in the past decade."[129] A team-centric leader creates the right climate for a team, and this increases followers' empowerment.[130] Leadership climate is effective when a team leader gives their team many responsibilities, asks the team for advice when making decisions, is not too controlling, allows the team to set its own goals, stays out of the way when the team works on its performance problems, tells the team to expect a lot from itself, and trusts the team. A study of 62 teams in a Fortune 500 company found leadership climate is related to team performance through team empowerment.[131] More-empowered teams are more productive and proactive than less-empowered teams and have higher levels of customer service, job satisfaction, and commitment. However, shared leadership is most strongly related to team performance when team members have high levels of task-related competence.[132] Empowerment is also related to lower employee cynicism and "time theft" (spending time on non-work-related activities during working hours).[133] A meta-analysis of relationships between leader behaviors and team performance found task-focused behaviors are moderately related to perceived team effectiveness and team productivity. However, person-focused behaviors are more related to perceived team effectiveness, team productivity, and team learning than task-focused behaviors. Examining specific leader behaviors, empowerment behaviors accounted for nearly 30% of the variance in team learning.[134] Empowerment seems to be a critical aspect of the development of highly effective teams. Team members need to feel that they have the power to make significant decisions about their work. Empowering leadership has also been found to increase the effectiveness of collaboration in virtual teams where members are geographically dispersed.[135] Empowering leaders act more like coaches than command-and-control formal leaders. A study[136] of 70 service teams compared formal team leaders to leaders that behaved as coaches and found that coaches significantly influence team empowerment, and thereby team processes and performance, whereas formal team leaders did not. Team coaches engaged in behaviors such as building teamwork and giving team members the technical information needed to do their jobs. Complete Self-Assessment 10.2 to learn about your team leadership style.

In some cases, empowerment takes the form of the team being SMWTs. SMWTs are teams that are empowered to lead themselves without a formal assigned leader. In SMWTs, decisions regarding the specific ways that tasks are performed are left up to the members of the team.[137] These teams are now common at the workplace, and they have been related to higher job satisfaction and commitment.[138] SMWTs are in place in 79% of Fortune 1000 companies and in 81% of manufacturing companies.[139] The role of the leader in SMWTs is to relate (build trust), scout (seek information and diagnose problems), persuade (gain external support and influence the team), and empower (delegate and coach). The research evidence on SMWTs reports mixed results, however. While members report that they are more satisfied, team performance may be more difficult to attain without a leader. For example, SMWTs' members don't manage conflict well, and this may result in an erosion of trust.[140] A study of SMWTs that compared them to traditional teams found that claims of the effectiveness of self-management may have been inflated; SMWTs did not perform better than traditional teams.[141]

Leadership matters for team performance in a number of ways. Leaders can move their team through the team development process by establishing SMART goals and having the team create a team charter to guide them. The team charter establishes team norms that can lead to higher levels of cohesion, which has been shown to impact team effectiveness. Leaders should pay attention to the metrics that the team uses to evaluate their performance and include task, process, and individual development measures to assess the team. A team leader needs to assess any challenges that the team may face such as social loafing, being virtual, and the degree of diversity. Diversity can benefit team process and performance but must be effectively managed. Finally, leaders should use a variety of team decision-making processes, including participation, brainstorming, consensus, NGT, and the stepladder technique. If a vote must be taken, a leader should consider using multivoting rather than a simple majority vote that creates winners and losers. For these techniques to work, it is important that the leader create the right leadership climate for the team and empower the team to act.

> **Critical Thinking Question:** Explain why the existence of SMWTs that also have a team leader poses a paradox for the leader. If a team is self-managed, what is the leader's role?

SAGE edge™

edge.sagepub.com/scandura2e

Want a better grade? **Go to edge.sagepub.com/scandura2e** for the tools you need to sharpen your study skills.

KEY TERMS

TOOLKIT ACTIVITY 10.1: The Team Charter

Getting Started: Developing Ground Rules

Anyone who plays sports has to learn the rules. Anyone who learns to play an instrument has to learn the techniques. The rules of "how we do things here" (the etiquette of the situation, the appropriate behaviors) are the ground rules.

Teams often begin making assumptions about ground rules. Members believe that everyone knows how it should be and how everyone should behave. When someone else's behavior fails to conform to one's own expectations, people tend to be surprised. Even more important, because the rules are not clear and because there has been no discussion as to how problems will be managed, unnecessary conflict follows. This assignment serves the following objectives:

- Gives you the opportunity to get to know your team members

- Provides a short but *important* task so that the team can learn to function quickly without a large portion of your grade resting on the initial outcome

- Enables the team to develop and understand the rules of conduct expected of each team member

Your team will be required to submit a team charter. The following points that must be included in your charter are listed next, with some examples of the kinds of questions that might be addressed. However, use these as starting points; be sure to address any other important issues that come up in your discussions.

Attendance

How often should we meet?

How long should our meetings be?

When is it okay to miss a meeting?

Lateness

Since team meetings should start on time, how do we deal with lateness?

What does "on time" mean?

Interruptions

How do we deal with interruptions?

What is allowed? Phone calls? Messages?

Food, Coffee, and Breaks

Do we have food or coffee?

Who cleans up?

How many breaks should we have?

How much socializing is permissible?

Participation

What do we mean by participation?

How do we encourage participation?

Are there group norms that we can establish to encourage participation?

Goals

What are the team's goals and objectives?

What is the team's mission?

How will the team keep members motivated?

How will the team reward itself (and individual members) for a job well done?

Norms

What behaviors are permissible?

How do we deal with people who dominate, resist, are too quiet, are too noisy, etc.?

How will we monitor our progress?

What important roles need to be assumed by team members during the semester? How will these roles be assigned?

Decision Making

How do we make decisions?

What decisions must be agreed to by all?

What does consensus mean?

Conflict

How will the team encourage positive (creative) conflict and discourage negative (dysfunctional) conflict?

How can the team encourage and manage differences of opinion and different perspectives?

Sanction Issues (What Will the Team Do With Deviates?)

How will the team deal with members who violate the agreed-upon norms of the team? For example, how will social loafing or inadequate participation be dealt with?

Firing Team Members

What are the specific rules or criteria for firing a team member? (You must give two written notices to the person and a copy to the professor prior to dismissal.)

Team Member Strengths and Weaknesses

Each team member should be identified (name, phone number, e-mail) along with an assessment of his or her strengths and his or her areas for improvement.

Other

Are there other issues that have a positive or negative impact on the team?

The Next Step: A Name and a Logo

After your team has prepared its team charter, create a name for your team and design a logo. The name and logo should be meaningful to the team, reflecting an attribute that the team members believe is important (humor is allowed and encouraged, but both the team logo and name should be meaningful). The name is limited to one or two words. Write a brief explanation of your name and logo choice. Give a copy to your instructor (along with your team charter). Your team charter should also include the following:

- A cover page with the following printed on it: the team name; team logo; team member names; and course name, number, and section

- A page with team member names, phone numbers, and e-mail addresses

- Team charter rules and expectations

- A brief explanation of your team name and logo choice

Discussion Questions

1. Which part(s) of the team charter was the most difficult for your team to reach agreement on? Why do you think this was the case?

2. What did you learn about your teammates by listing their strengths and weaknesses? How can you help them develop their weak areas?

3. How do you plan to use the team charter to keep your team on track toward accomplishing its goals?

Source: Adapted from Cox, P. L., & Bobrowski, P. E. (2000). The team charter assignment: Improving the effectiveness of classroom teams. *Journal of Behavioral and Applied Management, 1*(1), 92–103.

TOOLKIT ACTIVITY 10.2: The Marshmallow Challenge (Team Exercise)

The Marshmallow Challenge has been tested worldwide by consultant Tom Wujec. Wujec has run the challenge with different categories of teams such as CEO teams, teams of architects, teams of engineers, teams of business students, and teams of kindergarten children.

First, form teams of four people. Provide each team with a building kit containing 20 sticks of spaghetti, 1 yard of masking tape, 1 yard of string, and 1 marshmallow. You need a measuring tape and watch. Run the challenge with your group, and then watch the debriefing video provided at http://www.tomwujec.com/design-projects/marshmallow-challenge/

The goals and rules of the Marshmallow Challenge follow.

1. **Build the tallest freestanding structure:** The winning team is the one that has the tallest structure measured from the tabletop surface to the top of the marshmallow. That means the structure cannot be suspended from a higher structure, like a chair, ceiling, or chandelier.

2. **The entire marshmallow must be on top:** The entire marshmallow needs to be on the top of the structure. Cutting or eating part of the marshmallow disqualifies the team.

3. **Use as much or as little of the kit:** The team can use as many or as few of the 20 spaghetti sticks, as much or as little of the string or tape. The team cannot use the paper bag that the materials are in as part of their structure.

4. **Break up the spaghetti, string, or tape:** Teams are free to break the spaghetti, cut up the tape and string to create new structures.

5. **Observe the time limit:** You have 18 minutes to build your structure.

Discussion Questions

1. Was there a leader on your team? Who was this person, and who decided who the leader would be? If you had no leader, do you think having designated someone a leader would have helped?

2. Did you feel everyone's ideas were well received during the activity? How did you deal with frustration? Were all teammates included?

3. Did your team have a plan? Did the plan work? Did you veer from the plan at all? Why or why not? What worked? What didn't work?

Source: http://www.tomwujec.com/design-projects/marshmallow-challenge/

TOOLKIT ACTIVITY 10.3: How to Run an Effective Meeting (Checklist)

Research has demonstrated that running meetings effectively increases team performance. A study of 63 team meetings[142] including a total of 359 meeting participants from different organizations found that leaders must remember to show considerate leadership, which was positively related to satisfaction with meetings. Also, team leaders need to balance relational- and task-oriented meeting procedures. The following checklist is a useful guide to ensuring a successful meeting.

Before the meeting

- Set goals for the meeting, and prepare an agenda.

- Prioritize issues to be discussed, including carryover issues from previous meetings.

- Consult with team members to finalize the agenda.

- Research information necessary for making important decisions (or delegate this).

- Arrange logistics: date, time, place, catering. Select a comfortable and convenient meeting place.

- Send out announcements and reminders for the meeting, including the meeting agenda.

- Arrange for AV equipment, flip charts, markers, and other supplies.

- Arrive early to set up, and check for adequate lighting, ventilation, heating, or air-conditioning.

- Arrange seating, and post directional signs if needed.

- Prepare name tags or tent cards if needed.

During the meeting

- Greet people warmly as they arrive individually.
- Announce the nearest restrooms.
- Have the agenda at each person's place or projected on screen.
- Set a welcoming tone: introductions (you may want to include an icebreaker exercise if time permits).
- Review minutes from the previous meeting if appropriate.
- Provide background information, and review the meeting goals.
- Be courteous, respectful, and inclusive during the discussions.
- Start and finish the meeting on time.

Bring closure

- Make decisions.
- Prepare action plans and follow up.
- Summarize main points and what was accomplished during the meeting.
- Schedule the next meeting (if needed).

After the meeting

- E-mail participants, and thank them for their contributions.
- Distribute minutes of the meeting and action plans.
- Include a reminder about the next meeting.

Discussion Questions

1. From the checklist, identify which behaviors are task-related and which behaviors are relationship-related. Explain how you would set the tone for the meeting by being a considerate leader.

2. Discuss why it is important to have an agenda for the meeting. Should the leader set the agenda or have it created by the team? Explain.

3. Why is it important to start and finish the meeting on time? What should the leader do if the agenda is not completed by the end of the meeting time?

4. Why is it important to follow up after the meeting? Create one or two additional items that should be included in the follow-up after a meeting.

Source: Odermatt, I., König, C. J., Kleinmann, M., Nussbaumer, R., Rosenbaum, A., Olien, J. L., & Rogelberg, S. G. (2017). On leading meetings: Linking meeting outcomes to leadership styles. *Journal of Leadership & Organizational Studies, 24*(2), 189–200.

CASE STUDY 10.1: Problem Solving in Virtual Teams

Shelia works for General Electric's (GE) energy company in the wind turbine manufacturing division as an inventory controller. Her job duties include receiving the wind turbine components into GE's inventory when vendors provide the required documentation and then moving them out of inventory when the components reach the wind field site. She handles primarily the large components including tower segments, blades, machine heads, and hubs. The tower segments are made by firms in the United States and China and are received into inventory once the signed inspection tags are e-mailed to her. For the blades, they are shipped to the port of Houston, and once they are unloaded and pass inspection they are entered into inventory. The machine heads and hubs are made by GE at three different plants and go into inventory once completed and ready for shipment.

Sheila is based in the Greenville, NC, plant with two of the three-person buyer teams that handle the orders of the parts to make the machine heads and hubs. Another of the machine head teams is based in Schenectady, NY. She also works with a team based in Houston, TX, that handles the ordering of the wind turbine blades and the tower team that works in the plant in Pensacola, FL. She also works with a transportation specialist on each team to help with the shipment of these large wind turbine components to the client's site, and with up to two dozen wind farm site teams at any given time to capture the delivery and installation of the different wind turbine components in order to move items out of inventory and trigger billing to the client.

The majority of the work Sheila does with her teams is through the phone, e-mail, and occasional web meeting. Rarely does she get to see any of the teams outside of the two located at Greenville, as there is trust and respect among teammates as well as understanding of what is her role on these teams. However, working in such spread-out teams that span the globe as well as several organizations creates a number of challenges. Sometimes, there are issues with suppliers when they do not provide the proper documentation for completion and still are seeking payment. Sometimes, there are issues with working out replacement shipments when the blades and towers from overseas are damaged in transit. However, most of the time the job and relationship between team members goes smoothly thanks to a number of processes and procedures that have been set in place to help with those challenges.

Currently, a new team is being formed in the wind division. As can often happen when shipping goods, the hubs, machine heads, and towers frequently have components that are damaged in transit. In order to assist the wind farm sites to get the turbines up and running as fast as possible, they need all the parts fully functional. So a team is forming to help the wind farm sites quickly get the replacement parts that are needed. A ticket system has been set up for the wind farm site team to put in reports of damaged parts. The system then assigns each case to a different team member, who is responsible for finding the solution to the problem and getting the needed parts to the wind farm site as quickly as possible. In addition, there is a weekly web meeting on Wednesdays where the cases are discussed and everyone on the team is updated.

Sheila was assigned to work on this new team, but it has not been going as well as the work on her other teams. First, while she knows some of the larger components based upon the receiving she does, she does not have a clue as to the list of smaller components, cables, and wires used to make the larger components. While the on-ground crews provide pictures and a description, they don't provide the exact part number or name that is needed, and so for her first two cases she spent nearly a week hunting down schematics and talking with engineers in both Schenectady and Greenville to figure out what part is needed. She then spent 3 more days getting the purchase orders needed to order the parts (as receivers can't cut their own purchase orders for fraud prevention reasons), and shipping took another 2 days. The team leader was upset with the amount of time Sheila took to close the cases and reprimanded her on the weekly call. Sheila felt that this was unfair, as she does not have access to the knowledge and resources to get the job done as quickly as others. However, she still tried to do her best on her next case, getting replacement ladders for the towers at a couple different sites. However, that case took 3 weeks to close as a result of the ladders arriving damaged from transit and required Sheila to find another vendor to ship and deliver the ladders.

Discussion Questions

1. How does trust and respect facilitate the virtual teams' ability to operate?

2. What processes and procedures are important to making the teams work?

3. Why do you think Sheila is having trouble in her role on the new team?

4. What factors should you consider when putting together a virtual team?

SELF-ASSESSMENT 10.1: Teamwork Orientation

This self-assessment exercise identifies your propensity toward working in teams. The goal is for you to learn about yourself. There are no right or wrong answers, and this is not a test. You don't have to share your results with others unless you wish to do so.

Part I: Taking the Assessment

Statements	Strongly Disagree	Disagree	Neutral	Agree	Strongly Agree
1. The basic idea of the team concept is good.	1	2	3	4	5
2. Teams are essential for effective or organizational functioning.	1	2	3	4	5
3. I feel positive about working in a team.	1	2	3	4	5
4. Teams are good for organizations.	1	2	3	4	5
5. The team concept helps organizations.	1	2	3	4	5

Part II. Scoring Instructions

Add your responses to determine your total for team orientation. Higher scores suggest a higher propensity for teamwork. In general, scores from 5 to 12 indicate a lower interest in being on a team, and scores above 13 indicate a higher interest in being on a team.

Discussion Questions

1. Based on your results, are you a team-oriented person? How does this affect your attitude toward working in teams?

2. Compare your results to your teammates. Are there more people who are team-oriented compared to those who are not? How might this affect your team process?

3. How can a team leader motivate team members who don't value the team concept (in other words, lower scores on this assessment ranging from 5 to 12)? What can a leader do to convince such reluctant members to engage with the team?

Source: Adapted from Scandura, T. A. (1995). *Management practices survey.* Coral Gables, FL: University of Miami.

SELF-ASSESSMENT 10.2: Team Leadership Inventory (TLI)

To take this assessment, use the number 4 for the response that is **MOST** like you, a 3 for the one that is **MODERATELY** like you, a 2 for the one that is **LITTLE** like you, and a 1 for the response that is **LEAST** like you. **Do not repeat** any number when answering a given question. Use all four numbers when responding to a question. **There are no right or wrong answers,** so respond to what comes first to your mind.

Example:

I see my role as:	giving directions	4	expert	3	making goals exciting	1	listening to people	2

In the example above, giving directions is most like you, being expert is moderately like you, listening to people is a little like you, and making goals exciting is least like you. Note that all four numbers are used. Now, answer the following questions about yourself:

1.	The most critical team activity is:	goal setting		decision making		brainstorming		supporting one another
2.	I prefer a team:	that works hard		that is flexible		that creates something new		that gets along
3.	When a team has conflict:	stick to the goal		use logic to solve it		take risks		feelings should be protected
4.	To motivate a team, I would:	reward them as a team		explain why hard work is needed		focus on the overall mission		coach them
5.	From my team I expect:	commitment		rationality		change		caring
6.	I lead my team with:	confidence		decisiveness		a sense of mission		warmth
7.	Teams are:	goal-oriented		challenging		the future of work		social entities
8.	To improve teamwork, I:	reinforce deadlines		challenge the team		set stretch goals		encourage participation
9.	In a team, I am a(n):	take charge person		problem-solver		idea generator		conflict manager
10.	Teams require:	clear and specific tasks		planning		a meaningful goal		a supportive atmosphere
11.	To lead a team, it takes:	a proven track record		intelligence		flexibility		attention to each team member
12.	Teammates see me as:	task-oriented		logical		forward-looking		nice
13.	I am trying to improve my:	time management		decision processes		creativity		interpersonal skills
14.	In meetings, I prefer:	brevity		detail orientation		innovation		sensitivity
15.	The best team leaders are:	in the military		in large companies		entrepreneurs		in volunteer organizations
16.	Teams should:	have well- defined plans		be organized		explore new possibilities		build consensus
17.	When there is a deadline, I:	try to meet it		set up a timeline		consider it as a general guide only		see if others feel it can be met
18.	I admire teams that:	work hard		learn together		take risks		treat one another fairly
19.	In teams, I play the role of:	taskmaster		devil's advocate		cheerleader		clown
20.	Teams are needed:	to increase performance		to avoid errors		to build enthusiasm for the mission		because people like to interact
Totals:		C:___		L:___		V:___		R:___

Interpretation

Column 1 = Command and control (C)

You stick to deadlines and reinforce this with your team. You focus on individual accomplishments and take charge of the team in an efficient manner. You are results-oriented. Power base: Legitimate.

Column 2 = Logic and persuasion (L)

You are dependable, logical, and develop arguments that persuade others. You are an effective problem solver for your team and are valued for your expertise. You are thorough and painstakingly detail-oriented. Power base: Expert.

Column 3 = Visionary (V)

You focus on the big picture for the team and see your role as a change agent. You thrive on finding new opportunities and exploring options. You have a clear understanding of the organization's mission and translate this for your team. Power base: Charisma.

Column 4 = Relationship-oriented (R)

You focus on people and provide a supportive environment for your team. You are seen as a consensus-builder and participative manager. You are skilled in communication and listening, and develop a sense of trust in your team. Power base: Referent.

Discussion Questions

1. Which team leadership style is your dominant style (the highest score)? Are you strong in another type of team leadership? Are you balanced across three or all four?

2. Assess the basis of power you use with your team (refer back to the discussion of the French and Raven bases of power from Chapter 7). Would another power base be more effective? Explain why or why not.

3. Ask some of your team members to complete this assessment about you, and then compare your ratings to their ratings. Do you see yourself as your team members do? Can you explain why there is agreement or disagreement? How can you use this information to improve your team leadership?

CHAPTER ELEVEN

MANAGING CONFLICT AND NEGOTIATION

THE COSTS OF WORKPLACE CONFLICT

A study commissioned by Consulting Psychologists Press, Inc., publishers of the Myers-Briggs Type Assessment and the Thomas-Kilmann Conflict Mode Instrument, found that U.S. employees spend 2.1 hours per week involved with conflict, which amounts to approximately $359 billion in paid hours (based on average hourly earnings of $17.95), or the equivalent of 385 million working days. For the purposes of the study, the authors defined conflict as: "any workplace disagreement that disrupts the flow of work." According to the report, *Workplace Conflict and How Businesses Can Harness It to Thrive*, the following statistics demonstrate how pervasive conflict is in the workplace:

- 85% of employees deal with conflict on some level;
- 29% of employees deal with it almost constantly;
- 34% of conflict occurs among frontline employees;
- 49% of conflict is a result of personality clashes and "warring egos";
- 34% of conflict is caused by stress in the workplace; and
- 33% of conflict is caused by heavy workloads.

In addition to the dollar costs of conflict, employees report a number of negative outcomes, which are shown in Figure 11.1.

The inability for managers to effectively manage conflict and bring about positive resolution is costing them nearly one full day of productivity per month—about two-and-a-half weeks per year. Also, the study found that 70% believe managing conflict is a critically important leadership skill. And 54% of employees believe managers could handle disputes more effectively by addressing underlying tensions immediately when they surface.

Another poll conducted by Stanford University and the Miles Group asked CEOs two questions: What skills are you working on? and What skills do you think you need more development for? They also asked

Learning Objectives

After studying this chapter, you should be able to do the following:

11.1: Describe the causes of conflict in organizations and devise solutions for them.

11.2: Compare and contrast the five conflict resolution styles.

11.3: Explain how team conflict affects team performance.

11.4: Provide an example of how managing conflict differs across cultures.

11.5: Identify how third-party interventions can reduce conflict.

11.6: Describe the negotiation process, and explain the difference between integrative and distributive bargaining.

Get the edge on your studies at **edge.sagepub.com/scandura2e**

- Take the chapter quiz
- Review key terms with eFlashcards
- Explore multimedia resources, SAGE readings, and more!

Figure 11.1 Negative Outcomes of Workplace Conflict

What negative outcomes of workplace conflict have you witnessed?

Personal insults/attacks
27%

Sickness/absence
25%

Cross-departmental conflict
18%

Bullying
18%

People left the organization
18%

People were fired
16%

Employees were moved to different departments
13%

Project failure
9%

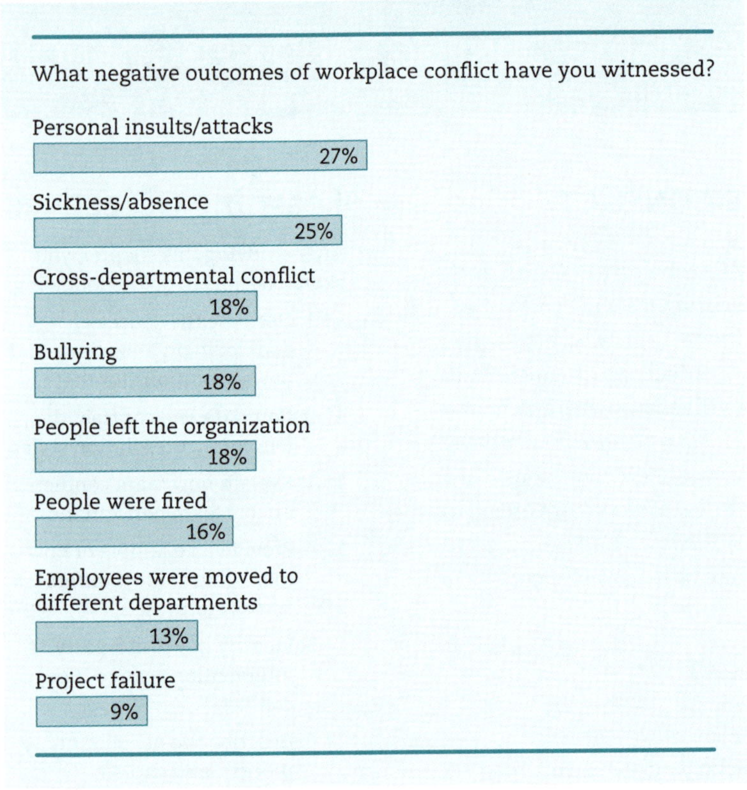

Source: Consulting Psychologists Press. (2008). Workplace conflict and how businesses can harness it to thrive. Retrieved from http://img.en25.com/Web/CPP/Conflict_report.pdf

their boards of directors what skills CEOs need development in. Conflict management skills were the most mentioned skill that CEOs believed they needed development in (42.9% reported needing to develop this skill). What is also interesting about these poll results is that CEOs also reported that they were working on skills related to conflict management such as listening (32.1%) and persuasion (14.3%). The results of this poll underscore the importance of the ability to manage **conflict** since it was mentioned as the number one skill needing development by top executives.[1]

This chapter reviews the research on conflict management in organizations. The relationship between conflict and performance is emphasized, with coverage of both interpersonal two-party and team conflict. Also, conflict resolution is needed for effective negotiation, and this core management competency is also covered in this chapter.

> **Critical Thinking Questions:** Do you agree that conflict resolution is the most important skill that leaders need? Which other skills do you think are most important?

WHAT IS CONFLICT?

Learning Objective 11.1: Describe the causes of conflict in organizations and devise solutions for them.

Conflict is defined as "the process that begins when one party perceives that the other has negatively affected, or is about to negatively affect, something that he or she cares about."[2] Note that conflict is a perception, and as discussed in Chapter 5, perceptions don't always line up with reality. However, they do influence behavior and they can be changed, which is essential for leaders to keep in mind as they approach conflict resolution in organizations. Managing conflict is a skill that managers at all levels need, not just CEOs. This suggests that managing conflict is an important aspect of a leader's job and that most leaders are not well equipped to deal with it. In this chapter, we review the evidence-based research on conflict and discuss how it can be effectively managed. First, it is important to understand what causes conflict in the first place (so that some conflict might be avoided).

Causes of Organizational Conflict

There are three general sources of organizational conflict:[3]

1. **Substantive conflict.** This occurs because people have different opinions on important issues in the organization that affect them. For example, there may be differences of opinion about which advertising campaign would best promote a new product. Such conflict can result in better decisions because both sides have to defend their position.

2. **Affective conflict.** This is conflict that engenders strong emotions such as anger or disgust. This may be due to personality differences or arguments. For example, two individuals in the organization escalate an argument to the level of shouting (it happens). This form of conflict may be highly disruptive to both parties and may even create stress for other members of the work group.

3. **Process conflict.** At times, people disagree on what course of action to pursue or the best way to operate even after a decision has been made. For example, team members may disagree on what aspects of a project should be assigned to specific individuals. This type of conflict reduces team performance.

> Critical Thinking Questions: How do the three forms of conflict relate to one another? For example, how might affective conflict affect process conflict?

Paul Endress, a nationally recognized consultant, provides some specific examples of where conflict in organizations may originate and recommends solutions a leader may follow to resolve each type:[4]

1. Personalities
   - Organizational strife is sometimes traced to personalities (as we learned in Chapter 2). This is one person differing with another based on how he or she feels about that person.
   - *Solution:* Train everyone to recognize the personality types along with their inherent strengths and weaknesses so that they understand one another. For example, the Big Five Personality Test (included in this textbook in Self-Assessment 2.1) can be given to team members. Based on the results, team members can discuss their personality differences and how they affect team interactions (extraverts may be dominating the team meetings, for example).

2. Sensitivity/hurt
   - This occurs when a person, because of low self-esteem, insecurity, or other factors in his or her personal life, sometimes feels attacked by perceived criticism.
   - *Solution:* Adopt the belief that even negative behaviors may have a positive intention. Use active listening, and ask questions to understand the root cause of the problem.

3. Differences in perception and values
   - Most conflict results from the varying ways people view the world. These incongruent views are traceable to differences in personality, culture, race, experience, education, occupation, and socioeconomic class, as examples.
   - *Solution:* A leader must set and communicate the values for the organization.

4. Differences over facts
   - A fact is a piece of data that can be quantified or an event that can be documented. Arguments over facts typically need not last very long since they are verifiable. But a statement like "It is a fact that you

are insensitive to my feelings" is neither documentable nor quantifiable and is actually a difference in perception.

- *Solution:* Have a neutral third party or expert arbitrate the dispute (third-party intervention is discussed later in this chapter).

5. Differences over goals and priorities

- This is a disagreement over strategy. For example, this may be an argument about whether a bank should focus more resources on international banking or on community banking. Another example would be whether or not to increase the amount of advanced professional training given to employees.

- *Solution:* A leader must set, communicate, and enforce the goals and values for the organization.

6. Differences over methods

- Two sides may have similar goals but disagree on how to achieve them. For example, a manager and their direct reports may not agree on how a training program should be conducted.

- *Solution:* Try seeing the other person's point of view by perspective taking. You can practice perspective taking in Case Study 11.1. Read the case study and practice perspective taking on a controversial issue where people have different points of view. Another alternative is to have a neutral third party or expert arbitrate the dispute (third-party alternative dispute resolution is covered later in this chapter).

7. Competition for scarce resources

- This occurs when there are limited resources that must be allocated in the organization. For example, two managers might argue over who has the greater need for an assistant, whose budget should be increased more, or how to allocate recently purchased computers.

- *Solution:* Upper-level management must set and communicate the values hierarchy for the organization. Resources can then be allocated based upon alignment with the organization's priorities.

8. Competition for supremacy

- This occurs when one person seeks to outdo or outshine another person. You might see it when two employees compete for a promotion or for power. Depending on personalities, this type of conflict can be visible or very subtle.

- *Solution:* A leader must set and communicate the values for the organization and emphasize that everyone's contribution matters.

9. Misunderstanding

- The majority of what looks like interpersonal conflict is actually a communication breakdown. Communication, if not attended to, is as likely to fail as to succeed. And when it does, a listener's incorrect inferences about a speaker's intent often create interpersonal conflict. Communication is discussed in more detail in Chapter 12.

- *Solution:* Ask this question—"What else could this mean?"—before assuming a negative intent of the other person.

10. Unfulfilled expectations

- Many of the causes listed previously can be linked to one person not fulfilling the expectations of another. Unfulfilled expectations are often the cause of firings and other forms of relational breakdown. Expectations go unfulfilled because they may be unreasonable, inappropriate, too numerous, or unstated.

- *Solution:* Use active listening and questioning techniques to set and clarify expectations on a regular basis. Active listening is discussed in detail in Chapter 12.

As these examples illustrate, a leader can take actions that affect whether conflict is dysfunctional or may become productive. It is also clear from the solutions suggested that conflict may result in either higher or lower performance in organizations. The next section discusses whether conflict can be good for an organization.

> Critical Thinking Question: How would you resolve a conflict between two of your direct reports who both want an office with a window when there is only one such office available? Identify the sources of the conflict from the list above and evaluate the recommended solutions.

Is Conflict Always Bad?

Organizational behavior (OB) research has recognized that there are some situations where conflict may have a positive effect on performance.[5] There is a difference between unproductive (dysfunctional) organizational conflict and functional (productive) conflict. Conflict may be productive if it aligns with the goals of the organization and improves performance.[6] Dysfunctional conflict can harm relationships between leaders and followers and among teammates, and ultimately harms performance.[7] A useful way to think about the relationship between conflict and performance is shown in Figure 11.2. As shown in the figure, on the left-hand side, if conflict is too low, there may be apathy and a lack of constructive discussion regarding important issues that need to be addressed. People may even be avoiding conflict, which is dysfunctional. As the level of conflict increases, performance increases as long as the conflict is aligned with the goals of the organization and does not become personal.

Productive (functional) conflict enhances organizational performance.[8] In fact, a study of 232 employees in a long-term health care organization found that more frequent mild task conflict resulted in more information being generated.[9] However, at a point, too much conflict may become unproductive or even dysfunctional, particularly if it brings

Figure 11.2 **The Relationship Between Conflict and Performance**

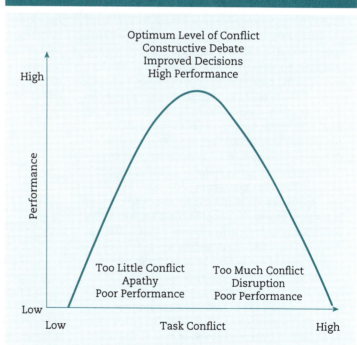

Source: Adapted from Duarte, M., & Davies, G. (2003). Testing the conflict–performance assumption in business-to-business relationships. *Industrial Marketing Management, 32*(2), 91–99.

affective conflict in which individuals become frustrated or angry. Performance may begin to suffer as the level of conflict becomes too much and begins to disrupt the work process. For example, people may become so involved with the conflict that they spend time complaining to one another rather than on work that needs to be performed. Thus, it is important to keep in mind that how conflict is managed by the leader plays a pivotal role in channeling conflict toward the organization's goals and ensuring that unproductive conflict is resolved before it harms performance. This approach focuses on **task conflict**, but this is only one form of conflict—**relationship conflict** exists in organizations as well, and research has shown that they may affect performance differently.

Task Versus Relationship Conflict

Conflict may focus on task-related issues or around relationship issues.[10,11] Disagreements about resource allocation, policies, or even interpretation of data are known as task conflict. A meta-analysis of the relationships of

BEST PRACTICES

Planned Conflict: The Devil Made Me Do It!

Kodak managers missed many opportunities in digital photography, a technology its employees invented. Steve Sasson, the Kodak engineer who invented the first digital camera in 1975, said management's reaction was "that's cute—but don't tell anyone about it" (reported in the *New York Times* on May 2, 2008). Kodak management had the technological breakthrough, but its senior managers were not able to assess its potential. Senior managers did not question their commitment to the production and marketing of film and did not see the technological disruption that unfolded in later years.[12] As the Kodak case illustrates, sometimes there needs to be planned conflict where differences of opinions are stated regardless of the preferred course of action of the decision makers. Devil's advocacy is a technique in which one member is assigned to play the role of the devil's advocate (DA) and critically evaluate the leader's (or a team's) decision. The role of the DA is "a procedure which involves the appointment of one or more persons to raise objections to favored alternatives, challenge assumptions underlying them, and possibly point out alternatives."[13] This is one of the recommended strategies for preventing groupthink (described in Chapter 10). The devil's advocate method is the application of critical thinking to decisions to uncover assumptions and provide a reality check. The DA approach improves critical thinking

because beliefs and assumptions are challenged to foster a better understanding about the complexity of decisions.[14] Devil's advocacy leads to higher-quality recommendations and assumptions compared to consensus decision making.[15] Appropriate application of the devil's advocate method may increase the creativity of decisions and avoid errors. The steps for the devil's advocacy approach are as follows:

1. Propose a course of action.
2. Assign a devil's advocate to critique the proposal.
3. Present the critique to the decision maker(s).
4. Gather additional information if the critique reveals it is needed.
5. Make a decision to adopt, modify, or end the proposed course of action.
6. Monitor the implementation of the decision.

The final step is an important one. A study found that teams that had a DA achieved higher decision quality than groups under open discussion. However, devil's advocacy teams also had higher levels of affective conflict. As a result, while they selected the best solution, devil's advocacy introduced some adverse conditions that hindered the implementation of a decision.[16]

Discussion Questions

1. Explain why assigning a devil's advocate during a decision-making meeting reduces groupthink.
2. Give an example of a decision you have been involved in that might have benefited from the assignment of a devil's advocate using the previously given steps.
3. Describe the steps that you would take to reduce the potential negative effect of conflict due to a devil's advocate to protect the implementation of a decision.

Sources: Cosier, R. A., & Schwenk, C. R. (1990). Agreement and thinking alike: Ingredients for improper decisions. *Academy of Management Executive, 4*(1), 72–73; Davis, J. R. (2013). Improving students' critical thinking and classroom engagement by playing the devil's advocate. *Academy of Management Learning Education, 11*(2), 228–243; Power, D. J., & Mitra, A. (2016). Reducing "bad" strategic business decisions. *Drake Management Review, 5*(1/2), 15–31; Schweiger, D. M., Sandberg, W. R., & Ragan, J. R. (1987). Group approaches for improving strategic decision making: A comparative analysis of dialectical inquiry, devil's advocacy, and consensus. *Academy of Management Journal, 29*(1), 51–71; Waddell, B. D., Roberto, M. A., & Yoon, S. (2013). Uncovering hidden profiles: Advocacy in team decision making. *Management Decision, 51*(2), 321–340.

task and relationship conflict with team performance and satisfaction found strong negative associations between relationship conflict, team performance, and team member satisfaction.[17] This study also found strong negative correlations between task conflict, team performance, and team member satisfaction. The number of people in a team that experience task conflict may make a difference. Task conflict may be positively related to team performance when a majority of members perceive lower levels of task conflict in the group while a minority perceives higher levels of task conflict.[18] Relationship conflict involves personality clashes or differences in values.[19] Relationship conflict may be particularly detrimental to new employees since they are unable to get needed information from their coworkers.[20]

Relationship conflict may have some benefits in certain circumstances. Experimental studies found that relationship conflict increased group creativity because it increased persistence.[21] Relationship conflict was also lower when followers reported that they had tenacity and passion for work. Passion is the willingness to engage in activities with the team that team members love and value (and thus find important), and in which they invest time and efforts together.[22] The more that team members identify with the goals of the team, the less relationship conflict they experience.[23] These studies on passion support research that found emotions play an important role in linking task and relationship conflict.[24] Group emotional intelligence (EI), good working relationships, and norms for suppressing negative emotions decrease the relationship between task and relationship conflict. In other words, regulating emotions may keep the conflict focused on the task so that it is not perceived as a personal attack on others.

Team leadership may buffer the effects of conflict on the team. A study[25] conducted in a large Mexican-based distributor of pharmaceutical products found that task conflict reduces job satisfaction, but this effect is weaker at higher levels of transformational leadership. Leaders should first diagnose the type of conflict (task or relationship) and then provide coaching on how to manage the conflict. When task conflicts emerge, team performance may benefit but only when the conflict is managed constructively by the leader. When relationship conflicts occur, performance and satisfaction may suffer and intervention is necessary. A study[26] of head-nurse–nurse relationships in 56 units of two major hospitals found that head nurses who had in-groups and out-groups experienced more relationship conflict in their units. The relationship conflict had a negative effect on customer service. This may be due to out-group members experiencing envy of the in-group. Another study found that relationship conflict exacerbated the effect of envy on team members undermining others on their team, which in turn related to lower job performance.[27] So leaders should pay attention to the potential downside of having better relationships with some followers than others. To summarize, in considering the potential for conflict to be productive, active conflict management by the leader to develop a climate of openness and trust is essential or conflict may harm performance.[28] In addition, helping followers feel passion and regulating negative emotions also helps focus the conflict on the task and not personal relationships.

> **Critical Thinking Questions:** What can a leader do specifically to keep followers focused on the task? How can a leader develop trust with followers so that conflict management is effective?

As this section has suggested, conflict at work may become personal. It may even escalate to more intense levels such as bullying.[29] **Workplace bullying** is an emergent phenomenon; it refers to "a social interaction through which one individual (seldom more) is attacked by one or more (seldom more than four) individuals almost on a daily basis and for periods of many months, bringing the person into an almost helpless position with potentially high risk of expulsion."[30] The next section discusses workplace aggression and violence, and how leaders should address it.

Workplace Incivility and Aggression

Workplace incivility is "low intensity deviant behavior with ambiguous intent to harm the target, in violation of workplace norms for mutual respect. Uncivil behaviors are characteristically rude and discourteous, displaying a lack of regard for others."[31] Workplace incivility may even extend to the classroom. Research has examined student perceptions of incivility of professors. Students' perceptions of incivility fall into two areas: a professor's competence and interest as well as respect for the individualism of students.[32] Workplace incivility appears to be on the rise (refer to the boxed insert). In some cases, incivility may escalate to aggression or even workplace violence.[33] **Workplace aggression** is defined as overt physical or nonphysical behavior that harms others at work (e.g., yelling or pushing).[34]

Workplace aggression can emanate from the culture of the organization and/or the behavior of supervisors. The next sections discuss abusive supervision and toxic organizational cultures as sources of workplace incivility and aggression.

Abusive Supervision

Incidences of harassment and bullying at work are rising. Having a "bad boss" may be a source of stress for employees. Supervisors have a lot of power over followers and control their work experiences to a great extent. Some supervisors engage in hostile behavior known as **abusive supervision**.[35] Supervisors may ridicule, spread rumors, take credit for work done by followers, give the "silent treatment," and/or withhold information.[36] Research has shown that such supervisory abuse is related to psychological distress, anxiety, and emotional exhaustion.[37] Research has also shown that abusive supervision may even evoke a "paranoid" reaction from followers that is characterized as hypervigilance, rumination, and sinister attributions about others.[38] Employees may be affected even when they are not the target of workplace abuse. For example, one study found that employees who watched their supervisor abuse customers were more likely to have intentions to leave their jobs.[39] Poor supervision is a root cause of stress at the workplace.[40] This occurs for two primary reasons: Abusive supervisors place additional job demands on employees, and they don't provide support to help employees cope. To address the problem of abusive supervision, organizations are encouraged to set up confidential (or even anonymous) reporting "hotlines" so that supervisory abuse can

> **Critical Thinking Questions:** Have you ever experienced (or observed) a situation of abusive supervision? What did you do about it? If you did nothing, what would you do differently?

be reported.[41] Also, training that focuses on appropriate supervisory behaviors may alleviate stress and improve employee well-being.[42]

Abusive supervision is a serious concern in organizations. But supervisors are not the only sources of stress due to work relationships. A review of the literature on "coworkers behaving badly" found that **deviant behavior** of coworkers violates organizational norms and may include "aggression, bullying, harassment, incivility and social undermining."[43] The literature on deviant behavior in organizations has documented negative impacts of deviance on attitudes, emotions, and performance. Deviant, dysfunctional, and counterproductive behavior of a coworker affects others in three ways. First, there are **direct effects** where the employee is the target of a coworker's deviant act. Second, there are **indirect effects**, or vicarious impact, in which an employee is affected by learning of another coworker's deviant behaviors. Third, there can also be **ambient impact** in which collective deviant behavior creates a hostile working environment. Coworker deviant behavior is considered a workplace demand and creates stress for the target. Being mistreated by one's coworkers creates emotional strain, which leads to lower morale and turnover.[44] Ambient effects may build and create what are known as **"toxic" workplaces**.

"Toxic" Workplaces

Employees lower in the hierarchy of bureaucratic organizations experience more frustration and anger compared to managers. A study found that employees who had jobs at lower levels in an organization's hierarchy felt more powerless and had less control over their work. They also report more emotional distress, medication use, cardiovascular disturbance, gastrointestinal disturbance, and allergy/respiratory disturbance.[45] A study of engineers found frustration was associated with anger reactions, latent hostility, job dissatisfaction, and work-related anxiety.[46] Toxic workplaces may be exacerbated by organizational politics. Political behavior may increase during times of organizational turmoil, and this represents an additional source of stress.

In many situations, it is necessary to engage in organizational politics to survive or advance in the organization. Highly political organizations reward employees who engage in hardball influence tactics, take credit for the work of others, join powerful coalitions, and have connections to high-ranking supporters in the organization.[47] This may place strain on employees who feel they must engage in these behaviors to succeed. Research has shown significant relationships between perceptions of organizational politics and psychological strain. For example, a study of Israeli employees found job distress was an immediate response to organizational politics. Also, organizational politics resulted in aggressive behavior by employees.[48] In politicized workplaces, there are less helping behaviors (organizational citizenship behavior) toward individuals and organizations.[49]

Workplace Violence

The U.S. Department of Labor reports that every year, 2 million people in the United States are victims of nonfatal violence at the workplace.[50] They cite data from the U.S. Department of Justice, which found violence to be a leading cause of fatal injuries at work with about 1,000 workplace homicides per year. This violence occurs in a variety of situations, including robberies and other crimes, actions by dissatisfied clients or customers, and acts perpetrated by disgruntled coworkers or coworkers who have been fired. It is difficult to profile the type of employee who may commit workplace violence, but a combination of personal and workplace factors must be considered. For example, alcohol use or a history of aggression may combine with perceived organizational injustice to evoke a violent response.[51] The term *going postal* denotes the situation in which organizational members suddenly become extremely violent, derived after several incidents in the U.S. Postal Service in the late 1980s involving workplace homicides. Another incident reported in the media was a Connecticut Lottery Corporation accountant who searched for and then killed the corporation's president and three of his supervisors before killing himself.[52] Despite such media accounts of workplace violence, most aggression experienced by employees emanates from unhappy clients or customers.[53]

RESEARCH IN ACTION

Is the Workplace Becoming More Uncivilized? Send in Miss Manners!

Examples of uncivil workplace behavior include making demeaning remarks, ignoring, and hostile looks. Results of public polls suggest that incivility at work is increasing, with four out of five employees viewing disrespect and a lack of courtesy as a serious problem.[54] Nearly three out of five believe that the problem of workforce incivility is getting worse, and a poll of 800 workers found that 10% witnessed incivility daily and 20% said that they personally were the direct targets of incivility at least once per week.[55] Another study of 603 nurses found 33% had experienced verbal abuse in the previous 5 days.[56] The source of incivility can be supervisors, coworkers, or customers.[57] The rise of incivility may be due to the increasing rates of change; people don't have the time to be "nice" anymore. Another explanation is generational differences; the "me generation" is focused more on their own concerns and lacks respect for others.[58] Workplace incivility has been linked to outcomes for individuals and the organization. For example, a study conducted in a large public-sector organization found workplace incivility is related to sexual harassment and that both were detrimental to female employees' well-being.[59] When employees experience incivility, they respond in various ways, including losing work time to avoid the uncivil person, decreasing their effort, thinking about quitting, and leaving the job to avoid the instigator.[60] Workplace incivility predicts burnout, which, in turn, predicts employees' intentions to quit.[61] In response to this growing concern, organizations are beginning to set zero-tolerance expectations for rude and disrespectful behavior at work.[62] Others are even implementing training in proper etiquette for managers.[63] A research study found that leaders can be proactive in reducing workplace incivility by taking actions such as describing the policies available in the organization for preventing aggression incidents between employees, encouraging employees to keep them updated regarding signs of potential coworker-initiated aggression, and assigning a victim of incivility to work with different coworkers.[64] Workplace incivility needs to be addressed to reduce the personal and professional impact on employees, and leaders need to take a proactive role to prevent it.

Discussion Questions

1. Provide an example of an incident that you have experienced that was rude and discourteous, displaying a lack of regard for others. This can be an example you or another person at work or school experienced.

2. How did the experience of incivility (previously described) make you feel? What did you do about it?

3. Which source of workplace incivility do you feel is most harmful and why (supervisors, coworkers, or customers)?

Sources: Andersson, L. M., & Pearson, C. M. (1999). Tit-for-tat? The spiraling effect of incivility in the workplace. *Academy of Management Review, 24*(3), 452–471; Coutu, D. L. (2003, September). In praise of boundaries: A conversation with Miss Manners. *Harvard Business Review,* 41–45; Graydon, J., Kasta, W., & Khan, P. (1994, November–December). Verbal and physical abuse of nurses. *Canadian Journal of Nursing Administration,* 70–89; Magley, V. J., Williams, J. H., & Langhout, R. D. (2001). Incivility in the workplace: Incidence and impact. *Journal of Occupational Health Psychology, 6,* 64–80; Pearson, C., Andersson, L., & Porath, C. (2000, Fall). Assessing and attacking workplace incivility. *Organizational Dynamics,* 123–137; Schilpzand, P., De Pater, I. E., & Erez, A. (2016). Workplace incivility: A review of the literature and agenda for future research. *Journal of Organizational Behavior, 37,* S57–S88; Taylor, S. G., Bedeian, A. G., Cole, M. S., & Zhang, Z. (2014). Developing and testing a dynamic model of workplace incivility change. *Journal of Management, 43*(3), 645–670; Yang, L. Q., & Caughlin, D. E. (2017). Aggression-preventive supervisor behavior: Implications for workplace climate and employee outcomes. *Journal of Occupational Health Psychology, 22*(1), 1–18.

Research has shown that leaders can reduce the exposure of their followers to workplace aggression and the strain it causes by directly or indirectly helping employees prevent aggression (e.g., stepping in to resolve disputes between employees before they escalate into aggressive incidents).[65] Therefore, one important way that a leader can avoid escalation of conflict into workplace incivility or aggression is to engage in effective conflict resolution. The following sections discuss different conflict-handling styles. It is important for a leader to recognize their own predisposition toward conflict as a first step to becoming effective at resolving conflicts at work. From the previously given discussion of workplace incivility and aggression and sources of conflict, it is clear that leaders need to take an active role in resolving workplace conflicts before they escalate.

A leader should be able to adapt to situations and adjust their conflict resolution style as needed. However, most people have a dominant style that they use, particularly when they are under stress. It's important to know what your tendencies are toward avoiding conflict. Complete Self-Assessment 11.1 to learn what your conflict resolution style is so that you are aware of how you approach conflict. Complete the assessment before you read further.

CONFLICT RESOLUTION STYLES

Learning Objective 11.2: Compare and contrast the five conflict resolution styles.

Conflict resolution can be seen as two dimensions in a space that reflect possible outcomes for handling interpersonal conflict.[66,67] First, a person involved in a conflict is concerned with the satisfaction of their *own* concerns in a dispute. Second, the person may or may not also be concerned with the satisfaction of the *other party's* concerns. This may be represented by two dimensions, thus combining concern for self and others. This conceptualization was refined,[68] and a measure of conflict-handling styles called the Rahim Organizational Conflict Inventory (ROCI-II) was developed.[69] This framework is shown in Figure 11.3, depicting "concern for self" on the horizontal axis from high to low and "concern for others" on the vertical axis from low to high. By combining these two concerns, different approaches toward resolving conflicts result: integrating, obliging, dominating, avoiding, and compromising.

These five conflict-handling styles are:[70,71]

- **Integrating**. Both parties confront the issue directly and discuss alternative courses of action. The

Figure 11.3 Two-Dimensional Model of the Styles of Handling Interpersonal Conflict

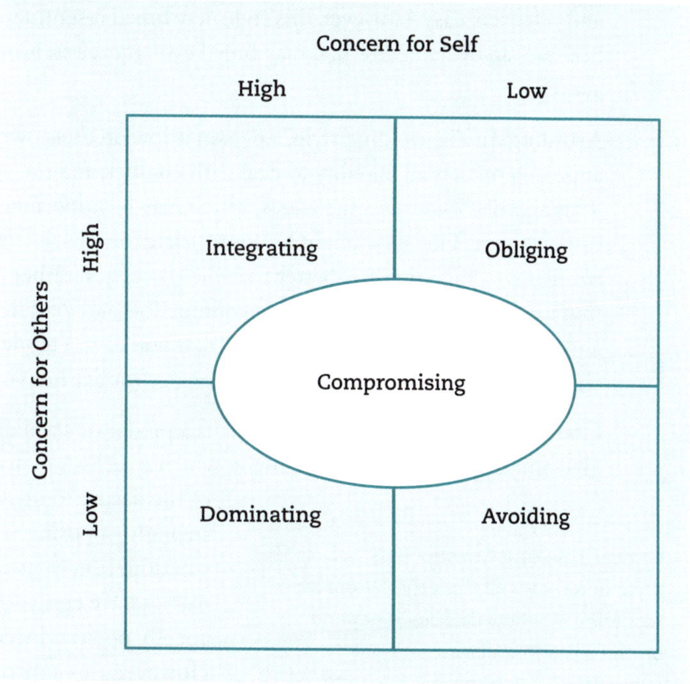

Source: Rahim, M. A. (1985). A strategy for managing conflict in complex organizations. *Human Relations, 38*(1), 81–89. p. 84.

strength of this approach is that it should provide a mutual benefits (win-win) solution and results in the conflict being resolved for the long term. The major drawback to this approach is that it is time consuming. This approach is the most appropriate for complex problems, strategic planning, and innovation.

- **Obliging**. In this approach, Figure 11.3 indicates that a person's concern for themselves is low but their concern for others is high. A person with a predisposition toward obliging "gives in" to the demands of others and may neglect his or her own concerns. It might be the best approach if the person is not sure they are right about a preferred course of action or it is politically best because the matter is so important to the other party. If used as a strategy, the person should consider requesting a reciprocated exchange in the future because they gave in the first time. It is not the best for complex problems and may result in a short-term solution. If it becomes a pattern, the obliging person may become resentful over time. The weakness of this strategy is that it is temporary, but its strength is that it will resolve the problem rather quickly.

- **Dominating**. In this approach, the individual is high with respect to his or her own concerns but low with respect to the concerns of others. People adopting this approach take a win-lose approach to problem solving, and their focus is on winning their position at the expense of others. The person using this approach may use their formal position to force others to comply (i.e., "do it because I am the boss"). It may be appropriate, however, for small decisions, or when the person knows the decision will be unpopular and discussion will not bring others on board. It may also be used when there is time pressure to make a decision, such as in a crisis situation. The primary strength of this approach is that it is quick and relatively easy. However, this style may breed resentment among those affected by decisions. If this becomes an overall pattern, it may breed even more resentment and attributions of a leader being an autocrat.

- **Avoiding**. In the avoiding style, a person is low on their own concerns and the concerns of others. This approach reflects an inability to deal with conflict, and the person withdraws from the conflict situation. This approach sidesteps the issues, which may be important, but there is no attempt to confront and resolve them. This style might be appropriate for trivial decisions or when the possibility of unproductive conflict is so high that it is better to avoid discussion rather than risk performance. The weakness of this approach is that by pretending conflict does not exist, it rarely goes away; it may be a temporary fix and the conflict will return in the future. If you have a tendency to avoid conflict, be sure to review the checklist for having difficult conversations in Toolkit Activity 11.1 at the end of this chapter.

- **Compromising**. This approach reflects a moderate level of concern for the self and for others. It is a give-and-take approach to conflict in which concessions are made in exchange for getting some aspects of the desired outcome. It is appropriate when parties have strongly opposing views and there is little hope of an integrative solution. It may also be the only possible approach when both parties have equivalent influence in the organization (e.g., two equally powerful vice presidents competing for resources). However, this approach may result in suboptimal or even strange solutions that try to include disparate views. The main strength is that everyone gets something in a compromise; however, it is important to keep in mind that no one is completely satisfied

> Critical Thinking Questions: Is one style better overall than the others for resolving conflict? Or does it depend on the situation, like situational leadership? If you think it depends, what are the situational factors that should be considered?

with the outcome. For this reason, it can be unproductive and worse than even the dominating or obliging styles. Also, with compromise, there is not creative problem solving or an attempt to come up with a win-win solution as in the integrating style.

Table 11.1 Conflict-Handling Strategies and Situations Where They Are Appropriate or Inappropriate

Conflict Style	Situations Where Appropriate	Situations Where Inappropriate
Integrating	1. Issues are complex. 2. Synthesis of ideas is needed to come up with better solutions. 3. Commitment is needed from other parties for successful implementation. 4. Time is available for problem solving. 5. One party alone cannot solve the problem. 6. Resources possessed by different parties are needed to solve their common problems.	1. The task or problem is simple. 2. Immediate decision is required. 3. Other parties are unconcerned about outcome. 4. Other parties do not have problem-solving skills.
Obliging	1. You believe that you may be wrong. 2. The issue is more important to the other party. 3. You are willing to give up something in exchange for something from the other party in the future. 4. You are dealing from a position of weakness. 5. Preserving a relationship is important.	1. The issue is important to you. 2. You believe that you are right. 3. The other party is wrong or unethical.
Dominating	1. The issue is trivial. 2. A speedy decision is needed. 3. An unpopular course of action is implemented. 4. It is necessary to overcome assertive subordinates. 5. An unfavorable decision by the other party may be costly to you. 6. Subordinates lack expertise to make technical decisions. 7. The issue is important to you.	1. The issue is complex. 2. The issue is not important to you. 3. Both parties are equally powerful. 4. The decision does not have to be made quickly. 5. Subordinates possess a high degree of competence.
Avoiding	1. The issue is trivial. 2. Potential dysfunctional effect of confronting the other party outweighs benefits of resolution. 3. A cooling-off period is needed.	1. The issue is important to you. 2. It is your responsibility to make a decision. 3. Parties are unwilling to defer; the issue must be resolved. 4. Prompt attention is needed.
Compromising	1. Goals of parties are mutually exclusive. 2. Parties are equally powerful. 3. Consensus cannot be reached. 4. Integrating or dominating style is not successful. 5. A temporary solution to a complex problem is needed.	1. One party is more powerful. 2. The problem is complex enough, needing problem-solving approach.

Source: Rahim, M. A. (2002). Toward a theory of managing organizational conflict. *International Journal of Conflict Resolution, 13*(3), 206–235.

While some early research suggested that the integrative style is best, later research suggests that the right conflict resolution style may depend upon the situation.[72,73] It is important to first correctly diagnose the conflict situation before selecting an intervention strategy. Generally, integrating is best for complex and strategic decisions, with compromise as a second option. The other styles may be effective to resolve smaller problems that occur on a day-to-day basis in the organization.[74] Table 11.1 lists the five conflict-handling styles and when they are appropriate or inappropriate.

This chapter has focused on interpersonal conflict to this point—conflict between two parties and strategies for conflict resolution. Conflict may also occur in teams; this situation may be among the most challenging for a leader to work through. Consider student teams that you have worked on during your undergraduate or graduate experience. Did they all run smoothly and free of conflict? If they did, you may consider yourself to be very lucky. Most students report that they have experienced dysfunctional and unproductive conflict that caused stress and perhaps even resulted in getting lower grades on team projects. Leaders in organizations have similar challenges with team conflict. Fortunately, the study of conflict at the team level has emerged as an important area of OB research that offers guidance for reducing team conflict.

TEAM CONFLICT AND PERFORMANCE

Learning Objective 11.3: Explain how team conflict affects team performance.

Conflict within teams produces stress and arguments that distract the team from working on the task and thus harms performance.[75] All types of conflict (task, relationship, and process) are detrimental to member satisfaction.[76,77] However, moderate levels of task conflict actually improve team performance because this stimulates information exchange among team members. Task conflict and differences of opinion may improve decision quality by forcing members to see other viewpoints and think creatively.[78,79,80] Effective teamwork results in higher performance when task conflict exists, and this is especially the case when team members trust one another.[81] Another study of 57 self-managed work teams (SMWTs; discussed in Chapter 10) found teams that improve or maintain top performance over time engage in three conflict resolution strategies:

1. They focus on the content of interactions rather than delivery style.

2. They explicitly discuss reasons behind any decisions in distributing work assignments.

3. They assign work to members who have the relevant task expertise rather than assigning by other common means such as volunteering, default, or convenience.[82]

Both task and relationship conflict can occur at the same time in teams.[83,84] Relationship conflict, as a hindrance, should always be avoided as a way to promote positive emergent team states. To do so, managers can provide communication training and engage in conflict resolution. At the same time, leaders should encourage their team to generate and express divergent opinions about what to do and about how to do it, ensuring a trustful environment without fear of negative consequences. In fact, leaders may want to encourage task conflict in teams where cohesion and team engagement have already been established.[85] In conflict situations, leaders can try to get team members to see both sides of an issue. Doing so increases creativity and job performance.[86] Leaders of high-performing teams are proactive in anticipating the need to resolve their conflicts and search for strategies that apply to all team members. Thus, the relationship between conflict and performance may depend upon how the team resolves conflict.

A meta-analysis found that the conflict to performance relationship in teams is more complex than previously assumed.[87] Task conflict and performance are more positively related when the association between task and relationship conflict is relatively weak. Also, the relationship of conflict to performance is stronger for top management teams rather than non-top management teams. Finally, when performance is measured by financial performance or decision quality rather than overall performance, there was a stronger effect of team conflict on performance. This meta-analysis provides support for the inverted-U relationship (refer back to Figure 11.2) at the team level.

The relationship of team conflict to performance appears to hold in other cultures. A test of the inverted-U relationship was conducted in two separate studies of work teams in Taiwan and Indonesia.[88] This study found the relationship between task conflict and team effectiveness outcomes varies as a function of the level of relationship conflict in the team. For team performance, the curvilinear relationship (inverted U) holds when relationship conflict is low but that task conflict is negatively related to performance when relationship conflict is high, as shown in Figure 11.4. The authors concluded the following: "Team members who have high relationship conflict and interpersonal tensions are more likely to bicker so intensely that the slightest task conflict is associated with performance declines."[89] Therefore, both task and relationship conflict matter in terms of understanding the impact of conflict on team performance. This study was conducted in Taiwan and Indonesia, and additional research has been conducted that examines conflict resolution across cultures.

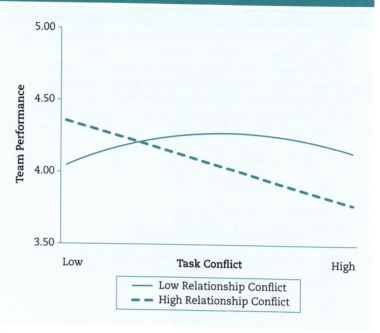

Figure 11.4 The Interaction of Task Conflict and Relationship Conflict in Predicting Team Performance

Source: Shaw, J. D., Zhu, J., Duffy, M. K., Scott, K. L., Shih, H. A., & Susanto, E. (2011). A contingency model of conflict and team effectiveness. *Journal of Applied Psychology, 96*(2), 391–400. p. 397.

Critical Thinking Questions: How would you address one essential team member who continually interrupts others, creating conflict within the team, which harms the team's productivity? Would your approach be different if this team member were from another culture (Taiwan, for example)?

RESOLVING CONFLICT ACROSS CULTURES

Learning Objective 11.4: Provide an example of how managing conflict differs across cultures.

Addressing conflict when working with a person from another culture requires knowledge of cultural differences (you will learn more about national culture values in Chapter 12). Research has shown that conflict resolution styles may differ by culture.[90] One study examined conflict resolution styles of MBA students from highly ranked programs in the United States, China, the Philippines, and India.[91] The study found that Chinese students are more likely to report an avoiding style, whereas the U.S. students were more likely to report a competing style. This is explained by the Chinese being more likely to value harmony over discord. In contrast, managers in the United States are more competitive and individualistic. Similar findings have been reported for U.S. students compared with Mexican students.[92]

Well-managed conflict contributes significantly to successful leadership in China.[93] Given China's emergence as a world market leader, they place an emphasis on openness and collaboration, which is consistent with their cultural values for group harmony. Another study compared conflict resolution styles for North American, Arab, and Russian negotiators.[94] This research found that North Americans tended to rely more on facts and logic. Arabs, in contrast, used emotional appeals to persuade others and made concessions during the bargaining process. Russians made few concessions and based their persuasion on ideal principles. Research conducted on 409 expatriates suggests the following guidelines for resolving cross-cultural conflict (ranked in order of importance):[95]

1. Be a good listener.

2. Be sensitive to the needs of others.

3. Be cooperative rather than overly competitive (tied with the #2 skill).

4. Advocate inclusive (participative) leadership.

5. Compromise rather than dominate.

6. Build rapport through conversations.

7. Be compassionate and understanding.

8. Avoid conflict by emphasizing harmony.

9. Nurture others (develop and mentor).

> Critical Thinking Question: How would you address conflict due to cultural differences in a team you lead that has members who are from China, Venezuela, and the United States?

The key takeaway from the research on cross-cultural conflict resolution is that the leader needs to consider the impact that national culture values may have on a person's perception of conflict and how to resolve it.

Despite attempts by leaders to facilitate conflict resolution, at times, conflict can continue for a long period of time and become complicated. There are situations where a third party must be called in to help resolve the conflict. This is sometimes done to avoid costly litigation. There are a number of options for resolving conflict using a third party. The next section discusses these options.

THIRD-PARTY INTERVENTIONS

Learning Objective 11.5: Identify how third-party interventions can reduce conflict.

Facilitation is when a leader intervenes to resolve a conflict. Leaders essentially play the role of an impartial mediator (discussed below) and engage in the following behaviors: taking the time to understand the employees' point of view, recognizing the employees' needs, taking the time to gain information on the conflict's context, giving employees a chance to express their emotions, showing understanding of what employees are going through, getting employees to understand other perspectives, encouraging the parties to propose solutions, getting employees to agree on concrete actions, does not take sides, and remains unbiased.[96] Before engaging in facilitation, leaders should ask the following questions when they are attempting to resolve a conflict:[97]

1. Is intervention necessary or appropriate?

2. If so, what type of intervention is most appropriate?

3. Is the leader the appropriate person to intervene?

4. If not, should the services of an independent resource person be provided? If so, how might the leader make use of the resource person?

If the answer to the third question above is *no*, then the leader needs to consider other options to resolve the conflict by bringing in an independent resource person. These options are known as **alternative dispute resolution**, which are methods to resolve conflict that both parties agree to without involving litigation. There are a variety of techniques available, which range from the leader bringing in a third party to restore damaged relationships to legally binding arbitration.[98] The most commonly used alternative dispute resolution approaches used by organizations follow. For example, your university may have an **ombudsperson**, who works for the university but hears grievances from students on an informal basis and attempts to resolve them. Your university may also have an honor code council, which is an example of a **peer review** process (or dispute resolution panel) for resolving cases of alleged cheating by students. In organizations, a leader may call in a neutral third party (e.g., another manager) to attempt to resolve the conflict (known as **conciliation**). Private-sector organizations including General Electric, Prudential, Johnson & Johnson, and Alcoa have in-house mediators, arbitrators, ombudspersons, and other conflict resolution specialists. Large federal agencies such as the U.S. Postal Service, the Department of the Interior, and the Departments of the Navy and Air Force have trained many of their own employees to become conflict resolution specialists.[99]

Sometimes, the conflict can become so complex that a more formalized dispute resolution method is needed. Conflicts sometimes escalate to legal action; however, **mediation** is a less adversarial and more personal process.[100] Mediation is when a third-party neutral person is called in to resolve the conflict. Mediation is the most common form of alternative dispute resolution because the fairness of the process results in people being satisfied with the outcome.[101] Mediation often results in an outcome that satisfies both parties. A study of 449 cases handled by four major alternative dispute resolution service providers in the United States that proceeded to mediation revealed that 78% were settled whether or not the parties had voluntarily participated in the process.[102] Mediation can result in improved workplace relationships, increased performance, improved morale, and less occupational stress.[103] Mediators are formally trained to perform this role; typically, they are outside of the organization in which the conflict has occurred. The mediator does not make a decision; their role is to help the parties reach an acceptable solution. In general, the steps in mediation are as follows:

- **Participation**—participants are actively involved in the decision-making process. By participating, it may be found that simple misunderstandings are at the heart of a dispute.

- **Representation/reparation**—parties are allowed to express their perspective and how they feel about what has occurred. One of the most powerful forms of reparation is an apology (research on apologies at work has found them to be effective in certain circumstances).

- **Validation/reintegration**—parties work to solve a dispute in a cooperative and respectful way. For example, in restorative justice, balance is achieved through forgiveness as the parties are reintegrated back into the original "community" (the team or organization they work for).[104]

In arbitration, both parties agree in advance to accept the decision, and it is made by a neutral third party. The decision of the arbitrator is legally binding on the parties. Mediation and arbitration are the most expensive, and thus, many organizations have ombudspersons or peer review available if the leader cannot resolve the conflict through facilitation or conciliation.

> **Critical Thinking Question: In the United States, employers have a legal right to require mandatory arbitration if their employees have a grievance. Do you agree or disagree? Explain your position.**

The process of alternative dispute resolution often involves negotiating a settlement that both parties will agree to. One of the most common conflict-laden situations a leader encounters involves negotiation. Negotiation is one of the key applications of conflict resolution techniques learned in this chapter. Conflict resolution styles, for example, may influence how a leader enters into a bargaining situation. For example, if a leader has a dominating style, they are only concerned about their own outcomes. With this style, it may be impossible to develop a win-win bargaining solution. In contrast, a negotiator with an integrating style may be able to claim value for themselves but also address the interests of their negotiating partner. The negotiation process is described in the following sections.

NEGOTIATION

Learning Objective 11.6: Describe the negotiation process, and explain the difference between integrative and distributive bargaining.

The steps involved in an ideal negotiation situation are shown in Figure 11.5. As shown in the figure, preparation for the negotiation is the first step. A leader needs to do their homework so they have all of the facts and possible options researched prior to negotiation. During the preparation, it is essential to gather good information, assess the bargaining position, and be creative about developing options.[105] Next, the process of building the relationship follows. Not all negotiations start out discussing business. Often, there is an exchange of personal greetings prior to the actual bargaining process. Also, developing rapport with the bargaining partner reduces the chances that they will get angry during the negotiation.[106] Building the relationship is an area to pay particular attention to in cross-cultural negotiations. For example, negotiators from the Middle East may be more relationship-oriented.[107] Negotiators in Costa Rica were found to be more likely to build the relationship through the expression of emotions.[108] Another study[109] compared negotiators in the United States, China, and Qatar. In the United States, negotiators based their negotiation behavior on *dignity*, which is deriving self-worth based on the individual achievements in pursuit of individual goals and values. In China, negotiators were influenced by *face*, in which self-worth is based on others' assessments of whether the individual is fulfilling stable social role obligations. In Qatar, negotiation was found to be based on *honor*, where self-worth is based on an individual's reputation and also the assessment of what others think of a person. These cultural orientations influence how negotiators approach a bargaining situation. The Chinese and Qatari negotiators were more competitive than the U.S. negotiators. This study demonstrates the nuances of cross-cultural negotiation. Some cultures build relationships; however, they may still be competitive. It's important to study the culture in detail prior to a cross-cultural negotiation.

Next, the process of gathering and using information follows. For example, in a real estate negotiation, the seller's agent often has conducted a market analysis of the value of the property so that the buyer gets the property at a fair price. This information is shared with the seller, particularly if the price the seller wants is significantly above

Figure 11.5   **Steps in the Negotiation Process**

Phase 1	Phase 2	Phase 3	Phase 4	Phase 5	Phase 6	Phase 7
Preparation →	Relationship building →	Information gathering →	Information using →	Bidding →	Closing the deal →	Implementing the agreement

Source: Thompson, L. (2012). *The mind and the heart of the negotiator* (5th ed.). Upper Saddle River, NJ: Prentice Hall.

the market. Also, research has shown that the process of asking questions and answering them builds trust during the negotiation.[110] The next step is the bidding process—offers and counteroffers are extended until a mutually agreeable solution is attained. However, this doesn't always go smoothly since emotions can become heightened during the bidding process. It's important to keep your emotions in check. Research has shown that displays of anger result in more impasses and less attractive outcomes during negotiations. Anger erodes trust and liking in the relationship. This is especially true if the anger is faked, known as the *blowback effect*.[111] Also, displays of anger create stress, and experimental research has shown that when negotiators experienced anxiety, they ended up with deals that were 12% less attractive than those who remained calm.[112] Finally, the implementation of the decision involves the execution of the contract. In a purchasing situation, this would be the transfer of money and goods and/or services. In some cases, implementation of an agreement involves a **contingency contract**. These contracts bridge concerns about future events that are brought up during the negotiation, and they become part of the agreement.[113] For example, an entrepreneur may sell an invention to venture capitalists, but their concerns about letting go of the future potential benefits could be addressed by including a contingency that they will receive 1% of all future revenues from the sales of the product.

There are two general types of negotiation—distributive and integrative—and these are discussed next. Generally, distributive bargaining is hardball, whereas integrative bargaining takes a softer approach to the deal. A meta-analysis of 34 studies analyzed the impact of hard and soft bargaining strategies on economic and emotional negotiation in distributive negotiations.[114] Hard bargaining led to higher economic outcomes, but soft bargaining led to higher emotional outcomes such as satisfaction and relationship development. Your approach to negotiation on these dimensions may determine how successful you are at getting the best deal. However, it is important to keep in mind what your goals are: getting the best deal, preserving the quality of the relationship, or both.

Distributive Bargaining

The distinction to remember about distributive bargaining is that the negotiator approaches the process as a zero-sum game. In other words, one person gains at the expense of the other. The negotiator views the possible outcome as a **fixed pie**, meaning that there is a limited amount of goods to be divided up, and the goal is to get the largest share. Each negotiator has a goal, or target point, of what they want to get from the bargaining process. They may also have a **best alternative to a negotiated agreement (BATNA)** if they have prepared properly. This concept was put forth in the best-selling book *Getting to Yes: How to Get What You Want Without Giving In*.[115] The BATNA is an alternative that negotiators will accept if the negotiation reaches an impasse and they can't get their ideal outcome. If neither the preferred alternative nor the BATNA is accepted, then there is no deal. The strategies the negotiator uses in distributive bargaining involve making the first offer to anchor the bargaining process, since people focus on the first information they see (recall the primacy effect discussed in Chapter 5).[116] Decades of research on negotiation has supported the *first-offer effect*, in which counteroffers and final offers correlate strongly with the first offer, making first offers among the best predictors of final prices. In other words, final prices often end up higher when sellers versus buyers go first in negotiations. On the other hand, prices are lower when the buyer makes the first offer. Follow these guidelines in making the first offer:

- **Be confident in your speech and demeanor**. Phrase your offer as a statement, not a question. Avoid terms like "somewhere around." Resist the temptation to immediately revise the number.

- **Be precise**—but not too precise. For example, if you are buying a used car, an offer such as $10,425 might work. It sounds like you've done your homework about the value of the car. However, $10,425.52 probably won't work. The seller may become suspicious because the offer looks fake.

- **Avoid ranges**. For example, if you say $10,000 to $12,000, the other side won't even hear the numbers; they'll just pick the part of the range they like.[117] If you do use a range, be sure that the endpoint of the range is your target.

- **Be aggressive but realistic**. A first offer that is too extreme can have a "chilling effect." This may make the bargaining partner angry and they walk away.[118]

Another tactic that research has shown to be effective is to use a deadline to put pressure on the person you are bargaining with to make a decision faster.[119] For example, an employer may make a job offer and request that the applicant respond within 1 week (known as an "exploding offer"). Research has shown that most negotiators begin the process with the fixed-pie bias—they assume it is a zero-sum game. However, experimental research has demonstrated that it is possible to change the mental model of the fixed pie to one that reflects win-win.[120] This is known as **integrative bargaining**.

Integrative Bargaining

Integrative bargaining differs from distributive bargaining in one significant way: The parties do not see the process as a zero-sum game, and they believe that an agreement can be reached that satisfies all concerns.[121] Thus, they view the possible outcome space as an **expanding pie** in which a win-win solution can be reached. In general, integrative bargaining is preferable, particularly when the parties value having a long-term relationship. No one walks away from the negotiation as a loser, so there are no hard feelings. Negotiators are more likely to want to bargain with one another again after an integrative bargain is reached—even the losing party.[122] For integrative bargaining to work, individuals need to be willing to share information (this is more difficult to achieve than it may seem because people tend to want to hide information on their goals and acceptable outcomes during negotiation). Another successful tactic is to put more issues out for discussion during a negotiation.[123] This is known as "sweetening the deal" with added incentives and different features. For example, when negotiating for a new car, dealers will often throw in extras such as an upgraded stereo system or sunroof to get the buyer focused on features other than the price of the car. To be effective in integrative bargaining, negotiators also need to get past the fixed position of one another and discuss what their real interests are.[124] This gets to what people really value since money has symbolic meaning in some cases (recall the discussion of the meaning of money from Chapter 9). For example, a person who is presenting their product on *Shark Tank*, a popular TV show where entrepreneurs pitch their products and services to investors, might really want to maintain control over their invention rather than make more money. Thus, they might accept an offer of less money but more control over their business in the long run. By focusing on interests, the investor might get a higher percentage of the profit by letting the inventor control their business. Finally, integrative bargaining requires creativity and the ability to think of novel solutions that can address the concerns of both parties.[125]

A review of research on negotiation found that the principles put forth in Fisher and Ury's *Getting to Yes* have generally been supported by research evidence.[126] This book is recommended reading for all leaders. Interest-based negotiation as presented in this book is based on four pillars:

- Focus on interests and not on positions;

- Imagine a wide range of solutions before making a decision. Explore solutions providing a mutual benefit;

- Resolve disputes and choose solutions based on objective criteria to which everyone agrees; and

- Distinctly address people issues and substantive issues.

Try to practice putting these principles into action by completing Toolkit Activity 11.2. This is an opportunity to practice win-win negotiating skills to negotiate a better employment package while creating a good working relationship with your future boss.

Union-Management Negotiations

Labor relations refer to activities that labor unions and managers engage in to resolve conflicts between employers and employees represented by a union that they have elected.[127] Historically, unions were created to counter the power of employers by giving employees more voice. Unionization occurs when employees are dissatisfied with wages, job security, and supervision.[128] Given that employees' motivation to unionize is to right what they view as wrongs, it isn't surprising that labor management negotiations are often adversarial. In the past, when negotiations took place between unions and management, distributive (win-lose) bargaining was often employed by both sides. Unions would stage strikes or walk-outs. Management would engage in strategic actions to lower a firm's perceived ability to meet wages or other demands. For example, they might hold less cash, cut dividends, and use other methods to present a negative picture to get a better negotiated agreement. Such managers are reluctant to share information on their organizations' financial health with labor so as to preserve bargaining power.[129]

During the 1990s, there was a decrease in the number of labor disputes. This was due to the economy, in part, and the rate of organizational change. Many organizations began implementing practices that improved job satisfaction. Scholars have noted a shift in the adversarial role of management toward unions to a more cooperative process that employs integrative bargaining, employing interest-based negotiation.[130] When top management teams realize they are facing a union movement capable of resistance, they adopt a strategy of cooperation rather than restriction of their bargaining options.[131] Being emotionally intelligent has been linked to successful negotiation and dispute resolution.[132,133] Leaders in a unionized environment are advised to show emotional intelligence, work with their unions, and show empathy for their workers rather than taking an adversarial role that may end up with costly work stoppages and bad press.

Successful integrative negotiation in all contexts requires a leader to be able to see things the way the other party sees them. Empathy is part of being emotionally intelligent (discussed in Chapter 3). Research has indicated that some individuals have a greater ability to engage in seeing another person's point of view than others. The concluding section discusses perspective taking and how it plays a key role in conflict resolution and negotiation.

LEADERSHIP IMPLICATIONS: PERSPECTIVE TAKING

Being emotionally intelligent is critical for resolving conflict and effective negotiation. To do this, a leader needs to be able to see the situation from the other party's point of view. This is called **perspective taking**, which is defined as a cognitive process in which an individual adopts another person's views to better understand their preferences, values, and needs.[134] In other words, it is the ability to see things from another person's perspective, even if it conflicts with their own. In a classic study, researchers found that when people were asked to give directions to a landmark in New York City, they changed the way they described how to get to the landmark depending on whether the person asking was from the city. For those that lived in the city, people gave less specific instructions because they assumed people would know basic aspects of navigating the city, like how to get uptown versus downtown.[135] For those who were not from the city, they provided more specific instructions and described buildings on the way to the landmark. These researchers also examined whether perspective taking was a single ability or a task that involves multiple different skill sets. They concluded that perspective taking is complex and involves a number of different abilities. People have to diagnose what information someone else has access to (or what information they are likely to have in the future) and then use that information to inform their decisions. Perspective taking requires good memory and imagination. And the skills needed may vary due to the situation and the task being performed. One review of perspective taking concluded: "The ability to intuit another person's thoughts, feelings, and inner mental states is surely among the most impressive of human mental faculties."[136] Perspective taking is a useful skill for a leader to develop, and it is also useful for those in sales positions because they can see their product the way that a customer sees it. It is also important for effective conflict resolution and negotiation.

There are two reasons why perspective taking helps resolve conflict.[137] First, when people engage in perspective taking, they are more likely to create a social bond with the other person.[138] Second, perspective taking creates positive attributions about another person's behavior, such as recognizing the effects of external circumstances on what they do. For example, if a person gets into an argument with another person, perspective taking helps the person resolving the conflict by providing insight into why they care so much about an issue that they will fight about it. Perspective taking enhances the ability to repair emotions and enables a person to forgive and problem solve during a conflict situation.[139] This results in a more integrating conflict resolution style as well as less use of the dominating style. Perspective taking has a number of other benefits. For example, it increases the relationship between intrinsic motivation and creativity, particularly for employees with prosocial motivation.[140] Entrepreneurs who are able to take the perspectives of customers are more likely to identify business opportunities.[141] Another study of 397 employees in 25 work teams found that perspective taking was related to knowledge sharing and better customer service climates.[142]

A negotiator that is able to take the perspective of the person they are bargaining with has an advantage. Research has demonstrated that perspective taking is related to effective integrative negotiation.[143] This is because taking the perspective of another person reduces the errors in misrepresenting their true interests. Another set of experiments[144] found that perspective taking increased individuals' ability to discover hidden agendas and to both create and claim resources at the bargaining table. However, empathy did not prove nearly as advantageous and at times was detrimental to discovering a possible deal and achieving individual profit. The authors conclude that it pays to get inside the head of your opponent in a negotiation situation. There is some evidence that leaders can create the right conditions for their followers to engage in perspective taking. For example, a research study found that when leaders are humble, followers are more likely to engage in perspective taking.[145] Team members who take the perspectives of their teammates are more likely to emerge as informal leaders.[146]

In this chapter, essential research evidence on identifying and resolving conflict has been reviewed. The sources of workplace conflict have been identified and solutions recommended. Five conflict resolution styles are described with an emphasis on the leader being able to adapt the style used to the situation. In general, the integrating style is best for complex problems. The role of conflict at the team level has been discussed, noting the importance of identifying task and relationship conflict so that a leader can manage the conflict appropriately. Sometimes, conflict escalates to workplace incivility and even aggression. This chapter also covers conflict resolution in the context of negotiations and compares distributive bargaining with integrative bargaining. The chapter ends with the leadership implication of perspective taking where you see things from another person's point of view. Research has demonstrated that perspective taking is essential for both conflict resolution and negotiation.

edge.sagepub.com/scandura2e

Want a better grade? Go to **edge.sagepub.com/scandura2e** for the tools you need to sharpen your study skills.

KEY TERMS

abusive supervision, 282
affective conflict, 277
alternative dispute resolution, 291
ambient impact, 283
arbitration, 292
best alternative to a negotiated
    agreement (BATNA), 293
conciliation, 291
conflict, 276
contingency contract, 293
deviant behavior, 283

direct effects, 283
expanding pie, 294
facilitation, 290
fixed pie, 293
indirect effects, 283
integrative bargaining, 294
labor relations, 295
mediation, 291
negotiation, 292
ombudsperson, 291
peer review, 291

perspective taking, 295
process conflict, 277
relationship conflict, 280
substantive conflict, 277
task conflict, 280
"toxic" workplaces, 283
workplace aggression, 282
workplace bullying, 282
workplace incivility, 282

TOOLKIT ACTIVITY 11.1: Checklist for Difficult Conversations

Before you jump into a difficult conversation, spend some private time to identify the difficulty and acknowledge different points of view.

- How do you see the situation?

- What assumptions are you making? What stories are you telling yourself?

- How might the other person perceive the same situation?

- What emotions are this problem stirring up for you?

- What is the impact of this situation on you, and what hypothesis do you have about the other person's intention?

Be certain this is a conversation that is worth having.

- What is your purpose in addressing this issue or having this conversation?

- What will likely happen if you ignore this problem? How will you feel?

- How is this problem affecting the productivity and morale of your unit?

Invite the other person to talk with you. Emphasize your interest in working well together and hearing their point of view. A couple of sentences you might consider using are as follows: "I would like to understand where you are coming from on . . ." or "Can you say a little more about how you see things regarding . . .?"

Start the conversation by "seeking first to understand." Ask the other person an open-ended question that will get him or her to describe how he or she sees the situation. Do your very best listening. Listen with empathy. Acknowledge the other person's feelings and point of view. Paraphrase to see if you got it right.

Share your own point of view, your intentions, and your feelings. Use *I* statements. Describe how you believe you got to where you are, including how you contributed to the problem. Take responsibility for your part.

Talk about the future and what can happen differently so you don't end up in the same place. Offer what you plan to do differently. Ask the person what suggestions they have to resolve the situation. Suggest what you think the other person could do.

Thank the other person for talking with you. Offer why it was important to resolve this conflict.

Discussion Questions

1. Recall a situation in which you needed to have a difficult conversation with another person and you avoided having it (this can also be a current situation). Why did you do so? What emotions were you feeling about the situation?

2. Imagine that you will have a conversation with the person about your concerns. Complete one of these sentences to begin the conversation: "I would like to

understand where you are coming from on . . ." or "Can you say a little more about how you see things regarding . . .?"

3. Next, write an open-ended question to follow up so that you would have listened and been able to empathize with the other person. If this is a current situation, consider having the conversation. What happened?

Source: Stone, D., Patton, B., & Heen, S. (1999). *Difficult conversations: How to discuss what matters most.* New York, NY: Penguin.

TOOLKIT ACTIVITY 11.2: Salary Negotiation

For this role-play exercise, you will find another classmate to negotiate with. Choose one of the roles (but don't look at the role of your negotiating partner, and don't show him or her the role you have been assigned).

Role of Pat (Boss)

You are the brand manager of a division of an organization that makes a variety of household products. You are in charge of a major brand of laundry detergent located in a downtown area in the Midwest. You have been having some trouble finding the right candidate for your open position in marketing research. While the job has been advertised, you have been taking on this responsibility in addition to your own job duties, so you are motivated to fill the position.

You are seriously considering the application of Terry, who is about to graduate with an MBA from a good school in Florida. You were impressed with Terry's assertiveness in pursuing the opportunity, and the interviews went well. Terry lacks specific marketing research experience, but he has a great personality that you feel will be a good fit with others in your division. You are concerned that Terry may not want to relocate from great weather in South Florida to dreary winter weather in the Midwest, but you are ready to make the job offer.

Your company does not pay high salaries but has a generous bonus plan that could be up to 10% of the base salary. Typically, someone with Terry's lack of experience would start between $80,000 and $85,000, and you are prepared to make an offer in this range. You have been working for the company for 3 years, and you make $115,000. You may also offer relocation expenses up to $5,000.

You have an alternative candidate who did not interview as well but has an MBA from Wharton and has done an internship in marketing research at a competitor. This applicant is asking for $105,000 to start, and you don't like his attitude about insisting on this salary level. You wonder if his personality will be a good fit with your team.

You need to meet with Terry and make a decision whether to make the offer and the terms.

Role of Terry (Applicant)

You are graduating from a good business school in South Florida with an MBA in management in late May. You took a variety of management electives (leadership and teams) and enjoyed them, but you also enjoyed your introduction to a marketing course where you did a marketing research project on preferences for soft drinks. Your fiancée lives in the Midwest and does not want to relocate too far from where the family lives. You have found what you think is a perfect job in marketing research as an entry-level position with great management potential for the future. The job is in a large metropolitan area that is listed in the top 10 in terms of quality of life due to major sports, a lively music scene, and fabulous restaurants. Based on your experience leading teams, you know this is the right job to really show your managerial skills.

You had two interviews that went well, and you liked Pat, who would be your boss. You feel that you would enjoy working with Pat and the division team members (some of whom you met during the interviews). You are sure that you made a positive impression on Pat although you lack specific experience in marketing research. You are good at statistics and feel that you can apply them in a marketing research position. You are expecting an offer from Pat in your next meeting, but you feel that you will have to negotiate for a good package.

You have done research at the career center at your school, and you know that this company has rather strict salary ranges for entry-level positions. You learned that starting salaries for management majors start at $80,000, but the average salaries for recent MBA graduates is around $100,000. You also learned that the company is doing well financially, and they can afford to pay well. You think you are above average in your leadership potential, and your friends are telling you not to accept an offer less than $100,000.

You have gotten a quote from a moving company from South Florida to the midwestern city where the company is located, and moving your furniture and car would cost around $9,000. You are hoping that the company can pay you in advance for the moving expenses.

You have another job offer with a small consulting firm in the Midwest. The offer is good at $100,000, including the bonus and stock options. You are certain that the potential for upward mobility would not be as good as it would be with a larger consumer products company. Also, the location is not as desirable as the consumer products company because it is a small city with limited quality of life opportunities.

Discussion Questions

Names (Roles): _____ (Pat: Boss)

_____ (Terry: Candidate)

1. Did you reach an agreement? _____ Yes _____ No

2. If not, why not? _____

_____

3. If so, what was the final agreement?

Salary _____

Benefits _____

Other terms _____

4. How satisfied are you with the agreement you made? (Each person rates on a scale of 1 to 10, with 1 being extremely dissatisfied and 10 being extremely satisfied).

Pat:

| 1 | 5 | 10 |
| Not at all satisfied | Somewhat satisfied | Very satisfied |

Terry:

| 1 | 5 | 10 |
| Not at all satisfied | Somewhat satisfied | Very satisfied |

5. Did you reach an integrative (win-win) agreement? Explain.

TOOLKIT ACTIVITY 11.3: Negotiation Style Assessment

Negotiating Partner's Name: _____

Your Name: _____

Instructions: Please rate your negotiating partner on the following aspects of performance in the negotiation you just completed. Do not be overly harsh or overly lenient.

Statements	Strongly Disagree	Disagree	Neutral	Agree	Strongly Agree
1. My negotiating partner understood my interests.	1	2	3	4	5
2. My negotiating partner saw things from my perspective.	1	2	3	4	5
3. My negotiating partner adapted to my negotiating style.	1	2	3	4	5
4. My negotiating partner was trustworthy.	1	2	3	4	5
5. My negotiating partner managed the negotiation process well.	1	2	3	4	5
6. My negotiating partner recognized opportunities for win-win outcomes.	1	2	3	4	5

Total: Add the responses for questions 1 through 6: _____ (scores range from 6 to 30). In general, a low score for integrative (win-win) bargaining style is between 6 and 19, and a high score for integrative bargaining style is above 19.

Discussion Questions

1. Compare your ratings of one another. Was one person a more effective negotiator? Why?

2. Were you able to engage in perspective taking during the negotiation exercise? In other words, did you see things from one another's point of view (review your answers to question 2 above)?

3. What role did trust play in the negotiation? Did you trust one another (review your answers to question 4 above). Do you think that you will be able to work together effectively as boss and follower in the future? Why or why not?

CASE STUDY 11.1: Perspective Taking: Captain Owen Honors

Naval captain Owen Honors was fired for the production of video skits with offensive content using navy equipment starring his crew members during 2006 and 2007. The following case study illustrates how different parties can view the same events differently, leading to conflict.

On January 1, 2011, Norfolk's newspaper the *Virginian-Pilot* greeted the new year with a story of videos produced, written, and featuring naval captain Owen Honors, at the time commander of the USS *Enterprise*. Four days later, Captain Honors, 49, had been relieved of his command and essentially put on desk duty pending further investigation. The cited reason was this: "profound lack of good judgment and professionalism."

The *Virginian-Pilot* article reported that anonymous men and women who served on the ship at the time the videos were created and aired complained immediately to no avail. In fact, Captain Honors stated this in the introduction of his "last video": "Over the years I've gotten several complaints about inappropriate material during these videos, never to me personally but, gutlessly, through other channels." He then suggests the following: "This evening, all of you bleeding hearts . . . why don't just go ahead and hug yourself for the next 20 minutes or so, because there's a really good chance you're gonna be offended."

Although it appears that Captain Honors's supervisors learned of the videos at the time, Captain Honors was not reprimanded—other than told to cease production of them—and was ultimately promoted to commander of the USS *Enterprise* in May of 2010. It is important to note that it is not public knowledge as to who knew about the videos prior to the *Virginian-Pilot* article.

As a result of the videos surfacing, the navy stripped Captain Honors of command of the USS *Enterprise*.

However, the "firing" of Captain Owen Honors has not quieted the public debate over the videos or the naval response.

To do nothing is to condone. By not acting at the time, the navy essentially condoned the videos and Captain Honors's making of them. Perhaps the current navy leadership's response is one impacted by public relations; perhaps the existence of the videos had been the secret of a select few who protected Captain Honors from being penalized in the past. Whatever the impetus for the action taken, at this point the navy has made a public decision not to condone the videos or the behavior.

The public debate, however, exemplifies what so often happens in a conflict: Each side demands that the other side admit defeat and agree that the other side is right. Regardless of an individual's perspective—one of support for Captain Honors, one of agreement with the navy's decision, seeing nothing objectionable in the videos, or finding the videos offensive—the discourse is one of proving the other side wrong. Once this happens, the conflict grows and the discussion becomes polarized, with each side refusing to consider how the other opinion is not wrong, just different.

As this scenario illustrates, the same events may be viewed and interpreted differently by different individuals who deeply care about an issue. Some support Captain Honors because he was attempting to entertain his crew members, and the videos had been shown for some time, airing on the closed-circuit televisions on the ship. Others view the content of the videos as repulsive sexual harassment and gay slurs, and feel that the navy was justified in removing Captain Honors from his post. This case brought forth strong emotions on either side, indicating that people really care about the outcome or the issues that surfaced from the production of the videos.

Discussion Questions

1. Do you think the navy was justified in firing Captain Honors? Explain your position.

2. How open are you to another point of view on this case?

3. Take the opposite position to your point of view and write a paragraph explaining the other point of view. For example, if you think the navy was wrong to fire Captain Honors, write a statement that supports firing him.

4. Think about the other alternatives to conflict—compromise and collaboration—that don't involve one side losing and the other winning. In situations like the one in the case, is it possible for both sides to come to a compromise or collaboration? Why or why not? How might the number of parties play a role in the type of solution generated?

Source: Johnston, E. (2011). Workplace conflict case study: The navy & Capt. Owen Honors. Retrieved on December 13, 2012, from http://cfrmediation.com/workplace-conflict-case-study-the-navy-capt-owen-honors

SELF-ASSESSMENT 11.1: Conflict Resolution Styles

This self-assessment exercise identifies your conflict resolution style. There are no right or wrong answers, and this is not a test. The purpose of this assessment is for you to learn about yourself. You don't have to share your results with other classmates unless you wish to do so.

Part I. Taking the Assessment

Purpose:

1. To identify your conflict style

2. To examine how your conflict style varies in different contexts or relationships

Directions:

1. Think of two different situations (A and B) where you have a conflict, a disagreement, an argument, or a disappointment with someone, such as a roommate or a work associate. Write the name of the person for each situation that follows.

2. According to the following scale, fill in your scores for Person A and Person B. For each question, you will have two scores. For example, on question 1, the scoring might look like this: 1. 2 | 5 (see the example below).

Directions for taking the conflict scale: Please respond to the following 25 items. Be honest. There are no right or wrong answers!

You will be presented with some questions representing your approach to conflict.

As an example, the answers to situations could look like this:

Person A: Miriam   (write first name) Person B: Jose   (write first name)

I try to resolve conflict constructively.

Statements	Never		Seldom		Occasionally		Often		Always	
Person	A	B	A	B	A	B	A	B	A	B
1. I try to resolve conflict constructively	1	1	2	2	3	3	4	4	5	5

Person A____2____ I Person B____5____

This response indicates that you seldom try to resolve conflict with Miriam constructively, but you always try to resolve conflict with Jose constructively.

Person A: _____ (write first name)   Person B _____ (write first name)

Statements	Never		Seldom		Occasionally		Often		Always	
Person	A	B	A	B	A	B	A	B	A	B
1. I avoid being put on the spot. I keep conflicts to myself.	1	1	2	2	3	3	4	4	5	5
2. I use my influence to get my ideas accepted.	1	1	2	2	3	3	4	4	5	5
3. I usually try to "split the difference" in order to resolve an issue.	1	1	2	2	3	3	4	4	5	5
4. I generally try to satisfy the other's needs.	1	1	2	2	3	3	4	4	5	5
5. I try to investigate an issue to find a solution acceptable to both of us.	1	1	2	2	3	3	4	4	5	5
6. I usually avoid open discussion of my differences with the other.	1	1	2	2	3	3	4	4	5	5
7. I use my authority to make a decision in my favor.	1	1	2	2	3	3	4	4	5	5
8. I try to find a middle course to resolve an impasse.	1	1	2	2	3	3	4	4	5	5
9. I usually accommodate the other's wishes.	1	1	2	2	3	3	4	4	5	5

(Continued)

(Continued)

| Statements | Never | | Seldom | | Occasionally | | Often | | Always | |
Person	A	B	A	B	A	B	A	B	A	B
10. I try to integrate my ideas with the other's to come up with a decision jointly.	1	1	2	2	3	3	4	4	5	5
11. I try to stay away from disagreement with the other.	1	1	2	2	3	3	4	4	5	5
12. I use my expertise to make a decision that favors me.	1	1	2	2	3	3	4	4	5	5
13. I propose a middle ground for breaking deadlocks.	1	1	2	2	3	3	4	4	5	5
14. I give in to the other's wishes.	1	1	2	2	3	3	4	4	5	5
15. I try to work with the other to find solutions that satisfy both of our expectations.	1	1	2	2	3	3	4	4	5	5
16. I try to keep my disagreement to myself in order to avoid hard feelings.	1	1	2	2	3	3	4	4	5	5
17. I generally pursue my side of an issue.	1	1	2	2	3	3	4	4	5	5
18. I negotiate with the other to reach a compromise.	1	1	2	2	3	3	4	4	5	5
19. I often go with the other's suggestions.	1	1	2	2	3	3	4	4	5	5
20. I exchange accurate information with the other so we can solve a problem together.	1	1	2	2	3	3	4	4	5	5
21. I try to avoid unpleasant exchanges with the other.	1	1	2	2	3	3	4	4	5	5
22. I sometimes use my power to win.	1	1	2	2	3	3	4	4	5	5
23. I use give-and-take so that a compromise can be made.	1	1	2	2	3	3	4	4	5	5
24. I try to satisfy the other's expectations	1	1	2	2	3	3	4	4	5	5
25. I try to bring all our concerns out in the open so that the issues can be resolved.	1	1	2	2	3	3	4	4	5	5

Part II. Scoring Instructions

Add up your scores on the following questions:

A | B	A | B	A | B	A | B	A | B
1. __|__	2. __|__	3. __|__	4. __|__	5. __|__
6. __|__	7. __|__	8. __|__	9. __|__	10. __|__
11. __|__	12. __|__	13. __|__	14. __|__	15. __|__
16. __|__	17. __|__	18. __|__	19. __|__	20. __|__
21. __|__	22. __|__	23. __|__	24. __|__	25. __|__
__|__	__|__	__|__	__|__	__|__
A | B	A | B	A | B	A | B	A | B
Avoiding Totals A__ | B__	Dominating Totals A__ | B__	Compromising Totals A__ | B__	Obliging Totals A__ | B__	Integrating Totals A__ | B__

Scoring Interpretation

This questionnaire is designed to identify your conflict style and examine how it varies in different relationships. By comparing your total scores for the different styles, you can discover which conflict style you rely most heavily upon and which style you use least. Furthermore, by comparing your scores for Person A and Person B, you can determine how your style varies or stays the same in different relationships. Your scores on this questionnaire are indicative of how you responded to a particular conflict at a specific time and therefore might change if you selected a different conflict or a different relationship. The conflict style questionnaire is not a personality test that labels or categorizes you; rather, it attempts to give you a sense of your more dominant and less dominant conflict styles.

Scores from 21 to 25 are representative of a very strong style.

Scores from 16 to 20 are representative of a strong style.

Scores from 11 to 15 are representative of an average style.

Scores from 5 to 10 are representative of a weak style.

Discussion Questions

1. Based on the results of this assessment, what is your primary conflict resolution style? What is your secondary (back-up) style?

2. Given your results on this assessment, is there anything that you would change in the future with respect to how you manage conflict? Explain.

3. Did you have a consistent conflict management style, or did you vary it depending on the person? Compare your responses for Person A and Person B and explain differences if you see any.

Source: Adapted from Rahim, M. A., & Magner, N. R. (1995). Confirmatory factor analysis of the styles of handling *interpersonal conflict:* First-Order factor model and its invariance across groups. In W. Wilmot & J. Hocker (2011), *Interpersonal conflict* (pp. 146–148). Washington, DC: American Psychological Association. (Reprinted from *Journal of Applied Psychology, 80*[1], 122–132.)

CHAPTER TWELVE

ORGANIZATIONAL COMMUNICATION

Learning Objectives

After studying this chapter, you should be able to do the following:

12.1: Describe the communication process, and discuss sources of noise in the process.

12.2: Identify how communication apprehension affects the communication process.

12.3: Compare and contrast different forms of communication networks.

12.4: Discuss the advantages and disadvantages of electronic communication.

12.5: Provide an example of how to communicate effectively across cultures.

12.6: Summarize the significance of the percentages of verbal and nonverbal face-to-face communication.

12.7: Explain why employees remain silent or withhold information and how to address this.

Get the edge on your studies at **edge.sagepub.com/scandura2e**

- Take the chapter quiz
- Review key terms with eFlashcards
- Explore multimedia resources, SAGE readings, and more!

"THIN SLICING" A CONVERSATION

Can the first few minutes of communication define the course of the conversation and the benefits or costs derived from it? These first few minutes are referred to as "thin slices" of behavior. Thin slices were studied by having college students evaluate 30-second video clips of instructors teaching a class.[1] These quick evaluations significantly predicted teacher ratings at the end of the semester. Research on thin slicing has shown that early interactions (minutes) predict conviction of criminals and divorce (in some cases, months or years in the future).[2] This fascinating line of research has revealed the surprising finding that observation of a thin slice of behavior (minutes or even seconds) predicts important outcomes such as professional competence as rated by a person conducting an employment interview. Early cues are often based on both verbal and nonverbal behaviors in communication. Another study[3] examined the accuracy of a 5-second thin slice of another person with respect to their personality characteristics. Results of this experiment found that negative affect, extraversion, conscientiousness, and intelligence were judged moderately well after just 5 seconds of exposure. However, positive affect, neuroticism, openness, and agreeableness required more exposure time to achieve similar levels of accuracy.

An experimental study examined whether conversational dynamics early in negotiation predict the attractiveness of an employment package.[4] Researchers examined four types of initial communication: activity level, conversational engagement, emphasis, and vocal mirroring. Activity level refers to how much time a person is speaking during the conversation. Conversational engagement is how much influence one person has on the turn-taking process of speaking. Emphasis is the variation in the person's tone, stress, and rhythm. Finally, vocal mirroring is copying of the others' behaviors (e.g., body movements, facial expressions, or speech). The results of this experiment showed that 30% of the variation in negotiators' success was due to these four conversational behaviors *during the first 5 minutes* of negotiation interactions that lasted up to 45 minutes. Negotiators that had high activity, engagement, emphasis, and mirroring during the first five minutes received better employment deals (salary, vacation days, job assignment, company car, signing bonus, moving expense reimbursement, and a preferable insurance provider). Another experiment[5] examined first impressions of job applicants in 163 mock interviews. The results suggest that a significant portion of initial impressions' influence overlaps with what questions applicants were asked in the interview. More important, these initial impressions were strongly related to interviewer evaluations of applicant responses earlier rather than later in the structured interview. While you might find this amazing, your communication in the first few minutes of a meeting may determine the benefits you derive from it. This research highlights the importance of communicating effectively at work. In this chapter, research on organizational communication is discussed—and this knowledge is essential for leaders.

WHAT IS ORGANIZATIONAL COMMUNICATION?

Learning Objective 12.1: Describe the communication process, and discuss sources of noise in the process.

Organizational communication is "the process by which individuals stimulate meaning in the minds of other individuals by means of verbal or nonverbal messages in the context of a formal organization."[6] As indicated in the research discussed in the previous section on thin slicing, communication is important for job interviews and negotiating the best deals. Also, positive organizational communication relates to both job performance and satisfaction.[7,8,9] One of the earliest statements regarding the importance of organizational communication is found in *The Functions of the Executive*: "The first function of the executive is to develop and maintain a system of communication."[10] Organizational communication is a specialized field today and emerged as a scientific discipline by the 1960s.[11] Organizational communication has been referred to as "the social glue that ties organizations together."[12] Entire books have been written on organizational communication. However, the purpose of this chapter is to provide you with the essential knowledge of communication needed to lead effectively.

The Communication Process

The **Shannon–Weaver model of communication** is essential to understanding the two-party communication process.[13] The key elements of the communication process are shown in Figure 12.1. These are described in the following sections.

1. **The sender.** This is the source transmission who selects a desired message out of a set of possible messages. The selected message may consist of written or spoken words, pictures, music, or combinations of these. The message may also contain nonverbal behaviors such as gestures. For example, a leader prepares a speech for her employees consisting of a written outline and a PowerPoint presentation that contains graphs and pictures.

2. **Encoding.** This is the transformation of the message into the signal, which is sent over the communication channel from the transmitter to the receiver. For example, if a leader makes a speech to employees, the leader is the encoder.

3. **The channel.** The channel is the medium that transmits the message. In the previously given example, the channels are the leader's voice and the projector that shows slides that accompany the speech. The choice of communication channel (or medium) is influenced by institutional conditions (e.g., incentives, trust, and physical proximity) and situational conditions (e.g., urgency, task), and by the routine use of the media over time.[14] Research has indicated that the choice of communication medium (e.g., e-mail versus face-to-face) affects both attitudes and behaviors of the receiver.[15]

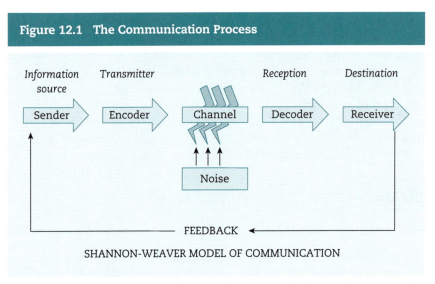

Figure 12.1 The Communication Process

Information source — Transmitter — Reception — Destination

Sender → Encoder → Channel → Decoder → Receiver

Noise

FEEDBACK

SHANNON-WEAVER MODEL OF COMMUNICATION

Source: Weaver, W. (1949). Recent contributions to the mathematical theory of communication. *The Mathematical Theory of Communication, 1,* 1–12.

4. **Decoding.** The receiver then decodes the message sent through the selected channel or channels by translating what is seen and heard into an understanding of the message. This is not a perfect process since there is **noise** in the communication process that affects the decoding process. Noise is any communication barrier that may affect how a person interprets a message. For example, perceptual biases, language choice, cultural differences, and the room being too hot may affect how a person decodes a message and result in errors. This is why feedback is so important in the communication process. A leader must check to see that the message was understood by followers. They need to know whether followers understood the speech. This might be accomplished by inviting followers to e-mail with questions and comments after the speech.

> Critical Thinking Question: Provide an example of noise in the communication process based on your experience. How could this noise have been reduced?

5. **The receiver.** The receiver is the person or persons who receive the message. There may be noise on the receiver's part as well. For example, the receiver may not be paying attention or they may be distracted by noise in the room.

Noise represents barriers to communication, as the previously given examples illustrate. There are other barriers to communicating effectively in organizations, and some of these are discussed next.

BARRIERS TO EFFECTIVE COMMUNICATION

Learning Objective 12.2: Identify how communication apprehension affects the communication process.

Communication Apprehension

Some people are uncomfortable communicating with others, and it seems clear that this imposes a significant barrier to their success as a leader. A classic definition of **communication apprehension (CA)** is "an individual's level of fear or anxiety with either real or anticipated communication with another person or persons."[16] A more recent and expanded definition of CA is "anxiety or fear suffered by an individual of either actual or anticipated communication, with a group or a person, that can profoundly affect their oral communication, social skills, and self-esteem."[17] There are two types of CA: trait-based and state-based. Trait-based CA affects a person's ability to communicate with others across a variety of situations.[18] State-based CA is triggered by specific situations, such as being required to give a speech.[19] Therefore, CA may affect communication between two parties, team participation, or giving presentations. A meta-analysis of 36 studies on CA found that it is negatively related to both the quality and quantity of communication behavior.[20] CA may affect numerous aspects of behavior in organizations. For example, people with high CA may seek jobs with lower communication requirements and would seek less advice or assistance from their managers.[21] Another study of found that students with high CA preferred to sit in the back or at the edges of a classroom to restrict their interaction with the professor.[22] A study of CA and leadership abilities of 263 students found CA was detrimental to performance although these students had high intellectual ability (their GPA was not a factor).[23] The research showed CA was negatively associated with students' perceptions of their adaptability, appreciation for a multicultural world, and willingness to take on leadership roles. The authors recommend self-awareness (being aware that you are high in CA) and assertiveness training to overcome this communication barrier. Leaders should be aware that some followers may have CA and carefully draw them out in one-on-one conversations before asking them to speak in a team meeting or make a presentation.

Language

Words may have different meanings to different people even if they are communicating in the same language. Slang, or colloquial terms, are used in organizations and can be bewildering to new employees or those outside of the organization. For example, a new employee may be told by her boss to "scale" her ideas for a new product implementation. What does it mean to scale something in business? Josh Lawry, general manager at 2nd Watch, a premier cloud partner for Amazon Web Services, noted that the word *scale* is often used in business and can have different meanings depending on the context.[24] Some common examples include the following: "Are we operating the business at scale?" (allocating and optimizing resources to drive the greatest results) or "Are we taking advantage of the scale of our business?" (another way to say size) or "Can the product scale up or scale down depending on demand?" (increasing or decreasing capacity). This example shows that beyond vocabulary, it is important to understand the context of business jargon and multiple meanings for the same phrase.

Due to noise and communication barriers, it is important for the receiver of a communication to provide feedback to the sender to ensure that the communicated message was understood correctly. This can be accomplished through **active listening**.

> **Critical Thinking Questions:** Provide an example of jargon or slang used in an organization that could be misinterpreted by a new employee. Then, provide an alternative way of stating this concept so that it is more easily understood.

Active Listening

In his impactful psychology book *A Way of Being*, Carl Rogers described "active listening" as the way of listening that is "a creative, active, sensitive, accurate, empathic, nonjudgmental listening."[25] Experimental research has shown study participants who receive active listening responses feel they are understood better than participants who receive either advice or a simple acknowledgment. This research also found participants with active listening responses were more satisfied with their conversations. Active listening has three components:

1. It demonstrates moderate to high nonverbal involvement.

2. It reflects the speaker's message using verbal paraphrasing.

3. It may include asking questions that encourage speakers to elaborate on his or her experiences.[26]

Leaders must become active listeners to be more effective since listening allows them to verify their communications, clarify messages, and encourage more two-way communication with followers.[27] Kevin Sharer, the former CEO of biotechnology giant Amgen, stated the following:

> As you become a senior leader, it's a lot less about convincing people and more about benefiting from complex information and getting the best out of the people you work with. Listening for comprehension helps you get that information, of course, but it's more than that: it's also the greatest sign of respect you can give someone.[28]

A study of 183 undergraduate students[29] found that mindfulness relates to active listening. This occurred because being mindful resulted in students observing their feelings, being able to describe them, and then being nonjudgmental about why they felt the way they did. This opened the pathway for them to be more empathetic and actively listen to others. Active listening is also a powerful tool used by effective salespeople—they do more listening than talking to their potential customers.[30] An interview study[31] of 43 middle managers found that effective managers engaged significantly more in positive relations-oriented "active listening" and "agreeing" behaviors, and significantly less in "task monitoring" and counterproductive work behaviors (such as "providing negative feedback" and "defending one's own position"). Based on research evidence, active-listening is a skill that effective leaders need to develop. Guidelines for active listening are provided in Table 12.1.

To develop your active listening skills, complete Toolkit Activity 12.1 at the end of this chapter. This is an active listening exercise that you can use to practice active listening and receive feedback on your listening accuracy. The exercise involves a dyadic (or two-party) conversation. However, in organizations, it is important to recognize that communication often occurs through networks that flow in all

Table 12.1 Guidelines for Active Listening in Organizations

1. Listen for Total Meaning

Any message a person tries to get across usually has two components: the content of the message and the feeling or attitude underlying this content. Both are important; both give the message meaning. It is this total meaning of the message that we try to understand.

2. Respond to Feelings

In some instances, the content is far less important than the feeling that underlies it. To catch the full flavor or meaning of the message, one must respond particularly to the feeling component. Each time, the listener must try to remain sensitive to the total meaning the message has to the speaker. What is he trying to tell me? What does this mean to him? How does he see this situation?

3. Note All Cues

Not all communication is verbal. The speaker's words alone don't tell us everything he is communicating. And, hence, truly sensitive listening requires that we become aware of several kinds of communication besides verbal. The way in which a speaker hesitates in his speech can tell us much about his feelings—so, too, can the inflection of his voice. He may stress certain points loudly and clearly, and may mumble others. We should also note such things as the person's facial expressions, body posture, hand movements, eye movements, and breathing. All of these help to convey his total message.

Source: Adapted from Rogers, C. R., & Farson, F. E. (1987). Active Listening. In R. G. Newman, M. A. Danzinger, & M. Cohen (Eds.), *Communicating in business today.* Washington, DC: Heath & Company.

directions (**upward communication**, **downward communication**, and **lateral communication**).

COMMUNICATION NETWORKS

Learning Objective 12.3: Compare and contrast different forms of communication networks.

Critical Thinking Questions: Why do you think that people in organizations have a difficult time listening? What can organizations do to increase the degree to which their leaders listen to their followers?

Communication flows through relatively reliable patterns in organizations. Figure 12.2 depicts some of the common communication networks. First, the **wheel network** indicates that all communication flows through one person, who is most likely the group leader. This is the most centralized communication network shown. The next one is the **circle** communication network in which each person can communicate with two others located adjacent to them. The **all-channel (or star)** pattern is more decentralized and allows a free flow of information among all group members. The **chain** gives a flow of information among members, although the people are at the end of the chain. Finally, the **Y-pattern** is slightly less centralized than the all-channel network since two persons are closer to the center of the network.

Research has shown that communication networks are an important way for job applicants to learn about job opportunities. The "strength of weak ties" thesis is that weak ties—especially bridging ties—help people tap into nonredundant pools of information.[32] For example, a weak tie when looking for a job would be a suggestion from your parents' neighbor about a job opening in the accounting firm she works for. An interesting study[33] was conducted

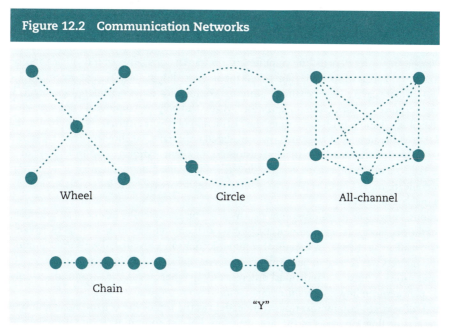

Figure 12.2   Communication Networks

Wheel

Circle

All-channel

Chain

"Y"

Source: Adapted from Leavitt, H. J. (1951). Some effects of certain communication patterns on group performance. *Journal of Abnormal and Social Psychology, 46,* 38–50.

by examining tie strength on Facebook by counting tagged photos, posts to others' walls, and the number of mutual friends that people had. Results showed that weak ties are important because of the quantity, but strong ties may also be important because of their quality. A study of 709 graduating MBA students[34] found that a search through social networks typically results in job offers with lower total compensation (for both strong and weak ties), compared with jobs found through on-campus recruiting. However, students were considerably more likely to *accept* offers found from weak ties. They did so because the referred jobs were perceived to have greater growth potential and other noncompensation value. This study supports the idea that communication networks provide value in a job search by facilitating access to information that is otherwise difficult to obtain rather than only relying on compensation information to decide which job to accept.

> **Critical Thinking Questions: Which communication network is the most effective in terms of an organization's ability to innovate? Why?**

Communication Flows in Organizations

Organizational communication may be external or internal. **External communication** refers to information that is shared with the public through marketing and public relations efforts.[35] These communication flows are important because leaders must create a positive impression with various stakeholders such as customers, shareholders, the government, and the general public. For example, when a flight from Fort Lauderdale, Florida, to Newark, New Jersey, left travelers stranded on the tarmac at the wrong airport for more than 7 hours in November 2011, Rob Maruster, JetBlue's CEO at the time, made an apology in a video message posted on blog.jetblue.com. More than 100 passengers on that flight were left on board the plane without food, water, or functioning bathrooms, causing a public relations nightmare for the airline. JetBlue has had difficulty shaking this image; Forbes named JetBlue one of the "worst airlines." JetBlue's troubles continue to be profiled in the media. In June 2014, a woman's young daughter urinated in her seat during a delay of a flight from New York to Boston. Flight attendants refused to let the child go to the restroom during the delay on the tarmac. JetBlue publicly apologized—again.[36]

Internal communication refers to "the communication transactions between individuals and/or groups at various levels and in different areas of specialization that is intended to design and redesign organizations, to implement designs, and to co-ordinate day-to-day activities."[37] Internal communication is considered a strategic business imperative due to the importance of sharing the organization's vision and helping employees cope with change (this is discussed in more detail in Chapter 15).[38] Over time, the distinction between external and internal communication has become blurred. This is because employees are now considered important stakeholders of an organization. Also, some employees communicate externally with suppliers, customers, or clients (known as **boundary spanners**). As a result, external and internal communications have now become fused into one function in most organizations, representing "integrated communications."[39] Thus, the patterns of information discussed in the following sections may refer to both external and internal communication.

In organizations, communications often flow downward. For example, the leader of an organization communicates the vision of the organization to the employees. Downward communication is essential to explain new policies or help an organization adapt to change. In a study of communications in a hospital, downward communication on task and administrative matters was related to performance of nurses, but the relationship was influenced by the tasks performed, the organization's context, and individual differences.[40] In other words, the organizational culture or follower personalities may play a role in how communications are *interpreted*.

In addition to downward communication from leaders at the top of the organization and bosses, communication may be lateral or flow sideways in the organization. Lateral communication takes place among peers or members of the same team or work group. This form of communication may either support or challenge the information received in downward communication. For example, a leader may communicate that all employees must be on time for work, but the members of a work group may challenge this by communicating an informal norm that it is acceptable to be late. Lateral communications may also reflect conflicts among team members that negatively impact satisfaction and performance. On the positive side, effective lateral communication in support of the organization's goals can enhance adaptability and effectiveness since peers may be more available to provide information quickly than superiors.

Upward communication refers to the process by which employees communicate with others who are higher in the organizational hierarchy.[41] Upward communication provides essential feedback to leaders regarding whether messages to employees have been understood. Upward communication is also important to assess the morale of employees and learn of their progress on goals. In some instances, a follower will offer an idea for improving something by communicating it to a person higher in the organization. Employees are closer to the work and the customers, and also learn more about what might be improved. It is important for leaders to encourage upward communication from their followers.

An experimental study found that followers' reputations and perceptions of their competence were affected by whether they communicated in a way that indicated the importance of their idea to the organization's goals. Also, the study found that supervisors were more likely to grant requests if the follower was not seen as aggressive or self-promoting in making it.[42] Thus, upward communication, if done effectively, may enhance a person's reputation in the organization.

Upward communication from subordinate to superior relates to (a) information about the subordinate himself, (b) information about coworkers and their problems, (c) information about organizational practices and policies, and (d) information about what needs to be done and how to do it.[43] This information is clearly essential for the leader to know; thus, accuracy is important. However, upward communication is more likely to be distorted than other directions of communication.[44] Ensuring truthful upward communication is recognized as a serious problem.[45,46] The accuracy of upward communication is improved if the followers trust their boss, believe the boss has influence over their career, and have high mobility aspirations.[47,48] Upward communication is essential for leaders to implement change for the following reasons:

- The promotion of shared leadership and an enhanced willingness by managers to act on employee suggestions

- A greater tendency by employees to report positive changes in their managers' behavior

- Actual rather than perceived improvements in management behavior following feedback

- A reduced gap between managers' self-ratings and those of their subordinates

- The creation of improved forums for obtaining information, garnering suggestions, defusing conflict, and facilitating the expression of discontent

- An enhancement of organizational learning

- Better decision quality (currently, it is estimated that about half of decisions in organizations fail—largely because of insufficient participation)

- Enhanced participation[49]

> Critical Thinking Questions: Why do you think followers distort information when they communicate with those higher in the organization? What can be done to address this concern?

The Grapevine

Much communication in organizations happens through the informal network known as the **grapevine**. The term *grapevine* is believed to have originated during the Civil War when messages were transmitted through telegraph lines strung from tree to tree resembling grapevines.[50] Information transmitted through grapevines is often rumor and gossip, but it is still an important source of information that leaders need to tap into. For example, a survey of

419 managers found 89% of those surveyed believed that the grapevine carried rumors that reflected a lack of trust in organizational leaders and their policies.[51]

Rumors that flow through the organizational grapevine can be destructive.[52] They "can drain productivity, reduce profits, create stress in the workplace, or sully a company's image. Some rumors tear at a company's credibility, with both personnel and customers. In other instances, rumors have catapulted firms into financial disaster."[53] This has become even more important due to the spread of information on social media as a grapevine. For example, a Domino's Pizza employee uploaded a video to YouTube that depicted a coworker doing unappetizing things to the pizzas he was preparing for delivery. The video was faked, but by the time Domino's was able to remove the video, it had been viewed over 1 million times. Their stock plummeted, and their brand was damaged as shocked customers reacted to the video.[54] Leaders should be aware that the grapevine may even lead to litigation if rumors and gossip contain defamation, fraud or misrepresentations, invasion of privacy, harassment, or discrimination, as well as cause emotional distress for an employee. In such cases, leaders are expected to take reasonable action to squelch the rumor mill.[55] An interview study of 15 top-ranked corporate executives found that employees engage in Internet grapevine behavior due to familiarity with the Internet, anonymity, the wide reach of the Internet, and opportunities for cyberloafing at work.[56]

Despite the evidence that the grapevine is often negative, some research has shown benefits. One study found that gossip is a powerful tool to control behavior in groups. Gossip kept group members in line by discouraging social loafing (refer back to Chapter 10 for a refresher on this team challenge).[57] Thus, while most see gossip as a negative force, it may have benefits. Another benefit is that information about working for an organization transmitted through the grapevine influences whether job applicants view employment opportunities as attractive and want to apply to work for a particular organization.[58]

Common internal corporate rumors include those connected with organizational change, such as layoffs, reorganizations, mergers, and changes in management.[59] The grapevine allows employees to vent during organizational change. In a study of a hospital undergoing change, there were more negative rumors than positive rumors in the grapevine. Also, employees exposed to negative rumors reported more stress.[60] Leaders should not ignore the grapevine; it can be an important part of the socialization of employees.[61] In sum, the grapevine is an important source of information in organizations that leaders need to monitor since it has been shown to have both negative and positive effects.

RESEARCH IN ACTION

Communication Networks and Ethics

The Enron Corporation was the seventh-largest business organization by 2001 and employed over 21,000 people in 40 countries with gross revenues of over $100 billion. Enron was "an exceedingly successful global financial powerhouse from very simple beginnings."[62] By the end of 2001, the organization was suddenly insolvent and filed for bankruptcy after the company admitted to inflating reports of earnings. Following investigations, the Federal Energy Regulatory Commission conducted investigations and released the e-mail records of 158 employees from the company over a period of 3.5 years to help the public understand what happened in what is now considered "one of the United States' most disastrous business failures."[63]

The e-mail communications analyzed by researchers found Enron executives' communication networks "lit up" with activity. As interpersonal communication became more intense and spread through the networks, formal chains of command previously in place were ignored. Executives deferred to others in the e-mails, resulting in "groupthink" (explained in Chapter 10). For example, peers of equal rank deferred to their peers to preserve their status by protecting themselves from being seen as "overstepping one's place."[64]

Could anything have been done to prevent the Enron meltdown? Executives failed to (a) communicate appropriate values to create a moral climate, (b) maintain adequate communication to be informed regarding organizational operations, and (c) maintain openness to signs of problems.[65] The lessons from Enron seem clear: Leaders must communicate their expectations for integrity for their followers as well as their peers.

Discussion Questions

1. Explain how the grapevine had both negative and positive effects in this case.
2. Discuss this case in terms of the characteristics of groupthink from Chapter 10 (group rationalization, direct pressure, suppression, and illusion of unanimity). What role do you think communication plays in the emergence of groupthink?
3. Provide some guidelines that organizations can implement to address the process of negative communication through the grapevine in an organization.

Sources: Diesner, J., Frantz, T. L., & Carley, K. M. (2005). Communication networks from the Enron email corpus: "It's always about the people. Enron is no different." Computational & Mathematical Organization Theory, 11(3), 201–228; Fragale, A. R., Sumanth, J. J., Tiedens, L. Z., & Northcraft, G. B. (2012). Appeasing equals: Lateral deference in organizational communication. Administrative Science Quarterly, 57(3), 373–406; O'Connor, M. A. (2002). Enron board: The perils of groupthink. University of Cincinnati Law Review, 71, 1233–1471; Seeger, M. W., & Ulmer, R. R. (2003). Explaining Enron communication and responsible leadership. Management Communication Quarterly, 17(1), 58–84.

The Research in Action box on Enron indicates that much communication in organizations is through electronic means. What is also clear is that organizations have the right to monitor the communications of their employees, and most employees feel that this is acceptable as long as they are notified in advance.[66] So a leader must be careful regarding what is transmitted in e-mails. The next section discusses the emerging importance of understanding the implications of electronic communication in its various forms, including e-mail, texting, social media, and videoconferencing.

> **Critical Thinking Questions:** Do you agree that organizations have the right to monitor employee e-mails and other forms of electronic communication? Why or why not?

ELECTRONIC COMMUNICATION

Learning Objective 12.4: Discuss the advantages and disadvantages of electronic communication.

E-mail

E-mail has become a primary mode for communicating in organizations. Even employees who work in offices next to one another often communicate by e-mail rather than face-to-face! A study of face-to-face and e-mail communication in a Fortune 500 office equipment firm employing over 100,000 people employed interviews, questionnaires, and actual e-mails. Researchers found that more information is conveyed in e-mail than other communication mediums: People paid less attention to social cues that suppress information and were more uninhibited in e-mails.[67] Due to this inhibition, harassment may be more likely to occur through e-mail compared to face-to-face interactions. In some cases, this harassment includes comments that are sexual in nature.[68] Organizations should have formal policies for harassment that include "e-harassment."[69]

Leaders should avoid e-harassment. However, some e-mail offenses are more subtle. The Internet has evolved over time, and there are now rules for how to be polite in e-mail. This is termed **netiquette** (e-mail etiquette). Whether you are communicating with a prospective employer or to others you work with, it is sound advice to show good manners. Without knowing netiquette, you might annoy or even offend someone unintentionally. These rules developed as norms (unwritten rules) over time, so everyone may not be aware of them (refer to Chapter 10 for a discussion of the powerful impact of norms). According to one communication expert, "Netiquette rules are based on common sense and respect, but since email is so quick, we often forget that we are still using a form of written communication."[70] Ten rules for netiquette are shown in Table 12.2. You should be familiar with these rules to avoid social blunders in e-mail communication. The lack of visual cues may lead to difficulty interpreting the meaning of e-mail communication. Miscommunications of emotion occur in e-mail messages more than face-to-face communications, and this affects both the relationships and the information conveyed. These miscommunications affect both satisfaction and performance.[71]

Research on e-mail usage and performance is mixed. The amount of e-mail sent and received is positively related to job performance.[72] Yet some research suggests checking e-mail frequently may result in interruptions that affect the flow of work.[73] Frequently checking e-mail has been related to information overload and stress.[74,75] High levels of e-mail use in the workplace relate to avoidant decisional styles such as procrastination.[76] A study[77] surveyed 341 employees over 7 days immediately after they received an electronic communication from work after they had left work. Researchers focused on key elements of the communication message. They asked questions about the time it took to read and address the e-mail, whether the e-mail was negative, and how it affected their emotional reactions (i.e., anger or happiness). Results showed that such e-mails were related to stress. In other words, employees felt angry that the e-mail was taking away from their time with family and friends. Another study of knowledge workers found employees adapt to e-mail interruptions through new work strategies as they negotiate the constant connectivity of

Table 12.2	Netiquette Rules
1.	Imagine your message on a billboard. Anything you send can be forwarded, saved, and printed by people it was never intended for. Never send anything that will reflect badly on you or anyone else.
2.	Remember that company e-mails are company property. Emails sent from your workplace can be monitored by people besides the sender and reader, and are technically company property.
3.	Avoid offensive comments. Anything obscene, libelous, offensive or racist does not belong in a company e-mail, even as a joke.
4.	Keep your message cool. E-mail messages can easily be misinterpreted because we don't have the tone of voice or body language to gives us further cues. Using multiple explanation points, emoticons, and words in all capital letters can be interpreted as emotional language.
5.	Be careful about forwarding messages. If you aren't sure if the original sender would want to forward the message, don't do it.
6.	Don't expect an answer right away. E-mail messages may be delivered quickly, but your recipient may not read it right away.
7.	Don't sacrifice accuracy for efficiency. Don't send sloppy, unedited e-mail. Experts say that for every grammar mistake in an e-mail, there's an average of three spelling mistakes. While the odd spelling mistake is overlooked, when your readers have to break communication to decipher a word or message, at best, you'll look sloppy, if not illiterate. At worst, they may stop reading.
8.	Include the message thread. Keep the original message for a record of your conversation. However, when sending a new message to the same person, start a new thread with a new subject line.
9.	Don't type in all CAPS. It's perceived as YELLING. However, don't write with only small letters, as this is perceived as your being lazy, because it makes it more difficult for people to read.
10.	Write clear, organized messages, with a subject line that gives enough information for the reader to file it and find it later.

Source: Goldman, L. (2007). Netiquette rules—10 best rules for email etiquette. Retrieved from http://ezinearticles.com/?Netiquette-Rules—10-Best-Rules-for-Email-Etiquette&id=785177

communication media. For example, employees find ways to leverage the importance of e-mail for environmental monitoring by setting aside uninterrupted work time by shutting off e-mail alerts.[78] Managers need to be mindful of employees' needs to "unplug" from work. Table 12.3 provides some guidelines for electronic communication at work.

Table 12.3   Questions to Consider for After-Hours Electronic Communication

	Organization	Manager (sender)	Employee (receiver)
IS after-hours communication appropriate?	• Establish clear policy for after-hour electronic communications • Consider ramifications of a ban on after-hours electronic communications (positive and negative)	• Reflect on how frequently after-hours communications are sent • Decide whether this communication can wait • Think about whether there is potential for the communication to be misinterpreted	• Communicate with others, including supervisor, on preferences for after-hour communication • Set boundaries (e.g,. temporal) when possible to avoid being compulsively connected • Be purposeful in disconnecting from work as much as allowed by organizational policy and culture
How will after-hours communication be received?	• Train supervisors and employees on effective communication within messages and best mediums to communicate • Provide guidelines on use of communication features to maximize communication effectiveness such as salutations, capitalization, response time, and even emoticons • Assess group/departmental and profession/industry norms around after-hours communication	• Use subject line to clarify purpose of communication and whether it needs to be read after-hours • Frame communication as positively as possible • Be clear about whether action is required by other party, and, if so, when • Be mindful of message length; longer messages are more taxing on the receiver	• Do not overreact to (or "read too much into") electronic communication messages • Seek clarification if unsure about whether action is required
How can the potential negative impact of after-hours communication be minimized?	• Conduct formal on-boarding and regular training for employees on after-hours communications policies and expectations • Conduct periodic audits of electronic communications and establish system for addressing policy violations • Provide HR legal guidance to managers regarding inappropriate electronic communications	• Consider nature of relationship with receiver • Seek out and consider the preferences of the receiver • If after-hours action is required, be clear about expectations and why; consider compensation for additional work hours for exempt employees and ensure appropriate compensation for non-exempt employees	• Be mindful of negative emotional responses to after-hours communications and resolve them before reengaging in non-work activities • Consider impact on non-work partner and others who may be impacted by after-hours work communication

Source: Boswell, W. R., Olson-Buchanan, J. B., Butts, M. M., & Becker, W. J. (2016). Managing "after hours" electronic work communication. *Organizational Dynamics, 45*(4), 291–297, p. 294.

Text Messages

With the ubiquitous use of smartphones and other mobile devices, employees can now check e-mail and send text messages more frequently than ever—even during evenings and weekends. Text messages are far more likely to be sent from handheld mobile devices than from desktop or laptop computers. The Cellular Telecommunications & Internet Association reports that in 2015, there were over 1.9 trillion text messages sent in the United States (that's over 4 million per minute).[79] For business communications, it is important to follow the rules of grammar and capitalization and avoid abbreviations (*brb* for "be right back," for example). Due to their brevity, text messages will probably never replace e-mail as the primary mode for electronic business communications. Also, there are concerns about the privacy of text messages. Finally, general business expectations are that sending text messages at work is not a good use of time or is undesirable behavior.[80] However, a recent study conducted found that the use of smartphones during working hours to take short breaks increased employee well-being. The authors believe that the use of smartphones may have benefits, but too much time using social media may harm productivity.[81] *When* smartphones are used seems to be an important consideration. An interview study conducted found mobile text and e-mail usage patterns "are dangerous, distracting, anti-social and . . . infringe on work-life boundaries."[82] This research also found that many employees check e-mail during their commutes to and from work.

> Critical Thinking Questions: List the advantages and disadvantages of being able to access work e-mail from a mobile device.

Social Networking

It is estimated that more than 2 billion people worldwide are making use of social media platforms.[83] You are probably familiar with social networking sites such as Facebook, Twitter, LinkedIn, and Instagram. As discussed earlier in this chapter, being central to a communication network may result in more power. But social networking has caveats. It is important to keep in mind that if your social media site such as Facebook is public, your current or prospective employers might check it. It's best to assume that what you post may become public, so discretion matters. For example, employees have been fired for writing about their employer in inappropriate ways in blogs (web logs).[84] The First Amendment does not protect employees by giving them the right to say whatever they want about their job or employer, and many employers now have specific blogging policies, including Cisco, IBM, Intel, and Microsoft.[85]

Could your social media account cost you a job? A clever study[86] captured Facebook profiles of college students who were applying for full-time jobs and then asked job recruiters to evaluate them. Next, researchers followed up with applicants in their new jobs. The results are interesting. Recruiter ratings of applicants' Facebook information were unrelated to supervisor ratings of job performance, turnover intentions, and actual turnover. This research also uncovered evidence of potential discrimination because the Facebook ratings tended to favor female and White applicants. The overall results suggest that organizations should be very cautious about using social media information such as Facebook to assess job applicants.

On the other hand, blogs have become popular as a way for leaders to promote their organization. Twitter is a microblog that limits messages to 140 characters called *tweets*. A social media strategist noted that "smart brands use Twitter in meaningful ways, and most of them use their brand name as a way to make sure customers can find and recognize them."[87] The strategist cited Chevrolet, Wachovia, The Home Depot, Zappos.com, and the Red Cross as some of the most successful Twitter brands. However, a study of university business deans found that posting on Twitter was not related to rankings of the school. The findings of the study suggest speaking *at* stakeholders from a public microblog may not be the most effective way for leaders to connect with followers.[88]

> Critical Thinking Question: Discuss the advantages and disadvantages of using social media to promote an organization's public image.

Another challenge for organizations due to the use of the Internet at work is **cyberslacking**. Research has documented an increase in the use of the Internet for personal use during working hours. This may include using social media, shopping, looking at pornography, and looking for another job while at work: "When employees use workplace PCs for personal reasons, the immediate effect is a loss of productivity. . . . Time is an asset and a misuse of that asset is just as wrong as the misuse of any other asset."[89] One study found that 60% of companies surveyed had disciplined employees for inappropriate use of the Internet during work.[90] Communication researchers offer the following guidelines for the use of social media by employees:[91]

- Recognize the inevitable presence of social media to avoid asserting impractical social media guidelines.

- Dialogue with employees with regard to social media demonstrates mutual trust and reciprocates employee dedication.

- Employees can be the best ambassadors and can create substantial stakeholder engagement. Encourage them to use social media to communicate about the organization they work for in a positive way.

- Social media guidelines create opportunity for employers in reducing risk exposure as well as for employees as a provision of information and a guide for behavior.

- Social media guidelines benefit from cross functional and professional input.

- The use of social media has maximum impact when coupled with positive employee–organization relationships.

Despite the persistence of e-mail as the main communication mode for organizations, there still appears to be a need for face-to-face contact. Being able to see another person is important since face-to-face contact is much richer due to the ability to read nonverbal messages that accompany the words. Thus, videoconferencing is now an important communication mode for organizations.

Videoconferencing

Videoconferencing (or conducting virtual meetings) has long been an important communication mode at the workplace. Virtual meetings may be through the telephone only (a conference call) or they may be face-to-face. Skype has made it possible to speak to one or more persons face-to-face nearly everywhere in the world. Videoconferencing is advantageous because you are able to discern emotions through the tone of voice and/or facial expressions. Most large organizations depend on videoconferencing to coordinate work among employees who are not co-located. Accenture, a technology consulting firm, installed 35 videoconferencing rooms at its offices around the world. In 1 month alone, its consultants used virtual meetings to avoid 240 international trips and 120 domestic flights for an annual saving of millions of dollars and countless hours of tiring travel for its workers.[92] Thus, there are cost savings plus reductions in employee travel stress that result from the use of videoconferencing. Videoconferencing has not replaced face-to-face meetings at companies such as IBM, but rather, it has reduced the number of travel days. For example, Darryl Draper, the national manager of customer service training for Subaru of America, used to travel 4 days a week for 9 months of the year. Now, much of her training is done online.[93]

Today, for most organizations, having a social media plan is an essential business strategy.[94] The landscape for social media in business is a new one, but it is clear that on both a personal and business level, social media will significantly impact organizational behavior (OB) in the years ahead. The use of the Internet at work has brought both opportunities for organizations and new challenges. Some challenges stem from the nature of the communication process itself and apply to both electronic and face-to-face communication.

The use of e-mail and videoconferencing has made it possible to communicate with employees and customers anywhere in the world. For example, many videoconference calls take place in globally distributed teams, where employees from a number of different countries participate. Thus, cross-cultural communication is now more important than ever, and this applies to electronic as well as face-to-face interactions.

CROSS-CULTURAL COMMUNICATION

Learning Objective 12.5: Provide an example of how to communicate effectively across cultures.

An executive from India referred to women in an organization as "females," and U.S. women in the organization thought this was an odd way to refer to them and were offended. As this example illustrates, the ability to communicate effectively with those from other cultures is now an essential leadership skill.[95] There is a difference between cross-cultural and intercultural communication. Cross-cultural communication compares one culture to another, and intercultural communication focuses on the behavior of two individuals' communication patterns.[96] For example, a cross-cultural communication study of 124 managers from the United States and Russia found cultural values affected communication competence and performance in teams.[97] Another study[98] examined the differences in the ways that CEOs of *Fortune's* Global 500 corporations in China and the United States communicated with shareholders by analyzing the wording they used in the annual letter to shareholders. The results showed significant differences in communication styles: Chinese leaders tend to be more instrumental, elaborate, and competitive, while U.S. leaders are more emotional, succinct, and harmonious. An example of an intercultural study examined business meetings between British and Chinese managers and found that mismatches in expectations regarding silence during meetings resulted in feelings of "uncomfortable silence."[99] These cultural differences can result in misunderstandings, even if communication is in English. Translation adds yet another layer of complexity that may lead to misunderstandings. An example of miscommunication due to literal translation in intercultural communication follows:

> In translating an English financial report, a translator from Xian, by taking the surface value of words, translated terms like red gold, green sheet, and white goods as chijin (gold in red color), ludan (paper in green color), and baihuo (goods in white color) literally so that the clients had no idea what the expressions referred to.[100]

Differences in language are only part of the challenge of communication with a person from another culture. It has been noted that "language-related inefficiencies take numerous forms: loss of information, added work, loss of learning opportunities, and disruption of the collaborative process."[101] Misunderstandings often occur due to cultural value differences. For example, perceptions of time, individualism, risk, relationship orientation, and power may affect intercultural communication.[102,103] The next chapter discusses cultural values in more detail (Chapter 13).

There are nine levels of differences on which cross-cultural communication can falter: when to talk; what to say; pacing and pausing; listenership; intonation; prosody; formality; indirectness, and coherence.[104] There are several ways to address such cross-cultural communication challenges. For example, emotional intelligence (EI; discussed in Chapter 3) has been positively associated with communication competence.[105] Preparation for cross-cultural communication challenges and active listening also improves communication with persons from a culture other than one's own.[106] Bilingualism has been shown to improve communication efficiency—especially when both parties are at least partially fluent with respect to the language of the person they are working with.[107] Finally, training in cross-cultural communication is also effective.[108,109]

Another important aspect of cross-cultural communication is nonverbal communication. Gestures may not mean the same thing in different cultures. For example, in the United States, not making eye contact may be associated with not telling the truth. However, in certain Arabic cultures, it may be viewed as rude and intrusive to look into another person's eyes. Another example is how close you should be to a person. In Japan, people are comfortable at about 30.2 inches apart; in Venezuela, it is 32.2 inches; and in the United States, it is 35.4.[110] For example, someone from Venezuela could make someone from the United States very uncomfortable by unknowingly invading their space. As these examples illustrate, knowledge of the meaning of nonverbal communication is essential in preparing for an

BEST PRACTICES

You Just Don't Understand: Women and Men in Conversation

Women and men communicate differently at the workplace.[111] This is in part due to fundamental differences in why men and women communicate in the first place. Most men see themselves as individuals in a hierarchically structured world where they are trying to get ahead. In contrast, most women see themselves as bringing closeness, confirmation, and support to the world. Hence, when women display *connection,* which they think is positive (i.e., thanking their boss for being a mentor), a male mentor might interpret this as *lack of independence* or insecurity. When presented with a problem, men often respond with "I'll fix it for you." Men see themselves as problem solvers and focus on solutions. Women are more likely to show empathy when a problem is brought to their attention: "I support you and want you to know you're not alone." Thus, in leadership positions, a man might interpret a woman showing empathy and listening as not being an active problem solver.

Other differences in communication styles at work have been found.[112] For example, women apologize more often. Also, women tend to have a more indirect communication style compared to men. Another example is that men and women have different views about giving praise. Many women believe that if their boss does not praise them, their work is not acceptable. Women appear to need more feedback (men believe that if their boss says nothing, then everything is fine).

Leaders must remember that understanding gender differences in communication is a two-way street. Leaders need to understand that men and women have different communication styles. The need for feedback or showing empathy is not a sign of weakness. In fact, women may be well-suited for organizations interested in a more emotionally intelligent workplace.

Discussion Questions

1. Explain how you could use active listening (discussed earlier in this chapter) to more effectively communicate with someone of the opposite gender.
2. This research is based upon generalizations, and leaders must be careful not to stereotype employees. Give an example of a man who exhibits a more female pattern of indirect communication. Give an example of a woman who exhibits a direct communication style (these examples can be from your experience or from leaders in the media).

Source: Tannen, D. (1990). *You just don't understand: Women and men in conversation.* New York, NY: William Morrow; Tannen, D. (1994). *Talking from 9 to 5: How women's and men's conversational styles affect who gets heard, who gets credit, and what gets done at work.* New York, NY: Simon & Schuster.

interaction with a person from another culture or an expatriate assignment (expatriation is discussed in more detail in the next chapter).

Nonverbal communication is important for all forms of face-to-face and telephone conversation. Even on the telephone, nonverbal communication, such as a sigh or grunt, will be interpreted by the receiver and may change the intended meaning of the message. People use emoticons (i.e., faces with emotional expressions) in their text messages to convey nonverbal sentiments. Next, we discuss the evidence on nonverbal communication in organizations.

NONVERBAL COMMUNICATION

Learning Objective 12.6: Summarize the significance of the percentages of verbal and nonverbal face-to-face communication.

Nonverbal communication is "the sending and receiving of thoughts and feelings via nonverbal behavior."[113] Nonverbal communication includes facial expressions, posture, gestures, and tone of voice. As shown in Figure 12.3, when it comes to face-to-face communication, approximately 7% of a person's understanding of others is attributed to words, whereas 38% is attributed to verbal tone and 55% is attributed to facial expressions.[114] The meaning of a message can even be negated by a facial expression or a person rolling their eyes. For example, if a person says, "I love my accounting class" and rolls their eyes, it means the opposite of what they are saying. If a verbal message contradicts a nonverbal message, the nonverbal message will carry the meaning. On the other hand, nonverbal messages can reinforce a verbal message.

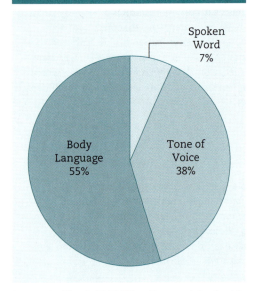

Figure 12.3 Elements of Face-to-Face Communication

Spoken Word 7%

Body Language 55%

Tone of Voice 38%

Sources: Ambler, G. (2013). When it comes to leadership everything communicates. Retrieved from http://www.georgeambler.com/when-it-comes-to-leadership-everything-communicates; Mehrabian, A. (1981). *Silent messages* (2nd ed.). Belmont, CA: Wadsworth.

For example, a leader can raise their voice slightly while speaking to emphasize a point they are making to the team. Leaders are observed constantly, and every action is analyzed by others.[115] So it's important to pay attention to nonverbal as well as verbal communication. Think of it this way: "Leaders are never *not* communicating. As a result, increasing their awareness of nonverbal communication may be a key factor in improving their communication skills and ultimately helping them to become better leaders."[116] Nonverbal communication serves the following functions in organizations.[117]

1. **Display of personal attributes.** Nonverbal communication reveals information about a person's personality, intentions, and attitudes. In other words, people "give off signals" to what they are really thinking and feeling.[118]

2. **Establishment of dominance and hierarchy.** Nonverbal cues of power are responded to with nonverbal cues that signify submission.[119] Other nonverbal behaviors associated with power include talking time and interruption. In addition to "power posing" (recall this research covered in Chapter 7), eye contact, tone of voice, and facial expressions are used to signal who is in control in organizations.

3. **Promotion of social functioning.** Beyond influencing others via dominance and power cues, followership and social coordination can be achieved via nonverbal displays of competence, prestige, and persuasion.

For example, people are more likely to follow those who exhibit charisma, and nonverbal behaviors are an effective tool in communicating these elements in charismatic leaders. For example, conveying passion through body language, such as animated body gestures and voice and message-appropriate expressions, contributes to a charismatic leader's effectiveness.[120]

4. **Fostering high-quality relationships.** Nonverbal behaviors such as eye contact and facial expressions increase the development of rapport between employees. Nonverbal messages that enhance coordination behaviors, such as mimicking another person's expressions, can also create affiliation and trust.[121] A study of leaders and their direct reports found that supervisors' nonverbal kinesics (e.g., nodding of the head appropriately) led to greater relational identification with the leader.[122]

5. **Display of emotions.** An employee's emotional displays influence the emotional experiences of other employees due to the emotional contagion process (discussed in Chapter 3). Emotions are manifested via facial expressions, bodily gestures, and tone of voice, which are processed by others. For example, authentic smiles as compared to inauthentic smiles lead to greater positive customer emotional reactions and good customer–employee rapport, which influence customer satisfaction.[123]

To this point, we have been discussing processes of communication where information is shared between and/or among employees in organizations. However, what happens when there is no communication? In other words, what are the consequences when employees remain silent? The next section summarizes the evidence on organizational silence and its implications for leadership.

SILENCE

Learning Objective 12.7: Explain why employees remain silent or withhold information and how to address this.

Employee silence is the intentional withholding of meaningful information from management, which includes asking questions, expressing concerns, and offering suggestions.[124] A diary study[125] conducted with professionals from diverse organizations found that employees with negative affect were more likely to be silent when they also had high levels of rumination. In other words, employees who have negative emotions and also worry about their job situation are more likely to withhold information. This effect was even stronger for employees whose jobs had high demands for problem solving. Another study found that employees' perceptions of procedural justice generated positive emotions, and thus, they were less likely to remain silent.[126]

Climates of organizational silence emerge due to organizational structures or policies, managerial practices, and degree of demographic dissimilarity between employees and top managers.[127] A sample of 461 MBAs and managers were asked if they had intentionally remained silent about an issue at work, and 95% stated that they had.[128] The types of incidents reported in the study are shown in Table 12.4. The most common type of silence incident was unfair treatment (21%). Given recent attention to ethics at the workplace, it is disturbing that the second most common silence incident was someone else behaving unethically (17.6%). Concerns about a coworker's competence or performance (16.8%) and operational process concerns and/or ideas for improvement (13.3%) were other areas where employees withheld information.

Withholding information by remaining silent is a barrier to organizational change and compromises the ability to hear different points of view on important organizational matters.[129] Organizational silence can have detrimental effects on decision making by blocking

> Critical Thinking Question: What are the potential costs of organizational silence? Give an example where an employee withholding information damages the performance of an organization.

Table 12.4	Types of Incidents to Which Respondents Reported Remaining Silent
Experienced unfair treatment	21.0%
Someone else behaving unethically	17.6%
Concerns about a coworker's competence or performance	16.8%
Operational process concern and/or idea for improvement	13.3%
Disagreement or concerns with company policies or decisions	6.5%
Personal performance issue	6.2%
Concerns about supervisor or management competence	6.0%
Someone else being treated unfairly	3.5%
Personal career issue or concern	1.9%
Unclear	7.2%

Source: Brinsfield, C. T. (2013). Employee silence motives: Investigation of dimensionality and development of measures. *Journal of Organizational Behavior, 34*(5), 671–697. p. 675.

alternative views, negative feedback, and accurate information.[130] Managerial secrecy combined with employee silence may combine to enable corruption.[131] Remaining silent has negative consequences for employees as well. Research has shown silence is negatively related to job satisfaction and organizational commitment.[132] In sum, organizational silence has numerous negative outcomes for both employees and the organization.

Can leaders take actions to reduce silence? Research on employee voice suggests formalized employee involvement and a participative climate both encourage employees to provide opinions, which reduce organizational silence.[133,134] For example, a study of police officers found building trust with higher-level managers and building communication bridges reduced officer silence.[135] Also, ethical leadership supports employees and encourages them be more confident to speak up in a constructive way.[136]

As the preceding discussion indicates, leaders have an influence on the degree to which employees voice their concerns and suggestions up the organizational hierarchy. There are additional ways that theories of communication inform leadership, and the next section addresses the power of framing, which is essential for leaders in communication with followers and others.

LEADERSHIP IMPLICATIONS: THE MANAGEMENT OF MEANING

In an influential *Harvard Business Review* article, Deborah Tannen stated, "Talk is the lifeblood of managerial work."[137] Without a doubt, spoken communication (i.e., face-to-face, phone, or videoconferencing) is a powerful way to influence others as a leader. But we have also learned in this chapter that "talk" does not only mean verbal face-to-face conversation but may also mean electronic communication and the powerful influence of nonverbal behavior. The knowledge and skills discussed in this chapter are essential for a leader to be effective. This is because leaders manage meaning for their followers. Leaders create a frame of reference for employees, particularly during times of organizational change.[138] Leadership scholar and former president of the University of Cincinnati Warren Bennis writes: "To make dreams apparent to others, and to align people with them, leaders must communicate their vision. Communication and alignment work together."[139] Regardless of the communication channel chosen (i.e., verbal, nonverbal, face-to-face, one-on-one, or formal presentations), leaders interpret what is happening in the organization and what it means for employees. Strategic leadership is the creation and maintenance of organizational systems that result in organized action toward goals.[140]

Communication scholars define leadership in terms of communication: "Leadership is human (symbolic) communication that modifies the attitudes and behaviors of others in order to meet shared group goals and needs."[141] This perspective implies that a failure to communicate is a failure in leadership.

Leaders, thus, frame organizational events. *Framing* is defined as:

the ability to shape the meaning of a subject, to judge its character and significance. To hold the frame of a subject is to choose one particular meaning (or set of meanings) over another. When we share our frames with others (the process of framing), we manage meaning because we assert that our interpretations should be taken as real over other possible interpretations.[142]

In other words, leaders manage meaning by using talk to get followers to act.[143] To do so, leaders may use metaphors, jargon, and stories in their communications. We are all familiar with "spin" during political campaigns. This is also employed by leaders to reframe a negative event that has occurred.[144] Leaders can't always control what happens in their environments or within their organizations, but they can control how events are interpreted.[145] Here are five communication guidelines for leaders to follow in the management of meaning:[146]

- Leaders "cannot not communicate."[147] While discussions of leadership communication typically focus on the creation and delivery of intentional, verbal messages with particular ends in mind, a leader's nonverbal behavior will be interpreted as well. Even not communicating is interpreted. For example, a leader not showing up at a meeting communicates that the meeting isn't important.

- Leadership communication is a process that involves the *negotiation* of meaning rather than the *transmission* of meaning. Leaders interpret events for followers and attach meaning to them.

- Communication creates a history that shapes and guides future influence efforts. The flow of messages, along with their interpretations, builds over time. This shapes current meanings and creates the foundation for future communications. The history provides a backdrop and context for the communications that follow.

- All leadership communication is intercultural. Leadership communication is essentially an intercultural phenomenon in which one's own personal experiences, language patterns, religion, family history, work history, values, and beliefs provide a unique set of cultural filters through which all messages flow and are interpreted.

- Leadership communication always has both content and relational consequences. What one says and does influences both the content of the messages sent and received, and the leader–follower relationship that is being formed through communication. In other words, when leaders communicate, it changes their relationships with their followers.

The creation of meaning applies to strategic leadership. However, the relationship with the boss also matters; research has shown that effective communication from leaders relates to follower satisfaction and motivation.[148] The quality of leader–member exchange (LMX; discussed in Chapter 6) strongly influences subordinates' satisfaction with personal feedback and supervisory communication. Good relationships with followers also positively influence team and organizational communication. One study concludes "the quality of LMX has a 'spillover' or 'ripple' effect on perceptions of communication satisfaction in other forms of communication interaction."[149] Thus, the context of a positive working relationship affects perceptions of communication and the meaning that is attached to them.

In sum, leaders influence followers through effective communication that helps them make sense of organizational events. They also use effective communication to give followers a sense of meaning in their work, which motivates them. In this chapter, the communication process has been presented, followed by discussion of barriers to effective communication, including communication apprehension. Communication in organizations flows in all directions through networks, including the grapevine. Finally, new forms of communication have been covered, including the emergence and power of electronic communication and social media. All communication is filtered by culture, and cross-cultural and intercultural communication has been discussed. Finally, organizational silence has been addressed since in some cases employees withhold information, which generally has negative consequences. Communication is fundamental to leadership since leaders are constantly communicating at all organizational levels within their organizations and to their constituents outside of it.

 **edge.sagepub.com/scandura2e**

Want a better grade? Go to **edge.sagepub.com/scandura2e** for the tools you need to sharpen your study skills.

KEY TERMS

active listening, 309
all-channel (or star) network, 311
boundary spanners, 312
chain network, 311
circle network, 311
communication apprehension
   (CA), 308
cross-cultural communication, 320
cyberslacking, 319

downward communication, 311
e-harassment, 315
external communication, 312
grapevine, 313
intercultural
   communication, 320
internal communication, 312
lateral communication, 311
netiquette, 316

noise, 308
nonverbal communication, 322
organizational communication, 307
Shannon–Weaver model of
   communication, 307
upward communication, 313
wheel network, 311
Y-pattern network, 311

TOOLKIT ACTIVITY 12.1: Active Listening Exercise

Asking about what causes negative emotions can provide much information about someone's values, beliefs, and needs. By asking questions, we increase our understanding. Increased understanding leads to compassion, empathy, and a sense of connection with others.

In this exercise, you will partner with another classmate. Ask them to tell you about a setback in their life that they felt strongly about. Listen for feelings, values, and beliefs. Make notes using the form in this activity.

Focus on the feelings and the causes of them, not the details of the story. Try to get to the underlying thoughts below the emotions. While listening, remember not to give advice or try to solve the person's problems.

How did this person feel (name at least five feelings)?

What does this person value?

What needs were not met?

What are some of the person's beliefs?

After you have noted the person's values, needs, and beliefs, share them with the person. Ask the person to circle on a scale from 1 to 10 how accurate you were in identifying them using the following scale.

	Not at all accurate			Moderately accurate				Extremely accurate		
Values	1	2	3	4	5	6	7	8	9	10
Needs	1	2	3	4	5	6	7	8	9	10
Beliefs	1	2	3	4	5	6	7	8	9	10

If time permits, switch roles and let the other person practice active listening.

Discussion Questions

1. Did you feel an increased level of empathy with the person as you were listening to them describe their experience? In other words, could you put yourself "in their shoes" and see the situation the way they did?

2. Was it difficult just to listen and not try to give advice? Why or why not?

3. How accurate were you in identifying the person's values, needs, and beliefs? Were you surprised at your feedback?

4. If you were the person describing the setback in your life, how did it feel to be listened to?

5. If you were the person describing the setback, what did the listener do that helped you continue speaking? Provide them with this feedback.

CASE STUDY 12.1: What's App-ening?

In order to better communicate and engage with employees, organizations are taking advantage of technology. What was once shared by posters, flyers, and word of mouth is now spread through company e-mails or notices on the company website. However, to Carla Jennison, head of human resources (HR) at the southern division of Hospital Care Corporation (HCC), that kind of communication has not been as effective as she would have liked. For instance, HCC rolled out a wellness program 4 months ago and let employees know through an e-mail. There have only been a few dozen sign-ups among several thousand employees at 12 different hospitals. However, when surveyed at trainings, only one or two participants had heard of the program. So Carla has decided that HCC definitely needs a new way to communicate with its employees.

Carla thinks that the problem may be that most hospital personnel don't have time to check e-mail on their shift and that the website is built more for other aspects of HR—like job applications or completing forms. In order to find a different solution, she begins looking into alternatives. After exploring recommendations and products both online and at the Society of Human Resource Management conference, Carla has narrowed it down to two options. The first comes from the company Straight to Text, which will send texts to employees' cell phones that let them know about things going on at HCC and where to go from there. It works similar to the emergency alert system that the hospital uses to notify employees of emergencies like bad weather or Amber Alerts. However, the one most intriguing to her was to get a cell phone app for employees that lets them learn about new benefits, receive benefit-related news, and even manage and make changes to their benefits from the company Katora Inc. For those employees that do not have phones that use apps or tablets, there is also a web-based option. After getting demos of each product and pricing the different package options, Carla decides to go with Katora's app for communicating with HCC's employees.

The app is rolled out over the next 6 months at the 12 different hospitals during different trainings and events. In order to get people to install the app, she uses three tactics: (1) require training attendees to log into the app at the training sessions in order to get credit for their training; (2) to log into the app to make an appointment to get service or help at the local HR office, including making adjustments to their benefits; and (3) new hires have to download it and log in to set up their benefit communication preferences at hire. She also puts the information in companywide e-mails and on the hospital websites under the employee information page. Carla figures that these methods should get the app out to employees, and from there, word of mouth can help drive employees to install the app and use it.

It has been a year since HCC's Southern Division started using Katora's employee benefits app. So far, about 87% of all employees have adopted the app and use it to get news and at least partially manage their benefits. It has been successful because it is easy and convenient to use, can be used when the employee has time either at work or off the clock, and has the right functionality to get the employees and HCC HR what it needs. In fact, it has been successful enough that the company is planning to extend the use of the app nationwide. While it has worked well for communicating information about benefits, Carla's bosses are now looking for something more. With the changes that have happened in health care over the last decade, it is more important to come up with ideas on how to be more competitive. Employees who work on the frontlines are a great resource in knowing what is going wrong, what is going right, and what can be done better. However, getting employees' input on these issues is currently time consuming and inefficient. Carla's boss, Devon, has asked her to look into other apps to see if there are any that might work for what they need.

Carla begins figuring out the criteria to evaluate the apps. Working with her boss and with her direct reports, she has determined that the app will need to have survey capability to poll employees about different ideas the company has, that allows written feedback to these surveys, that would integrate with several different systems like the facilities management system so repair requests could be input directly and pictures attached if needed, and would have a way for employees to provide anonymous feedback about others and themselves, and allow them to see and respond to anonymous feedback from supervisors, coworkers, and patients. She also creates a list of features and functions that would be nice for the app to have but could be passed on if the costs grew too high. After some research, Carla has found several companies that might have what the company needs. Now it is time to schedule demos and even see if she could trial the different apps on a larger scale.

Discussion Questions

1. What kind of communication would you say these apps would be?

2. What problems do you see with using an app for upward communication? For using an app for formal organization communication?

3. Do you have any concerns with the employees using their own cell phones or tablets to run the company apps? Why or why not?

4. What do you think a company should look for in terms of functionality for employee engagement and two-way communication? Explain your thoughts.

Source: This case is based upon actual companies; however, all names are fictitious.

SELF-ASSESSMENT 12.1: Quality of Communication Experience

This self-assessment exercise provides feedback on how you feel about communication with another person. There are no right or wrong answers, and this is not a test. You don't have to share your results with others unless you wish to do so.

Part I. Taking the Assessment

You will be presented with some questions representing how you feel about your communication with another person. Circle the response that indicates your agreement with each of the following statements.

Choose a person to rate that you communicate with on a regular basis. This should be a person that you communicate with at least five times during a typical week. Then think of a specific time when you communicated with them about something that was important to you for at least 30 minutes. For example, you could select a person that you are working with on a team project for a class. Write their first name or initials here: _____.

Statements	Strongly Disagree	Disagree	Neutral	Agree	Strongly Agree
1. I understood what the other side was saying.	1	2	3	4	5
2. I understood what was important to the other side.	1	2	3	4	5
3. We clarified the meaning if there was a confusion of the messages exchanged.	1	2	3	4	5
4. I think the other side understood me clearly.	1	2	3	4	5
5. The messages exchanged were easy to understand.	1	2	3	4	5
6. The other side responded to my questions and requests quickly during the interaction.	1	2	3	4	5
7. The conversation ran smoothly without any uncomfortable silent moments, or I did not notice any uncomfortable silent moments.	1	2	3	4	5
8. I was willing to listen to the other side's perspectives.	1	2	3	4	5
9. When the other side raised questions or concerns, I tried to address them immediately.	1	2	3	4	5

	Strongly Agree	Agree	Neutral	Disagree	Strongly Disagree
10. One or both of us kept silent from time to time.	1	2	3	4	5
11. I was nervous talking to the other side.	1	2	3	4	5

	Strongly Disagree	Disagree	Neutral	Agree	Strongly Agree
12. I felt the other side trusted me.	1	2	3	4	5
13. I felt the other side was trustworthy.	1	2	3	4	5
14. I felt comfortable interacting with the other side.	1	2	3	4	5
15. The other side seemed comfortable talking with me.	1	2	3	4	5

Part II. Scoring Instructions

Add the numbers you circled in each of the columns to derive your scores for the quality of communication experience.

Clarity	Responsiveness	Comfort
1. _____	6. _____	11. _____
2. _____	7. _____	12. _____
3. _____	8. _____	13. _____
4. _____	9. _____	14. _____
5. _____	10. _____	15. _____
Totals _____	_____	_____

Interpretation

Clarity—the degree of comprehension of the meaning being communicated. Meaning encompasses not only factual information but also ideas, emotions, and values conveyed through symbols and actions. Scores can range from 5 to 25. In general, scores from 5 to 14 are lower, and scores above 15 are higher.

Responsiveness—refers to how well the other party's communications meet expectations regarding how they react to you. Scores can range from 5 to 25. In general, scores from 5 to 14 are lower, and scores above 15 are higher.

Comfort—experienced by communicators, it reflects the affective aspect of communication, and it is the ease and pleasantness felt when interacting with the other person. Scores can range from 5 to 25. In general, scores from 5 to 14 are lower, and scores above 15 are higher.

Discussion Questions

1. Which of the dimensions of the Quality of Communication Experience was the highest one for you? Which was the lowest? Explain why you think this was the case based upon your interaction with the person you chose to complete the assessment about.

2. Do you think your results would differ if you had chosen another person? Explain how.

3. How could you use the results of this assessment to provide feedback to the person you chose to complete the assessment about? How can you use this information to improve your communication with them?

Source: Liu, L.A., Chua, C. H., & Stahl, G. (2010). Quality of communication experience: Definition, measurement, and implications for intercultural negotiations. *Journal of Applied Psychology, 95*(3), 469–487.

CHAPTER THIRTEEN

DIVERSITY AND CROSS-CULTURAL ADJUSTMENTS

DIVERSITY: A KEY WORKFORCE TREND

The term *diversity* was first used in the early 1990s following the passage of U.S. equal employment opportunity laws protecting certain classes of employees based upon their sex, race, and ethnicity.[1] Embracing diversity is now considered a competitive advantage, and organizations should include the following in their planning: cost, attraction of human resources, marketing success, creativity and innovation, problem-solving quality, and organizational flexibility.[2] These six dimensions of business performance are directly impacted by the management of diversity. Research evidence supports the argument that diversity increases performance and organizations that embrace diversity build more inclusive work environments. In fact, ignoring diversity may result in an apathetic or even resistant workforce. Also, by not allowing individuals to express their differences, creativity may be suppressed.

In today's multicultural and multinational context, leaders regularly interact with those whose assumptions about work behavior differ from their own. Global diversity is identified as a key workforce trend in a *Human Capital Trends* report:

> In the midst of ongoing global expansion and a worldwide shortage of critical talent, companies are stepping up efforts— at very different speeds and levels of investment—to recruit and retain a workforce diverse in both demographics and ideas.[3]

Being able to effectively engage diverse employees is now a necessary leadership skill. For example, unsuccessful cross-cultural interaction leads to "failed integration that can seriously affect the realization of desired organizational outcomes such as successful technology transfer, knowledge-sharing, and the general realization of global growth."[4]

Learning Objectives

After studying this chapter, you should be able to do the following:

13.1: Compare and contrast surface-level and deep-level diversity.

13.2: Name the characteristics of four generations at work, and describe how millennials will affect organizations.

13.3: Explain why culture is important for understanding organizational behavior (OB).

13.4: Summarize the key findings from the Global Leadership and Organizational Behavior Effectiveness (GLOBE) project international study of leadership effectiveness.

13.5: Discuss the importance of developing global leaders and the impact this has on an organization.

13.6: Devise a plan for coping with the symptoms of culture shock.

13.7: Explain the steps for an expatriate to take when adjusting to a cross-cultural assignment.

Get the edge on your studies at **edge.sagepub.com/scandura2e**

- Take the chapter quiz
- Review key terms with eFlashcards
- Explore multimedia resources, SAGE readings, and more!

One aspect of diversity is national culture. Culture is so ubiquitous that we rarely think about it until we travel to another country. Then it becomes obvious that our own culture influences the way we think because we are struck by the fact that people from other cultures dress, think, and behave differently than we do. Some characterize the French as rude for their abrupt attitudes toward Americans who are loud in restaurants. However, another explanation is that the physical space in many older French restaurants is smaller and customers are closer to one another. Many French people are brought up to be quiet in public spaces because they want to focus on the conversations of the people they are with and not everyone else in the restaurant. This preference is passed down from their grandparents and parents, and they don't question why it is not appropriate to be boisterous in places for intimate dining.

Fortunately, there has been a lot of research on diversity and how it influences the work environment. There are frameworks that guide the cross-cultural adjustment process, including adjustment for leaders on expatriate assignments. Thus, embracing diversity is important to being an effective leader both at home as well as abroad given the changing landscape of business. Multinational corporations are common, and many products are built either partly or entirely with contributions from other countries. Products and services are marketed abroad. The best-selling book *The World Is Flat* describes a new world where organizations are becoming global villages with contributors from anywhere in the world due to advances in technology and the Internet.[5] For example, many organizations employ workers in other countries to staff call centers. Your lab results may be read by a technician in Australia and sent back to your doctor while she is sleeping in the United States, and they will be waiting for her electronically at 6:00 a.m. As discussed in Chapter 12, multinational corporations require work to be geographically dispersed, and team members communicate with one another only through e-mail or teleconference meetings. With these global changes in work, the effective leader will be equipped with a sound understanding of culture, cultural differences, and how to adjust when other cultural values are encountered. This chapter covers research and practical applications of diversity, national culture, cross-cultural organizational behavior (OB), and the process of cross-cultural adjustment. Embracing diversity and leading across cultures has become an essential skill set in today's working world. Case Study 13.1 provides an example of how a multinational company, IBM, takes a proactive approach to managing their diverse workforce.

DIVERSITY

Learning Objective 13.1: Compare and contrast surface-level and deep-level diversity.

There are a number of challenges and values to having a diverse workforce. In the workplace, diversity is commonly referred to as "differences between individuals at work on any attribute that may evoke the perception that the other person is different from the self."[6] These differences pose a challenge for leaders who must unite their followers in the pursuit of common goals. One scholar notes that "Leadership is impossible outside of a community defined by shared values and vision."[7] Diversity poses some unique challenges for OB. On the one hand, the leader must articulate a shared vision that all followers can embrace (as we learned in Chapter 6). On the other hand, the leader must respect the differences of all followers.

We first must acknowledge the powerful North American culture largely rooted in a sense of independence. Leaders need to create a shared culture that all followers can embrace regardless of such attributes as gender, race or ethnicity, age, sexual orientation, or disability status. However, leaders must also show discretion when balancing the needs of the organization with the needs of employees. For example, members of some Latin American cultures are somewhat casual with respect to being on time. Leaders must ask themselves how it will affect their team if they allow some workers to habitually show up late for work. Leaders must enforce organizational policies but do so in a respectful way. They need to remember that human beings want to belong and have a shared sense of values in social groups. Hence, one of the leader's top goals is to integrate individuals with the organization's culture.

Organizational cultures can be powerful forces (you will learn more about this in Chapter 14), but for now, note that strong cultures can bind individuals together—even those with diverse backgrounds. Leaders may be able to build consensus among diverse followers by relating to values held in common by the majority of people in the world (e.g., justice or personal happiness). It has become part of the leader's job to help diverse employees (particularly recent immigrants) adjust to the job and the organization's culture. Leading diverse followers is thus a process of adjustment, taking into account demographic differences as well as values and reactions to work. But diversity goes beyond what can be seen and also includes deeper attitudes, values, and work habits, which are not visible.

Surface-Level and Deep-Level Diversity

The demographic attributes we typically think of when we think of "diversity" are called **surface-level diversity** because they are visible to observers. Surface-level diversity is defined as "differences among group members in overt, biological characteristics that are typically reflected in physical features."[8] A review of the research on surface-level diversity concluded that relationships of sex, race, and age had mixed results in the prediction of job performance and work attitude—that is, sometimes these demographic variables were related to performance and sometimes they were not. To fully understand diversity, we need to also consider **deep-level diversity**, which is defined as "differences among members' attitudes, beliefs, and values."[9] More recent research shows that prior studies that had predicted poor outcomes when groups were diverse should be interpreted with caution. This is because when deep-level diversity is considered, diversity may actually contribute positively to work group functioning and effectiveness. In other words, the values and attitudes of organizational members may matter more than surface characteristics. Another interesting diversity attribute is age; different generations have been shown by research to have different underlying mind-sets, and this may be a source of conflict at the workplace.

GENERATIONS AT THE WORKPLACE

Learning Objective 13.2: Name the characteristics of four generations at work, and describe how millennials will affect organizations.

Age is a demographic or surface-level diversity variable, but there are clear values and attitudes that have been shown to be related to what generation an employee belongs to. Much has been written about generations interacting at the workplace, and this poses some challenges for the leader. Generational differences affect everything, including recruiting, building teams, dealing with change, motivating, managing, and productivity.[10] Table 13.1 shows the four generations now at the workplace, their characteristics, career goals, and work–life balance attitudes. The **traditionalists** were born between 1900 and 1945 and are retiring or have passed on. However, trends indicate that people are retiring later than 65, so it can be expected that many will remain in the workforce for some time since retirement plans were dented by the great recession of 2007 to 2009. The **boomers** were born between 1946 and 1964 and are called this due to the baby boom that occurred after World War II (also called the "me" generation or yuppies for *young upwardly mobile professionals*). They had significant influence throughout their lives and brought about the social changes experienced in the 1960s. The **generation Xers**, or **gen Xers**, were born between 1965 and 1980 and are sometimes referred

Table 13.1 Four Generations at the Workplace

Generation	Traditionalists	Boomers	Gen Xers	Millennials
Birth Years	1900–1945	1946–1964	1965–1980	1981–1999
Current Ages	70+	51–69	35–50	16–34
Also known as...	Veterans WW II Generation The Silent Generation	Baby boomers 77 million	Xers 44 million Baby busters Post-boomers	Nexters Generation Y Nintendo Generation
On the Job	"Build a legacy" A lifetime career with one company	"Build a stellar career" Excel in career	"Build a portable career" A repertoire of skill, experience	"Build parallel careers" Several jobs simultaneously
Career Goals	Security and fair rewards Part-time schedule	Monetary gains and career progression Flexibility	Immediate rewards and career portability	Parallel careers and choice
Work/Life	Support me in maintaining balance.	Help me balance everyone else and find myself.	Give me balance now, not when I'm 65.	Work isn't everything. I need flexibility to balance all my activities.

Source: Adapted from Zemke, R., Raines, C., & Filipczak, B. (2000). *Generations at work: Managing the clash of Veterans, Boomers, Xers, and Nexters in your workplace.* New York, NY: American Management Association.

to as the "baby busters" or "latchkey kids" because many of them had to let themselves into their homes after school because their parents were both at work. Now the **millennials** are entering the workforce and having a clear impact on organizations (and they are the largest group in the general population). They were born between 1981 and 1999 and look for flexibility and choice. Due to their numbers and impact, employers need to transition "from a 'boomer-centric' workplace to a 'millennial-centric' workplace."[11]

Consider the following situations:

- At annual appraisal time, a manager from the traditionalist generation gives out a nice bonus for a project well done. The generation X employee is ungrateful and says, "Why didn't I get this 6 months ago, when the project was completed?" Gen X wants instant gratification, whereas a person in the traditionalist generation is happy to get money anytime. The solution here may be for the company to explore reward plans geared to the different generations, or things like monetary rewards and recognition given at the time when it is earned.

- A generation X manager tells a boomer he has been working too hard and should take time off to take the family on vacation. Instead of saying thanks, the boomer replies, "I work to get ahead, to get a promotion, not for a vacation." The next time that situation comes up, the manager might elect to give this particular employee a bonus rather than suggest a vacation.[12]

As these scenarios illustrate, the interactions of the different generations pose challenges for boomers, gen X, and millennials alike. As shown in Table 13.1, the four generations have different attitudes about work and the balance between work and home life. Gen X employees want portable skills that they can take with them to their next job. The boomers strive for monetary gain and mobility, whereas the millennial generation doesn't view work as the be-all and end-all of their existence. They are the children of the boomers, and most grew up more affluently than other generations. This generation is more interested in career options and choice rather than employment with one organization long term. There are important differences across the generations in the workforce. It's important to understand your own generation and how you fit in with others at the workplace. Toolkit Activity 13.1 provides you with an opportunity to reflect on your generation and how this may influence your approach to your work and career.

The Millennials

A recent study[13] found that millennials are the only generational group that does not conceptually link organizational commitment with workplace culture. Millennials think about work differently than members of the other generations, and managers need to understand their attitudes toward duty, drive, and reward. For example, most millennials received trophies for participation in high school sports, even if they didn't win.[14] An in-depth study of the personalities of millennials administered personality inventories online to more than 1,000 millennials (up to 29 years old) and more than 3,000 persons from other generations (above 29 years old). The results indicated that millennials are motivated by recognition, public acknowledgment, instant and frequent positive feedback, and instant gratification. A survey of undergraduates found that millennials want praise when they do a good job and rewards for hard work on occasion. They show a clear communication preference for one-on-one honest feedback from their bosses. They also enjoy communicating with coworkers and feel that they can learn from them.[15]

Millennials also state that they need to balance their personal and professional lives, and have a comfortable work environment. They want flexible work schedules; however, they resent having to stay at work after hours. In particular, they are motivated by work in a nonconformist environment without strict rules and traditional work approaches. They tend to challenge the status quo and they will not be patient to keep the same job many years.[16] Millennials are the first wave of the digital generation born into the high levels of technology. They are far more qualified in digital knowledge than the generations that preceded them, and they quickly acquire new information technology. They have wide networks of friends and nurture these relationships using social media platforms.[17]

Managers from other generations are sometimes surprised at the work habits of millennials. For example, a survey found that during interviews, millennials asked questions such as: "Do I have to show up every day for work?" "Do you drug test—*often?*" and "Can my *mom* call you about the benefits package?"[18] Despite the discomfort with these questions that may reflect underlying attitudes toward work, other generations can't simply avoid millennials; there are an estimated 40 million in the workforce today. The consulting firm that conducted this survey offers the following advice:

- **Make training and mentoring a priority.** Millennials respond to one-on-one attention.

- **Set clear objectives—from the start—with the different generations and diversity at the workplace.** Don't assume that millennials understand the ground rules.

- **Consider the medium.** Millennials grew up on the Internet and respond to YouTube, TED Talks, and blogs. They are used to accessing information in different ways though Google searches and Wikis, for example.

- **Provide feedback early and often.** Build it into the job for millennials. Feedback is important to all generations, but millennials grew up experiencing more from parents and online learning platforms.

- **Pause before reacting.** Think through your response to what might appear to be inappropriate workplace behavior, and choose your response carefully.

Building relationships to enhance effectiveness is a two-way street. If you are a millennial, organizational consultant Jeanne Meister offers the following advice:

- **Don't "friend" your boss on Facebook or other social media platforms.**

- **Remember that social media is forever**. Don't criticize your boss or employer on social media.

- **Keep your need to text in check.** You are used to sending as many as 1,500 text messages a month, but prior generations are not.

- **Become an expert on your generation**. Your perspective is valued, so offer your ideas on how to design a product or service to fit the needs of millennials.

- **View your manager as a role model.** Ask him or her to explain the corporate culture and what is (and is not) appropriate.

What's Next? Generation Z

Research is just beginning on the generation that will follow the millennials. The Z generation is comprised of individuals born between 1995 and 2010. Generation Z is the "net generation" due to the highly developed digital era they were born into. They are also referred to as the "Facebook generation," "digital natives," or sometimes the "iGeneration." The norms of generation Z are different from the norms of millennials. They tend to use slang and expressions that may seem strange to other generations, and this distances them from other groups. Since generation Z was born into technology, they feel good in the digital world and surround themselves in the online environment. They are constantly online on a variety of devices, with no interruptions. Other forms of socialization may be difficult for them. They are more impatient than their predecessors, and they look for new challenges continuously. They are not afraid of change. To solve problems, they try to find the solutions on the Internet.[19] While millennials were considered the first "global" generation with the development of the Internet, generation Z will become even more global in their outlook and interactions with others. A survey found that 58% of adults worldwide ages 35 or older agree that "kids today have more in common with their global peers than they do with adults in their own country."[20]

The generation you belong to is possibly one that already thinks globally; however, this perspective is becoming increasingly important for members of all generations. The next sections discuss research on cross-cultural adjustments, how national culture affects OB, and the requirements for effective leadership. First, the concept of culture is defined.

BEST PRACTICES

Understanding Millennials

An article with a provocative title appeared in *Time* magazine in May 2013.[21] According to research cited by Stein and conducted by the National Institutes of Health (NIH), there may be more to this than an older generation stereotyping a younger one: 58% more college students scored higher on a personality measure of narcissism in 2009 than in 1982. The study also indicated that 40% of millennials think "they should be promoted every two years, regardless of performance" (p. 28). Clearly, their personality characteristics and expectations will challenge leaders in the years ahead. But Stein also cited other research that shows some positive characteristics of this generation. He stated that they tend to be optimistic and crave new experiences (which may be more important than material things). And they are "pro-business" (p. 34), which should be a good thing for organizations. They have endured years of cynicism from baby boomers and gen Xers, who are both burnt out from overwork. Gen Xers were disengaged from work after the ethics scandals of the 1980s and 1990s. Millennials highly value their free time and do not define themselves through their job. Instead, they value the impact they are able to make on the community through their active involvement in things that matter to them.[22] So before reacting negatively to something a millennial says, it may be best to remember that (like all prior generations before them) they have a complex mix of values and attitudes (both positive and negative), and they are worth taking the time to understand.

Discussion Questions

1. What are some limits to using categorizations of generations such as millennials to understand behavior in organizations?
2. Can you think of people of this age group that don't fit the descriptions (i.e., they were born between 1981 and 1999)? What are they like, and why do you think they are different than how millennials are often described?
3. What is useful about these attempts to understand different generations at the workplace?

Sources: Kelly, C., Elizabeth, F., Bharat, M., & Jitendra, M. (2016). Generation gaps: Changes in the workplace due to differing generational values. *Advances in Management, 9*(5), 1–8; Stein, J. (2013, May). The me me me generation: Millennials are lazy, entitled narcissists who still live with their parents. Why they'll save us all. *Time,* 28–34.

WHAT IS CULTURE?

Learning Objective 13.3: Explain why culture is important for understanding organizational behavior (OB).

Before defining culture, it should be noted that the culture of an organization is also important to understand and is covered in Chapter 14 of this textbook. National culture is an elusive concept in terms of definition. Definitions typically employed in OB have their roots in sociology or anthropology. Sociologists define *culture* as follows:

- It is shared by almost all members of a social group.

- Older members of the group pass it on to younger members.

- It shapes behavior or structures one's perception of the world (such as morals, laws, and customs).[23]

A straightforward definition of culture is that it is the unstated standard operating procedures or ways of doing things.[24] As this definition implies, culture is comprised of things that we can see (e.g., the clothing a person wears or the objects they display in their home) and things we cannot see (e.g., how they define morality and what they value). It is important to bear in mind that culture is not the same thing as country.[25] Different countries may share cultural values. For example, Hong Kong and China are in the same country but have very distinct cultural values. Also, a meta-analytic study found that there is within-country variation on cultural values—approximately 80% of variation in cultural values reside within countries, confirming that country is not the same as culture.[26]

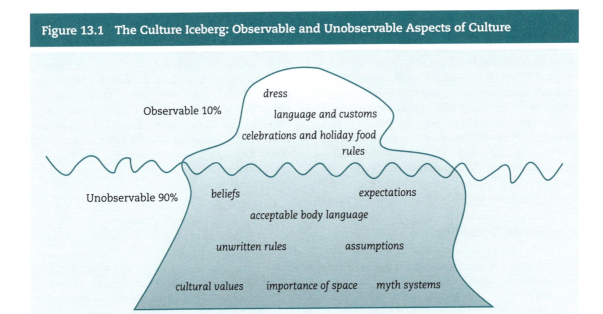

Figure 13.1 The Culture Iceberg: Observable and Unobservable Aspects of Culture

Observable 10%

dress

language and customs

celebrations and holiday food rules

Unobservable 90%

beliefs

expectations

acceptable body language

unwritten rules

assumptions

cultural values   importance of space   myth systems

Source: Adapted from Hall, E. T. (1977). *Beyond culture.* New York, NY: Random House.

A useful way to think about culture is the analogy of an iceberg (see Figure 13.1).[27] As shown in the figure, at the observable level, we can see dress, home or office décor, language, and even customs that are followed (what holidays are celebrated, as an example). However, under the surface, there are expectations of acceptable behavior, such as whether or not you should enter another's personal space. So what we can observe is only the tip of the iceberg, and leaders may make errors if they only rely upon what can be seen. These unobservable aspects' attributes of culture are often so deeply rooted in a person's worldview that they are not questioned by them. For example, some people have little respect for authority and even lampoon political leaders, whereas other cultures have such a high respect for authority that they don't question those in power. From the previously given examples, it is clear that cultural values affect OB. A leader can't assume that what works in their native culture will work everywhere in the world. And only viewing the tip of the iceberg can be treacherous when dealing with people of different cultural backgrounds. As with the iceberg, a leader may get into difficulties by not being able to see what is underneath the surface. Fortunately, today we have sonar and GPS to locate and estimate the size of what's underneath the surface of the ocean. Like sonar, there is research in OB that helps us to understand what's underneath the culture iceberg. This chapter provides evidence-based guidelines that are essential to a leader being effective in today's international context.

> Critical Thinking Question: Give an example of an assumption about another culture that may influence your working relationship with a person from that culture. What questions could you ask them to determine whether the person fits your assumption?

High-Context Versus Low-Context Cultures

High-context cultures rely heavily on situational cues for meaning when perceiving and communicating with others. For example, in a high-context culture, a person may need to get to know a negotiating partner as a person before proceeding to business. In **low-context cultures**, written and spoken words carry the burden of shared meanings. So when negotiating with a person from a low-context culture, you can expect that the person will want to see a written formal agreement early in the process as a reference. From these examples, it is clear that employees bring their national culture values with them to work every day and that understanding them is essential to succeed as a leader. Examples showing the range from high- and low-context cultures (from low to high) are shown in Figure 13.2.[28,29]

The situation with Brian and Chan described in Case Study 13.2 at the end of this chapter can be understood by considering that China is a high-context culture (Chan took extra meaning from Brian's words because he is from a culture that relies on situations to determine meaning). However, Brian is from a relatively low-context culture (the United States) in which his words were not meant to be a personal attack on Chan but rather about the work. A common phrase we hear in the

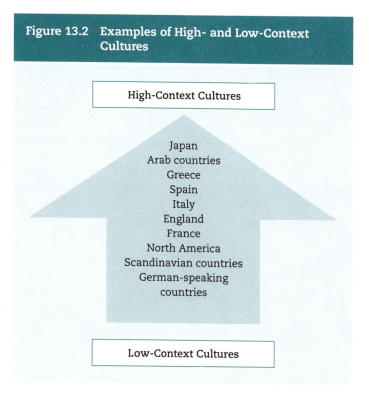

Figure 13.2   Examples of High- and Low-Context Cultures

High-Context Cultures

Japan
Arab countries
Greece
Spain
Italy
England
France
North America
Scandinavian countries
German-speaking
countries

Low-Context Cultures

United States is "it's not personal, it's just business." To an employee from a high-context culture, this might not make sense since they look to situations, including those at the workplace, to understand whether they are a worthy person.

One of the most often quoted definitions of culture is "the collective mental programming of the mind which distinguishes the members of one human group from another . . . the interactive aggregate of common characteristics that influence a human group's response to its environment."[30] This definition has become famous among managers, and its author is one of the most-cited researchers in the social sciences. In addition to offering a definition of culture, Hofstede articulated four cultural values that have received much research attention. In 1988, a fifth cultural value, time orientation (called Confucian dynamism), was added.[31] Thirty years after the initial research, the cultural value of indulgence versus restraint was added to the set. These cultural values remain the most well-known framework for understanding cross-cultural differences in a variety of disciplines, including management. Next, we review them and the research on these cultural values, which has had a large impact on how we view the effects on national culture in organizations.

Hofstede's Cultural Values

The five cultural values articulated by Hofstede and his colleagues follow, and their definitions are summarized in Table 13.2. Brief definitions and examples of countries with the United States as the referent culture for comparison purposes are provided next.

Table 13.2 Hofstede's Cultural Values

Low Score on Cultural Value	High Score on Cultural Value
Individualism: Social organization is loose, and people care for themselves and their immediate family.	**Collectivism:** Social organization is tight, and people are loyal to their in-group and/or organization.
Low Power Distance: People prefer that power be equally distributed in an egalitarian way.	**High Power Distance:** People accept power differences and respect authority.
Low Uncertainty Avoidance: People tolerate uncertainty and ambiguity. They are willing to take risks.	**High Uncertainty Avoidance:** People feel threatened by uncertainty and ambiguity. They are risk averse and create rules to create stability.
Masculinity: People value assertiveness and strive to acquire money and things.	**Femininity:** People value caring for one another and the quality of life.
Short-term oriented: People value the past and present, expecting short-term gain.	**Long-term oriented:** People plan for the future, persist, and value being thrifty.
Indulgence: How much each individual lacks control of their desires and impulses.	**Restraint:** Each individual controls their desires and impulses due to strong socialization to the societal norms.

Sources: Hofstede, G. (1980). *Culture's consequences: International differences in work-related values.* Beverly Hills, CA: Sage; Hofstede, G. (1991). *Culture's consequences: International differences in work-related values* (2nd ed.). Newbury Park, CA: Sage; Hofstede, G., & Bond, M. H. (1988). The Confucius connection: From cultural roots to economic growth. *Organizational Dynamics,* 16(4), 5–21: Hofstede, G., Hofstede, G. J., & Minkov, M. (2010). *Cultures and organizations, software of the mind: Intercultural cooperation and its importance for survival* (3rd ed.). New York, NY: McGraw-Hill.

Power distance—deference to authority (e.g., the United States is low, China is high)

Collectivism–individualism—group orientation (e.g., the United States is low, Russia is high)

Uncertainty avoidance—risk aversion (e.g., the United States is low, France is high)

Relationship orientation (masculinity–femininity)—a focus on people over material things (e.g., the United States is low and the Netherlands is high on femininity/relationship orientation)

Confucian dynamism (long-term orientation)—a focus on the future rather than the past and present[32] (e.g., the United States is low, Japan is high)

Indulgence—how much each individual lacks control of their desires and impulses compared with its opposite of restraint (being repressed) (e.g., China is low, the United States is high).[33]

Hofstede collected surveys from employees all over the world—initially from 40 countries.[34] His research was later expanded to 62 countries (116,000 managers and employees working for the large multinational company IBM were surveyed twice).[35] Hofstede found cultural values remained relatively stable over time. With this large database, he was able to create cultural clusters of countries. For example, Venezuela, Peru, Mexico, and Argentina are high power distance and collectivist cultures.[36] In contrast, the United States, Great Britain, Canada, and Australia are relatively lower on power distance and higher on individualism. Spain, France, Belgium, and Italy are higher on power distance but also relatively more individualistic cultures.

There has been a great deal of research interest in OB on the dimensions of national culture and collectivism in particular.[37,38] For example, being a loyal team member is expected to be more important in collectivist cultures compared to individualist cultures.[39,40] Research has linked collectivism to positive team outcomes.[41,42,43] The high level of individualism in the United States may help explain why teams have been more challenging to implement in the United States compared with some Asian cultures such as Japan. In individualistic cultures, employees' personal relationships with supervisors are important since they view the relationship as being tied to advancement and monetary rewards.[44] A recent meta-analysis showed that cooperation and performance were higher in collectivistic cultures compared to individualistic cultures.[45] On the other hand, individualism may have positive benefits. A study of 72 cultures found that individualism, long-term orientation, and indulgence were associated with innovation (creation of new technology and creativity).[46]

Power distance has been linked to leadership and team behavior. For example, for individuals with high power distance, high-quality relationships with their boss may not be expected, and they don't attempt to manage their boss because they tend to have unquestioning deference to authority.[47] In contrast, for employees with low power distance, relative position and status in the organizations are likely to be overlooked, and they may see themselves as equal to their supervisors.[48]

Hofstede's research has had a large effect on both research and practice in management. A review of impactful publications in the social sciences published by the London School of Economics and Political Science found his book *Culture's Consequences* to be one of the 25 most-cited books, with over 42,000 citations.[49] This cultural values framework has been instrumental in the overseas implementation of many business systems, including compensation, budget control, entrepreneurial behavior, training design, conflict resolution, work group dynamics, innovation, and leadership.[50,51]

> **Critical Thinking Questions:** Do you think that cultures around the world are becoming more "westernized" (in other words, like the United States)? Why or why not?

Criticisms and Usefulness of Hofstede's Research

Despite the high level of research interest and management application of these cultural values, the Hofstede model has been criticized for relevancy (i.e., the values and measures were developed in 1980). Other criticisms are that it is not possible to characterize all people in one culture the same way. Also, the use of nations for the study is a limitation of the research (i.e., the United States and Canada are similar). The Hofstede studies also lack attention to political influences on the data collected in the 1980s and the use of only one company (IBM) for the original research. Some scholars believe that culture is complex and cannot be captured in only four or five dimensions.[52] Hofstede's measures and statistical analyses have been criticized for their lack of validity and rigor.[53] Another criticism is that most research does not adopt a multiple levels perspective and analyze the effects of national culture on organizations and teams.[54] One review points out some strengths of Hofstede's work: The study was published when there was little work on culture and spurred a great deal of research interest, his approach was systematic and rigorous for the time, and other studies have generally confirmed the initial results.

A meta-analysis of research covering 30 years on the Hofstede cultural values analyzed 598 studies (and over 200,000 employees and managers). Hofstede's original four cultural value dimensions and work outcomes were equally important. Five cultural values (with the exception of indulgence, which was added later) were significantly and positively related to organizational commitment, identification, citizenship behavior, team-related attitudes, and feedback seeking. However, personality and demographics were better predictors of performance, absenteeism, and turnover than cultural values.[55]

A new approach to understanding cultural differences has emerged in recent years. Research on cultural tightness–looseness is intended to be complementary to the Hofstede values framework. For example, collectivist countries tend to be tighter compared to individualistic countries (e.g., China).[56] This perspective brings together the different cultural values and summarizes them in terms of how tight or loose a culture is with respect to how much people follow society's norms.

Cultural Tightness–Looseness

Cultural tightness–looseness is described as the strength of social norms and the level of sanctioning within societies.[57] **Tightness** is associated with order and efficiency, conformity, and low rates of change. In contrast, **looseness** is associated with social disorganization, deviance, innovation, and openness to change. Tightness–looseness is reflected by the clarity and pervasiveness of norms within societies and the degree of tolerance for deviation from these norms. The first factor delineating tight and loose societies is the level of accountability in organizations and the extent to which individuals have a sense of accountability. A large-scale study assessed cultural tightness–looseness in 33 cultures with the following survey questions (respondents were asked to agree or disagree with the questions on a 6-point scale):

1. There are many social norms that people are supposed to abide by in this country.

2. In this country, there are very clear expectations for how people should act in most situations.

3. People agree upon what behaviors are appropriate versus inappropriate in most situations in this country.

4. People in this country have a great deal of freedom in deciding how they want to behave in most situations (reverse-scored; higher scores indicate more cultural tightness).

5. In this country, if someone acts in an inappropriate way, others will strongly disapprove.

6. People in this country almost always comply with social norms.[58]

This research found the 33 cultures studied varied with respect to tightness–looseness. Tight cultures had more social controls and were more likely to be autocratic. They were also more likely to have more rules and laws, for instance. Examples of tight cultures are India, Malaysia, and Pakistan. Examples of relatively loose cultures are Hungary, Israel, and Ukraine. The United States had a score of 5.1, which was a bit below the overall average score of 6.5 across all respondents from all cultures. So the United States can be seen as somewhat loose.

Cultural tightness is likely a response to ecological and historical threats such as population density, conflict, natural disasters, and disease (as examples). Also, governments, the media, education, laws, and religion shape cultural tightness. These aspects relate to the structure of norms and tolerance for deviation from them, and this affects the degree of structure in everyday situations, including OB. Researchers conclude that "understanding tight and loose cultures is critical for fostering cross-cultural coordination in a world of increasing global interdependence."[59] Another research study[60] examined perceptions of leadership effectiveness in 29 different tight and loose cultures. Researchers found that tightness is positively related to perceptions that autonomous leadership is effective and negatively related to perceptions that team-oriented leadership is effective. In other words, employees in tight cultures prefer independent leaders who do not rely on others, perhaps because they prefer decisiveness. This study also found that tight cultures did not view charismatic leadership as effective, compared with loose cultures. Research on cultural tightness–looseness is relatively new, but this approach shows a great deal of promise for enhancing our understanding of cross-cultural OB.

Research on cultural values laid the foundations for understanding cross-cultural OB. Another large-scale study of cultural differences specifically focused on cultural values and leadership. The **Global Leadership and Organizational Behavior Effectiveness (GLOBE) project** at Wharton sought to understand differences in leader behaviors and relationships with relevant organizational outcomes worldwide. We review these studies next.

GLOBE STUDIES OF CROSS-CULTURAL LEADERSHIP

Learning Objective 13.4: Summarize the key findings from the Global Leadership and Organizational Behavior Effectiveness (GLOBE) project international study of leadership effectiveness.

The GLOBE project described and predicted the relationship of specific cultural variables to leadership and organizational processes and their effectiveness. The GLOBE researchers refined and extended the Hofstede cultural value framework. GLOBE involved 170 social scientists and management scholars from 61 cultures throughout the world to collect, analyze, and interpret data collected from employees and managers. This research identified nine cultural concepts that were shown to be relevant to perceptions of leadership. As with Hofstede, this research identified power distance and uncertainty avoidance as cultural values. Collectivism was split into two dimensions—loyalty to the group and loyalty to institutions (such as the organization you work for). In addition, the GLOBE project identified humane orientation, assertiveness, gender, egalitarianism, and future orientation, which is similar to Confucian dynamism and performance orientation. The nine GLOBE cultural dimension definitions and sample questionnaire items are shown in Table 13.3.

Table 13.3 GLOBE Cultural Dimensions and Sample Questionnaire Items

Culture Construct Definitions	Sample Questionnaire Item
Power distance: The degree to which members of a collective expect power to be distributed equally.	Followers are expected to obey their leaders without question.
Uncertainty avoidance: The extent to which a society, organization, or group relies on societal norms, rules, and procedures to alleviate unpredictability of future events.	Most people lead highly structured lives with few unexpected events.
Humane orientation: The degree to which a collective encourages and rewards individuals for being fair, altruistic, generous, caring, and kind to others.	People are generally very tolerant of mistakes. Aging parents generally live at home with their children.
Institutional collectivism: The degree to which organizational and societal institutional practices encourage and reward collective distribution of resources and collective action.	Leaders encourage group loyalty even if individual goals suffer.
In-group collectivism: The degree to which individuals express pride, loyalty, and cohesiveness in their organizations or families.	Aging parents generally live at home with their children.
Assertiveness: The degree to which individuals are assertive, dominant, and demanding in their relationships with others.	People are generally dominant.
Gender egalitarianism: The degree to which a collective minimizes gender inequality.	Boys are encouraged more than girls to attain a higher education. (reverse-scored)
Future orientation: The extent to which a collective encourages future-oriented behaviors such as delaying gratification, planning, and investing in the future.	More people live for the present than for the future. (reverse-scored)
Performance orientation: The degree to which a collective encourages and rewards group members for performance improvement and excellence.	Students are encouraged to strive for continuously improved performance.

Sources: Adapted from House, R., Javidan, M., Hanges, P., & Dorfman, P. (2002). Understanding cultures and implicit leadership theories across the globe: An introduction to project GLOBE. *Journal of World Business, 37*(1), 3–10.

Table 13.4 Examples of High- and Low-Scoring Countries on GLOBE Cultural Dimensions

Cultural Dimension	Highest	Lowest
Power distance	Argentina, Spain, Russia	Denmark, Israel, Costa Rica
Uncertainty avoidance	Switzerland, Denmark, Austria	Russia, Hungary, Venezuela
Humane orientation	Philippines, Ireland, Egypt	Spain, France, Singapore
Institutional collectivism	Sweden, South Korea, Japan	Greece, Argentina, Italy
In-Group collectivism	Iran, India, China	Finland, Netherlands, Sweden
Assertiveness	Germany (former East), Spain	New Zealand, Japan, Kuwait, United States
Gender egalitarianism	Hungary, Poland, Sweden	Morocco, India, China
Future orientation	Canada, Singapore, Denmark	Russia, Argentina, Italy
Performance orientation	Hong Kong, Taiwan, United States	Argentina, Greece, Venezuela

Sources: Adapted from House, R., Javidan, M., Hanges, P., & Dorfman, P. (2002). Understanding cultures and implicit leadership theories across the globe: An introduction to project GLOBE. *Journal of World Business, 37*(1), 3–10.

Based upon the GLOBE research and the 61 countries included in the study, cultures appear to vary on the nine dimensions. High- and low-scoring country examples are shown for each of the dimensions in Table 13.4.

In addition to refining cultural values, the GLOBE research team also examined the question of whether or not there were any leadership behaviors that appear to be effective across cultures. Their analysis found that there are certain culturally endorsed attributes of leadership that may be universal. This is known as the **culturally endorsed implicit leadership theory (CLT)**, which identified the following leadership behaviors that were perceived as effective across cultures.

1. **Charismatic/value-based**—the ability to inspire and motivate others to high performance

2. **Team-Oriented**—effective team building and implementing a common goal

3. **Participative**—involving others in decisions and implementations

4. **Humane-Oriented**—being supportive and showing consideration, compassion, and generosity

5. **Autonomous**—independent and individualistic leadership

6. **Self-protective**—ensuring safety and security of individuals, including face-saving

Thus, GLOBE research found that employees may have some similar conceptions of leadership based on implicit assumptions regarding what constitutes effective leadership. These belief systems affect the way that a person responds to directives from a leader. GLOBE uncovered some important underlying perceptions regarding what is deemed effective in terms of leadership and offers some practical advice for leaders operating abroad.[61] There appear to be some cultural "universals" according to GLOBE: having integrity, having vision, being inspirational, and building teams. Also, there are universal attributes of ineffective leadership: being a loner, being irritable, and being autocratic. Other attributes may depend on the culture: individualism, being conscious of status, and risk taking.

> Critical Thinking Questions: What are the advantages of knowing cultural values that generalize across cultures? Is it more useful to learn about cultural values that are unique to a culture? Why or why not?

Following this foundation in cultural value differences, we next turn to the development of global leaders. Experts have concluded that most of today's managers lack the global leadership skills needed to be effective in the multinational business context.[62] One study estimated that 85% of Fortune 500 companies have a shortage of global managers.[63] The critical skills needed for effective global leadership and how they can be developed are discussed in the following sections.

DEVELOPING GLOBAL LEADERS

Learning Objective 13.5: Discuss the importance of developing global leaders and the impact this has on an organization.

Carlos Ghosn, the chairman and CEO of the Renault-Nissan Alliance, was asked about the importance of cross-cultural management education for managers. Here is his reply:

> More and more, managers are dealing with different cultures. Companies are going global, and teams are spread across the globe. If you're head of engineering, you have to deal with divisions in Vietnam, India, China or Russia, and you have to work across cultures. You have to know how to motivate people who speak different languages, who have different cultural contexts, who have different sensitivities and habits. You have to get prepared to deal with teams who are multicultural, to work with people who do not all think the same way as you do.[64]

Ghosn's view is shared by other top executives who view the ability to influence people from other cultures as the most important skill required for their own success.[65] **Global mind-set** has been defined as a set of individual attributes that enhance a manager's ability to influence others who are different from them.[66]

The global mind-set is developed through three interrelated skills: **cultural intelligence (CQ)** and **integrative acculturation** (becoming bicultural). Also, the boxed insert describes the process of **cultural retooling**, which is the psychological process of adapting to another culture. The next sections elaborate on these leadership skills; all of them are needed to develop effective working relationships with others that result from a mutual adjustment process resulting in a third culture.

The Third Culture

The **third culture** has been defined as "the construction of a mutually beneficial interactive environment in which individuals from two different cultures can function in a way beneficial to all involved."[67] The third culture consists of shared frameworks, value systems, and communication patterns that emerge when people from different cultures interact. This is an important concept because it is through a mutual adjustment process over time that a third culture emerges, which has features of both so that both parties can be comfortable interacting. While this is a two-person example, third (or hybrid) cultures have also been shown to be important for team harmony and performance.[68] The process of the development of the third culture is shown in Figure 13.3. As shown in this figure, third cultures emerge over four phases as follows:

- **Phase 1.** Initial contact may result in the person withdrawing from the other person (or culture). For example, an expatriate travels to the city of Al Ain in the United Arab Emirates (UAE) from Argentina to develop a contract for oil exports. The expatriate insists that business colleagues taste wine brought as a gift from Argentina. The Arab executives are uncomfortable and limit their interactions after this exchange.

- **Phase 2.** The parties evaluate the need for continued interaction. As the discussions continue, the UAE representatives realize that a business between Argentina may open additional markets in Latin America,

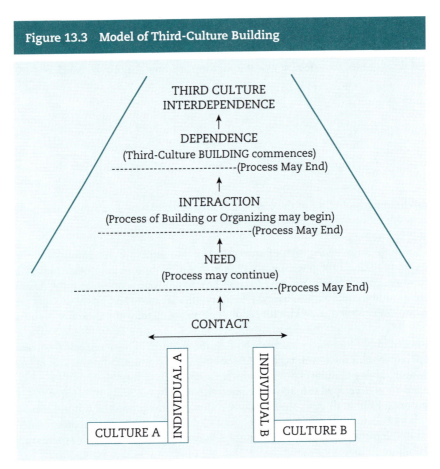

Figure 13.3 Model of Third-Culture Building

THIRD CULTURE
INTERDEPENDENCE

↑

DEPENDENCE
(Third-Culture BUILDING commences)
----------------------------(Process May End)

↑

INTERACTION
(Process of Building or Organizing may begin)
-----------------------------------(Process May End)

↑

NEED
(Process may continue)
--(Process May End)

↑

CONTACT

INDIVIDUAL A

INDIVIDUAL B

CULTURE A

CULTURE B

Source: Casmir, F. L. (1999). Foundations for the study of intercultural communication based on a third-culture building model. *International Journal of Intercultural Relations, 23*(1), 91–116.

and the executive from Argentina has valuable contacts. The parties have options at this point. They may choose to rely on their own cultural values and not adapt. At this point, the interaction might end, so the risk of staying with one's own values must be evaluated. For extended interactions, however, the parties begin a natural process of mutual adjustment. The need for ongoing and mutually beneficial interactions supports the cultural adjustment process.

- **Phase 3.** The dependence of the parties on one another is clear by this point. Norms for interaction have evolved to the point where they feel "natural" to both parties. Positive outcomes reinforce the motivations for continued adjustment, and a third culture emerges that accommodates both parties' cultures. Following the previously given example, the attractiveness of the Latin American market for oil exports motivates the UAE executives to explain why their religious and cultural beliefs don't allow them to drink alcohol. Both parties become accustomed to cultural differences in cultural values and a balanced approach emerges.

- **Phase 4.** Interdependence results in more nuanced development and maintenance of the third culture. There is a continued process of open communication, and the process becomes dependent on trust.

In the previously given example, the executive from Argentina contacts the home office and requests that alternative gifts of leather binders be sent immediately. This example illustrates that there is a type of intelligence that emanates from an interest in learning about other cultures and a willingness to make adjustments. The next section discusses research on cultural intelligence.

Cultural Intelligence

CQ has been defined as an individual's capabilities to function and manage effectively in culturally diverse settings.[69] The personality trait of openness to experience, combined with agreeableness, relates positively to CQ.[70] However, CQ does not appear to be a trait. Like emotional intelligence (EI; as discussed in Chapter 3), CQ can be cultivated by first assessing one's strengths and weaknesses in CQ, undergoing training in cross-cultural interactions, and then applying CQ learning to real-life cross-cultural situations to build confidence.[71] A study of 183 college-level business students who had recently completed study-abroad experiences found that CQ influenced the relationship between core self-evaluation and the success of the study-abroad experiences (i.e., their enjoyment, personal growth, and success).[72] Another study of 254 university students who were enrolled in an international exchange program were assessed at three points in time, and results of the study showed that positive cross-cultural adjustment experiences predicted CQ.[73]

CQ is composed of four dimensions: metacognitive, cognitive, motivational, and behavioral, as shown in Figure 13.4. **Metacognitive CQ** refers to the cognitive processing necessary to recognize and understand expectations appropriate for different cultural situations. **Cognitive CQ** refers to self-awareness and the ability to detect cultural patterns. **Motivational CQ** refers to persistence and goal setting for cross-cultural interactions. **Behavioral CQ** is the ability to adjust to others' cultural practices. To assess your CQ, complete Self-Assessment 13.1 in the Toolkit at the end of this chapter. The cognitive aspect of CQ predicts cultural judgment, whereas motivational CQ predicts cultural adaptation. Both cognitive and behavioral CQ predicts task performance.[74] A review of the research on CQ concluded that CQ positively relates to expatriate adjustment and leadership effectiveness.[75] But can CQ be acquired through training? Two multination studies compared students' CQ before taking cross-cultural management courses to their scores afterward. Student CQ was significantly higher after taking courses that included CQ, with stronger effects found for cognitive CQ than motivational or behavioral. Thus, there is some indication that CQ can be learned.[76] CQ training should include assessment and training on all facets of CQ:

- **Cognitive (and metacognitive)**—acquiring information on the new culture and engaging in self-reflection

- **Motivational**—developing culture-specific confidence (self-efficacy) and setting goals for cross-cultural adjustment

- **Behavioral**—includes role-plays to model and practice effective behaviors with those from another culture[77]

> Critical Thinking Questions: Explain whether or not you agree that CQ can be learned. What aspect of CQ do you feel is the most important for a leader to exhibit? Why?

Thus, CQ involves the ability to learn about other cultures and develop the confidence and skills to engage in new behaviors. Adaptation is a key aspect of success in working with others to achieve a third culture both one-on-one and in teams.

Cross-Cultural Adjustment Strategies

With respect to cross-cultural adjustment, four acculturation strategies are possible: assimilation, separation, marginalization, and integration.[78,79] Assimilation involves relinquishing cultural heritage and adopting the beliefs and behaviors of the new culture. For example, a Chinese person adopts an English name to better fit in with U.S. coworkers. Separation involves maintaining only the heritage culture without intergroup relations. For example, a Russian

Figure 13.4   Dimensions of Cultural Intelligence

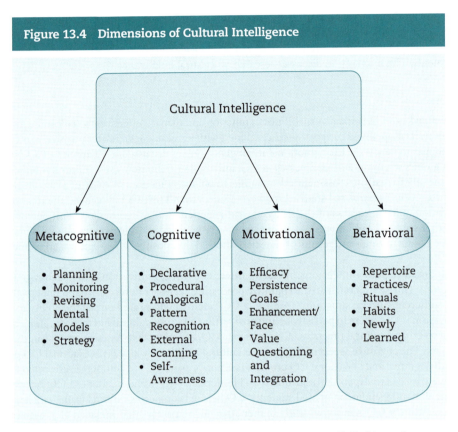

Source: Adapted from Earley, P. C., & Ang, S. A. (2003). *Cultural intelligence: Individual interactions across cultures.* Stanford, CA: Stanford University Press; Eisenberg, J., Lee, H., Bruck, F., Brenner, B., Claes, M., Mironski, J., & Bell, R. (2013). Can business schools make students culturally competent? Effects of cross-cultural management courses on cultural intelligence. *Academy of Management Learning & Education*, 12(4), 603–621.

scientist avoids contact with coworkers by eating lunch at his desk. Marginalization involves rejecting both the old and new culture. For example, an Indian expatriate working in Saudi Arabia does not celebrate Christmas or Ramadan. Integration (or biculturalism) involves maintaining one's cultural heritage and adopting a new cultural identity; the identities remain independent of one another. For example, a Cuban immigrates to the United States and speaks Spanish at home with her family but speaks English at work.

We have learned a lot about how people adjust to different cultures from the study of bicultural individuals. **Biculturals** are defined as "people who have internalized more than one cultural profile."[80] These individuals are therefore comfortable operating in two different cultures, and they have been found to have more cross-cultural adaptive skills compared to monoculturals (those comfortable with only one culture).

Integrative Acculturation: Biculturals

Biculturals have higher metacognitive CQ skills and have been shown by research to be more complex than those using other strategies.[81] This is referred to as **integrative complexity**, which is defined as follows:

RESEARCH IN ACTION

When in Rome . . . Cultural Retooling

The need to adapt to another culture is not new. You have probably heard the phrase, "When in Rome, do as the Romans do." This originated with an ancient Roman leader's need to adjust to another culture. Augustine, a native of Carthage serving as Bishop of Milan, wrote to Januarius, Bishop of Naples, with advice about an upcoming trip to their organization's headquarters in Rome. At the time, Christians in Rome fasted on Saturday, whereas Christians in other cities did not. To avoid scandal or offense, Augustine's approach was to fast when in Rome but not when at home in Milan, and he advised Januarius to adapt to local norms in the same way. Augustine had a long successful career, and it may have been due to his ability to adapt and do as the Romans did when in Rome.[82] Today's OB research has shed light on the process that individuals go through in adapting to another culture.

The psychological process of adaptation to another culture is called *cultural retooling*.[83] Using longitudinal data from foreign-born master's degree students in the United States, researchers found that during cultural retooling individuals experience internal conflicts. This conflict can be related to either values or disruptions in routines. Cultural retooling follows three distinct phases:

Phase 1. **Deep conflict**—feeling illegitimate and awkward (e.g., a Japanese student does not feel comfortable talking about her strengths at networking events)

Phase 2. **Ambivalence**—adjusting and not feeling as negative about the behavior (e.g., the Japanese student overcomes the strong negative reaction to "boasting" and begins to imitate others at networking events)

Phase 3. **Authenticity**—naturally engaging in the new behavior consistent with the new culture (e.g., the Japanese student experiences a shift in values that is consistent with talking about her strengths to others)

Not all of the participants in the study experienced the third phase of authenticity. They adapted using different strategies. Some took an integrative approach and allowed themselves to change (telling themselves it was okay to behave a certain way because it is acceptable in the new culture and personalizing experiences by making them more congruent with their home culture). Using an instrumental approach, those finding themselves in conflict recognize that it is necessary to adapt by switching their culture's behavior for a new one. Another strategy was to suppress their conflict by telling themselves they were just acting out a role. This research provides insight into the thought processes people go through when making cross-cultural adjustments.

Discussion Questions:

1. Explain why the instrumental approach is more effective in adapting to another culture than suppression.
2. Provide an example of a time when you experienced a conflict due to interaction with a person from another culture. Reflect on this experience. What did you learn from this?
3. How can you use knowledge of cultural retooling phases to help you adapt to another culture?

Sources: Molinsky, A. (2013). The psychological processes of cultural retooling. *Academy of Management Journal, 56*(3), 683–710; Morris, M. W., Savani, K., Mor, S., & Cho, J. (2014). When in Rome: Intercultural learning and implications for training. *Research in Organizational Behavior, 34,* 189–215.

The degree to which a person accepts the reasonableness of different cultural perspectives on how to live, both at the micro interpersonal level and at more macro organizational-societal levels and, consequently, is motivated to develop integrative schemas that specify when to activate different worldviews and/or how to blend them together into a coherent holistic mental representation.[84]

Research involving Asian American college students and Israelis working in the United States found that bicultural individuals are more integratively complex in both cultural and work situations compared to assimilated or separated individuals. Integrative complexity was assessed by asking study participants to write answers to questions like "What does it mean to you to be bicultural?" and then trained raters scored them for the degree to which they were able to recognize causality, see issues from different points of view, and show value trade-offs. This research also showed that pressure to acculturate drives individuals toward more integrative complexity.[85] Hence, integrative complexity might be developed rather than a completely inborn trait.

Research on acculturation suggests that it is possible to adjust to a new culture. This is important because many people experience **culture shock**, which is feeling stress and being uncomfortable when a new culture is experienced for the first time. It's important to remember that this is a normal reaction, and you can work through your feelings of stress in stages. In addition, as a leader, it's important to understand that some of your followers may be recent immigrants who may be experiencing such conflicts, and you can help them adjust through CQ.

CULTURE SHOCK

Learning Objective 13.6: Devise a plan for coping with the symptoms of culture shock.

Culture shock has become a common term, and most people are now familiar with the concept. The term was coined by an anthropologist who defined *culture shock* as the distress experienced by a traveler from the loss of familiar patterns of social interaction.[86] He described several "symptoms" of culture shock, including

1. stress due to the effort required to make necessary adjustments;

2. having a sense of loss from missing family and friends—"homesickness";

3. wanting to avoid interactions with persons from the host culture;

4. feeling helpless and wanting to depend on those from one's home country;

5. having a fear of being robbed or injured, or becoming ill;

6. being angry at delays and inconveniences experienced; and

7. feeling incompetent from not being able to cope with the new environment.

Culture shock is a series of phases a person goes through—particularly expatriates on assignment. First, the expatriate is excited and finds the new culture to be "exotic." Then, he begins to feel it is "wicked and silly." Finally, he sees it as "dissimilar and diverse."[87] The process of culture shock from predeparture to reentry is shown in Figure 13.5. As this figure illustrates, the impact of cultural transitions on well-being follows a W-shaped curve. During the predeparture phase, there is a sense of excitement and anticipation of experiencing a new adventure in another culture. On arrival, there is typically a sense of confusion due to jet lag and getting accommodated to one's surroundings. As noted previously, most expatriates experience a honeymoon period followed by a plunge when they begin to encounter difficulties in understanding cultural practices and values. Over time, reconciliation occurs, and the expatriate begins to adjust and accommodate to

Figure 13.5 Stages of Culture Shock

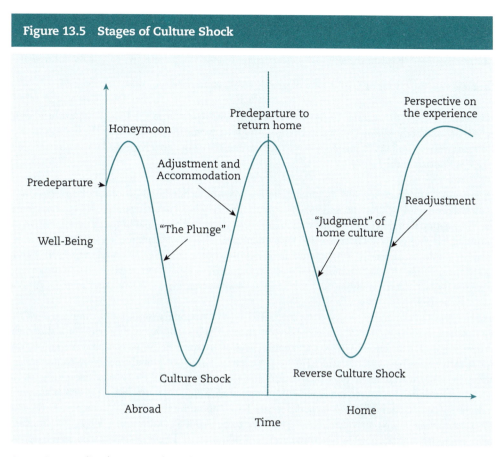

Source: Gaw, K. F. (2000). Reverse culture shock in students returning from overseas. *International Journal of Intercultural Relations, 24*(1), 83–104; Oberg, K. (1960). Culture shock adjustment to new cultural environments. *Practical Anthropology, 7,* 177–182.

the new environment. Nearing the time he will return home, there is a similar excitement as that of predeparture where the expatriate puts things in order in the host country and makes preparations to return to his home country.

It is important to keep this in mind and anticipate the "highs" and "lows" that will likely be experienced while on an expatriate assignment. Being able to work through culture shock is critical for expatriates since many organizations now expect significant international experience as a prerequisite to promotion to the highest rank. It has been reported that "companies like GE, Citigroup, Shell, Siemens, and Nokia are using international assignments of high potential employees as the means to develop their managers' global leadership mindset and competencies."[88] International assignments are the most effective source for developing global leaders.[89] So if you have aspirations to be an executive-level leader, it is important for you to understand the process of expatriate cross-cultural adjustment and be ready for the adjustment process of culture shock. Fortunately, OB researchers have been studying this process for a number of years.

> **Critical Thinking Question:** Give an example of when you found something troubling about a different culture. What did you do?

EXPATRIATE ADJUSTMENT

Learning Objective 13.7: Explain the steps for an expatriate to take when adjusting to a cross-cultural assignment.

Jack Welch stated that the CEOs of the future will be able to adjust to other cultures:

> The Jack Welch of the future cannot be like me. I spent my entire career in the U.S. The next head of General Electric will be somebody who spent time in Bombay, in Hong Kong, in Buenos Aires. We have to send our best and brightest overseas and make sure they have the training that will allow them to be the global leaders who will make GE flourish in the future.[90]

Welch was right. His successor, Jeffrey Immelt, held a series of leadership positions with GE that included marketing and global product development, and vice president of worldwide marketing and product management for GE Appliances. Multinational organizations need employees who are globally mobile in today's competitive global business environment. Global mobility occurs when individuals, and often their families, are relocated from one country to another by an employer, generally from a familiar situation (a home country) to a novel one (a host country) for a fixed period of time. These globally mobile employees, also known as expatriates, have grown in importance as firms expand their global reach. As the number of a firm's foreign subsidiaries grows, the number of expatriates working in them often grows as well.[91]

Despite the prevalence and importance of expatriates on international assignments, poor cross-cultural adjustment often results in dissatisfaction and lower performance.[92,93] This can be costly for organizations that make a significant investment in training, relocating, and compensating expatriates. Some estimate the failure rate (leaving an assignment early) to be between 8% and 12%.[94,95,96] Recently, a study of global leadership trends was released by the consulting firm Right Management, which found that managers still fail in overseas assignments. A survey of 202 CEOs and senior human resource management professionals found that just 58% of overseas assignments were considered to be successful, and there was little difference based upon the region.[97] With respect to the costs, for the United States, expatriate failure costs have been estimated to be about $1 million per failure,[98,99] and the total economic impact of failure ranges between $2 billion and $2.5 billion.[100,101] These costs have led to the development of sophisticated measures of the return on investment for expatriate assignments, which include such costs as selection, moving expenses, housing, compensation, bonuses, and readjustment costs after the assignment.[102] In addition to these costs, there are psychological effects on expatriates and decreased productivity that are not accounted for in these estimates.[103]

An expatriate assignment can be either self-initiated or assigned by the organization. Self-initiated expatriates (SIEs) choose to go abroad, and assigned expatriates (AEs) are offered the opportunity by their organization. A study of 193 expatriates (67 AEs and 126 SIEs)[104] indicates that self-initiated foreign work experience is significantly more likely to be chosen by women and those having lower job levels. Also, SIEs have higher organizational mobility. So there may be a difference in career outcomes for those who have the flexibility to volunteer for an expatriate assignment. But what makes people want to volunteer for an expatriate assignment? Based upon a study of 514 university students,[105] CQ influences the degree to which career adaptability relates to intentions to go abroad for their careers. In other words, being flexible and culturally intelligent seems to influence the intention to become an expatriate. CQ also has been related to the ability to adjust to the expatriate assignment in the host country.[106] Being an expatriate relates to compensation as well as career mobility. A study of 440 graduates of elite MBA programs from around the world[107] found that expatriates receive more total compensation but only if they have experienced more than one expatriate assignment and acquired knowledge and new skills utilized during postrepatriation. They also tend to be at higher organizational levels. In other words, expatriation relates to compensation attainment because it is an intense developmental experience and not merely a signaling mechanism for who is on the fast track.

What can organizations do to help expatriates adjust to their international assignments? A study of the adjustment experiences of 213 expatriates from three U.S.-based Fortune 500 companies found perceived support from the organization influenced their adjustment.[108] Expatriates' adjustment was, in turn, related to their performance as rated by their supervisors. Surface-level cultural differences (e.g., food, housing, and climate) were most strongly related to general adjustment. However, deep-level cultural differences (e.g., values and assumptions) affected work and interaction adjustment, and expatriates who reported self-transcendence had an easier time adjusting to their expatriate assignment. Self-transcendence includes universalism (understanding, appreciation, tolerance, and protection for the welfare of all people and for nature) and benevolence (preservation and enhancement of the welfare of people with whom one is in frequent personal contact).[109]

Expatriate managers need to realize that they don't have to go it alone. Adjustments in personal interactions with people from a host culture were a significant predictor of expatriate retention in a study of 321 U.S. expatriates assigned to the Pacific Rim or Western Europe.[110] Also, having a mentor provides both career and social support that are essential.[111] Mentors are key resources before, during, and after international assignments and are often indispensable for facilitating promotions after the assignment ends. Expatriates must think in terms of having a network of mentors who can provide support for adaptation in terms of host country culture, task assistance, and office culture (these may or may not be the same mentors and can be supervisors, peers, or someone outside of the organization).[112] Finally, training in cross-cultural interactions, culture, and language has been shown to improve adjustment for expatriates.[113]

At the end of the assignment, expatriates return to their home country. The process of returning to work and family life may also have shocks, known as "reverse culture shock" or "re-entry shock." As with expatriation, two research studies of international students and recent university graduates found that CQ can also ease the reverse culture shock when an expatriate returns.[114] Additional research on the process of repatriation will be discussed next.

Repatriation

Even when an expatriate has adjusted and performed well on assignment, he or she must also be prepared for **repatriation**. Repatriation, or reentry, refers to the transition when the expatriate has completed the international assignment and returns home.[115] Expatriates are at risk of leaving the organization after they return. It has been estimated that 10% of expatriates leave their firm shortly after completing an international assignment, and another 14% leave between 2 and 3 years of their return.[116] Expatriates may experience a similar sequence of culture shock feelings when they return to their home culture. Successful expatriates become accustomed to their host culture and are tolerant of unfamiliar situations and work habits. **Reverse culture shock** is the realization that time has moved on and things have not stood still while the expatriate was away from the home office.[117,118] The returning expatriate experiences confusion and disappointment that may lead to a temporary state of depression and a sense of loss. Upon return to the home country, they may even look judgmentally upon their home culture as they realize some of the negative aspects of their own national culture. They may be disappointed in the reactions of coworkers and superiors upon their return. Also, they feel that their work abroad is not understood or appreciated, and expected rewards and promotions may not follow.[119] Other employees who stayed home may have been promoted, and the expatriate was "out of sight, out of mind" in the eyes of their supervisor. Finally, there is a readjustment phase (whether the expatriate leaves the job or not) in which there is resolution of the reentry culture shock and the expatriate puts the experience into perspective.

As shown in Figure 13.5, the expatriate can expect a series of "culture bumps," and research suggests the following steps to cope with them:

1. Pinpoint the specific time when you felt different or uncomfortable.

2. Define the situation.

3. List the behaviors of the other person(s).

4. List your own behavior.

5. List your feelings in the situation.

6. List the behaviors you expect from people in your own culture in that same situation.

7. Reflect on the underlying value in your culture that prompts that behavior expectation.[120]

Communication and validation are important to successful repatriation.[121,122] Communication is how much information the expatriate has regarding what is happening at home while on assignment. With higher levels of communication, those who return are more proactive, effective, and satisfied with their jobs after they return.[123] Fortunately, today we have Skype and Google hangouts (virtual face-to-face chat rooms), which allow expatriates to have face-to-face contact with their families and colleagues while on assignment. If the family is living abroad with the expatriate, the spouse has a significant influence on the expatriate adjustment process.[124] Culture shock may be more difficult for the spouse, who may feel isolated while the expatriate has peers at work to interact with.[125] Validation refers to the amount of recognition the expatriate gets for success on the international assignment. This may include a promotion—those who are promoted after an expatriate assignment adjust better than those who are not.[126]

> **Critical Thinking Questions: Have you been on a study-abroad experience (or an expatriate assignment)? Describe your process of cultural adjustment and repatriation. If you have not been on a study-abroad experience (or expatriate assignment), explain why.**

LEADERSHIP IMPLICATIONS: BECOMING A GLOBAL LEADER

Diversity takes many forms, including surface- and deep-level diversity (which includes cultural values). Embracing diversity relates to organizational effectiveness. For example, a study of Standard & Poor's firms over a 15-year period showed that having women in top management teams improves firm performance for firms whose strategy is focused on innovation.[127] The study authors concluded that in a context of innovation, "the informational and social benefits of gender diversity and the behaviors associated with women in management are likely to be especially important for managerial task performance."[128] International management scholars have noted a shift from "international management" to "global leadership" being the required skill set in today's business environment.[129] It is imperative that leaders embrace all forms of diversity to enhance the engagement of a diverse and multinational workforce to harness their productive and creative work to meet organizational goals.

A convincing example of the power of diversity is from a study of NFL draft picks for 12 players by well-known sports analysts from *NFL Countdown*, *Sporting News*, *Sports Illustrated*, *CBS SportsLine*, About.com, and Fanball.com. Since their reputations depend on being right, the analysts care about whether or not they make the right predictions in the NFL draft. Researchers found that the average of all analysts was a better predictor of any individual analyst. Prediction diversity matters, and this example demonstrates that diverse points of view can enhance organizational functioning through better decisions: "*Diversity matters just as much as individual ability.* That is not a feel-good statement. It's a mathematical fact."[130] Thus, the field of OB recognizes that diversity is not something that must be "managed," but rather, it is something that must be embraced because it is a business imperative. Many organizations today reflect diversity in mission statements. For example, ESPN has won several awards for diversity, and their mission statement reflects the importance of valuing diversity to their profitability:

ESPN will embrace diversity to better serve our fans and customers. We strive to attract and retain talented and diverse people, and to create an inclusive environment where all employees can contribute to their fullest potential. In a changing world in which we endeavor to grow our business, it is imperative that ESPN's workforce reflects the diversity of cultures, thinking and perspectives of its current and prospective fans and customers. Tapping the skills, ideas and perspectives of a diverse workforce will make us a better and more profitable company, and is key to sustaining our continued growth. (Diversity at ESPN, 2013, http://espncareers.com/working-here/diversity.aspx)

This seems like a great vision statement, but what can organizations do specifically to develop an inclusive and diverse work environment? One thing is to apply critical thinking by asking key questions about diversity. Leading a diverse workforce does have some challenges, such as shifting power dynamics in the organization or employees not being willing to participate in diversity initiatives. A study of human resource managers revealed several questions that every leader should be asking themselves and others in their organization to promote open discussions about diversity:[131]

- Are there challenging or pressing issues in managing a diverse workforce? If so, which do you find to be most challenging?

- What are specific things you have done personally to ease those challenges?

- In regard to diversity, are there things you wish had been done differently? If so, what? And how would you have handled those things differently?

- What are specific things your company has done to ease those challenges?

- What are your (or your company's) future plans for diversity? Do you have specific plans that will be implemented in the near future? If so, what?

Asking such questions (and thinking thoughtfully about the answers) should help a leader identify what challenges the organization faces and what is (or is not) being done to address them. For example, pairing employees with different backgrounds in terms of age, gender, and race or ethnicity in a one-on-one coaching program might be something an organization could implement.

> **Critical Thinking Questions:** What do you think is the biggest challenge in leading a diverse workforce? How can a leader address this challenge?

A case study of a multicultural organization found that the organization implemented several key managerial actions:[132]

- CEO support of diversity initiatives

- Managerial accountability

- Fundamental change in human resource practices

- Employee involvement and buy-in

- Overarching corporate philosophy regarding diversity

- Ongoing monitoring and improvement of diversity climate

- Multiple measures of success

In terms of managerial accountability, 25% of the managers' salary increase was linked to interaction with diverse individuals as an example in the multicultural organization studied. These authors concluded that it is important to have a plan for diversity and inclusion initiatives, and to link them to hard organizational outcomes such as revenue.

The effective global leader must keep the phrase "explain before blame" in mind when interacting with people from other cultures—employees, supervisors, peers, customers, and negotiating partners. Culture, like personality, is something that is relatively stable, and the leader's best tools are to understand it and learn to develop mutually adjusted relationships with those from different cultures. The thought patterns and behaviors associated with CQ are helpful in implementing the idea of "explain before blame." It is important to keep an open mind and be curious about other cultures. It's fine to politely ask questions about other cultural values and practices. Try to focus on what people have in common rather than differences. For example, the GLOBE research reviewed in this chapter indicated that there are some cultural universals that define effective leadership. Focus on what you have learned from cross-cultural interactions, and support others by providing positive feedback when you see them trying to understand cultural differences.

In summary, the skills needed for successful interactions with another culture are CQ, cultural retooling, and an integrative approach to acculturation. It is also important to anticipate and develop a plan to cope with culture shock if you embark on an expatriate assignment. These guidelines are also helpful for the reentry process for those returning from an international assignment. This chapter has hopefully increased your awareness of the effects of culture on OB. The effective leader must be able to suspend judgment (explain before blame) and use their CQ to effectively adjust to those from other cultures whether assigned in the United States or abroad. Throughout this textbook, we have referenced research on how culture affects leader effectiveness with respect to perceptions, motivation, negotiation, teams, and more. By now, you realize that in today's global environment, cross-cultural differences affect every aspect of OB.

 **edge.sagepub.com/scandura2e**

Want a better grade? Go to **edge.sagepub.com/scandura2e** for the tools you need to sharpen your study skills.

KEY TERMS

assimilation, 347
behavioral CQ, 347
biculturals, 348
boomers, 333
cognitive CQ, 347
cultural intelligence (CQ), 345
cultural looseness, 342
cultural retooling, 345
cultural tightness, 342
cultural tightness–looseness, 341
culturally endorsed implicit
    leadership theory (CLT), 344

culture shock, 350
deep-level diversity, 333
generation Xers, or gen Xers, 333
Global Leadership and
    Organizational Behavior
    Effectiveness (GLOBE)
    project, 342
global mind-set, 345
global mobility, 352
high-context cultures, 338
integration, 347
integrative acculturation, 345

integrative complexity, 348
low-context cultures, 339
marginalization, 347
metacognitive CQ, 347
millennials, 334
motivational CQ, 347
repatriation, 353
reverse culture shock, 353
separation, 347
surface-level diversity, 333
third culture, 345
traditionalists, 333

TOOLKIT ACTIVITY 13.1: Generations at Work

Based on Table 13.1, identify which generation you are in: _____

What is your current age? _____

Answer the following questions. Then, join a group of four to five classmates and discuss how your answers are similar or different. Do they agree with the characterizations of your generation?

1. What is your preferred length of workday and the number of days worked per week?

   _____

2. Are you interested in flexible working hours? Working from home? Why or why not?

   _____

3. Do you multitask (do more than one thing at once)?

   _____

4. What frequency and form of team meetings do you prefer?

   _____

   _____

5. What style of leadership do you prefer? Why?

   _____

   _____

6. What organizational rewards are meaningful to you? Why?

   _____

   _____

7. How important is a balance between work and personal life to you? Explain.

   _____

TOOLKIT ACTIVITY 13.2: Journey to Sharahad

Background

This exercise simulates an intercultural exchange between Americans and a fictional culture. Participants role-playing either culture can learn from the experience. The task is simple, but the cultural barriers are considerable.

The briefing sheets for the roles are on the following pages. It is important that you do not read the briefing sheet for the other culture or the discussion questions following the briefing sheets. First, the Sharahadans and Americans will go to separate rooms to discuss how to role-play their cultures (10 minutes).

You will join a small group of four or five (more than one group can participate at once). Each group should have two "Americans" and two or three "Sharahadans." You will discuss the situation for 15 to 20 minutes and then return to the classroom for debriefing.

Situation: The Americans have proposed a business meeting in order to gather information on Mizar Marketing. The questions relate to what kind of performance the Sharahadans can promise the Americans as their distributors. If the information is favorable, they will propose a profitable deal for both sides.

Sharahadan Briefing Sheet

You are representatives of Mizar Marketing, Inc., a computer distributorship in the country of Sharahad. Mizar has been very successful marketing and distributing computers in this region for the last 12 years. Your company has witnessed steady double-digit growth every year it has been in business. You attribute this to your astute customer service skills and your ability to literally speak the language of all of your customers. Your company currently distributes 100,000 units a year (and earns a commission of 15% on each unit sold). You anticipate continued growth—but then, who can predict the future?

An American computer company has contacted Mizar and requested a meeting. You assume that this meeting is some kind of exploratory visit to see if Mizar can serve as the American company's distributor. You are looking forward to meeting the American representatives, even though you don't know much about American culture (although you do speak English).

Sharahadan culture exhibits very different communication patterns and values. Sharahadans pride themselves on their ability to speak expressively and to interact with others in a close personal manner. This involves using **intense eye contact and standing very close** to the person to whom they are speaking (6-12" distance is quite common). Sharahadans like to **establish personal relationships before conducting business** and prefer to discuss personal matters first. Sharahadans are also likely **to discuss multiple topics simultaneously**, switching back and forth to keep the conversion animated, and always interjecting personal matters into the business at hand. **Sharahadans do not speculate on future events**. Any kind of prediction or claim about what will be done in the future is foreign to Sharahadan ways. Sharahadans are also very humble, and never brag about their achievements (bragging is considered taboo), preferring instead to use such phrases as "I have been fortunate" or "God willing" to refer to past successes or future goals. Last, Sharahadans **often imply real meanings nonverbally, usually through their degree of enthusiasm**. For example, louder vocalizations, closer proximity, and physical contact (such as a hand on another person's shoulder) always accompany positive messages (such as agreement or when giving genuine compliments).

Mizar has two major competitors in the region: Altair Computers and Vega International. Both Altair and Vega sell fewer computers than your company does and have been in business for less time. They each sell about 50,000 units a year, and currently experience a 5% annual growth rate. However, you would consider it rude to point out their deficiencies so bluntly, preferring instead to let your judgment show in your lack of enthusiasm when you praise them.

Whatever behavior your American guests display, you will always treat them with respect and communicate with them for at least 15- to 20-minutes—even if they violate your cultural norms.

American Briefing Sheet

You and another business associate are sales representatives from an American computer company. You have been chosen to travel far away to the country of Sharahad. Your company has learned that Mizar Marketing, Inc. in Sharahad can distribute your computers in this region of the world for a much cheaper price than your current distributor, Altair Computers. **You have come to meet with the company's representatives. Your goal is to close a deal with them, asking them to sell 10,000 units a year, of which their commission will be 15%.** Your current distributor in this region (Altair Computers) can currently sell only 5,000 of your computers (at a commission rate of 25%). Any deal that increases your sales volume and reduces the current commission rate would be considered an improvement and should be accepted.

You did not want to come on this trip. You know very little about the Sharahadan culture. You have heard rumors that the Sharahadans are pushy and loud, have difficulty giving straight answers, and do not take business very seriously. You arrived on a flight late last night, and had a rough night of sleep at the hotel. You have seen little of the country yet. This meeting is your first real experience with the host culture. Fortunately, you know that the representatives at the meeting will speak English, although from your earlier communications, you get the impression that they are not well versed in American cultural norms.

Your plan is to start the meeting by getting right down to business and exploring whether Mizar can meet your needs. **Before you can propose any deals, however, you need to confirm the following about Mizar Marketing:** (1) Are they growing, and do they have a plan for continued expansion? (2) Can they sell an additional 10,000 units a year? (3) Are they committed to high standards of customer satisfaction? If the answers to these questions are unclear or unsatisfactory, there is little point in proposing a deal.

Because you cannot afford to alienate Altair (in case this deal doesn't go through), you would prefer not to mention who your current distributor is.

As you and your partner walk into Mizar's corporate headquarters, you are amazed at the surroundings: ornate Sharahadan office suites and conference rooms furnished with both traditional and modern fixtures. After making your introductions to the people in the outer offices, you are shown into a modest looking room. There, the representatives of Mizar await you. You approach them—ready to act in your most professional manner—and ready to close the deal in 15–20 minutes…

Discussion Questions

1. Did you come to an agreement? What was the agreement? If not, why not?

2. [For the Americans:] What kinds of cultural differences did you notice in your discussion with the Sharahadans?

3. [For the Sharahadans:] What things did your American guests do that you found confusing or frustrating?

4. What are the real-world implications of an exercise such as this one?

Source: Journey to Sharahad. Phil Darg. 1999, all rights reserved. Distributed by globalEDGE.

CASE STUDY 13.1: Managing Diversity at IBM Netherlands

A Vision on Managing Diversity

The multinational IT company IBM is convinced that it can only keep its current competitive edge by reflecting marketplace diversity in the workforce and by offering a safe work environment for all employees. The company considers workforce diversity as "the bridge between the workplace and the marketplace."

Ambition: An Inclusive Work Environment

In 1953, the CEO at that time published IBM's first equal opportunity policy letter. This letter stated simply that IBM will hire people based on their ability "regardless of race, color or creed." IBM's subsequent CEOs reinforced that policy throughout the years. Since then,

equal opportunity at IBM has been an evolutionary journey that underscores the company's commitment to an inclusive work environment where people's ideas and contributions are welcome—regardless of where they come from, what they look like, or what personal beliefs they hold.

Diversity in Leadership

To stress the importance of workforce diversity, IBM has a vice president of Global Workforce Diversity who formulates global policies on managing diversity. At regional headquarters, diversity managers translate the global policies on managing diversity into regional initiatives. Next, the executive management teams of every branch office formulate local actions in order to increase and to make full use of workforce diversity in that specific IBM establishment. An example of a local action is the adjustment of human resources policies and processes in each country's offices. Due to the differences in national legislation on employment and discrimination, IBM thinks it's best to do this at a country level.

Active Input From Managers and Employees

IBM's leadership underscores its commitment to an inclusive work environment through eight executive task forces, established in 1995:

- Asian
- Black
- Gay/Lesbian/Bisexual/Transgender
- Hispanic
- Men
- Native American
- People with disabilities
- Women

The mission of each task force is to increase the success of IBM in the marketplace by focusing on the various constituencies as customers. The task forces are chaired and staffed by executives and employees from that particular constituency. Each was formed to look at IBM through the lens of their group and answer these questions:

- What is required for your group to feel welcomed and valued at IBM?

- What can IBM, in partnership with your group, do to maximize your productivity?

- What courses of action can IBM take to influence the buying decisions of your group?

There are also global diversity networks where people from various underrepresented groups can meet each other and colleagues from other backgrounds.

Many subsidiaries have local chapters of these networks. IBM Netherlands has local chapters of the global diversity network groups for women (called Women in Blue) and for gays, lesbians, bisexuals, and transgenders (called EAGLE). In both cases, the initiative for the foundation of a local chapter was taken by employees.

The networks organize meetings, lectures, workshops, and social events for employees belonging to the specific underrepresented group or for those interested in managing diversity and learning more about the other. All network activities are aimed at enhancing people's personal strength. Another employee collects and distributes information via the intranet about people with disabilities. The company stimulates initiatives like this by allocating time, resources, and budget. The human resources department plays a supportive role: It organizes meetings for the initiators to exchange knowledge and ideas. It also gives them advice on how to use the intranet to draw attention for their subject and gives them information about (international) conferences on managing diversity.

Toward Inclusive Leadership

Throughout the years, global and local diversity network groups were founded for almost any of the traditionally underrepresented groups at IBM. Lately, a turn of opinion has evolved. The company now believes that the key to managing diversity is inclusive leadership. Inclusive leadership implies creating a corporate culture where people feel respected and rewarded, with all their differences and similarities. International training has been developed that focuses on this broad concept of managing diversity. Several senior managers and their advisers have already participated in the training program. Among them were some executives from the Dutch subsidiary and their local diversity coordinator. According to these participants, the training made them aware of the fact that you must focus on diversity management by including all employees.

One exercise showed that everybody sometimes feels excluded from a group and that almost everybody experiences exclusion negatively. Because of the training, they now understand that diversity concerns all employees and not just the ones belonging to a minority. IBM strongly believes that this greater understanding is the basis for realizing inclusive leadership.

Discussion Questions

1. What are the most important aspects of IBM Netherlands' vision for diversity?

2. This case study is set in the Netherlands. Do you think that the diversity initiatives could work anywhere? Why or why not?

3. The executive task forces for diverse groups focus on three questions: (1) What is required for your group to feel valued? (2) What is required to maximize productivity? (3) How do you influence the buying decisions of the group? What other questions should be asked?

4. What is "inclusive leadership" at IBM? How can diversity training increase this type of leadership?

Source: Diversity@Work (http://www.diversityatwork.net/EN/en_case_004.htm). Used with permission from Richard Wynne.

CASE STUDY 13.2: "A Person Needs Face, Like a Tree Needs Bark"

American Brian Cook meets with his Chinese change manager Chan Ling and his team at the Beijing office of a European corporation to discuss last month's delay in the change deadlines. He questions Chan Ling repeatedly about his team's underperformance. Brian openly states he believes the team is not pushing hard enough and that there is a lack of commitment. He stresses than Ling is accountable for the results of the team and that he should have informed him about the issues. Ling nods silently and peers out the window. He picks up his papers, walks through the door without further discussion, and never returns (actual example with fictitious names).

Chan Ling has lost face. The directness of Brian's questioning was interpreted by Chan as a personal insult. He saw Brian as rude, and their working relationship ended abruptly based on this incident. Chan also terminated his employment with the company at a time when he was really needed. What happened?

In China, as in other cultures around the world, "face" is more important than anything else. Face is related to the Western concept of dignity, but it goes much deeper than that. There is a Chinese proverb that reads *Ren yao lian, shu yao pi* ("A person needs face, like a tree needs bark"). Losing face has serious consequences for people from such cultures since there is a profound emotion of shame associated with losing face, and this may reflect on the person, their families, or even their entire community. Chan felt a deep sense of embarrassment from Brian's assertive questioning style, which is commonly accepted in the United States and many other Western cultures. What Brian didn't realize is that this is not acceptable in all cultures; thus, his leadership effectiveness was compromised.

Discussion Questions

1. How could Brian have prepared more effectively for his international assignment (refer to the guidelines for culture shock and cultural agility)?

2. What cultural values (Hofstede; GLOBE) help explain Chan's reaction? What are the differences between the United States and China?

3. What should Brian do now? Develop a plan for addressing the situation.

Source: Boot, A., & Siebelink, H. (2013). Cross-cultural leadership: How to avoid making people lose face. Retrieved from www.leadershipwatch-aadboot.com/2013/07/14/cross-cultural-leadership-how-to-avoid-making-people-lose-face. Reprinted with permission.

SELF-ASSESSMENT 13.1: What Is Your Cultural Intelligence?

This self-assessment exercise identifies your approach to interacting with people from different cultures. There are no right or wrong answers, and this is not a test. You don't have to share your results with others unless you wish to do so.

Part I. Taking the Assessment

You will be presented with some questions representing different situations involving cross-cultural interaction. Answer each question using the scale below each question.

Statements	Strongly disagree	Disagree	Neutral	Agree	Strongly agree
1. I am conscious of the cultural knowledge I use when interacting with people with different cultural backgrounds.	1	2	3	4	5
2. I know the legal and economic systems of other cultures.	1	2	3	4	5
3. I enjoy interacting with people from different cultures.	1	2	3	4	5
4. I change my verbal behavior (e.g., accent, tone) when a cross-cultural interaction requires it.	1	2	3	4	5
5. I adjust my cultural knowledge as I interact with people from a culture that is unfamiliar to me.	1	2	3	4	5
6. I know the rules (e.g., vocabulary, grammar) of other languages.	1	2	3	4	5
7. I am confident that I can socialize with locals in a culture that is unfamiliar to me.	1	2	3	4	5
8. I use pause and silence differently to suit different cross-cultural situations.	1	2	3	4	5
9. I am conscious of the cultural knowledge I apply to cross-cultural interactions.	1	2	3	4	5
10. I know the cultural values and religious beliefs of other cultures.	1	2	3	4	5
11. I am sure I can deal with the stresses of adjusting to a culture that is new to me.	1	2	3	4	5
12. I vary the rate of my speaking when a cross-cultural situation requires it.	1	2	3	4	5
13. I check the accuracy of my cultural knowledge as I interact with people from different cultures.	1	2	3	4	5
14. I know the marriage systems of other cultures.	1	2	3	4	5
15. I enjoy living in cultures that are unfamiliar to me.	1	2	3	4	5
16. I change my nonverbal behavior when a cross-cultural situation requires it.	1	2	3	4	5
17. I know the arts and crafts of other cultures.	1	2	3	4	5
18. I am confident that I can get accustomed to the shopping conditions in a different culture.	1	2	3	4	5

Statements	Strongly disagree	Disagree	Neutral	Agree	Strongly agree
19. I alter my facial expressions when a cross-cultural interaction requires it.	1	2	3	4	5
20. I know the rules of expressing nonverbal behaviors in other cultures.	1	2	3	4	5

Part II. Scoring and Interpretation

In Part I, you rated yourself on 20 questions. Add the numbers you circled in each of the columns to derive your score for the four aspects of CQ. These dimensions have been shown through research to be related to cross-cultural adjustment and leader effectiveness, and are described in the section on CQ in this chapter. For each dimension, scores can range from 5 to 25. If your score ranges from 5 to 12, you have a lower rating on the dimension, and if your score is above 13, you have a higher rating on the dimension.

Metacognitive	Cognitive	Motivational	Behavioral
1. _____	2. _____	3. _____	4. _____
5. _____	6. _____	7. _____	8. _____
9. _____	10. _____	11. _____	12. _____
13. _____	14. _____	15. _____	16. _____
17. _____	18. _____	19. _____	20. _____
Total _____	_____	_____	_____

Discussion Questions

1. Which of the dimensions did you score highest on? Lowest? What does this tell you about areas that you may need to improve?

2. Add the scores together for each dimension to compute an overall score for cultural intelligence. Scores can range from 20 to 100. In general, scores from 60 to 100 are very high, and scores less than 40 are considered low. Do you have a high degree of cultural intelligence?

3. Discuss how you can increase your cultural intelligence. List two or three specific action steps you will take to improve your scores.

Sources: Eisenberg, J., Lee, H. J., Brueck, F., Brenner, B., Claes, M. T., Mironski, J., & Bell, R. (2013). Can business schools make students culturally competent? Effects of cross-cultural management courses on cultural intelligence. *Academy of Management Learning and Education, 12*(4), 603–621. doi:10.5465/amle.2012.0022

SELF-ASSESSMENT 13.2: Do You Have a Global Mind-Set?

This self-assessment exercise identifies your approach to interacting with people from different cultures. There are no right or wrong answers, and this is not a test. You don't have to share your results with others unless you wish to do so.

Part I. Taking the Assessment

Ask another person in your class (preferably a person you work with in a team) to rate you with respect to your overall global outlook. Your rater will be presented with some questions representing different situations involving your interactions. Ask them to answer each question using the scale below each question.

Your Name: _____

Name of Person That Rated You: _____

Statements	Not at all	Very little	Occasionally	A little	A great deal
1. In interacting with others, did national origin have an impact on whether or not he/she assigned equal status to others?	1	2	3	4	5
2. Do you consider him/her as equally open to ideas from other countries and cultures as he/she is to ideas from their country and culture of origin?	1	2	3	4	5
3. Do you think finding himself/herself in a new cultural setting would cause excitement or fear and anxiety?	1	2	3	4	5
4. When he/she interacts with people from other cultures, what do you think he/she regards as more important: understanding them as individuals or viewing them as representatives of their national cultures?	1	2	3	4	5

Part II. Scoring and Interpretation

Add your responses to the four items. Your Total Score: _____.

Scores can range from 4 to 20. Scores over 10 suggest that you have a global mind-set.

Discussion Questions

1. Do you agree with how the person rated you? Why or why not?

2. What did you learn about yourself by having someone rate your global mind-set? Rate another person in your class using this assessment. What feedback do you want to provide them with so that they can improve their global mind-set?

3. Which questions were rated 3 or lower (if any)? How could you improve on those behaviors? Give two or three specific strategies. If all of your ratings were 3 or higher, describe how you would help another person to improve on their global mind-set. Give two or three specific strategies.

Source: Adapted from Gupta, A. K., & Govindarajan, V. (2002). Cultivating a global mindset. *Academy of Management Executive*, 16(1), 116–126.

LEADERS AS CHANGE AGENTS

CHAPTER 14 · Organizational Culture

CHAPTER 15 · Leading Change and Stress Management

Introduction

Chapter 1: What Is Organizational Behavior?

↓

Understanding Individuals in Organizations

Chapter 2: Personality and Person–Environment Fit

Chapter 3: Emotions and Moods

Chapter 4: Attitudes and Job Satisfaction

Chapter 5: Perception, Decision Making, and Problem Solving

Influencing and Motivating Employees

Chapter 6: Leadership

Chapter 7: Power and Politics

Chapter 8: Motivation: Core Concepts

Chapter 9: Motivation: Applications

Building Relationships

Chapter 10: Group Processes and Teams

Chapter 11: Managing Conflict and Negotiation

Chapter 12: Organizational Communication

Chapter 13: Diversity and Cross-Cultural Adjustments

Leaders as Change Agents

Chapter 14: Organizational Culture

Chapter 15: Leading Change and Stress Management

CHAPTER FOURTEEN

ORGANIZATIONAL CULTURE

Learning Objectives

After studying this chapter, you should be able to do the following:

14.1: Define *organizational culture,* and describe the seven characteristics.

14.2: Compare and contrast *market, bureaucracy,* and *clan cultures.*

14.3: Explain the relationship between national culture and organizational culture.

14.4: Demonstrate understanding of the two characteristics of strong cultures by providing examples.

14.5: Explain how employees learn organizational culture through the socialization process.

14.6: Discuss four ways that employees learn organizational culture.

14.7: Compare and contrast *organizational culture* and *climate.*

Get the edge on your studies at **edge.sagepub.com/scandura2e**

- Take the chapter quiz
- Review key terms with eFlashcards
- Explore multimedia resources, SAGE readings, and more!

CULTURE CHANGE AT VERIZON: CAN YOU HEAR ME NOW?*

Verizon Wireless has turned the cell phone into a necessity of modern life. It's easy to forget that cellphone users once faced sky-high roaming charges, dropped calls, and experienced such unreliable service that companies found themselves earning the same level of customer disdain as used-car salesmen. CEO Lowell McAdam recalled those early days: "It was a pretty ugly experience. There was a good opportunity for someone to come in and disrupt the environment—to consolidate and create scale." McAdam described how Verizon seized that opportunity by building Verizon Wireless, which has become the nation's largest wireless provider and broadband data network with revenues of over $32 billion in 2016. He described the effort that went into creating a unique corporate culture. McAdam served as Verizon's chief operating officer and then he was named Verizon CEO in 2011. McAdam, an engineer-turned-executive who still enjoys tinkering with cars, said the memorable "Can you hear me now?" test man advertisement created a unique brand for the company. Creating a strong corporate culture was next.

McAdam had plenty of expertise within Verizon to draw on. Not long after he joined Verizon, former CEO Denny Strigl put him in charge of creating a corporate culture for Verizon Wireless, betting that it would further set the company apart from its competition. In 2011, Strigl had coauthored a book on Verizon's culture change strategy with the subtitle "*Managers, can you hear me now*?" Strigl believed that Verizon's corporate culture would determine the longevity and the success of the company as much as the technology would. To effect the change, McAdam used employee surveys to develop the core values to define a company credo. One of the things management learned from those surveys was that Verizon employees wanted to be associated with

---

*Adapted from Verizon CEO brings Verizon Wireless case study to life for MBA students. Retrieved from http://www.business.rutgers.edu/news/verizon-ceo-brings-verizon-wireless-case-study-life-mba-students; We Are Verizon. Retrieved from https://www.verizon.com/about/sites/default/files/Verizon-Credo.pdf

a company consumers could depend on. "That was the essence of the company we wanted to be," McAdam said, adding that once management decided on a set of core values, it had to be "relentless" in defining itself by them. "It took four years before we really knew people got it," he said. The Verizon credo emphasizes the customer experience, growth and profitability, and building the V-team culture. McAdam, who admitted to being uncertain about the idea when Strigl assigned him the task of creating a new culture, urges students in the job market to "take a hard look" at a prospective employer's culture. He states, "I can't overemphasize how important the culture is to the business."

Verizon CEO Lowell McAdam is clear that the corporate culture at Verizon is one of its keys to success. This chapter addresses the organizational level of analysis and discusses what organizational culture is, and why it is so important to the bottom line. How employees learn the culture of an organization through the socialization process is also discussed. Organizational culture has different dimensions, and these are discussed first.

WHAT IS ORGANIZATIONAL CULTURE?

Learning Objective 14.1: Define *organizational culture*, and describe the seven characteristics.

Organizational culture is

the pattern of basic assumptions, that a given group has invented, discovered, or developed in learning to cope with its problems of external adaptation and internal integration, and that have worked well enough to be considered valid, and, therefore, to be taught to new members as the correct way to perceive, think, and feel in relation to those problems.[1]

This definition is rather complex; however, culture can be thought of as a set of shared meanings that people in organizations have with respect to how to adapt to the environments and cope with change. Norms emerge in the organization regarding what constitutes the culture (you learned about the power of group norms in Chapter 10). Organizational culture norms have three distinct dimensions: (1) the *content* or what is deemed important (e.g., teamwork, accountability, innovation), (2) the *consensus* or how widely shared norms are held across people in the organization, and (3) the *intensity* of feelings about the importance of the norm (e.g., are people willing to sanction others for violating culture norms?).[2] In addition to these dimensions, culture operates at different levels, as shown in Figure 14.1:

1. **Artifacts and creations**—for example, the architecture of the buildings, the office decoration including artwork, and the way

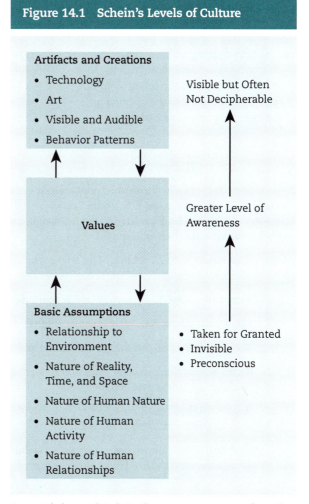

Figure 14.1   Schein's Levels of Culture

Source: Schein, E. H. (1984). Coming to a new awareness of organizational culture. *Sloan Management Review*, 25(2), 3–16. p. 4.

that people dress reflect the organization's culture. This can also include organization charts and new employee orientation materials.

2. **Values**—the reasons people give for their behavior. These values can be stated (or **espoused**), or they may be unconscious and people act them out (**enacted**). For example, a person may state that they believe in treating customers with respect (an **espoused value**). Treating customers with respect is an example of an enacted value.

3. **Assumptions**—underlie values and are often unconscious to people in organizations because they don't question them. For example, an assumption might be the view of the organization's relationship to the environment. Some view the environment as something to be exploited for financial gain, while others may view the environment as something that must be protected. Another example is the nature of human nature. Some may view employees as fundamentally lazy, and others may view employees as hard working and well intentioned (recall Theory X/Y assumptions from Chapter 1). To really understand an organization's culture, a person must go beyond what they can see and hear (artifacts and creations) and gain a deeper awareness of values first and then assumptions. What we can observe is an expression of values that are typically rooted in fundamental assumptions.

Critical Thinking Questions: Provide an example of an artifact found in an organization. Trace it to the underlying values and assumptions it represents.

The following sections review the research that examines what has been observed regarding different aspects of organizational culture.

Seven Characteristics of Culture

A research study compared the organizational cultures of 15 organizations in four industries in the service sector (public accounting, consulting, the U.S. Postal Service, and transportation of household goods). Cultural values differed across these sectors and were related to the levels of industry, technology, and growth. The seven characteristics and examples from this research follow.[3]

1. **Innovation and risk taking.** Most cultures in the service industries studied were average on this dimension, with transportation showing the highest score.

2. **Attention to detail.** Consulting and accounting firms were highest on this dimension.

3. **Outcome orientation.** All companies studied in the service industry were high on this dimension.

4. **People orientation.** All companies studied in the four industries were average on this dimension.

5. **Team orientation.** All companies studied were average, but consulting firms were slightly higher on working in teams as part of their culture.

6. **Aggressiveness (easygoingness reversed).** All industries were average; however, consulting firms were less easygoing than other companies.

7. **Stability.** Most industries were average on stability; however, the U.S. Postal Service was higher than other organizations on the need for stability as part of the organization's culture.

BEST PRACTICES

Is Your Culture in Trouble?

Management consultant Randy Pennington has worked with corporations like Procter & Gamble and Marriott in numerous industry sectors for over 20 years. In his book *Results Rule! Build a Culture That Blows the Competition Away,* he provided the following list of things to look for in an organization culture that limits results:[4]

- **High turnover and low morale.** Good employees decide to pursue other opportunities. Individuals remaining with the organization become demoralized and lethargic in the performance of their duties.
- **Ongoing inconsistency.** Everyone has an off-day occasionally. Performance that continually gyrates all over the map is a reflection on the culture. Consistency is one mark of a *Results Rule!* organization.
- **Lack of focus on the external environment.** Cultures in distress look internally at all the things that are going wrong. *Results Rule!* cultures focus on serving the customer. They compete against others in the marketplace rather than against themselves.
- **Short-term thinking.** Survival in today's competitive marketplace requires constant

attention to results. That, however, should not be an excuse for short-term thinking. *Results Rule!* cultures refuse to sacrifice long-term viability for short-term success. They look for both.
- **Rise of destructive subcultures.** Pride in one's team is admirable. Allowing team pride to deteriorate into impenetrable organizational silos is a sure sign of a fractured culture.
- **Undermining the success of others.** Disagreements that turn into vendettas and information purposely withheld are the symptoms of a culture where *team* is considered a four-letter word.
- **Increased cynicism.** Cultures that are in trouble look at all change—good or bad—through cynical eyes that assume the worst possible outcome.

Results Rule! cultures take a critical look at opportunities to improve and embrace cultural values that offer a satisfactory return on investment (ROI).

Discussion Questions

1. Which of the previously given challenges indicating a troubled culture are most important in your opinion? Explain why.
2. How can short-term and long-term thinking be accomplished at the same time? What

specifically can a leader do to keep employees focused on both?
3. What can leaders do to address the problem of cynicism of employees during times of change?

Source: Pennington, R. (2006). *Results rule! Build a culture that blows the competition away.* New York, NY: Wiley.

MARKETS, BUREAUCRACIES, AND CLANS

Learning Objective 14.2: Compare and contrast *market*, *bureaucracy*, and *clan cultures*.

Another approach to describing organizational cultures is by examining the mechanisms used for control when organizations are faced with *goal incongruence* and *performance ambiguity*. Goal incongruence exists when organizational members don't agree on what the goals of the organization are or should be. Performance ambiguity occurs when revenue streams are unpredictable or uneven.[5] These factors give rise to the need for organizational control, and organizations address the challenge of control in different ways. Table 14.1 shows the three ways that organizations address control according to a classic theory at the organizational level of analysis. **Market control** exists when prices determine how social interactions between people are formed. For example, you and your friends go for beverages and you choose the bar that has the best happy-hour prices. **Bureaucratic control** is when legitimate authority governs social interactions. An example of this is when you organize an end of the semester happy hour on campus, purchase food and beverages for a large group, and then charge them for attending; provide a wristband and only those with a wristband are served. There is a specific location predetermined as well as the hours for the event. The event must follow the rules and regulations of the university, and the rules must be followed by participants. **Clan control** occurs when shared values and beliefs govern how people interact socially. An example of clan control is when a group of friends just get together at one person's house and everyone chips in money for beverages and pizza. The group has this tradition at the end of every semester, and they know they can depend upon one another to share the costs and have a good time.

Differences in the emergent cultures have implications for how organizations are designed and employee performance.[6] Markets require only knowledge of prices and supply and demand. For example, the human resources department conducts a salary survey to determine how much to pay a new management trainee. Bureaucracies require the creation of rules and regulations (the employee handbook for a new employee, for example). Bureaucratic control also requires close surveillance and direction of employees by supervisors. Clans are more efficient in the sense that there is less need for information on pricing or rules, and norms and traditions that emerge over time are shared with a new

Table 14.1 Comparison of Market, Bureaucracy, and Clan Cultures

Control Challenges	Markets	Bureaucracies	Clans
Social Interaction Requirements	Reciprocity and exchange	Legitimate authority	Shared values and beliefs
Information Needs	Competitive pricing; supply and demand	Rules and regulations; created or designed	Implicit norms; traditions that emerge naturally over time
Employee Commitment	Low, self-interests based on price; compliance	Moderate, motivated by training, close supervision, and evaluation; identification	High, interest for the common good of the organization based on shared values; internalization
Method of Controlling People	Self-selected based on price mechanism	Select employees based on little screening, then train, monitor, and evaluate them	Carefully screen employees for fit to the clan culture; both skills and values
Cost of Maintaining the Control System	Low but market costs may vary	Moderate; high costs for training and supervision	High; high costs for job searches and training, but low costs for supervision

Sources: Adapted from Ouchi, W. G. (1980). Markets, bureaucracies, and clans. *Administrative Science Quarterly, 34,* 129–141; Ouchi, W. G. (1979). A conceptual framework for the design of organizational control mechanisms. *Management Science, 25*(9), 833–848.

employee. Control is more subtle but does exist since an employee might be ostracized from a group if they don't fit in with the norms. For example, a new employee does not stay late for work and coworkers let them know that everyone is "expected" to stay after regular working hours.

As shown in Table 14.1, employee organizational commitment is highest in the clan culture since they have internalized the organization's cultural value system. One reason that clans are more efficient is that the demands for control systems are less, and they cost less to maintain. The bureaucracy is moderately costly; the costs of selecting employees are low, but the costs of monitoring, evaluating, and supervising employees are high. The clan is high cost in terms of screening and selection, but once the right people are selected that best fit the cultural value system, the cost of maintaining the system is low because they don't need constant monitoring. For example, a computer software firm spends a great deal of money on sending recruiters to campuses to interview new programmers with high levels of skills that share the organization's entrepreneurial value system. Because they select the right people who are intrinsically motivated, they don't need as many supervisors and they don't need to maintain an elaborate performance management system.

NATIONAL CULTURE AND ORGANIZATIONAL CULTURE

Learning Objective 14.3: Explain the relationship between national culture and organizational culture.

Since the term *culture* is used for both national and organizational cultures, this may be a source of confusion. Results of the Global Leadership and Organizational Behavior Effectiveness (GLOBE) studies of leadership (discussed in Chapter 13) across cultures suggest that national culture has a strong influence on organizational culture.[7] A study of 10 European cultures found national culture values (power distance and collectivism) influence the development of organizational culture. However, the values of the founders of companies and key leaders also have an influence on organizational culture.[8] National culture constrains organizational culture, but only partially.[9]

A large-scale research program learned that four organizational culture values appear to be important in most cultures: **adaptability**, **involvement**, **mission**, and **consistency**. Adaptability is the ability to transfer the demands of the market into organizational actions. Involvement is building human capability, ownership, and responsibility. Mission is defining the meaningful long-term direction for the organization. Consistency is defining values and subsystems that are the basis of a strong culture. This model of organizational culture is shown in Figure 14.2.[10]

Mission and consistency are most related to profitability. Adaptability and mission are the best predictors of sales growth. Adaptability and involvement best predict innovation.[11] These organizational culture values appear relevant to all cultures; however, they are expressed differently in each culture.[12] For example, a study involving surveys from 179 foreign-owned firms operating in Russia and case studies found that all four values matter, but adaptability was most important for Russian organizations.[13] Another study[14] related the four Denison culture values to knowledge management in the Khorasan Province in Iran. This study found that all four cultural values contributed significantly to knowledge management (using knowledge to solve problems and make decisions). While what constitutes a strong culture may vary, research suggests that having a strong organizational culture makes a difference in terms of organizational effectiveness in all cultural contexts.

STRONG ORGANIZATIONAL CULTURES

Learning Objective 14.4: Demonstrate understanding of the two characteristics of strong cultures by providing examples.

Strong cultures are based on two characteristics: high levels of agreement among employees about what they value and high intensity toward these values. If both are high, a strong culture exists. Some organizations are characterized by high levels of intensity but low agreement. In this case, employees and/or groups are at war with one another over

Figure 14.2 The Denison Model of Organizational Culture

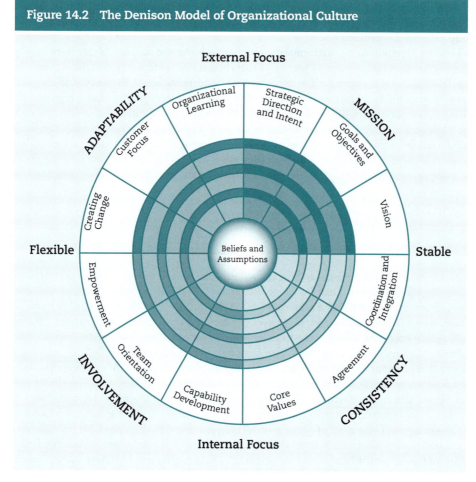

External Focus

ADAPTABILITY

Organizational Learning

Strategic Direction and Intent

MISSION

Customer Focus

Goals and Objectives

Creating Change

Vision

Flexible

Beliefs and Assumptions

Stable

Empowerment

Coordination and Integration

Team Orientation

Agreement

INVOLVEMENT

Capability Development

Core Values

CONSISTENCY

Internal Focus

Source: Denison, D. R., Haaland, S., & Goelzer, P. (2004). Corporate culture and organizational effectiveness: Is Asia different from the rest of the world? *Organizational Dynamics*, 33(1), 98–109. p. 101.

what is important for the organization to value.[15] For example, salespeople focus on customer-driven product features while accountants focus on cost containment. Thus, while both groups intensely value what they do, they disagree on priorities.

Strong organizational cultures are critical to bottom-line performance in large organizations.[16,17,18] Employee agreement on cultural values is also related to lower turnover among newly hired employees.[19,20] A study[21] of firms in a variety of industries found that strong cultures affect organizational learning in response to internal and external change. In this research, firm performance was assessed by using yearly return on invested capital (ROIC) and yearly operating cash flow. Results showed that strong-culture firms excelled at incremental change but encountered difficulties in more volatile economic environments. In other words, in relatively stable economic environments, strong-culture firms have more reliable performance.

You have probably heard of Zappos, the online seller of shoes and clothing. The CEO, Tony Hsieh (pronounced "Shay"), has developed a strong culture where employees very much agree on and are passionate about customer service.

The Zappos experience indicates that to build a culture that results in a great place to work, exceptional customer service, and impressive organizational performance requires specific drivers. The five drivers that Zappos uses to shape its culture are committed leaders, core values, customer-focused strategies, human resource practices, and management practices that align with core values.[22] At Zappos, employees are encouraged to express their uniqueness in executing on the mission of "delivering happiness." Zappos defines its culture in terms of these 10 core values:

1. Deliver wow through service.

2. Embrace and drive change.

3. Create fun and a little weirdness.

4. Be adventurous, creative, and open-minded.

5. Pursue growth and learning.

6. Build open and honest relationships with communication.

7. Build a positive team and family spirit.

8. Do more with less.

9. Be passionate and determined.

10. Be humble.

To Hsieh, the Zappos culture is about more than money: "It's not me saying to our employees, this is where our culture is. It's more about giving employees the permission and encouraging them to just be themselves."[23]

> Critical Thinking Questions: What role do you think the fact that Tony Hsieh founded Zappos plays in his ability to influence the culture? Would this be more difficult in an older organization? Explain.

In addition to understanding the strong overall culture in an organization, it is also important to recognize that organizations have subcultures. For example, the marketing department of an organization may have a risk-taking orientation, whereas the accounting department may not because they value stability. This is because a strong culture of stability may inhibit the marketing department's ability to be flexible. Organizations can increase flexibility without losing their strong overall culture by encouraging subcultures.[24] In this way, organizations reap the benefits of a strong culture while remaining responsive to change. For example, Procter & Gamble has a strong culture of attention to detail and outcome orientation, but their research departments encourage innovation and trial-and-error experimentation.

Organizational Subcultures

Three general subcultures exist in most organizations. **Operators** are the line managers and employees who are involved in making products, delivering services, and interacting with customers directly. The operators value teamwork and desire engagement with the work they do. **Engineers** represent the second type of organizational subculture, and this group focuses on designing systems to support the work of operations, such as employees who design a manufacturing facility. This may also include employees who design and implement information technology systems, financial analysis systems, and marketing research. The third group, **executives**, has worked their way up organizational career ladders, and they are financially responsible to their board of directors and shareholders. This group often has to "make the tough financial decisions based on imperfect information."[25] Executives manage large numbers of people and divisions, and rely on policies and reward systems to maintain control. They may lose touch with their customers and employees at lower levels in the organizational hierarchy.

In recent years, however, executive teams have become more enlightened regarding the importance of having a positive organizational culture that values employees. They also have found ways to stay in closer touch with their customers. For example, Amazon CEO Jeff Bezos has a public e-mail address, jeff@amazon.com. He reads many customer complaints and forwards them to the relevant employee at Amazon, with a one-character addition: a question mark.[26]

> **Critical Thinking Question:** Provide examples of how executives can stay in touch with their customers. How can executives promote an organizational culture that values employees?

As the previous discussion suggests, organizational culture has a significant impact on employee attitudes and behavior. For example, in a clan culture, employees act in ways that support the organizational goals because they have internalized the value system. It is important for a leader to understand the forces that shape organizational culture. The next sections discuss how employees learn organizational culture. First, the process of socialization is discussed, followed by ways that employees learn culture through stories, rituals, symbols, and language.

Figure 14.3   The Socialization Process

Anticipatory Socialization

⬇

Entry and Assimilation

⬇

Metamorphosis

⬇

Outcomes

- Job Performance
- Job Satisfaction
- Organizational Commitment
- Lower Turnover

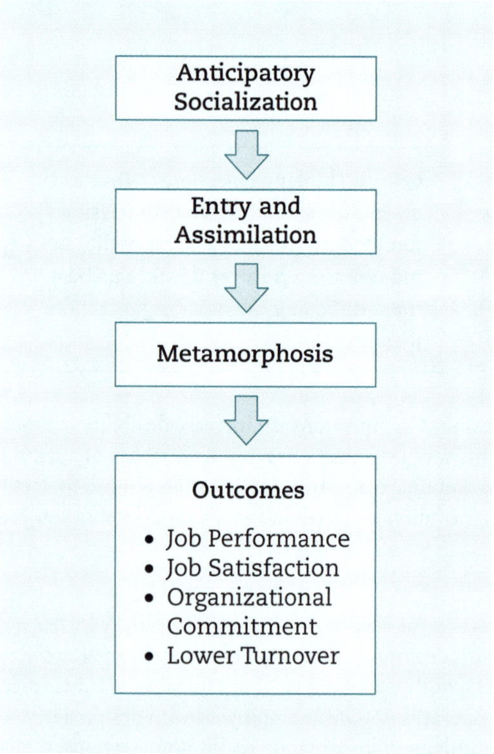

Source: Jablin, F. M. (1987). Organizational entry, assimilation, and exit. In L. L. Putnam, K. H. Roberts, & L. W. Porter (Eds.), *Handbook of organizational communication: An interdisciplinary perspective* (pp. 679–740). Beverly Hills, CA: Sage.

SOCIALIZATION

Learning Objective 14.5: Explain how employees learn organizational culture through the socialization process.

Organizational socialization is defined as the process an organization utilizes to ensure that new members acquire necessary attitudes, behaviors, knowledge, and skills to become productive organizational members.[27] When a new hire joins a company, the first 6 months on the job are characterized as a series of reality "shocks" as they are exposed to the unwritten rules defining the organizational culture in the organization.[28] For example, the job may be considered an 8-hour workday, but the new hire notices that everyone works at least 10 hours a day. The process of socialization follows these steps: organizational anticipatory socialization, organizational entry and assimilation, and metamorphosis.[29] This process is diagrammed in Figure 14.3, and these steps are discussed in the following sections.

Anticipatory Socialization

Organizational anticipatory socialization is the process an individual goes through as they attempt to find an organization to join. Organizational anticipatory socialization has two basic processes: recruiting and selection.[30] For example, as a student nears graduation, they visit the placement center at the university to learn about job opportunities and meet recruiters. The student then determines which jobs are the best fit to their college major, skills, and the type of organization they want to work for. For example, the student may want to work for a large organization as opposed to a small one. During the organizational anticipatory socialization stage, both the applicant and the organization are looking for evidence of a good person–organization fit. The recruitment process may involve psychological testing and interviews to determine how well a person will fit with the culture. HR expert Andrew Greenberg suggests asking the interview questions in Table 14.2 to assess an employee's fit with organizational culture.

Table 14.2   Interview Questions to Determine an Employee's Fit With a Strong Culture

Question	Purpose
1. If you could be doing anything, what would you do?	This question assesses passions and interests for culture fit.
2. What are your top three values?	This question helps you figure out if the candidate's values match those for the position, department, or team.
3. Have the candidate read the company's mission and value statements, and discuss how they fit with their personal values.	This question reveals how closely a candidate's personal values align with the company's values.
4. If hired, what would you accomplish in your first week on the job?	This question shows a candidate's expectations and organizational skills.

Source: Greenberg, A. (2014). Start asking unique interview questions. Retrieved from http://www.recruitingdivision.com/start-asking-unique-interview-questions-2

Entry and Assimilation

The **preentry** step occurs from the time someone is offered the job to when they actually start working. There are three important issues that arise during the preentry stage. First, the types of messages a new employee receives from the organization prior to starting work could include realistic job previews in which the members of the organization attempt to clarify what the job will be like. These might be different than what was discussed in the hiring process and may be either positive or negative surprises. Second, new employees are typically concerned about how they are seen by existing organizational members and engage in impression management (discussed in Chapter 7)—the process (either conscious or unconscious) where an individual deliberately attempts to influence the perceptions and opinions of others. For example, the new hire might mention the rankings of their university to enhance the perceptions of their qualifications for the job. Third, current organizational members form perceptions of the new hire and consider how well they will fit in. These perceptions may result in unrealistic expectations, so it's important to seek feedback in a new job to correct misconceptions. A four-phase longitudinal study of 273 new software engineers in an Indian company[31] found that when both new employees and their managers were proactive, they adjusted well to the culture, performed better, and mastered their tasks better. They were also less likely to be thinking of quitting. The results suggest that newcomers who proactively seek information from their coworkers are at an advantage because they are viewed as more committed to learning about the organization and fitting in. This in turn, motivates their managers and peers to share more information with them. The takeaway for a new employee is clear—be proactive in learning the organization's culture during the first weeks of employment.

Next, the **entry** phase occurs, which happens when the new member starts work. The new member begins to assimilate within the organizational culture. During the entry period, new employees begin to understand the organization's culture and work expectations. This may include a formal orientation program to help the new employee learn the rules and expectations of the organization—the explicit dictates that govern employee behavior within the organization. For example, an orientation program may include a session on the ethical code of the organization. **Onboarding** is the process of welcoming and orienting new organizational members to facilitate their adjustment to the organization, its culture, and its practices. It refers to the process of facilitating new members' adjustment to the organization and its culture.[32]

Employees have expectations regarding what the psychosocial contract is with the organization, and this influences the degree to which they view onboarding processes (such as an orientation training program) as being valuable. A longitudinal study of 144 recruits from a European army[33] found that when new employees have a psychological contract that involves a higher sense of personal obligation at entry, they perceived the orientation training as more useful. They also developed better relationships with their supervisors and peers, which in turn facilitated their adjustment to their work. In addition to orientation and new-hire training, the organization may assign a formal mentor or "buddy" during this phase to help the new employee learn the norms of the organization. The informal expectations about how new employees should behave within the organization are "unwritten rules" that govern how new employees should act. For example, employees may be expected to eat lunch at their desk while working, but this is not specifically written down anywhere.

Metamorphosis

The final stage of organizational entry and assimilation is the **metamorphosis** stage. During this stage, a person transforms from a new employee to an established contributor who is valued and trusted by other members of the organization. Metamorphosis completes the socialization process—the new employee is comfortable with the organization, their boss, and their work group. They have internalized the organizational culture and understand their job as well as the rules, procedures, and norms. Expectations are clear regarding what good performance means in the organization. Successful metamorphosis positively affects job performance, job satisfaction, and commitment to the organization. Also, there is a lower chance that the person will look for another job or quit.[34] Most often, this transition occurs over a long time period. However, the process may start over again (preentry and assimilation to metamorphosis) if a person gets a promotion to a new role in the organization.

> Critical Thinking Questions: How can you make your socialization process smoother when you enter into a new organization? What can you do now to prepare for the preentry and entry phases?

Attraction-Selection-Attrition (ASA)

The ASA approach suggests that applicants are attracted to organizations that match their personalities (recall the discussion of person–organization [PO] fit from Chapter 2). Some potential employees simply won't apply to an organization if they feel they won't fit in there.[35] Employees that choose to join an organization are more likely to share organizational values than those that do not (attraction-selection).[36] A study of 140 employees over a 2-year time period found that the lower the perceived match between one's own and the organizational values at entry, the more likely it was that someone left the organization over time (i.e., attrition).[37] Culture fit is becoming an important criterion for hiring because if the person doesn't fit the culture, they will leave. Based on the ASA framework, researchers have suggested using measures of PO fit for selection, especially in high-turnover jobs (e.g., call center employees).[38] An example of the ASA approach in practice is the recruitment and selection process at FedEx. As the company grew, they hired 25,000 people a year, according to one estimate. FedEx needed employees that were willing to take risks, entrepreneurial in nature, and ready to take on challenges. These attributes were carefully assessed using a 20-page application form and personal interview. Also, the company set up internships for college students to better socialize them into the FedEx culture prior to being hired full time.[39]

The process of assessing fit and then helping potential employees adjust to organizational culture through internships has been one of the keys to success at FedEx, a successful company that now employs over 400,000 people in 220 countries and territories.[40] As discussed previously, one of the important parts of the socialization process is a new employee learning the organizational culture. Culture is learned through a number of mechanisms including **stories**, **rituals**, **symbols**, and **language**. These are discussed in the following sections.

HOW EMPLOYEES LEARN CULTURE

Learning Objective 14.6: Discuss four ways that employees learn organizational culture.

Stories

Storytelling is now recognized as an important way to understand how employees make sense of what happens at work.[41] Storytelling is the sharing of knowledge and experiences through narrative and anecdotes to communicate lessons, complex ideas, concepts, and causal connections.[42] People try to understand complex events in ways that are integrated and make sense in the order they occurred. Stories are important because they aid comprehension and suggest a causal order for events. They convey shared meanings and values representing the organizational culture and guide behavior.[43] For example, stories told by charitable organizations are typically designed to evoke a series of emotions.[44] First, the potential donor feels negative emotions when they hear a story told about animals that are in need of rescue. Next, a story is told about animals being helped by the generosity of others, evoking a positive emotion and desire to help.

An example of an organizational story that is told at McDonald's about its founder Ray Kroc follows:

When Ray Kroc was running McDonald's from its Oakbrook, Illinois headquarters, he often drove by Chicago area McDonald's restaurants. Usually he asked his driver to stop so he could check things out. One sunny July afternoon, they were about to pass a McDonald's; Kroc told the driver, "We need to stop at this one." As they pulled into a parking space, he noticed that the flowering bushes were littered with shake cups, colorful Happy Meal boxes, messy napkins and other trash. Inside, Kroc asked for the manager. Only the assistant manager was there, so Kroc called the manager and waited for the anxious man to rush in after a speedy drive from his nearby home. "What can I do for you, sir?" the manager asked Kroc. Kroc led him to the parking lot, "Look. We don't want trash around our sites." So all three—driver, manager, and Ray Kroc—worked together to pick the trash out of the bushes. You'd better believe there was never again any trash in the parking lot of that location![45]

> **Critical Thinking Questions:** What have you learned about the organizational culture of McDonald's from this story? What did you learn about Kroc's leadership style?

Rituals

Rituals are defined as "a form of social action in which a group's values and identity are publicly demonstrated or enacted in a stylized manner, within the context of a specific occasion or event."[46] An example of a ritual is a graduation ceremony at a university. Rituals reinforce the cultural values of the organization by providing a tangible way for employees to see the values espoused. An interview study[47] of restaurant workers found that a small pizza restaurant had a ritual linked with family values and their emphasis on relationships created at work but extended to interactions outside work. Restaurant staff and managers engaged in social activities such as going to a regular "movie night" as a group. When probing on these patterns as to why this was important, the consistent response from the employees was "friendship." Another example is the Grammy Awards, a ritual that reinforces cultural values of the National Academy of Recording Arts and Sciences through performances, emotionally charged awards, legitimacy of artists, and creating links among the members.[48] Many organizations hold similar ceremonies and corporate dinners where top employees are rewarded for their contributions.

Symbols

Symbols represent the sharing of knowledge through access and exposure to images, diagrams, or objects that represent or illustrate a culture value or an idea. Examples include a map of a city, the alien emoji, or a corporate logo.[49] Symbols are important to organizations—they are not accidental; they are planned to communicate what the organizational culture represents.[50] Organizations make use of symbols in a variety of ways. Material symbols are office size and whether or not the office has a window.[51] The C-suite offices may be located on the top floor of the building to reinforce the idea that these individuals have attained the highest level in the organization. Symbols include how a leader is expected to dress at work.[52] For example, while it may not be written down as a policy, new managers may be expected to wear navy blue or gray suits. Another example of the power of symbols comes from the CEO of a hospital who wanted to reinforce the value of transparency in the organization. He had an open-door policy where literally anyone in the organization could come in and talk to him about their concerns. He created a symbol by having the doors of his office removed from their hinges and then hung up inside the lobby of the hospital so that everyone in the organization would see them and be reminded of his message every single day they walked in and out of the building. This symbol of his transparency was more effective than sending out an e-mail to communicate his open-door policy with the same message.[53]

Language

As discussed in Chapter 11, employees may communicate using culture-specific language, jargon, or acronyms that can be confusing to a new employee. These terms and usage may be unique to the organization and represent the organizational culture and how it is transmitted to newcomers. The language used to refer to employees reflects underlying values. For example, some organizations have stopped using the term *employees* in favor of *team members*. Another example is the manner in which employees at Disneyland are trained to refer to customers as "guests." Rides are referred to as "attractions." Disneyland is divided into "backstage," "on-stage," and "staging" regions.[54] The language used by Disneyland employees demonstrates is core values of valuing guests and providing a "magical experience" for them as part of its strong organizational culture. The use of organizational language reinforces who is in the culture and who is outside of it. Think about the extensive language developed by J. K. Rowling in the *Harry Potter* books that only the wizards and witches know. For example, a "muggle" is a person totally without magical powers—muggles live in ignorance of the world of wizards and witches. And "quidditch" is the wizarding national sport played on broomsticks by seven players. Those who know the language are in, and those who don't are lost in translation.

Organizational culture influences employee behaviors, as the previously given examples demonstrate. Organizational culture creates organizational climates. These concepts are related but not exactly the same. For example, understanding organizational culture relies primarily on qualitative methods such as case studies. On the other hand, research on **organizational climate** relies more on quantitative research and surveys that measure employee perceptions.[55] The distinction between culture and climate continues in the following section.

> **Critical Thinking Questions: Provide an example of storytelling, a ritual, a symbol, or language that you encountered when you learned an organizational culture based on your experience (this can be from your experience in a fraternity/sorority, sports team, or at work). Explain how this helped you understand what the expected behaviors were in the organization.**

ORGANIZATIONAL CLIMATE

Learning Objective 14.7: Compare and contrast *organizational culture* and *climate*.

Organizational climate has been defined as "shared perceptions of the way things are around here."[56] Organizational climate is the level of agreement in perceptions about the organization and work environment among employees. While the analysis of culture relies on understanding an organization's fundamental assumptions as discussed in the previous section, climate research is concerned with representing employees' shared perceptions of values in a static way as states that they experience at a point in time. Another key distinction between culture and climate is that culture is viewed as evolving over time and is studied from a sociology or anthropology viewpoint. Climate can be altered through management interventions.[57] In sum, the difference between culture and climate is that culture is an *evolved context* and climate is a *situation* that employees are in.[58]

Culture and climate aren't the same, but they are not completely different either. Culture results in climate by reinforcing the shared perceptions employees have about what is valued. The **climcult** perspective suggests that culture and climate work together to influence how people experience their work environment.[59] Climcult borrows from the research on climate and culture and has the following elements:

- A global climate or culture for well-being

- Strategy focused on policies, practices, procedures, and behaviors expected and rewarded

- Processes focused on policies, practices, procedures, and behaviors that are expected and rewarded

- Socialization practices through which values and beliefs for strategy and processes are transmitted

- Myths and stories used for transmitting those same beliefs and values[60]

The climcult perspective suggests combining survey measures of climate and culture to gain a more complete view of how people describe their organization's values and their work experiences.[61] For example, a measure of the climate for quality would have measures of how followers view their leader's support for quality initiatives (climate). Culture items would be added to reflect how the leader tells stories about things that went wrong when quality standards were not adhered to (culture). Climate focuses on perceptions, and culture focuses on the underlying assumptions and values. Both are important to understand the influence of organizational culture on employee behavior.

How Climate Influences Organizational Performance

Table 14.3 shows the dimensions of organizational climate. Climate significantly impacts on the dependent variables studied in organizational behavior (OB; refer back to Chapter 1 for a list of

---

Table 14.3 Dimensions of Organizational Climate

Affective facet—people involvement; interpersonal or social relations

- Participation: Perceived influence in a process of joint decision making; participation in setting goals and policies
- Warmth: Perceived feelings of good fellowship in workgroup; prevalence of friendly, informal social groups; perceived helpfulness of supervisors and coworkers; emphasis on mutual support
- Social rewards: Praise from others used to reward work, rewards based on effort and time spent on work; formal recognition and awards based on ability and effort
- Cooperation: Perceived helpfulness of supervisors and coworkers; emphasis on mutual support

Cognitive facet—psychological involvement; self-knowledge and development

- Growth: Perceived emphasis on personal growth and development on job; emphasis on skill improvement
- Innovation: Perceived emphasis on innovation and creativity in work
- Autonomy: Perceived freedom to be own boss; plan and control over work
- Intrinsic rewards: Formal recognition and awards based on ability and effort

Instrumental facet—task involvement and processes

- Hierarchy: Perceived emphasis on going through channels; locus of authority in supervisory personnel
- Structure: Perception of formality and constraint in the organization; orderly environment; emphasis on rules, regulations, and procedures
- Extrinsic rewards: Extrinsic rewards of pay, assignments, and advancement based on ability and time spent on work
- Achievement: Perception of challenge, demand for work, and continuous improvement of performance

Source: Ostroff, C. (1993). The effects of climate and personal influences on individual behavior and attitudes in organizations. *Organizational Behavior and Human Decision Processes, 56*(1), 56–90.

these variables). Also, research on climate summarizes much of what we have learned in this textbook regarding how attitudes of employees toward their work relate to work outcomes.

There are a number of facets of climate that have been studied including service, justice, safety, diversity, and innovation.[62,63,64,65,66] Some organizational climates are "toxic," and abusive supervision occurs in such climates. Toolkit Activity 14.1 is an exercise in which you compare two different organizations in terms of their service climate. Another specific type of organizational climate that has been studied is ethical climate, and the next section describes this line of research.

RESEARCH IN ACTION

Diversity Climate and Intentions to Quit

Diversity climate has been defined as "employees' shared perceptions of the policies, practices, and procedures that implicitly and explicitly communicate the extent to which fostering and maintaining diversity and eliminating discrimination is a priority in the organization."[67] The influence of diversity climate on turnover intentions was studied in a sample of managerial employees in a national retail organization.[68] Positive diversity climates were associated most negatively with turnover intentions among Blacks, followed in order of strength by Hispanics and then Whites. Organizational commitment (loyalty to the organization, as discussed in Chapter 4) alleviated the effect of race and diversity climate perceptions on turnover intentions. In other words, if managers are loyal to the organization, they are less likely to quit even if the diversity climate is poor. Results from a sample of 5,370 managers found the effect of a prodiversity climate was strongest among Blacks. Contrary to the hypotheses, however, White men and women exhibited slightly stronger effects than Hispanic personnel.

These results suggest that a prodiversity climate is not implemented at the expense of White employees. In fact, White men and women were also more likely to indicate lower intentions to quit when they perceived support for diversity. Although the strength of association varied by race, the total effect of diversity climate on turnover intentions was negative across all racial groups. Also, organizational commitment may reduce the effects of diversity climate on turnover intentions.

Discussion Questions

1. Explain why organizational commitment (loyalty, as discussed in Chapter 4) reduced the effects of a lesser diversity climate on intentions to quit.
2. Were you surprised by the study's findings? Why do you think White managers were also positively affected by prodiversity climates in their organizations?
3. This study was conducted using a sample of managers in retail organizations. How might the results be the same or different in a manufacturing organization, a hospital, or a university? Explain your answers.

Sources: Gelfand, M. J., Nishii, L. H., Raver, J., & Schneider, B. (2005). Discrimination in organizations: An organizational-level systems perspective. In R. Dipboye & A. Colella (Eds.), *Discrimination at work: The psychological and organizational bases* (pp. 89–116). Mahwah, NJ: Erlbaum; McKay, P. F., Avery, D. R., Tonidandel, S., Morris, M. A., Hernandez, M., & Hebl, M. R. (2007). Racial differences in employee retention: Are diversity climate perceptions the key? *Personnel Psychology, 60*(1), 35–62.

Ethical Climate

In Chapter 6, you learned that ethical leadership has emerged as an important new direction in OB research. Leaders influence an organization's ethical climate and employee attitudes. Leader moral development (i.e., the capacity for ethical reasoning) influences ethical climate, employee job satisfaction, and turnover intentions. This effect is stronger for younger organizations.[69] Research suggests the following five aspects of ethical climates:[70]

1. **Caring.** "Our major concern is always what is best for the other person."

2. **Law and Code.** "People are expected to comply with the law and professional standards over and above other considerations."

3. **Rules.** "Everyone is expected to stick by company rules and procedures."

4. **Instrumental.** "In this company, people are mostly out for themselves."

5. **Independence.** "Each person in this company decides for themselves what is right and wrong."

A survey of 872 employees of four firms found that organizations have distinct types of ethical climates, and the ethical climate is shaped by norms, bureaucracy, and the history of the organization.[71] Another study of 1,525 employees and their supervisors in 300 units in different organizations found that ethical climate made a difference in terms of the effects of ethical leadership and employee misconduct. Employees responded more to their leaders' ethical behaviors when the climate supported ethics.[72] An interesting study[73] was conducted using a sample of 2,192 employees from a public-sector city organization that related ethical climate to the number of sick days taken by employees. This research found that a strong ethical organizational climate was associated with less sickness absences. Ethical organizational culture plays a significant role in enhancing employee well-being measured as sickness absence. Emphasizing an ethical climate may be an important factor in preventing sickness absence at work. A meta-analysis of 42 studies of ethical climate found caring climates were related to job satisfaction and organizational commitment, whereas instrumental climates were negatively related to these outcomes.[74] Thus, ethical climates matter and leaders should develop the moral climate of the organization in addition to behaving ethically.

The ability of leaders to influence climate matters. A meta-analysis of 51 studies with 70 samples found climate affects individual-level outcomes through its impact on underlying cognitive and affective states. Three aspects of climate (affective, cognitive, and instrumental) significantly and positively impacted job performance, psychological well-being, and withdrawal (e.g., turnover intentions) through their impact on organizational commitment and job satisfaction.[75] Additional implications for leaders and guidelines for changing organizational culture follow.

LEADERSHIP IMPLICATIONS: CULTURE CHANGE

Lou Gerstner, the former chairman of IBM said, "Culture isn't just one aspect of the game—it is the game. In the end, an organization is no more than the collective capacity of its people to create value."[76] Culture is one of the key factors in *Fortune* magazine's ratings of the best companies to work for, since the ranking includes surveys of employees about the company culture. Leaders influence culture through their strategies, practices, values, leadership style, and setting an example.[77] For example, John Mackey, co-CEO of Whole Foods, capped his own salary at 19 times what the average employee makes.[78] A study of 114 CEOs[79] found that leadership is particularly critical when it provides psychological and motivational resources lacking in the organization's culture. For example, cultures that don't value employee empowerment and cohesiveness benefit from relationship-oriented leadership to build positive interpersonal relationships, employee cooperation, collaboration, and support.

Leaders need to understand how cultures develop because research has suggested that leaders can influence culture. Leaders can change organization culture through the following processes:

1. Make strategy and culture important leadership priorities.

2. Develop a clear understanding of the present culture.

3. Identify, communicate, educate, and engage employees in the cultural ideals.

4. Role model desired behaviors.

5. Recruit and develop for culture.

6. Align for consistency between strategy and culture.

7. Recognize and reward desired behaviors and practices.

8. Use symbols, ceremonies, socialization, and stories to reinforce culture.

9. Appoint a culture team.

10. Monitor and manage the culture.[80]

To effect these changes, there are three key managerial tools for leveraging culture for performance:[81]

Tool #1: Recruiting and Selecting People for Culture Fit

Selection is the process of choosing new members of the organization. This requires planning for what the organization will need to reward in the future in terms of knowledge, skills, and abilities of employees. Selection is linked to organizational culture because organizations strive to hire people who fit the culture. For example, candidates for flight attendant positions at Southwest Airlines were asked to read aloud a "Coat of Arms" where they finished statements like "One time my sense of humor helped me was . . ." and "My personal motto is . . ." In one interview, a man who said his personal motto was "I am the master of every situation"—a line that drew laughs—moved on to the next round in the interview process.[82] Southwest is known for fun in flight, and they are looking for applicants with a good sense of humor. In some cases, skills may be traded off for an applicant who fits the culture because skills are easier to learn than values.

Tool #2: Managing Culture Through Socialization and Training

As discussed earlier in this chapter, socialization is the process by which an individual learns the norms of the group and organization. The new employee learns the values, expectations, and what behaviors are needed to succeed in the organization. Two key aspects of effective socialization are ensuring that employees acquire cultural knowledge and that they bond with one another. During the socialization process, a new employee is exposed to stories, rituals, symbols, and language that transmit the organizational culture. For example, a new CEO was asked to choose the vehicle that he wanted to drive. Knowing that the other executives commonly drove luxury cars, he chose a mid-size Chevrolet. Although he never said a word about why he chose a much more modest car, he sent a strong message about desiring a culture in which leaders were good stewards and did not try to set themselves apart from the rest of the employees.[83] Most organizations have an orientation program for onboarding new employees and regular training programs that reinforce the organization's cultural values.

Tool #3: Managing Culture Through the Reward System

As discussed in Chapter 9, the reward system is one of the most important ways that leaders can influence employee behavior and performance. Rewards need to be clearly aligned with the organization's culture. Through rewards, employee behaviors that are consistent with the culture are reinforced. There should be a combination of extrinsic rewards (i.e., pay) and intrinsic rewards (i.e., interesting work). In a culture that values innovation and problem solving, employees need to be rewarded for voicing new ideas or even criticisms. For example, rewards are combined with rituals when an organization has a celebration that recognizes top sales performers for the year.

The previously given tools for changing organizational culture are important for the leader to know. This chapter reviews the research on organizational culture and discusses its relationship to national culture. The benefits of a strong organizational culture in terms of financial performance and employee attitudes are explained. Employees learn the organizational culture through the socialization process, which includes onboarding (orientation, training, and mentoring). The chapter also reveals the ways that organizational culture develops through stories, rituals, symbols, and language. Organizational culture influences the climate of an organization, and there are a number of aspects of climate, such as ethics, diversity, and service. Leaders shape and can change organizational culture. Culture is one aspect of OB that changes, but it is not the only one. Organizations today are undergoing rapid and frequent change, and leading organizational change is discussed in the next chapter.

 **edge.sagepub.com/scandura2e**

Want a better grade? Go to **edge.sagepub.com/scandura2e** for the tools you need to sharpen your study skills.

KEY TERMS

adaptability, 371
bureaucratic control, 370
clan control, 370
climcult, 379
consistency, 371
enacted values, 368
engineers, 373
entry, 375
espoused values, 368

ethical climate, 380
executives, 373
involvement, 371
language, 376
market control, 370
metamorphosis, 376
mission, 371
onboarding, 375
operators, 373

organizational anticipatory
    socialization, 374
organizational climate, 378
organizational culture, 367
organizational socialization, 374
preentry, 375
rituals, 376
stories, 376
symbols 376

TOOLKIT ACTIVITY 14.1: Comparing Organizational Cultures: IDEO and Amazon

IDEO and Amazon are both successful companies. Use the templates on the next pages to compare and contrast their organizational cultures. The information can be searched on the Internet using Google or some other search engine. Try to find the most specific information you can. For example, for artifacts, don't just state "open-plan offices." Describe what the offices look like and what is in them.

	IDEO	Amazon
Size		
Strategic Focus (cost minimization, innovation/creativity)		
Structural Design (simple, bureaucracy, matrix, boundary-less) Structural Elements: • Specialization • Departmentalization • Chain of command • Span of control • Centralization • Formalization		
Organizational Culture • Artifacts • Values • Assumptions		
Role of Human Resources in Shaping Culture? • How is "good performance" defined? • Recruitment/Selection • Training/Development • Rewarding/$$		
Role of the Leader in Shaping Culture?		
Impact: Employee Satisfaction & Turnover		
Impact: Organization Performance		

1. Compare the cultures of IDEO and Amazon. Which organization has a stronger culture? Or are they the same?

2. How are IDEO and Amazon different in their size and strategic focus?

3. What are some specific ways that the leader (i.e., CEO) for IDEO and Amazon influence the organizational culture?

Source: Developed by Marie Dasborough, University of Miami. Used with permission.

CASE STUDY 14.1: Changing Corporate Culture: The Case of B-MED

B-MED is a medical equipment distributor that sells and services General Electric Healthcare, Medtronic Corporation, Steris Corporation, and AGFA Healthcare medical equipment in the Caribbean and Latin American Region. B-MED was founded in 1984 by Bob Samuels and was run as a small family-owned business with fewer than 10 employees for 25 years. B-MED sold small medical equipment such as EKG machines, patient monitors, anesthesia machines, and defibrillators. As there were only a few products in these lines, B-MED only required a small staff that consisted of three sales persons, five administrative persons, and two engineers. The staff was mostly composed of Samuels's family members or friends of the family.

The company was a traditional vertical organization where Samuels made all decisions. As B-MED had strong financial performance, Samuels rewarded hard work with bonuses and commissions, and punished those who did not do as told. The employees were generally driven by extrinsic motives including fear of punishment and compensation, and lacked intrinsic motivation as they lacked a sense of responsibility and accomplishment. In addition, their input and suggestions were not valued by Samuels. However, the relatively small size of the company meant that B-MED's employees accepted the status quo and performed well enough to generate sufficient revenue to result in B-MED's profitability.

During the second quarter of 2010, everything changed for B-MED. Samuels received a call from the vice president of GE Healthcare informing Samuels that B-MED had been chosen to take on the full line of equipment GE Healthcare offered. B-MED would be taking the distribution rights from another company (MM Healthcare) because they were no longer meeting GE's performance goals. Samuels jumped at the opportunity without taking into account the large investment in capital, personnel, and equipment that would be required to successfully handle the entire GE line. After the call, Bob Samuels informed his son Craig about the good news. While Craig was excited, he also knew that his father's management style would have to change in order to be successful. He told Bob, "This could make us really rich, or really poor." Samuels didn't understand what his son was saying, as the potential profits blinded him of what was ahead.

The new line of GE equipment included MRI machines, CAT scanners, x-ray machines, nuclear medicine machines, and ultrasound machines, and with it, B-MED acquired an install base that consisted of hundreds of pieces of equipment. Most of the equipment carried service contracts, requiring B-MED to support a broader range of service capabilities. Eventually, B-MED started a new company in Trinidad and hired 12 new engineers to be able to service the existing customers. The majority of these engineers came from MM Healthcare. MM Healthcare was managed and organized much differently than B-MED. MM Healthcare had a modern structure that was flat with little middle management. This gave the employees of MM Healthcare a sense of ownership and had enhanced the company's culture to capitalize on employees feeling empowered and in control. When MM Healthcare's employees were hired by B-MED, they were extremely grateful and happy to have their jobs back, but these feelings of satisfaction quickly dissipated. The MM Healthcare employees found themselves in a traditional organization where their voices were not heard and their opinions did not matter. Further, B-MED's management did not have the proper tools, safety equipment, or safety procedures for these new jobs. The new employees immediately began to complain and voice their opinions to B-MED's existing employees. This caused tension between the two groups. B-MED not only grew in the amount of engineers but also hired additional sales staff and administrative staff. B-MED was now a company of more than 50 employees located in Trinidad and Miami. The original staff at B-MED began to blame the staff in Trinidad for all of the problems B-MED was facing. The staff in Trinidad would blame Samuels's bureaucratic style of management and his lack of commitment to his employees.

The tension between the two groups had a direct effect on the performance of the employees. The high level of tension created stress among the employees, creating an unpleasant work place. Samuels ignored stress levels in the company, the low job satisfaction, and the lack of intrinsic motivation in his employees. The turnover rate of employees began to increase at alarming rates, and the company's bottom line suffered substantially. Mr. Samuels was no longer able to meet commissions and bonuses that were promised, which took away his ability to extrinsically motivate the employees through compensation. All Mr. Samuels had was his coercive power over the employees. Needless to say, B-MED finds itself in a very bad financial state with unmotivated employees and unhappy customers.

Discussion Questions

1. There were a number of examples where opportunities for change existed but were not taken. Identify two different changes that were resisted. What could have been done differently to make the change happen?

2. Why were the existing B-MED employees willing to work for Mr. Samuels without any issues, yet the employees from MM Healthcare were having issues? How could Samuels have made this transition better?

3. Being that the two sets of employees came from different countries, what could have been done to ensure that both cultures (social and institutional) would mesh together?

4. What were some of the changes that you see are still needed?

SELF-ASSESSMENT 14.1: Comparing Service Climates

This assessment identifies an organization's service climate. Visit a local restaurant or retail establishment and rate their service climate by observing employees or asking employees these seven questions. Then visit another establishment of the same type (i.e., restaurant or retail) and perform the same rating. How do the service climates compare? You don't have to share your results with others unless you wish to do so. We will discuss the interpretations of this assessment in class.

Part I. Performing the Assessments

Instructions: Circle the response that best describes what employees experience in the organization.

Statements	Poor	Below Average	Average	Above Average	Excellent
1. How would you rate the job knowledge and skills of employees in this business to deliver superior quality work and service?	1	2	3	4	5

Statements	Poor	Below Average	Average	Above Average	Excellent
2. How would you rate efforts to measure and track the quality of the work and service in the business?	1	2	3	4	5
3. How would you rate the recognition and rewards employees receive for the delivery of superior work and service?	1	2	3	4	5
4. How would you rate the overall quality of service provided by the business?	1	2	3	4	5
5. How would you rate the leadership shown by management in the business in supporting the service quality effort?	1	2	3	4	5
6. How would you rate the effectiveness of communication efforts to both employees and customers?	1	2	3	4	5
7. How would you rate the tools, technology, and other resources provided to employees to support the delivery of superior quality work and service?	1	2	3	4	5

Part II. Scoring Instructions

Add up the scores for the items for each business you rated. Scores range from 7 (low service climate) to 35 (high service climate). Write the scores for the two businesses here:

Business A Service Climate

Business B Service Climate

_____

_____

Discussion Questions

1. Explain why you think the service climates were the same or different in the two businesses you observed.

2. List some specific behaviors that illustrate the service climate for each of the businesses.

3. Which business do you think had a stronger service climate? Explain why.

Source: Adapted from Schneider, B., White, S. S., & Paul, M. C. (1998). Linking service climate and customer perceptions of service quality: Test of a causal model. *Journal of Applied Psychology, 83*(2), 150–163.

CHAPTER FIFTEEN

LEADING CHANGE AND STRESS MANAGEMENT

Learning Objectives

After studying this chapter, you should be able to do the following:

15.1: Describe the forces driving organizational change.

15.2: Explain why planned organizational change is necessary.

15.3: Discuss the reasons why people resist organizational change.

15.4: Compare and contrast the models for leading organizational change (i.e., Lewin, Kotter).

15.5: Provide an example of the relationship between organizational change and stress.

15.6: Define *stress*, and discuss the estimated costs to business.

15.7: Develop a plan for coping with stress during change.

15.8: Identify organizational interventions and policies that help employees cope with stress.

Get the edge on your studies at **edge.sagepub.com/scandura2e**

- Take the chapter quiz
- Review key terms with eFlashcards
- Explore multimedia resources, SAGE readings, and more!

ING'S AGILE TRANSFORMATION

In the summer of 2015, the Dutch banking group ING embarked on a cultural change, shifting its traditional structure to an "agile" one inspired by companies such as Google, Netflix, and Spotify. Comprising about 350 nine-person "squads" in 13 so-called tribes, the new tribes encompassed a mix of marketing specialists, product and commercial specialists, user-experience designers, data analysts, and IT engineers—all focused on solving the client's needs and united by a common definition of success. Bart Schlatmann, the chief operating officer of ING Netherlands during the transformation, explained why the bank needed to change:

> We have been on a transformation journey for around ten years now, but there can be no let up. Transformation is not just moving an organization from A to B, because once you hit B, you need to move to C, and when you arrive at C, you probably have to start thinking about D. In our case, when we introduced an agile way of working in June 2015, there was no particular financial imperative, since the company was performing well, and interest rates were still at a decent level. Customer behavior, however, was rapidly changing in response to new digital distribution channels, and customer expectations were being shaped by digital leaders in other industries, not just banking. We needed to stop thinking traditionally about product marketing and start understanding customer journeys in this new omnichannel environment. It's imperative for us to provide a seamless and consistently high-quality service so that customers can start their journey through one channel and continue it through another—for example, going to a branch in person for investment advice and then calling or going online to make an actual investment. An agile way of working was the necessary means to deliver that strategy.[1]

Schlatmann further explained what agility meant for ING:

Agility is about flexibility and the ability of an organization to rapidly adapt and steer itself in a new direction. It's about minimizing handovers and bureaucracy, and empowering people. The aim is to build stronger, more rounded professionals out of all our people. Being agile is not just about changing the IT department or any other function on its own.[2]

ING's transformation is meeting their objectives to be quicker to market, increase employee engagement, reduce impediments and handovers, and, most important, to improve client experience. The executive team at ING knew that it needed to change to keep pace with a rapidly changing environment and increased customer demands. They learned from the best practices of successful IT companies and implemented an evidence-based management approach by adopting metrics to measure the success of their change efforts (e.g., time to market, employee engagement, reduced impediments, and client experience). Nearly all organizations today operate in a dynamic environment with forces that create the need for organizational change. These forces are reviewed next.

FORCES DRIVING ORGANIZATIONAL CHANGE

Learning Objective 15.1: Describe the forces driving organizational change.

There are numerous forces for change in organizations (see Table 15.1). For example, Chapter 13 discusses the impact of **workforce diversity** due to gender, race/ethnicity, and generations at work. Changes in the workforce as well as cultural differences will continue to be a force for organizational change. The economy represents a significant source for change. For example, economic recessions result in major changes such as downsizing and restructuring. Technology changes are rapid, and organizations must keep up with these advances. As we have discussed in Chapter 12, technology advances have resulted in changes in how people communicate inside and outside of the organization. Globalization represents a significant source of change for organizations with the rise of the multinational corporation. Increased globalization of markets has also given rise to competition from abroad in addition to competing with firms within a given country. As consumers, we enjoy a broader array of product options, lower prices, and increased attention to customer service. However, intense competition may lead to industry shakeouts, and we have seen some giants faltering, such as AOL who didn't see Google's competitive threat until it was too late.

Figure 15.1 shows key cultural shifts that have taken place in the evolution of work. For example, organizational hierarchies have been replaced with flatter organizational structures. In the past, employees worked 9:00 a.m. to 5:00 p.m. in offices, but there has been a shift toward flexible working hours and working from anywhere through mobile technology. Instead of information being held by the top executive team, information is shared with employees throughout organizations. Handheld mobile devices have become the primary means of communication in organizations. Leadership styles have shifted from command and control to inspirational. These changes are powerful forces that

Table 15.1 Forces Driving Organizational Change

Force for Change	Examples
Workforce diversity	Sex, race/ethnicity, cultural differences, LGBTQ, age/generation
The economy	Recession, government policy, rising health care costs
Technology	Mobile devices, social media, Internet security, robotics
Globalization	Multinational corporations, political instability, fair trade, sustainability, outsourcing, emerging markets
Competition	Global competition, mergers and acquisitions, customer standards, time to market

Figure 15.1 The Evolution of Work

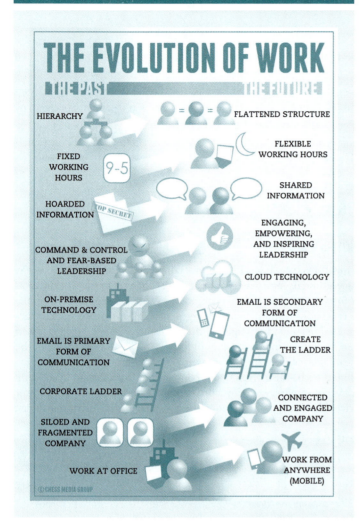

THE EVOLUTION OF WORK

THE PAST — THE FUTURE

HIERARCHY	= = FLATTENED STRUCTURE
FIXED WORKING HOURS	FLEXIBLE WORKING HOURS
HOARDED INFORMATION	SHARED INFORMATION
COMMAND & CONTROL AND FEAR-BASED LEADERSHIP	ENGAGING, EMPOWERING, AND INSPIRING LEADERSHIP
ON-PREMISE TECHNOLOGY	CLOUD TECHNOLOGY
EMAIL IS PRIMARY FORM OF COMMUNICATION	EMAIL IS SECONDARY FORM OF COMMUNICATION
CORPORATE LADDER	CREATE THE LADDER
SILOED AND FRAGMENTED COMPANY	CONNECTED AND ENGAGED COMPANY
WORK AT OFFICE	WORK FROM ANYWHERE (MOBILE)

©CHESS MEDIA GROUP

Source: Retrieved from http://www.forbes.com/sites/jacobmorgan/2013/09/10/the-evolution-of-work/. Courtesy of Jacob Morgan, principal and co-founder of Chess Media Group and best-selling author, most recently of *The Future of Work* (2013).

affect organizations, and leaders must help employees cope with them. The next section discusses how leaders implement planned organizational change in response to the forces that drive change.

PLANNED ORGANIZATIONAL CHANGE

Learning Objective 15.2: Explain why planned organizational change is necessary.

The forces for organizational change have resulted in the need for organizations to be **proactive** rather than **reactive** in reading the environment they operate in. Planned organizational change can have a number of targets including structure, technology, processes, teams, and people.[3] The idea of being proactive when it comes to change is not new and dates to the classic management book *Overcoming Organizational Defenses*.[4] Yet most organizations still are in reactive mode (i.e., "putting out fires") when it comes to change. Change may also be incremental (e.g., adding blue dots to a detergent) or radical (e.g., a major restructuring).[5,6] Incremental change is evolutionary, and radical change is revolutionary. Revolutionary and evolutionary change are different in terms of the size and rate of upheaval. Revolutionary change occurs quickly and affects virtually all parts of the organization at the same time, whereas evolutionary change occurs slowly and gradually, and may involve only one area of the organization at a time.[7] Putting these concepts together (reactive/proactive and incremental/radical) results in a useful framework for classifying the types of organizational change (see Figure 15.2). As shown in the figure, the most intense form of change is proactive and radical, and it is often when an organization engages in planned organizational change that affects all organizational subsystems, which is discussed next.

Figure 15.2   Types of Planned Organizational Change

	Reactive	Proactive
Incremental	**Put out small fires!** Solve problems on a day-to-day basis. Quick fixes to short-term concerns.	**Tweaking.** Anticipate and plan. Improve current ways of doing things. Fine tune. Guided evolution.
Radical	**Stop the bleeding!** Crisis management. Industry shakeups, economic turmoil, financial shocks.	**Transformation.** Do things fundamentally differently. Change basic assumptions. Revolution.

Organizational Subsystems Involved in Planned Change

Planned organizational change involves four organizational subsystems:

1. **Formal organization.** This provides the coordination and control necessary for organized activity; examples are formal structures and reward systems.

2. **Social factors.** These factors include individual differences, team interactions, and the organizational culture.

3. **Technology.** This is how raw materials and inputs transform into outputs, such as work flow design and job design.

4. **Physical setting.** These are the characteristics of the physical space and how it is arranged.[8]

An example of culture change implementation that is proactive and radical is the cultural change at Yum! Brands, Inc.[9] Yum! Brands (Pizza Hut, Taco Bell, and KFC) was able to create a new culture after the restaurants were spun off from PepsiCo, Inc. All three companies had strong founders, and changing and integrating the three cultures was a challenging task for the new vice chair, David Novak. Pizza Hut, Taco Bell, and KFC had been successful under the marketing and finance-driven culture of Pepsi, but they still had very different traditions and underlying assumptions about what success meant. The actions that Yum! took to create a new culture were as follows:

1. Starting with a set of shared values to define a culture across the three brands

2. Founding the new company in a way that that embodied the new culture

3. Using new titles to signal intentions and signify new cultural meanings

4. Creating a coaching management system to maximize restaurant performance

5. Developing a recognition culture to reinforce the new culture's values

6. Realigning reward systems to validate and "walk the talk" on values

7. Measuring the effectiveness and commitment of senior managers to the values

Organizational Development

Organizational development (OD) is a collection of social psychology methods employed to improve organizational effectiveness and employee well-being. OD reflects the insight that "there is nothing so practical as a good theory."[10] OB is an applied science, and theories of OB are applied in organizational settings through OD interventions. Also, the researchers of the Hawthorne studies (described in Chapter 1 of this book) found paying attention to workers increased productivity. Thus, organizational behavior (OB) can be considered to be the theory and research that underlies the practical application of OD interventions in the workplace. There is a difference between *theories of change* and *theories of changing*.[11] Theories of change try to answer the question of how and why change occurs (e.g., the impact of the Affordable Care Act on employee benefit plans). Theories of changing focus on how to implement successful organizational change (e.g., enhancing the ethical climate). Academics tend to write about theories of change, and management practitioners tend to write about theories of changing.[12] This chapter focuses on theories of changing with an emphasis on the leader's role in creating and sustaining organizational change. Organizational leaders and consultants have experimented with a variety of organizational change interventions. Specific examples of OD interventions follow.

Examples of Organizational Development Interventions

Survey feedback is one of the most commonly employed OD techniques. Throughout this textbook, you have taken a number of self-assessments at the end of the chapters that are the types of surveys that employees take (e.g., refer back to Table 4.1 in Chapter 4 for an example of a measure of job satisfaction). Data are collected from employees regarding their attitudes toward work, and their confidentiality is assured. These data are then analyzed and reported back to the organization as group averages. For example, a survey report might state that 55% of the employees surveyed indicate that they don't trust the top management team of the organization. This report becomes a starting point for further OD efforts, which may result in task forces to address the concerns identified in the survey. Most large organizations today conduct attitude surveys of their employees—typically on an annual basis. Participation in surveys should be organization-wide to ensure that the survey results accurately reflect employee attitudes.[13] Surveys are a key tool for understanding important organizational issues.

Workout was pioneered at General Electric (GE) and provided a method for employees to get new ideas heard by top management without having to go through hierarchical levels of bureaucracy. Other organizations have adopted this OD intervention.[14] Workout has several steps:[15]

1. The manager introduces a problem to a team of employees who have relevant expertise.

2. The manager leaves, and the employees work together for about 2 days on the problem.

3. The manager returns, and the employees report their proposals to solve the problem.

4. On the spot, the manager must accept the proposals, decline them, or ask for more information.

If more information is requested, a process to make a final decision must be articulated. Gary Kaplan, former president of construction at Zurich North America Commercial, was responsible for a wide range of operational transformation initiatives. He describes how the Workout method worked in his previous job:

When I was at Zurich Financial, I ran many Rapid Results projects. We achieved tremendous results and our people grew into stronger leaders. When I came to XL Group, I discovered we had a great deal of data analytics but weren't really using it to improve our underwriting results. To get things going we held a GE-style 'Workout' and launched eight projects, one for each business unit, aimed at reducing our loss ratio by 2 points. The projects achieved the result. We followed up with a second GE Workout and launched 14 more projects, with half of them focused on growing the portion of the businesses where we had improved the loss ratio and the other half focused on finding more opportunities for 2-point improvement in loss ratio. Most of them produced the targeted results. But beyond getting the results, a great deal of learning came out of it. For example, we hadn't utilized our actuaries effectively as team leaders. But we got them to play a very active lead role in the projects, and now their leadership roles are much stronger in the division.[16]

Sometimes, a leader needs an outside point of view on an organizational issue and hires a consultant with OD expertise who assists in a helping mode.[17] This is called process consultation and may focus on such matters as interpersonal relationships and communication. The consultant does not offer a solution to the problem but rather guides the leader to solve it through coaching. In this process, the leader develops their own skills in understanding and addressing the problem but may call upon the consultant later if needed for further coaching.

As you learned in Chapter 10, teams (when people work well together) can result in high levels of performance and learning for employees. Organizations are increasingly relying on teams to work on complex tasks and generate new ideas. Thus, team building emerged as an important OD intervention. Team building employs group activities that involve a great deal of interaction among team members to increase trust.[18] A meta-analysis showed that OD interventions do affect satisfaction and attitudes, with team building being one of the more effective interventions.[19] Despite the popularity of team building, research has not shown strong relationships to team performance. A meta-analysis of team-building interventions and performance found no overall effect. However, examination of the specific aspects of team building showed that interventions emphasizing role clarification were more likely to increase performance, and the effects of team building decreased as a function of the size of the team.[20] Team building seems to affect attitudes more than performance. Also, focusing on what roles members are playing in a team (e.g., leading, analyzing, presenting, supporting, and recording) within a small team is recommended for improved performance. One of the techniques used is known as "team building retreats." These meetings (often held off site) allow team members to become more cohesive, with the goal of increasing productivity when back on the job. Team-building retreat activities are often creative and memorable because they are entertaining.[21]

Appreciative inquiry (AI) is an OD intervention that is an example of action research (described in the Appendix of this textbook). AI is consistent with emerging ideas from positive psychology and OB.[22,23] The basic assumption is that people move in the direction that they visualize for the future. Participants begin the AI process by reflecting on a peak experience and then engage in conversation about it with others in a group setting. Questions are asked regarding why the moment was positive. Examples of topics in AI are learning, leadership, communication, or work relationships.[24] Individual reflections on the peak experience are then linked to develop a shared meaning for the group. AI is a process where the group learns what it has done well and focuses on strengths.[25,26] While AI has generated a lot of interest by practitioners, empirical support has been mixed.[27] However, a study[28] comparing groups with and without AI experience found that participating in AI unlocks and develops the human potential of employees. Those with AI experience had more confidence, hope, optimism, and resilience (psychological capital), particularly through satisfying the innate need to be competent and learn from others. AI may be an effective way to increase psychological capital as well as basic need satisfaction, both of which are conditions for creating new possibilities and effective systemic change. A field experiment[29] conducted in an urban transit organization found that AI generated more positive action ideas

Critical Thinking Questions: Which OD intervention(s) would you rely on for implementing a change in your organization's (or university's) approach to environmental conservation? Why?

compared with traditional problem solving. The results of the study suggest that not only does AI lead to more positive ideas but it leads to more creative ideas that focus on the specific area of managerial interest, while a problem-solving strategy may lead employees to use the opportunity to surface other issues that are "problems" for them. An example of how AI works is an application to your learning experiences in your OB course provided in Toolkit Activity 15.1.

More recently, **sustainability** has become a target of OD interventions with an emphasis on preserving the environment.[30] The World Commission on Environment and Development defines sustainability as "development that meets the needs of the present without compromising the ability of future generations to meet their own needs."[31] Most organizations now participate in recycling programs, and many adopt fair-trade practices in importing goods from other countries. For example, DuPont, a large science company, partnered with the Gift of the Givers Foundation, Africa's leading disaster relief organization, to advance women farmers in Malawi in terms of food security at household level. DuPont donated 1.5 tons of maize seed to 320 resource-poor women farmers in Malawi, Africa.[32] Such initiatives may require changes to the fundamental assumptions regarding the organization's culture, as discussed in Chapter 14.

Successful organizational change has people at the center. When human resource practices are aligned with organizational change strategies, the organization is more conducive to change.[33] Thus, OD interventions during organizational change must plan for employee resistance to change. The matter of why people resist change and strategies to address it are covered next.

RESISTANCE TO CHANGE

Learning Objective 15.3: Discuss the reasons why people resist organizational change.

When faced with an organizational change, employee reactions vary from resistance, compliance, or **commitment to change**. Resistance means that the employees fight the change and try to undermine it.[34] In compliance, they simply go along with the change but secretly hope that it is a program that will come to an end soon. Commitment to change is the most desirable reaction in which the employees support change and help the organization implement it.[35] Since resistance is the most difficult reaction for the leader to deal with, this section focuses on understanding and overcoming resistance to change.

Research on resistance to change dates back to a classic study of participative decision making conducted with a strong research design.[36] Employees were transferred to new jobs in which they encountered significant changes to their work. Interviews revealed employees resisted changes in their work methods due to resentment, frustration, and a loss of hope of regaining their former levels of proficiency. A second experiment was then conducted in which the control group was transferred to new jobs, but they were allowed to participate in the changes through chosen representatives; this group recovered rapidly and reached a higher level of productivity compared to the group that was not allowed to participate in the change. This study shows that OD can impact resistance to change through an intervention that increased employee participation in the process. A recent review of 70 years of research on resistance to change concluded that the findings of this classic study have held up over time and subsequent research studies.[37] Lack of participation and input to the change is one reason employees resist change. There are a number of additional reasons why people resist change that include both personal reasons and organizational reasons.[38,39,40] Personal reasons include habit, security, economic, and fear of the unknown. Organizational reasons for resistance are structural inertia (the structure is too rigid to support the change), group inertia, threats to expertise, and threats to established power relationships.

Resistance to change has a negative impact on employee health. It has been related to insomnia and lower employee well-being.[41] Using a longitudinal research design, a study[42] of 709 participants in 30 work units revealed that resistance to change predicted emotional exhaustion a year later. Organizations should offer coaching and training to cope with organizational change for employees who are highly change resistant. The next section discusses additional methods for overcoming resistance to change.

How to Overcome Resistance to Change

A *Harvard Business Review* article offers the following guidelines to help overcome resistance to change:[43]

1. **Being educated and communicating reduces misinformation about the change and helps convince employees that change is needed.**

2. **Participating matters, as demonstrated by the participative decision-making study described in the previous section.** People are more likely to accept changes that they help design.

3. **Building support and commitment reduces resistance because employees have the support through counseling or sabbaticals to ease the strain.** Commitment to the organization also increases commitment to change.

4. **Developing positive relationships through trust in management increases commitment to organizational change.** Research has shown that high-quality leader–member exchange (LMX) relationships reduce resistance.[44,45] Leaders provide explanations to followers that help them cope with change and commit to it.[46]

5. **Implementing changes fairly improves the chances that employees will accept change.** As reviewed in Chapter 8, organizational justice is a major concern of most employees, and it becomes even more important during change.

6. **Selecting people who accept change supports changes since research shows that people have personality traits that enable them to be more flexible when it comes to coping with change.**[47]

The article also includes the following tactics, but they may backfire and should only be used as last resorts:

7. **Manipulation and co-optation tactics are sometimes used in organizational transitions because they are relatively less expensive than the tactics listed previously.** Manipulation occurs when change agents use underhanded techniques such as the selective sharing of information and careful staging of events. Co-optation is basically "buying" the support of those who are needed. For example, members of a task force for change would be paid a bonus for serving on the task force.

8. **Coercion should be used rarely, if at all, as discussed in the leadership chapter of this book (Chapter 6).** Direct threats of loss of status, pay, or other things that employees care about may gain short-term compliance, but these tactics will rarely gain commitment to the change.

As the previous section indicates, real leadership is necessary to effectively implement organizational change. A study[48] of 40 health care clinics undergoing a 3-year period of significant organizational change found that resistance to change had increasingly negative relationships over time with two important consequences: employees' organizational commitment and perceptions of organizational effectiveness. These relationships became stronger over time, suggesting that resistance to change festers. However, this study also found that supportive leadership was increasingly impactful in reducing change resistance over time. The most effective tactics for overcoming resistance and gaining support are communication and building relationships that support the change. The next section discusses the models for leading change that have been shown to produce the best results.

> **Critical Thinking Question: Provide an example of manipulation, co-optation, or coercion during change. Evaluate the effectiveness of this tactic.**

RESEARCH IN ACTION

Ethical Leadership During Organizational Change

Research indicates that leaders play an important role during change by supporting the change and taking part in its implementation.[49] It has been argued that transformational leadership that is faked is not true transformational leadership. Leaders who lead transformation efforts exhibit leadership that depends upon "(1) the moral character of the leaders and their concerns for self and others; (2) the ethical values embedded in the leaders' vision, articulation, and program, which followers can embrace or reject; and (3) the morality of the processes of social ethical choices and action in which the leaders and followers engage and collectively pursue."[50] Thus, ethical behavior is an essential underpinning of transformational leadership. But does such ethical conduct by leaders make a difference in satisfaction and performance during organizational change?

A survey of 199 employees and their supervisors found ethical leadership matters in the context of organizational change.[51] Technology changes were the change that was most frequently listed as having the most impact, followed by downsizing, and then restructuring. Other changes reported were relocations, mergers, process changes, and people-centered changes. These changes have a significant impact on employees' regular work routines and cause stress. If an employee senses that their leader is behaving unethically, this may exacerbate the stress and result in lower performance. Followers need to be able to trust the integrity of their leaders during change. In addition, the degree to which employees felt that they were involved in the organization's change process made a difference as well. For example, having leaders discuss changes with employees results in higher job satisfaction, performance, and organizational citizenship behavior (OCB) during organizational change.

Discussion Questions

1. Do you agree or disagree with the statement that transformational leadership cannot be faked? Explain your position.

2. Explain why perceptions of leaders behaving unethically creates stress during organizational change. Consider the role of change uncertainty.

3. In addition to discussing changes with employees, describe some other actions that leaders can take to improve employee adjustment to organizational change.

Sources: Bass, B. M., & Steidlmeier, P. (1999). Ethics, character, and authentic transformational leadership behavior. *Leadership Quarterly, 10*(2), 181–217; Sharif, M. M., & Scandura, T. A. (2014). Do perceptions of ethical conduct matter during organizational change? Ethical leadership and employee involvement. *Journal of Business Ethics, 124*(2), 185–196; Whelen-Berry, K. S., Gordon, J. R., & Hinings, C. R. (2003). Strengthening organizational change processes: Recommendations and implications from a multi-level analysis. *Journal of Applied Behavioral Science, 39*(2), 186–207.

LEADING CHANGE

Learning Objective 15.4: Compare and contrast the models for leading organizational change (i.e., Lewin, Kotter).

After the issue of resistance to change is anticipated, analyzed, and addressed, the next step in changing organizations is to implement the change process through effective leadership. Next, the models of leading others through change are discussed.

Lewin's Three-Step Model

The three-step model is the starting point for understanding the fundamental process of leading change. As shown in Figure 15.3, there are three steps in the change process: **unfreezing, changing**, and **refreezing**. First, unfreezing challenges the status quo by shaking up assumptions; next, changing represents movement toward a new desired state. Finally, refreezing the changes by reinforcing and restructuring is the third phase to make the changes permanent. Think about an ice pack that you use when you have a sports injury. When you take it out of the freezer, it is hard and can't be changed much. As you use it, it becomes soft and malleable (this is the changing phase). After 20 minutes, you put it back in the freezer and it becomes solid again. Change is like this: When people and systems are in the frozen stage, you can't change them. You have to literally "heat things up" to soften the attitudes and assumptions about change so that the system is malleable like a defrosted ice pack. Once you have the changes you want in place, you reinforce the new behaviors with rewards or change the structure to support the change (refreezing).

Employees will tend toward the status quo or equilibrium, so there needs to be constant attention to refreezing the new system and behaviors after a change is implemented. For example, an organization that wants to implement teams must first challenge the old assumptions regarding working alone and getting rewarded for individual effort. A new organizational chart is presented to employees showing teams the new way that work will be organized. Some employees may resist the team concept and even leave the organization as the change is implemented. There may be storms and team conflict (things are heating up). Once there are successful teams in place, the new approach can be refrozen by offering team rewards and reinforcing the new organizational chart.

Leadership makes a difference: A study of a planned organizational change in a hospital system found that authentic leadership influenced the processes of unfreezing, change, and refreezing.[52] An interview study of 15 top executives who had been involved in significant organizational change found that it is necessary to balance the use of power with the autonomy of employees during change. One executive commented: "Leading change involves building social relationships to mobilize resources to create the power I need to make changes."[53] Change leaders should concentrate their

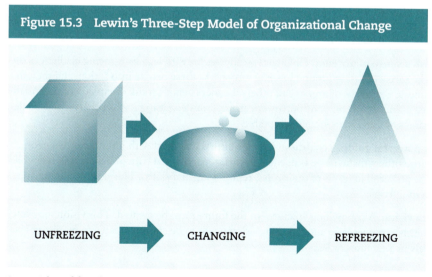

Figure 15.3 Lewin's Three-Step Model of Organizational Change

UNFREEZING   CHANGING   REFREEZING

Source: Adapted from http://www.mindtools.com/pages/article/newPPM_94.htm

resources on a few positively or negatively influential individuals and take advantage of communication networks to persuade and inform others to help with their change adoption. By partnering with opinion leaders in the organization, leaders can facilitate each player's proper role in the change effort.[54]

As this example illustrates, the Lewin model is still relevant today. A review of research evidence on organizational change over the past several decades concluded that "rather than being outdated or redundant, Lewin's approach is still relevant to the modern world."[55] Lewin's approach is based upon field theory and the analysis of forces for and against organizational change. This approach is discussed next.

Force Field Analysis

To implement organizational change using the three-step model, a **force field analysis** of the forces for and against an organizational change should be conducted.[56] The steps in force field analysis follow:

1. Define the problem (current state) and the target situation (target state).

2. List forces working for and against the desired changes.

3. Rate the strength of each force.

4. Draw a diagram (the length of line denotes strength of the force).

5. Indicate how important each force is.

6. List how to strengthen each important supporting force.

7. List how to weaken each important resisting force.

8. Identify resources needed to support forces for change and reduce forces against change.

9. Make an action plan: timing, milestones, and responsibilities.

Kotter's Eight-Step Model

Another important model for leading change is the Kotter eight-step model, which is shown in Figure 15.4. This model elaborates on the Lewin model of change and provides specific guidelines for changing organizations.[57] As the figure indicates, each step builds on the previous one, and descriptions of these steps follow.[58]

1. **Establish a sense of urgency.** Change typically begins with leaders noticing challenges the organization faces. The threat of losing ground in some way sparks these people into action, and they, in turn, try to communicate that sense of urgency to others. Leaders begin a frank discussion of potentially unpleasant facts such as increased competition, lower earnings, or decreasing market share. Most leaders are convinced that business as usual is no longer acceptable.

2. **Form a powerful guiding coalition.** Change efforts may start with just one or two people who begin to convince others that change is needed. In this step, an initial core of believers is assembled (this group should be powerful in terms of their roles, reputations, and skills). This coalition for change needs to have three to five people.

3. **Create a vision.** A compelling "picture" of the future must be created. This vision motivates people and keeps the change processes aligned. This vision needs to be communicated to employees clearly and effectively in 5 minutes or less.

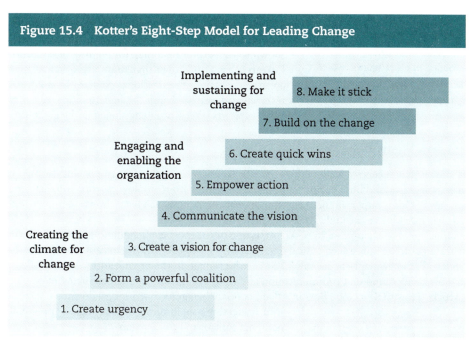

Figure 15.4   Kotter's Eight-Step Model for Leading Change

Implementing and sustaining for change

8. Make it stick

7. Build on the change

Engaging and enabling the organization

6. Create quick wins

5. Empower action

4. Communicate the vision

Creating the climate for change

3. Create a vision for change

2. Form a powerful coalition

1. Create urgency

Source: Kotter, J. P. (1995). Leading change: Why transformation efforts fail. *Harvard Business Review, 73*(2), 59–67. Reprinted with permission from *Harvard Business Review.*

4. **Communicate the vision.** Regardless of how much communication leaders think is needed, they should multiply that by 10. Every possible communication channel should be utilized including the CEO's speech, meetings, newsletters, e-mail, and face-to-face conversation as examples. Employees will be looking to see that the leaders in the organization are behaving consistently with the vision.

5. **Empower others to act on the vision.** Employees should be allowed to participate in making changes in their areas. This may require restructuring work and allowing key people the time to focus on the change effort. Also, this involves providing the money and support needed to bring about change.

6. **Plan for and create short-term wins.** Change takes time, and change efforts sometimes lose momentum as frustrations set in with employees. Plan and execute celebrations of short-term successes to reinforce people's efforts and maintain their commitment and motivation. This provides proof to employees that their efforts are working.

7. **Consolidate improvements and sustain the momentum for change.** A change process can take 5 to 10 years—as force field analysis shows, the forces against change such as resistance may result in regression to the prior ways of doing things. Leaders should resist the temptation to declare the change a success too soon. Leaders must enter the process believing that their efforts will take years.

8. **Institutionalize the new approaches.** A leader will know that the change is frozen in place when followers believe that it is "the way we do things around here." Employees understand that their efforts have led to a different outcome for the organization. The organization's leaders serve as role models for the new ways.

Critical Thinking Question: Show how
the Kotter model relates to the Lewin
three-step model. In other words, which
steps in the Kotter model represent
unfreezing, changing, and refreezing?

Despite some criticisms that the model has not kept pace with the current rate of organizational change, the Kotter model has been shown to be a useful road map for guiding organizational change.[59] Research has also shown that there are other elements that help ensure successful organizational change. In the next section, the research evidence on change implementation is reviewed, and it generally supports what Kotter envisioned in the eight-step model.

Effective Change Implementation

Research has shown that executive leadership—**top management support**—is important during organizational change.[60] A meta-analysis found little or no commitment to change from employees when top management support for change was low.[61] This is important because employee attitudes have also been shown to influence the success of organizational change.[62] One key attitude is commitment to change.[63]

Organizational **restructuring and downsizing** is one of the most challenging types of organizational change. Yet economic realities often require such radical organizational change for the organization to survive. These changes often result in layoffs that damage the morale of those who remain in the organization. A study of an organization undergoing a downsizing found that communication and fostering **innovation** helped maintain employee morale.[64] Bob Sutton's article "How to Be a Good Boss in a Bad Economy" suggests that during a downturn you need to rethink your leadership role in terms of focusing on "predictability, understanding, control and compassion."[65]

Critical Thinking Question: What
specific actions can a leader take to
maintain the morale of the survivors of
layoffs through showing compassion?

As this discussion suggests, organizational change may not only damage morale but it also creates stress for employees as the organization implements change. To be an effective change leader, managers need to understand stress and how to help employees cope with it. The next sections address this important organizational issue.

STRESS IN THE CONTEXT OF ORGANIZATIONAL CHANGE

Learning Objective 15.5: Provide an example of the relationship between organizational change and stress.

Stress has been rising at the workplace due to organizational change. Three research studies[66] conducted using different research methods found that change is more likely to lead to stress when the change has consequences that threaten employees' sense of identity. This effect is explained by employees' feelings of uncertainty. Change increases uncertainty and disrupts employees' regular work routines.[67] A qualitative interview study[68] conducted in a district health board undergoing change found that staff unhappiness with some organizational processes occurred when they were not consulted or informed, and where they suffered from uncertainty, heavy workloads, and inadequate support. The new organizational reality is one of competition with mergers, acquisitions, downsizings, and restructurings. These forces have increased psychological strain from work.[69] Uncertainty during organizational change may be related to layoffs, pay cuts, fewer promotion opportunities, and changes to the culture of the organization (the importance of organizational culture is discussed in Chapter 14).[70] **Change uncertainty** is defined as uncertain negative cognitive outcomes of a high level of perceived change excessiveness among employees.[71] It is created by strategic, structural, and job-related factors.[72] The uncertainty about outcomes and the perceived importance of these outcomes combine to produce this type of stress.[73] For example, a hospital was studied[74] as it underwent a major divisional consolidation. Employees were surveyed before and after the change was implemented; results showed stress was related to job dissatisfaction, intent to quit, and work-related irritation after the consolidation. However, organizational commitment reduced the stress effect.

Organizations are stressed due to environmental pressures to compete or even stay out of bankruptcy in some cases. This stress translates into stress experienced by individuals as organizations try to adapt to the demands of their environment. Organizational change affects all aspects of work design due to increases in shift work, night and weekend work, increases in overtime work, demands of employees being asked to work faster, and not having enough time to finish their work.[75] The intensification of work (fast pace and constant change) over the past 3 decades has also resulted in strained relationships with customers, coworkers, and supervisors.[76] It has been noted that

change is difficult for an institution and for its employees. There is uncertainty about the future, about what the organization will 'look like,' and how the employees feel they will fit into the new structure.[77]

Change creates job insecurity, which leads to emotional exhaustion during change.[78] Thus, employees may resist the change efforts. Such resistance is one of the most common sources of work stress.[79] A study followed the level of perceived stress over time and found that stress increased during the 2008–2009 economic recession, particularly for college-educated White men aged 45 to 64 years who were employed full time.[80] This may be due to threat of job loss, actual job loss, and/or the loss of retirement funds during the recession.

Both organizations and individuals can take actions to alleviate the stress due to change.[81] One study of a consolidation of human resource functions across divisions of an Australian public service organization found organizations can manage the frequency of change and the planning involved in change.[82] An important finding of this study was that supportive leadership made a difference in the reports of stress during the change. Managers need to understand how to deal with the acceleration of change to overcome the negative consequences for individuals.[83] Employees also need to develop coping mechanisms to deal with the stress of organizational change. Table 15.2 has tips for coping

Table 15.2 Surviving the Stress of Organizational Change

1. **Don't count on anyone else coming along to relieve your stress.**

   Put *yourself* in charge of managing the pressure. There's a good chance you're the only one in your work situation who will, or even *can*, do much to lighten your psychological load.

2. **The organization is going to change—it must—if it is to survive and prosper.**

   Rather than banging your head against the wall of hard reality and bruising your spirit, invest your energy in making quick adjustments. Turn when the organization turns. Practice instant alignment. Your own decisions may do more to determine your stress level than anything the organization decides to do.

3. **Accept fate, and move on.**

   Don't yield to the seductive pull of self-pity, at least for any extended period of time. Acting like a victim threatens your future. You're better off if you appear resilient and remain productive. Just stand proud, pick up the pieces, and start putting your career back together.

4. **Study the situation intently.**

   Figure out how the game has changed, how priorities have been reordered. Decide which aspects of your job you should focus on to leverage up your effectiveness the most.

5. **Don't fall into the trap of believing there's such a thing as a low-stress organization that's on track to survive.**

   In fact, just the opposite is true. You serve your best interests by aligning with an outfit that's got the guts to endure the pains of change and by avoiding those organizations destined to go belly-up because of their desire for short-term comfort.

(Continued)

Table 15.2 (Continued)

6. **Ask yourself if the struggle makes sense.**

   Are you really in a position to control the situation, or will you just get emotionally tired trying? Sometimes the most mature, most dignified, and most sensible move is to nobly accept what we can't change.

7. **Keep in step with the organization's intended rate of change.**

   March to the cadence that's being called by the people in charge instead of allowing yourself to take whatever amount of time you want or feel you need. Don't lag behind—there's little chance a lull will come along and give you a chance to play catch-up.

8. **Reengineer your job.**

   Eliminate unnecessary steps, get rid of busywork, and unload activities that don't contribute enough to the organization's current goals. Focus your efforts on doing the right things, and ditch those duties that don't count much, even if you can do them magnificently right.

9. **Speed up.**

   Cover more ground. Put your faith in action—in mobility—and maximize your personal productivity.

10. **Now's the time for some serious mind control.**

    Instead of worrying about bad things that might happen, get busy trying to create the kind of future you want. The best insurance policy for tomorrow is to make the most productive use of today.

11. **Remember the advice of Jonathan Kozol—"Pick battles big enough to matter, small enough to win."**

12. **Fall in love with your job, and keep the romance alive.**

    Don't let the stress of change drive a wedge between you and your work. Sure, your employer will benefit if you are committed, but not as much as you will. High job commitment is a gift you should give to yourself.

13. **Stretch yourself today so you'll be in better shape tomorrow.**

    Reach for new assignments that broaden your experience base. Remember that one of the best techniques for stress prevention is to keep updating your skills so you're highly employable.

14. **Develop a greater tolerance for constant changes in the game plan. For mid-course corrections. For raw surprise.**

    Allow a little more confusion in your life. Be willing to feel your way along, to wing it. Think of your job as having movable walls—flex to fit the immediate demands of the situation instead of struggling to make the job adapt to you.

15. **Be careful in what you use as evidence to evaluate how much the organization cares about people.**

    High stress and heavy pressure may provide the best proof that management's heart is in the right place. All things considered, trying to keep you comfortable could be the most cold-blooded management move of all.

Source: Pritchett, P., & Pound, R. (1995). A survival guide to the stress of organizational change. Used with full permission of PRITCHETT, LP. All rights are reserved. For more information, see www.pritchettnet.com and www.mergerintegration.com

with stress due to change. For example, try to become accustomed to change and increased pace of work to keep up with changes.

While change uncertainty is a major source of stress, it is not the only one. As noted previously, organizational change brings additional strains to roles and responsibilities. So in addition to uncertainty, change may bring about role conflicts and work overload. Next, stress is defined, followed by a discussion of the sources of work-related stress.

WHAT IS STRESS?

Learning Objective 15.6: Define *stress*, and discuss the estimated costs to business.

We all think we know what stress is and that we know how to cope. Take the following stress fact or fiction quiz to see how much you know about stress:

True or False?

1. People who feel stress are nervous to start with.

2. You always know when you are under stress.

3. Prolonged physical exercise will weaken your resistance to stress.

4. Stress is always bad.

5. Stress can cause unpleasant problems, but at least it can't kill you.

6. Stress can be controlled with medication.

7. Work-related stress can be left at the office and not brought home.

8. Stress is only in the mind; it's not physical.

9. Stress can be eliminated.

10. There's nothing you can do about stress without making drastic changes in your lifestyle.

The correct answer for all 10 questions is *false*. If you answered *true* to even one, you're a victim of a stress myth.[84] Psychological job strain is defined as the combination of greater psychological job demands and lower **job control**.[85] This results in **organizational stress**, which has been shown to have serious consequences to employees in terms of their well-being and health. In addition, stress costs organizations billions of dollars each year:

Nearly half of all workers suffer from moderate to severe stress while on the job, according to a recent survey. And 66 percent of employees report that they have difficulty focusing on tasks at work because of stress. Stress has been called the "health epidemic of the 21st century" by the World Health Organization and is estimated to cost American businesses up to $300 billion a year.[86]

One study of more than 46,000 U.S. employees found health care costs were 46% higher for workers who experienced high stress.[87] Also, it is estimated that half of the days employees are absent from work are due to stress.[88] The estimates for the cost of stress also include lower productivity due to **job burnout** as well as workplace accidents. Job burnout "is a prolonged response to chronic stressors on the job."[89] Symptoms of burnout are exhaustion, cynicism, detachment from work, and feelings of ineffectiveness or failure.[90] Burnout is a serious problem for many employees and affects their attitudes, motivation, and job performance. Toolkit Activity 15.2 contains a list of the warning signs of burnout to aid in the recognition of this serious condition in yourself and others.

> **Critical Thinking Questions:** How would you know if a coworker is experiencing burnout from work? What would you do about it?

Stress Episode

The stress response "is the generalized, patterned, unconscious mobilization of the body's natural energy resources when confronted with a demand or stressor."[91] The nervous and hormonal systems of an individual are activated

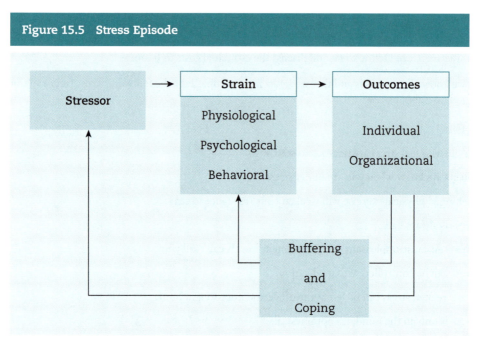

Figure 15.5 Stress Episode

Source: Viswesvaran, C., Sanchez, J. I., & Fisher, J. (1999). The role of social support in the process of work stress: A meta-analysis. *Journal of Vocational Behavior, 54*(2), 314–334.

producing adrenaline, and this may result in an elevated heart rate, perspiration, and tightening of the muscles. This is known as the **fight-or-flight response**, which is the result of human evolution in which the response was needed to attack predators or run away from them.

Strains resulting from the **stressors** reviewed in the previous section trigger a stress episode as depicted in Figure 15.5. Responses may be physiological, psychological, and/or behavioral.[92] These strains are listed next with examples found in research on stress at the workplace (however, one stressful event may trigger one, two, or all three of the following strains for an employee).

1. **Physiological**—high blood pressure, coronary heart disease, high cholesterol, stomach ulcers, compromised immune system

2. **Psychological**—anxiety, burnout, emotional exhaustion, fatigue, hostility, irritation, tension, lower self-confidence and self-esteem

3. **Behavioral**—accidents and errors, alcohol use, caffeine intake, drug use, smoking, workplace deviance (e.g., doing inferior work on purpose, stealing, damaging property)

Stress and Organizational Performance

A survey[93] of 1,950 adults found most are living with stress that is higher than what they believe to be healthy and that they are not having much success at managing or reducing their stress. Specific survey results included the following:

- Forty-two percent of adults report that their stress level has increased, and 36% say their stress level has stayed the same over the past 5 years (see Figure 15.6).

- Sixty-one percent of adults say that managing stress is extremely or very important, but only 35% report they are doing a very good or excellent job at this.

- Forty-four percent of adults say they are not doing enough (or are not sure how) to manage their stress, but 19% say they never engage in stress management activities.

- Money (71%), work (69%), and the economy (59%) continue to be the most commonly reported sources of stress.

These survey results show that work is one of the primary sources of stress in people's lives. But can stress have a positive side? Next, research on the negative and possible positive impacts of stress is discussed.

Stress can be performance enhancing or disruptive. A study of executive stress found that the experience of challenging or rewarding job experiences related differently to outcomes than stress from that associated with hindering or constraining job experiences. There are two general types of stress: challenge-related stress and hindrance-related stress. Challenge-related stress may be positive, or what is known as eustress, or "good stress" from the Greek root *eu* for "good."[94] Hindrance-related stress is excessive or undesirable constraints that interfere with an individual's ability to achieve goals, creating "negative stress."[95] A study of 270 U.S. Marines[96]

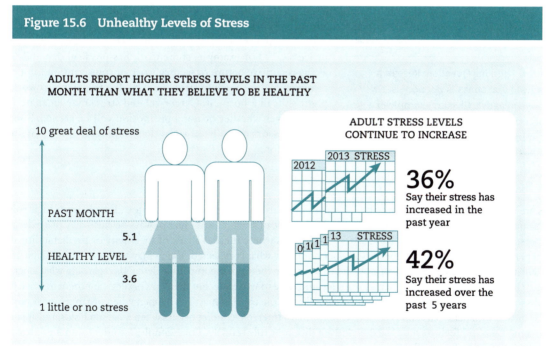

Figure 15.6   Unhealthy Levels of Stress

ADULTS REPORT HIGHER STRESS LEVELS IN THE PAST MONTH THAN WHAT THEY BELIEVE TO BE HEALTHY

10 great deal of stress

PAST MONTH

5.1

HEALTHY LEVEL

3.6

1 little or no stress

ADULT STRESS LEVELS CONTINUE TO INCREASE

2012   2013   STRESS

36%
Say their stress has increased in the past year

13   STRESS

42%
Say their stress has increased over the past 5 years

Source: Stress in America. (2013). American Psychological Association. Retrieved from http://www.stressinamerica.org

found that leadership (i.e., being a charismatic leader) increased the Marines' experience of stress as a challenge, and this predicted their task performance.

Some executives actually thrive on the good stress, and there may be an optimum level of stress for performance for some individuals, known as the Yerkes–Dodson law.[97,98] This law states that performance increases with increasing stress to an optimum point, but then the stress becomes too much and performance declines. Increased arousal can help improve performance but only to a certain point. At the point when arousal becomes excessive, performance diminishes. Psychologists Robert Yerkes and John Dillingham Dodson discovered that mild electrical shocks could be used to motivate rats to complete a maze, but when the electrical shocks became too strong, the rats would scurry around in random directions to escape. Increasing stress and arousal helps focus attention on tasks but only up to a certain point. For example, when you are studying for an exam, an optimal level of stress can help you concentrate and remember the correct answers while taking the exam. However, too much stress ("test anxiety") impairs your ability to focus and you start missing answers.

These forms of stress are not limited to executives, however. Both forms of stress relate to psychological strain, but one study found that hindrance-related stress is more related to lessened loyalty and intentions to quit.[99] Hindrance-related stress also negatively affects learning. However, a challenging learning environment increases learning.[100] A meta-analysis of 183 independent samples found support for the negative relationship of hindrance stress to job satisfaction and organizational commitment, and positive relationships with turnover intentions, turnover, and withdrawal behaviors (absenteeism and turnover).[101] Challenge stressors had the opposite effect on these outcomes.

Stress negatively impacts job performance and attitudes. Stress relates to lower job satisfaction, organizational commitment, and job involvement as well as higher frustration (these are psychological outcomes). Second, stress is related to more use of health care, sick days, and workers' compensation claims (physical outcomes). Third, stress is related to lower job performance, more counterproductive behavior, and accidents (behavioral outcomes).[102]

Stressors are situations and events that result in an employee experiencing strain.[103] The stressors found at work are physical, task related, role, social, work schedule related, career related, traumatic events, and stressful change processes.[104] For example, some work has physical demands such as the repetitive nature of factory work or transcription for a court reporter. Work schedule stress may be due to having to work the night shift in a hospital. Career-related stress may emanate from anxiety over whether or not a promotion will be earned. Some of these stressors come from roles that employees must play in the organization.

> Critical Thinking Question: Research suggests that stress is not necessarily always negative. Give an example of when stress can be a positive force in organizations.

Role Stress

Roles are the behaviors that are expected of a person in a particular organizational context. People learn their roles in organizations and "act" them out daily. Roles can be a source of stress in a number of ways because they place demands on a person to fulfill expectations. **Role ambiguity** occurs where there is a lack of specificity or predictability about what a person's role is.[105] In short, the person does not know what is expected, which may be due to not understanding what a boss requires, for example. **Role conflict** occurs when there are incompatible demands regarding what a person's role is.[106] For example, a person's boss may want an employee to work late, but their coworkers want them to leave when they do so they don't look bad (intersender role conflict). Role conflict may also happen when organizational requirements conflict with personal values (person–role conflict). Interrole conflict occurs when a person holds multiple roles at the same time and feels torn by the demands of different role senders. For example, a student wants to please the professor by studying for a midterm exam, but friends want to go out to dinner with them the night before the exam.

Role overload is a third form of role-related stress, and it is caused by too much work, time pressure, and deadlines that a person feels unable to meet.[107] Role overload may be quantitative (the number of demands) or qualitative, which refers to an employee not having the qualifications to perform their work role.[108] A study[109] of 210 managers found that reducing all three forms of role stress (role ambiguity, role conflict, and role overload) and having social support play a crucial role in increasing job satisfaction. Role stress may also cause employees to act out at work. For example, a study of sales and service representatives[110] found that role conflict had a positive relationship with both interpersonal (for example, making a racial joke at work) and organizational deviance (for example, taking property from work). Role ambiguity was positively related, while role overload was negatively related, to organizational deviance. Role stress also affects job performance. A study of 227 hotel employees in Turkey[111] found that role ambiguity and role conflict are negatively associated with job performance; however, role overload is positively associated with job performance. The effects of role stress can "add up" to produce higher stress. In other words, role conflict, ambiguity, and overload produce higher levels of stress when they are combined.[112]

Reconciling conflicts between work and family roles (known as **work–life balance**) is a specific form of interrole conflict that has received a great deal of research. Work–life balance is when work is compatible with participation in family life. This conflict can have an important effect on the quality of both work and family life.[113] Research has indicated that conflicts between work and family roles negatively affect employee well-being.[114,115] It is not uncommon for employees to carry stress home with them from the workplace (known as the **crossover stress effect**), and this affects family interactions. A study of 142 police couples found that police officers who were experiencing stress were more likely to display anger, spend time away from the family, be uninvolved in family matters, and have unsatisfactory marriages.[116] Other research on working couples found burnout in one partner affects the other.[117] There is also **family-to-work conflict**, another form of the crossover effect, which occurs when family problems crossover to work, and research has found this affects job performance, psychological distress, alcohol abuse, and physical health.[118]

Some students have to work while they are in school, and **work–school conflict** may occur, which is defined as "the extent to which work interferes with school-related demands/responsibilities and has been shown to be negatively related to school performance and satisfaction."[119] Of course, school and family conflict can combine to impact work outcomes. A study of 100 working married students[120] found that school-to-work and family-to-work conflict resulted in burnout and lower job satisfaction. This finding was more prevalent for women than men. However, the crossover from school to work may be beneficial. A study of 170 undergraduates[121] who were surveyed at several points in time during a semester found that having a good day at school was related to having a good day at work. Thus, employers may benefit from the performance gains and positive attitudinal shifts that stem from experiences of facilitation between roles.

A study of graduates in the early years of their career concluded that although graduates seek work–life balance, their concern for career success draws them into a situation where they work increasingly long hours and experience an increasingly unsatisfactory relationship between home and work.[122] This underscores the importance of organizational policy and practice to help employees manage the relationship between work and family. There are a number of sources of stress that come from outside the workplace, and Toolkit Activity 15.3 is an assessment where you can determine how much stress comes from events in your life.

There may be cultural differences in stress and coping, and research has been conducted in other countries. It is clear that the problem of workplace stress is now a global phenomenon, and the next section discusses international and cross-cultural research on stress.

> **Critical Thinking Questions: Which of the role-related stress sources do you think creates the most strain? Why?**

Stress Is a Global Concern

The prevalence of work stress has been documented in numerous countries, including the United Kingdom,[123] Germany,[124] Sicily,[125] Saudi Arabia,[126] and China,[127] to name a few. Stress has been related to outcomes of lower satisfaction and increased turnover intentions in other cultures as well. For example, a study of public-sector employees working in Botswana found stress related to turnover.[128] This has raised the question of whether the stressor-strain model reported in much of the literature is universal, prompting cross-cultural comparisons.

Relationships among role stressors, self-efficacy, and burnout were studied in nine countries (i.e., United States, Germany, France, Brazil, Israel, Japan, China, Hong Kong, and Fiji). Findings indicated self-efficacy had a universally negative association with burnout across all regions. Further, self-efficacy reduced the impact of role conflict and/or role ambiguity on burnout in eight of the nine cultures (the relationship did not hold for role ambiguity in the United States).[129] The relationship of job stress with burnout and turnover intentions among employees in Canada, China, Malaysia, and Pakistan examined four job stressors (i.e., work overload, conflict, ambiguity, and resource inadequacy) as well as burnout and turnover motivation. Overall, job stress and the four job stressors were significantly related to burnout and turnover motivation in all four countries.[130]

Two large-scale studies of cross-cultural stressors and cultural values found role conflict and role ambiguity to be related to power distance and individualism.[131,132] In terms of which country may experience the most stress, a review of cross-cultural research on stress suggests there are different sources of stress for people working in different countries.[133] For example, time pressure, deadlines, long working hours, and interpersonal problems are a source of stress for executives from Latin America and South Africa. In China and the United States, the most frequently reported stressors were poor working conditions, equipment failure, lack of training, difficulties with teamwork, and lack of structure. In the United States, the lack of adequate control was reported more frequently than in other countries. While cross-cultural research on stress is relatively new, evidence suggests that stress occurs worldwide.

There may be differences in how people cope with stress that depend on culture, however. For example, Indian and U.S. employees in similar jobs tend to use different coping strategies to deal with work-related strain. Indians preferred to talk with family members and close friends about their frustrations. U.S. employees engage in more action-oriented coping mechanisms to deal with the source of the stress.[134] This may be the result of having more job "decision" latitude, which is "the working individual's potential control over job-related decision making."[135] For example, problem-focused coping and job latitude reduced stress in a study of the United States, New Zealand, Germany, Spain, South Africa, and Japan.[136] The next section reviews coping mechanisms for job stress in more detail.

COPING

Learning Objective 15.7: Develop a plan for coping with stress during change.

Coping is defined as "constantly changing cognitive and behavioral efforts to manage specific external and/or internal demands that are appraised as taxing or exceeding the resources of the person."[137] There are two types of coping: behavioral methods (problem-solving behaviors) and cognitive methods (managing thoughts and emotions).[138] Examples of behavioral (or active) coping strategies are keeping a positive outlook, working harder, and seeking advice and help.[139] Examples of cognitive methods include reordering life priorities and convincing oneself that work isn't all that important. Men and women may cope differently. A meta-analysis found that women are more likely than men to engage in most forms of coping strategies. In particular, the strongest effects showed that women were more likely to use strategies that involved verbal expressions by seeking emotional support. For example, they were more likely than men to ruminate about problems and use positive self-talk.[140]

> **Critical Thinking Questions: Which coping strategies in Figure 15.7 work best for you and why? Are there any that don't work? Explain why. Develop a plan for coping with change that you are experiencing (or may experience in the future).**

An employee's ability to cope with stress relates to their well-being and job performance. For example, research has shown that active coping with organizational change has significant effects on extrinsic (higher salary, rank, and performance as well as lower career plateauing) and intrinsic career outcomes for employees (organizational commitment, job satisfaction).[141] Emotional strategies help as well. The ability to detach from work during off-job time is an important factor that helps to protect employee well-being and work engagement.[142] As Figure 15.7 suggests, one coping strategy is to ask for assistance or support when experiencing stress. The next section discusses research on the buffering effects of social support from others.

Figure 15.7   Coping Strategies

	Problem-Focused	Emotion-Focused
Behavioral Methods	Working harder Seeking assistance Acquiring more resources	Engaging in non-work activities Seeking support Venting anger

Cognitive Methods	Planning and organizing
	Focusing on job duties
	Take one step at a time
		Tell yourself you
		    always come through
		Escape and detachment
		Convince yourself
		    work doesn't matter

Source: Adapted from Latack, J. C., & Havlovic, S. J. (1992). Coping with job stress: A conceptual evaluation framework for coping measures. *Journal of Organizational Behavior, 13*(5), 479–508.

Social Support

Social support is the help that people receive when they experience job demands. Support during a stress episode is beneficial. This is called the **"buffering effect"** because help from others serves as a buffer from stress and strain.[143] Social support is a resource for coping with stress that comes from others—family, friends, coworkers, and supervisors. Social support may be emotional or **instrumental**.[144] Based on a longitudinal study of blue-collar workers, the buffering effect of social support on work hours, employee health, and well-being is a function of the pattern of exchange relations between an employee and his or her close support providers (friends and family).[145] Social support aids in stress management for the following reasons:[146]

- By building up the person's sense of identity and belonging

- By improving self-image

- By enhancing the sense of control and mastery over the stressful situation

A meta-analysis found social support is negatively related to both stressors and strains.[147] Social support may help prevent a stress episode as well as alleviate the stress when it occurs. Research has demonstrated that leaders play a key role in providing social support for employees experiencing stress.[148]

Given the high costs of stress, organizations have developed interventions and policies to help their employees cope with stress. In many of these interventions, the emphasis is on prevention, and these strategies are reviewed next.

PREVENTIVE STRESS MANAGEMENT IN ORGANIZATIONS

Learning Objective 15.8: Identify organizational interventions and policies that help employees cope with stress.

Given the rising costs of workplace stress, organizations have been addressing stress through a variety of policy changes and interventions. **Preventive stress management** is a set of methods that promote health at the workplace and avoid distress.[149] While organizations assume that employees will take some individual responsibility for preventing stress, it is a clear trend that organizations are being more proactive regarding stress management. Many organizations have **wellness programs** that offer workshops on time management, weight loss, alcohol and/or drug abuse, smoking cessation, and exercise. Reviews of the research on these organizational interventions have shown that they minimally impact employee well-being and performance.[150] Yet a more recent meta-analytic study of 36 wellness programs found they are effective in helping employees cope with workplace stress.[151]

BEST PRACTICES

Does Time Management Work?

There have been a number of popular books written about time management over the years. For example, *How to Get Control of Your Time and Your Life* has sold millions of copies and is considered a classic.[152] But is this supported by research evidence? Research shows that there are four aspects of time management: (1) setting goals and priorities (e.g., "I break down tasks"), (2) mechanics of planning and scheduling (e.g., "I write reminder notes"), (3) perceived control of time (e.g., "I am overwhelmed by tasks"—reversed), and (4) having a preference for disorganization (e.g., "I have a messy workspace"—reversed).[153]

The most predictive time management factor was the perceived control of time. The 165 students who completed a time management survey reported higher GPAs and work and life satisfaction, and lower stress (less role ambiguity, less role overload, and reported fewer job-related health issues such as headaches and insomnia) when they felt that they had more control over their time. A study of 353 government employees found that engaging in time management behaviors reduced tension and increased job satisfaction but did not relate to job performance. Also, employees that had attended time management training (a half-day seminar) did not report any significant differences in stress, satisfaction, or performance.[154] Time management may alleviate stress while you are a student and also on the job. Also, job and life satisfaction may be enhanced. However, the link to job performance is less clear. Time management training may not have the impact that much of the popular press claims. Following the general guidelines suggested by this research may be just as beneficial as training: Set goals and priorities, schedule tasks well, and stay organized.

Discussion Questions

1. One factor is the degree to which a person's work area is organized—that is, not messy. Is your work area organized? Do you think it makes a difference in your stress and performance?

2. Why do you think that time management is not related clearly to productivity (recall the discussion of the optimum level of stress for performance known as the Yerkes-Dodson law discussed earlier in this chapter)?

Sources: Macan, T. H. (1994). Time management: Test of a process model. *Journal of Applied Psychology, 79*(3), 381; Macan, T. H., Shahani, C., Dipboye, R. L., & Phillips, A. P. (1990). College students' time management: Correlations with academic performance and stress. *Journal of Educational Psychology, 82*(4), 760.

Employee Assistance Programs

When an employee exhibits a clear stress reaction that is affecting his relationships with coworkers and performance, a referral may be made for counseling through an **employee assistance program (EAP)**. These programs have become common in most large organizations. Although these counseling programs may be in-house, they are usually delivered through an outside agency. The employer typically offers the services of the EAP as an employee benefit. EAPs may provide counseling, information, and referrals appropriate for treatment and support services. For example, most universities offer free counseling services for students who may be experiencing stress in coping with the demands of school and/or work and family. An interview study of organizational leaders in Australia found that EAPs were an important source of support that can be offered by organizations to their staff for the management of both personal and professional concerns.[155] A longitudinal, matched-sample study[156] of 156 employees receiving EAP services with 188 non-EAP employees found that over time, EAP employees had significantly lower absenteeism and "presenteeism" (being at work but not working).

> **Critical Thinking Questions:** As this section indicates, organizations spend a lot of money helping employees cope with stress through prevention and wellness programs. Should they? In other words, do you think that employees should take responsibility for their own coping?

LEADERSHIP IMPLICATIONS: HELPING EMPLOYEES COPE

Most organizations today are undergoing changes that create stress for employees. A study was conducted by consulting firm McKinsey & Company to examine OB (people and processes) and how it relates to financial success from changes such as mergers and cost reduction strategies. The company studied change initiatives started by top management at 40 organizations, including banks, hospitals, and manufacturers. These change programs had specific financial targets that were expected to have a large economic impact on the organization. Some organizations (58%) failed to meet the financial goals of their organizational change initiative. The remaining 42% of these companies met their financial goals (or exceeded them—in some cases by as much as 200% to 300%). The companies with the lowest returns had poor change management practices, and companies that gained big returns had strong ones.[157] These change practices are shown for three levels of management in Table 15.3. While senior managers play a key role in articulating the need for change and leading the change process, this study also shows that managers play an important leadership role by providing feedback, skills, tools, and motivation for their followers to succeed.

As the McKinsey study indicates, effective leadership of organizational change can have significant bottom-line impact for organizations.

Workplace stress is a "leadership challenge," and "the challenge for leaders is to create organizational cultures and work environments in which people may produce, serve, grow, and be valued."[158] This chapter has reviewed various personality and organizational factors that may create anxiety for employees, especially organizational change, which is stressful for everyone. First, leaders need to develop plans for coping with stress themselves so that they are

Table 15.3 Factors for Successful Change

Senior managers	
Commitment	Put initiative at top of agenda
Communication	Relate single, clear, compelling story—no mixed messages
Financial incentives	Reward senior managers if initiative is successful
Nonfinancial incentives	Provide recognition for strong performance
Leadership	Identify owner/champion
Stretch targets	Upload goals with mantralike consistency; team "lives or dies" by the numbers
Middle managers	
Decision authority	Exercise consistent control over defined set of tasks
Skills in managing people	Provide feedback to employees on status of initiative
Skills in managing projects	Achieve measurable milestones in timely manner
Frontline staff	
Skills	Consider training key aspect of initiative
Tools	Make technology and techniques available to employees
Motivation	Clearly reward excellent performance to improve morale

Source: LaClair, J. A., & Rao, R. P. (2002). Helping employees embrace change. *McKinsey Quarterly, 4,* 17–20.

able to provide support to their followers. As noted previously, supervisors can provide social support for employees undergoing stress by listening to employees' concerns. Having a high-quality relationship with a boss who provides social support prevents burnout.[159] Leaders can provide emotional support by listening but can also help their followers actively problem solve to address the workplace stressors. Leaders should use both emotion-focused and problem-focused strategies with their followers to help them cope with change. A supervisor may also make appropriate referrals to an EAP or wellness program.

Ensuring the well-being of employees is essential to current thinking on positive organizational behavior (POB). During times of organizational change, it is important to ensure the well-being of followers. This requires the ability to show compassion for others at work. Compassion from a leader is noticing, feeling, and understanding the suffering of a follower. Based upon this understanding, the leader takes action to alleviate the person's suffering.[160] Thus, a leader should view followers as "whole people" who bring their emotions to the workplace with them, and assist with work–life balance concerns. Finally, leaders should promote compassionate organizational practices such as the prevention interventions discussed in this chapter.

edge.sagepub.com/scandura2e

Want a better grade? Go to **edge.sagepub.com/scandura2e** for the tools you need to sharpen your study skills.

KEY TERMS

appreciative inquiry (AI), 393
behavioral methods, 408
buffering effect, 409
challenge-related stress and
  eustress, 405
change uncertainty, 400
changing, 397
cognitive methods, 408
commitment to change, 394
compassion, 412
crossover stress effect, 407
employee assistance program
  (EAP), 411
family-to-work conflict, 407
fight-or-flight response, 404

force field analysis, 398
hindrance-related stress, 405
innovation, 400
instrumental support, 409
job burnout, 403
job control, 403
organizational development
  (OD), 392
organizational stress, 403
preventive stress management, 410
proactive, 390
process consultation, 393
reactive, 390
refreezing, 397
restructuring and downsizing, 400

role ambiguity, 406
role conflict, 406
role overload, 406
social support, 408
stressors, 404
survey feedback, 392
sustainability, 394
team building, 393
top management support, 400
unfreezing, 397
wellness programs, 410
workforce diversity, 389
work–life balance, 407
workout, 392
work–school conflict, 407

TOOLKIT ACTIVITY 15.1: Appreciative Inquiry

Think back on this course and the learning experiences that you participated in. Choose one that you think was a great learning experience. After answering the following four questions, create a small group with other students and discuss your experiences. Develop some suggestions for your professor to implement in future classes.

1. What happened that made it a great learning experience?

2. Describe the experience.

3. What did you learn?

4. What three wishes do you have that would make learning always like this?

Discussion Questions

1. What did you learn about yourself from the AI exercise?

2. What did you learn about how you learn best?

3. What did you learn about other students?

4. What new things did you learn about? _____ (insert the topics related to the lesson content—for example personality tests? Negotiation? Brainstorming?)

5. How could you use AI as a manager to learn about how your employees learn, what they like about their work, and what motivates them?

Source: Adapted from Conklin, T. A., & Hartman, N. S. (2013). Appreciative inquiry and autonomy—supportive classes in business education: A semi-longitudinal study of AI in the classroom. *Journal of Experiential Education, 37*(3), 285–309. doi:10.1177/1053825913514732

TOOLKIT ACTIVITY 15.2: Warning Signs of Burnout

Pay attention to your coworkers and/or classmates. If you see them exhibiting the following symptoms, they may be on the path to burnout. What can you do to help them?

Physical signs and symptoms of burnout

- Feeling tired and drained most of the time
- Lowered immunity, feeling sick a lot
- Frequent headaches, back pain, muscle aches
- Change in appetite or sleep habits

Emotional signs and symptoms of burnout

- Sense of failure and self-doubt
- Feeling helpless, trapped, and defeated
- Loss of motivation
- Increasingly cynical and negative outlook
- Detachment, feeling alone in the world
- Decreased satisfaction and sense of accomplishment

Behavioral signs and symptoms of burnout

- Withdrawing from responsibilities
- Isolating yourself from others
- Procrastinating, taking longer to get things done
- Using food, drugs, or alcohol to cope
- Taking out your frustrations on others
- Skipping work or coming in late and leaving early

Discussion Questions

1. Have you noticed any of the warning signs in yourself? If so, how many? What can you do to increase your coping?

2. Have you noticed any of the warning signs in a coworker or a classmate? If so, how many?

3. Write a paragraph stating what you will say to your coworker or classmate to help them cope.

Source: "Preventing Burnout." ©Helpguide.org. Retrieved from http://www.helpguide.org/mental/burnout_signs_symptoms.htm

TOOLKIT ACTIVITY 15.3: Stressful Life Events

Listed here are many of the events in life that have been found to produce individual stress reactions. The numerical value represents the degree of disruption that event causes in the average person's life. Some studies have found that people experiencing serious illnesses also had high scores on the life-event scale. Generally, the higher your score, the greater the probability you will experience a major health change in the near future. Since individuals differ in their abilities to handle stress, this score should be taken as a rough guide only.

For each of the events you have experienced during the past 12 months, transfer the value to the second column. Add all of your entries in the second column to obtain your total stress score.

Event	Stress value	Enter "stress value" if this event applies to me
1. My spouse/partner died.	100	
2. I got a divorce.	73	
3. I separated from my spouse/partner.	65	
4. I spent time in jail.	63	
5. A close family member died.	63	
6. I had a major illness or injury.	58	
7. I got married.	50	
8. I was fired at work.	47	
9. I had a marital reconciliation.	45	
10. I retired.	45	
11. I became pregnant.	40	
12. My family gained a new member.	39	
13. I changed to a different occupation.	36	
14. My son or daughter left home.	29	
15. I had trouble with my in-laws.	29	
16. I had an outstanding personal achievement.	28	
17. I started or finished high school or college.	26	
18. I had a change in my living conditions.	25	
19. I had trouble with my boss.	25	
20. My working hours or conditions changed.	20	
21. I had a change in my residence.	20	
22. I changed schools.	20	
23. My social activities changed.	18	
24. My sleeping habits changed.	16	

(Continued)

25. My eating habits changed.	15
26. I took a vacation.	13
27. I celebrated the holidays.	12
28. I had minor violations of the law (traffic or parking tickets, etc.).	11
MY TOTAL SCORE: _____	
Scoring:	
0–150: Low stress	
151–300: Moderate stress	
301+ : High or extreme stress	

Source: Adapted from Holmes, T. H., & Rahe, R. H. (1967). The social readjustment rating scale. *Journal of Psychosomatic Research, 11,* 213–218.

Discussion Questions

1. What is your overall level of stress due to life events (low, moderate, or high)? Did your results surprise you? Explain.

2. Based on completing the assessment, what is the most stressful thing that has happened to you in the past year? How can you focus on reducing the stress that this life event causes?

3. As a leader, explain how you could use the stressful life events assessment to help your employees cope with stress.

CASE STUDY 15.1: We Have to Change: Alighting Innovation in the Utility Industry

There are 3,200 utilities that make up the U.S. electrical grid that sell $400 billion worth of electricity a year. However, that's slowly changing. Companies like Comcast, NineStar Connect, and Vivint have started selling their customers electricity along with their services. Comcast offers its Xfinity customers in Pennsylvania the opportunity to purchase electricity as well as phone, Internet, and television services. NineStar Connect offers electricity, phone, broadband, and home security to customers in Indiana. Vivint, an alarm system company on the east coast, installs solar panels and alarms clients' homes for free, and then requires the homeowner to purchase the electricity that is generated. Any excess is sold to the local power company. Google, while it has not formally entered the market, has its own wholesale power license and has purchased Nest, which makes a "learning thermostat." Industry experts speculate that it will only be a matter of time before Google enters the market. Even individuals are getting in on going "off the electric grid" and making use of energy alternatives by erecting their own wind turbines, installing solar panels, and even hydroelectric systems.

Utilities lose revenues when businesses and residential customers switch to alternative energy sources, most often solar and wind power. Utilities have to maintain the power transmission lines across the grid, grid storage, and their own power generation operations. Customers often are assessed fees in their bills that help cover line and facilities maintenance, but those who are selling back power don't pay any of these fees while still using the power lines. They lose additional money from having to buy any excess electricity generated and from the increased grid storage capabilities that are needed to contain this extra generated power during lower use times.

Further, utility companies face a number of regulations and are limited in their actions. For instance, utilities in Louisiana, Idaho, and California have wanted to impose fees or taxes on solar users but have been rejected by regulators. It is unlikely that U.S. regulators will ever completely do away with electric companies, as there will always be a need to have a secure supply of power. However, it is unlikely that the government will help electric utility firms ensure they operate at highly profitable levels like the industry enjoyed for years after deregulation. Thus, these companies will always have to incur the expense of keeping up the power lines—and with a dwindling customer base.

With this influx of new competitors and poorly functioning operating model, utility companies are going to have to do something different in order to continue to be profitable and to combat the loss of customers. Michael Peevey, the president of the California Public Utilities Commission, states that these days utilities "hold their own fate in their hands. They can do nothing but complain or moan about technological change or they can try to adapt."

However, most utility companies are behind the times on technology. While there are smart meters, most utilities have a limited presence in customer homes with programmable thermostats. They could have a greater presence if they were to invest in developing better in-home energy management tools (like the thermostats offered by Nest). Nor have many utilities looked into apps for phones or tablets that can help consumers manage their electricity use.

Finally, the utility companies themselves have been getting in the way of their own success. Over a decade ago, Peevey recommended to the California utilities to get into the solar business. He suggested they put the solar panels on people's homes and put the cost of installation into the rate base. The CEOs of the companies balked at Peevey's calls for change. Most CEOs replied to his innovative ideas by saying, "It's not our culture," which is true, as most electric companies did not have a need to innovate its production processes or products for decades.

Anthony Earley Jr., CEO of Pacific Gas & Electric, realizes the seriousness of the threat these problems pose. He knows that his company needs to change, but where should they start?

Thus far, utility companies have tried to engage with customers through "energy audits," free consultations with homeowners to evaluate one's energy usage with suggestions on how to be more energy efficient. In addition, firms try to build relationships with customers through advertising and community sponsorships. What do you think of these ideas?

Discussion Questions

1. What changes will the company need to make? In what areas should the company start making changes?

2. Looking at the change models presented in the text, how might you roll out the changes you came up with? How can leaders help or hinder change?

3. How can planning for organizational change help the company adapt? Think of several specific functional areas or processes that can be used to help facilitate this planned change.

4. What can you do to help overcome employees' resistance to change both before the changes are implemented as well as during the change process? Is it simply behaviors that will need to change, or will attitudes need to change as well?

Sources: Developed from Martin, C., Chediak, M., & Wells, K. (2013, August 22). Why the U.S. power grid's days are numbered. Retrieved from http://www.businessweek.com/articles/2013-08-22/homegrown-green-energy-is-making-power-utilities-irrelevant#p1; Smith, S. J. (2014, May 28). Barclays warns that U.S. electric utilities are under solar threat. Retrieved from http://nextcity.org/daily/entry/barclays-downgrade-us-electric-utility-sector-solar-threat; Goossens, E., Chediak, M., & Polson, J. (2014, May 29). Technicians at the gate: How Google could become your next power company. Retrieved from http://www.bloomberg.com/news/2014-05-29/tv-web-phone-electricity-a-new-threat-to-utilities.html

CASE STUDY 15.2: The Price of Entrepreneurship

All jobs have stress, risk, and drama associated with them. Television programs from the last decade (*Deadliest Catch, Ax Men, Does Someone Have to Go? Kitchen Nightmares*, and *Restaurant Impossible*, to name a few) have captured a number of different challenges employees and business owners face on a daily basis. However, business owners have more stress and anxiety than other employees. Entrepreneurs have the double-edged sword of having to deal with stress from the problems that are happening and having to help their employees cope with stress. Sometimes the pressure is small, and other times the pressure overwhelming. Read the following situations and think about how you would handle the pressure.

Situation 1: A client called complaining that the merchandise he ordered from your firm arrived damage. He points out this is the second shipment he's received that has been damaged in the last 4 months. You offer a discount, but the client not only wants the discount, he wants replacement items. You agree, but are upset about how much it is costing you. You are also frustrated with needing to come up with a better way to ship your goods to this client in the future but are determined to find a way so you don't have these same losses again.

Situation 2: You and a friend from college own a restaurant. You started this business thinking that your management skills and your friend's culinary skills and experience would generate a great success. The first year things went pretty well, and while you weren't raking in the dough, you made enough to generally cover expenses. This year, however, things have changed, and the restaurant is now losing $1,000 a week. You realize this is a problem as you don't have a large cash reserve, as most of your and your partner's money went into starting up the restaurant. As you are struggling to pay your suppliers, employees, and other creditors, it's taking a toll on the relationship with your business partner as you are starting to fight more and more on money and strategy. For instance, you want to send out mailers with coupons, while your partner disagrees and instead wants to develop new specials to help drive traffic in the door. You two can't agree. Further, you and your spouse just found out that you two will be having a baby. What's worse, on your way in you passed a sign announcing that a new restaurant is opening up a few blocks away. Sadly, you can't call Gordon Ramsay as he's no longer filming *Kitchen Nightmares*, and Robert Irvine has turned into a daytime talk show host along the lines of Jerry Springer and Ricki Lake.

Situation 3: You run a management consulting firm that focuses on helping clients boost their output. For the last 10 years, things have been going well. You've developed a sound list of clients that engage in repeat business, and you and your staff are typically able to generate 10 to 20 new client projects a year. However, 5 years ago when the world entered into another global financial crisis, for the first 9 months you did not get any business. You've let go half of your staff, and in order to keep things afloat, you've exhausted your personal savings and assets—including your car and jewelry. Things have slowly gotten better; you get a few new small clients each year that help stop the hemorrhaging, but you're not profitable. In fact, you took a second mortgage out on your house and have taken a second job driving a cab to help make ends meet. You're finally at the point where you have decided to close the doors and walk away from the loss.

Situation 4: Last year, you started up an engineering technology firm. You've been in contract negotiations with a large oil manufacturing firm that is considering becoming a strategic investor. You're hoping that they sign the 400-page contract you sent them last month and deposit the $1 million due upon signing to your corporate account soon, but there has been no indication from the oil company if they will sign or not. Right now, you have exactly $7.85 in the bank. You are 60 days late on the car payment and 90 days behind on the mortgage. The IRS has filed a lien against you. Your home phone, cell phone, and cable TV have all been turned off. In less than a week, the natural gas company is scheduled to suspend service to your house, and then there will be no heat or way to prepare food.

Discussion Questions

1. In these scenarios, the personal life as well as the business life are both creating stress. How can the situation in your personal life make the stress in your business better or worse?

2. For each of these scenarios, you're definitely suffering a lot of stress. How might stress affect your attitude? What should you do to avoid creating a toxic work environment for your employees?

3. In some of these situations, the employees know things are bad and are likely feeling stressed and worried. What can you do to help employees cope with the situation? How can you keep your best employees committed and not jumping ship to other more stable firms?

4. How, with all this stress, might you motivate yourself to keep going? How do you balance the need to escape or hide from problems with the responsibility of giving it your all to keep the business going?

5. Sometimes, a business will fail. According to the Small Business Administration, more businesses close each month than open, and more than half of all businesses won't last 5 years (SBA.gov). If your business were to fail and close as in Situation 3, what would you do to cope with the stress and emotional turbulence from its closing? How could you turn such a negative experience into something positive?

Source: Developed from Bruder, J. (2013, September). The psychological price of entrepreneurship. Retrieved from https://www.inc.com/magazine/201309/jessica-bruder-psychological-price-of-entrepreneurship.html

SELF-ASSESSMENT 15.1: Leading Through Change Assessment

This self-assessment exercise identifies your approach(es) to leading through change. There is no "one best" approach—all have strengths and weaknesses. There are no right or wrong answers, and this is not a test. You don't have to share your results with others unless you wish to do so.

Part I. Taking the Assessment

You will be presented with some questions representing different approaches to leading through change. If you don't currently have direct reports ("followers"), answer the questions with respect to how you approach others (for example, your peers) during change.

Statements	Strongly Disagree	Disagree	Neutral	Agree	Strongly Agree
1. I assign tasks to followers to implement change.	1	2	3	4	5
2. I try to keep the morale of my followers high during change.	1	2	3	4	5
3. I set ground rules and leave it up to my followers to change.	1	2	3	4	5
4. I use logic to convince my followers to change.	1	2	3	4	5
5. I expect my followers to be committed to the goals of change.	1	2	3	4	5
6. I believe that change is best implemented when few people are involved.	1	2	3	4	5

(Continued)

Statements	Strongly Disagree	Disagree	Neutral	Agree	Strongly Agree
7. I try to emphasize that followers will be satisfied with the benefits of change.	1	2	3	4	5
8. I leave decisions on change and its implementation to my followers.	1	2	3	4	5
9. I explain the reasons for the change to my followers.	1	2	3	4	5
10. I communicate clear goals for change.	1	2	3	4	5
11. I demonstrate my expertise with respect to change to my followers.	1	2	3	4	5
12. I rely on good working relationships to get things done during change.	1	2	3	4	5
13. My followers decide what changes are needed.	1	2	3	4	5
14. I present the need for change logically to my followers.	1	2	3	4	5
15. I emphasize the rewards from commitment to change.	1	2	3	4	5
16. I ask my followers to complete tasks efficiently during change.	1	2	3	4	5
17. I explain how change will improve morale.	1	2	3	4	5
18. I allow my followers to follow their own course of action with respect to change.	1	2	3	4	5
19. I prefer to implement change slowly to allow followers to adjust to it.	1	2	3	4	5
20. I show followers how the goals of change positively impact our organization's performance.	1	2	3	4	5

Part II. Preliminary Scoring Instructions

In Part I, you rated yourself on 20 questions. Copy the numbers you circled in each of the columns to derive your score for the approaches to leading through change. During class, we will discuss each approach and its strengths and weaknesses, as well as discuss how you can be more effective in leading change. (If you have been given a peer form for others to rate you, score it as well and bring it with you.)

Approach A	Approach B	Approach C	Approach D	Approach E
1. _____	2. _____	3. _____	4. _____	5. _____
6. _____	7. _____	8. _____	9. _____	10. _____
11. _____	12. _____	13. _____	14. _____	15. _____
16. _____	17. _____	18. _____	19. _____	20. _____
Total _____	_____	_____	_____	_____

Now, enter your scores in high to low order in Column 2 of the following table. On the first line of Column 3, enter your difference score, which is obtained by subtracting Line 2 of Column 2 from Line 1 of Column 2. Then take the difference for your second and third choices and record it on the second line of Column 3. Continue taking differences between each of your scores and recording them. The difference between scores indicates the likelihood that a person will shift styles: a low score (1–5) suggests shifting; a high score (over 5) suggests resistance to shifting. We will discuss why it is important to be able to shift your style.

Your Choice	Leading Through Change Approach (LETTER)	Score (High to Low) (Column 2)	Differences Between Scores (Column 3)
1st primary			
2nd backup			
3rd backup			
4th backup			
5th backup			

Brief explanations of the five approaches to leading through change follow.

Directive controlling (A). The leader using this approach has maximum concern for efficient accomplishment of operational goals and little concern about whether followers are committed to change. This leader views followers as parts of a machine that must implement change. He or she believes that people must be directed and monitored because they don't have the willingness or ability to change. This leader relies on his or her own expertise. Maintaining control over the situation is important to this leader.

Relationship focused (B). The leader following this approach focuses on the followers' satisfaction and commitment to the change. The operational goals and outcomes from the change are not as important as the morale during change. Decisions about change are delegated to followers who are encouraged to design their own change process. Relationship development is important to this leader.

Status quo (C). This leader's approach to change shows little concern for either operational goals or people. The leader does not want to be involved in change and is "waiting it out" until the change passes and new directives are given from his or her superiors. This leader sees change as disruptive and would rather have a stable environment. Security is important to this leader.

Rational–incremental (D). This leader balances concerns for operational goals with people. This rational leader makes trade-offs between the organization's goals for change and followers' concerns about it. This leader views moderate change as the best course of action (i.e., evolution rather than revolution) and is concerned that changing systems too quickly will be disruptive and harm productivity. This leader will implement change in small increments to allow people to adjust slowly to change. Explaining the reasons for change to followers is important to this leader.

Goal setting (E). The leader using this approach focuses on communication and specific, measurable, actionable, relevant, and time-based (SMART) goals. He or she follows up to ensure that goals are met by followers. This leader also wants personal commitment from followers to the goals of change and his or her vision for the future. He or she makes the link between goal commitment, attainment, and organizational rewards. He or she tries to show how followers' actions impact the bottom-line performance of the organization. Goal acceptance is important to this leader.

You may have found that you use different approaches to change. In fact, most people have more than one approach to change, and this may depend upon the situation. The purpose of this assessment is to make you aware of different approaches to leading others during change and give you feedback on preferred approaches. The differences calculated in the assessment indicate how flexible you may be in changing your style (small differences between scores indicates a tendency to switch your approach if needed, whereas large differences suggest that you rely heavily on one approach). You may want to work on adding another approach (your second-highest score would be a good place to start).

This assessment may be used as a point of departure for further reflection and observation concerning the way you attempt to lead people through change. To obtain a better understanding of your change style, ask your followers, supervisor, and peers how they view you in terms of these five approaches.

Discussion Questions

1. What is your primary approach to leading change? How resistant are you to switching your style? Do you think it is important to stay with one style or be able to switch styles? Explain.

2. Have a peer complete the assessment about you. Is their assessment of the primary way you lead change the same or different than your self-assessment? Explain why it is the same or different.

3. Based on your results, write a brief description of how you would lead change through an organizational downsizing when there would be layoffs of employees.

SELF-ASSESSMENT 15.2: Perceived Stress Scale

This self-assessment exercise indicates how much stress you are experiencing. There is no "one best" answer to these questions, and the goal is for you to learn about yourself. There are no right or wrong answers, and this is not a test. You don't have to share your results with classmates unless you wish to do so.

Part I. Taking the Assessment

You will be presented with some questions representing different situations. Circle the response that indicates how often you experience the situation.

In the last month, how often have you . . .

Statements	Very often	Fairly often	Sometimes	Almost never	Never
1. Felt confident about your ability to handle your personal problems?	1	2	3	4	5
2. Felt that you were on top of things?	1	2	3	4	5
3. Been able to control irritations in your life?	1	2	3	4	5
4. Felt that things were going your way?	1	2	3	4	5
	Never	Almost never	Sometimes	Fairly often	Very often
5. Felt nervous and stressed?	1	2	3	4	5
6. Been angered because of things that were outside your control?	1	2	3	4	5
7. Been upset because of something that happened unexpectedly?	1	2	3	4	5

8. Felt difficulties were piling up so high that you could not overcome them?	1	2	3	4	5
9. Found that you could not cope with all the things that you had to do?	1	2	3	4	5
10. Felt that you were unable to control the important things in your life?	1	2	3	4	5

Part II. Scoring the Assessment

For each of the questions, write down your score based on the following scale:

Question	Score
1.	_____
2.	_____
3.	_____
4.	_____
5.	_____
6.	_____
7.	_____
8.	_____
9.	_____
10.	_____
Total:	_____
Total Score:	_____
37–50: indicates a high level of stress	
24–36: indicates a moderate level of stress	
10–23: indicates a low level of stress	

Source: Cohen, S., & Williamson, G. (1988). Perceived stress in a probability sample of the United States. In S. Spacapan & S. Oskamp (Eds.), *The social psychology of health: Claremont symposium on applied social psychology*. Newbury Park, CA: Sage.

Discussion Questions

1. Based on this assessment, how much stress have you been experiencing over the past month (low, moderate, or high)? Do you think that this would be the same if you had taken the self-assessment 6 months ago? Explain.

2. To what extent do you feel that you have control over circumstances in your life (low, moderate, or high)? If low or moderate, how can you increase your control? If high, explain why.

3. Provide an example of a time when difficulties piled up. What did you do to manage all of the things you needed to do?

APPENDIX

RESEARCH DESIGNS USED IN ORGANIZATIONAL BEHAVIOR

Organizational behavior (OB) researchers make choices regarding the type of study they will conduct. For example, a study of leader behavior and engagement could be conducted by collecting surveys from a sample of workers in an organization. All research designs have strengths and weaknesses. Therefore, you need to be aware of them so that you may critically evaluate research. The following types of research may be conducted in organizational settings.[1]

Qualitative and Quantitative Research

Qualitative research typically involves interviewing people in organizations and gathering detailed information through transcriptions of the interviews (data may also be gathered through observations or company documents). **Quantitative research** designs involve collecting data through organizational surveys containing measures of OB concepts. An example of a job satisfaction survey measure is found in Table 1.2 in Chapter 1.

Experimental and Quasi-Experimental Studies

Inferences of what causes what in organizations can be found in **experimental** studies, and they are the best way to determine what causes behavior in organizations.[2] Much is known about behavior in small groups—for example, from rigorous studies conducted with student samples in very controlled settings (laboratory experiments). In such studies, there is a control group (a group that receives attention but not the study focus) to guard against the Hawthorne effect we learned about earlier; you might get results due to the researchers paying attention to the subjects in the study. For example, the effects of creativity training on the creative output of engineers were studied in a quasi experiment.[3] The

engineers were randomly assigned to the two groups (experimental and control), and the level of divergent thinking was measured before and after creativity training was conducted. By controlling for alternative explanations with the control group, researchers could be reasonably certain that the increase in divergent thinking was due to the creativity training. The result of this study was an evaluation of how effective the creativity training was in changing the creative behavior of the engineers who were trained.

Correlational Field Study

This study is based on survey data collected in organizational settings. The **correlational field study** is the most common research design employed. Data are gathered by having organizational members complete survey forms, and then data are analyzed using statistical methods. It is desirable in a correlational field study to have data from multiple sources (from employees and their immediate supervisors, for example) to increase the value of the research to the organization. For example, a correlational field study may include measures of leader behavior rated by employees and ratings of performance provided by their supervisors and/or from company records.

Case Study

There are short case studies at the end of each chapter of this textbook. A **case study** is a description of a situation in an organization. The goal is to describe the situation in great detail, paying particular attention to the context. Due to the specificity of the case to a particular organization, it may not apply to other situations. Also, case studies cannot explain what causes behavior, and this is one of the biggest limitations of this research.

Action Research

Action research is the process of problem specification and then interventions (i.e., actions) until the researcher understands how the intervention is affecting the organization. Multiple cycles of interventions are conducted, and the next stage of diagnosis may result in the intervention changing on the next cycle. This requires a large commitment from the organization being studied due to the time invested and the potential disruption of organizational processes. Action research is valuable but is not as common as other types of OB research.

Mixed Methods Research

As noted earlier, there is a distinction between qualitative and quantitative research. However, some OB researchers combine both qualitative (e.g., interviews) and quantitative (e.g., surveys) in a single study that is called **mixed methods research**.[4] In doing so, they attempt to understand something that occurs in an organizational setting in depth by balancing the strengths and weaknesses of different research designs. For example, to understand the perceptions of the fairness of a new compensation plan, the researchers would first conduct interviews with 20 employees to understand the employees' feelings regarding fair pay. Based on these interviews, a survey would then be constructed and administered to a random sample of 300 employees to see how well the initial interviews with 20 employees' feelings about the pay plan represent all employees.

Meta-Analysis

Meta-analysis is a quantitative approach to literature review on a topic.[5] A meta-analysis allows the researcher to combine numerous studies conducted over a period of time to gain an overall summary of an area such as goal setting. The researchers gather a large pool of studies and look for overall trends. The studies in the pool have been conducted by different researchers in different organizations. This increases the confidence that the findings of the meta-analysis will generalize to new situations. Meta-analysis summarizes an entire field of study

Table A1 Strengths and Weaknesses of Different Research Designs

Research Design	Strengths	Weaknesses
Experimental	Can draw conclusions about causality; can maximize study control in the laboratory	May not accurately reflect organizational context; many studies use student subjects
Quasi-experimental	Can simulate benefits of experiments in a real-world setting	More difficult to justify causality than in true (laboratory) experiment
Correlational field study	Expedient way to examine hypothesized relationships in a real-world setting	Less control than experiment; difficult to rule out alternative explanations for findings
Case study	Provides in-depth understanding of real organizational problems	Difficult to generalize findings to other organizations; can't be used to test hypotheses
Action research	Real managers investigate important problems they face	Often not rigorous; generally not accepted by the research community
Mixed methods	Takes advantage of the strengths of qualitative and quantitative research	Difficult and time consuming to implement; costly, careful planning and design choices are required
Meta-analysis	Summarizes a large body of research of time and draws generalizable conclusions	There may be a bias because most studies published show significance; must find unpublished research

in an efficient way for students and researchers interested in a topic. In a sense, a meta-analysis can be thought of as a "study of studies," and this book often relies on them to provide you with an overview of a research area in OB.

In choosing a research design, OB researchers must make trade-offs. For example, the laboratory experiment provides the most rigorous test of hypotheses, but it often lacks the realism of organizational settings. Case studies, on the other hand, provide an in-depth quali-tative understanding of challenges managers face in the real world but lack the statistical rigor to be generalized to other organizations; however, they cannot be used to test hypotheses. The strengths and weaknesses of the various research designs discussed in this section are summarized in Table A1.

> **Critical Thinking Questions:** If you were going to study how to improve employee productivity, which research method would you use? Why?

action research, 425

case study, 424

correlational field study, 424

experimental, 424

meta-analysis, 425

mixed methods research, 425

qualitative research, 424

quantitative research, 424

GLOSSARY

A-B-C analysis: systematic planning in OB mod, examining antecedents, behaviors, and consequences

absenteeism: regularly staying away from work or school without good reason

abusive supervision: hostile behavior toward followers that may include ridiculing, spreading rumors, taking credit for work done by followers, giving the "silent treatment," and/or withholding information

achievement-oriented leadership: challenging followers to perform at high levels, setting standards for excellence, showing confidence in followers' ability to reach goals

action research: the process of problem specification and then interventions (i.e., actions) until the researcher understands how the intervention is affecting the organization

active: doing something about job dissatisfaction

active listening: way of listening that is "a creative, active, sensitive, accurate, empathic, nonjudgmental listening"[1]

adaptability: the ability to transfer the demands of the market into organizational actions

additive task: a performance goal that can be met by adding up individual contributions

adjourning: the team finalizes its work and disbands

affect: one's attitude comprised of both emotions and moods

affective: the emotional part of an attitude

affective climate: refers to the shared affective experience of a work group or team[2]

affective commitment: employee's emotional attachment to an organization

affective conflict: conflict that engenders strong emotions such as anger or disgust

affective neuroscience: the study of the neural mechanisms of emotion

affect spin: the ability to vary responses to emotional events by knowing which people are more reactive than others to both internal and external events

agreeableness: a characteristic in which one is affable, tolerant, sensitive, trusting, kind, and warm

all-channel (or star) network: more decentralized and allows a free flow of information among all group members

alternative dispute resolution: methods to resolve conflict that both parties agree to without involving litigation

ambient impact: collective deviant behavior that creates a hostile working environment

applied social psychology: the study of how people interact in groups

appreciative inquiry (AI): an OD intervention in which people reflect on peak experiences and visualize the future

apprising: persuading the target of influence that complying with the influencer will advance his or her career

arbitration: both parties agree in advance to accept a decision, and it is made by a neutral third party

assimilation: relinquishing cultural heritage and adopting the beliefs and behaviors of the new culture

attitude: "a psychological tendency that is expressed by evaluating a particular entity with some degree of favor or disfavor"[3]

attributions: a person's attempt to assign a cause to a behavior or event they observe

attribution theory: proposes that "the attributions people make about events and behavior can be either internal or external"[4]

authentic leadership: knowing oneself and behaving in a way that is consistent with what is intuitively right; this includes the four dimensions of self-awareness, relational transparency, internalized moral perspectives, and balanced processing

autonomy: ability to work alone without supervision

availability bias: readily available information that comes to a person's mind and affects a decision

behavioral: an intention to act based upon the cognitions and affect experienced

behavioral CQ: the ability to adjust to others' cultural practices

behaviorally anchored rating scales (BARS): a vertical scale presented with specific examples of performance

behavioral methods: problem-solving behaviors

belief updating: initial information affects the conclusion one draws, and this conclusion then impacts later judgments

best alternative to a negotiated agreement (BATNA): an alternative that negotiators will accept if the negotiation reaches an impasse and they can't get their ideal outcome

biculturals: "people who have internalized more than one cultural profile"[5]

boomers: born between 1946 and 1964; called this due to the baby boom that occurred after World War II

boundary spanners: individuals in an organization who link the organization's internal networks and/or external constituents together

bounded ethicality: an unconscious psychological process that hinders the quality of decision making

bounded rationality: when decision makers have limits on their ability to assimilate large amounts of information

brainstorming: generating a large quantity of ideas in a face-to-face team meeting

broaden-and-build model: a process by which emotions serve to both broaden employee experiences and then allow them to build better-functioning organizations

buffering effect: support during a stress episode that prevents stress

bureaucratic control: when legitimate authority governs social interactions

calculus-based trust (CBT): a form of trust based upon keeping records of

what another person does for you and what you do for them

career adaptability: defined as "a psychosocial construct that denotes an individual's resources for coping with current and anticipated tasks, transitions, traumas in their occupational roles"[6]

career indecision: "the difficulties preventing individuals from making a career decision"[7]

case study: a description of a situation in an organization

central tendency error: giving ratings that center in the middle of a scale

chain network: gives a flow of information among members, although the people are at the end of the chain

challenge-related stress and eustress: good stress

change uncertainty: uncertainty due to strategic, structural, and/or job-related change

changing: represents movement toward a new desired state

circle network: each person can communicate with two others located adjacent to them

clan control: occurs when shared values and beliefs govern how people interact socially

climcult: culture and climate work together to influence how people experience their work environment

coalition tactics: seek the aid or support others

coding: linking the information you need to remember to something familiar and easily retrievable

coercive power: the ability to punish

cognitive: a statement of belief about something

cognitive CQ: refers to self-awareness and the ability to detect cultural patterns

cognitive dissonance: incompatibility between two or more attitudes or between attitudes and behavior

cognitive evaluation theory: another term for self-determination theory

cognitive methods: managing thoughts and emotions

cohesion: team spirit experienced in high-performing teams

collaboration: offer to provide assistance or resources to the person being asked to do something

collective effort: a work project that reflects the contributions of everyone on the team

collectivism: group orientation

combining tasks: creating natural work units by putting tasks together to create a more challenging and complex work assignment

commitment: employees enthusiastically carry out the program.

commitment to change: employees support change and help the organization implement it

communication apprehension (CA): "an individual's level of fear or anxiety with either real or anticipated communication with another person or persons"[8]

compassion: noticing, feeling, and understanding the suffering of a follower

competence: "a cluster of related knowledge, skills and attitudes that affects a major part of one's job (a role or responsibility), that correlates with performance on the job, that can be measured against well-accepted standards, and that can be improved via training and development"[9]

complementary linkage: one individual identifies with another person, and this identification causes the emotions to spread, as in "misery loves company"

compliance: employees simply go along with the change but secretly hope that it is a program that will come to an end soon

conciliation: calling in a neutral third party to attempt to resolve the conflict

conflict: "the process that begins when one party perceives that the other has negatively affected, or is about to negatively affect, something that he or she cares about"[10]

conscientiousness: being organized, systematic, punctual, achievement oriented, and dependable

consensus: discussing ideas and deferring a final decision until everyone can say they have been heard and will support the final decision

consideration: the degree to which the leader shows trust, respect, and sensitivity to employees' feelings

consistency: defining values and subsystems that are the basis of a strong culture

constructive: a positive response to job dissatisfaction

consultation: invites the person to be involved with a proposed idea, and may be used in any direction as well

consultative: asking for input from team members one-on-one or as a group and then making the final decision

contingency contract: contracts that bridge concerns about future events that are brought up during the negotiation, and they become part of the agreement

continuance commitment: degree to which an employee is aware of the costs of leaving the organization

contrast effect: evaluation of a characteristic of an object or person affected by comparisons with other objects or people ranking higher or lower on the characteristic

convergent linkage: occurs when individuals share the interpretations of emotional events

core self-evaluation (CSE): "fundamental premises that individuals hold about themselves and their functioning in the world"[11]

correlational field study: data are gathered by having organizational members complete survey forms, and then data are analyzed using statistical methods

counterdependent: employees who resent authority and being told what to do

creativity: "production of a novel and appropriate response, product, or solution to an open-ended task"[12]

critical thinking: the objective analysis and evaluation of an issue in order to form a judgment

cross-cultural communication: compares one culture to another

crossover stress effect: a phenomenon that occurs when employees carry stress home with them from the workplace, which affects family interactions

cultural intelligence (CQ): an individual's capabilities to function and manage effectively in culturally diverse settings

cultural looseness: associated with social disorganization, deviance, innovation, and openness to change

culturally endorsed implicit leadership theory (CLT): a theory that identifies leadership behaviors perceived as effective and ineffective across cultures

cultural retooling: the psychological process of adaptation to another culture

cultural tightness: associated with order and efficiency, conformity, and low rates of change

cultural tightness–looseness: the strength of social norms and the level of sanctioning within societies

culture shock: the distress experienced by a traveler from the loss of familiar patterns of social interaction

cyberslacking: using the Internet for personal reasons during working hours

Dark Triad: "comprised of Machiavellianism, narcissism, and psychopathy"[13]

deep acting: when a desired emotional expression is achieved by changing one's underlying felt emotion

deep-level diversity: "differences among members' attitudes, beliefs, and values"[14]

delegating: allowing a team (or individual) to make a final decision

demands–abilities (DA) fit: the compatibility between the employee's knowledge, skills, and abilities, and the demands of the job. In other words, the job characteristics are neither too easy nor too difficult for the abilities of the employee; they match.

destructive: a negative response to job dissatisfaction

determinism: the belief that "people should not try to change the paths their lives are destined to take"

deviant behavior: "aggression, bullying, harassment, incivility and social undermining"[15]

direct effects: an employee is the target of a coworker's deviant act

directive leadership: giving followers specific instructions about their tasks, providing deadlines, setting standards for performance, and explaining rules

distributive justice: perceived fairness of how rewards are distributed

disturbance handler: one who resolves conflict and chooses strategic alternatives

divergent linkage: occurs when interpretations of emotional events differ

downward communication: the process by which employees communicate with others who are lower in the organizational hierarchy

e-harassment: e-mail or other electronic communication directed at a specific person that causes substantial emotional distress and serves no legitimate purpose

elaborative interrogation: people are asked to generate their own explanations of factual statements presented to them

emotional contagion: the negative mood of one employee spreads to others in their group

emotional dissonance: the result of the difference between the organizationally expected emotions and an employee's inner or "real" emotions[16]

emotional division of labor (EDOL): defined as any explicit or implicit division of roles in which individuals vary in their requirement to use emotional abilities[17]

emotional intelligence (EI): "ability to monitor one's own and others' feelings and emotions, to discriminate among them and to use this information to guide one's thinking and actions"[18]

emotional labor: the effort required to effectively manage emotions to be successful on the job

emotion regulation: ability to manage emotion in self and others (e.g., detaching from fear states that interfere with one's functioning)

emotions: brief but intense feelings triggered by specific events that disrupt a person's thinking

employability: "an attribution employers make about the probability that job candidates will make positive contributions to their organizations"[19]

employee assistance program (EAP): programs "designed to help

employees deal with problems that seriously affect job performance"[20]

employee engagement: "the investments of an individual's complete self into a role"[21]

employee well-being: lack of emotional exhaustion, psychosomatic health complaints, and physical health symptoms

enacted values: values that are acted out

engineers: this group focuses on designing systems to support the work of operations, such as employees who design a manufacturing facility

entrepreneur: one who looks for new ideas and opportunities

entry: when a new member starts work

equity theory: a theory that looks at how people compare their inputs to their outcomes

escalation of commitment: when individuals continue a failing course of action after receiving feedback that shows it isn't working

espoused values: values that are stated

ethical climate: the moral atmosphere of the work environment and the level of ethics practiced within an organization

ethical leadership: leadership that promotes honesty and acts based on moral values and beliefs

ethics of care: a normative ethical theory that holds interpersonal relationships and care or benevolence as a virtue central to moral action

evidence-based approach: integrating individual clinical expertise with the best available external clinical evidence from systematic research

evidence-based management (EBM): the ability to translate research to practice

exchange: persuasion based on a quid pro quo

executives: employees who have worked their way up organizational career ladders

and are financially responsible to their board of directors and shareholders

exemplification: when people self-sacrifice or go above and beyond the call of duty in order to gain the attribution of dedication from observers

expanding pie: enlarging the pool of resources so that a negotiation can end in a "win-win" agreement where both feel that they got the best possible outcome

experimental: rigorous studies conducted in controlled settings

expert power: the ability to influence others due to knowledge or a special skill set or expertise

external attribution: people believe that a person's behavior is due to situational factors

external communication: information that is shared with the public through marketing and public relations efforts

extraversion: a trait of a person who is outgoing, talkative, and sociable as well as enjoys social situations

extrinsic motivation: involves the performance → outcome instrumentality between the task and a tangible reward

"extrinsics in service of intrinsics": refers to how extrinsic rewards may support an employee's sense of competence if they don't undermine autonomy

facilitation: when a leader intervenes to resolve a conflict

facilitator: one who helps the team make a decision by asking questions and reflecting statements but not influencing the final decision

family-to-work conflict: family problems cross over to work

feedback: knowledge of results of a person's efforts

feedback seeking: an individual's general level of proactive activity with respect to obtaining feedback from the work environment

fight-or-flight response: the result of human evolution in which the response was needed to attack predators or run away from them

five-stage model: forming, storming, norming, performing, and adjourning

fixed: a specified amount of time or number of responses

fixed pie: only a limited amount of goods are divided, and the goal is to get the largest share

flexible job search behavior (FJSB): flexibility with respect to pay/hierarchical level, skill use, and commuting time

flexible working hours: hours may be formal (i.e., allowing employees to arrive later to work and stay later) or informal (i.e., a supervisor being flexible regarding an employee's need to pick up children from school)

flow: when a person experiences a challenging opportunity aligned with their skills

force field analysis: analyzing the forces for and against a change

forming: the first stage of team development when the team members meet for the first time

framing: whether questions are presented as gains or losses

fundamental attribution error: tendency to attribute other people's behavior to internal factors such as character traits or abilities, but when explaining one's own behavior, people tend to attribute the cause to the situation

gain-sharing plans: compensation is tied to unit-level performance, where revenue increases (or cost savings) are shared with employees

Galatea effect: when an individual sets high expectations for himself or herself and then performs to these expectations

generation Xers, or gen Xers: born between 1965 and 1980; sometimes referred to as the "baby busters" or "latchkey kids"

Global Leadership and Organizational Behavior Effectiveness (GLOBE) project: a large-scale research program that sought to understand differences in leader behaviors and relationships with relevant organizational outcomes worldwide

global mind-set: a set of individual attributes that enhance a manager's ability to influence others who are different from them

global mobility: occurs when individuals, and often their families, are relocated from one country to another by an employer, generally from a familiar situation (a home country) to a novel one (a host country) for a fixed period of time

Golem effect: when an individual sets low expectations for himself or herself and then performs to these expectations

grapevine: the circulation of unofficial information in an organization

gratitude: "a generalized tendency to recognize and respond with grateful emotion to the roles of other people's benevolence in the positive experiences and outcomes that one obtains"[22]

groupthink: the conformity-seeking tendency of a group

growth need strength: refers to a person's need to learn new things, grow, and develop from working

halo error: occurs when the rater's overall positive impression or evaluation strongly influences ratings of specific attributes

Hawthorne effect: positive responses in attitudes and performance when researchers pay attention to a particular group of workers

heuristic: decision rules

high-context cultures: cultures that rely heavily on situational cues for meaning when perceiving and communicating with others

hindrance-related stress: excessive or undesirable constraints that interfere with an individual's ability to achieve goals, creating "negative stress"

hindsight bias, or I-knew-it-all-along effect: the tendency for individuals with outcome knowledge (hindsight) to claim they would have estimated a probability of occurrence for the reported outcome that is higher than they would have estimated in foresight (without the outcome information)

horizontal: adding different tasks at the same level

horns error: occurs when the rater's overall negative impression or evaluation strongly influences ratings of specific attributes

humble leadership: a style of leadership where leaders tend to view themselves more objectively, others more appreciatively, and new information or ideas more openly

hygienes: things like supervision, pay, company policies, and the working conditions

idea evaluation: discussing the strengths and weaknesses of ideas

idea generation: creating new ideas

identification-based trust (IBT): form of trust characterized by the leader and follower sharing the same goals and objectives

imaging: linking verbal information to visual images

implicit leadership schemas: traits and characteristics a person thinks are linked to being a leader

implicit leadership theory (ILT): examines how attributions about leadership affect follower perceptions of who you are in the role of leader

impression management: set of behaviors that people use to protect their self-image or change the way they are seen by others (or both)

indirect effects: an employee is affected by learning of another coworker's deviant behaviors

individual level: the most basic level

individual rights: rights that protect an individual within an organization and guide ethical decision making

industry level: the aggregate of productive enterprises in a particular field, often named after its principal product or service (for example, the health care industry)

influence: the exercise of power to change the behavior, attitudes, and/or values of an individual or group

informational justice: refers to the perceived fairness of the communications made by leaders during a process

ingratiation: compliment-giving or acting deferential

in-group members: group members who perform to the specifications in their job descriptions and go above and beyond and take on extra work

initiating structure: defining tasks for employees and focusing on goals

innovation: the generation, acceptance, and implementation of new ideas, processes, products, or services

inspirational appeals: an appeal made to followers' values and ideals or seeks to arouse the target person's emotions to gain commitment for a request or proposal

instrumental support: focuses on problem solving during a stress episode

integration: maintaining one's cultural heritage and adopting a new cultural identity

integrative acculturation: becoming bicultural

integrative bargaining: parties do not see the process as a zero-sum game, and they believe that an agreement can be reached that satisfies all concerns

integrative complexity: "the degree to which a person accepts the reasonableness of different cultural perspectives on how to live, both at the micro interpersonal level and at more macro organizational-societal levels and, consequently, is motivated to develop integrative schemas that specify when to activate different worldviews and/ or how to blend them together into a coherent holistic mental representation"[23]

intercultural communication: focuses on the behavior of two individuals' communication patterns

interdependent: employees who depend on one another to get things done in the group and organization

internal attribution: people infer that an event or a person's behavior is due to his or her own character traits or abilities

internal communication: "the communications transactions between individuals and/or groups at various levels and in different areas of specialization that is intended to design and redesign organizations, to implement designs, and to co-ordinate day-to-day activities"[24]

interpersonal justice: refers to how employees are treated by their leaders, including respect and propriety

interval: provision of reinforcement based on time

intimidation: where people signal their power or potential to punish in order to be seen as dangerous by observers

intrinsic motivation: when someone works on a task because they find it interesting and gains satisfaction from the task itself

involvement: building human capability, ownership, and responsibility

job burnout: "a prolonged response to chronic stressors on the job"[25]

job control: "the degree to which an individual perceives that s/he can control where, when, and how s/he works"[26]

job crafting: extent to which individuals can demonstrate initiative in designing their own work

job enrichment: redesigning jobs so that they are more challenging to the employee and have less repetitive work

job involvement: how much an employee identifies with his or her job and views his or her performance at work as an essential part of his or her self-esteem

job performance: performance can be actual performance as collected in organizational records (e.g., the number of forms correctly processed in an insurance company) or it may be rated by supervisors and/or peers

job rotation: involves cross-training or allowing workers to do different jobs

job satisfaction: how content an individual is with his or her job, whether or not they like the job or aspects of it, such as the nature of work or supervision

job sharing: two part-time employees jointly do a full-time job, sharing the remuneration

justice: emphasizes fair treatment and the right to pursue happiness

just-world hypothesis: need to believe that the world is fair and that people get what they deserve

knowledge-based trust (KBT): trust grounded in experience of how predictable the other person is

labor relations: the study and practice of managing *unionized* employment situations

language: jargon or acronyms that may be unique to an organization and represent the organizational culture and how it is transmitted to newcomers

lateral communication: the process by which employees communicate with others at the same level in the organizational hierarchy

law of effect: past actions that led to positive outcomes tend to be repeated, whereas past actions that led to negative outcomes will diminish

law of reciprocity: universal belief that if someone does something for you, they should be paid back

leader–member exchange (LMX): the quality of the working relationship that is developed with each follower

leadership climate: effective behaviors, attitudes, and environmental conditions created by a leader that enhance team performance and increase empowerment

learning goal orientation (LGO): when individuals want to learn new things at work and see themselves as adaptable

legitimate power: the ability to make a request and get a response due to the nature of the roles between two people

legitimating tactics: the agent seeks to establish the legitimacy of a request or to verify authority to make it by referring to rules, policies, contracts, or precedent

low-context cultures: cultures in which written and spoken words carry the burden of shared meanings

Machiavellianism: refers to a person who believes that the "ends justify the means" mainly for university students,

based on the pressures and obligations from each domain

management by objectives (MBO): a performance appraisal program where leaders meet with their direct reports and set specific performance objectives jointly

marginalization: rejecting both the old and new culture

market control: exists when prices determine how social interactions between people are formed

mediation: when a third-party neutral person is called in to resolve a conflict

mentoring: intense developmental relationship whereby advice, counseling, and developmental opportunities are provided to a protégé by a mentor, which, in turn, shapes the protégé's career experiences

meta-analysis: a quantitative literature review on a topic

metacognitive CQ: the cognitive processing necessary to recognize and understand expectations appropriate for different cultural situations

metamorphosis: a person transforms from a new employee to an established contributor who is valued and trusted by other members of the organization

millennials: born between 1981 and 1999; look for flexibility and choice

mindfulness: a state of open attention on what is happening in the present without thinking about the past or worrying about the future

Minnesota twin studies: conducted from 1979 to 1999, which followed identical and fraternal twins who were separated at an early age

mission: defining the meaningful, long-term direction for the organization

mixed methods research: research that combines qualitative (e.g., interviews)

and quantitative (e.g., surveys) in a single study

moods: general feeling states that are not related to something that happens to a person but are not intense enough to interrupt regular thought patterns or work

moral outrage: severe reaction to perceived injustice

motivational CQ: refers to persistence and goal setting for cross-cultural interactions

motivation to lead (MTL): defined as "an individual differences construct that affects a leader's or leader-to-be's decisions to assume leadership training, roles, and responsibilities and that affect his or her intensity of effort at leading and persistence as a leader"[27]

motivation–work cycle match: understanding that innovation occurs in phases, and intrinsic motivation may be more important during the idea-generation phase

motivator–hygiene theory: another term for the Herzberg two-factor theory

motivators: factors that satisfy workers when they think about their job, such as advancement, recognition, and achievement

narcissism: the expression of grandiosity, entitlement, dominance, and superiority[28]

need for achievement (nAch): the drive to succeed at high levels

need for affiliation (nAff): the need for close personal relationships

need for power (nPow): the need to influence others to do what you want

needs–supplies (NS) fit: addresses whether the job fulfills the employee's needs for interesting work and a sense of meaning in their work

negative state affect: the experience of negative emotions and poor self-concept. Negative affectivity subsumes a variety of negative emotions, including anger, contempt, disgust, guilt, fear, and nervousness.

negotiation: discussion aimed at reaching an agreement

negotiator: one who protects the interests of the business by interacting within teams, departments, and the organization

netiquette: e-mail etiquette

neuroticism: represents a tendency to be anxious or moody

noise: any communication barrier that may affect how a person interprets a message

nominal group technique (NGT): group meets face-to-face, but discussion is more restricted than in brainstorming or consensus decision making

nonverbal communication: "the sending and receiving of thoughts and feelings via nonverbal behavior"[29]

normative commitment: moral obligation to stay with the organization—because it is the right thing to do

normative decision-making model: shows that team decisions fall on a continuum ranging from leaders making the decision themselves to delegating the decision to the team

norming: a stage of team development where members of the team form a cohesive unit and close relationships among team members develop

observational learning: learning from watching others

ombudsperson: a person who hears grievances on an informal basis and attempts to resolve them

onboarding: the process of welcoming and orienting new organizational members to facilitate their adjustment to the organization, its culture, and its practices

openness: a person's willingness to embrace new ideas and new situations

operant conditioning: a theory that proposes that behavior is a function of consequences

operators: the line managers and employees who are involved in making products, delivering services, and interacting with customers directly

organizational anticipatory socialization: the process an individual goes through as they attempt to find an organization to join

organizational behavior (OB): the study of individuals and their attitudes and behaviors at work

organizational behavior modification (OB mod): programs that apply reinforcement theory in organizations

organizational citizenship behavior (OCB): considered to be performance beyond the expectations of a person's job description—extrarole performance

organizational climate: level of agreement in perceptions about the organization and work environment among employees

organizational commitment: an employee's desire to remain a member of an organization

organizational communication: "the process by which individuals stimulate meaning in the minds of other individuals by means of verbal or nonverbal messages in the context of a formal organization"[30]

organizational culture: "the pattern of basic assumptions, that a given group has invented, discovered, or developed in learning to cope with its problems of external adaptation and internal integration, and that have worked well enough to be considered valid, and, therefore, to be taught to new members as the correct way to perceive, think, and feel in relation to those problems"[31]

organizational development (OD): a collection of social psychology methods employed to improve organizational effectiveness and employee well-being

organizational justice: overall perception of what is fair in an organization

organizational level: an entire entity structured and managed to pursue collective goals with a structure that determines relationships between the different activities and the members

organizational neuroscience: examines the potential of brain science to enhance prediction of OB

organizational politics: unsanctioned influence attempts that seek to promote self-interest at the expense of organizational goals

organizational socialization: defined as the process an organization utilizes to ensure that new members acquire necessary attitudes, behaviors, knowledge, and skills to become productive organizational members[32]

organizational stress: negative environmental factors or stressors associated with a particular job

out-group members: group members who perform to the specifications in their job descriptions but don't go above and beyond and don't take on extra work

overconfidence bias: hubris, or inflated confidence in how accurate a person's knowledge or estimates are

overdependent: employees who are compliant and give in all of the time

overpayment inequity: the perception that a person's outcomes are greater than they deserve compared to another person's outcomes, given their inputs

participative leadership: allowing followers to have a voice in decisions that affect them, sharing information, inviting followers' ideas and opinions

passive: not responding to job dissatisfaction

path–goal theory (PGT): leaders motivate followers to accomplish goals by establishing the *paths* to the *goals*.[33] Specifically, leaders increase the quality and number of payoffs from reaching goals and then make the path to the goals clear by removing obstacles.[34]

pay dispersion: how pay rates differ across individuals

pay inequity: perceived unfairness of how pay is distributed

peer review: a panel of a grievant's peers that hears the concern and attempts to resolve it

perceived organizational support (POS): "employees pay attention to whether the organization values their contributions and cares about their well-being"[35]

perception: process through which people organize and interpret sensory information to give meaning to their world

perceptions of organizational politics (POP): a person's perception of others' behavior strategically designed to maximize short-term or long-term self-interest

perceptual errors: flaws in perception due to mental shortcuts people make to simplify information that is processed

performing: the team meets its goals and completes tasks

personal appeals: asking someone to carry out a request or support a proposal out of friendship or asking for a personal favor before saying what it is

personality: "regularities in feeling, thought and action that are characteristic of an individual"[36]

personality–job fit theory: occurs when job characteristics are aligned with employees' personality, motivations, and abilities

personal power: influence over others, the source of which resides in the person instead of being vested by the position he or she holds

person–environment (PE) fit: the degree of congruence between the person and the work situation

person–job (PJ) fit: occurs when job characteristics are aligned with employees' personalities, motivations, and abilities

person–organization (PO) fit: the match between a person's individual values and those of the organization they work for

perspective taking: the ability to see things from another person's perspective that holds a view that conflicts with your own

political skill: ability to effectively understand others at work and to use such knowledge to influence others to act in ways that enhance one's personal and/or organizational objectives

position power: authority and influence bestowed by a position or office on whoever is occupying it

positive state affect: the extent to which an individual subjectively experiences positive moods such as joy, interest, and alertness

power: the potential of one person (or group) to influence another person or group

power distance: deference to authority

preentry: occurs from the time someone is offered the job to when they actually start working

pressure tactics: threats; relate to coercion

prevention-focused: a tendency to aim for getting to an end because of a fear of an undesirable alternative

preventive stress management: a set of methods that promote health at the workplace and avoid distress

primacy effect: perseverance of beliefs based upon what is observed first

proactive: actively attempting to make alterations to the workplace and its practices

proactive influence tactics: positive and negative ways of influencing others

procedural justice: perception of how fair the process was in making decisions that affect employees

process conflict: people disagree on what course of action to pursue or the best way to operate even after a decision has been made

process consultation: a consultant with OD expertise assists in a helping mode

profit-sharing plans: employee bonuses are based upon reaching a financial target such as return on assets or net income

promotion-focused: a need for achievement, focus on advancement, and set learning goals

prosocial motivation: new concept of motivation that assesses the degree to which employees behave in a way that benefits society as a whole

prospect theory: a perspective that highlights the importance of uncertainty and risk to the decision-making process

psychological capital (PsyCap): the value of individual differences, including efficacy, optimism, hope, and resiliency

psychological empowerment: "intrinsic task motivation manifested in a set of four cognitions reflecting an individual's orientation to his or her work role: competence, impact, meaning, and self-determination"[37]

psychological safety: shared belief that the team is safe for interpersonal risk taking. Being able to show and employ one's self without fear of negative consequences of self-image, status, or career.

psychopathy: impulsivity and thrill seeking combined with low empathy and anxiety[38]

punctuated equilibrium: transition between an early phase of inactivity followed by a second phase of significant acceleration toward task completion

Pygmalion effect: perceptions of performance expectations play a significant role in improving performance

qualitative research: interviewing people in organizations and gathering detailed information through transcriptions of interviews

quantitative research: collecting data through organizational surveys containing measures of OB concepts

ratio: provision of reinforcement is based on the number of responses (attempts)

rational persuasion: use of logic and facts, a tactic commonly employed by leaders

reactive: when an organization makes changes in its practices after some threat or opportunity has already occurred

recency effect: when people remember the most recently presented items or experiences

referent power: the ability to influence based upon others' identification with the individual and followers' desire to emulate them

refreezing: reinforcing and restructuring the changes

regulatory focus theory (RFT): an alternative approach to understanding how individuals strive to meet their goals

rehearsal: repetition of information

reinforcement theory: another term for operant conditioning

reinforcers: something that increases or decreases behavior

relationship conflict: personality clashes or differences in values

remote working: also known as telecommuting, or the ability to work from home—or anywhere

repatriation: the transition when the expatriate has completed the international assignment and returns home

resistance: employees fight the change and try to undermine it

resource allocator: one who decides how to prioritize the direction of resources

restructuring and downsizing: reorganization that includes laying off employees

reverse culture shock: the distress experienced by an expatriate when they assimilate to a foreign culture and have trouble adjusting to their native culture when they return home

reward power: the ability to provide incentives or other things valued

risk taking: a personality trait defined as "any purposive activity that entails novelty or danger sufficient to create anxiety in most people. Risk taking can be either physical or social, or a combination of the two"[39]

rituals: "a form of social action in which a group's values and identity are publicly demonstrated or enacted in a stylized manner, within the context of a specific occasion or event"[40]

role ambiguity: a lack of specificity or predictability about what a person's role is

role conflict: occurs when there are incompatible demands regarding what a person's role is

role overload: role-related stress caused by too much work, time pressure, and deadlines

romance of leadership: the tendency to view leadership as the most important factor for the success or failure of organizations; whereas the influence of other factors is de-emphasized, the influence of leadership is overemphasized

sabbaticals: a leave taken from work to "recharge one's batteries" or take care of family responsibilities

satisfice: making a decision that is satisfactory but perhaps not optimal

schedules of reinforcement: various ways in which reinforcers can be administered

self-actualization: the drive to meet our fullest capacity (e.g., growth and feeling fulfilled as a person)

self-awareness: seeks feedback to improve interactions with others

self-determination: a person's needs for autonomy and competence

self-efficacy: an individual's belief in his or her capacity to execute the behaviors necessary to produce specific performance levels

self-managed work team (SMWT): a team where there is typically no designated leader

self-monitoring: defined as "self-observation and self-control guided by situational cues to social appropriateness"[41]

self-promotion: individuals point out their abilities or accomplishments in order to be seen as competent by observers

self-serving bias: when a person attributes successes to internal factors and failures to situational factors

sense of meaning: how much work goals align with an employee's personal standards (i.e., how well the work "fits" the employee's values)

separation: maintaining only the heritage culture without intergroup relations

servant leadership: going beyond one's self-interest to help followers grow and to promote their well-being

Shannon–Weaver model of communication: framework describing the communication process including the sender, encoding, channel, noise, receiver, and decoding of a message

social identity: a way to explain how people view their own place in society through membership in various groups

social learning theory: extends operant conditioning to consider the fact that people can learn from watching other people succeed or fail

social loafing: the reduction in motivation and effort when individuals work collectively compared with when they work individually or coactively

social pressure: influence from peers that may strengthen the relationship of an attitude toward behavior

social support: help that people receive when they experience job demands

solution implementation: creating options in the form of actions that get results and gain acceptance

state affect: feelings experienced in the short term and fluctuate over time

state-like: characteristics that are relatively changeable and can be developed through awareness and/or training

stereotypes: judging a person based on their membership in a group

stock options: a variation of profit sharing where employees are given stock options as part of their compensation package

stories: "convey shared meanings and values representing the organizational culture and guide behavior"[42]

storming: a stage of team development where conflicts emerge regarding the goals and contributions of team members; and there may be challenges to the leader

stressors: demands

substantive conflict: occurs because people have different opinions on important issues in the organization that affect them

sunk costs fallacy: a person has already invested in this course of action and does not recognize what they invested initially is sunk (or gone)

supplication: "where individuals advertise their weaknesses or shortcomings in order to elicit an attribution of being needy from observers"[43]

supportive leadership: showing consideration, being friendly and approachable, and paying attention to the well-being of followers

surface acting: "producing a desired outward emotional expression without modifying the underlying emotions"[44]

surface-level diversity: "differences among group members in overt, biological characteristics that are typically reflected in physical features"[45]

survey feedback: data are collected from employees regarding their attitudes toward work, reports are created, and shared with the organization

sustainability: values, governance, transparency, and ethics, as well as such goals as diversity, social responsibility, supporting human and employee rights, protecting the environment, and contributing to the community

symbols: the sharing of knowledge through access and exposure to images, diagrams, or objects that represent or illustrate a culture value or an idea

synergy: the team can produce something beyond the sum of individual member contributions

task conflict: disagreements about resource allocation, policies, or even interpretation of data

team affect: team atmosphere

team building: group activities that involve a great deal of interaction among team members to increase trust

team charter: a document developed by a team that clarifies team direction and establishes ground rules

team level: the group level of analysis

team mental models (TMMs): shared understandings within teams

team norms: informal and interpersonal rules that team members are expected to follow

team performance curve: recognizes that team performance over the course of the life of the team is not always linear and performance does not always increase over time

team viability: collective sense of belonging similar to team cohesion

Theory X: leaders assume that people are basically lazy, don't like to work, and avoid responsibility

Theory Y: leaders assume that people are internally motivated, like to work, and will accept responsibility

third culture: "the construction of a mutually beneficial interactive environment in which individuals from two different cultures can function in a way beneficial to all involved"[46]

three "lines" of power: lines of supply, information, and support

360-degree performance appraisal: the input from a number of sources included to provide a more comprehensive view of an employee's performance

top management support: executive-level managers review plans, follow up on results, and facilitate change efforts

"toxic" workplaces: marked by significant drama and infighting, where personal battles often harm productivity

traditionalists: born between 1900 and 1945 and are retiring or have passed on

trait affect: stable individual differences

trait approach: it is believed that leaders are born with the talent and abilities for leadership

trait-like: personality characteristics that are relatively stable over time

transactional leadership: leadership behaviors that motivate followers through rewards and corrective actions

transformational leadership: leadership behaviors that mobilize extra effort from followers through emphasis on change through articulating a new vision for the organization

turnover: the rate at which employees leave a workforce and are replaced

turnover intentions: employees' thoughts about quitting their jobs

two-factor theory: relates to lower- and higher-order needs, and relates them to job satisfaction

Type A behavior: a behavior pattern characterized by hostility, time urgency, impatience, and a competitive drive

Type B behavior: a behavior pattern characterized by a relaxed demeanor, steady work habits, a noncompetitive nature, and a desire to be liked by others

Type C behavior: a behavior pattern characterized by predictability, loyalty, patience, thoughtfulness, an attention to detail, and seriousness.

Type D behavior: a behavior pattern characterized by an aversion to leading, punctuality, contentment, and giving support to others

underpayment inequity: the perception that a person's outcomes are not fair compared to another person's outcomes, given their inputs

unfreezing: challenges to the status quo through shaking up assumptions

upward communication: the process by which employees communicate with others who are higher in the organizational hierarchy

utilitarianism: consideration of decisions that do the most good for the most people

valences (Vs): the value an individual places on the rewards of an outcome (positive or negative)

variable: the timing of reinforcement varies

vertical: adding decision-making responsibility

virtual teams: defined as "functioning teams that rely on technology-mediated communication while crossing several different boundaries"[47]

wellness programs: workplace interventions that include time management, weight loss, alcohol and/or drug abuse, smoking cessation, and exercise

wheel network: all communication flows through one person who is most likely the group leader

wicked organizational problems: complex and changing decision scenarios

workforce diversity: sex, race/ethnicity, cultural differences, and age/generation as examples

work–life balance: when work is compatible with participation in family life

workout: a method for generating new ideas using employee participation and empowerment

workplace aggression: defined as overt physical or nonphysical behavior that harms others at work (e.g., yelling or pushing)[48]

workplace bullying: an emergent phenomenon; it refers to "a social interaction through which one individual (seldom more) is attacked by one or more (seldom more than four) individuals almost on a daily basis and for periods of many months, bringing the person into an almost helpless position with potentially high risk of expulsion"[49]

workplace incivility: "low intensity deviant behavior with ambiguous intent to harm the target, in violation of workplace norms for mutual respect. Uncivil behaviors are characteristically rude and discourteous, displaying a lack of regard for others"[50]

work redesign: load jobs with more of the core characteristics that have been shown to motivate

work–school conflict: situations in which work conflicts with the family role and school role,

work teams: a small number of people with complementary skills who are committed to a common purpose, performance goals, and approach for which they hold themselves mutually accountable

Y-pattern network: slightly less centralized than the all-channel network since two persons are closer to the center of the network

zone of indifference: the range in which attempts to influence a person will be perceived as legitimate and will be acted on without a great deal of thought

NOTES

Chapter 1

1. Gallup. (2016). Employee engagement in U.S. stagnant in 2015. Retrieved from http://www.gallup.com/poll/188144/employee-engagement-stagnant-2015.aspx

2. McKeefry, H. L. (2016). Engage employees in the supply chain. Retrieved from http://www.ebnonline.com/author.asp?section_id=3219&doc_id=282241

3. Taylor, F. W. (1911). *The principles of scientific management*. New York, NY: Harper.

4. Dipboye, R. L. (2016). Exploring industrial & organizational psychology: Work & organizational behavior. Retrieved from https://ssrn.com/abstract=2767463

5. Mayo, E. (1949). *Hawthorne and the Western Electric Company, The social problems of an industrial civilization*. New York, NY: Routledge.

6. Baron, J. N. (2013). Empathy wages? Gratitude and gift exchange in employment relationships. *Research in Organizational Behavior, 33,* 113–134.

7. Argyris, C. (1957). *Personality and organization: The conflict between system and the individual*. New York, NY: Harper. Contributed by J. Antonakis, in a post to the Organizational Behavior Division listserve, OB-LIST, on Tuesday, August 23, 2016.

8. Briner, R. B., Denyer, D., & Rousseau, D. M. (2009). Evidence-based management: Construct cleanup time? *Academy of Management Perspectives, 4,* 19–32.

9. Rousseau, D. M., & Gunia, B. C. (2016). Evidence-based practice: The psychology of EBP implementation. *Annual Review of Psychology, 67,* 667–692.

10. Wright, A. L., Zammuto, R. F., Liesch, P. W., Middleton, S., Hibbert, P., Burke, J., & Brazil, V. (2016). Evidence-based management in practice: Opening up the decision process, decision-maker and context. *British Journal of Management, 27*(1), 161–178.

11. Aasekjær, K., Waehle, H. V., Ciliska, D., Nordtvedt, M. W., & Hjälmhult, E. (2016). Management involvement—A decisive condition when implementing evidence-based practice. *Worldviews on Evidence-Based Nursing, 13*(1), 32–41.

12. HakemZadeh, F., HakemZadeh, F., Baba, V. V., & Baba, V. V. (2016). Toward a theory of collaboration for evidence-based management. *Management Decision, 54*(10), 2587–2616.

13. Pfeffer, J., & Sutton, R. (2006, January). Evidence-based management. *Harvard Business Review,* 1–16.

14. Sutton, R. (2006). Breakthrough business ideas? Retrieved from http://bobsutton.typepad.com/my_weblog/2006/07/breakthrough_bu.html

15. Surowiecki, J. (2004). *The wisdom of crowds*. New York, NY: Random House.

16. "Cocaine" drink is illegal too, FDA says. (2007). *Los Angeles Times*. Retrieved from http://articles.latimes.com/print/2007/apr/12/business/fi-cocaine12

17. Price, L. (2012). Former Circuit City chief tells all. *Richmond Business Sense*. Retrieved from http://www.richmondbizsense.com/2012/10/18/former-circuit-city-chief-tells-all

18. Glaser, E. M. (1941). *An experiment in the development of critical thinking*. New York, NY: Teachers College, Columbia University.

19. Paul, R., & Elder, L. (2010). *The miniature guide to critical thinking concepts and tools*. Dillon Beach, CA: Foundation for Critical Thinking Press.

20. Kurland, D. (2000). Critical thinking skills. Retrieved from www.criticalreading.com

21. Paul, R., & Elder, L. (2008). *The miniature guide to critical thinking concepts and tools*. Dillon Beach, CA: Foundation for Critical Thinking Press.

22. Stupple, E. J., Maratos, F. A., Elander, J., Hunt, T. E., Cheung, K. Y., & Aubeeluck, A. V. (2017). Development of the Critical Thinking Toolkit (CriTT): A measure of student attitudes and beliefs about critical thinking. *Thinking Skills and Creativity, 23,* 91–100.

23. Mitroff, I. (1998). *Smart thinking for crazy times: The art of solving the right problems*. San Francisco, CA: Berrett-Koehler.

24. Organ, D. W. (1988). *Organizational citizenship behavior: The good soldier syndrome*. Lexington, MA: Lexington Books.

25. Williams, L. J., & Anderson, S. E. (1991). Job satisfaction and organizational commitment as predictors of organizational citizenship and in-role behaviors. *Journal of Management, 17,* 601–617.

26. Podsakoff, N. P., Whiting, S. W., Podsakoff, P. M., & Blume, B. D. (2009). Individual- and organizational-level consequences of organizational citizenship behaviors: A meta-analysis. *Journal of Applied Psychology, 94,* 122–141.

27. Hoppock, R. (1935). *Job satisfaction*. New York, NY: Harper.

28. Cooper-Hakim, A., & Viswesvaran, C. (2005). The construct of work commitment: Testing an integrative framework. *Psychological Bulletin, 131*(2), 241–259.

29. Mathieu, J. E., & Zajac, D. M. (1990). A review and meta-analysis of the antecedents, correlates, and consequences of organizational commitment. *Psychological Bulletin, 108*(2), 171–194.

30. Meyer, J. P., Stanley, D. J., Herscovitch, L., & Topolnytsky, L. (2002). Affective, continuance, and normative commitment to the organization: A meta-analysis of antecedents, correlates, and

consequences. *Journal of Vocational Behavior, 61*(1), 20–52.

31. Meyer, J. P., & Allen, N. J. (1997). *Commitment in the workplace: Theory, research, and application.* Thousand Oaks, CA: Sage.

32. Klein, H. J., Becker, T. E., & Meyer, J. P. (2009). *Commitment in organizations: Accumulated wisdom and new directions.* New York, NY: Routledge/Psychology Press.

33. Macey, W., & Schneider, B. (2008). The meaning of employee engagement. *Industrial and Organizational Psychology, 1,* 3–30.

34. Christian, M. S., Garza, A. S., & Slaughter, J. D. (2011). Work engagement: A quantitative review and test of its relations with task and contextual performance. *Personnel Psychology, 64,* 89–136.

35. Karasek, R. A. (1998). Demand/Control Model: A social, emotional and physiological approach to stress risk and active behavior development. In Stellman, J. M. (Ed.), *Encyclopedia of occupational health and safety* (pp. 34.6-34.14). Geneva, Switzerland: International Labour Organization.

36. Barling, J., & Frone, M. R. (2016). If only my leader would just do something! Passive leadership undermines employee well-being through role stressors and psychological resource depletion. *Stress and Health.* doi:10.1002/smi.2697

37. Eatough, E. M., Meier, L. L., Igic, I., Elfering, A., Spector, P. E., & Semmer, N. K. (2016). You want me to do what? Two daily diary studies of illegitimate tasks and employee well-being. *Journal of Organizational Behavior, 37,* 108–127. (Quotation on p. 109.)

38. Deci, E. L., Koestner, R., & Ryan, R. M. (1999). A meta-analytic review of experiments examining the effects of extrinsic rewards on intrinsic motivation. *Psychological Bulletin, 125,* 627–668.

39. Grant, A. (2008). Does intrinsic motivation fuel the prosocial fire? Motivational synergy in predicting persistence, performance and productivity. *Journal of Applied Psychology, 93,* 48–58.

40. Hom, P. W., Caranikas-Walker, F., Prussia, G. E., & Griffeth, R. W. (1992). A meta-analytical structural equations analysis of a model of employee turnover. *Journal of Applied Psychology, 77,* 890–909.

41. McGregor, D. (1960). *The human side of enterprise.* New York, NY: McGraw-Hill.

42. Russ, T. L. (2011). Theory X/Y assumptions as predictors of managers' propensity for participative decision making. *Management Decision, 49*(5), 823–836.

43. Gürbüz, S., S¸ahin, F., & Köksal, O. (2014). Revisiting of Theory X and Y: A multilevel analysis of the effects of leaders' managerial assumptions on followers' attitudes. *Management Decision, 52*(10), 1888–1906.

44. Bobic, M. P., & Davis, W. W. (2003). A kind word for Theory X: Or why so many newfangled management techniques quickly fail. *Journal of Public Administration Research and Theory, 13*(3), 239–264.

45. Thomas, J. M., & Bennis, W. G. (1972). *The management of change and conflict: Selected readings.* Harmondsworth, England: Penguin.

46. Kopelman, R. E., Prottas, D. J., & Falk, D. W. (2012). Further development of a measure of Theory X and Y managerial assumptions. *Journal of Managerial Issues, 24*(4), 450–470.

47. Bedeian, A. G., & Wren, D. A. (2001). Most influential management books of the 20th century. *Organizational Dynamics, 29*(3), 221–225.

48. Carter, M. Z., Armenakis, A. A., Feild, H. S., & Mossholder, K. W. (2013). Transformational leadership, relationship quality, and employee performance during continuous incremental organizational change. *Journal of Organizational Behavior, 34*(7), 942–958.

49. Aslam, U., Ilyas, M., Imran, M. K., & Rahman, U. U. (2016). Detrimental effects of cynicism on organizational change: An interactive model of organizational cynicism (a study of employees in public sector organizations). *Journal of Organizational Change Management, 29*(4), 580–598.

50. Nilson, L. B. (2016, October 24). *Teaching critical thinking: Some practical points.* Retrieved from http://www.facultyfocus.com/articles/effective-teaching-strategies/teaching-critical-thinking-practical-points/

Chapter 2

1. Markowitz, E. (2013). Lesson from Zynga: Not all founders make good public company CEOs. Retrieved from http://www.inc.com/eric-markowitz/zynga-mark-pincus-not-all-founders-are-good-ceos.html

2. Wasserman, N. N. (2003). Founder–CEO succession and the paradox of entrepreneurial success. *Organization Science, 14*(2), 149–172.

3. Wingfield, N., & Isaac, M. (2015). Mark Pincus, Zyngas founder, returns as CEO. Retrieved from http://www.nytimes.com/2015/04/09/technology/mark-pincus-zyngas-founder-returns-as-ceo.html?_r=0

4. Weinberger, M. (2016, March 1). Mark Pincus is out as CEO of Zynga after less than a year — and a turnaround expert is in. Retrieved from http://www.businessinsider.com/marc-pincus-out-zynga-ceo-2016-3

5. Snyder, M., & Cantor, N. (1998). Understanding personality and social behavior: A functionalist strategy. In D. T. Gilbert, S. T. Fiske, & G. Lindzey (Eds.), *The handbook of social psychology* (4th ed., pp. 635–679). New York, NY: McGraw-Hill.

6. Waller, N. G., Kojetin, B. A., Bouchard, T. J., Lykken, D. T., & Tellegen, A. (1990). Genetic and environmental influences on religious interests, attitudes, and values: A study of twins reared apart and together. *Psychological Science, 1*(2), 138–142.

7. Lykken, D. T., Bouchard, T. J., McGue, M., & Tellegen, A. (1993). Heritability of interests: A twin study. *Journal of Applied Psychology, 78*(4), 649–661.

8. Keller, L. M., Bouchard, T. J., Arvey, R. D., Segal, N. L., & Dawis, R. V. (1992). Work values: Genetic and environmental influences. *Journal of Applied Psychology, 77*(1), 79–88.

9. Murray, J. B. (1990). Review of the Myers-Briggs Type Indicator.

Perceptual and Motor Skills, 70, 1187–1202.

10. Myers, I. B. (with Myers, P. B.). (1995). *Gifts differing.* Mountain View, CA: Consulting Psychologists Press.

11. Pittenger, D. J. (2005). Cautionary comments regarding the Myers-Briggs Type Indicator. *Consulting Psychology Journal: Practice and Research, 57*(3), 210–221.

12. Arnau, R. C., Green, B. A., Rosen, D. H., Gleaves, D. H., & Melancon, J. G. (2003). Are Jungian preferences really categorical? An empirical investigation using taxometric analysis. *Personality and Individual Differences, 34*(2), 233–251.

13. Myers, P. B., & Myers, K. D. (1998). *Introduction to type* (6th ed.). Mountain View, CA: Consulting Psychologists Press.

14. Barrick, M. R., & Mount, M. K. (1990). Another look at the validity of personality: A dimensional perspective. Presented at the annual meetings of the Society for Industrial and Organizational Psychology, Miami Beach, FL.

15. Barrick, M. R., Mount, M. K., & Judge, T. A. (2001). The FFM personality dimensionsand job performance: Meta-analysis of meta-analyses. *International Journal of Selection and Assessment, 9*(1–2), 9–30.

16. Judge, T. A., Higgins, C. A., Thoresen, C. J., & Barrick, M. R. (1999). The Big Five personality traits, general mental ability, and career success across the life span. *Personnel Psychology, 52*(3), 621–652.

17. Barrick, M. R., & Mount, M. K. (1993). Autonomy as a moderator of the relationships between the Big Five personality dimensions and job performance. *Journal of Applied Psychology, 78*(1), 111–118.

18. LePine, J. A., Colquitt, J. A., & Erez, A. (2000). Adaptability to changing task contexts: Effects of general cognitive ability, conscientiousness, and openness to experience. *Personnel Psychology, 53*(3), 563–595.

19. Booth-Kewley, S., & Friedman. H. S. (1987). Psychological predictors of heart disease: A quantitative review. *Psychological Bulletin, 101*(3), 343–362.

20. Riggio, R. E. (2012). Are you a Type A or Type B personality? Cutting edge leadership. Retrieved from https://www.psychologytoday.com/blog/cutting-edge-leadership/201206/are-you-type-or-b-personality

21. Miller, R., & Krauskopf, C. J. (1999). The personality assessment system as a conceptual framework for the Type A coronary-prone behavior pattern. *The Best of Personality Assessment System Journals,* 121–132.

22. Pedersen, S. S., Van Domburg, R., Theuns, D. A. M. J., Jordaens, L., & Erman, R. A. M. (2004). Type D personality is associated with increased anxiety and depressive symptoms in patients with an implantable cardioverter defibrillator and their partners. *Psychosomatic Medicine, 66,* 714–719.

23. Pedersen, S. S., & Denollet, J. (2003). Is Type D personality here to stay? Emerging evidence across cardiovascular disease patient groups. *Current Cardiology Reviews, 2*(3), 205–213.

24. Friedman, H. S., Hall, J. A., & Harris, M. J. (1985). Type A behavior, nonverbal expressive style, and health. *Journal of Personality and Social Psychology, 48*(5), 1299–1315.

25. Kobasa, S. C. (1979). Stressful life events, personality, and health: An inquiry into hardiness. *Journal of Personality and Social Psychology, 37*(1), 1–11.

26. Kobasa, S. C, Maddi, S. R., & Kahn, S. (1982). Hardiness and health: A prospective study. *Journal of Personality and Social Psychology, 42*(1), 168–177.

27. Uchino, B. N., Cacioppo, J. T., & Kiecolt-Glaser, J. K. (1996). The relationship between social support and physiological processes: A review with emphasis on underlying mechanisms and implications for health. *Psychological Bulletin, 119*(3), 488–531.

28. Machiavelli, N. (1952). *The Prince* (trans. Luigi Ricck). New York, NY: New American Library. (Original work published 1532).

29. Dahling, J. J., Whitaker, B. G., & Levy, P. E. (2009). The development and validation of a new Machiavellianism scale. *Journal of Management, 35*(2), 219–257.

30. Pilch, I., & Turska, E. (2015). Relationships between Machiavellianism, organizational culture, and workplace bullying: Emotional abuse from the target's and the perpetrator's perspective. *Journal of Business Ethics, 128*(1), 83–93.

31. Wisse, B., & Sleebos, E. (2016). When the dark ones gain power: Perceived position power strengthens the effect of supervisor Machiavellianism on abusive supervision in work teams. *Personality and Individual Differences, 99,* 122–126.

32. Kilduff, G. J., & Galinsky, A. D. (2016). The spark that ignites: Mere exposure to rivals increases Machiavellianism and unethical behavior. *Journal of Experimental Social Psychology, 69,* 156–162. https://doi.org/10.1016/j.jesp.2016.10.007

33. Paulhus, D. L., & Williams, K. (2002). The Dark Triad of personality: Narcissism, Machiavellianism, and psychopathy. *Journal of Research in Personality, 36,* 556–568.

34. Spain, S. M., Harms, P., & LeBreton, J. M. (2014). The dark side of personality at work. *Journal of Organizational Behavior, 35*(S1), S41–S60.

35. Morf, C. C., & Rhodewalt, F. (2001). Unraveling the paradoxes of narcissism: A dynamic self-regulatory processing model. *Psychological Inquiry, 12,* 177–196.

36. Hare, R. D. (1985). Comparison of procedures for the assessment of psychopathy. *Journal of Consulting and Clinical Psychology, 53,* 7–16.

37. Hare, R. D. (1999). *Without conscience: The disturbing world of the psychopaths among us.* New York, NY: Guilford.

38. Jonason, P. K., Slomski, S., & Partyka, J. (2012). The Dark Triad at work: How toxic employees get their way. *Personality and Individual Differences, 52*(3), 449–453.

39. Spurk, D., Keller, A. C., & Hirschi, A. (2016). Do bad guys get ahead or fall behind? Relationships of the Dark Triad of personality with objective and subjective career success. *Social Psychological and Personality Science, 7*(2), 113–121.

40. Snyder, M. (1974). Self-monitoring of expressive behavior. *Journal of Personality and Social Psychology, 30*(4), 526–537. (Quotation on p. 526.)

41. Snyder, M. (1987). *Public appearances/private realities: The psychology of self-monitoring.* New York, NY: W. H. Freeman.

42. Day, D. V., Shleicher, D. J., Unkless, A. L., & Hiller, N. J. (2002).

Self-monitoring personality at work: A meta-analytic investigation of construct validity. *Journal of Applied Psychology, 91*(2), 390–401.

43. Wang, S., Hu, Q., & Dong, B. (2015). Managing personal networks: An examination of how high self-monitors achieve better job performance. *Journal of Vocational Behavior, 91*, 180–188.

44. Fang, R., Landis, B., Zhang, Z., Anderson, M. H., Shaw, J. D., & Kilduff, M. (2015). Integrating personality and social networks: A meta-analysis of personality, network position, and work outcomes in organizations. *Organization Science, 26*(4), 1243–1260.

45. Oh, I. S., Charlier, S. D., Mount, M. K., & Berry, C. M. (2014). The two faces of high self-monitors: Chameleonic moderating effects of self-monitoring on the relationships between personality traits and counterproductive work behaviors. *Journal of Organizational Behavior, 35*(1), 92–111.

46. Levenson, M. R. (1990). Risk taking and personality. *Journal of Personality and Social Psychology, 58*(6), 1073–1080.

47. Stewart, W. H., Jr., & Roth, P. L. (2001). Risk propensity differences between entrepreneurs and managers: A meta-analytic review. *Journal of Applied Psychology, 86*(1), 145–153.

48. Mata, R., Josef, A. K., & Hertwig, R. (2016). Propensity for risk taking across the life span and around the globe. *Psychological Science, 27*(2), 231–243.

49. Luthans, F. (2002). Positive organizational behavior: Developing and managing psychological strengths. *Academy of Management Perspectives, 16*(1), 57–72. (Quotation on p. 59.)

50. Joo, B.-K., Lim, D. H., & Kim, S. (2016). Enhancing work engagement: The roles of psychological capital, authentic leadership, and work empowerment. *Leadership & Organization Development Journal, 37*(8), 1117–1134.

51. Luthans, F., Avey, J. B., Avolio, B. J., Norman, S. M., & Combs, G. M. (2006). Psychological capital development: Toward a micro-intervention. *Journal of Organizational Behavior, 27*(3), 387–393. (Quotation on p. 388.)

52. Luthans, F., Avolio, B. J., Avey, J. B., & Norman, S. M. (2007). Positive psychological capital: Measurement and relationships with performance and satisfaction. *Personnel Psychology, 60*(3), 541–572.

53. Ibid.

54. Peterson, S. J., Luthans, F., Avolio, B. J., Walumbwa, F. O., & Zhang, Z. (2011). Psychological capital and employee performance: A latent growth modeling approach. *Personnel Psychology, 64*(2), 427–450.

55. Luthans, F., Avey, J. B., Avolio, B. J., Norman, S. M., & Combs, G. M. (2006). Psychological capital development: Toward a micro-intervention. *Journal of Organizational Behavior, 27*(3), 387–393.

56. Luthans, F., & Youssef, C. M. (2004). Investing in people for competitive advantage. *Organizational Dynamics, 33*(2), 143–160.

57. Avey, J., Wernsing, T. S., & Luthans, F. (2008). Can positive employees help positive organizational change? Impact of psychological capital and emotions on relevant attitudes and behaviors. *Journal of Applied Behavioral Science, 44*(1), 48–70.

58. Judge, T. A., Erez, A., & Bono, J. E. (1998). The power of being positive: The relation between positive self-concept and job performance. *Human Performance, 11*(2–3), 167–187.

59. Srivastava, A., Locke, E. A., & Judge, T. A. (2002). Dispositional causes of task satisfaction: The mediating role of chosen level of task complexity. In R. Ilies (Chair), *Core self-evaluations: New developments and research findings.* Symposium presentation at the Society for Industrial and Organizational Psychology Annual Meetings, Toronto, Canada.

60. Aryee, S., Walumbwa, F. O., Mondejar, R., & Chu, C. W. (2017). Core self-evaluations and employee voice behavior: Test of a dual-motivational pathway. *Journal of Management, 43*(3), 946–966. doi:0149206314546192

61. Judge, T. A., & Bono, J. E. (2001). Relationship of core self-evaluations traits—self-esteem, generalized self-efficacy, locus of control, and emotional stability—with job satisfaction and job performance: A meta-analysis. *Journal of Applied Psychology, 86*(1), 80–92.

62. Salvaggio, A. N., Schneider, B., Nishii, L. H., Mayer, D. M., Ramesh, A., & Lyon, J. S. (2007). Manager personality, manager service quality orientation, and service climate: Test of a model. *Journal of Applied Psychology, 92*(6), 1741–1750.

63. Cheung, Y. H., Herndon, N. C., & Dougherty, T. W. (2016). Core self-evaluations and salary attainment: The moderating role of the developmental network. *International Journal of Human Resource Management, 27*(1), 67–87.

64. Wanberg, C. R., Glomb, T., Song, Z., & Sorenson, S. (2005). Job-search persistence during unemployment: A ten wave longitudinal study. *Journal of Applied Psychology, 90*(3), 411–430.

65. Judge, T. A., & Hurst, C. (2008). How the rich (and happy) get richer (and happier): Relationship of core self-evaluations to trajectories in attaining work success. *Journal of Applied Psychology, 93*(4), 849–863.

66. Kristof-Brown, A. L., Zimmerman, R. D., & Johnson, E. C. (2005). Consequences of individuals' fit at work: A meta-analysis of person-job, person-organization, person-group, and person-supervisor fit. *Personnel Psychology, 58*(2), 281–342.

67. Jansen, K. J., & Kristof-Brown, A. L. (2006). Toward a multidimensional theory of person-environment fit. *Journal of Managerial Issues, 18*(2), 193–212.

68. Cable, D. M., & Judge, T. A. (1997). Interviewers' perceptions of person-organization fit and organizational selection decisions. *Journal of Applied Psychology, 82*, 546–561.

69. Edwards, J. R., & Cable, D. M. (2009). The value of value congruence. *Journal of Applied Psychology, 94*(3), 654–677.

70. Cable, D. M., & Edwards, J. R. (2004). Complementary and supplementary fit: A theoretical and empirical integration. *Journal of Applied Psychology, 89*, 822–834.

71. Van Dyne, L., & Pierce, J. L. (2004). Psychological ownership and feelings of possession: Three field studies predicting employee attitudes and organizational citizenship behavior. *Journal of Organizational Behavior, 25*, 439–459.

72. Han, T. S., Chiang, H. H., McConville, D., & Chiang, C. L. (2015). A

longitudinal investigation of person–organization fit, person–job fit, and contextual performance: The mediating role of psychological ownership. *Human Performance, 28*(5), 425–439.

73. Boon, C., & Biron, M. (2016). Temporal issues in person–organization fit, person–job fit and turnover: The role of leader–member exchange. *Human Relations, 69*(12), 2177–2200.

74. Brandstätter, V., Job, V., & Schulze, B. (2016). Motivational incongruence and well-being at the workplace: Person–job fit, job burnout, and physical symptoms. *Frontiers in Psychology, 7.* https://doi.org/10.3389/fpsyg.2016.01153

75. Kristof-Brown, A. L., Zimmerman, R. D., & Johnson, E. C. (2005).

Consequences of individuals' fit at work: A meta-analysis of person-job, person-organization, person-group, and person-supervisor fit. *Personnel Psychology, 58*, 281–342.

76. Cable, D. M., & De Rue, D. S. (2002). The convergent and discriminant validity of subjective fit perceptions. *Journal of Applied Psychology, 87*, 875–884.

77. Tracey, T. J., & Rounds, J. (1993). Evaluating Holland's and Gati's vocational interest models: A structural meta-analysis. *Psychological Bulletin, 113*(2), 229–246.

78. Nye, C. D., Su, R., Rounds, J., & Drasgow, F. (2017). Interest congruence and performance: Revisiting recent meta-analytic

findings. *Journal of Vocational Behavior, 98*, 138–151.

79. Van Iddekinge, C. H., Putka, D. J., & Campbell, J. P. (2011). Reconsidering vocational interests for personnel selection: The validity of an interest-based selection test in relation to job knowledge, job performance, and continuance intentions. *Journal of Applied Psychology, 96*(1), 13–33.

80. Nye, C. D., Su, R., Rounds, J., & Drasgow, F. (2012). Vocational interests and performance: A quantitative summary of over 60 years of research. *Perspectives on Psychological Science, 7*(4), 384–403.

81. Merritt, C. (2010). Disarming difficult personalities at work. *Work & Family Life, 24*(6), 6.

Chapter 3

1. Pilcher, J. J., & Huffcutt, A. I. (1996). Effects of sleep deprivation on performance: A meta-analysis. *Sleep, 19*, 318–326.

2. Gordon, A. M. (2013). Up all night: The effects of sleep loss on mood. Retrieved from https://www.psychologytoday.com/blog/between-you-and-me/201308/all-night-the-effects-sleep-loss-mood

3. Wrzus, C., Wagner, G. G., & Riediger, M. (2014). Feeling good when sleeping in? Day-to-day associations between sleep duration and affective well-being differ from youth to old age. *Emotion, 14*, 624–628.

4. Gish, J. J., & Wagner, D. T. (2016). The affective implications of sleep. In J. Barling, C. M. Barnes, E. L. Carleton, & D. T. Wagner (Eds.), *Work and sleep: Research insights for the workplace.* New York, NY: Oxford University Press.

5. Christian, M. S., & Ellis, A. P. (2011). Examining the effects of sleep deprivation on workplace deviance: A self-regulatory perspective. *Academy of Management Journal, 54*(5), 913–934.

6. Barnes, C. M., Lucianetti, L., Bhave, D., & Christian, M. S. (2015). You wouldn't like me when I'm sleepy: Leader sleep, daily abusive supervision, and work unit engagement. *Academy of Management Journal, 58*, 813–845.

7. Scott, B. A., & Judge, T. A. (2006). Insomnia, emotions, and job satisfaction: A multilevel study. *Journal of Management, 32*, 622–645.

8. Lanaj, K., Johnson, R. E., & Barnes, C. M. (2014). Beginning the workday yet already depleted? Consequences of late-night smartphone use and sleep. *Organizational Behavior and Human Decision Processes, 124*(1), 11–23.

9. Hirshkowitz, M., Whiton, K., Albert, S., Alessi, C., Bruni, O., DonCarlos, L., . . . Adams Hillard, P. (2015). National Sleep Foundation's sleep time duration recommendations: Methodology and results summary. *Sleep Health: Journal of the National Sleep Foundation, 1*(1), 40–43.

10. Arvey, R. D., Renz, G., Watson, T. W., & Driskill, W. (1998). Feasibility of using individual differences in emotionality as predictors of job performance. *Research in Personnel and Human Resource Management, 16*, 103–147.

11. Barsade, S., Brief, A. P., Spataro, S. E., & Greenberg, J. (2003). The affective revolution in organizational behavior: The emergence of a paradigm. *Organizational Behavior: A Management Challenge, 1*, 3–50.

12. Watson, D. (2000). *Mood and temperament.* New York, NY: Guilford Press.

13. Lazarus, R. S. (1991). *Emotion and adaptation.* New York, NY: Oxford University Press.

14. Tangney, J. P. (1995). Shame and guilt in interpersonal relationships. In J. P. Tangney & K. W. Fisher (Eds.), *Self-conscious emotions: The psychology of shame, guilt, embarrassment, and pride* (pp. 114–139). New York, NY: Guilford Press.

15. Brief, A. P., & Weiss, H. M. (2002). Organizational behavior: Affect in the workplace. *Annual Review of Psychology, 53*(1), 379–307.

16. Ashkanasy, N. M., & Daus, C. S. (2002). Emotion in the workplace: The new challenge for managers. *Academy of Management Executive, 16*(1), 77.

17. Cropanzano, R., Dasborough, M., & Weiss, H. (2016). Affective events and the development of leader-member exchange. *Academy of Management Review.* doi:10.5465/amr.2014.0384

18. Weiss, H. M., & Beal, D. J. (2005). Reflections on affective events theory. In N. M. Ashkanasy, W. J. Zerbe, & C. E. J. Härtel (Eds.), *The effect of affect in organizational settings* (Vol. 1, pp. 1–21). San Diego CA: Emerald.

19. Fisher, C. D. 2003. Why do lay people believe that satisfaction and performance are correlated? Possible sources of a commonsense theory. *Journal of Organizational Behavior, 24*, 753–777.

20. Ohly, S., & Schmitt, A. (2015). What makes us enthusiastic, angry, feeling

at rest or worried? Development and validation of an affective work events taxonomy using concept mapping methodology. *Journal of Business and Psychology, 30*(1), 15–35.

21. Cropanzano, R., & Dasborough, M.T. (2015). Dynamic models of well-being: Implications of affective events theory for expanding current views on personality and climate. *European Journal of Work and Organizational Psychology, 24*(6), 844–847.

22. Menges, J. I., & Kilduff, M. (2016). Group emotions: Cutting the Gordian knots concerning terms, levels-of-analysis, and processes. *Academy of Management Annals, 9*, 845–938.

23. Dasborough, M.T., Ashkanasy, N. M., Tee, E. Y. J., & Tse, H. H. M. (2009). What goes around comes around: How meso-level negative emotional contagion can ultimately determine organizational attitudes toward leaders. *Leadership Quarterly, 20*, 571–585.

24. Carr, J. Z., Schmidt, A. M., Ford, J. K., & DeShon, R. P. (2003). Climate perceptions matter: A meta-analytic path analysis relating molar climate, cognitive and affective states, and individual level work outcomes. *Journal of Applied Psychology, 88,* 605–619. (Quotation on p. 618).

25. Warr, P. B. (1990). The measurement of well-being and other aspects of mental health. *Journal of Occupational Psychology, 63,* 193–210.

26. Gamero, N., González-Romá, V., & Peiró, J. M. (2008). The influence of intra-team conflict on work teams' affective climate: A longitudinal study. *Journal of Occupational and Organizational Psychology, 81*(1), 47–69. (Quotation on p. 50).

27. Herman, H. M., Dasborough, M.T., & Ashkanasy, N. M. (2008). A multi-level analysis of team climate and interpersonal exchange relationships at work. *Leadership Quarterly, 19*(2), 195–211.

28. Levecque, K., Roose, H., Vanroelen, C., & Van Rossem, R.(2014). Affective team climate: A multi-level analysis of psychosocial working conditions and psychological distress in team workers. *Acta Sociologica, 57*(2), 153–166.

29. Kim, M. J., Choi, J. N., & Lee, K. (2016). Trait affect and individual creativity: Moderating roles of

affective climate and reflexivity. *Social Behavior and Personality: An International Journal, 44*(9), 1477–1498.

30. Fredrickson, B. L. (2000). Why positive emotions matter in organizations: Lessons from the broaden-and-build model. *Psychologist-Manager Journal, 4*(2), 131–142.

31. Ibid.

32. Barsade, S. G. (2002). The ripple effect: Emotional contagion and its influence on group behavior. *Administrative Science Quarterly, 47*(4), 644–675.

33. Fredrickson, B. L. (2004). Gratitude, like other positive emotions, broadens and builds. In R. A. Emmons & M. E. McCullough (Eds.), *The psychology of gratitude* (pp. 145–166). New York, NY: Oxford University Press.

34. McCullough, M. E., Emmons, R. A., & Tsang, J. A. (2002). The grateful disposition: A conceptual and empirical topography. *Journal of Personality and Social Psychology, 82*(1), 112–127.

35. Scandura, T. A., & Sharif, M. M. (2017). Gratitude as a broaden-and-build emotion at work. In D. Stone & J. Dulebohn (Eds.), *Research in human resource management: Theory and research on new employment relationships* (pp. 75–108). Charlotte, NC: Information Age.

36. Hammett, Y. C. (2015). Kindness pays: Employee's act of compassion recognized with London trip. Retrieved from http://www.tbo.com/news/business/kindness-pays-employees-act-of-compassion-recognized-with-london-trip-20150311/

37. Grant, A. M., & Gino, F. (2010). A little thanks goes a long way: Explaining why gratitude expressions motivate prosocial behavior. *Journal of Personality and Social Psychology, 98*(6), 946–955.

38. Grant, A. M., & Wrzesniewski, A. (2010). I won't let you down . . . or will I? Core self-evaluations, other-orientation, anticipated guilt and gratitude, and job performance. *Journal of Applied Psychology, 95*(1), 108–121.

39. Davis, D. E., Choe, E., Meyers, J., Wade, N., Varjas, K., Gifford, A., . . . Worthington, E. L. (2016). Thankful for the little things: A meta-analysis of gratitude interventions. *Journal of Counseling Psychology, 63*(1), 20–31.

40. Watson, D., Clark, L. A., & Tellegen, A. (1988). Development and validation of brief measures of positive and negative affect: The PANAS scales. *Journal of Personality and Social Psychology, 54*(6), 1063–1070.

41. Lyubomirsky, S., King, L., & Diener, E. (2005). The benefits of frequent positive affect: Does happiness lead to success? *Psychological Bulletin, 131*(6), 803–855.

42. Staw, B. M., Sutton, R. I., & Pelled, L. H. (1994). Employee positive emotion and favorable outcomes in the workplace. *Organization Science, 5*(1), 51–71.

43. Wright, T. A., & Staw, B. M. (1999). Affect and favorable work outcomes: Two longitudinal tests of the happy-productive worker thesis. *Journal of Organizational Behavior, 20*(1), 1–23.

44. Rothbard, N. P., & Wilks, S. L. (2011). Waking up on the right or wrong side of the bed: Start-of-workday mood, work events, employee affect, and performance. *Academy of Management Journal, 54*(5), 959–980. Quotation on p. 963).

45. Hochschild, A. R. (1983). *The managed heart: Commercialization of human feeling.* Berkeley: University of California Press. (Quotation on p. 7.)

46. Yagil, D. (2012). The mediating role of engagement and burnout in the relationship between employees' emotion regulation strategies and customer outcomes, *European Journal of Work and Organizational Psychology, 21*(1), 150–168.

47. Hochschild, A. R. (1983). *The managed heart: Commercialization of human feeling.* Berkeley: University of California Press.

48. Rafaeli, A. (1989). When cashiers meet customers: An analysis of the role of supermarket cashiers. *Academy of Management Journal, 32*(2), 245–273.

49. Scott, B. A., & Barnes, C. M. (2011). A multilevel field investigation of emotional labor, affect, work withdrawal, and gender. *Academy of Management Journal, 54,* 116–136.

50. Gabriel, A. S., & Diefendorff, J. M. (2015). Emotional labor dynamics: A momentary approach. *Academy of Management Journal, 58*(6), 1804–1825.

51. Brotheridge, C., & Grandey, A. A. (2002). Emotional labor and burnout: Comparing two perspectives of

"people work." *Journal of Vocational Behavior, 60*(1), 17–39.

52. Grandey, A. A. (2003). When "the show must go on": Surface acting and deep acting as determinants of emotional exhaustion and peer-rated service delivery. *Academy of Management Journal, 46*(1), 86–96.

53. Elfenbein, H. A. (2016). Emotional division-of-labor: A theoretical account. *Research in Organizational Behavior, 36*, 1–26. (Quotation on p. 1). doi:http://dx.doi.org/10.1016/j .riob.2016.11.001 0191-3085/

54. Ibid.

55. Judge, T. A., Woolf, E. F., & Hurst, C. (2009). Is emotional labor more difficult for some than for others? A multilevel, experience-sampling study. *Personnel Psychology, 62*(1), 57–88.

56. Becker, W. J., & Cropanzano, R. (2015). Good acting requires a good cast: A meso-level model of deep acting in work teams. *Journal of Organizational Behavior, 36*(2), 232–249.

57. Ashkanasy, N. M., Dasborough, M. T., & Ascough, K. W. (2009). *Developing leaders: Teaching about emotional intelligence and training in emotional skills.* Thousand Oaks, CA: Sage.

58. Humphrey, R. H., Ashforth, B. E., & Diefendorff, J. M. (2015). The bright side of emotional labor. *Journal of Organizational Behavior, 36*(6), 749–769.

59. Goleman, D. (1995). *Emotional intelligence: Why it can matter more than IQ.* New York, NY: Bantam Books.

60. Salovey, P., & Mayer, J. D. (1990). Emotional intelligence. *Imagination, Cognition, and Personality, 9*(3), 185–211.

61. Antonakis J., Ashkanasy N. M., Dasborough M. T. (2009). Does leadership need emotional intelligence? *Leadership Quarterly, 20*, 247–261.

62. Mayer, J. D., Caruso, D. R., & Salovey, P. (2016). The ability model of emotional intelligence: Principles and updates. *Emotion Review, 8*(4), 290–300.

63. Law, K. S., Wong, C. S., & Song, L. J. (2004). The construct and criterion validity of emotional intelligence and its potential utility for management studies. *Journal of Applied Psychology, 89*(3), 483–496.

64. Jordan, P. J., Dasborough, M. T., Daus, C. S., & Ashkanasy, N. M.

(2010). A call to context. *Industrial and Organizational Psychology, 3*(2), 145–148.

65. Côté, S., & Miners, C. T. (2006). Emotional intelligence, cognitive intelligence, and job performance. *Administrative Science Quarterly, 51*(1), 1–28.

66. Dong, Y., Seo, M. G., & Bartol, K. M. (2014). No pain, no gain: An affect-based model of developmental job experience and the buffering effects of emotional intelligence. *Academy of Management Journal, 57*(4), 1056–1077.

67. Wilderom, C. P., Hur, Y., Wiersma, U. J., Berg, P. T. V., & Lee, J. (2015). From manager's emotional intelligence to objective store performance: Through store cohesiveness and sales-directed employee behavior. *Journal of Organizational Behavior, 36*(6), 825–844.

68. Bar-On, R., Handley, R., & Fund, S. (2005). The impact of emotional intelligence on performance. In V. Druskat, F. Salas, & G. Mount (Eds.), *Linking emotional intelligence and performance at work: Current research evidence* (pp. 3–20). Mahwah, NJ: Erlbaum.

69. Cavallo, K., & Brienza, D. (2004). *Emotional competence and leadership excellence at Johnson & Johnson: The emotional intelligence and leadership study.* New Brunswick, NJ: Consortium for Research on Emotional Intelligence in Organizations (Rutgers University).

70. Miao, C., Humphrey, R. H., & Qian, S. (2016). Leader emotional intelligence and subordinate job satisfaction: A meta-analysis of main, mediator, and moderator effects. *Personality and Individual Differences, 102*, 13–24.

71. Miao, C., Humphrey, R. H., & Qian, S. (2016). Leader emotional intelligence and subordinate job satisfaction: A meta-analysis of main, mediator, and moderator effects. *Personality and Individual Differences, 102*, 13–24.

72. Joseph, D. L., Jin, J., Newman, D. A., & O'Boyle, E. H. (2015). Why does self-reported emotional intelligence predict job performance? A meta-analytic investigation of mixed EI. *Journal of Applied Psychology, 100*(2), 298–342.

73. Parke, M. R., Seo, M. G., & Sherf, E. N. (2015). Regulating and facilitating: The role of emotional intelligence

in maintaining and using positive affect for creativity. *Journal of Applied Psychology, 100*(3), 917–934.

74. Farh, C. I., Seo, M., & Tesluk, P. E. (2012). Emotional intelligence, teamwork effectiveness, and job performance: The moderating role of job context. *Journal of Applied Psychology, 97*(4), 890–900.

75. Hopkins, M. M., & Yonker, R. D. (2015). Managing conflict with emotional intelligence: Abilities that make a difference. *Journal of Management Development, 34*(2), 226–244.

76. Joseph, D. L., & Newman, D. A. (2010). Emotional intelligence: An integrative meta-analysis and cascading model. *Journal of Applied Psychology, 95*(1), 54–78.

77. Ashkanasy, N. M., Dasborough, M. T., & Ascough, K. W. (2009). Developing leaders: Teaching about emotional intelligence and training in emotional skills. In S. J. Armstrong & C. V. Fukami (Eds.), *The Sage handbook of management learning, education and development* (pp. 161–183). Thousand Oaks, CA: Sage.

78. Kirk, B. A., Schutte, N. S., & Hine, D. W. (2011). The effect of an expressive writing intervention for employees on emotional self-efficacy, emotional intelligence, affect, and workplace incivility. *Journal of Applied Social Psychology, 41*(1), 179–195.

79. Slaski, M., & Cartwright, S. (2003). Emotional intelligence training and its implications for stress, health, and performance. *Stress and Health, 19*(4), 233–239.

80. Thory, K. (2013). Teaching managers to regulate their emotions better: Insights from emotional intelligence training and work-based application. *Human Resource Development International, 16*(1), 4–21.

81. Schutte, N. S., Malouff, J. M., & Thorsteinsson, E. B. (2013). Increasing emotional intelligence through training: Current status and future directions. *International Journal of Emotional Education, 5*(1), 56–72.

82. Mayer, J. D., Salovey, P., & Caruso, D. R. (2000). Models of emotional intelligence. In R. J. Sternberg (Ed.), *Handbook of intelligence* (pp. 392–420). Cambridge, England: Cambridge University Press.

83. Petrides, K. V., & Furnham, A. (2001). Trait emotional intelligence: Psychometric investigation with reference to established trait taxonomies. *European Journal of Personality, 15,* 425–448.

84. Mayer, J. D., & Salovey, P. (1997). What is Emotional Intelligence? In P. Salovey & D. J. Sluyter (Eds.) *Emotional development and emotional intelligence: Educational implications* (pp. 3–31). New York, NY: Basic Books.

85. Joseph, D. L., & Newman, D. A. (2010). Emotional intelligence: An integrative meta-analysis and cascading model. *Journal of Applied Psychology, 95*(1), 54–78.

86. Davies, M., Stankov, L., & Roberts, R. D. (1998). Emotional intelligence: In search of an elusive construct. *Journal of Personality and Social Psychology, 75*(4), 989–1015.

87. Landy, F. J. (2005). Some historical and scientific issues related to research on emotional intelligence. *Journal of Organizational Behavior, 26*(4), 411–424.

88. Locke, E. A. (2005). Why emotional intelligence is an invalid concept. *Journal of Organizational Behavior, 26*(4), 425–431.

89. Zeidner, M., Matthews, G., & Roberts, R. D. (2004). Emotional intelligence in the workplace: A critical review. *Applied Psychology: An International Journal, 53*(3), 371–399.

90. Cooper, R. K. (1997). Applying emotional intelligence in the workplace. *Training and Development, 51*(12), 31–33.

91. Cherniss, C. (1999). *The business case for emotional intelligence.* The consortium for research on emotional intelligence in organizations. Retrieved from http://www.eiconsortium.org

92. Freedman, J. (2014). Case study: Emotional intelligence for people-first leadership at FedEx Express. Retrieved from http://www.6seconds.org/2014/01/14/case-study-emotional-intelligence-people-first-leadership-fedex-express/

93. Ashkanasy, N. M., & Daus, C. S. (2002). Emotion in the workplace: The new challenge for managers. *Academy of Management Perspectives, 16*(1), 76–86.

94. Gooty, J., Gavin, M. B., Ashkanasy, N. M., & Thomas, J. S. (2014). The wisdom of letting go and performance: The moderating role of emotional intelligence and discrete emotions. *Journal of Occupational and Organizational Psychology, 87*(2), 392–413.

95. Gross, J. J. (1998). The emerging field of emotion regulation: An integrative review. *Review of General Psychology, 2*(5), 271–299. (Quotation on p. 275.)

96. Grandey, A. A. (2000). Emotional regulation in the workplace: A new way to conceptualize emotional labor. *Journal of Occupational Health Psychology, 5*(1), 95–110.

97. Beal, D. J., Trougakos, J. P., Weiss, H. M., & Dalal, R. S. (2013). Affect spin and the emotion regulation process at work. *Journal of Applied Psychology, 98*(4), 593–605.

98. Burklund, L. J., Creswell, J. D., Irwin, M., & Lieberman, M. (2014). The common and distinct neural bases of affect labeling and reappraisal in healthy adults. *Frontiers in Psychology, 5.* https://doi.org/10.3389/fpsyg.2014.00221

99. Barsade, S. G. (2002). The ripple effect: Emotional contagion and its influence on group behavior. *Administrative Science Quarterly, 47*(4), 644–675.

100. George, J. M. (1990). Personality, affect, and behavior in groups. *Journal of Applied Psychology, 75*(2), 107–116.

101. Elfenbein, H. A. (2014). The many faces of emotional contagion: An Affective Process Theory for affective linkage. *Organizational Psychology Review, 4,* 326–362.

102. Tee, E. Y. J. (2016). The emotional link: Leadership and the role of implicit and explicit emotional contagion processes across multiple organizational levels. *Leadership Quarterly, 26,* 654–670.

103. Barsade, S. G. (2002). The ripple effect: Emotional contagion and its influence on group behavior. *Administrative Science Quarterly, 47,* 644–675.

104. Pugh, D. (2001). Service with a smile: Emotional contagion in service encounters. *Academy of Management Journal, 44*(5), 1018–1027.

105. Barger, P. B., & Grandey, A. A. (2006). Service with a smile and encounter satisfaction: Emotional contagion and appraisal mechanisms. *Academy of Management Journal, 49*(6), 1229–1238.

106. Torrente, P., Salanova, M., & Llorens, S. (2013). Spreading engagement: On the role of similarity in the positive contagion of team work engagement. *Journal of Work and Organizational Psychology, 29,* 153–159.

107. Sy, T., & Choi, J. N. (2013). Contagious leaders and followers: Exploring multistage mood contagion in a leader activation and member propagation (LAMP) model. *Organizational Behavior and Human Decision Processes, 122*(2), 127–140.

108. Fowler, J. H., & Christakis, N. A. (2008). Dynamic spread of happiness over a large social network: Longitudinal analysis over 20 years of the Framingham Heart Study. *British Medical Journal, 337,* 1–9.

109. Jiang, L., & Probst, T. M. (2016). A multilevel examination of affective job insecurity climate on safety outcomes. *Journal of Occupational Health Psychology, 21*(3), 366–377.

110. Brown, N. (2015). Lessons of the brain: The Phineas Gage story. Retrieved from http://news.harvard.edu/gazette/story/2015/10/lessons-of-the-brain-the-phineas-gage-story/

111. Panksepp, J. (1992). A role for "affective neuroscience" in understanding stress: The case of separation distress circuitry. In S. Puglisi-Allegra & A. Oliverio (Eds.), *Psychobiology of Stress* (pp. 41–58). Dordrecht, Netherlands: Kluwer Academic.

112. Becker, W. J., Cropanzano, R., & Sanfey, A. G. (2011). Organizational neuroscience: Taking organizational theory inside the neural black box. *Journal of Management, 37*(4), 933–961.

113. Kringelbach, M. L., & Berridge, K. C. (2016). Neuroscience of reward, motivation, and drive. In S. Kim, J. Reeve, & M. Bong (Eds.), *Recent developments in neuroscience research on human motivation* (Vol. 19, pp. 23–35). Bingley, England: Emerald Group.

114. Posner, J., Russell, J. A., & Peterson, B. S. (2005). The circumplex model of affect: An integrative approach to affective neuroscience, cognitive development, and psychopathology. *Development and Psychopathology, 17*(3), 715–734.

115. Berridge, K. C., & Kringelbach, M. L. (2013). Neuroscience of affect: Brain mechanisms of pleasure and displeasure. *Current Opinion in Neurobiology, 23*(3), 294–303.

116. Lindebaum, D. (2013). Ethics and the neuroscientific study of leadership: A synthesis and rejoinder to Ashkanasy, Cropanzano and Becker, and McLagan. *Journal of Management Inquiry, 22*(3), 317–323.

117. Antonakis, J. (2011). Predictors of leadership: The usual suspects and the suspect traits. In A. Bryman, D. Collinson, K. Grint, B. Jackson, & M. Uhl-Bien (Eds.), *SAGE handbook of leadership* (pp. 269–285). Thousand Oaks, CA: Sage.

118. Creswell, J. D., Way, B. M., Eisenberger, N. I., & Lieberman, M. D. (2007). Neural correlates of dispositional mindfulness during affect labeling. *Psychosomatic Medicine, 69*(6), 560–565.

119. Seltzer, L. F. (2011). Why we hide emotional pain. Retrieved from https:www.psychologytoday.com/blog/evolution-the-self/201109/why-we-hide-emotional-pain

120. Gelles, D. (2015). At Aetna, a CEOs management by mantra. Retrieved from https://www.nytimes.com/2015/03/01/business/at-aetna-a-ceos-management-by-mantra.html?_r=0

121. Hülsheger, U. R., Alberts, H. J., Feinholdt, A., & Lang, J. W. (2013). Benefits of mindfulness at work: The role of mindfulness in emotion regulation, emotional exhaustion, and job satisfaction. *Journal of Applied Psychology, 98*(2), 310.

122. Brown, K. W., & Ryan, R. M. (2003). The benefits of being present: Mindfulness and its role in psychological well-being. *Journal of Personality and Social Psychology, 84*(4), 822–848.

123. Winning, A. P., & Boag, S. (2015). Does brief mindfulness training increase empathy? The role of personality. *Personality and Individual Differences, 86,* 492–498.

124. Riddle, D. (2012). Three keys to mindful coaching. Retrieved from www.forbes.com/sites/ccl/2012/01/23/three-keys-to-mindful-leadership-coaching

125. Ibid.

126. Jha, A., Krompinger, J., & Baime, M. J. (2007). Mindfulness training modifies subsystems of attention. *Cognitive, Affective, & Behavioral Neuroscience, 7*(2), 109–119.

Chapter 4

1. Thurstone, L. L. (1928). Attitudes can be measured. *American Journal of Sociology, 33*(4), 529–554.

2. Allport, G. (1935). Attitudes. In C. Murchison (Ed.), *A handbook of social psychology* (pp. 789–844). Worcester, MA: Clark University Press.

3. Eagly, A. H., & Chaiken, S. (1993). *The psychology of attitudes.* New York, NY: Harcourt Brace Jovanovich College Publishers.

4. Rosenberg, M. J., & Hovland, C. I. (1960). Cognitive, affective and behavioral components of attitudes. In M. J. Rosenberg & C. I. Hovland (Eds.), *Attitude organization and change: An analysis of consistency among attitude components.* New Haven, CT: Yale University Press.

5. Breckler, S. J. (1984). Empirical validation of affect, behavior, and cognition as distinct components of an attitude. *Journal of Personality and Social Psychology, 47*(6), 1191–1205.

6. Crites, S. L., Jr., Fabrigar, L. R., & Petty, R. E. (1994). Measuring the affective and cognitive properties of attitudes: Conceptual and methodological issues. *Personality and Social Psychology Bulletin, 20*(6), 619–663.

7. Bagozzi, R. (1992). The self-regulation of attitudes, intentions, and behavior. *Social Psychology Quarterly, 55*(2), 178–204.

8. Festinger, L. (1957). *A theory of cognitive dissonance.* Stanford, CA: Stanford University Press.

9. Ibid.

10. Harrison, D. A., Newman, D. A., & Roth, P. L. (2006). How important are job attitudes? Meta-analytic comparisons of integrative behavioral outcomes and time sequences. *Academy of Management Journal, 49*(2), 305–325.

11. Riketta, M. (2008). The causal relation between job attitudes and performance: A meta-analysis of panel studies. *Journal of Applied Psychology, 93*(2), 472–481.

12. Ajzen, I., & Fishbein, M. (1977). Attitude-behavior relations: A theoretical analysis and review of empirical research. *Psychological Bulletin, 84*(5), 888–918.

13. Glasman, L. R., & Albarracin, D. (2006). Forming attitudes that predict future behavior: A meta-analysis of the attitude-behavior relation. *Psychological Bulletin, 132*(5), 778–822.

14. Locke, E. A. (1976). The nature and causes of job satisfaction. In M. D. Dunnette (Ed.), *Handbook of industrial and organizational psychology* (pp. 1297–1349). Chicago, IL: Rand McNally. (Quotation on p. 1300.)

15. Smith, P. C. (1992). In pursuit of happiness: Why study general job satisfaction? In C. J. Cranny, P. C. Smith, & E. F. Stone (Eds.), *Job satisfaction: How people feel about their jobs and how it affects their performance* (pp. 5–20). New York, NY: Lexington Books.

16. Wright, T. A. (2003). Positive organizational behavior: An idea whose time has truly come. *Journal of Organizational Behavior, 24*(4), 437–442.

17. Van Ryzin, G. G. (2014). The curious case of the post 9-11 boost in government job satisfaction. *American Review of Public Administration, 44*(1), 59–74.

18. Zablah, A. R., Carlson, B. D., Donavan, D. T., Maxham, J. G., III, & Brown, T. J. (2016). A cross-lagged test of the association between customer satisfaction and employee job satisfaction in a relational context. *Journal of Applied Psychology.* doi:http://dx.doi.org/10.1037/apl0000079

19. Boswell, W. R., Shipp, A. J., Payne, S. C., & Culbertson, S. S. (2009). Changes in newcomer job satisfaction over time: Examining the pattern of honeymoons and hangovers. *Journal of Applied Psychology, 94*(4), 844–858.

20. Bianchi, E. C. (2013). The bright side of bad times. The affective advantages of entering the workforce in a recession. *Administrative Science Quarterly, 58*(4), 587–623.

21. Riza, S. D., Ganzach, Y., & Liu, Y. (2016). Time and job satisfaction: A longitudinal study of the differential roles of age and tenure. *Journal of Management.* doi:0149206315624962.

22. Andreassi, J. K., Lawter, L., Brockerhoff, M., & Rutigliano, P. (2012). Job satisfaction determinants:

A study across 48 nations. *Business Faculty Publications,* Paper 220. Retrieved from http://digitalcommons .sacredheart.edu/wcob_fac/220

23. Judge, T. A., Thoresen, J. E., Bono, J. E., & Patton, G. K. (2001). The job satisfaction-job performance relationship: A qualitative and quantitative review. *Psychological Bulletin, 127*(3), 376–407.

24. Smith, P. C., Kendall, L. M., & Hulin, C. L. (1985). *The job descriptive index.* Bowling Green, OH: Department of Psychology, Bowling Green State University.

25. Ironson, G. H., Smith, P. C., Brannick, M.T., Gibson, W. M., & Paul, K. B. (1989). Construction of a job in general scale: A comparison of global, composite, and specific measures. *Journal of Applied Psychology, 74*(2), 193–200.

26. Russell, S. S., Spitzmuller, C., Lin, L. F., Stanton, J. M, Smith, P. C., & Ironson, G. H. (2004). Shorter can also be better: The abridged job in general scale. *Educational and Psychological Measurement, 64*(5), 878–893.

27. Parker, K. N., & Brummel, B. J. (2016). Examining the curvilinear relationship between income, job and pay satisfaction. *Journal of Personnel Psychology, 15*, 164–173. https://doi. org/10.1027/1866-5888/a000162

28. Judge, T. A., Thoresen, J. E., Bono, J. E., & Patton, G. K. (2001). The job satisfaction-job performance relationship: A qualitative and quantitative review. *Psychological Bulletin, 127*(3), 376–407.

29. Rusbult, C. E., Farrell, D., Rogers, G., & Mainous, A. G., III. (1988). Impact of exchange variables on exit, voice, loyalty, and neglect: An integrative model of responses to declining job satisfaction. *Academy of Management Journal, 31*(3), 599–627.

30. McClean, E. J., Burris, E. R., & Detert, J. R. (2013). When does voice lead to exit? It depends on leadership. *Academy of Management Journal, 56*(2), 525–548.

31. Burris, E. R., Detert, J. R., & Romney, A. C. (2013). NOTES 455 Speaking up vs. being heard: The disagreement around and outcomes of employee voice. *Organization Science, 24*(1), 22–38.

32. Wanberg, C. R., Zhu, J., & Van Hooft, E. A. J. (2010). The job search grind:

Perceived progress, self-reactions, and self-regulation of search effort. *Academy of Management Journal, 53*(4), 788–807.

33. Savickas, M. L., & Porfeli, E. J. (2012). Career adapt-abilities scale: Construction, reliability, and measurement equivalence across 13 countries. *Journal of Vocational Behavior, 80*(3), 661–673.

34. Guan, Y., Deng, H., Sun, J., Wang, Y., Cai, Z., Ye, L., . . . Li, Y. (2013). Career adaptability, job search self-efficacy and outcomes: A three-wave investigation among Chinese university graduates. *Journal of Vocational Behavior, 83*(3), 561–570.

35. Rudolph, C. W., Lavigne, K. N., & Zacher, H. (2017). Career adaptability: A meta-analysis of relationships with measures of adaptivity, adapting responses, and adaptation results. *Journal of Vocational Behavior, 98*, 17–34.

36. Vansteenkiste, S., Verbruggen, M., & Sels, L. (2016). Flexible job search behaviour among unemployed jobseekers: Antecedents and outcomes. *European Journal of Work and Organizational Psychology,* 1–21.

37. Cooper-Hakim, A., & Viswesvaran, C. (2005). The construct of work commitment: Testing an integrative framework. *Psychological Bulletin, 131*(2), 241–259.

38. Mathieu, J. E., & Zajac, D. M. (1990). A review and meta-analysis of the antecedents, correlates, and consequences of organizational commitment. *Psychological Bulletin, 108*(2), 171–194.

39. Meyer, J. P., Stanley, D. J., Herscovitch, L., & Topolnytsky, L. (2002). Affective, continuance, and normative commitment to the organization: A meta-analysis of antecedents, correlates, and consequences. *Journal of Vocational Behavior, 61*(1), 20–52.

40. Klein, H. J., Becker, T. E., & Meyer, J. P. (2009). *Commitment in organizations: Accumulated wisdom and new directions.* New York, NY: Routledge/ Psychology Press.

41. Meyer, J. P., & Allen, N. J. (1997). *Commitment in the workplace: Theory, research, and application.* Thousand Oaks, CA: Sage.

42. Judge, T. A., & Kammeyer-Mueller, J. D. (2012). Job attitudes. *Annual Review of Psychology, 63*, 341–367.

43. Meyer, J. P., & Allen, N. J. (1991). A three-component conceptualization of organizational commitment. *Human Resource Management Review, 1*(1), 61–89.

44. Guay, R. P., Choi, D., Oh, I. S., Mitchell, M. S., Mount, M. K., & Shin, K. H. (2016). Why people harm the organization and its members: Relationships among personality, organizational commitment, and workplace deviance. *Human Performance, 29*(1), 1–15.

45. Blau, G. J., & Boal, K. B. (1989). Using organizational commitment and job involvement interactively to predict turnover. *Journal of Management, 15*(1), 115–127.

46. Diefendorff, J. M., Brown, D. J., Kamin, A. M., & Lord, R. G. (2002). Examining the roles of job involvement and work centrality in predicting organizational citizenship behaviors and job performance. *Journal of Organizational Behavior, 23*(1), 93–108.

47. Blau, G. J., & Boal, K. B. (1987). Conceptualizing how job involvement and organizational commitment affect turnover and absenteeism. *Academy of Management Review, 12*(2), 288–300.

48. Rich, B. L., Lepine, J. A., & Crawford, E. R. (2010). Job engagement: Antecedents and effects on job performance. *Academy of Management Journal, 53*(3), 617–635. (Quotation on p. 617.)

49. Harter, J. K., Schmidt, F. L., & Hayes, T. L. (2002). Business-unit-level relationships between employee satisfaction, employee engagement, and business outcomes: A meta-analysis. *Journal of Applied Psychology, 87*(2), 268–279.

50. Gallup. (2013). State of the American workforce: Employee engagement insights for U.S. business leaders. Retrieved from http://www.gallup.com/ strategicconsulting/163007/ state-american-workplace.aspx.

51. Gallup. (2016). The relationship between engagement at work and organizational outcomes. 2016 Q12 meta-analysis (9th Ed.). Retrieved on January 11, 2017 from http://www .gallup.com/services/191489/q12-meta-analysis-report-2016.aspx

52. Minkara, O. (2015). Employee engagement and customer satisfaction: "Why" and "how" to bridge the gap. Retrieved from http://v1.aberdeen.com/launch/report/research_report/13091-RR-Employee-Engagement.asp

53. Rhoades, L., & Eisenberger, R. (2002). Perceived organizational support: A review of the literature. *Journal of Applied Psychology, 87*(4), 698–714.

54. Schaufeli, W. B., & Bakker, A. B. (2004). Job demands, job resources, and their relationship with burnout and engagement: A multi-sample study. *Journal of Organizational Behavior, 25*(3), 293–315.

55. Bakker, A. B., Hakanen, J. J., Demerouti, E., & Xanthopoulou, D. (2007). Job resources boost work engagement, particularly when job demands are high. *Journal of Educational Psychology, 99*(2), 274–284.

56. Eisenberger, R., Huntington, R., Hutchison, S., & Sowa, D. (1986). Perceived organizational support. *Journal of Applied Psychology, 71*(3), 500–507.

57. Shore, L. M., & Shore, T. H. (1995). Perceived organizational support and organizational justice. In R. S. Cropanzano & K. M. Kacmar (Eds.), *Organizational politics, justice, and support: Managing the social climate of the workplace* (pp. 149–164). Westport, CT: Quorum.

58. Rhoades, L., Eisenberger, R., & Armeli, S. (2001). Affective commitment to the organization: The contribution of perceived organizational support. *Journal of Applied Psychology, 86*(5), 825–836.

59. Eisenberger, R., Stinglhamber, F., Vandenberghe, C., Sucharski, I., & Rhoades, L. (2002). Perceived supervisor support: Contributions to perceived organizational support and employee retention. *Journal of Applied Psychology, 87*(3), 565–573.

60. Eder, P., & Eisenerger, R. (2008). Perceived organizational support: Reducing the negative influence of coworker withdrawal behavior. *Journal of Management, 34*(1), 55–68.

61. Riggle, R. J., Edmondson, D. R., & Hansen, J. D. (2009). A meta-analysis of the relationship between perceived organizational support and job outcomes: 20 years of research. *Journal of Business Research, 62*(10), 1027–1030.

62. Eisenberger, R., Malone, G. P., & Presson, W. D. (2016). *Optimizing perceived organizational support to enhance employee engagement* [White paper]. Retrieved from http://www.siop.org/SIOP-SHRM/SHRM-SIOP%20POS.pdf

63. Spreitzer, G. M. (1995). Psychological empowerment in the workplace: Dimensions, measurement, and validation. *Academy of Management Journal, 38*(4), 1442–1465.

64. Ibid.

65. Joo, B.-K., & Shim, J. H. (2010). Psychological empowerment and organizational commitment: The moderating effect of organizational learning culture. *Human Resource Development International, 13*(4), 425–441.

66. Spreitzer, G. M. (1996). Social structural characteristics of psychological empowerment. *Academy of Management Journal, 39*(2), 483–504.

67. Spreitzer, G. M., Kizilos, M. A., & Nason, S. W. (1997). A dimensional analysis of the relationship between psychological empowerment and effectiveness, satisfaction, and strain. *Journal of Management, 23*(5), 679–704.

68. Spreitzer, G. M. (2008). Taking stock: A review of more than twenty years of research on empowerment at work. In J. Barling & C. Cooper (Eds.), *The SAGE handbook of organizational behavior* (pp. 54–72). Thousand Oaks, CA: Sage.

69. Rapp, T. L., Gilson, L. L., Mathieu, J. E., & Ruddy, T. (2016). Leading empowered teams: An examination of the role of external team leaders and team coaches. *Leadership Quarterly, 27*(1), 109–123.

70. Duffy, R. D., Allan, B. A., Autin, K. L., & Douglass, R. P. (2014). Living a calling and work well-being: A longitudinal study. *Journal of Counseling Psychology*, *61*(4), 605–615.

71. Praskova, A., Hood, M., & Creed, P. A. (2014). Testing a calling model of psychological career success in Australian young adults: A longitudinal study. *Journal of Vocational Behavior*, *85*(1), 125–135.

72. Steger, M. F., Dik, B. J., & Duffy, R. D. (2012). Measuring meaningful work: The work and meaning inventory (WAMI). *Journal of Career Assessment, 20*(3), 1–16.

73. Bono, J. E., & Judge, T. A. (2003). Self-concordance at work: Toward understanding the motivational effects of transformational leaders. *Academy of Management Journal, 46*(5), 554–571.

74. Piccolo, R. F., & Colquitt, J. A. (2006). Transformational leadership and job behaviors: The mediating role of core job characteristics. *Academy of Management Journal, 49*(2), 327–340.

75. Rosso, B. D., Dekas, K. H., & Wrzesniewski, A. (2012). On the meaning of work: A theoretical integration and review. *Research in Organizational Behavior, 30,* 91–127. (Quotation on p. 101.)

76. Lee, M. C. C., Idris, M. A., & Delfabbro, P. H. (2016). The linkages between hierarchical culture and empowering leadership and their effects on employees' work engagement: Work meaningfulness as a mediator. *International Journal of Stress Management.* Advance online publication. http://dx.doi.org/10.1037/str0000043

77. Dulebohn, J. H., Bommer, W. H., Liden, R. C., Brouer, R. L., & Ferris, G. R. (2012). A meta-analysis of antecedents and consequences of leader–member exchange: Integrating the past with an eye toward the future. *Journal of Management, 38*(6), 1715–1759.

78. Ibid.

79. Kipfelsberger, P., Raes, A., Herhausen, D., & Bruch, H. (2015). Trickle down effects of work meaningfulness through visionary leadership. *Academy of Management Proceedings, 2015*(1), 10801.

80. Avolio, B. J., Zhu, W., Koh, W., & Bhatia, P. (2004). Transformational leadership and organizational commitment: Mediating role of psychological empowerment and moderating role of structural distance. *Journal of Organizational Behavior, 2*(8), 951–968.

81. Peng, A. C., Lin, H. E., Schaubroeck, J., McDonough, E. F., Hu, B., & Zhang, A. (2016). CEO intellectual stimulation and employee work meaningfulness: The moderating role of organizational context. *Group & Organization Management, 41*(2), 203–231.

82. Shamir, B., Zakay, E., Breinin, E., & Popper, M. (1998). Correlates of charismatic leader behavior in military units: Subordinates' attitudes, unit characteristics and superiors' appraisal of leader performance. *Academy of Management Journal, 41*(4), 387–409.

83. KPMG Healthcare & Pharmaceutical Institute. (2011, April). KPMG's 2011 U.S. Hospital Nursing Labor Costs Survey. Retrieved from http://www.natho.org/pdfs/KPMG_2011_Nursing_LaborCostStudy.pdf

84. Kovner, C. T., Brewer, C. S., Fairchild, S., Poormina, S., Kim, H., & Djukic, M. (2007). Newly licensed RN's characteristics, work attitudes, and intentions to work. *American Journal of Nursing, 107*(9), 58–70.

85. KPMG Healthcare & Pharmaceutical Institute. (2011, April). KPMG's 2011 U.S. Hospital Nursing Labor Costs Survey. Retrieved from http://www.natho.org/pdfs/KPMG_2011_Nursing_LaborCostStudy.pdf

86. Jones, C. B. (2008). Revisiting nurse turnover costs: Adjusting for inflation. *Journal of Nursing Administration, 38*(1), 11–18.

Chapter 5

1. Kahneman, D., Krueger, A. B., Schkade, D., Schwarz, N., & Stone, A. A. (2006). Would you be happier if you were richer? A focusing illusion. *Science, 30*(312), 1908–1910.

2. Nisbet, R. E., & Ross, L. (1980). *Human inference: Strategies and shortcomings of social judgment.* Englewood Cliffs, NJ: Prentice Hall.

3. Luchins, A. S. (1942). Mechanization in problem solving: The effect of Einstellung. *Psychological Monographs, 54*(6), 1–95.

4. Allport, G. W. (1979). *The nature of prejudice.* Cambridge, MA: Addison-Wesley.

5. Asch, S. E. (1946). Forming impressions of personality. *Journal of Abnormal and Social Psychology, 41*(3), 258–290.

6. Nisbett, R. E., & Wilson, T. D. (1977). Telling more than we can know: Verbal reports on mental processes. *Psychological Review, 84*(3), 231–259.

7. Dennis, M. J., & Ahn, W. K. (2001). Primacy in causal strength judgments: The effect of initial evidence for generative versus inhibitory relationships. *Memory & Cognition, 29*(1), 152–164.

8. Willis, J., & Todorov, A. (2006). First impressions making up your mind after a 100-ms exposure to a face. *Psychological Science, 17*(7), 592–598.

9. Tetlock, P. (1983). Accountability and the perseverance of first impressions. *Social Psychology Quarterly, 46*(4), 285–292.

10. Murdock, B. B. (1962). The serial position effect of free recall. *Journal of Experimental Psychology, 64*(5), 482–488.

11. Greene, R. L. (1986). Sources of recency effects in free recall. *Psychological Bulletin, 99*(2), 221–228.

12. Highouse, S., & Gallo, A. (1997). Order effects in personnel decision making. *Human Performance, 10*(1), 31–46.

13. Atkinson, R. C., & Shiffrin, R. M. (1971). The control processes of short-term memory [Technical Report 173, Psychology Series]. Stanford, CA: Institute for Mathematical Studies in the Social Sciences. Retrieved on September 8, 2013 from www.suppesscorpus.stanford.edu/techreports/IMMS_173.pdf

14. Ibid.

15. Tversky, A., & Kahneman, D. (1973). Availability: A heuristic for judging frequency and probability. *Cognitive Psychology, 5*(2), 207–232.

16. Ibid.

17. Levy, B. (2002). *Remember every name, every time: Corporate America's memory master reveals his secrets.* New York, NY: Fireside Books.

18. Schwartz, N., Bless, H., Strack, F., Klumpp, G., Rittenauer-Schatka, H., & Simons, A. (1991). Ease of retrieval as information: Another look at the availability heuristic. *Journal of Personality and Social Psychology, 61*(2), 195–202.

19. Anderson, C. A. (1982). Inoculation and counterexplanation: Debiasing techniques in the perseverance of social theories. *Social Cognition, 1*(2), 126–139.

20. Slusher, M. P., & Anderson, C. A. (1996). Using causal persuasive arguments to change beliefs and teach new information: The mediating role of explanation availability and evaluation bias in the acceptance of knowledge. *Journal of Educational Psychology, 88*(1), 110–122.

21. Pressley, M., Symons, S., McDaniel, M. A., Snyder, B. L., & Turnure, J. E. (1988). Elaborative interrogation facilitates acquisition of confusing facts. *Journal of Educational Psychology, 80*(3), 268–278.

22. Goodstadt, B., & Kipnis, D. (1970). Situational influences on the use of power. *Journal of Applied Psychology, 54*(3), 201–207.

23. Kipnis, D., & Vanderveer, R. (1971). Ingratiation and the use of power. *Journal of Personality and Social Psychology, 17*(3), 280–286.

24. Ivancevich, J. M. (1983). Contrast effects in performance evaluation and reward practices. *Academy of Management Journal, 26*(3), 465–476.

25. Latham, G. P., Wexley, K. N., & Pursell, E. D. (1975). Training managers to minimize rating errors in the observation of behavior. *Journal of Applied Psychology, 60*(5), 550–555.

26. Chapman, D. S., & Zweig, D. I. (2005). Developing a nomological network for interview structure: Antecedents and consequences of the structured selection interview. *Personnel Psychology, 58*(3), 673–702.

27. Rosenzweig, P. (2007). *The halo effect.* New York, NY: Free Press.

28. Thorndike, E. L. (1920). A constant error in psychological ratings. *Journal of Applied Psychology, 4*(1), 25–29.

29. Balzer, W. K., & Sulsky, L. M. (1992). Halo and performance appraisal research: A critical examination. *Journal of Applied Psychology, 77*(6), 975–985.

30. Saal, F. E., Downey, R. G., & Lahey, M. A. (1980). Rating the ratings: Assessing the psychometric quality of rating data. *Psychological Bulletin, 88*(2), 413–428.

31. Cooper, W. H. (1981). Ubiquitous halo. *Psychological Bulletin, 90*(2), 218–244.

32. Viswesvaran, C., Schmidt, F. L., & Ones, D. S. (2005). Is there a general

factor in ratings of job performance? A meta-analytic framework for disentangling substantive and error influences. *Journal of Applied Psychology, 90*(1), 108–131.

33. Hartwell, C. J., & Campion, M. A. (2016). Getting on the same page: The effect of normative feedback interventions on structured interview ratings. *Journal of Applied Psychology, 101*(6), 757–778.

34. Fugate, M., Kinicki, A. J., & Ashforth, B. E. (2004). Employability: A psycho-social construct, its dimensions, and applications. *Journal of Vocational Behavior, 65*(1), 14–38.

35. Hogan, R., Chamorro-Premuzic, T., & Kaiser, R. B. (2013). Employability and career success: Bridging the gap between theory and reality. *Industrial and Organizational Psychology, 6*(1), 3–16.

36. Bozionelos, N., Kostopoulos, K., Van Der Heijden, B., Rousseau, D. M., Bozionelos, G., Hoyland, T., . . . Mikkelsen, A. (2016). Employability and job performance as !inks in the relationship between mentoring receipt and career success: A study in SMEs. *Group & Organization Management, 41*(2), 135–171.

37. Fugate, M., & Kinicki, A. J. (2008). A dispositional approach to employability: Development of a measure and test of implications for employee reactions to organizational change. *Journal of Occupational and Organizational Psychology, 81*(3), 503–527.

38. Harnish, V. (2012). *The greatest business decisions of all time: How Apple, Ford, IBM, Zappos, and others made radical choices that changed the course of business.* New York, NY: Fortune.

39. Dean, J. W., & Sharfman, M. P. (1996). Does decision process matter? A study of strategic decision-making effectiveness. *Academy of Management Journal, 39*(2), 368–396.

40. Mintzberg, H. (1975, July–August). The manager's job: Folklore and fact. *Harvard Business Review,* 49–61.

41. Mintzberg, H. (1988). *Mintzberg on management: Inside our strange world of organizations.* New York, NY: Free Press.

42. Tasler, N. (2013). *Why quitters win.* Henderson, NV: Motivational Press. Retrieved from http://www.nicktasler.com/author

43. Potworowski, G. (2010). *Varieties of indecisive experience: Explaining the tendency to not make timely and stable decisions* (Unpublished doctoral dissertation). University of Michigan, Ann Arbor.

44. Bacanli, F. (2006). Personality characteristics as predictors of personal indecisiveness. *Journal of Career Development, 32*(4), 320–332.

45. Gati, I., Gadassi, R., Saka, N., Hadadi, Y., Ansenberg, N., Friedmann, R., & Asulin-Peretz, L. (2010). Emotional and personality-related aspects of career decision-making difficulties: Facets of career indecisiveness. *Journal of Career Assessment, 19*(1), 3–20.

46. Germeijs, V., & De Boeck, P. (2002). A measurement scale for indecisiveness and its relationship to career indecision and other types of indecision. *European Journal of Psychological Assessment, 18*(2), 113–122.

47. Shafir, E., & LeBoeuf, R. A. (2002). Rationality. *Annual Review of Psychology, 53*(1), 491–495.

48. Simon, H. A. (1986). Rationality in psychology and economics. *Journal of Business,* S209–S224.

49. Nutt, P. (1984). Types of organizational decision processes. *Administrative Science Quarterly, 29*(3), 414–450.

50. Mitroff, I. (1998). *Smart thinking for crazy times: The art of solving the right problems.* San Francisco, CA: Berrett-Koehler.

51. Russo, J. E., Carlson, K. A., & Meloy, M. G. (2006). Choosing an inferior alternative. *Psychological Science, 17*(10), 899–904.

52. Thompson, L., & Hrebec, D. (1986). Lose-lose agreements in interdependent decision making. *Psychological Bulletin, 120*(3), 396–409.

53. Hallen, B., & Pahnke, E. C. (2016). When do entrepreneurs accurately evaluate venture capital firms' track records? A bounded rationality perspective. *Academy of Management Journal, 59*(5), 1535–1560.

54. Simon, H. A. (1977). *The new science of management decisions* (2nd ed.). Englewood Cliffs, NJ: Prentice Hall.

55. Augier, M. (2001). Simon says: Bounded rationality matters. *Journal of Management Inquiry, 10*(3), 268–275.

56. Plous, S. (1993). *The psychology of judgment and decision making.* New York, NY: McGraw-Hill.

57. March, J. G. (1978). Bounded rationality and the psychology of choice. *The Bell Journal of Economics, 9*(2), 587–608.

58. Kahneman, D., & Tversky, A. (1979). Prospect theory: An analysis of decision under risk. *Econometrica, 47*(2), 263–291.

59. Järrehult, B. (2013). The importance of stupid, irrational decisions. *Innovation Management.* Retrieved from http://www.innovationmanagement.se/2013/09/06/the-importance-of-stupid-irrational-decisions/

60. Taleb, N. N. (2010). *The black swan: The impact of the highly improbable fragility.* New York, NY: Random House.

61. Joslyn, S., & LeClerc, J. (2013). Decisions with uncertainty: The glass half full. *Current Directions in Psychological Science, 22*(4), 308–315. (Quotation on p. 314.)

62. Stanovich, K. E., & West, R. F. (2000). Individual differences in reasoning: Implications for the rationality debate? *Behavioral & Brain Sciences, 23*(5), 645–665.

63. Gladwell, M. (2007). *Blink: The power of thinking without thinking.* New York, NY: Little, Brown.

64. Hogarth, R. M. (2010). Intuition: A challenge for psychological research on decision making. *Psychological Inquiry, 21*(4), 338–353. p. 339

65. Dane, E., & Pratt, M. (2007). Exploring intuition and its role in managerial decision making. *Academy of Management Review, 32*(1), 33–54. p. 36.

66. Simon, H. A. (1987). Making management decisions: The role of intuition and emotion. *Academy of Management Executive, 1*(1), 57–64. (Quotation on p. 63).

67. Zhao, S. (2009). The nature and value of common sense to decision making. *Management Decision, 47*(3), 441–453.

68. Hayashi, A. (2001, February). When to trust your gut. *Harvard Business Review,* 59–65.

69. Burke, L. A., & Miller, M. K. (1999). Taking the mystery out of intuitive decision making. *Academy of Management Executive, 13*(4), 91–99. p. 95

70. Hogarth, R. M. (2010). Intuition: A challenge for psychological research on decision making. *Psychological Inquiry, 21*(4), 338–353.

71. Waddock, S., Meszoely, G. M., Waddell, S., & Dentoni, D. (2015). The

complexity of wicked problems in large scale change. *Journal of Organizational Change Management*, 28(6), 993–1012.

72. Wood, G. (1978). The knew-it-all-along effect. *Journal of Experimental Psychology, Human Perception and Performance,* 4(2), 345–353.

73. Hawkins, S. A., & Hastie, R. (1990). Hindsight: Biased judgments of past events after the outcomes are known. *Psychological Bulletin, 107*(3), 311–327. p. 311.

74. Guilbault, R. L., Bryant, F. B., Brockway, J. H., & Posavac, E. J. (2004). A meta-analysis of research on hindsight bias. *Basic and Applied Social Psychology, 26*, 103–117.

75. Burdeau, C., & Mohr, H. (2010, May 1). BP didn't plan for major oil spill. Retrieved from http://www .businessweek.com/ap/financialnews/ D9FDULS81.htm

76. Sadler-Smith, E., Akstinaite, V., Robinson, G., & Wray, T. (2016). Hubristic leadership: A review. *Leadership.* doi:10.1177/1742715016680666

77. Russo, J. E., & Schoemaker, P. J. (1992). Managing overconfidence. *Sloan Management Review, 33*(2), 7–17.

78. Shipman, A. S., Byrne, C. L., & Mumford, M. D. (2010). Leader vision formation and forecasting: The effects of forecasting extent, resources, and timeframe. *Leadership Quarterly, 21*(3), 439–456.

79. Fast, N. J., Sivanathan, N., Mayer, N. D., & Galinsky, A. D. (2012). Power and overconfident decision making. *Organizational Behavior and Human Decision Processes, 117*(2), 249–260.

80. Camerer, C. F., & Johnson, E. J. (1997). The process-performance paradox in expert judgment: How can experts know so much and predict so badly? In W. M. Goldstein & R. M. Hogarth (Eds.), *Research on judgment and decision making: Currents, connections, and controversies* (pp. 342–364). Cambridge, England: Cambridge University Press.

81. McKenzie, C. R. M., Liersch, M. J., & Yaniv, I. (2008). Overconfidence in interval estimates: What does expertise buy you? *Organizational Behavior and Human Decision Processes, 107*(2), 179–191.

82. Fast, N. J., Sivanathan, N., Mayer, N. D., & Galinsky, A. D. (2012). Power and overconfident decision making.

Organizational Behavior and Human Decision Processes, 117(2), 249–260.

83. Ronay, R., Oostrom, J. K., Lehmann-Willenbrock, N., & Van Vugt, M. (2017). Pride before the fall: (Over) confidence predicts escalation of public commitment. *Journal of Experimental Social Psychology, 69*, 13–22.

84. Staw, B. M. (1981). The escalation of commitment to a course of action. *Academy of Management Review, 6*(4), 577–587.

85. Staw, B. M. (1976). Knee-deep in the big muddy: A study of escalating commitment to a chosen course of action. *Organizational Behavior and Human Performance, 16*(1), 27–44.

86. Brockner, J. (1992). The escalation of commitment to a failing course of action: Toward theoretical progress. *Academy of Management Review, 17*(1), 39–61.

87. Montealegre, R., & Keil, M. (2000). Deescalating information technology projects: Lessons from the Denver International Airport. *MIS Quarterly, 24*(3), 417–447.

88. Arkes, H. R., & Blumer, C. (1985). The psychology of sunk costs. *Organizational Behavior and Human Decision Processes, 35*(1), 124–140.

89. Moon, H. (2001). Looking forward and looking back: Integrating complete and sunk-cost effects within an escalation-of-commitment progress decision. *Journal of Applied Psychology, 86*(1), 104–113.

90. Khanin, D., & Mahto, R. V. (2013). Do venture capitalists have a continuation bias? *Journal of Entrepreneurship, 22*(2), 203–222.

91. Schoorman, F. D. (1988). Escalation bias in performance appraisals: An unintended consequence of supervisor participation in hiring decisions. *Journal of Applied Psychology, 73*(1), 58–62.

92. Staw, B. M., Barsade, S. G., & Koput, D. W. (1997). Escalation at the credit window: A longitudinal study of bank executives' recognition and write-off of problem loans. *Journal of Applied Psychology, 82*(1), 130–142.

93. Beshears, J., & Milkman, K. L. (2011). Do sell-side stock analysts exhibit escalation of commitment? *Journal of Economic Behavior & Organization, 77*(3), 304–317.

94. Wong, K. F. E., & Kwong, J. Y. Y. (2007). The role of anticipated regret in escalation of commitment. *Journal of Applied Psychology, 9*(2), 545–554.

95. Grant, A. (2013). How to escape from bad decisions. Retrieved from www .psychologytoday.com/blog/give-and-take/201307/ how-to-escape-bad-decisions

96. Franken, R. E. (1994). *Human motivation* (3rd ed.). Belmont, CA: Brooks/Cole.

97. Kabanoff, B., & Rossiter, J. R. (1994). Recent developments in applied creativity. In C. L. Cooper & L. T. Robertson (Eds.), *International review of industrial and organizational psychology* (Vol. 9, pp. 283–324). New York, NY: Wiley.

98. Amabile, T. M. (2012). *Componential theory of creativity* (Working Paper No. 12-096). Cambridge, MA: Harvard Business School. Retrieved from http://www.hbs.edu/faculty/ Publication%20Files/12-096.pdf

99. Tierney, P., Farmer, S. M., & Graen, G. B. (1999). An examination of leadership and employee creativity: The relevance of traits and relationships. *Personnel Psychology, 52*(3), 591–620.

100. George, J. M., & Zhou, J. (2001). When openness to experience and conscientiousness are related to creative behavior: An interactional approach. *Journal of Applied Psychology, 86*(3), 513–524.

101. Kuncel, N. R., Hezlett, S. A., & Ones, D. S. (2004). Academic performance, career potential, creativity, and job performance: Can one construct predict them all? *Journal of Personality and Social Psychology, 86*(1), 148–161.

102. Csikszentmihalyi, M. (1975). *Beyond boredom and anxiety.* San Francisco, CA: Jossey-Bass.

103. Csikszentmihalyi, M., & LeFevre, J. (1989). Optimal experience in work and leisure. *Journal of Personality and Social Psychology, 56*(5), 815–822.

104. De Fraga, D., & Moneta, G. B. (2016). Flow at work as a moderator of the self-determination model of work engagement. In L. Harmat, F. Ørsted Andersen, F. Ullén, J. Wright, & G. Sadlo (Eds.), *Flow experience: Empirical research and applications* (pp. 105–123). New York, NY: Springer.

105. Ibid.

106. Amabile, T. M. (1998). How to kill creativity. *Harvard Business Review, 76*(5), 76–87.

107. Basadur, M. (2004). Leading others to think innovatively together: Creative leadership. *Leadership Quarterly, 15*(1), 103–121.

108. Burkus, D. (2013*). The myths of creativity: The truth about how innovative companies and people generate great ideas.* San Francisco, CA: Jossey-Bass.

109. Amabile, T. M. (1998). How to kill creativity. *Harvard Business Review, 76*(5), 76–87.

110. Zeni, T. A., Buckley, M. R., Mumford, M. D., & Griffith, J. A. (2016). Making "sense" of ethical decision making. *Leadership Quarterly, 27*(6), 838–855.

111. Basadur, M. (2004). Leading others to think innovatively together: Creative leadership. *Leadership Quarterly, 15*(1), 103–121.

112. Basadur, M. S., Graen, G. B., & Green, S. G. (1982). Training in creative problem solving: Effects on ideation and problem finding in an applied research organization. *Organizational Behavior and Human Performance, 30*, 41–70.

113. Basadur, M. S., Runco, M. A., & Vega, L. A. (2000). Understanding how creative thinking skills, attitudes and behaviors work together: A causal process model. *Journal of Creative Behavior, 34*(2), 77–100.

114. Basadur, M. S. (1995). *The power of innovation.* London, England: Pitman Professional.

115. Cavanagh, G., Moberg, D., & Valasquez, M. (1981). The ethics of organizational politics. *Academy of Management Review, 6*(3), 363–374.

116. Gilligan, C. (1977). In a different voice. *Harvard Educational Review, 47*(3), 365–378.

117. Fritzsche, D. J., & Becker, H. (1984). Linking management behavior to ethical philosophy: An empirical investigation. *Academy of Management Journal, 27*(1), 166–175.

118. Stead, W. E., Worrell, D. L., & Stead, J. G. (1990). An integrative model for understanding and managing ethical behavior in business organizations. *Journal of Business Ethics, 9*(3), 233–242.

119. Noval, L. J. (2016). On the misguided pursuit of happiness and ethical decision making: The roles of focalism and the impact bias in unethical and selfish behavior. *Organizational Behavior and Human Decision Processes, 133*, 1–16.

120. Chugh, D., Bazerman, M. H., & Banaji, M. R. (2005). Bounded ethicality as a psychological barrier to recognizing conflicts of interest. In *National Science Foundation/Carnegie Bosch Institute Conference on Conflicts of Interest, Tepper School of Business.* Pittsburgh, PA: Carnegie Mellon University. Portions of this research were presented at the aforementioned conference. Cambridge: Cambridge University Press.

121. Shalvi, S., Dana, J., Handgraaf, M. J., & De Dreu, C. K. (2011). Justified ethicality: Observing desired counterfactuals modifies ethical perceptions and behavior. *Organizational Behavior and Human Decision Processes, 115*(2), 181–190.

122. Bazerman, M. H., & Sezer, O. (2016). Bounded awareness: Implications for ethical decision making. *Organizational Behavior and Human Decision Processes, 136*, 95–105.

123. Lattall, D. (2013). Ethical decision making in the workplace. Retrieved from http://aubreydaniels.com/pmezine/ethical-decision-making-workplace

Chapter 6

1. Edelman, R. (2016). 2016 Edelman Trust Barometer Global Results. http://www.edelman.com/insights/intellectual-property/2016-edelman-trust-barometer/global-results/

2. Northouse, P. G. (2016). *Leadership: Theory and practice* (7th ed.). Thousand Oaks, CA: Sage.

3. Yukl, G. (2013). *Leadership in organizations* (8th ed.). Boston, MA: Pearson. (Quotation on p. 7.)

4. Bennis, W. (1989). *On becoming a leader.* New York, NY: Basic Books.

5. Zaleznik, A. (2004, January). Managers and leaders—Are they different? *Harvard Business Review: Best of HBR,* 74–81.

6. Stogdill, R. M. (1974). *Handbook of leadership: A survey of theory and research.* New York, NY: Free Press.

7. Kirkpatrick, S. A., & Locke, E. A. (1991). Leadership: Do traits matter? *The Executive, 5*(2), 48–60.

8. Colbert, A. E., Judge, T. A., Choi, D., & Wang, G. (2012). Assessing the trait theory of leadership using self and observer ratings of personality: The mediating role of contributions to group success. *Leadership Quarterly, 23*(4), 670–685.

9. Zaccaro, S. J. (2007). Trait-based perspectives of leadership. *American Psychologist, 62*(1), 6–16.

10. Korman, A. K. (1966). "Consideration," "initiating structure," and organizational criteria: A review. *Personnel Psychology, 19*(4), 349–361.

11. Stogdill, R. M., & Coons, A. E. (1951). *Leader behavior in description and measurement* [Research Monograph No. 88]. Columbus: Ohio State University Bureau of Business Research.

12. Judge, T. A., Piccolo, R. F., & Ilies, R. (2004). The forgotten ones? The validity of consideration and initiating structure in leadership research. *Journal of Applied Psychology, 89*(1), 36–51.

13. Behrendt, P., Matz, S., & Göritz, A. S. (2017). An integrative model of leadership behavior. *Leadership Quarterly, 28*, 229–244.

14. Hersey, P., & Blanchard, K. H. (1988). *Management of organizational behavior: Utilizing human resources.* Englewood Cliffs, NJ: Prentice Hall.

15. House, R. J. (1971). A path-goal theory of leadership effectiveness. *Administrative Science Quarterly, 16*(3), 321–328.

16. House, R. J., & Mitchell, T. R. (1974). Path-goal theory of leadership. *Journal of Contemporary Business, 3*(4), 81–97.

17. Wofford, J. C., & Liska, L. Z. (1993). Path-goal theories of leadership: A meta-analysis. *Journal of Management, 19*(4), 857–876.

18. Schriesheim, C. A., & Neider, L. L. (1996). Path-goal leadership theory: The long and winding road. *Leadership Quarterly, 7*(3), 317–321.

19. Scandura, T. A., Graen, G. B., & Novak, M. A. (1986). When managers decide not to decide autocratically: An investigation of leader-member exchange and decision influence in managerial dyads. *Journal of Applied Psychology, 71*, 484–491.

20. Erdogan, B., & Bauer, T. N. (2010). Differentiated leader–member exchanges: The buffering role of justice climate. *Journal of Applied Psychology, 95*(6), 1104–1120.

21. Henderson, D. J., Liden, R. C., Glibkowski, B. C., & Chaudhry, A. (2009). LMX differentiation: A multilevel review and examination of its antecedents and outcomes. *Leadership Quarterly, 20*(4), 517–534.

22. Martin, R., Guillaume, Y., Thomas, G., Lee, A., & Epitropaki, O. (2016). Leader–member exchange (LMX) and performance: A meta-analytic review. *Personnel Psychology, 69*(1), 67–121.

23. Gottfredson, R. K., & Aguinis, H. (2016). Leadership behaviors and follower performance: Deductive and inductive examination of theoretical rationales and underlying mechanisms. *Journal of Organizational Behavior.* doi:10.1002/job.2152

24. Graen, G. B., & Scandura, T. A. (1987). Toward a psychology of dyadic organizing. In B. Staw & L. L. Cummings, *Research in organizational behavior* (Vol. 9, pp. 175–208). Greenwich, CT: JAI Press.

25. Bauer, T. N., & Green, S. G. (1996). Development of leader-member exchange: A longitudinal test. *Academy of Management Journal, 39*(6), 1538–1567.

26. Gabarro, J., & Kotter, J. (2005). Managing your boss. *Harvard Business Review: Best of HBR,* 90–99.

27. Vehar, J. (2016). *Manage your boss.* Greensboro, NC: Center for Creative Leadership.

28. Kelley, J. (2013). How to manage your boss. Retrieved from www.Amanet.org/training/articles/printverson/how-to-manage-Your-Boss.aspx

29. Graen, G. B., Cashman, J., Ginsburgh, S., & Schiemann, W. (1977). Effects of linking-pin quality upon the quality of working life of lower participants: A longitudinal investigation of the managerial understructure. *Administrative Science Quarterly, 22*(3), 491–504.

30. Heider, F. (1958). *The psychology of interpersonal relations.* Hillsdale, NJ: Erlbaum.

31. Miner, J. B. (2015). Attribution theory—Managerial perceptions of the poor performing subordinate. In J. Miner (Ed.), *Organizational behavior 1: Essential theories of motivation and leadership* pp. 184–206).

32. Ross, L. (1977). The intuitive psychologist and his shortcomings: Distortions in the attribution process. In L. Berkowitz (Ed.), *Advances in experimental social psychology* (Vol. 10, pp. 173–220). New York, NY: Academic Press.

33. Martinko, M. J., & Gardner, W. L. (1987). The leader member attribution process. *Academy of Management Review, 12*(2), 235–249.

34. Harvey, P., Madison, K., Martinko, M.,

35. Crook, T. R., & Crook, T. A. (2014). Attribution theory in the organizational sciences: The road traveled and the path ahead. *Academy of Management Perspectives, 28*(2), 128–146.

36. Eberly, M. B., Holley, E. C., Johnson, M. D., & Mitchell, T. R. (2011). Beyond internal and external: A dyadic theory of relational attributions. *Academy of Management Review, 36*(4), 731–753.

37. Eby, L. T. (1997). Alternative forms of mentoring in changing organizational environments: A conceptual extension of the mentoring literature. *Journal of Vocational Behavior, 51*(1), 125–144.

38. Scandura, T. A., & Schriesheim, C. A. (1994). Leader-member exchange and supervisor career mentoring as complementary constructs in leadership research. *Academy of Management Journal, 37*(6), 1588–1602.

39. Kram, K. E. (1988). *Mentoring at work: Developmental relationships in organizational life.* Lanham, MD: University Press of America.

40. Allen, T. D., Eby, L., Poteet, M., Lentz, E., & Lima, L. (2004). Career benefits associated with mentoring for protégés: A meta-analysis. *Journal of Applied Psychology, 89,* 127–136.

41. Higgins, M. C., & Kram, K. E. (2001). Reconceptualizing mentoring at work: A developmental network perspective. *Academy of Management Review, 26*(2), 264.

42. Green, S. G., & Bauer, T. N. (1995). Supervisory mentoring by advisers—relationships with doctoral-student potential, productivity, and commitment. *Personnel Psychology, 48*(3), 537–561.

43. Ragins, B. R. (2016). From the ordinary to the extraordinary: High-quality mentoring relationships at work. *Organizational Dynamics, 45*(3), 228–244.

44. Fleig-Palmer, M. M., Rathert, C., & Porter, T. H. (2016). Building trust: The influence of mentoring behaviors on perceptions of health care managers' trustworthiness. *Health Care Management Review.* doi:10.1097/HMR.0000000000000130

45. Mayer, R. C., Davis, J. H., & Schoorman, F. D. (1995). An integrative model of organizational trust. *Academy of Management Review, 20,* 709–734.

46. Colquitt, J., Scott, B. A., & LePine, J. A. (2007). Trust, trustworthiness, and trust propensity: A meta-analytic test of their unique relationships with risk taking and job performance. *Journal of Applied Psychology, 92,* 909–927.

47. Rousseau, D. M., Sitkin, S. B., Burt, R. S., & Camerer, C. (1998). Not so different after all: A cross-discipline view of trust. *Academy of Management Review, 23*(3), 393–404.

48. Dirks, K. T., & Ferrin, D. L. (2002). Trust in leadership: Meta-analytic findings and implications for research and practice. *Journal of Applied Psychology, 87*(4), 611–628.

49. Shapiro, D., Sheppard, B. H., & Cheraskin, L. (1992). Business on a handshake. *Negotiation Journal, 8*(4), 365–377.

50. Lewicki, R. J., & Bunker, B. B. (1996). Developing and maintaining trust in work relationships. In R. M. Kramer & T. R. Tyler (Eds.), *Trust in organizations: Frontiers of theory and research* (pp. 114–139). Thousand Oaks, CA: Sage.

51. van der Werff, L., & Buckley, F. (2017). Getting to know you: A longitudinal examination of trust cues and trust development during socialization. *Journal of Management.* doi:0149206314543475

52. Scandura, T. A., & Pellegrini, E. K. (2008). Trust and leader-member exchange: A closer look at relational

vulnerability. *Journal of Leadership and Organization Studies, 15*(2), 100–101.

53. Kim, P. H., Dirks, K.T., & Cooper, C. D. (2009). The repair of trust: A dynamic bilateral perspective and multilevel conceptualization. *Academy of Management Review, 34*(3), 401–422.

54. Kim, P. H., Ferrin, D. L., Cooper, C. D., & Dirks, K. T. (2004). Removing the shadow of suspicion: The effects of apology versus denial for repairing competence- versus integrity-based trust violations. *Journal of Applied Psychology, 89*(1), 104–118.

55. Ferrin, D. L., Kim, P. H., Cooper, C. D., & Dirks, K. T. (2007). Silence speaks volumes: The effectiveness of reticence in comparison to apology and denial for responding to integrity- and competence-based trust violations. *Journal of Applied Psychology, 92*(4), 893–908.

56. Kim, P. H., Dirks, K. T., Cooper, C. D., & Ferrin, D. L. (2006). When more blame is better than less: The implications of internal vs. external attributions for the repair of trust after a competence- vs. integrity-based trust violation. *Organizational Behavior and Human Decision Processes, 99*(1), 49–65.

57. Shapiro, D. L. (1991). The effects of explanations on negative reactions to deceit. *Administrative Science Quarterly, 36*(4), 614–630.

58. Bottom, W. P., Gibson, K., Daniels, S. W., & Murnighan, J. K. (2002). When talk is not cheap: Substantive penance and expressions of intent in rebuilding cooperation. *Organization Science, 13*(5), 497–513.

59. Gibson, K., Bottom, W., & Murnighan, J. K. (1999). Once bitten: Defection and cooperation in a cooperative enterprise. *Business Ethics Quarterly, 9*(1), 69–85.

60. Schweitzer, M. E., Hershey, J. C., & Bradlow, E. T. (2006). Promises and lies: Restoring violated trust. *Organizational Behavior and Human Decision Processes, 101*(1), 1–19.

61. Dirks, K. T., Kim, P. H., Ferrin, D. L., & Cooper. C. D. (2011). Understanding the effects of substantive responses on trust following a transgression. *Organizational Behavior and Human Decision Processes, 114*(2), 87–103.

62. Bass, B. M. (1985). *Leadership and performance beyond expectations.* New York, NY: Free Press.

63. Bass, B. M., & Avolio, B. J. (1990). *Transformational leadership development: Manual for the multifactor leadership questionnaire.* Palo Alto, CA: Consulting Psychologists Press.

64. Avolio, B. J. (2011). *Full range leadership development* (2nd ed.). Thousand Oaks, CA: Sage.

65. Ibid., p. 65.

66. Bono, J. E., & Judge, T. A. (2004). Personality and transformational and transactional leadership: A meta-analysis. *Journal of Applied Psychology, 89*(5), 901–910.

67. Qu, R., Janssen, O., & Shi, K. (2015). Transformational leadership and follower creativity: The mediating role of follower relational identification and the moderating role of leader creativity expectations. *Leadership Quarterly, 26*(2), 286–299.

68. Brown, M. E., & Treviño, L. K. (2006). Ethical leadership: A review and future directions. *Leadership Quarterly, 17*(6), 595–616.

69. Mayer, D. M., Aquino, K., Greenbaum, R., & Kuenzi, M. (2012). Who displays ethical leadership, and why does it matter? An examination of antecedents and consequences of ethical leadership. *Academy of Management Journal, 55*(1), 151–171.

70. Den Hartog, D. N. (2015). Ethical leadership. *Annual Review of Organizational Psychology & Organizational Behavior, 2*(1), 409–434. (Quotation on p. 428.)

71. Mayer, D. M., Kuenzi, M., Greenbaum, R., Bardes, M., & Salvador, R. (2009). How low does ethical leadership flow? Test of a trickle-down model. *Organizational Behavior and Human Decision Processes, 108*(1), 1–13.

72. Russell, R. F., & Stone, A. G. (2002). A review of servant leadership attributes: Developing a practical model. *Leadership & Organization Development Journal, 23*(3), 145–157.

73. George, B., Sims, P., & McLean, A. (2007). Discovering your authentic leadership. *Harvard Business Review,* 129–138.

74. Walumbwa, F., Avolio, B., Gardner, W., Wernsing, T., & Peterson, S. (2008). Authentic leadership: Development and validation of a theory-based measure. *Journal of Management, 34*(1), 89–126.

75. Kidder, R. M. (2003). *How good people make tough choices: Resolving the dilemmas of ethical living.* New York, NY: HarperCollins.

76. Barbuto, J. E., & Wheeler, J. W. (2006). Scale development and construct clarification of servant leadership. *Group & Organization Management, 31*(3), 300–326.

77. Liden, R. C., Wayne, S. J., Zhao, H., & Henderson, D. (2008). Servant leadership: Development of a multidimensional measure and multilevel assessment. *Leadership Quarterly, 19*(2), 161–177.

78. Liden, R. C., Wayne, S. J., Liao, C., & Meuser, J. D. (2014). Servant leadership and serving culture: Influence on individual and unit performance. *Academy of Management Journal, 37*(5), 1434–1452.

79. Hu, J., & Liden, R. C. (2011). Antecedents of team potency and team effectiveness: An examination of goal and process clarity and servant leadership. *Journal of Applied Psychology, 96,* 851–862.

80. Owens, B. P., & Hekman, D. R. (2012). Modeling how to grow: An inductive examination of humble leader behaviors, contingencies, and outcomes. *Academy of Management Journal, 55*(4), 787–818.

81. Chiu, C. Y. C., Owens, B. P., & Tesluk, P. E. (2016). Initiating and utilizing shared leadership in teams: The role of leader humility, team proactive personality, and team performance capability. *Journal of Applied Psychology, 101*(12), 1705–1720.

82. George, B., Sims, P., McLean, A., & Mayer, D. (2007, February). Discovering your authentic leadership. *Harvard Business Review,* 129–138.

83. Neider, L. L., & Schriesheim, C. A. (2011). The authentic leadership inventory (ALI): Development and empirical tests. *Leadership Quarterly, 22*(6), 1146–1164.

84. Steffens, N. K., Mols, F., Haslam, S. A., & Okimoto, T. G. (2016). True to what we stand for: Championing collective interests as a path to authentic leadership. *Leadership Quarterly, 27*(5), 726–744.

85. Hoch, J. E., Bommer, W. H., Dulebohn, J. H., & Wu, D. (2016). Do ethical, authentic, and servant leadership

explain variance above and beyond transformational leadership? A meta-analysis. *Journal of Management.* doi:0149206316665461

86. Phillips, J. S., & Lord, R. G. (1981). Causal attributions and perceptions of leadership. *Organizational Behavior and Human Performance, 28*(2), 143–163.

87. Lord, R. G., Foti, R. J., & Phillips, J. S. (1982). A theory of leadership categorization. In J. G. Hunt, U. Sekaran, & C. Schriesheim (Eds.), *Leadership: Beyond establishment views* (pp. 104–121). Carbondale: Southern Illinois University Press.

88. Phillips, J. S., & Lord, R. G. (1982). Schematic information processing and perceptions of leadership in problem-solving groups. *Journal of Applied Psychology, 67*(4), 486–492.

89. Lord, R. G. (1985). An information processing approach to social perceptions, leadership perceptions and behavioral measurement in organizational settings. In B. M. Staw & L. L. Cummings (Eds.), *Research in organizational behavior* (Vol. 7, pp. 85–128). Greenwich, CT: JAI Press.

90. Engle, E. M., & Lord, R. G. (1997). Implicit theories, self-schemas, and

leader-member exchange. *Academy of Management Journal, 40*(4), 988–1010.

91. Meindl, J. R., Ehrlich, S. B., & Dukerich, J. M. (1985). The romance of leadership. *Administrative Science Quarterly, 30*(1), 78–102.

92. Berson, Y., Halevy, N., Shamir, B., & Erez, M. (2015). Leading from different psychological distances: A construal-level perspective on vision communication, goal setting, and follower motivation. *Leadership Quarterly, 26*(2), 143–155.

Chapter 7

1. Flynn, F. J., Gruenfeld, D., Molm, L. D., & Polzer, J. T. (2011). Social psychological perspectives on power in organizations. *Administrative Science Quarterly, 56*, 495–500. (Quotation on p. 495.)

2. Berdahl, J., & Martorana, P. (2006). Effects of power on emotion and expression during a controversial group discussion. *European Journal of Social Psychology, 36*, 497–509.

3. Bendahan, S., Zehnder, C., Pralong, F. P., & Antonakis, J. (2015). Leader corruption depends on power and testosterone. *Leadership Quarterly, 26*(2), 101–122.

4. Carney, D. (2010, May). Power people are better liars. *Harvard Business Review*, 32–33.

5. Hildreth, J. A. D., & Anderson, C. (2016). Failure at the top: How power undermines collaborative performance. *Journal of Personality and Social Psychology, 110*(2), 261–286.

6. Mourali, M., & Yang, Z. (2013). The dual role of power in resisting social influence. *Journal of Consumer Research, 40*, 539–554.

7. Guinote, A. (2017). How power affects people: Activating, wanting, and goal seeking. *Annual Review of Psychology, 68*, 353–381.

8. Russell, B. (1938). *Power, a new social analysis.* New York, NY: Norton. (Quotation on p. 10.)

9. Farmer, S. M., & Aguinis, H. (2005). Accounting for subordinate perceptions of supervisor power: An identity-dependence model. *Journal of Applied Psychology, 90*(6), 1069–1083.

10. Uhl-Bien, M., & Pillai, R. (2007). The romance of leadership and the social construction of followership. In B. Shamir, R. Pillai, M. Bligh, & M. Uhl-Bien (Eds.), *Follower-centered perspectives on leadership: A tribute to the memory of James R. Meindl* (pp. 187–210). Charlotte, NC: Information Age. (Quotation on p. 196.)

11. Kanter, R. M. (1979, July-August). Power failure in management circuits. *Harvard Business Review*, 65.

12. Sturm, R. E., & Antonakis, J. (2015). Interpersonal power: A review, critique, and research agenda. *Journal of Management, 41*(1), 136–163. (Quotation on p. 136.)

13. Hill, L. (1994). Power dynamics in organizations. *Harvard Business School Note, 9*, 1–13.

14. French, J. R. P., & Raven, B. (1960). The bases of social power. In D. Cartwright & A. Zander (Eds.), *Group Dynamics* (2nd ed., pp. 607–623). New York, NY: Harper & Row.

15. Ward, E. A. (2001, February). Social power bases of managers: Emergence of a new factor. *Journal of Social Psychology*, 144–147.

16. Rylander, P. (2016). Coaches' bases of power and coaching effectiveness in team sports. *International Sport Coaching Journal, 3*(2), 128–144.

17. Junaimah, J., See, L. P., & Bashawir, A. G. (2015). Effect of manager's bases of power on employee's job satisfaction: An empirical study of satisfaction with supervision. *International Journal of Economics, Commerce and Management, 3*(2), 1–14.

18. Carson, P. P., Carson, K. D., & Roe, C. W. (1993). Social power bases: A meta-analytic examination of interrelationships and outcomes. *Journal of Applied Social Psychology, 23*(14), 1150–1169.

19. Yukl, G. (2013). *Leadership in organizations* (8th ed.). Boston, MA: Pearson.

20. Barnard, C. (1938). *Functions of the executive.* Cambridge, MA: Harvard University Press.

21. Emerson, R. M. (1962). Power-dependence relations. *American Sociological Review, 27*, 31–41.

22. Farmer, S. M., & Aguinis, H. (2005). Accounting for subordinate perceptions of supervisor power: An identity-dependence model. *Journal of Applied Psychology, 90*(6), 1069–1083.

23. Kanter, R. M. (1979). Power failure in management circuits. *Harvard Business Review, 57*(4), 65–75.

24. Pfeffer, J. (2013). You're still the same: Why theories of power hold over time and across contexts. *Academy of Management Perspectives, 27*(4), 269–280.

25. Strauss, G. (1962). Tactics of lateral relationship: The purchasing agent. *Administrative Science Quarterly, 7*, 161–186.

26. Pfeffer, J. (1981). *Power in organizations* (Vol. 33). Marshfield, MA: Pitman.

27. Emerson, R. E. (1962, February). Power-dependence relations. *American Sociological Review, 27*(1), 31–41.

28. Cohen, A. R., & Bradford, D. L. (2005). *Influence without authority* (2nd ed.). New York, NY: Wiley.

29. Gouldner, A. W. (1960). The norm of reciprocity: A preliminary statement. *American Sociological Review, 25*(2), 161–178.

30. Mintzberg, H. (1983). *Power in and around organizations.* Upper Saddle River, NJ: Prentice Hall.

31. Triplett, N. (1898). The dynamogenic factors in pacemaking and competition. *American Journal of Psychology, 9*, 507–533.

32. Ferris, G. R., Perrewé, P. L., Daniels, S. R., Lawong, D., & Holmes, J. J. (2016). Social influence and politics in organizational research: What we know and what we need to know. *Journal of Leadership & Organizational Studies.* doi: 1548051816656003

33. Kipnis, D., Schmidt, S. M., & Wilkinson, I. (1980). Intraorganizational influence tactics: Explorations in getting one's way. *Journal of Applied Psychology, 65*(4), 440–452.

34. Yukl, G. (2013). *Leadership in organizations* (8th ed.). New York, NY: Pearson.

35. Yukl, G., Lepsinger, R., & Lucia, T. (1992). Preliminary report on the development and validation of the influence behavior questionnaire. In K. Clark, M. B. Clark, & D. P. Campbell (Eds.), *Impact of leadership* (pp. 417–427). Greensboro, NC: Center for Creative Leadership.

36. Yukl, G., Seifert, C. F., & Chavez, C. (2008). Validation of the extended influence behavior questionnaire. *Leadership Quarterly, 19*(5), 609–621.

37. Falbe, C. M., & Yukl, G. (1992). Consequences for managers of using single influence tactics and combinations of tactics. *Academy of Management Journal, 35*(3), 638–652.

38. Fu, P. P., Kennedy, J., Tata, J., Yukl, G., Bond, M. H., Peng, T. K., . . . Boonstra, J. J. (2004). The impact of societal cultural values and individual social beliefs on the perceived effectiveness of managerial influence strategies: A meso approach. *Journal of International Business Studies, 35*(4), 284–305.

39. Fu, P. P., & Yukl, G. (2000). Perceived effectiveness of influence tactics in the United States and China. *Leadership Quarterly, 11*(2), 251–266.

40. Yukl, G., & Tracey, J. B. (1992). Consequences of influence tactics used with subordinates, peers, and the boss. *Journal of Applied psychology, 77*(4), 525–535.

41. Yukl, G., Kim, H., & Chavez, C. (1999). Task importance, feasibility, and agent influence behavior as determinants of target commitment. *Journal of Applied Psychology, 84*(1), 137–143.

42. Higgins, C. A., Judge, T. A., & Ferris, G. R. (2003). Influence tactics and work outcomes: A meta-analysis. *Journal of Organizational Behavior, 24*(1), 89–106.

43. Lee, S., Han, S., Cheong, M., Kim, S. L., & Yun, S. (2017). How do I get my way? A meta-analytic review of research on influence tactics. *Leadership Quarterly, 28*, 210–228.

44. Goffman, E. (1959). *The presentation of self in everyday life.* New York, NY: Overlook Press.

45. Schlenker, B. R. (1980). *Impression management: The self-concept, social identity, and interpersonal relations* (pp. 21–43). Monterey, CA: Brooks/Cole.

46. Wayne, S. J., & Liden, R. C. (1995). Effects of impression management on performance ratings: A longitudinal study. *Academy of Management Journal, 38*(1), 232–260.

47. Gardner, W. L., & Martinko, M. J. (1988). Impression management in organizations. *Journal of Management, 14*(2), 321–338.

48. Bolino, M., Long, D., & Turnley, W. (2016). Impression management in organizations: Critical questions, answers, and areas for future research. *Annual Review of Organizational Psychology and Organizational Behavior, 3*, 377–406.

49. Ham, J., & Vonk, R. (2011). Impressions of impression management: Evidence of spontaneous suspicion of ulterior motivation. *Journal of Experimental Social Psychology, 47*(2), 466–471.

50. Lafrenière, M. A. K., Sedikides, C., Van Tongeren, D. R., & Davis, J. (2016). On the perceived intentionality of self-enhancement. *Journal of Social Psychology, 156*(1), 28–42.

51. Bolino, M. C., Kacmar, K. M, Turnley, W. H., & Gilstrap, J. B. (2008). A multi-level review of impression management motives and behaviors. *Journal of Management, 34*(6), 1080–1109.

52. Ibid.

53. Jones, E. E., & Pittman, T. S. (1982). Toward a general theory of strategic self-presentation. In J. Suls (Ed.), *Psychological perspectives on the self,* (pp. 231–261). Hillsdale, NJ: Erlbaum.

54. Bolino, M. C., Kacmar, K. M, Turnley, W. H., & Gilstrap, J. B. (2008). A multi-level review of impression management motives and behaviors. *Journal of Management, 34*(6), 1080–1109.

55. Wayne, S. J., & Ferris, G. (1990). Influence tactics, affect, and exchange quality in supervisor-subordinate interactions: A laboratory experiment and field study. *Journal of Applied Psychology, 75*(5), 487–499.

56. Yukl, G. (2013). *Leadership in organizations* (8th ed.). Boston, MA: Pearson.

57. Aguinis, H., Simonsen, M. M., & Pierce, C. A. (1998). Effects of nonverbal behavior on perceptions of power bases. *Journal of Social Psychology, 138*(4), 455–469.

58. Carney, D. R., Cuddy, A. J. C., & Yap, A. J. (2010). Power posing: Brief nonverbal displays affect neuroendocrine levels and risk tolerance. *Psychological Science, 21*(10), 1363–1368.

59. Rosenberg, R. S. (2011). The superheroes: Inside the mind of batman and other larger-than-life-heroes. Retrieved from www.psychologytoday.com/blog/the-superheroes/201107/superherostance

60. Cuddy, A. J., Wilmuth, C. A., Yap, A. J., & Carney, D. R. (2015). Preparatory power posing affects nonverbal presence and job interview performance. *Journal of Applied Psychology, 100*(4), 1286–1295.

61. Cuddy, A., Schultz, J., & Fosse, N. E. (2017). P-curving a more comprehensive body of research on postural feedback reveals clear evidential value for "Power Posing" effects: Reply to Simmons and Simonsohn. Forthcoming in *Psychological Science.* Available at SSRN: https://ssrn.com/abstract=3054952

62. Murphy, K. (2013). The right stance can be reassuring. Retrieved from www.nytimes.com/2013/05/05/fashion/the-right-stance-can-be-reassuring-studied.html?ref=fashion&_r=1&&

63. Kidder, R. M. (2003). *How good people make tough choices: Resolving the dilemmas of ethical living.* New York, NY: HarperCollins.

64. Drory, A., & Romm, T. (1990). The definition of organizational politics: A review. *Human Relations*, 1133–1154.

65. Cropanzano, R. S., Kacmar, K. M., & Bozeman, D. P. (1995). The social setting of work organizations: Politics, justice, and support. In R. S. Cropanzano & K. M Kacmar (Eds.), *Organizational politics, justice, and support: Managing the social climate of the workplace*, (pp. 1–18). Westport, CT: Quorum Books.

66. Randall, M. L., Cropanzano, R., Bormann, C. A., & Birjulin, A. (1999). Organizational politics and organizational support as predictors of work attitudes, job performance, and organizational citizenship behavior. *Journal of Organizational Behavior*, 20, 159–174.

67. Williams, M., & Dutton, J. E. (1999). Corrosive political climates: The heavy toll of negative political behavior in organizations. In R. E. Quinn, R. M. O'Neill, & L. St. Clair (Eds.), *Pressing problems of modern organizations (that keep us up at night): Transforming agendas for research and practice* (pp. 3–30). New York, NY: American Management Association.

68. Ferris, G. R., Harrell-Cook, G., & Dulebohn, J. H. (2000). Organizational politics: The nature of the relationship between politics perceptions and political behavior. In S. B. Bacharach & E. J. Lawler (Eds.), *Research in the sociology of organizations* (pp. 89–130). Stamford, CT: JAI Press.

69. Kacmar, K. M., & Ferris, G. R. (1993). Politics at work: Sharpening the focus of political behavior in organizations. *Business Horizons, 36*, 70–74.

70. Kacmar, K. M., & Carlson, D. S. (1997). Further validation of the perceptions of politics scale (POPS): A multiple sample investigation. *Journal of Management, 23*(5), 627–658.

71. Kacmar, K. M., Bozeman, D. P., Carlson, D. P., & Anthony, W. P. (1999). An examination of the perceptions of organizational politics model: Replication and extension. *Human Relations, 52*(3), 383–416.

72. Miller, B. K., Rutherford, M. A., & Kolodinsky, R. W. (2008). Perceptions of organizational politics: A meta-analysis of outcomes. *Journal of Business and Psychology, 22*(3), 209–222.

73. Bedi, A., & Schat, A. C. (2013). Perceptions of organizational politics: A meta-analysis of its attitudinal, health, and behavioral consequences. *Canadian Psychology, 54*(4), 246–259.

74. Poon, J. M. (2003). Situational antecedents and outcomes of organizational politics perceptions. *Journal of Managerial Psychology, 18*(2), 138–155.

75. Atinc, G., Darrat, M., Fuller, B., & Parker, B. W. (2010). Perceptions of organizational politics: A meta-analysis of theoretical antecedents. *Journal of Managerial Issues*, 494–513.

76. Biberman, G. (1985). Personality and characteristic work attitudes of persons with high, moderate, and low political tendencies. *Psychological Reports, 57*(3_suppl.), 1303–1310.

77. O'Connor, W. E., & Morrison, T. G. (2001). A comparison of situational and dispositional predictors of perceptions of organizational politics. *Journal of Psychology, 135*(3), 301–312.

78. Ferris, G. R., Perrewé, P. L., Daniels, S. R., Lawong, D., & Holmes, J. J. (2016). Social influence and politics in organizational research: What we know and what we need to know. *Journal of Leadership & Organizational Studies*. doi:1548051816656003

79. Valle, M., & Perrewé, P. L. (2000). Do politics perceptions relate to political behaviors? Tests of an implicit assumption and expanded model. *Human Relations, 53*(3), 359–386.

80. Ferris, G. R., Frink, D. D., Galang, M. C., Zhou, J., Kacmar, K. M., & Howard, J. L. (1996). Perceptions of organizational politics: Prediction, stress-related implications, and outcomes. *Human Relations, 49*(2), 233–266.

81. Kostigan, T. (2009). The 10 most unethical people in business. Retrieved from http://www.marketwatch.com/story/the-10-most-unethical-people-in-business

82. Kacmar, K. M., Andrews, M. C., Harris, K. J., & Tepper, B. J. (2013). Ethical leadership and subordinate outcomes: The mediating role of organizational politics and the moderating role of political skill. *Journal of Business Ethics, 115*(1), 33–44.

83. Ahearn, K. K., Ferris, G. R., Hochwarter, W. A., Douglas, C., & Ammeter, A. P. (2004). Leader political skill and team performance. *Journal of Management, 30*(3), 309–327.

84. Ferris, G. R., Treadway, D. C., Kolodinsky, R. W., Hochwarter, W. A., Kacmar, C. J., Douglas, C., & Frink, D. D. (2005). Development and validation of the political skill inventory. *Journal of Management, 31*(1), 126–152.

85. Munyon, T. P., Summers, J. K., Thompson, K. M., & Ferris, G. R. (2015). Political skill and work outcomes: A theoretical extension, meta-analytic investigation, and agenda for the future. *Personnel Psychology, 68*(1), 143–184.

86. Epitropaki, O., Kapoutsis, I., Ellen, B. P., Ferris, G. R., Drivas, K., & Ntotsi, A. (2016). Navigating uneven terrain: The roles of political skill and LMX differentiation in prediction of work relationship quality and work outcomes. *Journal of Organizational Behavior, 37*(7), 1078–1103.

87. Harris, K. J., Kacmar, K. M., Zivnuska, S., & Shaw, J. D. (2007). The impact of political skill on impression management effectiveness. *Journal of Applied Psychology, 92*(1), 278.

88. Jawahar, I. M., & Liu, Y. (2016). Proactive personality and citizenship performance: The mediating role of career satisfaction and the moderating role of political skill. *Career Development International, 21*(4), 378–401.

89. Shaughnessy, B. A., Treadway, D. C., Breland, J. W., & Perrewé, P. L. (2016). Informal leadership status and individual performance: The roles of political skill and political will. *Journal of Leadership & Organizational Studies, 24*(1), 83–94. http://dx.doi.org/10.1177%2F1548051816657983

90. Harris, J. N., Maher, L. P., & Ferris, G. R. (2016). The roles of political skill and political will in job performance prediction: A moderated nonlinear perspective. In E. Vigoda-Gadot & A. Drory (Eds.), *Handbook of organizational politics: Looking back and to the future* (pp. 15–39). Northampton, MA: Edward-Elgar.

91. Pfeffer, J. (1992). *Managing with power*. Boston, MA: Harvard Business School Press.

Chapter 8

1. Duckworth, A. L., Peterson, C., Matthews, M. D., & Kelly, D. R. (2007). Grit: Perseverance and passion for long-term goals. *Journal of Personality and Social Psychology, 92*(6), 1087–1101. (Quotation on p. 1087).

2. Eskresis-Winkler, L., Shulman, E. P., Beal, S. A., & Duckworth, A. L. (2014). The grit effect: Predicting retention in the military, the workplace, school and marriage. *Frontiers in Psychology*, 5(36), 1–12. doi:10.3389/fpsyg.2014.00036

3. Judge, T. A., & Ilies, R. (2002). Relationship of personality to performance motivation: A meta-analytic review. *Journal of Applied Psychology, 87*(4), 797–807.

4. Credé, M., Tynan, M. C., & Harms, P. D. (2016). Much ado about grit: A meta-analytic synthesis of the grit literature. *Journal of Personality and Social Psychology*. Retrieved from https://www.ncbi.nlm.nih.gov/pubmed/27845531

5. Packard, E. (2007). Grit: It's what separates the best from the merely good. Retrieved from http://www.apa.org/monitor/nov07/grit.aspx

6. Steers, R., Mowday, R., & Shapiro, D. (2004). The future of work motivation theory. *Academy of Management Review, 29*(3), 379–387.

7. Kanfer, R. (1990). Motivation theory and industrial and organizational psychology. In M. D. Dunnette (Ed.), *Handbook of industrial and organizational psychology* (Vol. 1, 2nd ed., pp. 75–170). Palo Alto, CA: Consulting Psychologists Press.

8. Maslow, A. (1954). *Motivation and personality*. New York, NY: Harper & Row.

9. Wahba, M. A., & Bridwell, L. G. (1976). Maslow reconsidered: A review of research on the need hierarchy theory. *Organizational Behavior and Human Performance, 15*(2), 212–240.

10. McClelland, D. C. (1961). *The achieving society*. New York, NY: Van Nostrand Reinhold.

11. Miner, J. B., Smith, N. R., & Bracker, J. S. (1994). Role of entrepreneurial task motivation in the growth of technologically innovative firms: Interpretations from follow-up data. *Journal of Applied Psychology, 79*(4), 627–630.

12. Herzberg, F., Mausner, B., & Snyderman, B. (1959). *The motivation to work*. New York, NY: Wiley.

13. House, R. J., & Wigdor, L. A. (1967). Herzberg's dual-factor theory of job satisfaction and motivations: A review of the evidence and criticism. *Personnel Psychology, 20*(4), 369–389.

14. Herzberg, F., Mausner, B., & Snyderman, B. (1959). *The motivation to work*. New York, NY: Wiley.

15. Locke, E. A. (1968). Toward a theory of task motivation and incentives. *Organizational Behavior and Human Performance, 3*(2), 157–189.

16. Locke, E. A., & Latham, G. P. (2002). Building a practically useful theory of goal setting and task motivation: A 35-year odyssey. *American Psychologist, 57*(9), 705–717.

17. Tubbs, M. E. (1986). Goal setting: A meta-analytic examination of the empirical evidence. *Journal of Applied Psychology, 71*(3), 474–483.

18. Carroll, S. J., & Tosi, H. L. (1973). *Management by objectives*. New York, NY: Macmillan.

19. Wofford, J. C., Goodwin, V. L., & Premack, S. (1992). Meta-analysis of the antecedents of personal goal level and of the antecedents and consequences of goal commitment. *Journal of Management, 18*(3), 595–615.

20. Latham, G. P., Erez, M., & Locke, E. A. (1988). Resolving scientific disputes by the joint design of crucial experiments by the antagonists: Application to the Erez–Latham dispute regarding participation in goal setting. *Journal of Applied Psychology, 73*(4), 753.

21. Crowe, E., & Higgins, E. T. (1997). Regulatory focus and strategic inclinations: Promotion and prevention in decision-making. *Organizational Behavior and Human Decision Processes*, 69, 117–132.

22. Brockner, J., & Higgins, E. T. (2001). Regulatory focus theory: Implications for the study of emotions at work. *Organizational Behavior and Human Decision Processes, 86*(1), 35–66.

23. Dweck, C. S. (1986). Motivational processes affecting learning. *American Psychologist, 41*, 1040–1048.

24. VandeWalle, D. (1997). Development and validation of a work domain goal orientation instrument. *Educational and Psychological Measurement*, 57, 995–1015.

25. Payne, S. C., Youngcourt, S. S., & Beaubien, J. M. (2007). A meta-analytic examination of the goal orientation nomological net. *Journal of Applied Psychology, 92*(1), 128–150.

26. Janssen, O., & Van Yperen, N. (2004). Employee's goal orientations, the quality of leader member exchange and the outcomes of job performance and job satisfaction. *Academy of Management Journal, 47*, 368–384.

27. Brett, J. F., Uhl-Bien, M., Huang, L., & Carsten, M. (2016). Goal orientation and employee resistance at work: Implications for manager emotional exhaustion with the employee. *Journal of Occupational and Organizational Psychology, 89*(3), 611–633.

28. Shaw, K. N. (2004). Changing the goal-setting process at Microsoft. *Academy of Management Executive, 18*(4), 139–142.

29. Ibid., pp. 140–141.

30. Latham, G. P., Brcic, J., & Steinhauer, A. (2017). Toward an integration of goal setting theory and the automaticity model. *Applied Psychology, 66*(1), 25–48.

31. Tubbs, M. E. (1986). Goal setting: A meta-analytic examination of the empirical evidence. *Journal of Applied Psychology, 71*(3), 474–483.

32. Ivancevich, J. M., & McMahon, J. T. (1982). The effects of goal setting, external feedback and self-generated feedback on outcome variables: A field experiment. *Academy of Management Journal, 25*(2), 359–372.

33. Ordonez, L. D., Schweitzer, M. E., Galinsky, A. D., & Bazerman, M. (2009). Goals gone wild: The systemic side effects of overprescribing goal setting. *Academy of Management Perspectives, 23*(1), 6–16.

34. Locke, E. A., & Latham, G. P. (2009). Has goal setting gone wild, or have its attackers abandoned good scholarship? *Academy of Management Perspectives, 23*(1), 17–23.

35. Hackman, J. R., & Oldham, G. R. (1976). Motivation through the design of work: Test of a theory. *Organizational*

*Behavior and Human Performance,
16*(2), 250–279.

36. Bond, F. W., Flaxman, P. E., & Bunce, D. (2008). The influence of psychological flexibility on work redesign: Mediated moderation of a work reorganization intervention. *Journal of Applied Psychology, 93*(3), 645.

37. Hackman, J. R., & Oldham, G. R. (1980). *Work redesign*. Reading, MA: Addison-Wesley.

38. Hackman, J. R., & Suttle, J. L. (Eds.). (1977). *Improving life at work: Behavioral science approaches to organizational change*. Santa Monica, CA: Goodyear.

39. Erskine, L., & Howell, J. (2010). Spar Applied Systems: Anna's challenge. Ivey Management Services. In W. G. Rowe & L. Guerrero (Eds.), *Cases in leadership* (3rd ed.), Thousand Oaks, CA: Sage. (Original work published 1997)

40. Grant, A. M. (2007). Relational job design and the motivation to make a prosocial difference. *Academy of Management Review, 32*(2), 393–417.

41. Ibid., p. 65.

42. Grant, A. M. (2008). The significance of task significance: Job performance effects, relational mechanisms, and boundary conditions. *Journal of Applied Psychology, 93*(1), 108–124.

43. Grant, A. M., & Parker, S. K. (2009). Redesigning work design theories: The rise of relational and proactive perspectives. *Academy of Management Annals, 3*(1), 317–375.

44. Humphrey, S. E., Nahrgang, J. D., & Morgeson, F. P. (2007). Integrating motivational, social, and contextual work design features: A meta-analytic summary and theoretical extension of the work design literature. *Journal of Applied Psychology, 92*(5), 1332–1356.

45. Campion, M. A., & McClelland, C. L. (1993). Follow-up and extension of the interdisciplinary costs and benefits of enlarged jobs. *Journal of Applied Psychology, 78*(3), 339–351.

46. Fried, Y., & Ferris, G. R. (1987). The validity of the job characteristics model: A review and meta-analysis. *Personnel Psychology, 40*(2), 287–322.

47. Griffin, R. W. (1983). Objective and social sources of information in task redesign: A field experiment. *Administrative Science Quarterly, 28*(2), 184–200.

48. Orpen, C. (1979). The effects of job enrichment on employee satisfaction, motivation, involvement, and performance: A field experiment. *Human Relations, 32*(3), 189–217.

49. Pritchard, R. D., Harrell, M. M., Diaz-Grandos, D., & Guzman, M. J. (2008). The productivity measurement and enhancement system: A meta-analysis. *Journal of Applied Psychology, 93*(3), 540–567.

50. Subramony, M. (2009). A meta-analytic investigation of the relationship between HRM bundles and firm performance. *Human Resource Management, 48*(5), 745–768.

51. Theorell, T. (1999). How to deal with stress in organizations. A health perspective on theory and practice. *Scandinavian Journal of Work, Environment & Health, 25*(6), 616–624.

52. Daniels, K., Beesley, N., Wimalasiri, V., & Cheyne, A. (2013). Problem solving and well-being: Exploring the instrumental role of job control and social support. *Journal of Management, 39*(4), 1016–1043.

53. Wrzesniewski, A., & Dutton, J. E. (2001). Crafting a job: Revisioning employees as active crafters of their work. *Academy of Management Review, 26*, 179–201. (Quotation on p. 180.)

54. Ibid.

55. Petrou, P., Demerouti, E., & Schaufeli, W. B. (2016). Crafting the change: The role of employee job crafting behaviors for successful organizational change. *Journal of Management*. Retrieved from http://dx.doi.org/10.1177%2F0149206315624961

56. Oldham, G. R., & Hackman, J. R. (2010). Not what it was and not what it will be: The future of job design research. *Journal of Organizational Behavior, 31*(2–3), 463–479. (Quotation on p. 470.)

57. Lind, E. A., & Tyler, T. R. (1988). *The social psychology of procedural justice*. New York, NY: Springer.

58. Adams, J. S. (1965). Inequity in social exchange. In L. Berkowitz (Ed.), *Advances in experimental social psychology* (Vol. 2, pp. 267–299). New York, NY: Academic Press.

59. Ambrose, M. L., & Kulik, C. T. (1999). Old friends, new faces: Motivation in the 1990s. *Journal of Management, 25*, 231–292.

60. Greenberg, J. (1990). Employee theft as a reaction to underpayment inequity: The hidden cost of pay cuts. *Journal of Applied Psychology, 75*, 561–568.

61. Blakely, G. L., Andrews, M. C., & Moorman, R. H. (2005). The moderating effects of equity sensitivity on the relationship between organizational justice and organizational citizenship behaviors. *Journal of Business & Psychology, 20*(2), 259–273.

62. Moorman, R. H. (1991). Relationship between organizational justice and organizational citizenship behaviors: Do fairness perceptions influence employee citizenship? *Journal of Applied Psychology, 76*, 845–855.

63. Sherf, E. N., & Venkataramani, V. (2015). Friend or foe? The impact of relational ties with comparison others on outcome fairness and satisfaction judgments. *Organizational Behavior and Human Decision Processes, 128*, 1–14.

64. Greenberg, J. (1987). A taxonomy of organizational justice theories. *Academy of Management Review, 12*(1), 9–22.

65. Cropanzano, R., Bowen, D. E., & Gilliland, S. W. (2007). The management of organizational justice. *Academy of Management Perspectives, 21*(4), 34–48. (Quotation on p. 34.)

66. Bies, R. J. (1987). The predicament of injustice: The management of moral outrage. *Research in Organizational Behavior, 9*, 289–319.

67. Ambrose, M. L., Seabright, M. A., & Schminke, M. (2002). Sabotage in the workplace: The role of organizational justice. *Organizational Behavior and Human Decision Processes, 89*(1), 947–965.

68. Tyler, T. R., & Caine, A. (1981). The role of distributive and procedural fairness in the endorsement of formal leaders. *Journal of Personality and Social Psychology, 41*(4), 643–655.

69. Colquitt, J. A. (2001). On the dimensionality of organizational justice: A construct validation of a measure. *Journal of Applied Psychology, 86*(3), 386–400.

70. Adams, J. S. (1965). Inequity in social exchange. In L. Berkowitz (Ed.), *Advances in experimental social psychology* (Vol. 2, pp. 267–299). New York, NY: Academic Press.

71. Leventhal, G. S. (1980). What should be done with equity theory? New

approaches to the study of fairness in social relationships. In K. Gergen, M. Greenberg, & R. Willis (Eds.), *Social exchange: Advances in theory and research* (pp. 27–55). New York, NY: Plenum Press.

72. Thibaut, J., & Walker, L. (1975). *Procedural justice: A psychological analysis*. Hillsdale, NJ: Erlbaum.

73. Colquitt, J. A. (2001). On the dimensionality of organizational justice: A construct validation of a measure. *Journal of Applied Psychology, 86*(3), 386–400.

74. Cohen-Charash, Y., & Spector, P. (2001). The role of justice in organizations: A meta-analysis. *Organizational Behavior and Human Decision Processes, 86*(2), 278–321.

75. Bies, R. J., & Moag, J. S. (1986). Interactional justice: Communication criteria of fairness. *Research on negotiation in organizations, 1*(1), 43–55.

76. Colquitt, J. A. (2001). On the dimensionality of organizational justice: A construct validation of a measure. *Journal of Applied Psychology, 86*(3), 386–400.

77. Bies, R. J., & Moag, J. S. (1986). Interactional justice: Communication criteria of fairness. *Research on negotiation in organizations, 1*(1), 43–55.

78. Bies, R. J., & Shapiro, D. L. (1988). Voice and justification: Their influence on procedural fairness judgments. *Academy of Management Journal, 31*(3), 676–685.

79. Huseman, R. C., Hatfield, J. D., & Miles, E. W. (1987). A new perspective on equity theory: The equity sensitivity construct. *Academy of Management Review, 12*(2), 222–234.

80. Miles, E. W., Hatfield, J. D., & Huseman, R. C. (1994). Equity sensitivity and outcome importance. *Journal of Organizational Behavior, 15*(7), 585–596.

81. Bing, M. N., & Burroughs, S. M. (2001). The predictive and interactive effects of equity sensitivity in teamwork-oriented organizations. *Journal of Organizational Behavior, 22*(3), 271–290.

82. Blakely, G. L., Andrews, M. C., & Moorman, R. H. (2005). The moderating effects of equity sensitivity on the relationship between organizational justice and organizational citizenship behaviors. *Journal of Business & Psychology, 20*(2), 259–273.

83. Shore, T. H. (2004). Equity sensitivity theory: Do we all want more than we deserve? *Journal of Managerial Psychology, 19*(7), 722–772.

84. Scandura, T. A. (1999). Rethinking leader-member exchange: An organizational justice perspective. *Leadership Quarterly, 10*(1), 25–40.

85. Erdogan, B., & Bauer, T. N. (2010). Differentiated leader-member exchanges: The buffering role of justice climate. *Journal of Applied Psychology, 95*(6), 1104–1120.

86. Li, N., Liang, J., & Crant, J. M. (2010). The role of proactive personality in job satisfaction and organizational citizenship behavior: A relational perspective. *Journal of Applied Psychology, 95*(2), 395–404.

87. Cooper, C. D., & Scandura, T. A. (2012). Was I unfair? Antecedents and consequences of managerial perspective taking in a predicament of injustice. In C. A. Schriesheim & L. L. Neider (Eds.), *Research in management: Perspectives on trust and justice* (Vol. 9). Greenwich, CT: Information Age.

88. Dewhurst, M. (2009). Motivating people: Getting beyond money [Commentary]. Retrieved from http://www.mckinsey.com/insights/organization/motivating_people_getting_beyond_money

89. Kanfer, R., & Chen, G. (2016). Motivation in organizational behavior: History, advances and prospects. *Organizational Behavior and Human Decision Processes, 136*, 6–19.

90. Ambrose, M. L., & Kulik, C. T. (1999). Old friends, new faces: Motivation in the 1990s. *Journal of Management, 25*(3), 231–292. (Quotation on p. 240.)

91. Porter, L. W., & Lawler, E. E., III. (1968). *Managerial attitudes and performance.* Homewood, IL: Irwin.

92. Vroom, V. H. (1964). *Work and motivation.* New York, NY: Wiley.

93. Ibid.

94. Mitchell, T. R. (1974). Expectancy models of job satisfaction, occupational preference and effort: A theoretical, methodological, and empirical appraisal. *Psychological Bulletin, 81*(12), 1053–1077.

95. Van Eerde, W., & Thierry, H. (1996). Vroom's expectancy models and work-related criteria: A meta-analysis. *Journal of Applied Psychology, 81*(5), 575–586.

96. Bandura, A. (1994). *Self-efficacy.* New York, NY: Wiley.

97. Pinder, C. C. (1991). Valence-instrumentality-expectancy theory. *Motivation and work behavior*, 144–164.

98. Bono, J. E., & Judge, T. A. (2003). Self-concordance at work: Toward understanding the motivational effects of transformational leaders. *Academy of Management Journal, 46*(5), 554–571.

99. Rosenthal, R., & Jacobson, L. (1968). *Pygmalion in the classroom: Teacher expectation and pupils' intellectual development.* New York, NY: Holt, Rinehart & Winston.

100. Riggio, R. E. (2009). Pygmalion leadership: The power of positive expectations. Retrieved from http://www.psychologytoday.com/blog/cutting-edge-leadership/200904/pygmalion-leadership-the-power-positive-expectations

101. Eden, D. (1993). Leadership and expectations: Pygmalion effects and other self-fulfilling prophecies in organizations. *Leadership Quarterly, 3*(4), 271–305.

102. Bezuijen, X. M., van den Berg, P. T., van Dam, K., & Thierry, H. (2009). Pygmalion and employee learning: The role of leader behaviors. *Journal of Management, 35*(5), 248–267.

103. Eden, D., & Shani, A. B. (1982). Pygmalion goes to boot camp: Expectancy, leadership, and trainee performance. *Journal of Applied Psychology, 67*(2) 194–199.

104. McNatt, D. B. (2000). Ancient Pygmalion joins contemporary management: A meta-analysis of the result. *Journal of Applied Psychology, 85*(2), 314–322.

105. Davidson, O. B., & Eden, D. (2000). Remedial self-fulfilling prophecy: Two field experiments to prevent Golem effects among disadvantaged women. *Journal of Applied Psychology, 85*(3), 386–398.

106. Nanatovich, G., & Eden, D. (2008). Pygmalion effects among outreach

supervisors and tutors: Extending sex generalizability. *Journal of Applied Psychology, 93*(6), 1382–1389.

107. Rosenthal, R. (1973). The mediation of Pygmalion effects: A four factor "theory." *Papua New Guinea Journal of Education, 9,* 1–12.
108. McNatt, D. B., & Judge, T. A. (2004). Boundary conditions of the Galatea Effect: A field experiment and constructive replication. *Academy of Management Journal, 47*(4), 550–565.
109. Manzoni, J. F., & Barsoux, J. L. (1997). The set-up-to-fail syndrome. *Harvard Business Review, 76*(2), 101–113.
110. Davidson, O. B., & Eden, D. (2000). Remedial self-fulfilling prophecy: Two field experiments to prevent Golem effects among disadvantaged women. *Journal of Applied Psychology, 85*(3), 386–398.

111. Oz, S., & Eden, D. (1994). Restraining the Golem: Boosting performance by changing the interpretation of low scores. *Journal of Applied Psychology, 79*(5), 744–754.
112. Chan, K. Y., & Drasgow, F. (2001). Toward a theory of individual differences and leadership: Understanding the motivation to lead. *Journal of Applied Psychology, 86*(3), 481–498. (Quotation on p. 482.)
113. Ibid.
114. Kark, R., & Van Dijk, D. (2007). Motivation to lead, motivation to follow: The role of the self-regulatory focus in leadership processes. *Academy of Management Review, 32*(2), 500–528.
115. Hong, Y., Catano, V. M., & Liao, H. (2011). Leader emergence: The role of emotional intelligence and motivation to lead. *Leadership & Organization Development Journal, 32*(4), 320–343.

116. Luria, G., & Berson, Y. (2013). How do leadership motives affect informal and formal leadership emergence? *Journal of Organizational Behavior, 34*(7), 995–1015.
117. Hendricks, J. W., & Payne, S. C. (2007). Beyond the Big Five: Leader goal orientation as a predictor of leadership effectiveness. *Human Performance, 20,* 317–343.
118. DeRue, D. S., & Ashford, S. J. (2010). Who will lead and who will follow? A social process of leadership identity construction in organizations. *Academy of Management Review, 35*(4), 627–647.
119. Guillén, L., Mayo, M., & Korotov, K. (2015). Is leadership a part of me? A leader identity approach to understanding the motivation to lead. *Leadership Quarterly, 26*(5), 802–820.

Chapter 9

1. Kube, S., Maréchal, M. A., & Puppe, C. (2012). The currency of reciprocity: Gift-exchange in the workplace. *American Economic Review, 102*(4), 1644–1662.
2. Gilchrist, D. S., Luca, M., & Malhotra, D. (2016). When 3+ 1> 4: Gift structure and reciprocity in the field. *Management Science, 62*(9), 2639–2650.
3. Tang, T. L. P. (1992). The meaning of money revisited. *Journal of Organizational Behavior, 13*(2), 197–202.
4. Thorndike, E. L. (1911). *Animal intelligence.* New York, NY: Macmillan.
5. Skinner, B. F. (1971). *Contingencies of reinforcement.* East Norwalk, CT: Appleton-Century-Crofts.
6. Latham, G. P., & Huber, V. L. (1991). Schedules of reinforcement: Lessons from the past and issues for the future. *Journal of Organizational Behavior Management, 12*(1), 125–149.
7. Pinder, C. (2008). *Work motivation in organizational behavior.* New York, NY: Psychology Press.
8. Komacki, J. L., Coombs, T., & Schepman, S. (1996). Motivational implications of reinforcement theory. In R. M. Steers, L. W. Porter, & G. Bigley (Eds.), *Motivation and work*

behavior (6th ed., pp. 87–107). New York, NY: McGraw-Hill.
9. Conard, A. L., Johnson, D. A., Morrison, J. D., & Ditzian, K. (2016). Tactics to ensure durability of behavior change following the removal of an intervention specialist: A review of temporal generality within Organizational Behavior Management. *Journal of Organizational Behavior Management, 36*(2-3), 210–253.
10. Welsh, D. H. B., Luthans, F., & Sommer, S. M. (1993). Organizational behavior modification goes to Russia: Replicating an experimental analysis across cultures and tasks. *Journal of Organizational Behavior Management, 13*(2), 15–35.
11. Stajkovic, A. D., & Luthans, F. (1997). A meta-analysis of the effects of organizational behavior modification on task performance, 1975–95. *Academy of Management Journal, 40*(5), 1122–1149.
12. Locke, E. A. (1980). Latham vs. Komaki: A tale of two paradigms. *Journal of Applied Psychology, 65*(1), 16–23.
13. Bandura, A. (1977). *Social learning theory.* Upper Saddle River, NJ: Prentice Hall.
14. Porter, L. W., & Lawler, E. E. III. (1968). *Managerial attitudes and performance.* Homewood, IL: Irwin-Dorsey.

15. Vroom, V. H. (1964). *Work and motivation.* New York, NY: John Wiley.
16. Porter, L. W., & Lawler, E. E. III. (1968). *Managerial attitudes and performance.* Homewood, IL: Irwin-Dorsey.
17. Barbuto, J. E., Jr., & Scholl, R. W. (1998). Motivation sources inventory: Development and validation of new scales to measure an integrative taxonomy of motivation. *Psychological Reports, 82*(3), 1011–1022.
18. Deci, E. L. (1972). Intrinsic motivation, extrinsic reinforcement, and inequity. *Journal of Personality and Social Psychology, 22*(1), 113–120.
19. Deci, E. L., Connell, J. P., & Ryan, R. M. (1989). Self-determination in a work organization. *Journal of Applied Psychology, 74*(4), 580–590.
20. Amabile, T. M. (1993). Motivational synergy: Toward new conceptualizations of intrinsic and extrinsic motivation in the workplace. *Human Resource Management Review, 3*(3), 185–201.
21. Leong, K. C. (2013). Google reveals its 9 principles of innovation. Retrieved from http://www.fastcompany.com/3021956/how-to-be-a-success-at-everything/googles-nine-principles-of-innovation

22. Deci, E. L., Connell, J. P., & Ryan, R. M. (1989). Self-determination in a work organization. *Journal of Applied Psychology, 74*(4), 580–590.

23. Gilson, L. L., & Madjar, N. (2011). Radical and incremental creativity: Antecedents and processes. *Psychology of Aesthetics, Creativity and the Arts, 5*, 21–28.

24. Cerasoli, C. P., Nicklin, J. M., & Ford, M. T. (2014). Intrinsic motivation and extrinsic incentives jointly predict performance: A 40-year meta-analysis. *Psychological Bulletin, 140*(4), 980–1008.

25. Deci, E. L., Koestner, R., & Ryan, R. M. (1999). A meta-analytic review of experiments examining the effects of extrinsic rewards on intrinsic motivation. *Psychological Bulletin, 125*(6), 627–668.

26. Deci, E. L., & Ryan, R. M. (1985). *Intrinsic motivation and self-determination in human behavior.* New York, NY: Plenum.

27. Van den Broeck, A., Ferris, D. L., Chang, C. H., & Rosen, C. C. (2016). A review of self-determination theory's basic psychological needs at work. *Journal of Management, 42*(5), 1195–1229.

28. Koestner, R., Ryan, R. M., Bernieri, F., & Holt, K. (1984). Setting limits on children's behavior: The differential effects of controlling versus informational styles on intrinsic motivation and creativity. *Journal of Personality, 52*(3), 233–248.

29. Deci, E. L., Connell, J. P., & Ryan, R. M. (1989). Self-determination in a work organization. *Journal of Applied Psychology, 74*(4), 580–590.

30. Gagné, M., & Deci, E. L. (2005). Self-determination theory and work motivation. *Journal of Organizational Behavior, 26*(4), 331–362.

31. Aguinis, H., Joo, H., & Gottfredson, R. K. (2013). What monetary rewards can and cannot do: How to show employees the money. *Business Horizons, 56*(2), 241–259.

32. Brown, M. P., Sturman, M. C., & Simmering, M. J. (2003). Compensation policy and organizational performance: The efficiency, operational, and financial implications of pay levels and pay structure. *Academy of Management Journal, 46*(6), 752–762.

33. Kerr, S. (2009). *Reward systems: Does yours measure up?* Cambridge, MA: Harvard Business School Press.

34. Aguinis, H., Joo, H., & Gottfredson, R. K. (2013). What monetary rewards can and cannot do: How to show employees the money. *Business Horizons, 56*(2), 241–259.

35. Ibid.

36. Rynes, S. L., Gerhart, B., & Park, L. (2005). Personnel psychology: Performance evaluation and pay for performance. *Annual Review of Psychology, 56*, 571–600.

37. Viswesvaran, C., & Ones, D. (2000). Perspectives on models of job performance. *International Journal of Selection and Assessment, 8*(4), 216–226. (Quotation on p. 224.)

38. Cascio, W. F., & Aguinis, H. (2010). *Applied psychology in human resource management* (7th ed.). Upper Saddle River, NJ: Prentice Hall.

39. Heidemeier, H., & Moser, K. (2009). Self-other agreement in job performance ratings: A meta-analytic test of a process model. *Journal of Applied Psychology, 94*(2), 353–370.

40. Atwater, L. E., Brett, J. F., & Charles, A. C. (2007). Multisource feedback: Lessons learned and implications for practice. *Human Resource Management, 46*(2), 285–307.

41. Brett, J. F., & Atwater, L. E. (2001). 360° feedback: Accuracy, reactions, and perceptions of usefulness. *Journal of Applied Psychology, 86*(5), 930–942.

42. Fedor, D. B., Bettenhausen, K. L., & Davis, W. (1999). Peer reviews: Employees' dual roles as raters and recipients. *Group and Organization Management, 24*(1), 92–120.

43. Ng, K., Koh, C., Ang, S., Kennedy, J. C., & Chan, K. (2011). Rating leniency and halo in multisource feedback ratings: Testing cultural assumptions of power distance and individualism-collectivism. *Journal of Applied Psychology, 96*(5), 1033–1044.

44. Caruso, J. (2011). Case study: Starwood Hotels takes 360-degree feedback to a new level. Retrieved from http://web.viapeople.com/viaPeople-blog/bid/65018/Case-Study-Starwood-Hotels-Takes-360-Degree-Feedback-to-a-New-Level

45. Locher, A. H., & Teel, K. S. (1988, September). Appraisal trends. *Personnel Journal,* 139–145.

46. Kerr, S. (2009). *Reward systems: Does yours measure up?* Cambridge, MA: Harvard Business School Press.

47. McGregor, J. (2013). For whom the bell curve tolls. Retrieved from http://www.washingtonpost.com/blogs/on-leadership/wp/2013/11/20/for-whom-the-bell-curve=tolls

48. Mount, M. K., & Scullen, S. E. (2001). Multisource feedback ratings: What do they really measure? In M. London (Ed.), *How people evaluate others in organizations* (pp. 155–176). Mahwah, NJ: Erlbaum.

49. Murphy, K. R., & Balzer, W. K. (1989). Rater errors and rating accuracy. *Journal of Applied Psychology, 74*(4), 619–624.

50. Ng, K., Koh, C., Ang, S., Kennedy, J. C., & Chan, K. (2011). Rating leniency and halo in multisource feedback ratings: Testing cultural assumptions of power distance and individualism-collectivism. *Journal of Applied Psychology, 96*(5), 1033–1044.

51. Rynes, S. L., Gerhart, B., & Park, L. (2005). Personnel psychology: Performance evaluation and pay for performance. *Annual Review of Psychology, 56*, 571–600.

52. Kerr, S. (2009). *Reward systems: Does yours measure up?* Cambridge, MA: Harvard Business School Press.

53. Gallo, A. (2013). How to make a job sharing situation work. Retrieved from https://hbr.org/2013/09/how-to-make-a-job-sharing-situation-work

54. de Menezes, L. M., & Kelliher, C. (2016). Flexible working, individual performance and employee attitudes: Comparing formal and informal arrangements. *Human Resource Management.* doi:10.1002/hrm.21822

55. Shen, L. (2016). These 19 great employers offer paid sabbaticals. Retrieved from http://fortune.com/2016/03/07/best-companies-to-work-for-sabbaticals//

56. Boswell, W. R., & Boudreau, J. W. (2002). Separating the developmental and evaluative performance appraisal uses. *Journal of Business Psychology, 16*(3), 391–412.

57. Culbertson, S. S., Henning, J. B., & Payne, S. C. (2013). Performance

appraisal satisfaction. *Journal of Personnel Psychology, 12*(4), 189–195.

58. Deming, W. E. (1986). *Out of the crisis.* Cambridge, MA: MIT Center for Advanced Engineering Study.

59. Pfeffer, J. (1998). Six dangerous myths about pay. *Harvard Business Review, 76*(3), 108–120.

60. Cable, D. M., & Judge T. A. (1994). Pay preferences and job search decisions: A person-organization fit perspective. *Personnel Psychology, 47*(2), 317–348.

61. Trevor, C. O., Gerhart B., & Boudreau, J. W. (1997). Voluntary turnover and job performance: Curvilinearity and the moderating influences of salary growth and promotions. *Journal of Applied Psychology, 82*(1), 44–61.

62. Rynes, S. L., Gerhart, B., & Park, L. (2005). Personnel psychology: Performance evaluation and pay for performance. *Annual Review of Psychology, 56*, 571–600.

63. Ramirez, J. C. (2013). Rethinking the review: After 50 years of debate, has the time come to chuck the performance review? Retrieved from www.hronline.com/HRE/view/story.jhtmal?id=534355695&

64. McGregor, J. (2013). For whom the bell curve tolls. Retrieved from http://www.washingtonpost.com/blogs/on-leadership/wp/2013/11/20/for-whom-the-bell-curve=tolls

65. Ramirez, J. C. (2013). Rethinking the review: After 50 years of debate, has the time come to chuck the performance review? Retrieved from www.hronline.com/HRE/view/story.jhtmal?id=534355695&

66. Morris, D. (2013). Forget reviews, let's look forward. Retrieved from http://blogs.adobe.com/conversations/tag/donna-morris

67. Bersin, J. (2013). Is it time to scrap performance appraisals? Retrieved from http://www.forbes.com/sites/joshbersin/2013/05/06/time-to-scrap-performance-appraisals

68. Ewenstein, B., Hancock, B., & Komm, A. (2016). Ahead of the curve: The future of performance management. Retrieved from http://www.mckinsey.com/business-functions/organization/our-insights/ahead-of-the-curve-the-future-of-performance-management

69. Romero, J. L. (2016, May). Re-examine perspective on performance appraisals: Design and rename process with a focus on helping employees grow. *Healthcare Registration, 7–8.*

70. Silver, E. (2016). 8 tips for successful performance management. Retrieved from http://www.hrreporter.com/article/28069-8-tips-for-successful-performance-management

71. Ashford, S. J., & Cummings, L. L. (1983). Feedback as an individual resource: Personal strategies of creating information. *Organizational Behavior and Human Performance, 32*(3), 370–398.

72. Ashford, S. J., Blatt, R., & Vandewalle, D. (2003). Reflections on the looking glass: A review of research on feedback-seeking behavior in organizations. *Journal of Management, 29*(6), 773–779.

73. Pichler, S., Varma, A., Michel, J. S., Levy, P. E., Budhwar, P. S., & Sharma, A. (2016). Leader-member exchange, group- and individual-level procedural justice and reactions to performance appraisals. *Human Resource Management, 55*(5), 871–883.

74. Ibid., p. 880.

75. Levy, P. E., & Williams, J. R. (2004). The social context of performance appraisal: A review and framework for the future. *Journal of Management, 30*(6), 881–905.

76. Elicker, J. D., Levy, P. E., & Hall, R. J. (2006). The role of leader-member exchange in the performance appraisal process. *Journal of Management, 32*(4), 531–551.

77. Mani, B. G. (2002). Performance appraisal systems, productivity, and motivation: A case study. *Public Personnel Management, 31*(2), 141–159.

78. Buckingham, M., & Goodall, A. (2015). Reinventing performance management. Retrieved from https://hbr.org/2015/04/reinventing-performance-management

79. Ewenstein, B., Hancock, B., & Komm, A. (2016). Ahead of the curve: The future of performance management. Retrieved from http://www.mckinsey.com/business-functions/organization/our-insights/ahead-of-the-curve-the-future-of-performance-management

80. Wright, G. (2015). Employee feedback apps on the rise. Retrieved from https://www.shrm.org/resourcesandtools/hr-topics/technology/pages/employee-feedback-apps.aspx

81. Council of Economic Advisors. (2016, January). The gender pay gap on the anniversary of the Lilly Ledbetter Fair Pay Act. Retrieved from: http://digitalcommons.ilr.cornell.edu/key_workplace/1580/

Chapter 10

1. De Jong, B. A., Dirks, K. T., & Gillespie, N. (2016). Trust and team performance: A meta-analysis of main effects, moderators, and covariates. *Journal of Applied Psychology, 101*(8), 1134–1150.

2. Mathieu, J. E., Hollenbeck, J. R., van Knippenberg, D., & Ilgen, D. R. (2017). A century of work teams in the Journal of Applied Psychology. *Journal of Applied Psychology, 102*(3), 452–467.

3. Ibid.

4. Cross, R., Rebele, R., & Grant, A. (2016). Collaboration overload. Retrieved from https://hbr.org/2016/01/collaborative-overload

5. Gostick, A., & Elton, C. (2010). *The orange revolution: How one great team can transform an entire organization.* New York, NY: Free Press.

6. Katzenbach, J. R., & Smith, D. K. (1993). *The wisdom of teams: Creating the high-performance organization.* New York, NY: Harper Business. (Quotation on p. 45.)

7. Kozlowski, S. W. J., & Ilgen, D. R. (2006). Enhancing the effectiveness of work groups and teams. *Psychological Science in the Public Interest, 7*, 77–124. (Quotation on p. 79.)

8. Katzenbach, J. R., & Smith, D. K. (1993). *The wisdom of teams: Creating the high-performance organization.* New York, NY: Harper Business.

9. Ibid.

10. Weldon, E., & Weingart, L. R. (1993). Group goals and group performance. *British Journal of Social Psychology, 32*(4), 307–334.

11. DeShon, R. P., Kozlowski, S. W., Schmidt, A. M., Milner, K. R., & Wiechmann, D. (2004). A multiple-goal,

multilevel model of feedback effects on the regulation of individual and team performance. *Journal of Applied Psychology, 89*(6), 1035–1056.

12. Hogg, M. A., & Reid, S. A. (2006). Social identity, self-categorization, and the communication of group norms. *Communication Theory, 16*(1), 7–30.

13. Duhigg, C. (2016). What Google learned from its quest to build the perfect team. Retrieved from https://www.nytimes.com/2016/02/28/magazine/what-google-learned-from-its-quest-to-build-the-perfect-team.html?_r=0

14. Mathieu, J. E., & Rapp, T. L. (2009). Laying the foundation for successful team performance trajectories: The roles of team charters and performance strategies. *Journal of Applied Psychology, 94*(1), 90–103.

15. Mohammed, S., Ferzandi, L., & Hamilton, K. (2010). Metaphor no more: A 15-year review of the team mental model construct. *Journal of Management, 36*(4), 876–910. (Quotation on p. 897.)

16. Klimoski, R., & Mohammed, S. (1994). Team mental model: Construct or metaphor? *Journal of Management, 20*(2), 403–437.

17. Rouse, W. B., Cannon-Bowers, J. A., & Salas, E. (1992). The role of mental models in team performance in complex systems. *IEEE Transactions on Systems, Man, & Cybernetics, 22,* 1296–1308.

18. Mohammed, S., Ferzandi, L., & Hamilton, K. (2010). Metaphor no more: A 15-year review of the team mental model construct. *Journal of Management, 36*(4), 876–910.

19. DeChurch, L. A., & Mesmer-Magnus, J. R. (2010). The cognitive underpinnings of effective teamwork: A meta-analysis. *Journal of Applied Psychology, 95*(1), 32–53.

20. Tuckman, B. (1965). Developmental sequence in small groups. *Psychological Bulletin, 63,* 384–399.

21. Tuckman, B., & Jensen, M. (1977). Stages of small group development. *Group and Organizational Studies, 2,* 419–427.

22. Gersick, C. J. G. (1988). Time and transition in work teams: Toward a new model of group development. *Academy of Management Journal, 31*(1), 9–41.

23. Seers, A., & Woodruff, S. (1997). Temporal pacing in task forces: Group development or deadline pressure? *Journal of Management, 23*(2), 169–187.

24. Katzenbach, J. R., & Smith, D. K. (1993). *The wisdom of teams: Creating the high-performance organization.* New York, NY: Harper Business.

25. Webber, S. S., & Webber, D. S. (2015). Launching and leading intense teams. *Business Horizons, 58*(4), 449–457.

26. Sharp, J., Hides, M., Bamber, C., & Castka, P. (2000). Continuous organisational learning through the development of high performance teams. Retrieved from http://citeseerx.ist.psu.edu/viewdoc/download?doi=10.1.1.92.3903&rep=rep1&type=pdf

27. McGrath, J. E. (1984). *Groups: Interaction and performance* (Vol. 14). Englewood Cliffs, NJ: Prentice Hall.

28. Barrick, M. R., Stewart, G. L., Neubert, M. J., & Mount, M. K. (1998). Relating member ability and personality to work-team processes and team effectiveness. *Journal of Applied Psychology, 83*(3), 377–391.

29. Edmondson, A. (1999). Psychological safety and learning behavior in work teams. *Administrative Science Quarterly, 44*(2), 350–383.

30. Marks, M. A., Sabella, M. J., Burke, C. S., & Zaccaro, S. J. (2002). The impact of cross-training on team effectiveness. *Journal of Applied Psychology, 87*(1), 3–13.

31. Hackman, J. R. (1987). The design of work teams. In J. W. Lorsch (Ed.), *Handbook of organizational behavior* (pp. 315–342). Englewood Cliffs, NJ: Prentice Hall.

32. Cohen, S. G., & Bailey, D. E. (1997). What makes teams work: Group effectiveness research from the shop floor to the executive suite. *Journal of Management, 23*(3), 239–290.

33. Li, N., Zhao, H. H., Walter, S. L., Zhang, X. A., & Yu, J. (2015). Achieving more with less: Extra milers' behavioral influences in teams. *Journal of Applied Psychology, 100*(4), 1025–1039.

34. LePine, J. A., Piccolo, R. F., Jackson, C. L., Mathieu, J. E., & Saul, J. R. (2008). A meta-analysis of teamwork processes: Tests of a multidimensional model and relationships with team effectiveness criteria. *Personnel Psychology, 61*(2), 273–307.

35. Katzenbach, J. R., & Smith, D. K. (1993). *The wisdom of teams: Creating the high-performance organization.* New York, NY: Harper Business.

36. Senge, P. M. (1990). *The fifth discipline: The art and practice of the learning organization.* New York, NY: Currency Doubleday. (Quotation on p. 13.)

37. Argote, L., Gruenfeld, D., & Naquin, C. (2001). Group learning in organizations. In M. E. Turner (Ed.), *Groups at work: Theory and research* (pp. 369–409). Mahwah, NJ: Erlbaum.

38. Edmondson, A. (1999). Psychological safety and learning behavior in work teams. *Administrative Science Quarterly, 44*(2), 350–383.

39. Pearsall, M. J., & Venkataramani, V. (2015). Overcoming asymmetric goals in teams: The interactive roles of team learning orientation and team identification. *Journal of Applied Psychology, 100*(3), 735–748.

40. Lankau, M. J., & Scandura, T. A. (2002). An investigation of personal learning in mentoring relationships: Content, antecedents, and consequences. *Academy of Management Journal, 45,* 779–790. (Quotation on p. 780.)

41. Jiang, Y., Jackson, S. E., & Colakoglu, S. (2015). An empirical examination of personal learning within the context of teams. *Journal of Organizational Behavior, 37,* 654–672.

42. Kostopoulos, K. C., Spanos, Y. E., & Prastacos, G. P. (2013). Structure and function of team learning emergence: A multilevel empirical validation. *Journal of Management, 39*(6), 1430–1461.

43. Edmondson, A. (1999). Psychological safety and learning behavior in work teams. *Administrative Science Quarterly, 44*(2), 350–383.

44. Kurtzberg, T. R., & Amabile, T. M. (2001). From Guilford to creative synergy: Opening the black box of team level creativity. *Creativity Research Journal, 13*(4), 285–294.

45. Wuchty, S., Jones, B. F., & Uzzi, B. (2007). The increasing dominance of teams in production of knowledge. *Science, 316*(5827), 1036–1039.

46. Gilson, L. L., & Shalley, C. E. (2004). A little creativity goes a long way: An examination of teams' engagement in creative processes. *Journal of Management, 30*(4), 453–470.

47. Gilson, L. L. (2001). *Diversity, dissimilarity and creativity: Does group composition or being different enhance or hinder creative performance.* Academy of Management Meetings, Washington, DC.

48. Madrid, H. P., Totterdell, P., Niven, K., & Barros, E. (2016). Leader affective presence and innovation in teams. *Journal of Applied Psychology*, 101(5), 673–686.

49. To, M. L., Herman, H. M., & Ashkanasy, N. M. (2015). A multilevel model of transformational leadership, affect, and creative process behavior in work teams. *Leadership Quarterly*, 26(4), 543–556.

50. Gilson, L. L., & Shalley, C. E. (2004). A little creativity goes a long way: An examination of teams' engagement in creative processes. *Journal of Management*, 30(4), 453–470.

51. Vera, D., Nemanich, L., Vélez-Castrillón, S., & Werner, S. (2016). Knowledge-based and contextual factors associated with R&D teams' improvisation capability. *Journal of Management*, 42(7), 1874–1903.

52. Edmondson, A. C., & Harvey, J. F. (2017). Cross-boundary teaming for innovation: Integrating research on teams and knowledge in organizations. *Human Resource Management Review.* http://dx.doi.org/10.1016/j.hrmr.2017.03.002

53. Gumusluoglu, L., Karakitapoğlu-Aygün, Z., & Scandura, T. A. (in press). Benevolent leadership and innovative behavior in R&D contexts: A social identity approach. *Journal of Leadership & Organizational Studies.*

54. Mathieu, J., Maynard, M.T., Rapp, T., & Gilson, L. (2008). Team effectiveness 1997–2007: A review of recent advancements and a glimpse into the future. *Journal of Management*, 34(3), 410–476.

55. Festinger, L. (1950). Informal social communication. *Psychological Review*, 57, 271–282. (Quotation on p. 274.)

56. Tekleab, A. G., Quigley, N. R., & Tesluk, P. E. (2009). A longitudinal study of team conflict, conflict management, cohesion, and team effectiveness. *Group & Organization Management*, 34, 170–205.

57. Evans, C. R., & Jarvis, P. A. (1980). Group cohesion: A review and re-evaluation. *Small Group Behavior*, 11, 359–370.

58. De Cooman, R., Vantilborgh, T., Bal, M., & Lub, X. (2016). Creating inclusive teams through perceptions of supplementary and complementary person–team fit: Examining the relationship between person–team fit and team effectiveness. *Group & Organization Management*, 41(3), 310–342.

59. Drescher, S., Burlingame, G., & Fuhriman, A. (2012). Cohesion: An odyssey in empirical understanding. *Small Group Research*, 43(6), 662–689.

60. Cartwright, D. (1968). The nature of group cohesiveness. In D. Cartwright & A. Zander (Eds.), *Group dynamics: Research and theory* (3rd ed., pp. 91–109). New York, NY: Harper & Row.

61. Rodríguez-Sánchez, A. M., Devloo, T., Rico, R., Salanova, M., & Anseel, F. (2016). What makes creative teams tick? Cohesion, engagement, and performance across creativity tasks a three-wave study. *Group & Organization Management*, 42(4), pp. 521–547.

62. Neal, D. J., Cohen, R. R., Burke, M. J., & McLendon, C. L. (2003). Cohesion and performance in groups: A meta-analytic clarification of construct relations. *Journal of Applied Psychology*, 88(6), 989–1004.

63. Gully, S. M., Devine, D. J., & Whitney, D. J. (1995). A meta-analysis of cohesion and performance: Effects of level of analysis and task interdependence. *Small Group Research*, 26(4), 497–520.

64. Evans, C. R., & Dion, K. L. (1991). Group cohesion and performance: A meta-analysis. *Small Group Research*, 22(2), 175–186.

65. Mathieu, J. E., Kukenberger, M. R., D'Innocenzo, L., & Reilly, G. (2015). Modeling reciprocal team cohesion–performance relationships, as impacted by shared leadership and members' competence. *Journal of Applied Psychology*, 100(3), 713–734.

66. Lee, C., & Fahr, J.-L. (2004). Joint effects of group efficacy and gender diversity on group cohesion and performance. *Applied Psychology: An International Review*, 53(1), 136–154.

67. Hogg, M. A. (2001). A social identity theory of leadership. *Personality and Social Psychology Review*, 5(3), 184–200.

68. Tajfel, H. (1972). Social categorization. English manuscript of 'La catégorisation sociale.' In S. Moscovici (Ed.), *Introduction à la Psychologie Sociale* (Vol. 1, pp. 272–302). Paris, France: Larousse. (Quotation on p. 292.)

69. Hogg, M. A., Terry, D. J., & White, K. M. (1995). A tale of two theories: A critical comparison of identity theory with social identity theory. *Social Psychology Quarterly*, 58(4), 255–269.

70. Ibid.

71. Ashforth, B. E., & Mael, F. (1989). Social identity theory and the organization. *Academy of Management Review*, 14(1), 20–39.

72. Van Knippenberg, D., & Hogg, M. A. (2003). A social identity model of leadership effectiveness in organizations. *Research in Organizational Behavior*, 25, 243–295.

73. Pescosolido, A. T., & Saavedra, R. (2012). Cohesion and sports teams: A review. *Small Group Research*, 43(6), 744–758.

74. Widmeyer, W. N., Carron, A. V., & Brawley, L. R. (1993). Group cohesion in sport and exercise. *Handbook of Research on Sport Psychology*, 672–692.

75. Jowett, S., & Chaundy, V. (2004). An investigation into the impact of coach leadership and coach-athlete relationship on group cohesion. *Group Dynamics: Theory, Research and Practice*, 8(4), 302–331.

76. Turman, P. D. (2003). Coaches and cohesion: The impact of coaching techniques on team cohesion in the small group sport setting. *Journal of Sport Behavior*, 26(1), 86–104.

77. Kim, H. D., & Cruz, A. B. (2016). The influence of coaches' leadership styles on athletes' satisfaction and team cohesion: A meta-analytic approach. *International Journal of Sports Science & Coaching*, 11(6), 900–909.

78. Janis, I. L. (1972). *Victims of groupthink: A psychological study of foreign-policy decisions and fiascoes.* Boston, MA: Houghton Mifflin.

79. Goncalo, J. A., Polman, E., & Maslach, C. (2010). Can confidence come too soon? Collective efficacy, conflict

and group performance over time. *Organizational Behavior and Human Decision Processes, 113*(1), 13–24.

80. Janis, I. L. (1972). *Victims of groupthink: A psychological study of foreign-policy decisions and fiascoes.* Boston, MA: Houghton Mifflin.

81. Esser, J. K. (1998). Alive and well after 25 years: A review of groupthink research. *Organizational Behavior and Human Decision Processes, 73*(2), 116–141.

82. Leana, C. R. (1985). A partial test of Janis' groupthink model: Effects of group cohesiveness and leader behavior on defective decision making. *Journal of Management, 11*(1), 5–18.

83. Moorhead, G., Ference, R., & Neck, C. P. (1991). Group decision fiascoes continue: Space shuttle *Challenger* and a revised groupthink framework. *Human Relations, 44*(6), 539–550.

84. Vroom, V. H., & Yetton, P. W. (1973). *Leadership and decision making.* Pittsburgh, PA: University of Pittsburgh Press.

85. Vroom, V. H. (2003). Educating managers for decision making and leadership. *Management Decision, 41*(10), 968–978.

86. Scully, J. A., Kirkpatrick, S. A., & Locke, E. A. (1995). Locus of knowledge as a determinant of the effects of participation on performance, affect, and perceptions. *Organizational Behavior and Human Decision Processes, 61*(3), 276–288.

87. Vroom, V. H., & Jago, A. G. (1988). *The new leadership: Managing participation in organizations.* Englewood Cliffs, NJ: Prentice Hall.

88. Vroom, V. H. (2003). Educating managers for decision making and leadership. *Management Decision, 41*(10), 968–978.

89. Miller, K. I., & Monge, P. R. (1986). Participation, satisfaction, and productivity: A meta-analytic review. *Academy of Management Journal, 29*(4), 727–753.

90. Wagner, J. A. (1994). Participation's effects on performance and satisfaction: A reconsideration of research evidence. *Academy of Management Review, 19*(2), 312–330.

91. Nutt, P. C. (2002). *Why decisions fail: Avoiding the blunders and traps that lead to debacles.* Williston, VT: Berrett-Koehler.

92. Osborn, A. F. (1979). *Applied imagination: Principles and procedures of creative thinking* (3rd ed.). New York, NY: Scribner.

93. Bressen, T. (2012). Consensus decision-making: What, why, how. In J. Orsi & J. Kassan (Eds.), *Practicing law in the sharing economy: Helping people build cooperatives, social enterprise, and local sustainable economies.* Chicago, IL: ABA Books.

94. Tague, N. R. (2004). *The quality toolbox* (2nd ed.). Milwaukee, WI: ASQ Quality Press.

95. Faure, C. (2004). Beyond brainstorming: Effects of different group procedures on selection of ideas and satisfaction with the process. *Journal of Creative Behavior, 38*(1), 13–34.

96. Delbecq, A. L., Van de Ven, A. H., & Gustafson, D. H. (1975). *Group techniques for program planning: A guide to nominal group and Delphi processes.* Glenview, IL: Scott, Foresman.

97. Mind Tools. (n.d.). The stepladder technique: Making better group decisions. Retrieved from http://www.mindtools.com/pages/article/newTED_89.htm#sthash.c6PFOpJh.dpuf

98. Rogelberg, S. G., Barnes-Farrell, J. L., & Lowe, C. A. (1992). The stepladder technique: An alternative group structure facilitating effective group decision making. *Journal of Applied Psychology, 77*(5), 730–737.

99. Comer, D. R. (1995). A model of social loafing in real work groups. *Human Relations, 48*(6), 647–667.

100. Liden, R. C., Wayne, S. J., Jaworski, R. A., & Bennett, N. (2004). Social loafing: A field investigation. *Journal of Management, 30*(2), 285–304.

101. Karau, S. J., & Williams, K. D. (1993). Social loafing: A meta-analytic review and theoretical integration. *Journal of Personality and Social Psychology, 65*(4), 681.

102. Martins, L. L., Gilson, L. L., & Maynard, M. T. (2004). Virtual teams: What do we know and where do we go from here?

Journal of Management, 30(6), 805–835. (Quotation on p. 807.)

103. Maynard, M. T., & Gilson, L. L. (2014). The role of shared mental model development in understanding virtual team effectiveness. *Group & Organization Management, 39*(1), 3–32.

104. Hollingshead, A. B., McGrath, J. E., & O'Connor, K. M. (1993). Group task performance and communication technology: A longitudinal study of computer-mediated versus face-to-face work groups. *Small Group Research, 24*(3), 307–333.

105. Charlier, S. D., Stewart, G. L., Greco, L. M., & Reeves, C. J. (2016). Emergent leadership in virtual teams: A multilevel investigation of individual communication and team dispersion antecedents. *Leadership Quarterly, 27*(5), 745–764.

106. Hollingshead, A. B., & McGrath, J. E. (1995). Computer-assisted groups: A critical review of the empirical research. In R. A. Guzzo & E. Salas (Eds.), *Team effectiveness and decision making in organizations* (pp. 46–78). San Francisco, CA: Jossey-Bass.

107. Liu, Y. C., & Li, F. C. (2012). Exploration of social capital and knowledge sharing: An empirical study on student virtual teams. *International Journal of Distance Education Technologies, 10*, 17–38.

108. Wilson, J. M., Straus, S. G., & McEvily, B. (2006). All in due time: The development of trust in computer-mediated and face-to-face teams. *Organizational Behavior and Human Decision Processes, 99*(1), 16–33.

109. Mesmer-Magnus, J. R., & DeChurch, L. A. (2009). Information sharing and team performance: A meta-analysis. *Journal of Applied Psychology, 94*(2), 535–546.

110. Griffith, T. L., Sawyer, J. E., & Neale, M. A. (2003). Virtualness and knowledge in teams: Managing the love triangle of organizations, individuals, and information technology. *MIS Quarterly, 27*(2), 265–287.

111. Gilson, L. L., Maynard, M. T., Young, N. C. J., Vartiainen, M., & Hakonen, M. (2015). Virtual teams research 10 years, 10 themes, and 10 opportunities. *Journal of Management, 41*(5), 1313–1337.

112. Carte, T. A., Chidambaram, L., & Becker, A. (2006). Emergent leadership in self-managed virtual teams. *Group Decision and Negotiation, 15*(4), 323–343.

113. Malhotra, A., Majchrzak, A., & Rosen, B. (2007). Leading virtual teams. *Academy of Management Perspectives, 21*(1), 60–70.

114. Brahm, T., & Kunze, F. (2012). The role of trust climate in virtual teams. *Journal of Managerial Psychology, 27,* 595–614.

115. Avolio, B. J., Kahai, S., & Dodge, G. E. (2001). E-leadership: Implications for theory, research, and practice. *Leadership Quarterly, 11*(4), 615–668.

116. Mayo, M., Kakarika, M., Mainemelis, C., & Deuschel, N. T. (2016). A metatheoretical framework of diversity in teams. *Human Relations, 70*(8), 911–939. http://dx.doi.org/10.1177%2F0018726716679246

117. Kirkman, B. L., & Shapiro, D. L. (2001). The impact of cultural values on job satisfaction and organizational commitment in self-managing work teams: The mediating role of employee resistance. *Academy of Management Journal, 44*(3), 557–569.

118. Elenkov, D. S. (1998). Can American management concepts work in Russia? *California Management Review, 40*(4), 133–156.

119. Nicholls, C. E., Lane, H. W., & Brechu, M. B. (1999). Taking self-managed teams to Mexico. *Academy of Management Executive, 13*(3), 15–25.

120. Cheng, C. Y., Chua, R. Y., Morris, M. W., & Lee, L. (2012). Finding the right mix: How the composition of self-managing multicultural teams' cultural value orientation influences performance over time. *Journal of Organizational Behavior, 33*(3), 389–411.

121. Ibid.

122. Gassmann, O. (2001). Multicultural teams: Increasing creativity and innovation by diversity. *Creativity and Innovation Management, 10*(2), 88–95.

123. Lisak, A., Erez, M., Sui, Y., & Lee, C. (2016). The positive role of global leaders in enhancing multicultural team innovation. *Journal of International Business Studies, 47*(6), 655–673.

124. Cox, T., & Blake, S. (1991). Managing cultural diversity: Implications for organizational competitiveness. *Academy of Management Executive, 5*(3), 45–56.

125. Horwitz, S. K., & Horwitz, I. B. (2007). The effects of team diversity on team outcomes: A meta-analytic review of team demography. *Journal of Management, 33*(6), 987–1015.

126. Stahl, G. K., Maznevski, M. L., Voigt, A., & Jonsen, K. (2009). Unraveling the effects of cultural diversity in teams: A meta-analysis of research on multicultural work groups. *Journal of International Business Studies, 41*(4), 690–709.

127. Egan, T. M. (2005). Creativity in the context of team diversity: Team leader perspectives. *Advances in Developing Human Resources, 7*(2), 207–225.

128. Homan, A. C., Buengeler, C., Eckhoff, R. A., van Ginkel, W. P., & Voelpel, S. C. (2015). The interplay of diversity training and diversity beliefs on team creativity in nationality diverse teams. *Journal of Applied Psychology, 100*(5), 1456–1467.

129. Kozlowski, S. W., Mak, S., & Chao, G. T. (2016). Team-centric leadership: An integrative review. *Annual Review of Organizational Psychology and Organizational Behavior, 3,* 21–54. (Quotation on p. 47.)

130. Kirkman, B. L., & Rosen, B. (1999). Beyond self-management: Antecedents and consequences of team empowerment. *Academy of Management Journal, 42*(1), 58–74.

131. Chen, G., Kirkman, B. L., Kanfer, R., Allen, D., & Rosen, B. (2007). A multilevel study of leadership, empowerment, and performance in teams. *Journal of Applied Psychology, 92*(2), 331–346.

132. Chiu, C. C., Owens, B. P., & Tesluk, P. E. (2016). Initiating and utilizing shared leadership in teams: The role of leader humility, team proactive personality, and team performance capability. *Journal of Applied Psychology, 101*(12), 1705–1720.

133. Lorinkova, N. M., & Perry, S. J. (2014). When is empowerment effective? The role of leader-leader exchange in empowering leadership, cynicism, and time theft. *Journal of Management, 43*(5), 1631–1654. http://dx.doi.org/10.1177%2F0149206314560411

134. Burke, C. S., Stagl, K. C., Klein, C., Goodwin, G. F., Salas, E., & Halpin, S. M. (2006). What type of leadership behaviors are functional in teams? A meta-analysis. *Leadership Quarterly, 17*(3), 288–307.

135. Hill, N. S., & Bartol, K. M. (2016). Empowering leadership and effective collaboration in geographically dispersed teams. *Personnel Psychology, 69*(1), 159–198.

136. Rapp, T. L., Gilson, L. L., Mathieu, J. E., & Ruddy, T. (2016). Leading empowered teams: An examination of the role of external team leaders and team coaches. *Leadership Quarterly, 27*(1), 109–123.

137. Erez, A., Lepine, J. A., & Elms, H. (2002). Effects of rotated leadership and peer evaluation on the functioning and effectiveness of self-managed teams: A quasi-experiment. *Personnel Psychology, 55*(4), 929–948.

138. Cordery, J. L., Mueller, W. S., & Smith, L. M. (1991). Attitudinal and behavioral effects of autonomous group working: A longitudinal field study. *Academy of Management Journal, 34*(2), 464–476.

139. Druskat, V. U., & Wheeler, J. V. (2003). Managing from the boundary: The effective leadership of self-managing work teams. *Academy of Management Journal, 46*(4), 435–457.

140. Langfred, C. W. (2007). The downside of self-management: A longitudinal study of the effects of conflict on trust, autonomy, and task interdependence in self-managing teams. *Academy of Management Journal, 50*(4), 885–900.

141. DeVaro, J. (2008). The effects of self-managed and closely managed teams on labor productivity and product quality: An empirical analysis of a cross-section of establishments. *Industrial Relations: A Journal of Economy and Society, 47*(4), 659–697.

142. Odermatt, I., König, C. J., Kleinmann, M., Nussbaumer, R., Rosenbaum, A., Olien, J. L., & Rogelberg, S. G. (2017). On leading meetings: Linking meeting outcomes to leadership styles. *Journal of Leadership & Organizational Studies, 24*(2), 189–200.

Chapter 11

1. Gavett, G. (2013). Research: What CEOs really want from coaching. Retrieved from http://blogs.hbr.org/2013/08/research-ceos-and-the-coaching

2. Thomas, K. W. (1992). Conflict and negotiation processes in organizations. In M. D. Dunnette & L. M. Hough (Eds.), *Handbook of industrial and organizational psychology* (2nd ed., Vol. 3, pp. 651–717). Palo Alto, CA: Consulting Psychologists Press. (Quotation on p. 653.)

3. Dirks, K. T., & McLean Parks, J. (2003). Conflicting stories: The state of the science of conflict. In J. Greenberg (Ed.), *Organizational behavior: The state of the science* (2nd ed., pp. 283–324). Mahwah, NJ: Erlbaum.

4. Maximum Advantage. (2013). Ten causes of interpersonal conflict. Retrieved from http://www.maximumadvantage.com/ten-causes-of-conflict.html

5. Tjosvold, D. (2006). Defining conflict and making choices about its management: Lighting the dark side of organizational life. *International Journal of Conflict Resolution, 17*(2), 87–95.

6. Robbins, S. P. (1978). "Conflict management" and "conflict resolution" are not synonymous terms. *California Management Review, 21*(2), 67–75.

7. Jehn, K. A., & Mannix, E. A. (2001). The dynamic nature of conflict: A longitudinal study of intragroup conflict and group performance. *Academy of Management Journal, 44*(2), 238–251.

8. Amason, A. C. (1996). Distinguishing the effects of functional and dysfunctional conflict on strategic decision making: Resolving a paradox for top management teams. *Academy of Management Journal, 39*(1), 123–148.

9. Todorova, G., Bear, J. B., & Weingart, L. R. (2014). Can conflict be energizing? A study of task conflict, positive emotions, and job satisfaction. *Journal of Applied Psychology, 99*(3), 451–467.

10. Jehn, K. A. (1995). A multimethod examination of the benefits and detriments of intragroup conflict.

11. Jehn, K. A. (1997). A qualitative analysis of conflict types and dimensions in organizational groups. *Administrative Science Quarterly, 42*(3), 530–557.

12. Power, D. J., & Mitra, A. (2016). Reducing "bad" strategic business decisions. *Drake Management Review, 5*(1/2), 15–31.

13. Schwenk, C. R. (1984). Devil's advocacy in managerial decision-making. *Journal of Management Studies, 21*(2), 153–168. (Quotation on p. 158.)

14. Davis, J. R. (2013). Improving students' critical thinking and classroom engagement by playing the devil's advocate. *Academy of Management Learning Education, 11*(2), 228–243.

15. Schweiger, D. M., Sandberg, W. R., & Ragan, J. R. (1987). Group approaches for improving strategic decision making: A comparative analysis of dialectical inquiry, devil's advocacy, and consensus. *Academy of Management Journal, 29*(1), 51–71.

16. Waddell, B. D., Roberto, M. A., & Yoon, S. (2013). Uncovering hidden profiles: Advocacy in team decision making. *Management Decision, 51*(2), 321–340.

17. De Dreu, C. K. W., & Weingart, L. R. (2003). Task versus relationship conflict, team performance, and team member satisfaction: A meta-analysis. *Journal of Applied Psychology, 88*(4), 741–749.

18. Sinha, R., Janardhanan, N. S., Greer, L. L., Conlon, D. E., & Edwards, J. R. (2016). Skewed task conflicts in teams: What happens when a few members see more conflict than the rest? *Journal of Applied Psychology, 101*(7), 1045–1055.

19. De Dreu, C. K. W., & Van de Vliert, E. (Eds.). (1997). *Using conflict in organizations.* Thousand Oaks, CA: Sage.

20. Nifadkar, S. S., & Bauer, T. N. (2016). Breach of belongingness: Newcomer relationship conflict, information, and task-related outcomes during organizational socialization. *Journal of Applied Psychology, 101*(1), 1–13.

21. Jung, E. J., & Lee, S. (2015). The combined effects of relationship conflict and the relational self on creativity. *Organizational Behavior and Human Decision Processes, 130*, 44–57.

22. Lin, C. P., & Chen, Y. F. (2016). Modeling team performance: The moderating role of passion. *Journal of Leadership & Organizational Studies, 23*(1), 96–107.

23. Schaeffner, M., Huettermann, H., Gebert, D., Boerner, S., Kearney, E., & Song, L. J. (2015). Swim or sink together: The potential of collective team identification and team member alignment for separating task and relationship conflicts. *Group & Organization Management, 40*(4), 467–499.

24. Yang, J., & Mossholder, K. W. (2004). Decoupling task and relationship conflict: The role of intragroup emotional processing. *Journal of Organizational Behavior, 25*(5), 589–605.

25. De Clercq, D., & Belausteguigoitia, I. (2017). Overcoming the dark side of task conflict: Buffering roles of transformational leadership, tenacity, and passion for work. *European Management Journal, 35*(1), 78–90.

26. Auh, S., Bowen, D. E., Aysuna, C., & Menguc, B. (2016). A search for missing links: Specifying the relationship between leader-member exchange differentiation and service climate. *Journal of Service Research, 19*(3), 260–275.

27. Eissa, G., & Wyland, R. (2016). Keeping up with the Joneses: The role of envy, relationship conflict, and job performance in social undermining. *Journal of Leadership & Organizational Studies, 23*(1), 55–65.

28. Cobb, A. T., & Lau, R. S. (2015). Trouble at the next level: Effects of differential leader–member exchange on group-level processes and justice climate. *Human Relations, 68*(9), 1437–1459.

29. Leon-Perez, J. M., Medina, F. J., Arenas, A., & Munduate, L. (2015). The relationship between interpersonal conflict and workplace bullying. *Journal of Managerial Psychology, 30*(3), 250–263.

30. Leymann, H. (1996). The content and development of mobbing at

Administrative Science Quarterly, 40(2), 256–282.

work. *European Journal of Work and Organizational Psychology, 5*(2), 165–184. (Quotation on p. 168.)

31. Andersson, L. M., & Pearson, C. M. (1999). Tit-for-tat? The spiraling effect of incivility in the workplace. *Academy of Management Review, 24*(3), 452–471. (Quotation on p. 457.)

32. Stork, E., & Hartley, N. T. (2011). Classroom incivilities: Students' perceptions about professors' behaviors. *Contemporary Issues in Education Research (CIER), 2*(4), 13–24.

33. Barling, J., Dupré, K. E., & Kelloway, E. K. (2009). Predicting workplace aggression and violence. *Annual Review of Psychology, 60,* 671–692.

34. Neuman, J. H., & Baron, R. A. (2005). Aggression in the workplace: A social-psychological perspective. In S. Fox & P. E. Spector (Eds.), *Counterproductive work behavior: Investigations of actors and targets* (pp. 13–40). Washington, DC: American Psychological Association. http://dx.doi.org/10.1037/10893-001

35. Vroom, V. H. (2003). Educating managers for decision making and leadership. *Management Decision, 41*(10), 968–978.

36. Miller, K. I., & Monge, P. R. (1986). Participation, satisfaction, and productivity: A meta-analytic review. *Academy of Management Journal, 29*(4), 727–753.

37. Wagner, J. A. (1994). Participation's effects on performance and satisfaction: A reconsideration of research evidence. *Academy of Management Review, 19*(2), 312–330.

38. Nutt, P. C. (2002). *Why decisions fail: Avoiding the blunders and traps that lead to debacles.* Williston, VT: Berrett-Koehler.

39. Osborn, A. F. (1979). *Applied imagination: Principles and procedures of creative thinking* (3rd ed.). New York, NY: Scribner.

40. Bressen, T. (2012). Consensus decision-making: What, why, how. In J. Orsi & J. Kassan (Eds.), *Practicing law in the sharing economy: Helping people build cooperatives, social enterprise, and local sustainable economies.* Chicago, IL: ABA Books.

41. Tague, N. R. (2004). *The quality toolbox* (2nd ed.). Milwaukee, WI: ASQ Quality Press.

42. Faure, C. (2004). Beyond brainstorming: Effects of different group procedures on selection of ideas and satisfaction with the process. *Journal of Creative Behavior, 38*(1), 13–34.

43. Delbecq, A. L., Van de Ven, A. H., & Gustafson, D. H. (1975). *Group techniques for program planning: A guide to nominal group and Delphi processes.* Glenview, IL: Scott, Foresman.

44. Mind Tools. (n.d.). The stepladder technique: Making better group decisions. Retrieved from http://www.mindtools.com/pages/article/newTED_89.htm#sthash.c6PFOpJh.dpuf

45. DeChurch, L. A., & Mesmer-Magnus, J. R. (2010). The cognitive underpinnings of effective teamwork: A meta-analysis. *Journal of Applied Psychology, 95*(1), 32–53.

46. Vroom, V. H., & Yetton, P. W. (1973). *Leadership and decision making.* Pittsburgh, PA: University of Pittsburgh Press.

47. Vroom, V. H. (2003). Educating managers for decision making and leadership. *Management Decision, 41*(10), 968–978.

48. Scully, J. A., Kirkpatrick, S. A., & Locke, E. A. (1995). Locus of knowledge as a determinant of the effects of participation on performance, affect, and perceptions. *Organizational Behavior and Human Decision Processes, 61*(3), 276–288.

49. Vroom, V. H., & Jago, A. G. (1988). *The new leadership: Managing participation in organizations.* Englewood Cliffs, NJ: Prentice Hall.

50. U.S. Department of Labor. (2014). DOL Workplace Violence Program. Retrieved from http://www.dol.gov/oasam/hrc/policies/dol-workplace-violence-program.htm

51. Barling, J. (1996). The prediction, experience, and consequences of workplace violence. In G. R. VandenBos & E. Q. Bulatao (Eds.), *Violence on the job: Identifying risks and developing solutions* (pp. 29–49). Washington, DC: American Psychological Association.

52. Springer, J. (1998, March 7). Worker kills 4 bosses, self at lottery headquarters. Retrieved from http://www.courant.com/breaking-news/hc-lottery-shooting-newington-1998-story.html

53. Barling, J., Dupré, K. E., & Kelloway, E. K. (2009). Predicting workplace aggression and violence. *Annual Review of Psychology, 60,* 671–692.

54. Pearson, C., Andersson, L., & Porath, C. (2000, Fall). Assessing and attacking workplace incivility. *Organizational Dynamics,* 123–137.

55. Pearson, C. M., & Porath, C. L. (2005). On the nature, consequences and remedies of workplace incivility: No time for "nice"? Think again. *Academy of Management Executive, 19*(1), 7–18.

56. Graydon, J., Kasta, W., & Khan, P. (1994, November–December). Verbal and physical abuse of nurses. *Canadian Journal of Nursing Administration,* 70–89.

57. Schilpzand, P., De Pater, I. E., & Erez, A. (2016). Workplace incivility: A review of the literature and agenda for future research. *Journal of Organizational Behavior, 37,* S57–S88.

58. Andersson, L. M., & Pearson, C. M. (1999). Tit-for-tat? The spiraling effect of incivility in the workplace. *Academy of Management Review, 24*(3), 452–471.

59. Lim, S., & Cortina, L. M. (2005). Interpersonal mistreatment in the workplace: The interface and impact of general incivility and sexual harassment. *Journal of Applied Psychology, 90*(3), 483–496.

60. Cortina, L. M., Magley, V. J., Williams, J. H., & Langhout, R. D. (2001). Incivility in the workplace. *Journal of Occupational Health Psychology, 6*(1), 64–80.

61. Taylor, S. G., Bedeian, A. G., Cole, M. S., & Zhang, Z. (in press). Developing and testing a dynamic model of workplace incivility change. *Journal of Management, 43*(3), 645–670. http://dx.doi.org/10.1177%2F0149206314535432

62. Pearson, C. M., & Porath, C. L. (2005). On the nature, consequences and remedies of workplace incivility: No time for "nice"? Think again. *Academy of Management Executive, 19*(1), 7–18.

63. Coutu, D. L. (2003, September). In praise of boundaries: A conversation with Miss Manners. *Harvard Business Review,* 41–45.

64. Yang, L. Q., & Caughlin, D. E. (2017). Aggression-preventive

supervisor behavior: Implications for workplace climate and employee outcomes. *Journal of Occupational Health Psychology, 22*(1), 1–18.

65. Yang, L. Q., & Caughlin, D. E. (2017). Aggression-preventive supervisor behavior: Implications for workplace climate and employee outcomes. *Journal of Occupational Health Psychology, 22*(1), 1–18.

66. Kilmann, R. H., & Thomas, K. W. (1977). Developing a forced-choice measure of conflict-handling behavior: The "MODE" instrument. *Educational and Psychological Measurement, 37*(2), 309–325.

67. Thomas, K. W. (1992). Conflict and negotiation processes in organizations. In M. D. Dunnette & L. M. Hough (Eds.), *Handbook of industrial and organizational psychology* (2nd ed., Vol. 3, pp. 651–717). Palo Alto, CA: Consulting Psychologists Press.

68. Rahim, M. A. (1985). A strategy for managing conflict in complex organizations. *Human Relations, 38*(1), 81–89.

69. Rahim, A., & Magner, N. (1995). Confirmatory factor analysis of the styles of handling interpersonal conflict: First-order factor model and its invariance across groups. *Journal of Applied Psychology, 80*(1), 122–132.

70. Ibid.

71. Rahim, M. A. (2002). Toward a theory of managing organizational conflict. *International Journal of Conflict Resolution, 13*(3), 206–235.

72. Blake, R. R., & Mouton, J. S. (1964). *The managerial grid.* Houston, TX: Gulf.

73. Rahim, M. A., & Bonoma, R. V. (1979). Managing organizational conflict: A model for diagnosis and intervention. *Psychological Reports, 44,* 1323–1344.

74. Rahim, M. A. (2002). Toward a theory of managing organizational conflict. *International Journal of Conflict Resolution, 13*(3), 206–235.

75. Hackman, J. R., & C. G. Morris. (1975). Group tasks, group interaction process, and group performance effectiveness: A review and proposed integration. In L. Berkowitz (Ed.), *Advances in experimental social psychology* (pp. 45–99). San Diego, CA: Academic Press.

76. Jehn, K. A. (1995). A multimethod examination of the benefits and detriments of intragroup conflict. *Administrative Science Quarterly, 40*(2), 256–282.

77. Jehn, K. A. (1997). A qualitative analysis of conflict types and dimensions in organizational groups. *Administrative Science Quarterly, 42*(3), 530–557.

78. Amason, A. C. (1996). Distinguishing the effects of functional and dysfunctional conflict on strategic decision making: Resolving a paradox for top management teams. *Academy of Management Journal, 39*(1), 123–148.

79. Hollenbeck, J. R., Ilgen, D. R., Sego, D. J., Hedlund, J., Major, D. A., & Phillips, J. (1995). Multilevel theory of team decision making: Decision performance in teams incorporating distributed expertise. *Journal of Applied Psychology, 80*(2), 292–316.

80. Schwenk, C. (1990). Conflict in organizational decision making: An exploratory study. *Management Science, 36*(4), 436–449.

81. Lee, C. C., Lin, Y. H., Huang, H. C., Huang, W. W., & Teng, H. H. (2015). The effects of task interdependence, team cooperation, and team conflict on job performance. *Social Behavior and Personality: An International Journal, 43*(4), 529–536.

82. Behfar, K. J., Peterson, R. S., Mannix, E. A., & Trochim, W. M. K. (2008). The critical role of conflict resolution in teams: A close look at the links between conflict type, conflict management strategies, and team outcomes. *Journal of Applied Psychology, 93*(2), 170–188. (Quotation on p. 170.)

83. Behfar, K., Friedman, R., & Brett, J. (2016). Managing co-occurring conflicts in teams. *Group Decision and Negotiation, 25*(3), 501–536.

84. O'Neill, T. A., McLarnon, M. J., Hoffart, G. C., Woodley, H. J., & Allen, N. J. (2015). The structure and function of team conflict state profiles. *Journal of Management.* http://dx.doi.org/10.1177%2F0149206315581662

85. Costa, P. L., Passos, A. M., & Bakker, A. B. (2015). Direct and contextual influence of team conflict on team resources, team work engagement, and team performance. *Negotiation and Conflict Management Research, 8*(4), 211–227.

86. Bai, Y., Harms, P., Han, G., & Cheng, W. (2015). Good and bad simultaneously? Leaders using dialectical thinking foster positive conflict and employee performance. *International Journal of Conflict Management, 26*(3), 245–267.

87. DeWit, F. R. C., Greer, L. L., & Jehn, K. A. (2012). The paradox of intragroup conflict: A meta-analysis. *Journal of Applied Psychology, 97*(2), 360–390.

88. Shaw, J. D., Zhu, J., Duffy, M. K., Scott, K. L., Shih, H. A., & Susanto, E. (2011). A contingency model of conflict and team effectiveness. *Journal of Applied Psychology, 96*(2), 391–400.

89. Ibid., p. 398.

90. Gelfand, M. J., Higgins, M., Nishii, L. H., Raver, A., Dominguez, A., Murakami, F., . . . Toyama, M. (2002). Culture and egocentric perceptions of fairness in conflict and negotiation. *Journal of Applied Psychology, 87*(5), 833–845.

91. Morris, M. W., Williams, K. Y., Leung, K., Larrick, R., Mendoza, M. T., Bhatnagar, D., . . . Hu, J.-C. (1998). Conflict management style: Accounting for cross-national differences. *Journal of International Business Studies, 29*(4), 729–747.

92. Gabrielidis, C., Stephan, W. G., Ybarra, O., Dos Santos Pearson, V. M., & Villareal, L. (1997). Preferred styles of conflict resolution: Mexico and the U.S. *Journal of Cross-Cultural Psychology, 28*(6), 661–677.

93. Tjosvold, D., Hui, C., & Law, K. S. (2001). Constructive conflict in China: Cooperative conflict as a bridge between East and West. *Journal of World Business, 36*(2), 166–183.

94. Glenn, J., Witmeyer, D., & Stevenson, K. A. (1977). Cultural styles of persuasion. *Journal of Intercultural Relations, 1*(3), 52–66.

95. Tung, R. L. (1998). American expatriates abroad: From neophytes to cosmopolitans. *Journal of World Business, 33*(2), 125–144.

96. Poitras, J., Hill, K., Hamel, V., & Pelletier, F. B. (2015). Managerial mediation competency: A mixed-method study. *Negotiation Journal, 31*(2), 105-129.

97. Nugent, P. S., & Broedling, L. A. (2002). Managing conflict: Third-party interventions for managers. *Academy of Management Executive, 16*(1), 139–154.

98. U.S. Office of Personnel Management. (2012). Alternative dispute resolution: A resource guide (pp. I-1 to 1-6). Retrieved from http://www.au.af.mil/au/awc/awcgate/dispute_resolution/opm_adrguide.pdf

99. Katz, N. H., & Flynn, L. T. (2013). Understanding conflict management systems and strategies in the workplace: A pilot study. *Conflict Resolution Quarterly, 30*(4), 393–410.

100. McKenzie, D. M. (2015). The role of mediation in resolving workplace relationship conflict. *International Journal of Law and Psychiatry, 39*, 52–59.

101. Bingham, L.B. (2004). Employment dispute resolution: The case for mediation. *Conflict Resolution Quarterly, 22*, 145–174.

102. Brett, J. M., Barsness, Z. I., & Goldberg, S. B. (1996). The effectiveness of mediation: An independent analysis of cases handled by four major service providers. *Negotiation*, 259–269.

103. Tallodi, T. (2015). Mediation's potential to reduce occupational stress: A new perspective. *Conflict Resolution Quarterly, 32*(4), 361–388.

104. Kidder, D. L. (2007). Restorative justice: Not "rights," but the right way to heal relationships at work. *International Journal of Conflict Management, 18*, 4–22.

105. Kolb, D. M. (2015, November). Managing yourself: Be your own best advocate. *Harvard Business Review*, 130–133.

106. Brooks, A. W. (2015). Emotion and the art of negotiation. *Harvard Business Review, 93*(12), 57–64.

107. Brett, J. M., Teucher, B. M., & Gunia, B. C. (2016). Culture and negotiation: Resolving three enigmas. *Current Opinion in Psychology, 8*, 78–83.

108. Ogliastri, E., & Quintanilla, C. (2016). Building cross-cultural negotiation prototypes in Latin American contexts from foreign executives' perceptions. *Journal of Business Research, 69*(2), 452–458.

109. Aslani, S., Ramirez-Marin, J., Brett, J., Yao, J., Semnani-Azad, Z., Zhang, Z. X., . . . Adair, W. (2016). Dignity, face, and honor cultures: A study of negotiation strategy and outcomes in three cultures. *Journal of Organizational Behavior, 37*(8), 1178–1201.

110. Yao, J., Zhang, Z. X., & Brett, J. M. (2016). Understanding trust development in negotiations: An interdependent approach. *Journal of Organizational Behavior*. doi:10.1002/job.2160

111. Campagna, R. L., Mislin, A. A., Kong, D. T., & Bottom, W. P. (2016). Strategic consequences of emotional misrepresentation in negotiation: The blowback effect. *Journal of Applied Psychology, 101*(5), 605.

112. Brooks, A. W., & Schweitzer, M. E. (2011). Can Nervous Nelly negotiate? How anxiety causes negotiators to make low first offers, exit early, and earn less profit. *Organizational Behavior and Human Decision Processes, 115*(1), 43–54.

113. Bazerman, M. H., & Gillespie, J. J. (1998). Betting on the future: the virtues of contingent contracts. *Harvard Business Review, 77*(5), 155–60.

114. Hüffmeier, J., Freund, P. A., Zerres, A., Backhaus, K., & Hertel, G. (2011). Being tough or being nice? A meta-analysis on the impact of hard- and softline strategies in distributive negotiations. *Journal of Management, 40*(3), 866–892.

115. Fisher, R., & Ury, W. (1981). *Getting to yes: Negotiating agreement without giving in*. Boston, MA: Houghton Mifflin.

116. Magee, J. C., Galinsky, A. D., & Gruenfeld, D. H. (2007). Power, propensity to negotiate, and moving first in competitive interactions. *Personality and Social Psychology Bulletin, 33*(2), 200–212.

117. Gunia, B. C. (2017). To move or to wait? Everything you need to know about making the first offer. *Business Horizons, 60*(1), 15–18.

118. Schweinsberg, M., Ku, G., Wang, C. S., & Pillutla, M. M. (2012). Starting high and ending with nothing: The role of anchors and power in negotiations. *Journal of Experimental Social Psychology, 48*(1), 226–231.

119. Moore, D. A. (2004). Myopic prediction, self-destructive secrecy and the unexpected benefits of revealing final deadlines in negotiation. *Organizational Behavior and Human Decision Processes, 94*(2), 125–139.

120. Liu, W., Liu, L. A., & Zhang, J. D. (2016). How to dissolve fixed-pie bias in negotiation? Social antecedents and the mediating effect of mental-model adjustment. *Journal of Organizational Behavior, 37*(1), 85–107.

121. Fisher, R., & Ury, W. (1981). *Getting to yes: Negotiating agreement without giving in*. Boston, MA: Houghton Mifflin.

122. Curhan, J. R., Elfenbein, H. A., & Xu, H. (2006). What do people value when they negotiate? Mapping the domain of subjective value in negotiation. *Journal of Personality and Social Psychology, 91*(3), 493–512.

123. Naquin, C. E. (2003). The agony of opportunity in negotiation: Number of negotiable issues, counterfactual thinking, and feelings of satisfaction. *Organizational Behavior and Human Decision Processes, 91*(1), 97–107.

124. Ten Velden, F. S., Beersma, B., & De Dreu, C. K. W. (2010). It takes two to tango: The effect of dyads' epistemic motivation composition in negotiation. *Personality and Social Psychology Bulletin, 36*(11), 1454–1466.

125. De Dreu, C. K. W., Weingart, L. R., & Kwon, S. (2000). Influence of social motives on integrative negotiation: A meta-analytic review and test of two theories. *Journal of Personality and Social Psychology, 78*(5), 889–905.

126. Thompson, L., & Leonardelli, G. J. (2004). The big bang: The evolution of negotiation research. *Academy of Management Executive, 18*(3), 113–117.

127. Fossum, J. A. (2014). *Labor relations*. New York, NY: McGraw-Hill Higher Education.

128. Brett, J. M. (1980). Why employees want unions. *Organizational Dynamics, 8*(4), 47–59.

129. Chung, R., Lee, B. B. H., Lee, W. J., & Sohn, B. C. (2015). Do managers withhold good news from labor unions? *Management Science, 62*(1), 46–68.

130. Tremblay, J. F. (2016). From principled negotiation to interest-based bargaining. *Universal Journal of Industrial and Business Management, 4*(2), 71–79.

131. Barrett, J. (2015). The interest-based bargaining story at the Federal Mediation and Conciliation Service. *Negotiation Journal, 31*(4), 431–435.

132. Kelly, E. J., & Kaminskiene, N. (2016). Importance of emotional intelligence in negotiation and mediation. *International Comparative Jurisprudence, 2*(1), 55–60.

133. Sharma, S., Bottom, W. P., & Elfenbein, H. A. (2013). On the role of personality, cognitive ability, and emotional intelligence in predicting negotiation outcomes: A meta-analysis. *Organizational Psychology Review, 3*(4), 293–336.

134. Parker, S. K., & Axtell, C. M. (2001). Seeing another viewpoint: Antecedents and outcomes of employee perspective taking. *Academy of Management Journal, 44*, 1085–1100.

135. Markman, A. (2015). Is perspective-taking a skill? Retrieved from https://www.psychologytoday.com/blog/ulterior-motives/201510/is-perspective-taking-skill

136. Epley, N., & Caruso, E. M. (2008). Perspective taking: Misstepping into others' shoes. In K. D. Markman, W. M. P. Klein, & J. A. Suhr (Eds.), *Handbook of imagination and mental simulation* (pp. 297–311). New York, NY: Psychology Press.

137. Parker, S. K., & Axtell, C. M. (2001). Seeing another viewpoint: Antecedents and outcomes of employee perspective taking. *Academy of Management Journal, 44*(6), 1085–1100.

138. Galinsky, A. D., Ku, G., & Wang, C. S. (2005). Perspective-taking and self-other overlap: Fostering social bonds and facilitating social coordination. *Group Processes & Intergroup Relations, 8*(2), 109–124.

139. Rizkalla, L., Wertheim, E. H., & Hodgson, L. K. (2008). The roles of emotion management and perspective taking in individuals' conflict management styles and disposition to forgive. *Journal of Research in Personality, 42*(6), 1594–1601.

140. Grant, A. M., & Berry, J. W. (2011). The necessity of others is the mother of invention: Intrinsic and prosocial motivations, perspective taking, and creativity. *Academy of Management Journal, 54*(1), 73–96.

141. Prandelli, E., Pasquini, M., & Verona, G. (2016). In user's shoes: An experimental design on the role of perspective taking in discovering entrepreneurial opportunities. *Journal of Business Venturing, 31*(3), 287–301.

142. Flinchbaugh, C., Li, P., Luth, M. T., & Chadwick, C. (2016). Team-level high involvement work practices: Investigating the role of knowledge sharing and perspective taking. *Human Resource Management Journal, 26*(2), 134–150.

143. Galinsky, A. D., & Mussweiler, T. (2001). First offers as anchors: The role of perspective-taking and negotiator focus. *Journal of Personality and Social Psychology, 81*(4), 657–669.

144. Galinsky, A. D., Maddux, W. W., Gilin, D., & White, J. B. (2008). Why it pays to get inside the head of your opponent: The differential effects of perspective taking and empathy in negotiations. *Psychological science, 19*(4), 378–384.

145. Wang, J., Zhang, Z., & Jia, M. (2016). Understanding how leader humility enhances employee creativity: The roles of perspective taking and cognitive reappraisal. *Journal of Applied Behavioral Science, 53*(1), 5–31. http://dx.doi.org/10.1177%2F0021886316678907

146. Wolff, S. B., Pescosolido, A. T., & Druskat, V. U. (2002). Emotional intelligence as the basis of leadership emergence in self-managing teams. *Leadership Quarterly, 13*(5), 505–522.

Chapter 12

1. Ambady, N., & Rosenthal, R. (1993). Half a minute: Predicting teacher evaluations from thin slices of nonverbal behavior and physical attractiveness. *Journal of Personality and Social Psychology, 64*(3), 431–441.

2. Ambady, N., & Rosenthal, R. (1992). Thin slices of expressive behavior as predictors of interpersonal consequences: A meta-analysis. *Psychological Bulletin, 111*(2), 256–274.

3. Carney, D. R., Colvin, C. R., & Hall, J. A. (2007). A thin slice perspective on the accuracy of first impressions. *Journal of Research in Personality, 41*(5), 1054–1072.

4. Curhan, J. R., & Pentland, A. (2007). Thin slices of negotiation: Predicting outcomes from conversational dynamics within the first 5 minutes. *Journal of Applied Psychology, 92*(3), 802–811.

5. Swider, B. W., Barrick, M. R., & Harris, T. B. (2016). Initial impressions: What they are, what they are not, and how they influence structured interview outcomes. *Journal of Applied Psychology, 101*(5), 625–638.

6. Richmond, V. P., McCroskey, J. C., & McCroskey, L. L. (2005). *Organizational communication for survival: Making work, work.* New York, NY: Allyn & Bacon. (Quotation on p. 20.)

7. O'Reilly, C. A. (1980). Individuals and information overload in organizations: Is more necessarily better? *Academy of Management Journal, 23*(4), 684–696.

8. Pincus, J. D. (1986). Communication satisfaction, job satisfaction, and job performance. *Human Communication Research, 12*(3), 395–419.

9. Pincus, J. D., Knipp, J. E., & Rayfield, R. E. (1990). Internal communication and job satisfaction revisited: The impact of organizational trust and influence on commercial bank supervisors. *Journal of Public Relations Research, 2*(1–4), 173–191.

10. Barnard, C. I. (1938). *The functions of the executive.* Cambridge, MA: Harvard University Press. (Quotation on p. 236.)

11. Redding, W. C. (1985). Stumbling toward identity: The emergence of organizational communication as a field of study. In R. D. McPhee & P. K. Tompkins (Eds.), *Organizational communication: Traditional themes and new directions* (pp. 15–54). Beverly Hills, CA: Sage.

12. Blair, R., Roberts, K. H., & McKechnie, P. (1985). Vertical and network communication in organizations: The present and the future. *Organizational communication: Traditional themes and new directions* (pp. 55–77). Beverly Hills, CA: Sage. (Quotation on p. 55.)

13. Weaver, W. (1949). Recent contributions to the mathematical theory of communication. *The Mathematical Theory of Communication, 1,* 1–12.

14. Watson-Manheim, M. B., & Bélanger, F. (2007). Communication media repertoires: Dealing with the multiplicity of media choices. *MIS Quarterly, 31*(2), 267–293.

15. Treviño, L. K., Webster, J., & Stein, E. W. (2000). Making

connections: Complementary influences on communication media choices, attitudes, and use. *Organization Science, 11*(2), 163–182.

16. McCroskey, J. C. (1977). Oral communication apprehension: A summary of recent theory and research. *Human Communication Research, 4*(1), 78–96. (Quotation on p. 78.)

17. Horowitz, B. (2002). *Communication apprehension: Origins and management.* Albany, NY: Singular Thomas Learning. (Quotation on p. 1.)

18. McCroskey, J. C. (1983). The communication apprehension perspective. *Communication, 12*(1), 1–25.

19. Friedman, P. G. (1980). *Shyness and reticence in students.* Washington, DC: National Education Association.

20. Allen, M. T., & Bourhis, J. (1996). The relationship of communication apprehension to communication behavior: A meta-analysis. *Communication Quarterly, 44*, 214–225.

21. Pate, L. E., & Merker, G. E. (1978). Communication apprehension: Implications for management and organizational behavior. *Journal of Management, 4*(2), 107–119.

22. McCroskey, J. C., & McVetta, R. W. (1978). Classroom seating arrangements: Instructional communication theory versus student preferences. *Communication Education 27*(2), 99–111.

23. Blume, B. D., Baldwin, T. T., & Ryan, K. C. (2013). Communication apprehension: A barrier to students' leadership, adaptability, and multicultural appreciation. *Academy of Management Learning & Education, 12*(2), 158–172.

24. Lawry, J. (2012). What does scale mean in business? Retrieved from http://joshlowryblog.com/2012/03/15/what-does-scale-mean-in-business

25. Rogers, C. R. (1980). *A way of being.* Boston, MA: Houghton Mifflin.

26. Weger, H., Jr., Castle Bell, G., Minei, E. M., & Robinson, M. C. (2014). The relative effectiveness of active listening in initial interactions. *International Journal of Listening, 28*(1), 13–31.

27. Knippen, J. T., & Green, T. B. (1994). How the manager can use active listening. *Public Personnel Management, 23*(2), 357–359.

28. Fleming, T. (2012). Why I'm a listener: Amgen CEO Kevin Sharer. Retrieved from http://www.mckinsey.com/insights/leading_in_the_21st_century/why_im_a_listener_amgen_ceo_kevin_sharer

29. Jones, S. M., Bodie, G. D., & Hughes, S. D. (2016). The impact of mindfulness on empathy, active listening, and perceived provisions of emotional support. *Communication Research, 1*, 1–28.

30. Brooks, B. (2003). The power of active listening. *American Salesman, 48*(6), 12–14.

31. van Dun, D. H., Hicks, J. N., & Wilderom, C. P. (2016). Values and behaviors of effective lean managers: Mixed-methods exploratory research. *European Management Journal, 35*, 174–186.

32. Granovetter, M. S. (1995). *Getting a job: A study of contacts and careers* (2nd ed.). Chicago, IL: University of Chicago Press.

33. Burke, M., Jones, J. J., & Gee, L. L. (2016). How strong and weak ties help you find a job. Retrieved from: https://research.fb.com/how-strong-and-weak-ties-help-you-find-a-job/

34. Greenberg, J., & Fernandez, R. M. (2016). The strength of weak ties in MBA job search: A within-person test. *Sociological Science, 3*, 296–316.

35. Van Riel, C. B. M. (1995). *Principles of corporate communication.* Upper Saddle River, NJ: Prentice Hall.

36. Burton, P. (2014). Mom: Flight attendant refused bathroom access, 3-year-old forced to urinate in seat. Retrieved from http://boston.cbslocal.com/2014/06/13/mom-flight-attendant-refused-bathroom-access-3-year-old-forced-to-urinate-in-seat

37. Frank, A., & Brownell, J. (1989), *Organizational communication and behavior: Communicating to improve performance.* Orlando, FL: Holt, Rinehart & Winston. (Quotation on pp. 5–6.)

38. Dolphin, R. A. (2005). Internal communications: Today's strategic imperative. *Journal of Marketing Communications, 11*(3), 171–190.

39. Miller, D. A., & Rose, P. B. (1994). Integrated communications: A look at reality instead of theory. *Public Relations Quarterly, 39*, 13–16.

40. Anderson, J., & Level, D. A. (1980). The impact of certain types of downward communication on job performance. *Journal of Business Communication, 17*(4), 51–59.

41. Waldron, V. R. (1999). Communication practices of followers, members, and protégés: The case of upward influence tactics. *Communication Yearbook, 22*, 251–300.

42. Foste, E. A., & Botero, I. C. (2012). Personal reputation effects of upward communication on impressions about new employees. *Management Communication Quarterly, 26*(1), 48–73.

43. Jablin, F. M. (1979). Superior–subordinate communication: The state of the art. *Psychological Bulletin, 86*(6), 1201–1222.

44. Gaines, J. H. (1980). Upward communication in industry: An experiment. *Human Relations, 33*(12), 929–942.

45. Chow, C., Hwang, R., & Liao, W. (2000). Motivating truthful upward communication of private information: An experimental study of mechanisms from theory and practice. *Abacus, 36*, 160–179.

46. Tourish, D., & Robson, P. (2006). Sensemaking and the distortion of critical upward communication in organizations. *Journal of Management Studies, 43*(4), 711–730.

47. Read, W. (1962). Upward communication in industrial hierarchies. *Human Relations, 15*, 3–16.

48. Roberts, K. H., & O'Reilly, C. A. (1974). Failures in upward communication in organizations: Three possible culprits. *Academy of Management Journal, 17*(2), 205–215.

49. Tourish, D. (2005). Critical upward communication: Ten commandments for improving strategy and decision making. *Long Range Planning, 38*(5), 485–503. (Quotation on p. 488.)

50. Crampton, S. M., Hodge, J. W., & Mishra, J. M. (1998). The informal communication network: Factors influencing grapevine activity. *Public Personnel Management, 27*(4), 569–584.

51. Ibid.

52. Baker, J. S., & Jones, M. A. (1996). The poison grapevine: How destructive are gossip and rumor in the workplace? *Human Resource Development Quarterly, 7*(1), 75–86.

53. DiFonzo, N., Bordia, P., & Rosnow, R. L. (1994). Reining in rumors. *Organizational Dynamics, 23*(1), 47–62. (Quotation on p. 47.)

54. Clifford, S. (2009). Video prank at Domino's taints brand. Retrieved from http://www.nytimes.com/2009/04/16/business/media/16dominos.html

55. Zachary, M. K. (1996). The office grapevine: A legal noose? *Getting Results . . . For the Hands-On Manager: Plant Edition, 41*(8), 6–7.

56. Banerjee, P., & Singh, S. (2015). Managers' perspectives on the effects of online grapevine communication: A qualitative inquiry. *Qualitative Report, 20*(6), 765.

57. Beersma, B., & Van Kleef, G. A. (2011). How the grapevine keeps you in line: Gossip increases contributions to the group. *Social Psychological and Personality Science, 2*(6), 642–649.

58. Van Hoye, G., & Lievens, F. (2009). Tapping the grapevine: A closer look at word-of-mouth as a recruitment source. *Journal of Applied Psychology, 94*(2), 341–352.

59. DiFonzo, N., & Bordia, P. (2002). Rumors and stable-cause attribution in prediction and behavior. *Organizational Behavior and Human Decision Processes, 88*(2), 785–800.

60. Bordia, P., Jones, E., Gallois, C., Callan, V. J., & DiFonzo, N. (2006). Management are aliens! Rumors and stress during organizational change. *Group & Organization Management, 31*(5), 601–621.

61. Nicoll, D. C. (1994). Acknowledge and use your grapevine. *Management Decision, 32*(6), 25–30.

62. Diesner, J., Frantz, T. L., & Carley, K. M. (2005). Communication networks from the Enron email corpus: "It's always about the people. Enron is no different." *Computational & Mathematical Organization Theory, 11*(3), 201–228. (Quotation on p. 201.)

63. O'Connor, M. A. (2002). Enron board: The perils of groupthink. *University of Cincinnati Law Review, 71*, 1233–1471. (Quotation on p. 1233.)

64. Fragale, A. R., Sumanth, J. J., Tiedens, L. Z., & Northcraft, G. B. (2012). Appeasing equals: Lateral deference in organizational communication. *Administrative Science Quarterly, 57*(3), 373–406. (Quotation on p. 373.)

65. Seeger, M. W., & Ulmer, R. R. (2003). Explaining Enron communication and responsible leadership. *Management Communication Quarterly, 17*(1), 58–84.

66. Hoffman, W. M., Hartman, L. P., & Rowe, M. (2003). You've got mail . . . and the boss knows: A survey by the Center for Business Ethics of companies' email and Internet monitoring. *Business and Society Review, 108*(3), 285–307.

67. Sproull, L., & Kiesler, S. (1986). Reducing social context cues: Electronic mail in organizational communication. *Management Science, 32*(11), 1492–1512.

68. Whitty, M. T., & Carr, A. N. (2006). New rules in the workplace: Applying object-relations theory to explain problem Internet and email behaviour in the workplace. *Computers in Human Behavior, 22*(2), 235–250.

69. Borstorff, P., Graham, G., & Marker, M. (2006). E-harassment: Employee perceptions of e-technology as a source of harassment. *Journal of Applied Management & Entrepreneurship, 11*(3), 51–67.

70. Goldman, L. (2007). Netiquette rules—10 best rules for email etiquette. Retrieved from http://ezinearticles.com/?Netiquette-Rules—10-Best-Rules-for-Email-Etiquette&id=785177

71. Byron, K. (2008). Carrying too heavy a load? The communication and miscommunication of emotion by email. *Academy of Management Review, 33*(2), 309–327.

72. Mano, R. S., & Mesch, G. S. (2010). E-mail characteristics, work performance and distress. *Computers in Human Behavior, 26*(1), 61–69.

73. Jackson, J., Dawson, R., & Wilson, D. (2003). Reducing the effect of e-mail interruptions on employees. *International Journal of Information Management, 23*(1), 55–65.

74. Jackson, T., Dawson, R., & Wilson, D. (2003). Understanding e-mail interaction increases organizational productivity. *Communications of the ACM, 48*(6), 80–84.

75. Szóstek, A. M. (2011). Dealing with my emails: Latent user needs in email management. *Computers in Human Behavior, 27*(2), 723–729.

76. Phillips, J. G., & Reddie, L. (2007). Decisional style and self-reported email use in the workplace. *Computers in Human Behavior, 23*(5), 2414–2428.

77. Butts, M. M., Becker, W. J., & Boswell, W. R. (2015). Hot buttons and time sinks: The effects of electronic communication during nonwork time on emotions and work–nonwork conflict. *Academy of Management Journal, 58*(3), 763–788.

78. Wajcman, J., & Rose, E. (2011). Constant connectivity: Rethinking interruptions at work. *Organization Studies, 32*(7), 941–961.

79. Cellular Telecommunications & Internet Association. (2015). Americans' wireless data usage continues to skyrocket. Retrieved from http://www.ctia.org/industry-data/ctia-annual-wireless-industry-survey

80. Herbsleb, J. D., Atkins, D. L., Boyer, D. G., Handel, M., & Finholt, T. A. (2002). Introducing instant messaging and chat in the workplace. *Proceedings of the SIGCHI conference on Human factors in computing systems, 4*(1), 171–178.

81. Kim, S., & Niu, Q. (2014). Smartphone: It can do more than you think. Presented at the annual meeting of the Society for Industrial & Organizational Psychology, Honolulu, HI.

82. Middleton, C. A., & Cukier, W. (2006). Is mobile email functional or dysfunctional? Two perspectives on mobile email usage. *European Journal of Information Systems, 15*(3), 252–260. (Quotation on p. 252.)

83. Cervellon, M.-C., & Lirio, P. (2017). When employees don't "like" their employers on social media. *MIT Sloan Management Review, 58*(2), 63–70.

84. Crawford, K. (2005). Have a blog, lose your job? *CNN/Money*, 15.

85. Black, T. (2010). How to handle employee blogging. Retrieved from http://www.inc.com/guides/2010/04/employee-blogging-policy.html

86. Van Iddekinge, C. H., Lanivich, S. E., Roth, P. L., & Junco, E. (2016). Social media for selection? Validity and adverse impact potential of a Facebook-based assessment. *Journal of Management, 42*(7), 1811–1835.

87. Van Grove, J. (2009). 40 of the best Twitter brands and

the people behind them. Retrieved from http://mashable.com/2009/01/21/best-twitter-brands

88. Naidoo, J., & Dulek, R. (2017). Leading by tweeting: Are deans doing it? An exploratory analysis of tweets by SEC business school deans. *International Journal of Business Communication, 54*(1), 31–51.

89. Johnson, P. R., & Indvik, J. (2004). The organizational benefits of reducing cyberslacking in the workplace. *Journal of Organizational Culture, Communications, and Conflict, 8*(2), 55–62. (Quotation on p. 56.)

90. Greenfield, D., & Davis, R. (2002). Lost in cyberspace: The web @work. *CyberPsychology & Behavior, 5*(4), 347–353.

91. Opgenhaffen, M., & Claeys, A.-S. (2017). Between hope and fear: Developing social media guidelines. *Employee Relations, 39*(2), 130–144. doi:10.1108/er-04-2016-0086

92. Lohr, S. (2008). As travel costs rise, more meetings go virtual. Retrieved from http://www.nytimes.com/2008/07/22/technology/22meet.html?_r=0&page wanted=print

93. Ibid.

94. Burgess, C., & Burgess, M. (2014). *The social employee: Success lessons from IBM, AT&T, Dell and Cisco on building a social culture.* New York, NY: McGraw-Hill.

95. Macnamara, J. R. (2004). The crucial role of research in multicultural and cross-cultural communication. *Journal of Communication Management, 8*(3), 322–334.

96. Levine, T. R., Park, H. S., & Kim, R. K. (2007). Some conceptual and theoretical challenges for cross-cultural communication research in the 21st century. *Journal of Intercultural Communication Research, 36*(3), 205–221.

97. Matveev, A. V., & Nelson, P. E. (2004). Cross cultural communication competence and multicultural team performance perceptions of American and Russian managers. *International Journal of Cross Cultural Management, 4*(2), 253–270.

98. Ngai, C. S. B., & Singh, R. G. (2017). Move structure and communication style of leaders' messages in corporate discourse: A cross-cultural

perspective. *Discourse & Communication, 11*(3), 276–295. http://dx.doi.org/10.1177%2F1750481317697860

99. Spencer-Oatey, H., & Xing, J. (2003). Managing rapport in intercultural business interactions: A comparison of two Chinese-British welcome meetings. *Journal of Intercultural Studies, 24*(1), 33–46.

100. Lohr, S. (2008). As travel costs rise, more meetings go virtual. Retrieved from http://www.nytimes.com/2008/07/22/technology/22meet.html?_r=0&pagewanted=print

101. Levine, T. R., Park, H. S., & Kim, R. K. (2007). Some conceptual and theoretical challenges for cross-cultural communication research in the 21st century. *Journal of Intercultural Communication Research, 36*(3), 205–221.

102. Gudykunst, W. B., Matsumoto, Y., Ting-Toomey, S., Nishida, T., Kim, K., & Heyman, S. (1996). The influence of cultural individualism-collectivism, self construals, and individual values on communication styles across cultures. *Human Communication Research, 22*(4), 510–543.

103. Zhang, T., & Zhou, H. (2008). The significance of cross-cultural communication in international business negotiation. *International Journal of Business and Management, 3*(2), 103–109.

104. Tannen, D. T. (1984). The pragmatics of cross-cultural communication. *Applied Linguistics, 5*(3), 189–195.

105. Washington, M. C., Okoro, E. A., & Okoro, S. U. (2013). Emotional intelligence and cross-cultural communication competence: An analysis of group dynamics and interpersonal relationships in a diverse classroom. *Journal of International Education Research, 9*(3), 241–246.

106. Huang, L. (2010). Cross-cultural communication in business negotiations. *International Journal of Economics & Finance, 2*(2), 196–199.

107. Burgess, C., & Burgess, M. (2014). *The social employee: Success lessons from IBM, AT&T, Dell and Cisco on building a social culture.* New York, NY: McGraw-Hill.

108. Littrell, L. N., & Salas, E. (2005). A review of cross-cultural training: Best practices, guidelines, and research

needs. *Human Resource Development Review, 4*(3), 305–334.

109. Nixon, J. C., & Dawson, G. A. (2002). Reason for cross-cultural communication training. *Corporate Communications: An International Journal, 7*(3), 184–191.

110. Sussman, N., & Rosenfeld, H. (1982). Influence of culture, language and sex on conversational distance. *Journal of Personality and Social Psychology, 42*(1), 67–74.

111. Tannen, D. (1990). *You just don't understand: Women and men in conversation.* New York, NY: William Morrow.

112. Tannen, D. (1994). *Talking from 9 to 5: How women's and men's conversational styles affect who gets heard, who gets credit, and what gets done at work.* New York, NY: Simon & Schuster.

113. Ambady, N., & Weisbuch, M. (2010). Nonverbal behavior. In S. T. Fiske, D. T. Gilbert, & G. Lindzey (Eds.), *Handbook of social psychology* (pp. 464–497). Hoboken, NJ: Wiley. (Quotation on p. 465.)

114. Mehrabian, A. (1981). *Silent messages* (2nd ed.). Belmont, CA: Wadsworth.

115. Ambler, G. (2013). When it comes to leadership everything communicates. Retrieved from http://www.georgeambler.com/when-it-comes-to-leadership-everything-communicates

116. Gentry, W. A., & Kuhnert, K. W. (2007). Sending signals: Nonverbal communication can speak volumes. *Leadership in Action, 27*(5), 3–7. (Quotation on p. 4.)

117. Bonaccio, S., O'Reilly, J., O'Sullivan, S. L., & Chiocchio, F. (2016). Nonverbal behavior and communication in the workplace: A review and an agenda for research. *Journal of Management, 42*(5), 1044–1074.

118. Goffman, E. (1959). *The presentation of self in everyday life.* London, England: Penguin.

119. Tiedens, L. Z., & Fragale, A. R. (2003). Power moves: Complementarity in dominant and submissive nonverbal behavior. *Journal of Personality and Social Psychology, 84*, 558–568.

120. Bono, J. E., & Ilies, R. (2006). Charisma, positive emotions and mood contagion. *Leadership Quarterly, 17*, 317–334.

121. Tickle-Degnen, L. (2006). Nonverbal behavior and its functions in the ecosystem of rapport. In V. Manusov & M. L. Patterson (Eds.), *The Sage handbook of nonverbal communication* (pp. 381–401). Thousand Oaks, CA: Sage.

122. Bellou, V., & Skemperis, N. (2015). Nonverbal communication and relational identification with the supervisor. *Management Decision, 53*(5), 1005–1022.

123. Hennig-Thurau, T., Groth, M., Paul, M., & Gremler, D. D. (2006). Are all smiles created equal? How emotional contagion and emotional labor affect service relationships. *Journal of Marketing, 70*(3), 58–73.

124. Tangirala, S., & Ramanujam, R. (2008). Employee silence on critical work issues: The cross level effects of procedural justice climate. *Personnel Psychology, 61*(1), 37–68.

125. Madrid, H. P., Patterson, M. G., & Leiva, P. I. (2015). Negative core affect and employee silence: How differences in activation, cognitive rumination, and problem-solving demands matter. *Journal of Applied Psychology, 100*(6), 1887.

126. Huang, L., & Huang, W. (2016). Interactional justice and employee silence: The roles of procedural justice and affect. *Social Behavior and Personality: An International Journal, 44*(5), 837–852.

127. Park, C., & Keil, M. (2009). Organizational silence and whistle-blowing on IT projects: An integrated model. *Decision Sciences, 40*(4), 901–918.

128. Brinsfield, C. T. (2013). Employee silence motives: Investigation of dimensionality and development of measures. *Journal of Organizational Behavior, 34*(5), 671–697.

129. Morrison, E. W., & Milliken, F. J. (2000). Organizational silence: A barrier to change and development in a pluralistic world. *Academy of Management Review, 25*(4), 706–725.

130. Bies, R. J., & Tripp, T. M. (1999). Two faces of the powerless: Coping with tyranny. In R. M. Kramer & M. A. Neale (Eds.), *Power and influence in organizations* (pp. 203–219). Thousand Oaks, CA: Sage.

131. De Maria, W. (2006). Brother secret, sister silence: Sibling conspiracies against managerial integrity. *Journal of Business Ethics, 65*(3), 219–234.

132. Nikolaou, I., Vakola, M., & Bourantas, D. (2011). The role of silence on employees' attitudes "the day after" a merger. *Personnel Review, 40*(6), 723–741.

133. Huang, X., Vliert, E. V. D., & Vegt, G. V. D. (2005). Breaking the silence culture: Stimulation of participation and employee opinion withholding cross-nationally. *Management and Organization Review, 1*(3), 459–482.

134. Van Dyne, L. V., Ang, S., & Botero, I. C. (2003). Conceptualizing employee silence and employee voice as multidimensional constructs. *Journal of Management Studies, 40*(6), 1359–1392.

135. Karaca, H. (2013). An exploratory study on the impact of organizational silence in hierarchical organizations: Turkish national police case. *European Scientific Journal, 9*(23), 38–50.

136. Zehir, C., & Erdogan, E. (2011). The association between organizational silence and ethical leadership through employee performance. *Procedia-Social and Behavioral Sciences, 24*, 1389–1404.

137. Tannen, D. (1995). The power of talk: Who gets heard and why. *Harvard Business Review, 73*(5), 138–148. (Quotation on p. 148.)

138. Smircich, L., & Morgan, G. (1982). Leadership: The management of meaning. *Journal of Applied Behavioral Science, 18*(3), 257–273.

139. Bennis, W. (1984). The four competencies of leadership. *Training and Development Journal, 38*(8), 14–19.

140. Smircich, L., & Stubbart, C. (1985). Strategic management in an enacted world. *Academy of Management Review, 10*(4), 724–736.

141. Hackman, M. Z., & Johnson, C. E. (2013). *Leadership: A communication perspective* (6th ed.). Long Grove, IL: Waveland Press. (Quotation on p. 11.)

142. Fairhurst, G. T., & Sarr, R. (1996). *The art of framing: Managing the language of leadership*. San Francisco, CA: Jossey-Bass. (Quotation on p. 3.)

143. Fairhurst, G. T. (2010). *The power of framing: Creating the language of leadership*. New York, NY: Wiley.

144. Fairhurst, G. T. (2016). Echoes of the vision when the rest of the organization talks total quality. *Management Communication Quarterly, 6*(4), 331–371. http://dx.doi.org/10.1177%2F0893318993006004001

145. Fairhurst, G. T. (2009). Considering context in discursive leadership research. *Human Relations, 62*, 1607–1633.

146. Ruben, B. D., & Gigliotti, R. A. (2016). Leadership as social influence: An expanded view of leadership communication theory and practice. *Journal of Leadership & Organizational Studies, 23*(4), 467–479.

147. Watzlawick, P., Beavin, J., & Jackson, D. (1967). *Pragmatics of human communication: A study of interactional patterns, pathologies, and paradoxes*. New York, NY: Norton.

148. Richmond, V. P., & McCroskey, J. C. (2000). The impact of supervisor and subordinate immediacy on relational and organizational outcomes. *Communication Monographs, 67*(1), 85–95.

149. Mueller, B. H., & Lee, J. (2002). Leader-member exchange and organizational communication satisfaction in multiple contexts. *Journal of Business Communication, 39*(2), 220–244. (Quotation on p. 235.)

Chapter 13

1. Roberson, Q., Ryan, A. M., & Ragins, B. R. (2017). The evolution and future of diversity at work. *Journal of Applied Psychology, 102*(3), 483–499.

2. Cox, T. H., & Blake, S. (1991). Managing cultural diversity: Implications for organizational competitiveness. *Academy of Management Executive, 5*(3), 45–56.

3. Deloitte Consulting. (2013). Resetting horizons: Human capital trends report. Retrieved from http://www.deloitte.com/view/en_US/us/Services/consulting/human-capital/human-capital-trends/index.htm (Quotation on p. 3.)

4. Brannen, M. Y., & Peterson, M. F. (2009). Merging without

alienating: Interventions promoting cross-cultural organizational integration and their limitations. *Journal of International Business Studies, 40*(3), 468–489. (Quotation on p. 468.)

5. Friedman, T. L. (2006). *The world is flat: A brief history of the twenty-first century.* New York, NY: Macmillan.

6. Guillaume, Y. R., Dawson, J. F., Woods, S. A., Sacramento, C. A., & West, M. A. (2013). Getting diversity at work to work: What we know and what we still don't know. *Journal of Occupational and Organizational Psychology, 86*(2), 123–141. (Quotation on p. 124.)

7. Fairholm, G. W. (1994). Leading diverse followers. *Journal of Leadership Studies, 1,* 82–93.

8. Harrison, D. A., Price, K. H., & Bell, M. P. (1998). Beyond relational demography: Time and the effects of surface-and deep-level diversity on work group cohesion. *Academy of Management Journal, 41*(1), 96–107.

9. Ibid.

10. Kelly, C., Elizabeth, F., Bharat, M., & Jitendra, M. (2016). Generation gaps: Changes in the workplace due to differing generational values. *Advances in Management, 9*(5), 1–8.

11. Ferri-Reed, J. (2014). Millennializing the workplace. *Journal for Quality & Participation, 37*(1), 13–14. (Quotation on p. 13.)

12. Kelly, C., Elizabeth, F., Bharat, M., & Jitendra, M. (2016). Generation gaps: Changes in the workplace due to differing generational values. *Advances in Management, 9*(5), 1–8.

13. Stewart, J. S., Oliver, E. G., Cravens, K. S., & Oishi, S. (2017). Managing millennials: Embracing generational differences. *Business Horizons, 60*(1), 45–54.

14. Ibid.

15. Hall, A. (2016). Exploring the workplace communication preferences of millennials. *Journal of Organizational Culture, Communication and Conflict, 20,* 35–44.

16. Pînzaru, F., Vatamanescu, E. M., Mitan, A., Savulescu, R., Vitelar, A., Noaghea, C., & Balan, M. (2016). Millennials at work: Investigating the specificity of generation Y versus other generations. *Management Dynamics in the Knowledge Economy, 4*(2), 173–192.

17. Bencsik, A., Horváth-Csikós, G., & Juhász, T. (2016). Y and Z generations at workplaces. *Journal of Competitiveness, 8*(3), 90–106.

18. Meister, J. (2013). The boomer-millennial workplace clash: Is it real? Retrieved from www.forbes.cm/sites/jeannemeister/2013/2013/06/04/the-boomer-millennial-workplace-clash-is-it-real. (Quotation on p. 1.)

19. Bencsik, A., Horváth-Csikós, G., & Juhász, T. (2016). Y and Z generations at workplaces. *Journal of Competitiveness, 8*(3), 90–106.

20. Beall, G. (2016). 8 key differences between Gen Z and Millennials. Retrieved from http://www.huffingtonpost.com/george-beall/8-key-differences-between_b_12814200.html

21. Stein, J. (2013, May). The me me me generation: Millennials are lazy, entitled narcissists who still live with their parents. Why they'll save us all. *Time,* pp. 28–34.

22. Kelly, C., Elizabeth, F., Bharat, M., & Jitendra, M. (2016). Generation gaps: Changes in the workplace due to differing generational values. *Advances in Management, 9*(5), 1–8.

23. Adler, N. J. (1997). *International dimensions of organizational behavior* (3rd ed.). Cincinnati, OH: South-Western. (Quotation on p. 19.)

24. Gelfand, M. J., Erez, M., & Aycan, Z. (2007). Cross-cultural organizational behavior. *Annual Review of Psychology, 58,* 479–514.

25. Beugelsdijk, S., Kostova, T., & Roth, K. (2017). An overview of Hofstede-inspired country-level culture research in international business since 2006. *Journal of International Business Studies, 48*(1), 30–47.

26. Taras, V., Steel, P., & Kirkman, B. L. (2016). Does country equate with culture? Beyond geography in the search for cultural boundaries. *Management International Review, 56*(4), 455–487.

27. Hall, E. T. (1977). *Beyond culture.* New York, NY: Random House.

28. Hall, E. T. (2000). Context and meaning. *Intercultural communication: A Reader, 9,* 34–43.

29. Hall, E. T., & Hall, M. R. (1990). *Understanding cultural differences.* Boston: MA: Intercultural Press.

30. Hofstede, G. (1980). *Culture's consequences: International differences in work-related values.* Beverly Hills, CA: Sage. (Quotation on p. 25.)

31. Hofstede, G., & Bond, M. H. (1988). The Confucius connection: From cultural roots to economic growth. *Organizational Dynamics, 16*(4), 5–21.

32. Ibid.

33. Hofstede, G., Hofstede, G. J., & Minkov, M. (2010). *Cultures and organizations, software of the mind: Intercultural cooperation and its importance for survival* (3rd ed.). New York, NY: McGraw-Hill.

34. Hofstede, G. (1980). *Culture's consequences: International differences in work-related values.* Beverly Hills, CA: Sage. (Quotation on p. 25.)

35. Hofstede, G. (1991). *Culture's consequences: International differences in work-related values* (2nd ed.). Newbury Park, CA: Sage.

36. Hofstede, G. (1980). *Culture's consequences: International differences in work-related values.* Beverly Hills, CA: Sage.

37. Gelfand, M. J., Erez, M., & Aycan, Z. (2007). Cross-cultural organizational behavior. *Annual Review of Psychology, 58,* 479–514.

38. Oyserman, D., Coon, H. M., & Kemmelmeier, M. (2002). Rethinking individualism and collectivism: Evaluation of theoretical assumptions and meta-analyses. *Psychological Bulletin, 128*(1), 3–72.

39. Markus, H. R., & Kitayama, S. (1991). Culture and the self: Implications for cognition, emotion, and motivation. *Psychological Review, 98*(2), 224–253.

40. Triandis, H. C. (1995). *Individualism and collectivism.* Boulder, CO: Westview Press.

41. Eby, L. T., & Dobbins, G. H. (1997). Collectivistic orientation in teams: an individual and group-level analysis. *Journal of Organizational Behavior, 18*(3), 275–295.

42. Erez, M., & Somech, A. (1996). Is group productivity loss the rule or the exception? Effects of culture and group-based motivation. *Academy of Management Journal, 39*(6), 1513–1537.

43. Gibson, C. B. (1999). Do they do what they believe they can? Group efficacy and group effectiveness across tasks

and cultures. *Academy of Management Journal, 42*(2), 138–152.

44. Triandis, H. C., & Gelfand, M. J. (1998). Converging measurement of horizontal and vertical individualism and collectivism. *Journal of Personality and Social Psychology, 74*(1), 118–128.

45. Marcus, J., & Le, H. (2013). Interactive effects of levels of individualism-collectivism on cooperation: A meta-analysis. *Journal of Organizational Behavior, 34*(6), 813–834.

46. Prim, A. L., Filho, L. S., Zamur, G. A. C., & Di Serio, L. C. (2017). The relationship between national culture dimensions and degree of innovation. *International Journal of Innovation Management, 21*(1). https://doi.org/10.1142/S136391961730001X

47. Chen, Y., Friedman, R., Yu, E., Fang, W., & Lu, X. (2009). Supervisor–subordinate guanxi: Developing a three dimensional model and scale. *Management and Organization Review, 5*(3), 375–399.

48. Fischer, R., & Mansell, A. (2009). Commitment across cultures: A meta-analytical approach. *Journal of International Business Studies, 40*(8), 1339–1358.

49. Green, E. (2016). What are the most-cited publications in the social sciences according to Google Scholar? Retrieved from: http://blogs.lse.ac.uk/impactofsocialsciences/2016/05/12/what-are-the-most-cited-publications-in-the-social-sciences-according-to-google-scholar/

50. Michael, J. (1997). A conceptual framework for aligning managerial behaviors with cultural work values. *International Journal of Commerce and Management, 7*(3), 81–101.

51. Smith, P. (1998). *The new American cultural sociology.* New York, NY: Cambridge University Press.

52. Jones, M. (2007, June 24–26). *Hofstede—Culturally questionable?* Presentation at the Oxford Business & Economics Conference, Oxford, England.

53. Dorfman, P. W., & Howell, J. P. (1988). Dimensions of national culture and effective leadership patterns: Hofstede revisited. *Advances in International Comparative Management, 3,* 127–150.

54. Kirkman, B. L., Lowe, K. B., & Gibson, C. B. (2016). A retrospective on culture's consequences: The 35-year journey. *Journal of International Business Studies,* 1–18.

55. Taras, V., Kirkman, B. L., & Steel, P. (2010). Examining the impact of culture's consequences: A three-decade, multilevel, meta-analytic review of Hofstede's cultural value dimensions. *Journal of Applied Psychology, 95*(3), 405–439.

56. Yates, J. F., & de Oliviera, S. (2016). Culture and decision making. *Organizational Behavior and Human Decision Processes, 136,* 106–118.

57. Gelfand, M. J., Nishii, L. H., & Raver, J. L. (2006). On the nature and importance of cultural tightness-looseness. *Journal of Applied Psychology, 91*(6), 1225–1244.

58. Gelfand, M. J., Raver, J. L., Nishii, L., Leslie, L. M., Lun, J., Lim, B. C., . . . Yamaguchi, S. (2011). Differences between tight and loose cultures: A 33-nation study. *Science, 332,* 1100–1104.

59. Ibid., p. 1104.

60. Aktas, M., Gelfand, M. J., & Hanges, P. J. (2016). Cultural tightness–looseness and perceptions of effective leadership. *Journal of Cross-Cultural Psychology, 47*(2), 294–309.

61. Javidan, M., Dorfman, P. W., Sully de Luque, M., & House, R. J. (2006). In the eye of the beholder: Leadership lessons from project GLOBE. *Academy of Management Perspectives, 20*(1), 67–90.

62. Hollenbeck, G. P., & McCall, M. W. (2003). Competence, not competencies: Making global executive development work. In W. Mobley & P. Dorfman (Eds.), *Advances in global leadership* (Vol. 3). Oxford, England: JAI Press.

63. Gregersen, H. B., Morrison, A., & Black, J. S. (1998). Developing leaders for the global frontier. *Sloan Management Review, 40,* 21–32.

64. Stahl, G., & Brannen, M. Y. (2013). Building cross-cultural leadership competence: An interview with Carlos Ghosn. *Academy of Management Learning & Education, 12*(3), 494–502. (Quotation on p. 495.)

65. Smith, A., Caver, K., Saslow, S., & Thomas, N. (2009). *Developing the global executive: Challenges and opportunities in a changing world.*

Pittsburgh, PA: Development Dimensions International, Inc.

66. Beechler, S., & Javidan, M. (2007). Leading with a global mindset. In M. Javidan, R. M. Steers, & M. A. Hitt (Eds.), *The global mindset (advances in international management)* (Vol. 19, pp. 131–169). New York, NY: Emerald Group.

67. Casrnir, F. L. (1999). Foundations for the study of intercultural communication based on a third-culture building model. *International Journal of Intercultural Relations, 23*(1), 91–116. (Quotation on p. 92.)

68. Earley, P. C., & Mossakowski, E. (2004, October). Cultural intelligence. *Harvard Business Review,* 139–146.

69. Earley, P. C., & Ang, S. A. (2003). *Cultural intelligence: Individual interactions across cultures.* Stanford, CA: Stanford University Press.

70. Li, M., Mobley, W. H., & Kelly, A. (2016). Linking personality to cultural intelligence: An interactive effect of openness and agreeableness. *Personality and Individual Differences, 89,* 105–110.

71. Earley, P. C., & Mossakowski, E. (2004, October). Cultural intelligence. *Harvard Business Review,* 139–146.

72. Barbuto, J. E., Beenen, G., & Tran, H. (2015). The role of core self-evaluation, ethnocentrism, and cultural intelligence in study abroad success. *International Journal of Management Education, 13*(3), 268–277.

73. Chao, M., Takeuchi, R., & Farh, J. L. (2017). Enhancing cultural intelligence: The roles of implicit culture beliefs and adjustment. *Personnel Psychology, 70,* 257–292.

74. Ang, S., Van Dyne, L., Kohl, C., Ng, K. Y., Templer, K. J., Tayl, C., & Chandrasekar, N. A. (2007). Cultural intelligence: Its measurement and effects on cultural judgment and decision making, cultural adaptation and task performance. *Management and Organization Review, 3*(3), 335–371.

75. Ott, D. L., & Michailova, S. (2016). Cultural intelligence: A review and new research avenues. *International Journal of Management Reviews, 00,* 1–21.

76. Eisenberg, J., Lee, H., Bruck, F., Brenner, B., Claes, M., Mironski, J., & Bell, R. (2013). Can business schools make students culturally competent? Effects of cross-cultural management

courses on cultural intelligence. *Academy of Management Learning & Education, 12*(4), 603–621.

77. Earley, P. C., & Peterson, R. S. (2004). The elusive cultural chameleon: Cultural intelligence as a new approach to training for the global manager. *Academy of Management Learning & Education, 3*(1), 100–115.

78. Berry, J. W. (1980). Acculturation as varieties of adaptation. In A.M. Padilla (Ed.), *Acculturation theory, models and some new findings* (pp. 9–25). Boulder, CO: Westview.

79. Bourhis, R. Y., Moise, L. C., Perreault, S., & Senecal, S. (1997). Towards an interactive acculturation model: A social psychological approach. *International Journal of Psychology, 32*(6), 369–386.

80. Thomas, D. C., Brannen, M. Y., & Garcia, D. (2010). Bicultural individuals and intercultural effectiveness. *European Journal of Cross-Cultural Competence and Management, 1,* 315–333. (Quotation on p. 315.)

81. Ibid.

82. Morris, M. W., Savani, K., Mor, S., & Cho, J. (2014). When in Rome: Intercultural learning and implications for training. *Research in Organizational Behavior, 34,* 189–215.

83. Molinsky, A. (2013). The psychological processes of cultural retooling. *Academy of Management Journal, 56*(3), 683–710.

84. Tadmor, C. T., & Tetlock, P. E. (2006). Biculturalism: A model of the effects of second-culture exposure on acculturation and integrative complexity. *Journal of Cross-Cultural Psychology, 37*(2), 173–190. (Quotation on p. 174.)

85. Tadmor, C. T., Tetlock, P. E., & Peng, K. (2009). Acculturation strategies and integrative complexity: The cognitive implications of biculturalism. *Journal of Cross-Cultural Psychology, 40*(1), 105–139.

86. Oberg, K. (1960). Culture shock adjustment to new cultural environments. *Practical Anthropology, 7,* 177–182.

87. Young, R. (2011). Cross-cultural skills: Essential for expatriate success. Retrieved from http://www.chronicle.com/article/Cross-Cultural-Skills-/128782

88. Javidan, M., Dorfman, P. W., Sully de Luque, M., & House, R. J. (2006). In the eye of the beholder: Leadership lessons from project GLOBE. *Academy of Management Perspectives, 20*(1), 67–90.

89. Conner, J. (2000, Summer–Fall). Developing the global leaders of tomorrow. *Human Resource Management, 39*(2&3), 146–157.

90. Black, J. S., Gregersen, H. B., Mendenhall, M., & Stroh, L. K. (1999). *Globalizing people through international assignments.* New York, NY: Addison-Wesley. (Quotation on p. 1.)

91. Caligiuri, P., & Bonache, J. (2016). Evolving and enduring challenges in global mobility. *Journal of World Business, 51*(1), 127–141.

92. Kraimer, M. L., Wayne, S. J., & Jaworski, R. A. (2001). Sources of support and expatriate performance: The mediating role of expatriate adjustment. *Personnel Psychology, 54*(1), 71–99.

93. Shaffer, M. A., & Harrison, D. A. (1998). Expatriates' psychological withdrawal from international assignments: Work, nonwork, and family influences. *Personnel Psychology, 51*(1), 87–118.

94. Harzing, A. W. K. (1995). The persistent myth of high expatriate failure rates. *International Journal of Human Resource Management, 6*(2), 457–474.

95. Forster, N. (1997). The persistent myth of high expatriate failure rates: A reappraisal. *International Journal of Human Resource Management, 8*(4), 414–433.

96. Daniels, J. D., & Insch, G. (1998). Why are early departure rates from foreign assignments lower than historically reported? *Multinational Business Review, 6*(1), 13–23.

97. Right Management. (2013). Many managers found to fail in overseas assignments. Retrieved from www.right.com/news-and-events/press-releases/2013-press-releases/item25142.aspx

98. Torbiörn, I. (1994). Operative and strategic use of expatriates in new organizations and market structures. *International Studies of Management & Organization, 24*(3), 5–17.

99. Shannonhouse, R. (1996). Overseas-assignment failures. *USA Today/International Edition,* p. 8.

100. Harrison, J. (1994). Developing successful expatriate managers: A framework for the structural design and strategic alignment of cross-cultural training programs. *Human Resource Planning, 17,* 17–35.

101. Kotabe, M., & Helsen, K. (1998). *Global marketing management* (2nd ed.). New York, NY: Wiley.

102. Nowak, C., & Linder, C. (2016). Do you know how much your expatriate costs? An activity-based cost analysis of expatriation. *Journal of Global Mobility, 4*(1), 88–107.

103. Forster, N. (1997). The persistent myth of high expatriate failure rates: A reappraisal. *International Journal of Human Resource Management, 8*(4), 414–433.

104. Andresen, M., Biemann, T., & Pattie, M. W. (2015). What makes them move abroad? Reviewing and exploring differences between self-initiated and assigned expatriation. *International Journal of Human Resource Management, 26*(7), 932–947.

105. Presbitero, A., & Quita, C. (2017). Expatriate career intentions: Links to career adaptability and cultural intelligence. *Journal of Vocational Behavior, 98,* 118–126.

106. Zhang, Y., & Oczkowski, E. (2016). Exploring the potential effects of expatriate adjustment direction. *Cross Cultural & Strategic Management, 23*(1), 158–183.

107. Ramaswami, A., Carter, N. M., & Dreher, G. F. (2016). Expatriation and career success: A human capital perspective. *Human Relations, 69*(10), 1959–1987.

108. Kraimer, M. L., Wayne, S. J., & Jaworski, R. A. (2001). Sources of support and expatriate performance: The mediating role of expatriate adjustment. *Personnel Psychology, 54*(1), 71–99.

109. Van Vianen, A. E., De Pater, I. E., Kristof-Brown, A. L., & Johnson, E. C. (2004). Fitting in: Surface-and deep-level cultural differences and expatriates' adjustment. *Academy of Management Journal, 47*(5), 697–709.

110. Gregersen, H. B., & Black, J. S. (1990). A multifaceted approach to expatriate retention in international assignments. *Group & Organization Management, 15*(4), 461–485.

111. Feldman, D. C., & Thomas, D. C. (1992). Career issues facing expatriate managers. *Journal of International Business Studies, 23*(2), 271–294.

112. Mezias, J. M., & Scandura, T. A. (2005). A needs-driven approach to expatriate adjustment and career development: A multiple mentoring perspective. *Journal of International Business Studies, 36*(5), 519–538.

113. Black, J. S., & Mendenhall, M. (1990). Cross-cultural training effectiveness: A review and theoretical framework for future research. *Academy of Management Review, 15*(1), 113–136.

114. Presbitero, A. (2016). Culture shock and reverse culture shock: The moderating role of cultural intelligence in international students' adaptation. *International Journal of Intercultural Relations, 53*, 28–38.

115. Adler, N. J. (1981). Re-entry: Managing cross-cultural transitions. *Group & Organization Studies, 6*(3), 341–356.

116. Dolins, I. L. (1999). 1998 global relocation survey: Current trends regarding expatriate activity. *Employment Relations Today, 25*(4), 1–11.

117. Gaw, K. F. (2000). Reverse culture shock in students returning from overseas. *International Journal of Intercultural Relations, 24*(1), 83–104.

118. Hsiaoying, T. (1995). Sojourner adjustment: The case of foreigners in Japan. *Journal of Cross-Cultural Psychology, 26*(5), 523–536.

119. Feldman, D. C., & Tompson, H. B. (1992). Entry shock, culture shock: Socializing the new breed of global managers. *Human Resource Management, 31*(4), 345–362.

120. Archer, C. M. (1986). Culture bump and beyond. In J. M. Valdes (Ed.), *Culture bound: Bridging the cultural gap in language teaching*. Cambridge, England: Cambridge University Press.

121. Black, J. S., & Gregersen, H. B. (1992). When Yankee comes home: Factors related to expatriate and spouse repatriation adjustment. *Journal of International Business Studies, 22*(4), 671–695.

122. Black, J. S., Gregersen, H. B., & Mendenhall, M. E. (1992). *Global assignments: Successfully expatriating and repatriating international managers*. San Francisco, CA: Jossey-Bass.

123. Gregersen, H. B., & Black, J. S. (1990). A multifaceted approach to expatriate retention in international assignments. *Group & Organization Management, 15*(4), 461–485.

124. Black, J. S., & Stephens, G. K. (1989). The influence of the spouses on American expatriate adjustment in overseas assignments. *Journal of Management, 15*(4), 529–544.

125. Adler, N. J. (2008). *International dimensions of organizational behavior* (5th ed.). Mason, OH: Thomson.

126. Gregersen, H. B., & Black, J. S. (1992). Antecedents to commitment to a parent company and a foreign operation. *Academy of Management Journal, 35*(1), 65–90.

127. Dezso, C. L., & Ross, D. G. (2012). Does female representation in top management improve firm performance? A panel data investigation. *Strategic Management Journal, 33*(9), 1072–1089.

128. Ibid., p. 1072.

129. Bird, A., & Mendenhall, M. E. (2016). From cross-cultural management to global leadership: Evolution and adaptation. *Journal of World Business, 51*(1), 115–126.

130. Page, S. E. (2007). Making the difference: Applying a logic of diversity. *Academy of Management Perspectives, 21*(4), 6–20.

131. Joplin, J. R. W., & Daus, C. S. (1997). Challenges of leading a diverse workforce. *Academy of Management Executive, 11*(3), 32–45.

132. Gilbert, J. A., & Ivancevich, J. (2000). Valuing diversity: A tale of two organizations. *Academy of Management Executive, 14*(1), 93–105.

Chapter 14

1. Schein, E. H. (1984). Coming to a new awareness of organizational culture. *Sloan Management Review, 25*(2), 3–16. (Quotation on p. 3.)

2. Chatman, J. A., & O'Reilly, C. A. (2016). Paradigm lost: Reinvigorating the study of organizational culture. *Research in Organizational Behavior, 36*, 199–224.

3. Chatman, J. A., & Jehn, K. A. (1994). Assessing the relationship between industry characteristics and organizational culture: How different can you be? *Academy of Management Journal, 37*(3), 522–553.

4. Pennington, R. (2006). *Results rule! Build a culture that blows the competition away*. New York, NY: Wiley.

5. Ouchi, W. G. (1980). Markets, bureaucracies, and clans. *Administrative Science Quarterly*, 129–141.

6. Ouchi, W. G. (1979). A conceptual framework for the design of organizational control mechanisms. *Management Science, 25*(9), 833–848.

7. House, R. J., Hanges, P. J., Javidan, M., Dorfman, P. W., & Gupta, V. (Eds.). (2004). *Culture, leadership, and organizations: The GLOBE study of 62 societies*. Thousand Oaks, CA: Sage.

8. Van Muijen, J. J., & Koopman, P. L. (1994). The influence of national culture on organizational culture: A comparative study between 10 countries. *European Journal of Work and Organizational Psychology, 4*(4), 367–380.

9. Gerhart, B. (2009). How much does national culture constrain organizational culture? *Management and Organization Review, 5*(2), 241–259.

10. Denison, D. R., Haaland, S., & Goelzer, P. (2004). Corporate culture and organizational effectiveness: Is Asia different from the rest of the world? *Organizational Dynamics, 33*(1), 98–109.

11. Denison, D. R., & Mishra, A. K. (1995). Toward a theory of organizational culture and effectiveness. *Organization Science, 6*(2), 204–223.

12. Denison, D. R., Haaland, S., & Goelzer, P. (2004). Corporate culture and organizational effectiveness: Is Asia different from the rest of the world? *Organizational Dynamics, 33*(1), 98–109.

13. Fey, C. F., & Denison, D. R. (2003). Organizational culture and effectiveness: Can American theory be applied in Russia? *Organization Science, 14*(6), 686–706.

14. Siadat, S. H., Abdollahi, A., & Mohseni, M. (2016). Impact of organizational culture on knowledge management. *Management and Administrative Sciences Review, 5*, 1–12.

15. O'Reilly, C. (1989). Corporations, culture, and commitment: Motivation and social control in organizations.

California Management Review, 31(4), 9–25.

16. Barney, J. B. (1986). Organizational culture: Can it be a source of sustained competitive advantage? *Academy of Management Review, 11*(3), 656–665.

17. Gordon, G. G., & DiTomaso, N. (1992). Predicting corporate performance from organizational culture. *Journal of Management Studies, 29*(6), 783–798.

18. Sørensen, J. B. (2002). The strength of corporate culture and the reliability of firm performance. *Administrative Science Quarterly, 47*(1), 70–91.

19. O'Reilly, C. A., Chatman, J. A., & Caldwell, D. F. (1991). People and organizational culture: A profile comparison approach to assessing person-organization fit. *Academy of Management Journal, 34*(3), 487–516.

20. Vandenberghe, C. (1999). Organizational culture, person-culture fit, and turnover: A replication in the health care industry. *Journal of Organizational Behavior, 20*(2), 175–184.

21. Sørensen, J. B. (2002). The strength of corporate culture and the reliability of firm performance. *Administrative Science Quarterly, 47*(1), 70–91.

22. Warrick, D. D., Milliman, J. F., & Ferguson, J. M. (2016). Building high performance cultures. *Organizational Dynamics, 45*(1), 64–70.

23. Rosenbaum, S. (2010). The happiness culture: Zappos isn't a company, it's a mission. Retrieved from http://www.fastcompany.com/1657030/happiness-culture-zappos-isnt-company-its-mission

24. Boisnier, A., & Chatman, J. (2003). Cultures and subcultures in dynamic organizations. In E. Mannix & R. Petersen (Eds.), *The dynamic organization* (pp. 87–114). Mahwah, NJ: Erlbaum.

25. Schein, E. H. (1996). Culture: The missing concept in organization studies. *Administrative Science Quarterly, 41*(2), 229–240. (Quotation on p. 237.)

26. Stone, B. (2013). The secrets of Bezos: How Amazon became the everything store. Retrieved from http://www.businessweek.com/articles/2013-10-10/jeff-bezos-and-the-age-of-amazon-excerpt-from-the-everything-store-by-brad-stone

27. Wanberg, C. R. (2012). Facilitating organizational socialization: An introduction. In C. R. Wanberg (Ed.), *The Oxford handbook of organizational socialization* (pp. 17–21). New York, NY: Oxford University Press.

28. Schein, E. H. (2003). Organizational socialization and the profession of management. In L. W. Porter, H. L. Angle, & R. W. Allen (Eds.), *Organizational influence processes* (pp. 283–294). New York, NY: M. E. Sharpe.

29. Jablin, F. M. (1987). Organizational entry, assimilation, and exit. In L. L. Putnam, K. H. Roberts, & L. W. Porter (Eds.), *Handbook of organizational communication: An interdisciplinary perspective* (pp. 679–740). Newbury Park, CA: Sage.

30. Kramer, M. W. (2010). *Organizational socialization: Joining and leaving organizations.* Malden, MA: Polity.

31. Ellis, A. M., Nifadkar, S. S., Bauer, T. N., & Erdogan, B. (2017). Newcomer adjustment: Examining the role of managers' perception of newcomer proactive behavior during organizational socialization. *Journal of Applied Psychology, 102*(6), 993–1001. http://dx.doi.org/10.1037/apl0000201

32. Bauer, T. N., & Erdogan, B. (2011). Organizational socialization: The effective onboarding of new employees. In S. Zedeck (Ed.), *APA handbook of industrial and organizational psychology, Vol. 3: Maintaining, expanding, and contracting the organization* (pp. 51–64). Washington, DC: American Psychological Association.

33. Delobbe, N., Cooper-Thomas, H. D., & De Hoe, R. (2016). A new look at the psychological contract during organizational socialization: The role of newcomers' obligations at entry. *Journal of Organizational Behavior, 37*(6), 845–867.

34. Bauer, T. N., Bodner, T., Erdogan, B., Truxillo, D. M., & Tucker, J. S. (2007). Newcomer adjustment during organizational socialization: A meta-analytic review of antecedents, outcomes, and methods. *Journal of Applied Psychology, 92*(3), 707–721.

35. Schneider, B., Goldstein, H. W., & Smith, D. B. (1995). The ASA framework: An update. *Personnel Psychology, 48*(4), 747–773.

36. Bretz, R. D., Ash, R. A., & Dreher, G. F. (1989). Do people make the place? An examination of the attraction-selection-attrition hypothesis. *Personnel Psychology, 42*(3), 561–581.

37. De Cooman, R., De Gieter, S., Pepermans, R., Hermans, S., Du Bois, C., Caers, R., & Jegers, M. (2009). Person–organization fit: Testing socialization and attraction–selection–attrition hypotheses. *Journal of Vocational Behavior, 74*(1), 102–107.

38. McCulloch, M. C., & Turban, D. B. (2007). Using person–organization fit to select employees for high-turnover jobs. *International Journal of Selection and Assessment, 15*(1), 63–71.

39. Prashanth, K. (2003). *Human resource management: Best practices at FedEx Corporation.* IBS Center for Management. Retrieved from http://www.academia.edu/9031020/Human_Resource_Management_Best_Practices_at_FedEx_Corporation

40. FedEx (2017). FedEx Corporate Fact Sheet. Retrieved from http://about.van.fedex.com/our-story/company-structure/corporate-fact-sheet/

41. Boje, D. M. (1995). Stories of the storytelling organization: A postmodern analysis of Disney as "*Tamara*-Land." *Academy of Management Journal, 38*(4), 997–1035.

42. Sole, D., & Wilson, D. G. (2002). *Storytelling in organizations: The power and traps of using stories to share knowledge in organizations.* LILA, Harvard, Graduate School of Education. Retrieved from http://www.providersedge.com/docs/km_articles/Storytelling_in_Organizations.pdf

43. Weick, K. (1995). *Sensemaking in organizations.* Thousand Oaks, CA: Sage.

44. Merchant, A., Ford, J. B., & Sargeant, A. (2010). Charitable organizations' storytelling influence on donors' emotions and intentions. *Journal of Business Research, 63*(7), 754–762.

45. Morgan, S., & Dennehy, R. F. (1995). Organizational storytelling: Telling tales in the business classroom. *Developments in Business Simulation & Experiential Exercises, 22,* 160–165.

46. Islam, G., & Zyphur, M. J. (2009). Rituals in organizations: A review and expansion of current theory. *Group & Organization Management, 34*(1), 114–139. (Quotation on p. 116.)

47. Erhardt, N., Martin-Rios, C., & Heckscher, C. (2016). Am I doing the right thing? Unpacking workplace rituals as mechanisms for strong organizational culture. *International Journal of Hospitality Management, 59,* 31–41.

48. Rafaeli, A., & Pratt, M. G. (Eds.). (2013). *Artifacts and organizations: Beyond mere symbolism.* New York, NY: Psychology Press.

49. Anand, N., & Watson, M. R. (2004). Tournament rituals in the evolution of fields: The case of the Grammy Awards. *Academy of Management Journal, 47*(1), 59–80.

50. Sole, D., & Wilson, D. G. (2002). *Storytelling in organizations: The power and traps of using stories to share knowledge in organizations.* LILA, Harvard, Graduate School of Education. Retrieved from http://www.providersedge.com/docs/km_articles/Storytelling_in_Organizations.pdf

51. Rafaeli, A., & Worline, M. (2000). Symbols in organizational culture. In N. M. Ashkanasy, C. P. M. Wilderom, and M. F. Peterson (Eds.), *Handbook of organizational culture and climate.* Thousand Oaks, CA: Sage.

52. Rafaeli, A., & Pratt, M. G. (1993). Tailored meanings: On the meaning and impact of organizational dress. *Academy of Management Review, 18*(1), 32–55.

53. Schleckser, J. (2015). Use stories and symbols to build a powerful culture. Retrieved from https://www.inc.com/jim-schleckser/use-stories-and-symbols-to-build-a-powerful-culture.html

54. Van Maanen, J. (1996). The smile factory: Work at Disneyland. In P. J. Frost, L. F. Moore, M. R. Louis, & C. C. Lundberg, *Reframing organizational culture* (pp. 58–76). Newbury Park, CA: Sage.

55. Denison, D. R. (1996). What is the difference between organizational culture and organizational climate? A native's point of view on a decade of paradigm wars. *Academy of Management Review, 21*(3), 619–654.

56. Reichers, A. E., & Schneider, B. (1990). Climate and culture: An evolution of constructs. *Organizational Climate and Culture, 1,* 5–39. (Quotation on p. 22.)

57. Denison, D. R. (1996). What is the difference between organizational culture and organizational climate? A native's point of view on a decade of paradigm wars. *Academy of Management Review, 21*(3), 619–654.

58. Ostroff, C., Kinicki, A. J., & Tamkins, M. M. (2003). *Organizational culture and climate.* New York, NY: Wiley.

59. Schneider, B., Ehrhart, M. G., & Macey, W. H. (2013). Organizational climate and culture. *Annual Review of Psychology, 64,* 361–388.

60. Schneider, B., Ehrhart, M. G., & Macey, W. H. (2011). Organizational climate research: Achievements and the road ahead. In N. M. Ashkanasy, C. P. M. Wilderom, & M. F. Peterson (Eds.), *The handbook of organizational culture and climate* (2nd ed., pp. 29–49). Thousand Oaks, CA: Sage. (Quotation on p. 42.)

61. Ibid.

62. Ehrhart, K. H., Witt, L. A., Schneider, B., & Perry, S. J. (2011). Service employees give as they get: Internal service as a moderator of the service climate–service outcomes link. *Journal of Applied Psychology, 96*(2), 423–431.

63. Gonzalez-Roma, V., Peiro, J. M., & Tordera, N. (2002). An examination of the antecedents and moderator influences of climate strength. *Journal of Applied Psychology, 87*(3), 465–473.

64. Naumann, S. E., & Bennett, N. (2000). A case for procedural justice climate: Development and test of a multilevel model. *Academy of Management Journal, 43*(5), 881–889.

65. Pugh, S. D., Dietz, J., Brief, A. P., & Wiley, J. W. (2008). Looking inside and out: The impact of employee and community demographic composition on organizational diversity climate. *Journal of Applied Psychology, 93*(6), 1422–1428.

66. Wallace, J. C., Popp, E., & Mondore, S. (2006). Safety climate as a mediator between foundation climates and occupational accidents: A group-level investigation. *Journal of Applied Psychology, 91*(3), 681–688.

67. Gelfand, M. J., Nishii, L. H., Raver, J., & Schneider, B. (2005). Discrimination in organizations: An organizational level systems perspective. In R. Dipboye & A. Colella (Eds.), *Discrimination at work: The psychological and organizational bases* (pp. 89–116). Mahwah, NJ: Erlbaum. (Quotation on p. 104.)

68. McKay, P. F., Avery, D. R., Tonidandel, S., Morris, M. A., Hernandez, M., & Hebl, M. R. (2007). Racial differences in

69. Schminke, M., Ambrose, M. L., & Neubaum, D. O. (2005). The effect of leader moral development on ethical climate and employee attitudes. *Organizational Behavior and Human Decision Processes, 97*(2), 135–151.

70. Victor, B., & Cullen, J. B. (1988). The organizational bases of ethical work climates. *Administrative Science Quarterly, 33*(1), 101–125.

71. Ibid.

72. Mayer, D. M., Kuenzi, M., & Greenbaum, R. L. (2010). Examining the link between ethical leadership and employee misconduct: The mediating role of ethical climate. *Journal of Business Ethics, 95*(1), 7–16.

73. Kangas, M., Muotka, J., Huhtala, M., Mäkikangas, A., & Feldt, T. (2015). Is the ethical culture of the organization associated with sickness absence? A multilevel analysis in a public sector organization. *Journal of Business Ethics,* 1–15.

74. Martin, K. D., & Cullen, J. B. (2006). Continuities and extensions of ethical climate theory: A meta-analytic review. *Journal of Business Ethics, 69*(2), 175–194.

75. employee retention: Are diversity climate perceptions the key? *Personnel Psychology, 60*(1), 35–62.

76. Carr, J. Z., Schmidt, A. M., Ford, J. K., & DeShon, R. P. (2003). Climate perceptions matter: A meta-analytic path analysis relating molar climate, cognitive and affective states, and individual level work outcomes. *Journal of Applied Psychology, 88*(4), 605.

77. Gerstner, L. V., Jr. (2002). *Who says elephants can't dance? Inside IBM's historic turnaround.* New York, NY: HarperCollins. (Quotation on p. 182.)

78. Steers, R. M., & Shim, W. S. (2013). Strong leaders, strong cultures: Global management lessons from Toyota and Hyundai. *Organizational Dynamics, 42*(3), 217–227.

79. Levering, R. (2016). This year's best employers have focused on fairness. Retrieved from http://fortune. com/2016/03/03/best-companies-2016-intro/

80. Hartnell, C. A., Kinicki, A. J., Lambert, L. S., Fugate, M., & Doyle Corner, P. (2016). Do similarities or differences between CEO leadership and organizational culture have a more positive effect on firm performance? A

test of competing predictions. *Journal of Applied Psychology*, *101*(6), 846–861.

81. Warrick, D. D. (2017, May–June). What leaders need to know about organizational culture. *Business Horizons, 60*(3), 395–404. http://dx.doi.org/10.1016/j.bushor.2017.01.011

82. Chatman, J. A., & Cha, S. E. (2003). Leading by leveraging culture. *California Management Review, 45*(4), 20–34.

83. VoiceGlance. (2014). How Southwest hires: Taking fun seriously. Retrieved from http://voiceglance.com/how-southwest-hires-taking-fun-seriously/

84. Warrick, D. D. (2017, May–June). What leaders need to know about organizational culture. *Business Horizons, 60*(3), 395–404. http://dx.doi.org/10.1016/j.bushor.2017.01.011

Chapter 15

1. Jacobs, P., Schlatmann, B., & Mahadevan, D. (2017). ING's agile transformation. Retrieved from http://www.mckinsey.com/industries/financial-services/our-insights/ings-agile-transformation

2. Ibid.

3. Beer, M., Eisenstat, R. A., & Spector, B. (1993). Why change programs don't produce change. In C. Mabey & B. Mayon-White (Eds.), *Managing change*. London, England: P.C.P.

4. Argyris, C. (1990). *Overcoming organizational defenses*. Boston, MA: Allyn & Bacon.

5. Oswick, C., Grant, D., Michelson, G., & Wailes, N. (2005). Looking forwards: Discursive directions in organizational change. *Journal of Organizational Change Management, 18*(4), 383–390.

6. Weick, K. E., & Quinn, R. E. (1999). Organizational change and development. *Annual Review of Psychology, 50*(1), 361–386.

7. Malhotra, N., & Hinings, C. B. (2015). Unpacking continuity and change as a process of organizational transformation. *Long Range Planning, 48*(1), 1–22.

8. Robertson, P. J., Roberts, D. R., & Porras, J. I. (1993). Dynamics of planned organizational change: Assessing empirical support for a theoretical model. *Academy of Management Journal, 36*(3), 619–634.

9. Mike, B., & Slocum, J. W. (2003). Slice of reality-changing culture at Pizza Hut and Yum! Brands, Inc. *Organizational Dynamics, 32*(4), 319–330.

10. Lewin, K. (1951). *Field theory in social science*. New York, NY: Harper & Row. (Quotation on p. 169.)

11. Bennis, W. G. (1966). *Changing organizations*. New York, NY: McGraw-Hill.

12. Austin, J. R., & Bartunek, J. M. (2006). Theories and practices of organizational development. In J. Gallos (Ed.), *Organization development* (pp. 89–128). San Francisco, CA: Jossey-Bass.

13. Edwards, J. E., & Thomas, M. D. (1993). The organizational survey process: General steps and practical considerations. *American Behavioral Scientist, 36*(4), 419–442.

14. Austin, J. R., & Bartunek, J. M. (2006). Theories and practices of organizational development. In J. Gallos (Ed.), *Organization development* (pp. 89–128). San Francisco, CA: Jossey-Bass.

15. Bunker, B. B., & Alban, B. T. (1997). *Large group interventions*. San Francisco, CA: Jossey-Bass.

16. Schaffer, R. H., & Stearn, J. M. (2015). The rapid results package: Better performance/stronger managers. *Business Horizons, 58*(6), 687–695. (Quotation on p. 690.)

17. Schein, E. H. (1990). A general philosophy of helping: Process consultation. *Sloan Management Review, 31*(3), 57–64.

18. Dyer, W. G., Jr., Dyer, J. H., & Dyer, W. G. (2013). *Team building: Proven strategies for improving team performance*. New York, NY: Wiley.

19. Neuman, G. A., Edwards, J. E., & Raju, N. S. (1989). Organizational development interventions: A meta-analysis of their effects on satisfaction and other attitudes. *Personnel Psychology, 42*(3), 461–489.

20. Salas, E., Rozell, D., Mullen, B., & Driskell, J. E. (1999). The effect of team building on performance: An integration. *Small Group Research, 30*(3), 309–329.

21. Sparks, G. A., Herman, R., Wolfe, P., & Zurick, A. (2015). Leading through

the complexities of team dynamics to achieve and sustain organizational goals. *Journal of Behavioral Studies in Business, 8*, 1–12.

22. Cooperrider, D. L., & Srivastva, S. (1987). Appreciative inquiry in organizational life. *Research in Organizational Change and Development, 1*(1), 129–169.

23. Luthans, F., & Church, A. H. (2002). Positive organizational behavior: Developing and managing psychological strengths. *Academy of Management Executive, 16*(1), 57–75.

24. Conklin, T. A., & Hartman, N. S. (2014). Appreciative inquiry and autonomy-supportive classes in business education: A semi-longitudinal study of AI in the classroom. *Journal of Experiential Education, 37*(3), 285–309.

25. Bushe, G. R. (1999). Advances in appreciative inquiry as an organization development intervention. *Organization Development Journal, 17*(2), 61–68.

26. Bushe, G. R., & Coetzer, G. (1995). Appreciative inquiry as a team-development intervention: A controlled experiment. *Journal of Applied Behavioral Science, 31*(1), 13–30.

27. Bushe, G. R., & Kassam, A. F. (2005). When is appreciative inquiry transformational? A meta-case analysis. *Journal of Applied Behavioral Science, 41*(2), 161–181.

28. Verleysen, B., Lambrechts, F., & Van Acker, F. (2015). Building psychological capital with appreciative inquiry: Investigating the mediating role of basic psychological need satisfaction. *Journal of Applied Behavioral Science, 51*(1), 10–35.

29. Bushe, G. R., & Paranjpey, N. (2015). Comparing the generativity of problem

solving and appreciative inquiry: A field experiment. *Journal of Applied Behavioral Science, 51*(3), 309–335.

30. Benn, S., Dunphy, D., & Griffiths, A. (2014). *Organizational change for corporate sustainability* (3rd ed.). New York, NY: Routledge.

31. World Commission on Environment and Development. (1987). *Our common future.* Oxford, England: Oxford University Press.

32. Weber, S. (2014). Seed donation: DuPont and Gift of the Givers collaborate to advance women farmers in Malawi. Retrieved from http://us.vocuspr.com/Newsroom/MultiQuery.aspx?SiteName=Dupont EMEA&Entity=PRAsset&SF_PRAssetPRAssetID_EQ=129627&XSL=NewsRelease&IncludeChildren=True&Lang=English

33. Sahoo, C. K., & Sharma, R. (2015). Managing grass root-level change in an Indian PSU: The role of people-centric strategies. *South Asian Journal of Management, 22*(3), 28–47.

34. Lines, R. (2004). Influence of participation in strategic change: Resistance, organizational commitment and change goal achievement. *Journal of Change Management, 4*(3), 193–215.

35. Herscovitch, L., & Meyer, J. P. (2002). Commitment to organizational change: Extension of a three-component model. *Journal of Applied Psychology, 87*(3), 474–487.

36. Coch, L., & French, J. R. (1948). Overcoming resistance to change. *Human Relations, 1*(4), 512–532.

37. Burnes, B. (2015). Understanding resistance to change—building on Coch and French. *Journal of Change Management, 15*(2), 92–116.

38. Burke, W. W. (2010). *Organization change: Theory and practice.* Thousand Oaks, CA: Sage.

39. Katz, D., & Kahn, R. L. (1978). *The social psychology of organizations* (2nd ed.). New York, NY: Wiley.

40. Nadler, D. A. (1987). The effective management of organizational change. *Handbook of organizational behavior* (pp. 358–369). Englewood Cliffs, NJ: Prentice Hall.

41. Rafferty, A. E., & Jimmieson, N. L. (2016). Subjective perceptions of organizational change and employee resistance to change: Direct and mediated relationships with employee

well-being. *British Journal of Management, 28,* 248–264.

42. Turgut, S., Michel, A., Rothenhöfer, L. M., & Sonntag, K. (2016). Dispositional resistance to change and emotional exhaustion: Moderating effects at the work-unit level. *European Journal of Work and Organizational Psychology, 25*(5), 735–750.

43. Kotter, J. P., & Schlesinger, L. A. (1978). Choosing strategies for change. *Harvard Business Review, 57*(2), 106–114.

44. Furst, S. A., & Cable, D. M. (2008). Employee resistance to organizational change: Managerial influence tactics and leader-member exchange. *Journal of Applied Psychology, 93*(2), 453–462.

45. Tierney, P. (1999). Work relations as a precursor to a psychological climate for change: The role of work group supervisors and peers. *Journal of Organizational Change Management, 12*(2), 120–134.

46. Rousseau, D. M., & Tijoriwala, S. A. (1999). What's a good reason to change? Motivated reasoning and social accounts in promoting organizational change. *Journal of Applied Psychology, 84*(4), 514–528.

47. Oreg, S. (2006). Personality, context, and resistance to organizational change. *European Journal of Work and Organizational Psychology, 15*(1), 73–101.

48. Whelen-Berry, K. S., Gordon, J. R., & Hinings, C. R. (2003). Strengthening organizational change processes: Recommendations and implications from a multi-level analysis. *Journal of Applied Behavioral Science, 39*(2), 186–207.

49. Bass, B. M., & Steidlmeier, P. (1999). Ethics, character, and authentic transformational leadership behavior. *Leadership Quarterly, 10*(2), 181–217. (Quotation on p. 181.)

50. Sharif, M. M., & Scandura, T. A. (2014). Do perceptions of ethical conduct matter during organizational change? Ethical leadership and employee involvement. *Journal of Business Ethics, 124*(2), 185–196.

51. Jones, S. L., & Van de Ven, A. H. (2016). The changing nature of change resistance: An examination of the moderating impact of time. *Journal of Applied Behavioral Science, 52*(4), 482–506.

52. Bakari, H., Hunjra, A. I., & Niazi, G. S. K. (2017). How does

authentic leadership influence planned organizational change? The role of employees' perceptions: Integration of theory of planned behavior and Lewin's three step model. *Journal of Change Management, 17*(2), 155–187.

53. Espedal, B. (2017). Understanding how balancing autonomy and power might occur in leading organizational change. *European Management Journal, 35*(2), 155–163. (Quotation on p. 159.)

54. Kim, T. (2015). Diffusion of changes in organizations. *Journal of Organizational Change Management, 28*(1), 134–152.

55. Burnes, B. (2004). Kurt Lewin and the planned approach to change: A re-appraisal. *Journal of Management Studies, 41*(6), 977–1002. (Quotation on p. 977.)

56. Lewin, K. (1951). *Field theory in social science.* New York, NY: Harper & Row.

57. Hughes, M. (2016). Leading changes: Why transformation explanations fail. *Leadership, 12*(4), 449–469.

58. Kotter, J. P. (1995). Leading change: Why transformation efforts fail. *Harvard Business Review, 73*(2), 59–67.

59. Hughes, M. (2016). Leading changes: Why transformation explanations fail. *Leadership, 12*(4), 449–469.

60. Nadler, D. A., & Tushman, M. L. (1990). Beyond the charismatic leader: Leadership and organizational change. *California Management Review, 32*(2), 77–97.

61. Rodgers, R., Hunter, J. E., & Rogers, D. L. (1993). Influence of top management commitment on management program success. *Journal of Applied Psychology, 78*(1), 151–155.

62. Neuman, G. A., Edwards, J. E., & Raju, N. S. (1989). Organizational development interventions: A meta-analysis of their effects on satisfaction and other attitudes. *Personnel Psychology, 42*(3), 461–489.

63. Herscovitch, L., & Meyer, J. P. (2002). Commitment to organizational change: Extension of a three-component model. *Journal of Applied Psychology, 87*(3), 474–487.

64. Mishra, A. K., Mishra, K. E., & Spreitzer, G. M. (2009). Downsizing the company without downsizing morale. *MIT Sloan Management Review, 50*(3), 39–44.

65. Sutton, R. I. (2009, June). How to be a good boss in a bad economy. *Harvard Business Review,* pp. 42–50. (Quotation on p. 44.)

66. Wisse, B., & Sleebos, E. (2016). When change causes stress: Effects of self-construal and change consequences. *Journal of Business and Psychology, 31*(2), 249–264.

67. Ashford, S. J. (1988). Individual strategies for coping with stress during organizational transitions. *Journal of Applied Behavioral Science, 24*(1), 19–36.

68. Smollan, R. K. (2015). Causes of stress before, during and after organizational change: A qualitative study. *Journal of Organizational Change Management, 28*(2), 301–314.

69. Quick, J. C., Quick, J. D., Nelson, D. L., & Hurrell J. J., Jr. (1997). *Preventive stress management in organizations.* Washington, DC: American Psychological Association.

70. Schweiger, D. M., & Denisi, A. S. (1991). Communication with employees following a merger: A longitudinal field experiment. *Academy of Management Journal, 34*(1), 110–135.

71. Johnson, K. J. (2016). The dimensions and effects of excessive change. *Journal of Organizational Change Management, 29*(3), 445–459.

72. Bordia, P., Hobman, E., Jones, E., Gallois, C., & Callan, V. J. (2004). Uncertainty during organizational change: Types, consequences, and management strategies. *Journal of Business and Psychology, 18*(4), 507–532.

73. Beehr, T. A., & Bhagat, R. S. (1985). *Human stress and cognition in organizations: An integrated perspective.* New York, NY: Wiley.

74. Begley, T. M., & Czajka, J. M. (1993). Panel analysis of the moderating effects of commitment on job satisfaction, intent to quit, and health following organizational change. *Journal of Applied Psychology, 78*(4), 552–556.

75. Theorell, T. (1999). How to deal with stress in organizations? A health perspective on theory and practice. *Scandinavian Journal of Work, Environment & Health, 25*(6), 616–624.

76. Parker, D. F., & DeCotiis, T. A. (1983). Organizational determinants of job stress. *Organizational Behavior and Human Performance, 32*(2), 160–177.

77. Manning, D., & Preston, A. (2003). Organizational stress: Focusing on ways to minimize distress. *CUPA HR Journal, 54*, 15–18. (Quotation on p. 16.)

78. Schumacher, D., Schreurs, B., van Emmerik, H., & de Witte, H. (2016). Explaining the relation between job insecurity and employee outcomes during organizational change: A multiple group comparison. *Human Resource Management, 55*(5), 809–827.

79. Pritchett, P., & Pound, R. (1995). *A survival guide to the stress of organizational change.* New York, NY: Pritchett & Associates.

80. Cohen, S., & Janacki-Deverts, D. (2012). Who's stressed? Distributions of psychological stress in the United States in probability samples from 1983, 2006, and 2009. *Journal of Applied Social Psychology, 42*(6), 1320–1334.

81. Callan, V. J. (1993). Individual and organizational strategies for coping with organizational change. *Work & Stress, 7*(1), 63–75.

82. Rafferty, A. E., & Griffin, M. A. (2006). Perceptions of organizational change: A stress and coping perspective. *Journal of Applied Psychology, 91*(5), 1154–1162.

83. Pluta, A., & Rudawska, A. (2016). Holistic approach to human resources and organizational acceleration. *Journal of Organizational Change Management, 29*(2), 293–309.

84. Matteson, M. T., & Ivancevich, J. M. (1987). *Controlling work stress: Effective human resource and management strategies.* New York, NY: Jossey-Bass. (Quotation on p. 7.)

85. Karasek, R. A. (1979). Job demands, job decision latitude, and mental strain: Implications for job redesign. *Administrative Science Quarterly, 24*, 285–308.

86. Smith, N. (2012). Employees reveal how stress affects their jobs . Retrieved from http://www .businessnewsdaily.com/2267-workplace-stress-health-epidemic-perventable-employee-assistance-programs.html

87. Goetzel, R. Z., Anderson, D. R., Whitmer, R. W., Ozminkowski, R. J., Dunn, R. L., Wasserman, J., & Health Enhancement Research Organization (HERO) Research Committee. (1998). The relationship between modifiable health risks and health care expenditures: An analysis of the multi-employer HERO health risk and cost database. *Journal of Occupational and Environmental Medicine, 40*(10), 843–854.

88. Cooper, C. L., Liukkonen, P., & Cartwright, S. (1996). *Stress prevention in the workplace: Assessing the costs and benefits to organizations.* Dublin, Ireland: European Foundation for the Improvement of Living and Working Conditions.

89. Maslach, C. (1998). A multidimensional theory of burnout. In C. L. Cooper (Ed.), *Theories of organizational stress.* (pp. 68–85). Oxford, England: Oxford University Press. (Quotation on p. 68.)

90. Maslach, C., & Leiter, M. P. (2008). *The truth about burnout: How organizations cause personal stress and what to do about it.* New York, NY: Wiley.

91. Quick, J. C., Quick, J. D., Nelson, D. L., & Hurrell J. J., Jr. (1997). *Preventive stress management in organizations.* Washington, DC: American Psychological Association. (Quotation on p. 3.)

92. Kahn, R. L., & Byosiere, P. (1992). Stress in organizations. In M. D. Dunette & L. M. Hough (Eds.), *Handbook of industrial & organizational psychology* (2nd ed., Vol. 3, pp. 571–650). Palo Alto, CA: Consulting Psychologists Press.

93. American Psychological Association. (2014). *Stress in America.* Retrieved from http://www.apa.org/news/press/releases/stress/2013/stress-report.pdf

94. Selye, H. (1976). Forty years of stress research: Principal remaining problems and misconceptions. *Canadian Medical Association Journal, 115*(1), 53–56.

95. Cavanaugh, M. A., Boswell, W. R., Roehling, M. V., & Boudreau, J. W. (2000). An empirical examination of self-reported work stress among U.S. managers. *Journal of Applied Psychology, 85*(1), 65–74.

96. LePine, M. A., Zhang, Y., Crawford, E. R., & Rich, B. L. (2016). Turning their pain to gain: Charismatic leader influence on follower stress appraisal and job performance. *Academy of Management Journal, 59*(3), 1036–1059.

97. Diamond, D. M., Campbell, A. M., Park, C. R., Halonen, J., & Zoladz, P. R. (2007). The temporal dynamics model of emotional memory processing: A

synthesis on the neurobiological basis of stress-induced amnesia, flashbulb and traumatic memories, and the Yerkes-Dodson law. *Neural Plasticity, (2007)*, 1–33. https://doi.org/10.1155/2007/60803

98. Yerkes, R. M., & Dodson, J. D. (1908). The relation of strength of stimulus to rapidity of habit-formation. *Journal of Comparative Neurology and Psychology*, 18(5), 459–482.

99. Boswell, W. R., Olson-Buchanan, J. B., & LePine, M. A. (2004). Relations between stress and work outcomes: The role of felt challenge, job control, and psychological strain. *Journal of Vocational Behavior*, 64(1), 165–181.

100. LePine, J. A., LePine, M. A., & Jackson, C. L. (2004). Challenges and hindrance stress: Relationships with exhaustion, motivation to learn and learning performance. *Journal of Applied Psychology*, 89, 883–891.

101. Podsakoff, N. P., LePine, J. A., & LePine, M. A. (2007). Differential challenge stressor-hindrance stressor relationships with job attitudes, turnover intentions, turnover, and withdrawal behavior: A meta-analysis. *Journal of Applied Psychology*, 92(2), 438–454.

102. Jex, S. M., & Crossley, C. D. (2005). Organizational consequences. In J. Barling, E. K. Kelloway, & M. R. Frone (Eds.), *Handbook of work stress* (pp. 575–599). Thousand Oaks, CA: Sage.

103. Kahn, R. L., & Byosiere, P. (1992). Stress in organizations. In M. D. Dunette & L. M. Hough (Eds.), *Handbook of industrial & organizational psychology* (2nd ed., Vol. 3, pp. 571–650). Palo Alto, CA: Consulting Psychologists Press.

104. Sonnentag, S., & Frese, M. (2003). Stress in organizations. In W. C. Borman, D. R. Ilgen, & R. J. Klimoski (Eds.), *Handbook of psychology* (pp. 453–491). New York, NY: Wiley.

105. Rizzo, J. R., House, R. J., & Lirtzman, S. I. (1970). Role conflict and ambiguity in complex organizations. *Administrative Science Quarterly*, 150–163.

106. House, R. J., & Rizzo, J. R. (1972). Role conflict and ambiguity as critical variables in a model of organizational behavior. *Organizational Behavior and Human Performance*, 7(3), 467–505.

107. Kahn, R. L. (1980). Conflict, ambiguity, and overload: Three elements in job stress. In D. Katz, R. Kahn, & J. Adams (Eds.), *The study of organizations* (pp. 418–428). San Francisco, CA: Jossey-Bass.

108. Beehr, T. A. (1985). Organizational stress and employee effectiveness. In T. A. Beehr & R. S. Bhagat (Eds.), *Human stress and cognition in organizations: An integrated perspective* (pp. 57–81). New York, NY: Wiley.

109. Singh, A. P., & Singhi, N. (2015). Organizational role stress and social support as predictors of job satisfaction among managerial personnel. *Journal of Psychosocial Research*, 10(1), 1–10.

110. Chiu, S. F., Yeh, S. P., & Huang, T. C. (2015). Role stressors and employee deviance: The moderating effect of social support. *Personnel Review*, 44(2), 308–324.

111. Akgunduz, Y. (2015). The influence of self-esteem and role stress on job performance in hotel businesses. *International Journal of Contemporary Hospitality Management*, 27(6), 1082–1099.

112. Leischnig, A., Ivens, B. S., & Henneberg, S. C. (2015). When stress frustrates and when it does not: Configural models of frustrated versus mellow salespeople. *Psychology & Marketing*, 32(11), 1098–1114.

113. Adams, G. A., King, L. A., & King, D. W. (1996). Relationships of job and family involvement, family social support, and work–family conflict with job and life satisfaction. *Journal of Applied Psychology*, 81(4), 411–420.

114. Edwards, J. R., & Rothbard, N. P. (1999). Work and family stress and well-being: An examination of person-environment fit in the work and family domains. *Organizational Behavior and Human Decision Processes*, 77(2), 85–129.

115. Greenhaus, J. H., & Parasuraman, S. (1987). A work-nonwork interactive perspective of stress and its consequences. *Journal of Organizational Behavior Management*, 8(2), 37–60.

116. Jackson, S. E., & Maslach, C. (1982). After-effects of job-related stress: Families as victims. *Journal of Organizational Behavior*, 3(1), 63–77.

117. Westman, M., & Etzion, D. (1995). Crossover of stress, strain and resources from one spouse to another. *Journal of Organizational Behavior*, 16(2), 169–181.

118. Frone, M. R., (2003). Work–family balance. In J. Quick & L. E. Tetrick (Eds.), *Handbook of occupational health psychology* (pp. 143–162). Washington, DC: American Psychological Association.

119. Park, Y., & Sprung, J. M. (2013). Work-school conflict and health outcomes: Beneficial resources for working college students. *Journal of Occupational Health Psychology*, 18(4), 384–394. (Quotation on p. 385.)

120. Kremer, I. (2016). The relationship between school-work-family-conflict, subjective stress, and burnout. *Journal of Managerial Psychology*, 31(4), 805–819

121. Wyland, R., Lester, S. W., Ehrhardt, K., & Standifer, R. (2016). An examination of the relationship between the work–school interface, job satisfaction, and job performance. *Journal of Business and Psychology*, 2(31), 187–203.

122. Sturges, J., & Guest, D. (2004). Working to live or living to work? Work/life balance early in the career. *Human Resource Management Journal*, 14(4), 5–20.

123. Daley, A. J., & Parfitt, G. (1996). Good health—Is it worth it? Mood states, physical well-being, job satisfaction and absenteeism in members and non-members of a British corporate health and fitness club. *Journal of Occupational and Organizational Psychology*, 69(2), 121–134.

124. Kirkcaldy, B. D., & Cooper, C. L. (1992). Cross-cultural differences in occupational stress among British and German managers. *Work & Stress*, 6(2), 177–190.

125. Lavanco, G. (1997). Burnout syndrome and type A behavior in nurses and teachers in Sicily. *Psychological Reports*, 81(2), 523–528.

126. Ben-Bakr, K. A., Al-Shammari, I. S., & Jefri, O. A. (1995). Occupational stress in different organizations: A Saudi Arabian survey. *Journal of Managerial Psychology*, 10(5), 24–28.

127. Xie, J. L. (1996). Karasek's model in the People's Republic of China: Effects of job demands, control, and individual differences. *Academy of Management Journal*, 39(6), 1594–1618.

128. Ongori, H., & Agolla, J. E. (2008). Occupational stress in organizations and its effects on organizational performance. *Journal of Management Research*, 8(3), 123–135.

129. Perrewé, P. L., Hochwarter, W. A., Rossi, A. M., Wallace, A., Maignan, I., Castro, S. L., . . . Wan, P. (2002). Are work stress relationships universal? A nine-region examination of role stressors, general self-efficacy, and burnout. *Journal of International Management*, 8(2), 163–187.

130. Jamal, M. (2010). Burnout among Canadian, Chinese, Malaysian and Pakistani employees: An empirical examination. *International Management Review*, 6(1), 31–41.

131. Peterson, M. F., Smith, P. B., Akande, A., Ayestaran, S., Bochner, S., Callan, V., . . . Viedge, C. (1995). Role conflict, ambiguity and overload: A 21-nation study. *Academy of Management Journal*, 38(2), 429–542.

132. Spector, P. E., Cooper, C. L., Sanchez, J., I., O'Driscoll, M., Sparks, K., Bernin, P., . . . Yu, S. (2002). Locus of control and well-being at work: How generalizable are western findings? *Academy of Management Journal*, 45(2), 453–466.

133. Bhagat, R. S., Segovis, J. C., & Nelson, T. A. (2012). *Work stress and coping in the era of globalization*. New York, NY: Routledge.

134. Narayanan, L., Menon, S., & Spector, P. E. (1999). A cross-cultural comparison of job stressors and reactions among employees holding comparable jobs in two countries. *International Journal of Stress Management*, 6, 197–212.

135. Karasek, R., Baker, D., Marxer, F., Ahlbom, A., & Theorell, T. (1981). Job decision latitude, job demands, and cardiovascular disease: A prospective study of Swedish men. *American Journal of Public Health*, 71(7), 694–705. (Quotation on p. 697.)

136. Bhagat, R. S., O'Driscoll, M. P., Babakus, E., Frey, L., Chokkar, J., Ninokumar, B., . . . Mahanyele, M. (1994). Organizational stress and coping in seven national contexts: A cross-cultural investigation. In G. Keita & J. J. Hurrel (Eds.), *Job stress in a changing workforce* (pp. 93–105). Washington, DC: American Psychological Association.

137. Lazarus, R. S., & Folkman, S. (1984). *Stress, appraisal and coping*. New York, NY: Springer. (Quotation on p. 141.)

138. Latack, J. C., & Havlovic, S. J. (1992). Coping with job stress: A conceptual evaluation framework for coping measures. *Journal of Organizational Behavior*, 13, 479–508.

139. Ito, J. K., & Brotheridge, C. M. (2003). Resources, coping strategies, and emotional exhaustion: A conservation of resources perspective. *Journal of Vocational Behavior*, 63(3), 490–509.

140. Tamres, L. K., Janicki, D., & Helgeson, V. S. (2002). Sex differences in coping behavior: A meta-analytic review and an examination of relative coping. *Personality and Social Psychology review*, 6(1), 2–30.

141. Judge, T. A., Thoresen, C. J., Pucik, V., & Welbourne, T. M. (1999). Managerial coping with organizational change: A dispositional perspective. *Journal of Applied Psychology*, 84(1), 107–122.

142. Sonnentag, S., Binnewies, C., & Mojza, E. J. (2010). Staying well and engaged when demands are high: The role of psychological detachment. *Journal of Applied Psychology*, 95(5), 965–976.

143. LaRocco, J. M., House, J. S., & French, J. R., Jr. (1980). Social support, occupational stress, and health. *Journal of Health and Social Behavior*, 202–218.

144. Beehr, T. A., & McGrath, J. E. (1992). Social support, occupational stress and anxiety. *Anxiety, Stress, and Coping*, 5(1), 7–19.

145. Nahum-Shani, I., & Bamberger, P. A. (2011). Explaining the variable effects of social support on work-based stressor–strain relations: The role of perceived pattern of support exchange. *Organizational Behavior and Human Decision Processes*, 114(1), 49–63.

146. Thoits, P. A. (1995). Stress, coping and social support processes: Where are we? What next? *Journal of Health and Social Behavior*, 35, 53–79.

147. Viswesvaran, C., Sanchez, J. I., & Fisher, J. (1999). The role of social support in the process of work stress: A meta-analysis. *Journal of Vocational Behavior*, 54(2), 314–334.

148. Kang, S. W., & Kang, S. D. (2016). High-commitment human resource management and job stress: Supervisor support as a moderator. *Social Behavior and Personality: An International Journal*, 44(10), 1719–1731.

149. Quick, J. C., Quick, J. D., Nelson, D. L., & Hurrell, J. J., Jr. (1997). *Preventve stress management in organizations*. Washington, DC: American Psychological Association.

150. Briner, R. B., & Reynolds, S. (1999). The costs, benefits, and limitations of organizational level stress interventions. *Journal of Organizational Behavior*, 20(5), 647–664.

151. Richardson, K. M., & Rothstein, H. R. (2008). Effects of occupational stress management intervention programs: A meta-analysis. *Journal of Occupational Health Psychology*, 13(1), 69–93.

152. Lakein, A. (1973). *How to get control of your time and your life*. New York, NY: Signet.

153. Macan, T. H., Shahani, C., Dipboye, R. L., & Phillips, A. P. (1990). College students' time management: Correlations with academic performance and stress. *Journal of Educational Psychology*, 82(4), 760.

154. Macan, T. H. (1994). Time management: Test of a process model. *Journal of Applied Psychology*, 79(3), 381.

155. Joseph, B., & Walker, A. (2017). Employee assistance programs in Australia: The perspectives of organizational leaders across sectors. *Asia Pacific Journal of Human Resources*, 55(2), 177–191.

156. Richmond, M. K., Pampel, F. C., Wood, R. C., & Nunes, A. P. (2017). The impact of employee assistance services on workplace outcomes: Results of a prospective, quasi-experimental study. *Journal of Occupational Health Psychology*, 22(2), 170–179.

157. LaClair, J. A., & Rao, R. P. (2002). Helping employees embrace change. *McKinsey Quarterly, 4*, 17–20.

158. Quick, J. C., Quick, J. D., Nelson, D. L., & Hurrell, J. J., Jr. (1997). *Preventive stress management in organizations*. Washington, DC: American Psychological Association. (Quotation on pp. 12–13.)

159. Thomas, C. H., & Lankau, M. J. (2009). Preventing burnout: The effects of LMX and mentoring on socialization, role stress, and burnout. *Human Resource Management*, 48(3), 417–432.

160. Dutton, J. E., Workman, K. M., & Hardin, A. E. (2014). Compassion at work. *Annual Review of Organizational Psychology and Organizational Behavior, 1*, 277–304.

Appendix

1. Tharenou, P., Donohue, R., & Cooper, B. (2007). *Management research methods.* Cambridge, England: Cambridge University Press.
2. Cook, T. D., & Campbell, D. T. (1979). *Quasi-experimentation: Design and analysis issues for field settings.* Boston, MA: Houghton Mifflin.
3. Basadur, M., Graen, G. B., & Scandura, T. A. (1986). Training effects on attitudes toward divergent thinking among manufacturing engineers. *Journal of Applied Psychology, 71*(4), 612–617.
4. Creswell, J. (2003). *Research design: Qualitative, quantitative, and mixed methods approaches* (2nd ed.). Thousand Oaks, CA: Sage.
5. Glass, G. V., McGaw, B., & Smith, M. L. (1981). *Meta-analysis in social research.* Beverly Hills, CA: SAGE.

Glossary

1. McCroskey, J. C. (1977). Oral communication apprehension: A summary of recent theory and research. *Human Communication Research, 4*(1), 78–96.
2. Cropanzano, R., & Dasborough, M. T. (2015). Dynamic models of well-being: Implications of affective events theory for expanding current views on personality and climate. *European Journal of Work and Organizational Psychology, 24*(6), 844–847.
3. Eagly, A. H., & Chaiken, S. (1993). *The psychology of attitudes.* New York, NY: Harcourt Brace Jovanovich College Publishers.
4. Miner, J. B. (2015). Attribution theory—Managerial perceptions of the poor performing subordinate. In J. Miner (Ed.), *Organizational behavior 1: Essential theories of motivation and leadership* (pp. 184–206).
5. Thomas, D. C., Brannen, M. Y., & Garcia, D. (2010). Bicultural individuals and intercultural effectiveness. *European Journal of Cross-Cultural Competence and Management, 1,* 315–333. (Quotation on p. 315.)
6. Savickas, M. L., & Porfeli, E. J. (2012). Career adapt-abilities scale: Construction, reliability, and measurement equivalence across 13 countries. *Journal of Vocational Behavior, 80*(3), 661–673.
7. Gati, I., Gadassi, R., Saka, N., Hadadi, Y., Ansenberg, N., Friedmann, R., & Asulin-Peretz, L. (2010). Emotional and personality-related aspects of career decision-making difficulties: Facets of career indecisiveness. *Journal of Career Assessment, 19*(1), 3.
8. McCroskey, J. C. (1977). Oral communication apprehension: A summary of recent theory and research. *Human Communication Research, 4*(1), 78–96.
9. Parry, S. B. (1996). The quest for competencies: Competency studies can help you make HR decisions, but the results are only as good as the study. *Training, 33,* 50.
10. Thomas, K. W. (1992). Conflict and negotiation processes in organizations. In M. D. Dunnette & L. M. Hough (Eds.), *Handbook of industrial and organizational psychology* (2nd ed., Vol. 3, pp. 651–717). Palo Alto, CA: Consulting Psychologists Press.
11. Judge, T. A., Erez, A., & Bono, J. E. (1998). The power of being positive: The relation between positive self-concept and job performance. *Human Performance, 11*(2–3), 167–187.
12. Amabile, T. M. (2012). *Componential theory of creativity* [Working Paper #12-096]. Cambridge, MA: Harvard Business School. Retrieved from http://www.hbs.edu/faculty/Publication%20Files/12-096.pdf
13. Paulhus, D. L., & Williams, K. (2002). The Dark Triad of personality: Narcissism, Machiavellianism, and psychopathy. *Journal of Research in Personality, 36,* 556–568.
14. Harrison, D. A., Price, K. H., & Bell, M. P. (1998). Beyond relational demography: Time and the effects of surface-and deep-level diversity on work group cohesion. *Academy of Management Journal, 41*(1), 96–107.
15. Robinson, S. L., Wang, W., & Kiewitz, C. (2014). Coworkers behaving badly: The impact of coworker deviant behavior upon individual employees. *Annual Review of Organizational Psychology and Organizational Behavior, 1,* 123–143.
16. Yagil, D. (2012). The mediating role of engagement and burnout in the relationship between employees' emotion regulation strategies and customer outcomes, *European Journal of Work and Organizational Psychology, 21*(1), 150–168.
17. Elfenbein, H. A. (2016). Emotional division-of-labor: A theoretical account. *Research in Organizational Behavior, 36,* 1–26. (Quotation on p. 1). doi:http://dx.doi.org/10.1016/j.riob.2016.11.001 0191-3085/
18. Salovey, P., & Mayer, J. D. (1989). Emotional intelligence. *Imagination, Cognition and Personality, 9*(3), 185–211.
19. Hogan, R., Chamorro-Premuzic, T., & Kaiser, R. B. (2013). Employability and career success: Bridging the gap between theory and reality. *Industrial and Organizational Psychology, 6*(1), 3–16.
20. Colantonio, A. (1989). Assessing the effects of employee assistance programs: A review of employee assistance program evaluations. *Yale Journal of Biology and Medicine, 62*(1), 13.
21. Rich, B. L., Lepine, J. A., & Crawford, E. R. (2010). Job engagement: Antecedents and effects on job performance. *Academy of Management Journal, 53*(3), 617–635.
22. McCullough, M. E., Emmons, R. A., & Tsang, J. A. (2002). The grateful disposition: A conceptual and empirical topography. *Journal of Personality and Social Psychology, 82*(1), 112–127.
23. Tadmor, C. T., & Tetlock, P. E. (2006). Biculturalism: A model of the effects of second-culture exposure on acculturation and integrative complexity. *Journal of Cross-Cultural Psychology, 37*(2), 173–190.
24. Frank, A., & Brownell, J. (1989). *Organizational communication and behavior: Communicating to improve performance.* Orlando, FL: Holt, Rinehart & Winston. (Quotation on pp. 5–6.)

25. Maslach, C. (1998). *A multidimensional theory of burnout*. In C. L. Cooper (Ed.), *Theories of organizational stress*. Oxford, England: Oxford University Press. (Quotation on p. 68.)

26. Kossek, E. E., Lautsch, B. A., & Eaton, S. C. (2006). Telecommuting, control, and boundary management: Correlates of policy use and practice, job control, and work–family effectiveness. *Journal of Vocational Behavior, 68*(2), 350.

27. Chan, K. Y., & Drasgow, F. (2001). Toward a theory of individual differences and leadership: Understanding the motivation to lead. *Journal of Applied Psychology, 86*(3), 481–498. (Quotation on p. 482.)

28. Spain, S. M., Harms, P., & LeBreton, J. M. (2014). The dark side of personality at work. *Journal of Organizational Behavior, 35*(S1), S41–S60.

29. Ambady, N., & Weisbuch, M. (2010). Nonverbal behavior. In S. T. Fiske, D. T. Gilbert, & G. Lindzey (Eds.), *Handbook of social psychology* (pp. 464–497). Hoboken, NJ: Wiley. (Quotation on p. 465.)

30. Richmond, V. P., McCroskey, J. C., & McCroskey, L. L. (2005). *Organizational communication for survival: Making work, work*. New York, NY: Allyn & Bacon. (Quotation on p. 20.)

31. Schein, E. H. (1984). Coming to a new awareness of organizational culture. *Sloan Management Review, 25*(2), 3–16.

32. Wanberg, C. R. (2012). Facilitating organizational socialization: An introduction. In C. R. Wanberg (Ed.), *The Oxford handbook of organizational socialization* (pp. 17–21). New York, NY: Oxford University Press.

33. House, R. J. (1971). A path-goal theory of leadership effectiveness. *Administrative Science Quarterly, 16*(3), 321–328.

34. House, R. J., & Mitchell, T. R. (1974). Path-goal theory of leadership. *Journal of Contemporary Business, 3*(4), 81–97.

35. Eisenberger, R., Huntington, R., Hutchison, S., & Sowa, D. (1986). Perceived organizational support. *Journal of Applied Psychology, 71*(3), 500–507.

36. Snyder, M., & Cantor, N. (1998). Understanding personality and social behavior: A functionalist strategy. In D. T. Gilbert, S. T. Fiske, & G. Lindzey (Eds.), *The handbook of social psychology* (4th ed., pp. 635–679). New York, NY: McGraw-Hill.

37. Spreitzer, G. M. (1995). Psychological empowerment in the workplace: Dimensions, measurement, and validation. *Academy of Management Journal, 38*(4), 1442–1465.

38. Hare, R. D. (1985). Comparison of procedures for the assessment of psychopathy. *Journal of Consulting and Clinical Psychology, 53*, 7–16.

39. Levenson, M. R. (1990). Risk taking and personality. *Journal of Personality and Social Psychology, 58*(6), 1073–1080.

40. Islam, G., & Zyphur, M. J. (2009). Rituals in organizations: A review and expansion of current theory. *Group & Organization Management, 34*(1), 114–139.

41. Snyder, M. (1974). Self-monitoring of expressive behavior. *Journal of Personality and Social Psychology, 30*(4), 526–537. (Quotation on p. 526.)

42. Weick, K. (1995). *Sensemaking in organizations*. Thousand Oaks, CA: Sage.

43. Jones, E. E., & Pittman, T. S. (1982). Toward a general theory of strategic self-presentation. In J. Suls (Ed.), *Psychological perspectives on the self*, (pp. 231–261). Hillsdale, NJ: Erlbaum.

44. Scott, B. A., & Barnes, C. M. (2011). A multilevel field investigation of emotional labor, affect, work withdrawal, and gender. *Academy of Management Journal, 54*, 116–136.

45. Harrison, D. A., Price, K. H., & Bell, M. P. (1998). Beyond relational demography: Time and the effects of surface-and deep-level diversity on work group cohesion. *Academy of Management Journal, 41*(1), 96–107.

46. Casrnir, F. L. (1999). Foundations for the study of intercultural communication based on a third-culture building model. *International Journal of Intercultural Relations, 23*(1), 91–116.

47. Martins, L. L., Gilson, L. L., & Maynard, M. T. (2004). Virtual teams: What do we know and where do we go from here? *Journal of Management, 30*(6), 805–835. (Quotation on p. 807.)

48. Neuman, J. H., & Baron, R. A. (2005). Aggression in the workplace: A social-psychological perspective. In S. Fox & P. E. Spector (Eds.), *Counterproductive work behavior: Investigations of actors and targets* (pp. 13–40). Washington, DC: American Psychological Association. http://dx.doi.org/10.1037/10893-001

49. Leymann, H. (1996). The content and development of mobbing at work. *European Journal of Work and Organizational Psychology, 5*(2), 165–184. (Quotation on p. 168.)

50. Andersson, L. M., & Pearson, C. M. (1999). Tit-for-tat? The spiraling effect of incivility in the workplace. *Academy of Management Review, 24*(3), 452–471. (Quotation on p. 457.)

INDEX